Sleeping price codes

LL	over US$200
L	US$151-200
AL	US$101-150
A	US$66-100
B	US$46-65
C	US$31-45
D	US$21-30
E	US$12-20
F	US$7-11
G	US$6 and under

Prices given are based on two people sharing a double room (including taxes) in high season. Note that the dollar/soles exchange rate can fluctuate substantially.

Eating price codes

♜♜♜	over US$12
♜♜	US$7-12
♜	US$6 and under

Prices are for a two-course meal for one person, excluding drinks or service charge.

Footprint story

It was 1921

Ireland had just been partitioned, the British miners were striking for more pay and the federation of British industry had an idea. Exports were booming in South America – how about a handbook for businessmen trading in that far away continent? The Anglo-South American Handbook was born that year, written by W Koebel, the most prolific writer on Latin America of his day.

1924

Two editions later the book was 'privatized' and in 1924, in the hands of Royal Mail, the steamship company for South America, it became The South American Handbook, subtitled 'South America in a nutshell'. This annual publication became the 'bible' for generations of travellers to South America and remains so to this day. In the early days travel was by sea and the Handbook gave all the details needed for the long voyage from Europe. What to wear for dinner; how to arrange a cricket match with the Cable & Wireless staff on the Cape Verde Islands and a full account of the journey from Liverpool up the Amazon to Manaus: 5898 miles without changing cabin!

1939

As the continent opened up, the South American Handbook reported the new Pan Am flying boat services, and the fortnightly airship service from Rio to Europe on the Graf Zeppelin. For reasons still unclear but with extraordinary determination, the annual editions continued through the Second World War.

1970s

Many more people discovered South America and the backpacking trail started to develop. All the while the Handbook was gathering fans, including literary vagabonds such as Paul Theroux and Graham Greene (who once sent some updates addressed to "The publishers of the best travel guide in the world, Bath, England").

1990s

During the 1990s the company set about developing a new travel guide series using this legendary title as the flagship. By 1997 there were over a dozen guides in the series and the Footprint imprint was launched.

2000s

The series grew quickly and there were soon Footprint travel guides covering more than 150 countries. In 2004, Footprint launched its first thematic guide: *Surfing Europe*, packed with colour photographs, maps and charts. This was followed by further thematic guides such as *Diving the World, Snowboarding the World, Body and Soul escapes, Travel with Kids and European City Breaks.*

2011

Today we continue the traditions of the last 90 years that have served legions of travellers so well. We believe that these help to make Footprint guides different. Our policy is to use authors who are genuine experts who write for independent travellers; people possessing a spirit of adventure, looking to get off the beaten track.

Cuzco & the Inca Heartland

Ben Box
Sarah Cameron

Can you imagine a city laid out in the shape of a puma; a stone to tie the sun to; a city of fleas? Are you willing to meet the Earth Changer, Our Lord of the Earthquakes and Mother Earth? If so, prepare to follow the pilgrimage to Cuzco, the place that every Inca endeavoured to visit once in a lifetime. Navel of the world, Spanish colonial showpiece, gringo capital of South America, Cuzco is all these things and more.

Cuzco's position, high up in the Andes, kept it largely isolated until the beginning of the 20th century when the railway arrived. As a result, although it has grown into a city of almost 300,000 inhabitants, its centre still has the feel of a colonial town. But don't be lulled into thinking that a holiday here is going to be a stroll back in time. Cuzco is alive with the traditions of the Incas' descendants and the legacy of 300 years of Spanish rule – most visible in its long list of festivals – but the latest trends of 21st-century adventure tourism, hotel fashion, nightlife and internet culture also give the city a vibrancy that's hard to match.

The quintessential South American tourist site, Machu Picchu, is a mere train ride away from Cuzco – or a four-day hike along the Inca Trail. In recent years, the trail has become a victim of its own success, eroded by countless pairs of boots, but the development of alternative, equally challenging Inca routes has widened the perspectives that you can get on this historic landscape. Also within easy reach of Cuzco are Andean markets selling essentials to the locals and handicrafts to the tourist, hot springs, charming places to stay and thrilling hikes that traverse 4000-m passes to reach lost cities. What's more, you have access to those features that make Peru one of the eight 'mega-diverse' countries on earth. Below snow-covered peaks, roads and trails drop into river canyons or descend the eastern slopes of the Andes to the vast lowlands of the Amazon.

This page Andes landscape near Moray in the Sacred Valley of the Incas.
Previous page For several days in June, the virgins and saints of the city are paraded through the streets of Cuzco as part of the Corpus Christi festival.

Highlights

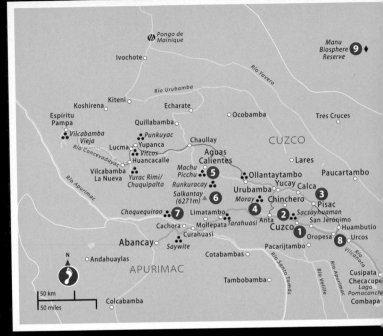

Pongo de Mainique

Ivochote

Manu Biosphere Reserve ⑨ ◆

Río Yavero

Río Urubamba

Kiteni
Koshirena
Echarate
Ocobamba
Tres Cruces

Espíritu Pampa
Quillabamba
CUZCO

Vilcabamba Vieja
Punkuyac
Chaullay
Aguas Calientes
Lares

Lucma Yupanca
Vitcos

Río Concevadayac
Huancacalle
Machu Picchu ⑤
Ollantaytambo
Yucay Calca
Paucartambo

Vilcabamba La Nueva
Yurac Rimi/ Chuquipalta
Runkuracay
Urubamba
Chinchero
③ Pisac

Río Apurímac
Salkantay (6271m) ▲ ⑥
Moray ④
Sacsayhuaman
San Jerónimo

Choquequirao ⑦
Limatambo
Anta ②
Cuzco ①
Huambutío

Cachora
Mollepata Tarahuasi
Oropesa ⑧ Urcos

Abancay
Curahuasi
Pacarijtambo

Saywite
Cotabambas
Río Santo Tomás

Andahuaylas
APURIMAC
Tambobamba
Cusipata
Checacupe
Lago Pomacanchi
Combapa

50 km
50 miles
Colcabamba

① The **Inca Temple of the Sun**, Qoricancha, is hidden within a Catholic church in Cuzco. ▶▶ page 77.

② Striking zigzag walls and massive masonry define the Inca ceremonial site of **Sacsayhuaman**. ▶▶ page 82.

③ Don't miss the market in **Pisac**, with great Inca ruins above. ▶▶ page 132.

④ Huge depressions become crop laboratories at **Moray**, while salt pans tumble down a hillside at **Salineras**. ▶▶ page 142.

⑤ **Machu Picchu**, one of the finest archaeological ruins in the world, is the focus for most people's visit to Peru. ▶▶ page 161.

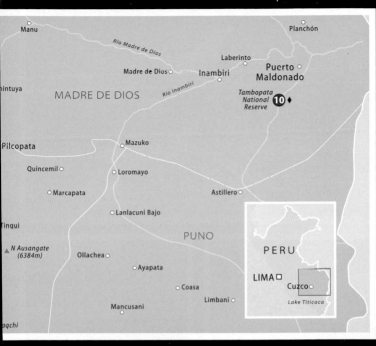

6 Hike around the mountain of **Salkantay** on two alternative treks to Machu Picchu. ▶▶ page 175.

7 **Choquequirao**: another lost city, another hard walk - but what a reward when you get there. ▶▶ page 232.

8 **Andahuaylillas**, the Sistine Chapel of the Andes, is a simple 17th-century church with the most amazing frescoes. ▶▶ page 217.

9 No rainforest reserve can compete for the diversity of life forms found in **Manu Biosphere Reserve**. ▶▶ page 247.

10 **Tambopata National Reserve** is another great place for wildlife. ▶▶ page 254.

Clockwise from top

Pisac.

Sacsayhuaman.

Manu Biosphere Reserve.

Salkantay.

Choquequirao.

Contents

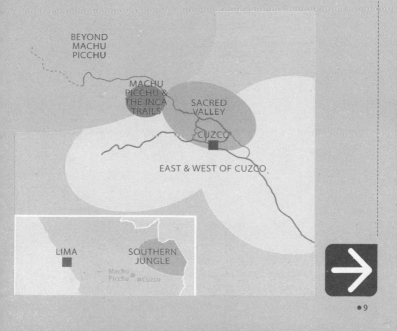

BEYOND MACHU PICCHU

MACHU PICCHU & THE INCA TRAILS

SACRED VALLEY

CUZCO

EAST & WEST OF CUZCO

LIMA

SOUTHERN JUNGLE

Machu Picchu ■ Cuzco

→

Contents

Footprint features

Essentials

Planning your trip

To see Cuzco and the surrounding area properly you'll need between 10 and 14 days. This would allow you to explore the city, enjoy its nightlife, visit the towns and villages of the Urubamba Valley – including Pisac, Ollantaytambo, Urubamba and Chinchero – and, of course, hike one of the Inca trails, many of which lead to Machu Picchu (about four days). Added to that, you'll need at least four or five days for a jungle trip to Manu or Tambopata, plus a few more for mountain biking and whitewater rafting. Three or four weeks, therefore, would allow you to enjoy the region to its full, but the one problem with Cuzco is that it is all too easy to find a colonial café with a balcony, toss the guidebook aside and sit back in the blazing sun to watch the world go by.

Where to go

Your first port of call should be Cuzco's **Plaza de Armas**, heart of the city since Inca times, and it is here that you will get an immediate feel for the city. Two grand churches and a series of arcades surround this great colonial space, which is filled with eating places, tourist businesses and people on the move. Behind the facade, you will gaze amazed at the gold altars of churches such as **La Compañía**, though even these will fade into insignificance on entering the complex of the **Temple of the Sun**. Here the Spanish *conquistadores* found so much gold it took them three months to melt it down. It takes only a little imagination to picture the solar garden as it once was: filled with life-sized replicas of men, women and children, insects, plants and flowers – all made from gold. The 700 gold and silver plates that once covered the temple walls here may have gone, but their disappearance has revealed the stunning craftsmanship of the Inca stonemasons whose blocks fit together so perfectly it is impossible to slide even a razorblade into the joints – and that after two major earthquakes.

Out of the city you have to travel only a few hours to discover the wonderful **Sacred Valley**. Take a one-day bus trip if you are on a tight schedule, otherwise see the spectacular Inca ruins, busy indigenous markets and beautiful scenery under your own steam and at your own pace. Some choose to take the bus, others to go off-road on a mountain bike. If you have the stomach for it, sign up for a condor's-eye view and paraglide in tandem with a professional.

For many, Cuzco means one thing: **Machu Picchu**, one of only three places in the Americas that has been declared a World Heritage Site for both its natural beauty *and* its history (the other two are Palenque in Mexico and Tikal in Guatemala). Its global fame was assured in 2007 when it was voted one of the New Seven Wonders of the World.

The ancient **Inca Trail** is one of the world's classic trekking routes. After four days of climbing through dizzying 4000-m-plus mountain passes, the weary hiker emerges at the Sun Gate to look down at last on one of the most awe-inspiring sights in the world. And its wonder is not confined to the young and fit. The site is accessible by luxury train followed by a bus ride up a switchback road.

It has however been realized that the Inca Trail was not built for thousands of hiking boots and camping sites, and the authorities have been forced to reduce degradation by limiting the number of trekkers through strict controls and high prices. Fortunately, there are many other equally challenging trails which lead to Machu Picchu, or other remarkable Inca sites: to **Choquequirao** over the **Vilcabamba** mountain range; to the last

Packing for Peru

Everybody has their own preferences, but listed here are the most often mentioned. These include: an inflatable travel pillow for neck support; hiking boots; waterproof clothing; wax earplugs (vital for noisy hotels); rubber sandals (to wear in showers to avoid athlete's foot; a sheet sleeping bag to avoid sleeping on filthy sheets in cheap hotels; a clothes line; a water bottle; a universal bath – and basin – plug of the flanged type that will fit any wastepipe; Swiss Army knife (do not carry it in your hand luggage on flights); an alarm clock for those early morning departures;

candles and/or a torch/flashlight; an adaptor, or the necessary equipment for recharging cameras, laptops, etc; padlocks (for doors of the cheapest hotels, tent zips, and backpacks as a deterrent to thieves); a small first aid kit; and a sun hat.

A list of useful medicines and health-related items is given in the Health section, see page 44. To these might be added some lip salve, with sun protection, and pre-moistened wipes (such as Wet Ones). Always carry toilet paper, which is especially important on long bus trips. Contact lens solution is readily available in pharmacies.

Inca stronghold at **Espíritu Pampa**; or around – and up! – ice-capped **Ausangate**, the mountain that dominates Cuzco's eastern skyline. The passes here are over 5000 m. Thrill-seekers can combine a jungle experience with rafting the turbulent waters of the **Apurímac**, the true source of the Amazon. There cannot be many places in the world where you can cast off amid snow-capped mountain scenery and take a trip that later leaves you bumping through caiman-infested jungle. The rivers around Cuzco are between a gentle Grade II to a heady Grade V.

No trip of more than two weeks would be complete without discovering the beauty of the jungle in the **Manu Biosphere Reserve**, one of the largest conservation areas on earth, or the **Tambopata National Reserve**. Over 10% of all the species of birds in the world can be found at Manu. Your trip will take you through cloudforest on the eastern slopes of the Andes, past the upper tropical zone where blue-headed and military macaws can be found, to the untouched forests of the western Amazon.

When to go

There is no time of year when you will have Cuzco and Machu Picchu to yourself. Having said that, Peru's high season is from June to September and, at that time, Cuzco is bursting at the seams. This also happens to be the time of year which enjoys the most stable weather for hiking the Inca Trail or trekking and climbing elsewhere. The days are generally clear and sunny, but nights can be very cold at high altitude. The highlands can be visited at other times of the year, though during the wettest months from November to April some roads become impassable and hiking trails can be very muddy. April and May, at the tail end of the highland rainy season, is a beautiful time to see the Peruvian Andes, but the rain may linger, so be prepared.

On the coast, the summer months are from December to April. If you arrive in Lima between May and October you will find the area covered with what's known locally as *la garúa*, a thick blanket of cloud and mist. As your plane heads towards Cuzco in the *garúa* season, you will soon be into clear skies and the mountains below can be seen rising like a new coastline out of the sea of fog.

The best time to visit the jungle is during the dry season, from April to October. During the wet season, November to April, it is oppressively hot (40°C and above) and while it only rains for a few hours at a time, which is not enough to spoil your trip, it is enough to make some roads virtually impassable.

What to do

This is one of the very best parts of the world for a number of adventure sports, including trekking and climbing, whitewater rafting and mountain biking. Facilities for adventure tourism tend to develop in correlation with general tourist services so always make sure the infrastructure and equipment is adequate before signing up for a potentially dangerous activity. Also check the experience and qualifications of operators and guides. Peru also offers probably the greatest wildlife viewing opportunities on the planet and it is unmatched anywhere for the sheer scale of its ancient ruins.

Birdwatching

Peru is the number one country in the world for birds. Its varied geography and topography have endowed Peru with the greatest biodiversity and variety of birds on earth. About 20% of all the bird species in the world and 45% of all neotropical birds occur in Peru. More new species have been described in Peru in the last 30 years than any other country in the world: on average 2 new species a year. This is why Peru is the best South American destination for birds, on a continent that is itself dubbed 'the bird continent' by professional ornithologists.

A birding trip to Peru is possible during any month of the year, as birds breed all year round. There is, however, a definite peak in breeding activity – and consequently birdsong – just before the rains come in Oct, and this makes it rather easier to locate many birds between Sep and Christmas.

Rainwear is recommended for the mountains, especially during the rainy season between Dec and Apr. But in the tropical lowlands an umbrella is the way to go. Lightweight hiking boots are probably the best general footwear, but wellingtons (rubber boots) are preferred by many neotropical birders for the lowland rainforests.

Apart from the usual binoculars, a telescope is helpful in many areas, whilst a tape recorder and shotgun microphone can be very useful for calling out skulking forest birds, although experience in using this type of equipment is recommended, particularly to limit disturbance to the birds.

A great 3-week combination is about 16 days in Manu, then 2-3 days in the highlands at Abra Málaga. You can extend this by including one or more of the other highly recommended spots outside the scope of this guidebook.

The birds

If your experience of neotropical birding is limited, the potential number of species which may be seen on a 3- or 4-week trip can be daunting. A 4-week trip can produce over 750 species, and some of the identifications can be tricky! You may want to take an experienced bird guide with you who can introduce you to, for example, the mysteries of foliage-gleaner and woodcreeper identification, or you may want to 'do it yourself' and identify the birds on your own.

Machu Picchu may be a nightmare for lovers of peace and solitude, but the surrounding bamboo stands provide excellent opportunities for seeing the Inca wren. A walk along the railway track near Puente Ruinas station can produce species which are difficult to see elsewhere. This is *the* place in Peru to see white-capped dipper and torrent duck.

The most accessible *polylepsis* woodlands in the Andes is only 2 hrs' drive from Ollantaytambo, whilst the humid temperate forest of Abra Málaga is only 45 mins further on. In the *polylepsis* some very rare birds can easily be seen, including royal cinclodes and white-browed tit-spinetail (the latter being one of the 10 most endangered birds on earth). The humid temperate forest is laden with moss and bromeliads, and mixed species flocks of multi-coloured tanagers and other birds are common.

See also Wildlife and vegetation, page 342.

★ **Head for ...**
Abra Málaga, page 195.
Machu Picchu, page 164.
Manu Biosphere Reserve, page 247.
Tambopata National Reserve, page 254.

Climbing and trekking

While Peru has some of the best climbing in the world, Cuzco is not developed for the sport. Peru has some outstanding trekking circuits around the *nevados*, its snowcapped mountains. Among the best known is the Ausangate circuit. The other type of trekking for which Peru is justifiably renowned is walking among ruins, the prime example being the Inca Trail. Other exciting walks of this type in a region rich in archaeological heritage are being developed and you are encouraged to try them, if for no other reason than to protect the fragile Inca Trail.

Most walking is on clear trails well trodden by *campesinos* who populate most parts of the Peruvian Andes. If you camp on their land, ask permission first and, of course, do not leave any litter. Tents, sleeping bags, mats and stoves can easily be hired in Cuzco but check carefully for quality.

Trekking and climbing conditions
May to Sep is the dry season in the Cordillera. Oct, Nov and Apr can be fine, particularly for trekking. Most bad weather comes from the east and temperatures plummet around twilight. The optimum months for extreme ice climbing are from late May to mid-Jul. In early May there is a risk of avalanche from sheered *neve* ice layers. It is best to climb early in the day as the snow becomes slushy later on. After Jul successive hot sunny days will have melted some of the main support (compacted ice) particularly on north-facing slopes. On the other hand, high altitude rock climbs are less troubled by ice after Jul. On south-facing slopes, the ice and snow never consolidates quite as well.

Maps
The following are the IGN 1:100,000 topographical sheets which apply to the treks. All sheets can be obtained through **South American Explorers** in Cuzco, see page 66. All names of mountains and other features given in the trek descriptions have been checked by the authors, even if they differ from those given on IGN or other sources.

Ausangate: Ocongate sheet (ref: 28-T). Choquequirao to Machu Picchu: Machu Picchu sheet (ref: 27-Q). Salkantay to Santa Teresa: Machu Picchu sheet (ref: 27-Q). Salkantay to Machu Picchu: Machu Picchu sheet plus Urubamba sheet (27-Q and 27-R). Espíritu Pampa: Machu Picchu sheet plus sheets to the west and northwest (27-Q, 27-P and 26-P). Ancascocha Trek: Urubamba sheet (27-R).

★ **Head for ...**
Choquequirao, page 232.
Cordillera Vilcabamba for Salkantay (6271 m) peak, page 175, and **Cordillera Vilcanota**, for Ausangate (6398 m) peak, page 219.
Inca Trail, page 171.
Vilcabamba traverse trek, page 197.

Cultural tourism

This covers more esoteric pursuits such as archaeology and mystical tourism. Several of the tour operators listed on page 53 offer customized packages for special interest groups. Local operators offering these more specialized tours are listed in the travelling text under the relevant location. Cultural tourism is a rapidly growing niche market.

Details of specialized shamanic healing and mystical tourism are listed under Cuzco Cultural tours, page 118.

★ Head for ...
Cuzco, page 64.

Contact
PromPerú, www.peru.info, has 5 interesting community-based tourism projects around the country. Click on 'What to do?' on the home page, then Culture, and then choose Experiential tourism. In the Cuzco area, the project involves activities in villages in the Sacred Valley and Raqchi.

Kayaking

Peru offers outstanding whitewater kayaking for all standards of paddlers from novice to expert. Many first descents remain unattempted due to logistical difficulties, though they are slowly being ticked off by a dedicated crew of local and internationally renowned kayakers. For the holiday paddler, you are probably best joining up with a raft company who will gladly carry all your gear (plus any non-paddling companions) and provide you with superb food while you enjoy the river from an unladen kayak. There is a surprising selection of latest-model kayaks available in Peru for hire for US$20-30 a day.

For complete novices, some companies offer 2- to 3-day kayak courses on the Urubamba and Apurímac that can be booked locally. For expedition paddlers, bringing your own canoe is the best option

though it is getting increasingly expensive to fly around Peru with your boats. A knowledge of Spanish is indispensable.

Mountain biking

With its amazing diversity of trails, tracks and rough roads, Peru is surely one of the last great mountain bike destinations yet to be fully discovered. Whether you're into a 2-day downhill blast from the Andes to the Amazon jungle or an extended off-road journey, Peru has some of the world's best biking opportunities. The problem is finding the routes as trail maps are virtually nonexistent and the few main roads are often congested with traffic and far from fun to travel along. A few specialist agencies run by dedicated mountain bikers are now exploring the intricate web of paths, single tracks and dirt roads that criss-crosses the Andes, putting together exciting routes to suit everyone from the weekend warrior to the long-distance touring cyclist, the extreme downhiller to the casual day tripper.

If you are considering a dedicated cycling holiday, then it is best to bring your bike from home. It's pretty easy, just get a bike box from your local shop, deflate the tyres, take the pedals off and turn the handlebars. It is worth checking first that your airline is happy to take your bike: some are, some will want to charge. Make sure your bike is in good condition before you depart as spares and repairs are hard to come by, especially if your bike is very complicated (eg: XT V-brake blocks are virtually impossible to find and rear suspension/disc brakes parts are totally unavailable). A tip from a Peruvian mountain bike guide: take plenty of inner tubes, brake blocks, chain lube and a quick release seat. Leave all panniers at home and rely on the support vehicle whenever you get tired as there will be plenty more riding later.

If you are hiring a bike, be it for one day or longer, the basic rule is that you get what you pay for. For as little as US$5-10 a day you can get a cheap imitation of a mountain bike that will be fine on a paved road, but will almost certainly not stand up to the rigours of off-roading. For US$20-25 you should be able to find something half-decent with front shocks, V-brakes, helmet and gloves. Bear in mind high-quality, well-maintained bikes are rare in Peru so you should check any hire bike thoroughly before riding it.

Choosing the right tour

When signing up for a mountain bike trip, remember that you are in the Andes so if you are worried about your fitness and the altitude, make sure you get a predominantly downhill route.

There are now a couple of companies offering imported high-quality, full-suspension mountain bikes with superb hydraulic disc brakes. Valued at over US$2500 each, these bikes are a dream to ride, for the novice and the expert alike. The guides at these companies are experts in making sure you get the very best out of these state-of-the-art machines. Whatever the quality of the bike, check that it is regularly maintained and that the guide gives you a full explanation on its use. In the wrong hands, or poorly maintained, bikes can cause problems and you may have very little come back, especially if booking and paying from overseas. Other things to check: the company must be operating in Peru legally. Trips should have a support vehicle for the duration, not just dropping you off and meeting you at the end. Guides should carry a first aid kit, at the very least a puncture repair kit (preferably a comprehensive tool kit) and be knowledgeable about bike mechanics. Bikes do go wrong, punctures are frequent and people do fall off, so it is essential that your guide provides this minimum cover.

On longer trips ask for detailed trip dossiers, describing the ups and downs and total distances of the routes, check how much is dirt road (suitable for anyone of reasonable fitness) and how much is single track (often requiring considerable experience and fitness). Also, find out what support will be provided in the way of experienced bike guides (they should have an official certificate of qualification), trained bike mechanics on hand, radio communications, spare bikes, cooking, dining and toilet facilities, etc.

★ Head for ...

All ideally require a guide as it's very easy to get lost in the Andes.

Abra Málaga, page 195. From 4200 m, an 80-km descent to the jungle or a radical Inca trail back to Ollantaytambo, both great rides.

Chinchero–Moray–Maras–Las Salineras–Urubamba, page 143. One of the finest day trips in Peru. Largely downhill on a mixture of dirt road and single track, this trip takes you to the interesting circular ruins of Moray and into the spectacular salt pans below Maras on an awesome mule track (watch out for mules!). Maras Moray Biking appears on the Urubamba Sheet (27-R); however, road information on this sheet is not accurate and to find the best off-road sections we recommend hiring a guide.

Cuzco ruins Cheat by taking a taxi to Puka Pukara and then enjoy a tarmac descent (if unguided) via Tambo Machay (page 90), Qenqo (page 84) and Sacsayhuaman (page 82) – don't forget your combined entrance ticket; see box, page 65. Or, with a guide, explore some of Cuzco's less visited ruins, following the mass of old Inca tracks accessible only to those in the know.

Cuzco–Puerto Maldonado Possibly the greatest Trans-Andean challenge on a bike: 550 km of hard work up to 4700 m and down to 230 m on one of the roughest roads there is (with the odd full-on single track thrown in for good measure). Be prepared to get wet as there are a lot of river crossings, sometimes up to waist deep. Either a 9-day epic, or cheat on the hills and enjoy some of the biggest downhills out (3-4 days).

Huchuy Cuzco, page 135. For biking experts only, this unbelievable trip is best described as 'trekking with your bike'. Various routes, again hard to find, are followed by what must be one of the hairiest single tracks in the world, along the top of and down into the Sacred Valley of the Incas.

Lares Valley, page 136. This offers some incredible down and uphill options on 2- or 3-day circuits including a relaxing soak in the beautiful Lares hot springs. Lares Biking appears on the IGN Urubamba and Calca Sheets (27-R and 27-S); however, the trip stays fairly close to the road so IGN is perhaps not essential.

Pisac–Tres Cruces–Manu From Pisac to Manu is a 250-km, beautiful dirt road ride offering big climbs and an even bigger (2-day) descent. A side trip to Tres Cruces to see the sunrise is a must if time permits. Remember that the road to Manu only operates downhill every other day, so be sure to check you've got it right or else beware irate truck drivers not giving way on a very narrow road!

Contact

Amazonas Explorer, Cuzco, www.amazonas-explorer.com. **Perú Bike**, Lima, www.perubike.com.

Parapenting and hang-gliding

Vuelo libre is its name in Peru. The season in the sierra is May-Oct, with the best months being Aug and Sep. Some flights in Peru have exceeded 6500 m.

While the attraction of parapenting or hang-gliding in the sierras is very great, with mountains on all sides and steep valleys below, most pilots are to be found in Lima. Arranging a tandem jump or a course is easy: just go to Parque del Amor in Miraflores in the afternoon and see who is hanging around waiting for the thermals and the breeze. Jumping off the cliff gives a completely different perspective on the city as you fly

above the Pacific breakers and the traffic on the coastal boulevard, with a pelican's view of the blocks of flats and offices.

★ Head for ...

Cerro Sacro (3797 m), Pampa de Chincheros, 45 km from Cuzco, with 550 m clearance at take-off. Launch site for cross-country flights over the Sacred Valley, Sacsayhuaman and Cuzco.

Mirador de Urubamba, 38 km from Cuzco, at 3650 m, with 800 m clearance and views over Pisac. Particularly good for parapenting.

Sacred Valley, page 129, excellent launch sites, thermals and reasonable landing sites.

Contact

Andean Trail Perú, Lima, www.andeantrailperu.com. **Peru Fly**, Lima, www.perufly.com. Make sure the operator has the backing of the **Asociación Peruana de Vuelo Libre (APVL)**, http://apvl.pe/.

Rafting

Peru is rapidly becoming one of the world's premier destinations for whitewater rafting. Several of its rivers are rated in the world's top 10 and a rafting trip is now high on any adventurer's list of activities while travelling in Peru. It is not just the adrenaline rush of big rapids that attracts, it is the whole experience of accessing areas beyond the reach of motor vehicles, whether tackling sheer-sided, mile-deep canyons, travelling silently through pristine rainforest, or canoeing across the stark Altiplano, high in the Andes.

Before you leap in the first raft that floats by, a word of warning and a bit of advice will help you ensure that your rafting trip of a lifetime really is as safe, as environmentally friendly and as fun as you want it to be.

The very remoteness and amazing locations that make Peruvian whitewater rivers so attractive mean that dealing with an emergency (should it occur) can be difficult, if impossible. As the sport of rafting has increased in popularity over the last few years, so too have the number of accidents (including fatalities). How then, do you ensure your safety on what are some of the best whitewater runs anywhere in South America if not the whole world? In 2010 a new regulatory body for rafting operators was set up to ensure that companies are able to run professional trips, that they employ international-standard safety techniques, that guides are adequately qualified and legally allowed to work in Peru and that equipment is regularly checked. It is hoped that, once fully in place in 2011, this body will weed out the poor practices, equipment and guides that have undermined this fun and exciting sport. Class 4+ guides must hold the internationally recognized qualification of Swift Water Rescue Technician and hold a current first aid certificate. All rafting equipment will be checked regularly to ensure it meets basic safety standards, eg life jackets that actually float, etc.

If you are keen on rafting and are looking to join a rafting expedition of some length, then it is worth signing up in advance before you set foot in Peru. Some long expeditions have only a few scheduled departures a year and the companies that offer them only accept bookings well in advance as the trips are logistically extremely difficult to organize. For the popular day trips and expeditions on the Apurímac there are regular departures (the latter in the dry season only, see below). If you can spare a few days to wait for a departure then it's fine to book in Cuzco. It also gives you the chance to talk to the company who will be operating your tour and to meet the guides. There are day trip departures all year and frequent multi-day departures in the high season. Note that the difficulty of the sections changes between the dry and rainy seasons. Some become extremely difficult or impossible in the rainy season. The dry season is Apr/May to Sep

(but can be as late as Nov), the rainy season Dec-Mar.

At present (and probably in the foreseeable future), as with many of Peru's adventure options, it simply boils down to you get what you pay for. Rafting is an inherently dangerous sport and doing it in Peru with the wrong operator can seriously endanger your life. If price is all that matters bear in mind the following comments: the cheaper the price, the less you get, be it with safety cover, experience of guides, quality of equipment, quantity of food, emergency back-up and environmental awareness.

You will often be required to show proof that your **travel insurance** will cover you for whitewater rafting (occasionally you may be asked to sign an insurance disclaimer). If you are unsure about it, and are planning to go rafting, it is worth checking with your insurance company before you leave, as some policies have an additional charge. Very few policies cover Grade V rafting so read the small print.

When signing up you should ask about the experience of the **guides** or, if possible, meet them. Firstly, find out their command of English (or whatever language; there are a few German-speaking guides available), essential if you are going to understand commands. Find out about their experience. How many times have they done this particular stretch of river? Many Peruvian guides have worked overseas. The more international experience a guide has, the more aware they will be of international safety practices. All guides should have some experience in rescue techniques. All guides must have knowledge of first aid. Ask when they last took a course and what level they are at.

Good **equipment** is essential for your safe enjoyment of your trip. If possible ask to see some of the gear provided. Essentials include self-bailing rafts for all but the calmest of rivers. Check how old your raft is and where it was made. Satellite phones are an indispensable piece of safety equipment on long trips in remote areas: does the company use them (they are not yet standard on the Apurímac)? Paddles should be of plastic and metal construction. Wooden paddles can snap, but a few companies use locally made ones which can be excellent, but expensive (in either case, losing a paddle should be of less importance to the company than the safety of the rafter). Helmets should always be provided and fit correctly (home-made fibreglass copies are inadequate). Life jackets must be of a lifeguard-recognized quality and be replaced regularly as they have a tendency to lose their flotation; locally made jackets don't float as well. Does your company provide wetsuits (some of the rivers are surprisingly cold), or, at the very least, quality splash jackets, as the wind can cause you to chill rapidly? On the longer trips, dry bags are provided – what state are these in? How old are they? Do they leak? There is nothing worse than a soggy sleeping bag at the end of a day's rafting. Are tents provided? And, most importantly for the jungle, do the zips on the mosquito net work and is it rain proof? Does the company provide mosquito netting dining tents? Tables? Chairs? These apparent excesses are a bonus when camping for some time at the bottom of a sandfly-infested canyon!

Ask to see the **first aid kit** and find out what is in there and, most importantly, do they know how to use it? When was it last checked? Or updated?

Ask about **food**. Good, wholesome food is relatively cheap in Peru and can make all the difference on a long trip. Once again, you pay for what you get. Ask if there's a vegetarian option. On the food preparation, simple precautions will help you stay healthy. Are all vegetables soaked in iodine before serving? Do the cooks wash their hands and is there soap available for the clients? Are the plates, pots and cutlery

washed in iodine or simply swilled in the river? (Stop and think how many villages upstream use that river as their main sewage outlet.)

On the Apurímac, the operator should provide a chemical **toilet** and remove all toilet paper and other rubbish. In the past, certain beaches have been subject to a completely uncaring attitude over toilet paper and human excrement. At the very least your company should provide a lighter for burning the paper and a trowel to dig a hole; always bury it deep and watch out when burning the paper so as not to start a fire. It is normal practice for guides to check the campsite on arrival and then again before leaving to ensure it is clean. If your company does not, make it your responsibility to encourage other members of the group to keep the campsites clean of **rubbish**. When cooking, bottled gas is used; neither driftwood nor cut trees should be burnt.

Above all it is your **safety** on the river that is important. Some companies are now offering safety kayaks as standard, as well as safety catarafts on certain rivers. This is open to misuse. Sometimes safety kayakers have little or no experience of what they are required to do and are just along for the ride; sometimes they are asked to shoot video (rendering the safety cover useless). A safety cataraft is useless if weighed down with equipment. All companies should carry at the very least a wrap kit, consisting of static ropes, carabiners, slings and pulleys should a raft get stuck. But check if the guides know how to use it.

If this has not put you off, you are now equipped to go out there and find the company that offers what you are looking for at a price you think is reasonable. Bear in mind a basic day's rafting in the USA can cost between US$75-120. In Peru you might get the same for just US$25, but ask yourself what you are getting for so little. As it is, rafts and equipment cost more in Peru.

★ Head for ...

The Abyss Below Puente Cunyac is a section of rarely run whitewater. This extreme expedition involves days of carrying rafts around treacherous rapids; few have attempted it.

Choquequirao, page 232. Another rarely run section, this 10-day adventure involves a walk in with mules, a chance to visit the amazing ruins of Choquequirao and raft huge rapids in an imposing sheer-sided canyon all the way to the jungle basin.

Chuquicahuana (rainy season, Grade IV to V+; dry season, Grade II to IV.) In the rainy season, this is a technically demanding day trip for genuine adrenaline junkies. In the dry season this section makes a good alternative from the now terribly polluted sections further downstream (Huambutío–Pisac, Ollantaytambo–Chilca, see above) and provides several hours of fun, with 3 km of rapids (technical) with much cleaner water and all in a very pretty canyon. Strict safety procedures are needed all year round.

Cusipata, page 224. (Rainy season, Grade III to IV; dry season Grade II to III.) Often used as a warm-up section in high water before attempting Chuquicahuana. This section has fun rapids and a beautiful mini-canyon, which, in low water, is ideal for inflatable canoes (duckies). Again the water purity is much better than the lower sections.

Cuzco region, page 64. This is probably the rafting capital of Peru, with more whitewater runs on offer than anywhere else in the country.

Huambutío–Pisac, page 212. (All year availability, Grade II.) A scenic half-day float with a few rapids to get the adrenaline flowing, right through the heart of the Sacred Valley of the Incas. Fits in perfectly with a day trip to Pisac market. A sedate introduction to rafting for all ages.

Huarán Canyon, page 136. (All year, Grade III+ to V+ depending on season.) A short section of fun whitewater that is occasionally rafted and used as the site of the Peruvian National Whitewater Championships for

kayaking and rafting. Definitely not for beginners in the rainy season.

Kiteni–Pongo Mainique (the bit made famous by Michael Palin). An interesting jungle gorge, but logistically hard to reach and technically pretty average except in the rainy season.

Ollantaytambo–Chilca (all year availability, Grade III to IV+ depending on season). A fun half-day introduction to the exciting sport of whitewater rafting with a few challenging rapids and some beautiful scenery near the Inca 'fortress' of Ollantaytambo. This trip also fits in perfectly with the start of the Inca Trail. Try to go early in the morning as a strong wind picks up in the late morning.

Pinipampa (all year availability, Grade I to II). A fun and beautiful section, rarely paddled but relatively clean; no major rapids but a fun canoeing or ducky trip for beginners. Get out at the Huambutío start point, before the Huatanay disgorges Cuzco's raw sewage into the Urubamba.

Puente Hualpachaca–Puente Cunyac (May-Nov, Grade IV to V). 3-4 days of non-stop whitewater adventure through an awesome gorge just 5 hrs' drive from Cuzco. Probably the most popular multi-day trip, this is one to book with the experts as there have been fatalities on this stretch.

Río Apurímac, page 231. Technically the true source of the Amazon, the Apurímac cuts a 2000-m-deep gorge through incredible desert scenery and offers some of the finest whitewater rafting on the planet.

Santa María–Quillabamba (dry season, Grade III to IV). A rarely rafted 2-day high jungle trip. A long way to go for some fairly good whitewater but mediocre jungle.

Tambopata, page 254. (Jun-Oct, Grade III to IV.) Wilderness, wildlife and whitewater, the Tambopata is the ultimate jungle adventure for those looking to get away from the standard organized jungle package. Starting with a drive from the shores of Lake Titicaca to the end of the road, the Tambopata travels through the very heart of the Tambopata

National Reserve. 4 days of fun whitewater followed by 2 days of gentle meandering through virgin tropical rainforest where silent rafts make perfect wildlife watching platforms. The final stage is a visit to the world's largest macaw clay lick and a short flight out from Puerto Maldonado.

Urubamba, page 141. Perhaps the most popular day run Peru, but sadly one heavily affected in parts by pollution both from Cuzco (the Río Huatanay joins the Urubamba by Huambutio and is one of the main sewage outlets of Cuzco) and from the towns of the Sacred Valley, who regularly dump their waste directly into the river. A recent clean-up campaign organized by various rafting companies removed 16 tons of rubbish, predominantly plastic bags and bottles, but it just touched the surface of the problem. See also box, page 135.

Getting there

Air

Unless you are flying from Bolivia, it is not possible to take an international flight direct to Cuzco; you have to fly via Lima. While it may be possible to make a connection to get you to Cuzco the same day you land in Peru, as often as not you will have to spend some time in the capital before flying up to the highlands. Many organized tours include a day or so in Lima as a matter of course. This allows you to get your bearings after your flight and see a bit of the city.

Airport information Lima's Jorge Chávez Airport will be your point of entry into Peru, see page 270.

Airport departure tax There is a US\$31 departure tax for international flights. For national flights the airport tax is US\$7. From 1 January 2011 both international and domestic airport taxes will be included in the price of flight tickets, not paid at the airport. Tickets purchased in Peru also include the 19% state tax.

From Europe and the Middle East There are direct flights to Lima only from Amsterdam (**KLM** via Bonaire) and Madrid (**Iberia**, **Air Europa** and **LAN**). **Air France** is due to start Paris–Lima flights in 2011. From London, Frankfurt, Rome, Milan, Lisbon or other European cities, the best connections are made in Madrid, or via Brazilian or US gateways. From Tel Aviv, make connections in either Madrid or Miami.

From North America Miami is the main gateway to Peru, together with Atlanta, Dallas, Houston, Los Angeles and New York. Airlines, not all direct, include **American Airlines**, **Continental**, **Delta**, **LAN**, **TACA**, **Copa** and **AeroMéxico**. Daily connections can be made from almost all major North American cities. From Toronto, **Air Canada** flies to Lima, but not daily. From Vancouver, there are no direct flights or connections; fly via one of the above gateways.

From Australia, New Zealand or South Africa There are no obvious connecting flights from either Australia or New Zealand to Lima. One option would be to go to Buenos Aires from Sydney or Auckland (four flights a week with **Aerolíneas Argentinas**) and fly on from there (several flights daily). Alternatively, fly to Los Angeles and travel down from there. From Johannesburg, make connections in Buenos Aires or São Paulo.

From Latin America There are regular flights (daily in many cases) to Peru from most South American countries. The **LAN** group has the most routes to Lima within the continent. The **TACA** group also has quite extensive coverage, including to Central America and Mexico.

From Asia From Hong Kong, Seoul and Singapore, connections have to be made in Los Angeles. Make connections in Los Angeles or Miami if flying from Tokyo.

Baggage allowance There is always a weight limit for your baggage, but there is no standard baggage allowance to Peru. If you fly via the USA you are allowed two pieces of luggage up to 32 kg per case. The American airlines are usually a bit more expensive but if you are travelling with a 40-kg bag of climbing gear, it may be worth looking into. On flights from Europe there is a weight allowance of 20 kg or 23 kg, although some carriers out of Europe use the two-piece system, but may not apply it in both directions. The two-piece system is gaining wider acceptance, but it is always best to check in advance. At busy times of the year it can be very difficult and expensive to bring items such as bikes and surfboards along. Many airlines will let you pay a penalty for overweight baggage – often this is US$5 per kg – but this usually depends on how full the flight is. Check first before you assume you can bring extra luggage. The weight limit for internal flights is often 20 kg or less per person.

Reconfirming flights

It is very important to reconfirm your flights when flying internally in Peru or leaving the country. This can be done in the case of e-tickets by checking-in online, 24-48 hours in advance. Otherwise, phone or visit the airline office directly 48-72 hours in advance. Some travel agents may reconfirm a flight, but you may have to pay a service charge. If you do not reconfirm your internal or international flight, you may not get on the plane.

Prices and discounts Most airlines offer discounted fares on scheduled flights through agencies who specialize in this type of fare. The very busy seasons are from 7 December to 15 January and from 10 July to 10 September. If you intend travelling during those times, book as far ahead as possible. From February to May and from September to November special offers may be available. Examples of fares on scheduled airlines are: from the UK a return with flexible dates will cost about £620, low season 2010 prices. A low season return from Miami to Lima cost from US$590 in 2010. From Sydney, Australia, return fares start at US$1600. Note that taxes and fuel surcharges may apply to these fares.

If you buy discounted air tickets always check the reservation with the airline concerned to make sure the flight still exists. Also remember the IATA airlines' schedules change in March and October each year, so if you're going to be away a long time it's best to leave return flight coupons open. In addition, check whether you are entitled to any refund or re-issued ticket if you lose, or have stolen, a discounted air ticket. Some airlines require the repurchase of a ticket before you can apply for a refund, which will not be given until after the validity of the original ticket has expired. Travel insurance in some cases covers lost tickets.

Discount flight agents

In the UK and Ireland
Journey Latin America, 12-13 Heathfield Terr, London W4 4JE, T020-8747 8315, www.journeylatinamerica.co.uk.
STA Travel, T0871-230 0040, www.statravel.co.uk. 45 branches in the UK, including many university campuses. Specialists in low-cost flights and tours, good for student IDs and insurance.
Trailfinders, 194 Kensington High St, London W8 7RG, T020-7938 3939, www.trailfinders.com. 22 branches in London and throughout the UK. Also 2 branches in Ireland (Dublin, Cork) and 2 travel centres in Australia (Brisbane, Sydney, www.trailfinders.com.au).
Trips Worldwide, 14 Frederick Pl, Clifton, Bristol BS8 1AS, T0800-840 0850, www.tripsworldwide.co.uk.

In North America
Discount Airfares Worldwide On-Line, www.etn.nl/discount.htm. A hub of consolidator and discount agent links.
eXito, 108 Rutgers Av, Fort Collins, CO 80525, USA, T1-800-655 4053 (USA), T800-670 2605 (Canada), www.exitotravel.com.
STA Travel, T1-800-781-4040, www.statravel.com. 18 branches in the USA, including university campuses.
Travel CUTS, in all major Canadian cities and on university and college campuses, T1-866-246-9762, www.travelcuts.com. Specialist in student discount fares, IDs and other travel services.

In Australia and New Zealand
Flight Centre, with offices throughout Australia and other countries. In Australia call T133 133 or www.flightcentre.com.au.
STA Travel, see above. In NZ: 130 Cuba St, Wellington, T04-385 0561, T0800-474400, www.statravel.co.nz. Also in major towns and university campuses.
Travel.com.au, Level 10, 17 York St, Sydney, NSW 2000, T1300 130 481, www.travel.com.au.

Note Using the internet for booking flights, hotels and other services directly is increasingly popular and you can get some good deals this way. But don't forget that a travel agent can find the best flights to suit your itinerary, as well as providing advice on documents, insurance, safety, routes, lodging and times of year to travel. A reputable agent will also be bonded to give you some protection if things go wrong.

Road
There are bus services from neighbouring countries to Peru. If coming from Bolivia, there are direct buses to Cuzco and Puno from La Paz. On rare occasions, customs officials at international borders may ask for a forward ticket out of the country. This means you'll have to buy the cheapest bus ticket out of Peru before they let you in. Note that these tickets are not transferable or refundable.

Getting around

Air

Low promotional tariffs are renewed monthly; often it is best to wait to purchase internal flights until your arrival. There are no deals for round-trip tickets and prices can rise within four days of the flight.

Lima to Cuzco is the main tourist axis in Peru and there are plenty of flights between the two cities. Most flights are in the morning, giving people in organized groups and independent travellers an early start. If you're on a tight schedule, then by far the best option is to fly from Lima to **Cuzco** (55 minutes, daily services), and then from Cuzco to **Puerto Maldonado**, if you're planning a trip to Tambopata (30 minutes, also daily services). Flights to **Boca Manu** for Manu are normally arranged through a tour operator (also 30 minutes). ▶ *For details of Cuzco airport, see page 64.*

Airlines and tickets The main national airlines serving the most travelled routes (of which Cuzco is the prime example) are **Star Perú** (www.starperu.com), **LAN** (www.lan.com) and **Peruvian Airlines** (www.peruvianairlines.pe). **Grupo TACA**, (www.grupotaca.com), offers a service on the Lima–Cuzco route. Flights start at about US$100 one-way anywhere in the country from Lima, but prices vary greatly between airlines, with **LAN** being the most expensive for non-Peruvians. Prices often increase at holiday times (Semana Santa, May Day, Inti Raymi, 28-29 July, Christmas and New Year), and for elections. During these times and the northern hemisphere summer, seats can be hard to come by, so book early. There are no deals for round-trip tickets. Internal flight prices are given in US dollars but can be paid in soles and the price should include the 19% general sales tax. Tickets are not interchangeable between companies but sometimes exceptions will be made in the case of cancellations. Do check with companies for special offers. If the price sounds too good to be true, double check your ticket to make sure you are not being sold a ticket for Peruvian nationals; these tickets are often half price but you need to show Peruvian ID to get on the plane.

Advice and information On the Cuzco–Lima route there is a high possibility of cancelled flights during the wet season; tourists are sometimes stranded for several days. It is possible for planes to leave early if the weather is bad. Always give yourself an extra day between national and international flights to allow for any schedule changes. Flights are often overbooked so it is very important to reconfirm your tickets at least 24 hours in advance of your flight and, in the high season, make sure you arrive at the airport two hours before departure to avoid problems. By law, the clerk can start to sell reserved seats to stand-by travellers 30 minutes before the flight. To save time and hassle, travel with carry-on luggage only (48 cm x 24 cm x 37 cm). This will guarantee that your luggage arrives at the airport when you do.

Road

Peru's road network is being upgraded and better roads mean better bus services and improved conditions for drivers. However, Peru is no different from other Latin American countries in that travelling by road at night or in bad weather should be treated with great care. It is also true that there are many more unpaved than paved roads, so overland travel is not really an option if you only have a few weeks' holiday.

Domestic airlines

LAN Perú, Av José Pardo 513, Miraflores, Lima, T01-213 8200, www.lan.com. Flights from Lima to Arequipa, Cajamarca, Chiclayo, Cuzco, Iquitos, Juliaca, Pucallpa, Piura, Puerto Maldonado, Tacna, Tarapoto and Trujillo and from Cuzco to Arequipa, Juliaca, Lima, Puerto Maldonado and Tacna.

LC Busre, Los Tulipanes 218, Urb San Eugenio, Lima 14, T01-619 1313, www.lcbusre.com.pe. Flights from Lima to Andahuaylas, Ayacucho, Cajamarca, Huancayo, Huánuco and Huaraz.

Star Perú, Av Comandante Espinar 331, Miraflores, Lima 18, T01-705-9000, www.starperu.com. Flights from Lima to Andahualas, Arequipa, Ayacucho, Chiclayo, Cuzco, Huánuco, Iquitos, Juliaca, Pucallpa, Puerto Maldonado, Talara, Tarapoto and Trujillo.

Taca Perú, Av Pardo 811, Miraflores, Lima, T01-511 8222 or T01-800-1TACA (8222), www.grupotaca.com. Flights between Lima and Cuzco, Juliaca, Tarapoto and Trujillo.

Getting around the country overland can be a difficult task and this is to be expected in a country whose geography is dominated by the Andes, one of the world's major mountain ranges. Great steps have been taken to improve major roads and enlarge the paved network linking the Pacific coast with the Highlands. It is worth taking some time to plan a journey in advance, checking which roads are finished, which have roadworks and which will be affected by the weather. The highland and jungle wet season, from mid-October to late March, can seriously hamper travel. It is important to allow extra time if planning to go overland at this time.

The Pan-American Highway runs north–south through the coastal desert and is mostly in good condition. From Nazca to Abancay and on to Cuzco is paved. This is now the main route from Lima to Cuzco. The main roads in and to the Sacred Valley from Cuzco are also paved. The Cuzco–Puno highway is fully paved and is a fast, comfortable journey to rival the train. The paved road continues along the south shore of Lake Titicaca to Desaguadero on the Bolivian border. In the main, mountain roads are of dirt, some good, some very bad. Each year they are affected by heavy rain and mud slides, especially those on the eastern slopes of the mountains. Repairs can be delayed because of a shortage of funds. This makes for slow travel and frequent breakdowns. Note that some of these roads can be dangerous or impassable in the rainy season. Check beforehand with locals (not with bus companies, who only want to sell tickets) as accidents are common at these times.

Bus Services along the coast to the north and south as well as inland are generally good, but since 2008 the number of accidents and hold-ups on buses has increased. You should also be prepared for blockades of highways by strikes and protests, which may cause delays. On long-distance journeys it is advisable to pay a bit extra and take a reliable company. All major bus companies operate modern buses with two decks on interdepartmental routes. The first deck is called *bus-cama*, the second *semi-cama*. Both have seats that recline, *bus-cama* further than *semi-cama*. These buses usually run late at night and are more expensive than ordinary buses, which tend to run earlier in the day. Many buses have toilets and show movies. Each company has a different name for its regular and *cama* or *ejecutivo* services. In the text below prices give only a general idea of bus fares; there is great variation between companies and between days of the week. Look out for promotional offers.

Cruz del Sur and **Ormeño** are bus lines covering most of the country. **Cruz del Sur**, generally regarded as a class above the others, accepts Visa cards and gives 10% discount to ISIC and Under26 cardholders (you may have to insist). There are many smaller but still excellent bus lines that run only to specific areas. An increasing number accept bookings on the internet. ►► *For contact details of national bus companies, see Lima Transport, page 302.*

With the better companies you will get a receipt for your luggage, it will be locked under the bus and you shouldn't have to worry about it at stops because the storage is not usually opened. On local buses there will be lots of people getting on and off the buses, loading and unloading bags, so it's best to watch your luggage. It will provide you with a good excuse to get off the bus and stretch anyway. Do not put your day bag above your head or on the floor inside the bus; keep it on your lap or beside you. It is too easy for someone to grab your bag and get off without your realizing. If you decide to get off the bus at a stop, take all your carry-on items with you. If you want to buy a return ticket from Lima, it is quite often cheaper to wait and buy the return portion when you arrive at your destination. This isn't always the case, but on the major lines things seem to cost more from the capital.

For long journeys be sure to take water and possibly a bit of food, although it is always possible to buy food at the stops along the way. See the warning under Safety, page 50, about not accepting food or drinks from fellow passengers. For mountain routes, have a blanket or at least a jacket handy as the temperature at night can drop quite low. Once you get off the beaten track, the quality of buses and roads deteriorates and you should stick to day buses. If your bus breaks down and you have to get on another bus, you will probably have to pay for the ticket, but keep your old ticket as some bus companies will give refunds. The back seats tend to be the most bumpy and the exhaust pipe is almost always on the left-hand side of the bus.

It is best to try to arrive at your destination during the day; it is safer and easier to find accommodation. Prices of tickets are raised by 60-100% during Semana Santa (Easter), Fiestas Patrias (Independence Day – 28 and 29 July), Navidad (Christmas) and special local events. Prices will usually go up a few days before the holiday and possibly remain higher a few days after. Tickets also sell out during these times so if travelling then, buy your ticket as soon as you know what day you want to travel.

Car hire The airport in Lima is the best and most cost-effective place to arrange car hire (see page 303). The minimum age for renting a car is 25. If renting a car, your home driving licence will be accepted for up to six months. Car hire companies are given in the text. They do tend to be very expensive, reflecting the high costs and accident rates. Hotels and tourist agencies will tell you where to find cheaper rates, but you will need to check that you have such basics as spare wheel, tool kit and functioning lights, etc.

Check exactly what the hirer's insurance policy covers. In many cases it will only protect you against minor bumps and scrapes, not major accidents, nor 'natural' damage (eg flooding). Ask if extra cover is available. Also find out, if using a credit card, whether the card automatically includes insurance. Beware of being billed for scratches which were on the vehicle before you hired it.

Touring y Automóvil Club del Perú ① *Av Trinidad Morán 698, Lince, T01-614 9999, www.touringperu.com.pe,* offers help to tourists and particularly to members of the leading motoring associations. The Club publishes touring guides and maps to northern, central and southern Peru (available as pdf on their website).

Maps Good maps are available from street sellers in the centre of Lima, or in better bookshops (published by **Lima 2000**, T01-440 3486, www.lima2000.com.pe). Lima 2000's *Mapa Vial del Perú* (1:2,200,000) is probably the best and most correct road map available for the country. The **Instituto Geográfico Nacional** in Lima sells a selection of good, accurate country and regional maps. **South American Explorers**, who will give good advice on road conditions, stock an excellent collection of maps. In the UK, **Stanfords** ① *12-14 Longacre, London WC2E 9LP, T020-78361321, www.stanfords. co.uk, with a branch in Bristol*, stocks an excellent range.

Fuel 84 octane petrol/gasoline costs US$3.95 per gallon; 90 octane, US$4.20; 95 octane, US$5.15; 98 octane, US$5.40. Diesel costs US$4. Unleaded fuel is available in large cities and along the Panamericana, but rarely in the highlands.

Combis, colectivos and trucks Combis operate between most small towns in the Andes on one- to three-hour journeys. This makes it possible, in many cases, just to turn up and travel within an hour or two. On rougher roads, combis are minibuses, while on better roads there are also slightly more expensive and much faster car colectivos, often called *autos*, or *cars*. Both operate in the Sacred Valley area. Colectivos are shared taxis that usually charge twice the bus fare and leave only when full. Most firms have offices. If you book one day in advance, they will pick you up at your hotel or in the main plaza. Trucks are not always much cheaper than buses. They charge 75% of the bus fare, but are wholly unpredictable. They are not recommended for long trips and comfort depends on the load.

Cycling Unless you are planning a journey almost exclusively on paved roads, a mountain bike is strongly recommended. The good-quality ones (and the cast-iron rule is never to skimp on quality) are incredibly tough and rugged, with low gear ratios for difficult terrain, wide tyres with plenty of tread for good road-holding, V brakes, sealed hubs and bottom bracket and a low centre of gravity for improved stability. A chrome-alloy frame is a desirable choice over aluminium as it can be welded if necessary. Once an aluminium frame breaks, it's broke. Although touring bikes, and to a lesser extent mountain bikes and spares are available in the larger cities, remember that most locally manufactured goods are shoddy and rarely last. (Shimano parts are generally the easiest to find.) Buy everything you possibly can before you leave home.

Remember that you can always stick your bike on a bus, canoe or plane to get yourself nearer to the heart of where you want your wheels to take you. This is especially useful when there are long stretches of major road ahead, where all that awaits you are hours of turbulence as the constant stream of heavy trucks and long-haul buses zoom by. It is possible to rent a bike for a few days, or join an organized tour for riding in the mountains. You should check, however, that the machine you are hiring is up to the conditions you will be encountering, or that the tour company is not a fly-by-night outfit without back-up, good bikes or maintenance.

South American Explorers have valuable cycling information that is continuously updated. Visit **www.warmshowers.org** for a hospitality exchange for touring cyclists. A related organization is **Cyclo-Camping International** ① *25 rue Ramus, 75020 Paris, France, T01-4797 6218, www.cci.asso.fr*.

Hitchhiking Hitchhiking in Peru is neither easy, owing to the lack of private vehicles, nor entirely risk-free. For obvious reasons, a lone female should not hitch by herself. Besides, you are more likely to get a lift if you are with a partner, whether they are male or female. The best combination is a male and female together. Positioning is also key. Freight traffic in Peru has to stop at the police *garitas* outside each town and these are the best places to try (also toll points, but these are further out of town).

Note Drivers usually ask for money but they don't always expect to get it. In mountain and jungle areas you usually have to pay drivers of lorries, vans and even private cars; ask the driver first how much they are going to charge, and then doublecheck with the locals.

Motorcycling The motorcycle should be off-road capable. A road bike can go most places an off-road bike can go. Get to know the bike before you go, ask the dealers in your country what goes wrong with it and arrange a link whereby you can get parts flown out to you. Get the book for international dealer coverage from your manufacturer, but don't rely on it. They frequently have few or no parts for modern, large machinery. An Abus D or chain will keep the bike secure. A cheap alarm gives you peace of mind if you leave the bike outside a hotel at night. Most hotels will allow you to bring the bike inside (see accommodation listings in the travelling text for details). Look for hotels that have a courtyard or more secure parking and never leave luggage on the bike overnight or whilst unattended. Passport, international driving licence and bike registration document are necessary. Riders fare much better with a *carnet de passages* than without it.

Taxis Taxi prices are fixed and cost around US$0.75-1.20 in the urban areas. In Lima prices range from US$2-4, but fares are not fixed. Some drivers work for companies that do have standard fares. Ask locals what the price should be and always set the price beforehand. Taxis at airports are often a bit more expensive, but ask locals what the price should be as taxi drivers may try to charge you three times the correct price. Many taxi drivers work for commission from hotels and will try to convince you to go to that hotel. Feel free to choose your own hotel and go there. If you walk away from the Arrivals gate a bit, the fares should go down to a price that is reasonable.

Another common form of public transport is the *mototaxi*, or *motocarro*. This is a three-wheel motorcycle with an awning covering the double-seat behind the driver. Fares are about US$1.

Train

Peru's national rail service was privatized in 1999. The lines of major interest to the traveller are Cuzco–Machu Picchu, on which three companies operate services (see page 64) and Puno–Juliaca–Cuzco, run by **PerúRail**, www.perurail.com. Train schedules may be cut in the rainy season.

Sleeping

Cuzco is full of excellent-value hotels throughout the price ranges and finding a room to suit your budget should not present any problems. The exception to this is during Christmas and Easter, Carnival in June and Independence celebrations at the end of July, when all hotels seem to be crowded. It's advisable to book in advance at these times and during school holidays and local festivals (see page 37).

Accommodation, as with everything else, is more expensive in Lima, where good budget hotels are fewer and therefore tend to be busy. Remote jungle towns such as Puerto Maldonado also tend to be more expensive than the norm. And if you want a room with air conditioning expect to pay around 30% extra. All hotels in the upper price brackets charge 19% general sales tax (IGV) and 10% service on top of prices (foreigners should not have to pay the sales tax on hotel rooms; neither tax is included in prices given in the accommodation listings, unless specified). The more expensive hotels also charge in dollars according to the rate of exchange at midnight.

By law all places that offer accommodation now have a plaque outside bearing the letters **H** (**Hotel**), **Hs** (**Hostal**), **HR** (**Hotel Residencial**) or **P** (**Pensión**) according to type. A hotel has 51 rooms or more, a *hostal* 50 or fewer, but the categories do not describe quality or facilities. Generally speaking, though, a *pensión* or *hospedaje* will be cheaper than a hotel or *hostal*. Most mid-range hotels have their own restaurants serving lunch and dinner, as well as breakfast. Many budget places serve breakfast – almost invariably continental breakfast. Many hotels have safe parking for motor cycles. Most places are friendly, irrespective of the price, particularly smaller *pensiones* and *hospedajes*, which are often family run and will treat you as another member of the family. Cheaper places don't always supply soap, towels and toilet paper. In colder (higher) regions they may not supply enough blankets, so take your own or a sleeping bag.

Youth hostels

The office of the Youth Hostel Association of Peru, **Asociación Peruana de Albergues Turísticos Juveniles** and **Administradora Peruana Hostelling International** ⓘ *Av Casimiro Ulloa 328, Miraflores, Lima T01-446 5488, www.hostellingperu.com.pe or www.limahostell.com.pe*, has information about youth hostels. For information about International Student Identity Cards (ISIC) and lists of discounts available to cardholders contact **Intej**, see page 52.

Camping

This normally presents no problems in Peru. There can, however, be problems with robbery when camping close to a small village. Avoid such a location, or ask permission to camp in a backyard or *chacra* (farmland). Most Peruvians are used to campers. Be casual about it, do not unpack all your gear, leave it inside your tent (especially at night) and never leave a tent unattended.

Camping gas in little blue bottles is available. Those with stoves designed for lead-free gasoline should use *ron de quemar*, available from hardware shops (*ferreterías*). White gas is called *bencina*, also available from hardware stores. If you use a stove system that uses canisters make sure you dispose of the empty canisters properly; the same goes for all rubbish. Keep in mind that you are responsible for the trash that your group, guide or mule driver may drop and it is up to you to say something and pick

Sleeping price codes

LL over US$200		**L** US$151-200		**AL** US$101-150	
A US$66-100		**B** US$46-65		**C** US$31-45	
D US$21-30		**E** US$12-20		**F** US$7-11	
G US$6 and under					

Prices given are for two people sharing a double room with bathroom (shower and toilet), unless the establishment charges per person, including taxes. If travelling alone, it's usually cheaper to share with others in a room with three or four beds. Prices are for the busy seasons (May-September, Christmas-February and Holy Week). During the low season, when many places may be half empty, it's often possible to bargain the room rate down. Note that the dollar/soles exchange rate can fluctuate substantially.

LL, L, AL and **A** Hotels in these categories are usually only found in the largest cities and main tourist centres. They should offer extensive leisure and business facilities, plus restaurants and bars. Most will provide a safe box in each room. Credit cards are usually accepted.

B and **C** These hotels range from very good to functional. You can expect breakfast, your own bathroom, a/c in tropical areas, plenty of hot water and towels, soap, shampoo, cable TV, a sitting area and a comfortable room.

D and **E** These are the most common categories and some offer very good value for money. Expect cleanliness, a private bathroom, hot water in the highlands, a/c or fan in the tropics, TV, maybe a simple breakfast, but no other frills.

F and **G** A room in these price ranges is small and consists of little more than a bed and walls. The bathroom is shared and soap, towels, toilet paper or a toilet seat are seldom supplied. In the highlands they may not have enough blankets, so take a sleeping bag. In the lowlands insects are common, use the mosquito net or bring your own, and ignore the cockroaches – they're harmless.

In shared rooms expect to pay from **G** to **E** per person, depending on the number of people sharing and the type of hostel. These range from the very basic to the 'boutique'. Many places offer single-sex dormitories. Some shared rooms have their own bath, others use communal showers. Almost all provide lockers for your belongings.

it up. Often the rubbish that is on the trails is blamed on locals and this is not usually the case; low-impact travel is everyone's responsibility and while you are picking up your own trash, pick up other people's too.

Advice and suggestions

If travelling alone, it's usually cheaper to share with others in a room with three or four beds. If breakfast is included in the price, it will almost invariably mean continental breakfast. During the low season, when many places may be half empty, it's often possible to bargain the room rate down. Reception areas in hotels may be misleading, so it is a good idea to see the room before booking. Many hoteliers try to offload their least desirable rooms first. If you're shown a dark box without any furniture, ask if there's another room with a window or a desk for writing letters. The difference is often surprising.

When booking a hotel from an airport or station by phone, always talk to the hotel yourself; do not let anyone do it for you (except an accredited hotel booking service). You will be told the hotel of your choice is full and be directed to a more expensive one.

Bathrooms and toilets

The electric showers used in many hotels (basic up to mid-range) are a health and safety nightmare. Avoid touching any part of the shower while it is producing hot water and always get out before you switch it off.

Except in the most upmarket hotels and restaurants, most Peruvian toilets are barely adequate at best. The further you go from the main population and tourist centres, the poorer the facilities, so you may require a strong stomach and the ability to hold your breath for a long time. Almost without exception used toilet paper or feminine hygiene products should not be flushed down the pan, but placed in the receptacle provided. This applies even in quite expensive hotels. Failing to observe this custom will block the pan or drain, which can be a considerable health risk.

Eating and drinking

Peruvian cuisine

Not surprisingly for a country with such a diversity of geography and climates, Peru boasts the continent's most extensive menu. Its cuisine varies from region to region, but basically can be divided into coastal, highland and tropical. Peru also prides itself on its new, fusion cuisine, claiming for itself the title 'gastronomic capital of South America'. Many if the dishes include native ingredients and pre-Hispanic recipes which are combined with better-known ingredients in innovative and delicious ways. The commonly applied term for this type of food is *novo andino*. Chefs such as Gastón Acurio, who has opened Peruvian restaurants in many countries, is gaining for Peruvian food a worldwide reputation

Coastal cuisine

With a coastline of more than 1800 km, the fruits of the sea are almost limitless. Sea bass, flounder, salmon, red snapper, sole and shellfish are all in abundance. The best coastal dishes are those with seafood bases, with the most popular being the jewel in the culinary crown, *ceviche*. This delicious dish of raw white fish marinated in lemon juice, onion and hot peppers can be found in neighbouring countries, but Peruvian is best. Ask for 'sin picante' if you don't want it hot. Traditionally, *ceviche* is served with corn-on-the-cob, *cancha* (toasted corn), yucca and sweet potatoes. Another mouth-watering fish dish is *escabeche* – fish with onions, hot green pepper, red peppers, prawns (*langostinos*), cumin, hard-boiled eggs, olives, and sprinkled with cheese. For fish on its own, don't miss the excellent *corvina*, or white sea bass. You should also try *chupe de camarones*, which is a shrimp stew made with varying and somewhat surprising ingredients. Other fish dishes include *parihuela*, a popular bouillabaisse that includes *yuyo de mar*, a tangy seaweed, and *aguadito*, a thick rice and fish soup said to have rejuvenating powers.

Fish isn't the only thing eaten on the coast. A favourite northern coastal dish is *seco de cabrito*, roasted kid (baby goat) served with beans and rice, or *seco de cordero,* which uses lamb instead. Also good is *ají de gallina*, a rich and spicy creamed chicken, and duck is excellent.

A limp excuse

Did you know there is a potato that has the opposite effect of Viagra? It's a tuber named *año* and Cuzqueña women have been known to use it to take revenge on cheating husbands. If a man is unfaithful, his wife will boil his trousers in a vat containing the potato – enough to stop him rising to any occasion!

Stories like these are part of the fun of discovering Cuzco's markets. Wandering round one is a great experience, packed with new sights, smells and the bright colours of unknown fruit and veg. At San Jerónimo you'll find *huacatay* (a mint grown at high altitude and used in the preparation of guinea pig), bulls' testicles (boiled, sliced and used in salads), huge sacks of dirt-cheap garlic, massive 20-25 kg pumpkins, *pepiño* (which has a creamy-coloured skin and is very refreshing), as well as strawberries from the coast, basil, coriander, green chilli peppers and spinach.

There is *caihua*, from the cucumber family, which grows only in sub-tropical valleys and which can be stuffed or chopped for stir-fry or salad. Then there is a dried black potato which smells of bad feet when it is cooked, but is favoured by locals nevertheless; they grind it up and add it to food.

Then there are potatoes frozen overnight as hard as rocks to bring out their flavour; these are mixed with salt and eaten with cheese. These, together with olives, oranges and tomatoes piled high in large mounds, are weighed out by indigenous women who proudly show off their region of origin by the different hats they wear.

Most Westerners will shrink from ever sampling these foodstuffs – especially when a lamb's head, complete with lipless, grinning teeth bobs to the surface of *caldo de cabeza*, the favourite soup here. (Locals pay a premium for this if it includes brain and tongue.) However, the sight of so much variety, of bright yellow bananas balanced chest-high, of brown guinea pigs scurrying around cages and of heady herbs sold by the sackful, is one worth seeking out. Just don't try the tuber named *año*!

People on the coast are referred to as *criollos* (see page 330) and *criollo* cooking can be found throughout the country. A dish almost guaranteed to appear on every restaurant menu is *lomo saltado*, a kind of stir-fried beef with onions, vinegar, ginger, chilli, tomatoes and fried potatoes, served with rice. Other popular examples are *cau cau*, made with tripe, potatoes, peppers and parsley, served with rice, and *anticuchos*, which are shish kebabs of beef heart with garlic, peppers, cumin seeds and vinegar. *Rocoto relleno* is spicy bell pepper stuffed with beef and vegetables, *palta rellena* is avocado filled with chicken or Russian salad, *estofado de carne* is a stew that often contains wine and *carne en adobo* is a cut and seasoned steak. Two good dishes that use potatoes are *causa* and *carapulca*. On coastal menus *causa* is made with mashed potato wrapped around a filling, which often contains crabmeat. On other occasions, *causa* has yellow potatoes, lemons, pepper, hard-boiled eggs, olives, lettuce, sweet cooked corn, sweet cooked potato, fresh cheese, and served with onion sauce.

Highland cuisine

The staples of highland cooking, corn and potatoes, date back to Inca times and are found in a remarkable variety of shapes, sizes and colours. A popular potato dish is *papa a la huancaína*, which is topped with a spicy sauce made with milk and cheese. The most commonly eaten corn dishes are *choclo con queso*, corn on the cob with cheese, and *tamales*, boiled corn dumplings filled with meat and wrapped in a banana leaf. Most typical of highland food is *pachamanca*, a combination of meats (beef, lamb, pork, chicken), potatoes, sweet potatoes, corn, beans, cheese and corn *humitas*, all slow-cooked in the ground, again dating back to Inca times.

Meat dishes are many and varied. *Ollucos con charqui* is a kind of potato with dried meat, *sancochado* is meat and all kinds of vegetables stewed together and seasoned with ground garlic and *lomo a la huancaína* is beef with egg and cheese sauce. Others include *fritos*, fried pork, usually eaten in the morning, *chicharrones*, deep fried chunks of pork ribs and chicken, and *lechón*, suckling pig. And not forgetting that popular childhood pet, *cuy* (guinea pig), which is considered a real delicacy.

Very filling and good value are the many soups on offer, such as *caldos* (broths): eg *de carnero*, *verde*, or *de cabeza*, which includes a sheep's head cooked with corn and tripe. Also *yacu-chupe*, a green soup that has a base of potato, with cheese, garlic, coriander leaves, parsley, peppers, eggs, onions, and mint, and *sopa a la criolla* containing thin noodles, beef heart, bits of egg and vegetables and pleasantly spiced. And not to be outdone in the fish department, *trucha* (trout) is delicious, particularly from Lake Titicaca.

Tropical cuisine
The main ingredient in much jungle cuisine is fish, especially the succulent, dolphin-sized *paiche*, which comes with the delicious *palmito*, or palm-hearts, and the ever-present yucca and fried bananas. *Tocacho* is green banana, cooked and ground to a chunky paste, usually served with pork (*cecina*) and sausage (*chorizo*). *Juanes* are a jungle version of *tamales*, stuffed with chicken and rice. A common dish to start the day is *chapo*, banana porridge, delicious with evaporated milk.

Desserts and fruits
The Peruvian sweet tooth is evident in the huge number of desserts and confections from which to choose. These include: *cocada al horno* – coconut, with yolk of egg, sesame seed, wine and butter; *picarones* – frittered cassava flour and eggs fried in fat and served with honey; *mazamorra morada* – purple maize, sweet potato starch, lemons, various dried fruits, sticks of ground cinnamon and cloves and perfumed pepper; *manjar blanco* – milk, sugar and eggs; *maná* – an almond paste with eggs, vanilla and milk; *alfajores* – shortbread biscuit with *manjar blanco*, pineapple, peanuts, etc; *pastelillos* – yuccas with sweet potato, sugar and anise fried in fat and powdered with sugar and served hot; and *zango de pasas*, made with maize, syrup, raisins and sugar. *Turrón*, the Lima nougat, is worth trying. *Tejas* are pieces of fruit or nut enveloped in *manjar blanco* and covered in chocolate or icing sugar – delicious.

The various Peruvian fruits are wonderful. They include bananas, the citrus fruits, pineapples, dates, avocados (*paltas*), eggfruit (*lúcuma*), the custard apple (*chirimoya* – the 'sweet of the gods' in Quechua) which can be as big as your head, quince, papaya, mango, guava, passion-fruit (*maracuyá*), prickly pear (*tuna*) and the soursop (*guanábana*). These should be tried as juices or ice cream – an unforgettable experience.
▸▸ *For a food and drink glossary, see page 354.*

Eating out
Lunch is the main meal, and apart from the most exclusive places, most restaurants have one or two set lunch menus, called *menú ejecutivo* or *menú económico*. The set menu has

Eating price codes

¶¶¶ Over US$12	¶¶ US$7-12	¶ US$6 and under

Prices are for a two-course meal for one person, excluding drinks or service charge.

the advantage of being ready and is served almost immediately and it is usually cheap. The *menú ejecutivo* costs US$2 or more for a three-course meal with a soft drink and it offers greater choice and more interesting dishes than the *menú económico*, which costs US$1.50-2.50. Don't leave it too late, though, as most Peruvians eat lunch around 1230-1400. There are many Chinese restaurants (*chifas*) that serve good food at reasonable prices, and the *comedores populares* found in the markets of most cities offer a standard three-course meal for as little as US$1 (but keep an eye on cleanliness and hygiene). Buying food on the street is generally best left until your stomach has acclimatized, but avoid hamburgers sold at stalls anywhere in Peru (guaranteed to upset even the hardiest of constitutions).

For those who wish to eschew such good value, the menu is called *la carta*. An *à la carte* lunch or dinner costs US$5-8, but can go up to an expensive US$30 in a first-class Cuzco restaurant, with drinks and wine included (US$80 in Lima). Middle- and high-class restaurants may add 10% service, but do add the 19% sales tax to the bill (which foreigners do have to pay). This is not shown on the price list or menu, so check in advance. Less fancy restaurants charge only the tax, while cheap, local restaurants charge no taxes. Dinner in restaurants is normally about 1900 onwards, but choice may be more limited than lunchtime.

The situation for vegetarians is improving, but slowly. In Cuzco you should have no problem finding a vegetarian restaurant (or a restaurant that has vegetarian options), and the same applies to Lima. Elsewhere, choice is limited and you may find that, as a non-meat eater, you are not understood. Vegetarians and people with allergies should be able to list (in Spanish) all the foods they cannot eat. By saying *No como carne* (I don't eat meat), people may assume that you eat chicken and eggs. If you do eat eggs, make sure they are cooked thoroughly. Restaurant staff will often bend over backwards to get you exactly what you want but you need to request it.

Drink

Peru's most famous drink is *pisco*, a grape brandy, used in the wonderful pisco sour, a deceptively potent cocktail which also includes egg whites and lime juice. The most renowned brands come from the Ica Valley. Other favourites are *chilcano*, a longer refreshing drink made with *guinda*, a local cherry brandy, and *algarrobina*, a sweet cocktail made with the syrup from the fruit of the carob tree, egg whites, evaporated milk, *pisco* and cinnamon.

Some Peruvian **wines** are good, others are acidic and poor. The best are the Ica wines Tabernero, Tacama (especially its Selección Especial and Terroix labels), Ocucaje and Santiago Queirolo (in particular its Intipalka label). Red, white and rosé, sweet and dry varieties can be found. Prices for a reasonable bottle start at around US$4.75, rising to US$18 for the best wines. Note that some Peruvian bodegas import Argentine wines and bottle them under their own label.

Peruvian **beer** is good, especially the *Cusqueña* and *Arequipeña* brands (lager) and *Trujillo Malta* (porter). In Lima *Cristal* and *Pilsen* are readily available. Other brands, including some Brazilian beers, are coming onto the market. Look out for the sweetish 'maltina' brown ale, which makes a change from the ubiquitous pilsner-type beers.

Chicha de jora is a strong but refreshing **maize beer**, usually homemade and not easy to come by, and *chicha morada* is a soft drink made with purple maize. **Coffee** in Peru is usually brought to the table in a small jug accompanied by a mug of hot water to which you add the coffee essence. If you want coffee with milk, a mug of milk is brought. The number of cafés serving good, fresh coffee is growing rapidly. There are many different kinds of herb **tea**: the commonest are *manzanilla* (camomile), *hierbaluisa* (lemongrass) and *mate de coca*. Although a stimulant, the latter is frequently served in the highlands to stave off the discomforts of altitude sickness. Try tea from another herb from the sierras, *muña*, instead, which is a relaxant and may be more effective.

Entertainment

Lima
The chances are you won't have much time in Lima and will want to move on to Cuzco as soon as possible. But if you do have a free night before flying you should check out the nightlife in Barranco, a pleasant, bohemian, seaside suburb of the capital. It's only a short taxi ride from Miraflores and at weekends is positively throbbing with young *limeños* out for a good time. It's also a great place for a romantic early evening drink while you watch the sun slip into the Pacific Ocean. There are lots of trendy bars and nightclubs in Miraflores, too. ›› *For listings, see Bars and clubs, page 295, and Entertainment, page 296.*

Cuzco → *Look out for the vast range of flyers, which give you free entry plus a complimentary drink.*
One of Cuzco's main attractions – apart from Inca ruins, colonial architecture, great trekking, wonderful scenery and wild adventure sports – is its nightlife. There is a staggering selection of bars to suit all tastes and dispositions, all crammed into a few streets on and around the main Plaza de Armas. You can large it up in the frenzied atmosphere of the **Cross Keys**, get blissed out in the laid-back **Los Perros**, or go all Oirish in **Paddy Flaherty's**. The choice, as they say, is yours. After the bars close the nightclubs kick into action. The old favourites such as **Mama Africa** and **Ukuku's** have been joined by a rash of new pretenders, some with decent sound systems and DJs spinning the latest happening tunes. But it's not all techno and thumping drum 'n' bass. There are also places where you can wiggle your hips to the sensuous sounds of salsa and merengue. If all that brings you out in a cold sweat, there are *peñas* offering relatively sedate folklore shows. A side effect of all the competition to entertain you is that establishments may come and go, or reinvent themselves as something new. The main places tend to stay constant, but this season's favourite may have moved on next year, or vanished altogether. Be warned that Cuzco's nightlife is so prolific you may be so off your face every night that you won't even have the energy to do the Inca Trail. More seriously, though, take it easy on the booze when you first arrive. Having altitude sickness and a hangover is no joke. Also be aware of the potential dangers of trying to score drugs in nightclubs (see page 43). ›› *For listings, see Bars and clubs, page 106, and Entertainment, page 108.*

Festivals and events

Festivals

Every bit as important as knowing where to go and what the weather will be like, is Peru's festival calendar. At any given time of the year there'll be a festival somewhere in the country, at which time even the sleepiest little town or village is transformed into a raucous mixture of drinking, dancing and water throwing (or worse). Not all festivals end up as choreographed drunken riots, however. Some are solemn and ornate holy processions. All draw people from miles around; it helps a great deal to know about these festivals and when they take place.

Two of the major festival dates are **Carnaval**, which is held over the weekend before **Ash Wednesday**, and **Semana Santa** (Holy Week), which ends on **Easter Sunday**. Carnaval is celebrated in most of the Andean regions and Semana Santa throughout most of Peru. Accommodation and transport is heavily booked at these times and prices rise accordingly.

Another important festival is **Fiesta de la Cruz**, held on the first of May in much of the central and southern highlands and on the coast. In Cuzco, the entire month of June is one huge fiesta, culminating in **Inti Raymi**, on 24 June, one of Peru's prime tourist attractions. Accommodation can be very hard to find at this time in Cuzco.

The two main festivals in Lima are **Santa Rosa de Lima**, on 30 August, and **Señor de los Milagros**, held on several dates throughout October. Another national festival is **Todos los Santos** (All Saints) on 1 November, and on 8 December is **Festividad de la Inmaculada Concepción**. For more dates, check the websites of **PromPerú** and **South American Explorers** (see page 66).

National holidays

Apart from the festivals listed above, the main holidays are: 1 January (New Year); 6 January (Bajada de Reyes/Epiphany); 1 May (Labour Day); 28-29 July (Fiestas Patrias/Independence); 7 October (Battle of Angamos); 24-25 December (Navidad/Christmas).

Most businesses such as banks, airline offices and tourist agencies close for the official holidays while supermarkets and street markets may be open. This depends a lot on where you are so ask around before the holiday. Sometimes holidays that fall during mid-week will be moved to the following Monday. Find out what the local customs and events are. Often there are parades, processions, special types of food or certain traditions (like yellow underwear at New Year) that characterize the event. The high season for foreign tourism in Peru is June to September while national tourism peaks on certain holidays eg Navidad, Semana Santa and Fiestas Patrias. Prices rise and accommodation and bus tickets are harder to come by. If you know when you will be travelling buy your ticket in advance.

Shopping

Almost everyone who visits Cuzco will end up buying a souvenir from the vast array of arts and crafts (*artesanía*) on offer. The best, and cheapest, place to shop for souvenirs, and almost anything else, is in the street markets which can be found everywhere.

Bargaining

Sooner or later almost everyone has to bargain in Peru. Only the rich and famous can afford to pay the prices quoted by taxi drivers, receptionists and self-proclaimed guides. The great majority of Peruvians are honest and extremely hard working, but their country is poor and often in turmoil, the future is uncertain and the overwhelming majority of people live below the poverty line. Foreigners are seen as rich, even if they are backpackers or students. In order to bring prices down, it is extremely helpful to speak at least some Spanish and/or to convince locals that you live, work or study in Peru and therefore know the real price.

You will not have to bargain in restaurants, department stores, expensive hotels or airline offices. However, almost all the rest is negotiable. Almost all better-class hotels have 'corporate' rates. Just say that you work for some company, that you are a journalist (they never check ID), or you are a researcher. This way you can usually get a reduction. If you think a lower price is appropriate in a cheaper hotel, ask for *'una rebajita, por favor'* ('a discount, please'). You can negotiate the price of a tour booked through a travel agency, but not an aeroplane, bus or train ticket. In fact, you will probably get a better price directly from the airline ticket office.

Bargaining is expected when you are shopping for artwork, handicrafts, souvenirs, or even food in the market. Remember, though, that most handicrafts, including alpaca and woollen goods, are made by hand. Ask yourself if it is worth taking advantage of the piteous state of the people you are buying from. Keep in mind, these people are making a living and the 50 centavos you save by bargaining may buy the seller two loaves of bread. You want the *fair* price not the lowest one, so bargain only when you feel you are being ripped off. Remember that some Peruvians are so desperate that they will have to sell you their goods at *any* price, in order to survive. Please, don't take advantage of it.

What to buy

Good buys are: silver and gold handicrafts; hand-spun and hand-woven textiles; manufactured textiles in traditional designs; llama and alpaca wool products such as ponchos, rugs, hats, blankets, slippers, coats and sweaters; *arpilleras* (appliqué pictures of Peruvian life), which are made with great skill and originality by women in the shanty towns; and fine leather products which are mostly hand-made. Another good buy is clothing made from high quality Pima cotton, which is grown in Peru.

The *mate burilado*, or engraved gourd, found in every tourist shop, is cheap and one of the most genuine expressions of folk art in Peru. Alpaca clothing, such as sweaters, hats and gloves, is cheaper in the sierra, the best value being found in Puno. Nevertheless, Cuzco is one of the main weaving centres and a good place to shop for textiles, as well as excellent woodcarvings (see the Shopping section on page 111). **Note** Genuine alpaca is odourless wet or dry, wet llama 'stinks'. ▶ *For a more detailed look at Peruvian arts and crafts, see page 331.*

Responsible travel

Sustainable or ecotourism has been described as "ethical, considerate or informed tourism where visitors can enjoy the natural, historical and social heritage of an area without causing adverse environmental, socio-economic or cultural impacts that compromise the long-term ability of that area and its people to provide a recreational resource for future generations and an income for themselves". Peru is a beautiful, fascinating country but also a living, working landscape and a fragile place. By observing certain guidelines outlined in the box opposite and behaving responsibly, you can help to minimize your impact and protect the natural and cultural heritage of this wonderful country.

Environmental legislation plays its part in protecting tourist destinations. CITES (Convention on International Trade in Endangered Species of Wild Fauna and Flora) aims to control the trade in live specimens of endangered plants and animals and also "recognizable parts or derivatives" of protected species. If you feel the need to purchase souvenirs derived from wildlife, it would be prudent to check whether they are protected. Importation of CITES-protected species can lead to heavy fines, confiscation of goods and even imprisonment.

While the authenticity of some ecotourism operators' claims need to be interpreted with care, there is clearly both a huge demand for this type of activity and also significant opportunities to support worthwhile conservation and social development initiatives. If you are concerned about the application of the principles of ecotourism, in Peru as elsewhere, you need to make an informed choice by finding out in advance how establishments such as jungle lodges cope with waste and effluent disposal, whether they create the equivalent of 'monkey islands' by obtaining animals in the wild and putting them in the lodge's property, what their policy is towards employing and training local staff, and so on. See also Voluntourism, page 59.

Local customs and laws

Codes of conduct
Politeness – even a little ceremoniousness – is much appreciated in Peruvian society. Men should always remove any headgear and say 'con permiso', when entering offices, and shake hands with other men. Women or men meeting women usually greet each other with one kiss on the cheek. When introduced, Peruvians will probably expect to greet visitors in the same way. Always say 'buenos días' (until midday) or 'buenas tardes' and wait for a reply before proceeding further. Business cards are commonly used.

When dealing with officials, always remember to be friendly and courteous no matter how trying the circumstances. Never be impatient and do not criticize situations in public (the officials may know more English than you think and they can certainly interpret gestures and facial expressions). In some situations, however, politeness can be a liability. Most Peruvians are disorderly queuers. In commercial transactions (buying a meal, goods in a shop, etc) politeness should be accompanied by firmness, and always ask the price first.

Politeness should also be extended to street traders. Saying 'no, gracias' with a smile is better than an arrogant dismissal. Whether you give money to beggars is a personal matter, but your decision should be influenced by whether a person is begging out of need or trying to cash in on the tourist trail. In the former case, local people giving may provide an indication. Giving money to children is a separate issue, upon which most

How big is your footprint?

- Where possible choose a destination, tour operator or hotel with a proven ethical and environmental commitment – if in doubt, ask.
- Spend money on locally produced (rather than imported) goods and services, buy directly from the producer or from a 'fair trade' shop, and use common sense when bargaining – the few dollars you save may be a week's salary to others.
- Use water and electricity carefully – travellers may receive preferential supply while the needs of local communities are overlooked.
- Learn about local etiquette and culture – consider local norms and behaviour and dress appropriately for local cultures and situations.
- Protect wildlife and other natural resources – don't buy souvenirs or goods unless they are clearly sustainably produced and are not protected under CITES legislation.
- Always ask before taking photographs or videos of people.
- Consider staying in local accommodation rather than foreign-owned hotels; the economic benefits for host communities are far greater, and there are more opportunities to learn about local culture.
- Make a voluntary contribution to **Climate Care**, www.co2.org, to help counteract the pollution caused by tax-free fuel on your flight.

Further information

The following organizations have begun to develop and/or promote ecotourism projects and destinations; their websites are an excellent source of information:

- **Conservation International**, T703-341 2400, www.ecotour.org.
- **International Ecotourism Society**, T001-202-506 5033, www.ecotourism.org.
- **Planeta**, www.planeta.com.
- **Tourism Concern**, T44-20-7133 3800, www.tourismconcern.org.uk.
- Organizations such as **Earthwatch**, www.earthwatch.org, and **Discovery Initiatives**, www.discoveryinitiatives. co.uk, offer opportunities to participate directly in scientific research and development projects in the region.

agree: don't do it. There are occasions where giving some healthy food may be appropriate, but first inform yourself of local practice.

In Peru it is common for locals to throw their rubbish, paper, wrappers and bottles into the street. Sometimes when asking a local where the rubbish bin is, they will indicate to you that it is the street. This does not give you the right to apply the 'when in Rome' theory. There are rubbish bins in public areas in many centres and tourists should use them.

Dress

Most Latin Americans, if they can afford it, devote great care to their clothes and appearance. It is appreciated if visitors do likewise. How you dress is mostly how people will judge you. This is particularly important when dealing with officials. Women should pack at least one medium- to long-length skirt and men might want to consider bringing a smart sweater or jacket. Wool sweaters and shawls can be easily purchased in Peru and make good additions to your wardrobe.

In general, clothing is less formal in the tropical lowlands, where men and women do wear shorts. In the highlands, people are more conservative, though wearing shorts is acceptable on hiking trails. Men should not be seen bare-chested in populated areas.

Essentials A-Z

Accident and emergency

Contact the relevant emergency service and your embassy (see pages 44 and 124). Make sure you obtain police/medical reports in order to file insurance claims.

Emergency services

Ambulance T01-225 4040 in Lima.
Emergency medical attention T117.
Fire T116, www.bomberosperu.gob.pe.
Police T105, www.pnp.gob.pe (PNP, Policía Nacional del Perú), for police emergencies nationwide. **Tourist police** Jr Moore 268, Magdalena, 38th block of Av Brasil, Lima, T01-460 1060, daily 24 hrs; for public enquiries, etc, Av España con la Av Alfonso Ugarte, Lima, and Colón 246, Miraflores, T01-243 2190. Go there if you have had property stolen. They are friendly, helpful and speak English and some German. **Consumer Protection Bureau (Indecopi)** hotline for travellers' complaints T/F01-224 7777, outside Lima T0800-44040 (not from pay phones), daily 0830-1630, www.indecopi.gob.pe. This body (with offices, kiosks and information stands in every town) will help with complaints regarding customs, airlines, travel agencies, accommodation, restaurants, public authorities or if you have lost, or had stolen, documents.

Children

Travel with children can bring you into closer contact with local families and, generally, presents no special problems – in fact the path is often smoother for family groups. Officials tend to be more amenable where children are concerned and they are pleased if your child knows a little Spanish. For more detailed advice, see *Travel with Kids* by William Gray (Footprint, 2007) and www.babygoes2.com.

Bus travel Remember that a lot of time can be spent waiting for and riding buses. You should take reading material with you as it is difficult to find and expensive. Also look for the locally available comic strip *Condorito*, which is popular and a good way for older children to learn a bit of Spanish. On long-distance buses you pay for each seat, and there are no half fares. For shorter trips it is cheaper, if less comfortable, to seat small children on your knee. Sometimes there are spare seats which children can occupy after tickets have been collected. In city buses, small children generally do not pay a fare, but are not entitled to a seat when paying customers are standing. On most domestic flights, children under 12 pay less than adults, the exact discounts vary. Make sure that children accompanying you are fully covered by your travel insurance policy.

Food This can be a problem if the children are not adaptable. It is easier to take food with you on longer trips than to rely on meal stops where the food may not be to taste. Avocados are safe, readily available, easy to eat and nutritious; they can be fed to babies as young as 6 months and most older children like them. Best stick to simple things like bread, bananas and tangerines while you are actually on the road. Biscuits, packaged junk food and bottled drinks abound. A small immersion heater and jug for making hot drinks is invaluable, but remember that electric current is 220 v in Peru. In restaurants, you can try to order a *media porción* (half portion), or divide a full-sized helping between 2 children.

In all hotels, try to negotiate family rates. If charges are per person, always insist that 2 children will occupy 1 bed only, therefore counting as 1 tariff. You can almost always get a reduced rate at cheaper hotels. For details of health issues, see page 44.

See also box, page 42.

A child's survival guide to Peru

I went to Peru for three months and loved it. We lived in a place in Urubamba called K'uychi Rumi, which was brilliant because it shared a big garden with the other houses and we visited Cuzco a lot.

The ruins are interesting to visit but you don't want to spend your whole time trudging up and down them. There is plenty else to do.

I really liked the horse riding. To start, try riding from Sacsayhuaman to the X-Zone (I love that name!) and around to Qenqo. This was my first horse-riding trip ever, so if you haven't been before, don't worry. It was quite flat and even my seven-year-old brother Owen managed on his own horse. My other brother Leo, who's four, rode with Dad.

The next ride wasn't flat at all. We went up a very steep hill in the Sacred Valley, from Lamay to a ruin called Huchuy Cuzco. It was amazing. We went up a steep windy path between two hills and when I was on the path, I looked up and couldn't believe that I was going to do that – but we did.

After these trips you are fully prepared for camping in the High Andes. We went up to, wait for it, 4200 m and it was cool in every sense, including temperature. The two nights in a tent were the coldest I have ever been in my life – but don't let me put you off because it was great fun and it warmed up during the day.

River-rafting on the Urubamba was fab. The first bit was gentle, but the second part near Ollantaytambo got rough, including a Grade III bit, which had a 2-m waterfall that we went over.

After all that exercise you might need some food. The place to go in Cuzco is Jack's Café, which has toasted sandwiches, big breakfasts, chips and milkshakes. For a more fancy dessert, try the Dolce Vita ice cream place in Santa Catalina Ancha. My favourite flavour was *naranja* (orange)-split, and there are a lot of unusual flavours like *lúcuma* (egg-fruit) and *maracuyá*.

In Urubamba, Quinta Los Geranios is recommended, as is anywhere which does fried chicken, which luckily is very popular around Cuzco.

By Daisy Thomson (aged nine)

Customs and duty free

Duty-free allowance When travelling into Peru you can bring 20 packs of cigarettes (400 cigarettes), 50 cigars or 500 g of tobacco, 3 litres of alcohol and new articles for personal use or gifts valued at up to US$300. There are certain items that cannot be brought in duty free: these include computers (but laptops are OK). The value-added tax for items that are not considered duty free but are still intended for personal use is generally 20%. Personal items such as laptops, cameras, bicycles, hiking and climbing equipment and anything else necessary for adventure sports are exempt from taxes and should be regarded as personal effects that will not be sold or left in Peru. All customs agents should be satisfied by this and allow you to pass. Anything that looks like it's being brought in for resale, however, could give you trouble.

Goods shipped to you Except for documents, customs duties must be paid on all goods shipped to Peru. Better to bring anything you think you will need with you when you travel, rather than having it sent later on.

On departure All airline baggage is inspected by security personnel and sniffed by dogs for drugs. Never transport anything you have not packed yourself, as you will be held responsible for the contents.

Export ban It is illegal to take items of archaeological interest or specimens of wild plants or animals without a permit out of Peru. This means that any pre-Columbian pottery or Inca artefacts cannot leave the country. If you are buying extremely good replicas make sure the pieces have the artist's name on them or that they have a tag which shows that they are not originals. No matter how simple it seems, it is not worth your time to try and take anything illegal out of the country – this includes drugs. The security personnel and customs officials are experts at their job. Understand that this is a foolhardy idea and save yourself the horror of 10 years in jail.

Disabled travellers

As with most underdeveloped countries, facilities for the disabled traveller are sadly lacking. Wheelchair ramps are a rare luxury and getting a wheelchair into a bathroom or toilet is virtually impossible, except in some of the more upmarket hotels. The entrance to many cheap hotels is up a narrow flight of stairs. Pavements are often in a poor state of repair (even able-bodied people need to look out for uncovered manholes and other unexpected traps). Visually and hearing-impaired travellers are similarly poorly catered for, as a rule, but experienced guides can often provide tours with individual attention. Disabled Peruvians obviously have to cope with these problems and mainly rely on the help of others to get on and off public transport and generally move around.

The **Ministerio de la Mujer y Desarrollo Social** (Ministry for Women and Social Development) incorporates a **National Council for the Integration of Disabled People** (CONADIS, www.conadisperu. gob.pe, in Spanish only). CONADIS, together with PromPerú, SATH (see below) and Kéroul of Québec, has been involved in a project called *Peru: Towards an Accessible Tourism*; the first report on 'Accessibility in Peru for Tourists with Disabilities' was published in 2001. The report identifies many challenges in a selected number of major tourist sites. For instance, archaeological sites such as Machu Picchu, being a World Heritage Site, may not be altered for accessibility. Specially trained personnel, however, can provide assistance to those with disabilities in these cases. The project can be accessed through the PromPerú website www.peru.info, click on Turismo accesible/Accessible tourism.

Some travel companies are beginning to specialize in exciting holidays, tailor made for individuals depending on their level of disability. The **Global Access Disabled Travel Network Site**, www.globalaccessnews.com, is dedicated to providing information for 'disabled adventurers' and includes a number of reviews and tips from members of the public. Another informative site, www.sath.org, belongs to the **Society for Accessible Travel and Hospitality (SATH)**, and has lots of advice on how to travel with specific disabilities, plus listings and links. Also see **www.access-able.com**. One company in Cuzco which offers tours for disabled people is **Apumayo**, see Cuzco Activities and tours, page 121.

Drugs

Illegal drugs are the most common way for foreigners to get into serious trouble in this part of the world. Some people come specifically to consume or buy drugs and may have the false impression that the country is currently permissive in this regard. This is not the case. While drugs are easily available, anyone caught in possession will be assumed to be a trafficker. Drug use or purchase is punishable by up to 15 years' imprisonment and the number of foreigners in Peruvian prisons on drug charges is still increasing. If arrested on any charge the wait for trial in prison can take up to a year and is particularly unpleasant. Be wary of anyone approaching you in a club and asking where they can score – the chances are they'll be a plain-clothes cop. If you are asked to have your bags searched, insist on having a witness present at all times. Never respond to offers by anyone selling drugs on the street anywhere, as they may be a plain-clothes officer.

Electricity

220 volts, 60 cycles (Arequipa 50 cycles). Most 4- and 5-star hotels have 110 volts AC. Plugs are either American flat-pin or twin flat and round pin combined.

Embassies and consulates

Australia, 40 Brisbane Av, Barton, ACT 2600, Canberra, T02-6273 7351, www.embaperu.org.au.
Austria, Mahlerstrasse 7/22, A-1010, Vienna, T1-713 4377, www.embaperuaustria.at.
Belgium (consulate), rue de Praetere 2, 1050 Brussels, T32-2-641 8760, consulate.peru@conperbruselas.be.
Bolivia (consulate), Av 6 de Agosto 2455, of 402, Sopocachi, La Paz, T591-2-244 0631, conperlapaz@acelerate.com.
Canada, 130 Albert St, Suite 1901, Ottawa, Ontario K1M 1W5, T1-613-238 1777, www.embassyofperu.ca.
France, 50 ave Kleber, 75116 Paris, T33-1-5370 4200, www.amb-perou.fr.
Germany, Mohrenstrasse 42, 10117 Berlin, T49-30-229 1455, www.embaperu.de.
Israel, 60 Medinat Hayehudin St, Herzliya Pituach, T972-9-9957 8835, consuladop@hotmail.com.
Italy, Via Siacci 2B, 2nd floor, 00197 Roma, T39-06-8069 1510, www.ambasciataperu.it.
Japan, 4-4 -27 Higashi Shibuya-Ku, Tokyo 150-0011, T081-3-3406 4243, www.embajadadelperuenjapon.org.
Netherlands (consulate), Amsteldijk 166-7E 1079 LH, Amsterdam, T31-20-622 8580, http://consuladoperuamsterdam.com.

New Zealand, Level 8, 40 Mercer St, Cigna House, Wellington, T64-4-499 8087, frojas@embassyofperu.org.nz.
South Africa (consulate), 200 Saint Patricks St, Muckleneuk Hill, Pretoria, T27-12-440 1030, embaperu6@telkomsa.net.
Spain, C Príncipe de Vergara 36, 5 to Derecha, 28001 Madrid, T34-91-431 4242, www.embajadaperu.es.
Sweden, Brunnsgatan 21 B, 111 38 Stockholm, T46-8-440 8740, www.peruembassy.se. Also for Denmark and Norway.
Switzerland, Thunstrasse No 36, CH-3005 Berne, T41-31-351 8555, www.embajadaperu.ch.
UK, 52 Sloane St, London SW1X 9SP, T020-7235 1917, www.peruembassy-uk.com.
USA, 1700 Massachusetts Av NW, Washington DC 20036, T1-202-833 9860, www.peruvianembassy.us.

Health

Cuzco stands at 3310 m, so you'll need time to acclimatize to the high altitude. If flying from Lima, don't underestimate the shock to your system of going from sea level to over 3000 m in 1 hr – see also acute mountain sickness below. If you're arriving in Cuzco by air, it makes a lot of sense to get down to the Urubamba Valley, at 2800 m, 510 m lower than Cuzco itself, and make the most of your first couple of days. At this relatively low altitude you will experience no headaches and you can eat and sleep comfortably. There are doctors who speak English (and other foreign languages) in Cuzco and Lima who have particular experience in dealing with locally occurring diseases, but don't expect good facilities away from the major centres.

Before you go

See your GP or travel clinic at least 6 weeks before departure for general advice on travel risks and vaccinations. Try phoning a specialist travel clinic if your own doctor is unfamiliar with health in the region. Make sure you have sufficient medical travel insurance, get a dental check, know your own blood group and, if you suffer a long-term condition such as diabetes or epilepsy, obtain a **Medic Alert** bracelet (www.medicalalert.co.uk).

Vaccinations and anti-malarials

Confirm that your primary courses and boosters are up to date. It is advisable to vaccinate against polio, tetanus, typhoid, hepatitis A and, for more remote areas, rabies. Yellow fever vaccination is obligatory for tropical lowland areas but not the Pacific coast, nor the highlands. Specialist advice should be taken on the best anti-malarials to take before you leave.

Health risks

The major risks posed in the region are those caused by insect disease carriers such as mosquitoes and sandflies. The key parasitic and viral diseases are malaria, dengue fever, and in some areas South American trypanosomiasis (Chagas' disease). **Malaria** is a danger throughout the lowland tropics and coastal regions. **Dengue fever** is particularly hard to protect against as the mosquitoes can bite throughout the day as well as night (unlike those that carry malaria). Try to wear clothes that cover arms and legs and also use effective mosquito repellent. Mosquito nets dipped in permethrin provide a good physical and chemical barrier at night. **Chagas' disease** is spread by faeces of a bug called the *vinchuca* or *chirimacha* which occurs in the north-central highlands and, with a much greater prevalence, in southwestern Peru. Sandflies spread **leishmaniasis**, a serious skin disease; it is called *uta* in northern Peru.

Some form of **diarrhoea** or intestinal upset is almost inevitable, the standard advice is always to wash your hands before eating and to be careful with drinking water and ice. If you have any doubts about the water then boil it or filter and treat it. In a restaurant buy bottled water or ask where the water has come from. Food can also pose a problem. Be wary of salads if you don't know whether they have been washed or not, undercooked meat, reheated foods or food that has been left out in the sun having been cooked earlier in the day. There is a simple adage that says 'wash it, peel it, boil it or forget it'. The key treatment for diarrhoea is rehydration. Try to keep hydrated by taking the right mixture of salt and water. This is available as oral rehydration salts (ORS) in ready-made sachets, or can be made up by adding a teaspoon of sugar and half a teaspoon of salt to a litre of clean water. If diarrhoea persists for several days or you develop additional symptoms, see a doctor.

There is a constant threat of **tuberculosis** (TB) and although the BCG vaccine is available, it is still not guaranteed protection. It is best to avoid unpasteurized dairy products and try not to let people cough and splutter all over you.

One of the most common problems for travellers in the region is **altitude sickness**. Acute mountain sickness can strike from about 3000 m upwards and in general is more likely to affect those who ascend rapidly (for example by plane) and those who over-exert themselves. Smokers and those with underlying heart and lung disease are often hardest hit. The sickness presents with headache, lassitude, dizziness, loss of appetite, nausea and vomiting. Insomnia is common and often associated with a suffocating feeling when lying down in bed. If the symptoms are mild, the treatment is to rest from your trip, take it easy for the first few days and drink plenty of water. Should symptoms be severe and prolonged it is best to descend to a lower altitude immediately and re-ascend, if necessary, slowly and in stages.

It is essential to get acclimatized to the thin air of the Andes before undertaking long treks or arduous activities. No one should attempt to climb over 5000 m until they have spent at least a week at around 3000 m and then a couple of nights at 4000 m. Agencies who offer 2-day climbs without adequate acclimatization are not to be trusted.

The altitude of the Andes also means that strong **protection from the sun** is always needed, regardless of how cool it may feel. Always use sunblock and a hat. Mountaineers should use glasses that provide 100% UV protection. In fact a good pair of sunglasses and a high-factor sunscreen are recommended in all parts of Peru.

Further information
Websites
Centres for Disease Control and Prevention (USA), www.cdc.gov.
Department of Health advice for travellers, www.dh.gov.uk/en/Policyandguidance/Healthadvicefortravellers/index.htm.
Fit for Travel (UK), www.fitfortravel.scot.nhs.uk, a site from Scotland providing a quick A-Z of vaccine and travel health advice requirements for each country.
National Travel Health Network and Centre (NaTHNaC), www.nathnac.org.
Prince Leopold Institute for Tropical Medicine, www.itg.be.
World Health Organisation, www.who.int.

Books
Dawood, R, editor, *Travellers' health*, 3rd ed, Oxford: Oxford University Press, 2002.
Johnson, Chris, Sarah Anderson and others, *Oxford Handbook of Expedition and Wilderness Medicine*, OUP 2008.
Wilson-Howarth, Jane. *Bugs, Bites and Bowels: the essential guide to travel health*, Cadogan 2009.

Insurance

We strongly recommend that you invest in a good insurance policy that covers you for theft or loss of possessions and money, the cost of medical and dental treatment, cancellation of flights, delays in travel arrangements, accidents, missed departures, lost baggage, lost passport and personal liability and legal expenses. Also check on inclusion of 'dangerous activities' if you plan on doing any. These generally include climbing, diving, skiing, horse riding, parachuting, even trekking. You should always read the small print carefully. Not all policies cover ambulance, helicopter rescue or emergency flights home.

There are a variety of policies to choose from, so it's best to shop around. Your travel agent can advise on the best deals available. Reputable student travel organizations often offer good-value policies. Travellers from North America can try the **International Student Insurance Service (ISIS)**, which is available through **STA**, T800-7814040, www.statravel.com. Companies worth trying in Britain include **Direct Line Insurance**, T0845-246 8704, www.directline.com, and the **Flexicover Group**, T0800-093 9495, www.flexicover.net. Some companies will not cover those over 65. The best policies for older travellers are through **Age UK**, T0845-600 3348, www.ageuk.org.uk.

Internet

You can find internet access everywhere. Cuzco has internet cafés on every corner; many of them have **net2phone**. Internet cafés are incredibly cheap to use, normally about US$0.60-1 per hr. When they first open in the morning is often a good time to use cyber cafés, as they are less busy then. Access is generally quick. Internet is more expensive in hotel business centres and in out-of-the-way places.

Language

The official language is **Spanish**. **Quechua**, an Andean language that predates the Incas, has been given some official status and there is much pride in its use, but despite the fact that it is spoken by millions of people in the sierra who have little or no knowledge of Spanish, it is not used in schools. Another important indigenous language is **Aymara**, used in the area around Lake Titicaca. The jungle is home to a plethora of languages but Spanish is spoken in all but the remotest areas. **English** is not spoken widely, except by those employed in the tourism industry (eg hotel, tour agency and airline staff). See page 348 for basic Spanish words and phrases and page 353 for pronunciation.

AmeriSpan, 1334 Walnut St, 6th floor, Philadelphia PA 19107, USA, T1-800-879 6640 (USA and Canada), T215-751 1100 (worldwide), SKYPE: amerispan, www.amerispan.com, organizes programmes throughout Latin America. They also have lots of information about travelling in the region. **Languages Abroad.com**, 386 Ontario St, Toronto, Ontario, Canada, M5A 2V7, T1-800-219 9924, in UK T0800-404 7738, www.languages abroad.com, offer Spanish and Portuguese programmes in most South American countries. They also have language immersion courses throughout the world. Similarly, there is **Cactus**, in the UK T0845-130 4775, www.cactuslanguage.com, and **Spanish Abroad**, 3219 East Camelback Rd No 806, Phoenix, AZ 85018, USA, T1-888-722 7623, or T602-778 6791 (UK T0800-028 7706), www.spanishabroad.com.

Courses of 1-4 weeks in Spanish language with cultural and/or volunteer programmes are offered in Cuzco by **Càlédönià**, The Clockhouse, Bonnington Mill, 72 New Haven Rd, Edinburgh, EH6 5QG, Scotland, T0131-621 7721, www.caledonialanguages.com.

LGBT (lesbian, gay, bisexual, transgendered) travellers

Movimiento Homosexual de Lima (MHOL), C Mcal Miller 828, Jesús María, T01-433 5314, www.mhol.org.pe, is a great contact for the gay community in Lima. Online resources for gay travellers in Peru are http://lima. queercity.info/index.html (a good site, in English, with lots of links and information), www.deambiente.com/web and www.gayperu.com (both in Spanish). The latter also has a tour operator in Miraflores, T01-447 3366, www.gayperutravel.com.

In the Lima section we include the names of gay-friendly establishments. There are also gay-friendly places in Cuzco, but the scene is not very active there. This does not mean, however, that there is hostility towards gay and lesbian travellers. As a major tourist centre that welcomes a huge variety of visitors, Cuzco is probably more open than anywhere in Peru.

Media

Newspapers and magazines
Lima has several daily papers. The most informative are *El Comercio*, www.elcomercio peru.com.pe, and *La República*, www.larepublica.com.pe. Also with an online edition is *Expreso*, www.expreso.com.pe. *Gestión*, www.gestion.com.pe, is a business daily. Very popular are the sensationalist papers, written in raunchy slang and featuring acres of bare female flesh on their pages. The main provincial cities have at least 1 newspaper each. There are a number of websites that provide regular news updates, including www.yachay.com.pe and www.peru.com.

The most widely read magazine is the weekly news magazine *Caretas*, www.caretas.com.pe, which gives a very considered angle on current affairs and is often critical of government policy.

Radio
Radio is far more important in imparting news to Peruvians than newspapers, partly due to the fact that limited plane routes make it difficult to get papers to much of

the population on the same day. There are countless local and community radio stations that cover even the most far-flung places. A popular station is *Radioprogramas del Perú* (www.rpp.com.pe), which features round-the-clock news.

A shortwave radio will allow you to absorb local culture, as well as pick up the **BBC World Service** (www.bbc.co.uk/worldservice) or the **Voice of America** (www.voa.gov).

Money → *Exchange rates: £1=S/.4.48, US$1=S/.2.76, €1=S/.3.82. (Feb 2011).*

Currency
Exchange rates For up-to-the-minute exchange rates visit www.xe.com.

The **nuevo sol** (new sol, S/.) is the official currency of Peru. It is divided in 100 *céntimos* (cents) with coins valued at S/.5, S/.2, S/.1 and 50, 20, 10 and 5 *céntimo* pieces although the latter is being phased out as it is virtually worthless. Notes in circulation are S/.200, S/.100, S/.50, S/.20 and S/.10.

Prices of airline tickets, tour agency services, non-backpacker hotels and hostels, among others, are almost always quoted in dollars. You can pay in soles or dollars but it is generally easiest to pay dollars when the price is in dollars and in soles when the price is in soles. This will save you from losing on exchange rates. In major tourist centres such as Lima and Cuzco dollars are frequently accepted.

Almost no one, certainly not banks, will accept dollar bills that are ripped, taped, stapled or torn. Do not accept damaged dollars from anyone; simply tell them you would like another bill. Likewise, ask your bank at home to give you only nice, crisp, clean dollars and keep your dollars neat in your money belt or wallet so they don't accidentally tear.

Forgeries of dollars and soles are not uncommon. Always check the sol notes you have received, even at the bank. Money changers, especially at borders, mix fake notes with genuine bills when giving wads of soles for other currencies. Information on notes and coins in circulation, including forgeries, can be found on **www.bcrp.gob.pe**, under **Billetes y Monedas**. Hold the bills up to the light to check the watermark and that the colours change according to the angle of the light. The line down the side of the bill in which the amount of the money is written should appear green, blue and pink at different angles; fake bills are only pink and have no hologram properties. There should be tiny pieces of thread in the paper (not glued on). Check to see that the faces are clear. Also, the paper should not feel smooth like a photocopy but rougher and fibrous. Try not to accept brand-new notes, especially if changing on the street, slightly used notes are less likely to be forgeries. There are posters in public places explaining what to look for in forged sol notes. In parts of the country, forged 1- and 5-sol coins are in circulation. They are slightly off-colour, the surface copper can be scratched off and they tend to bear a recent date.

Banks and ATMs
BCP opens Mon-Fri 0900-1800 and Sat 0900-1300, changes US$ cash to soles. Cash advances on Visa in soles only. VíaBCP ATM for Visa/Plus, MasterCard/Cirrus, Amex. **BBVA Continental** changes US$ cash to soles, US$12 commission per transaction for TCs at selected branches. B24 ATM for Visa/Plus. **Interbank**, open Mon-Fri 0900-1815, Sat 0900-1230, changes US$ cash and TCs to soles, TCs to US$ cash for US$5 per transaction up to US$500. GlobalNet ATM (see below). **Scotiabank**, open Mon-Fri 0915-1800, Sat 0915-1230, changes US$ cash to soles, cash advances on MasterCard, ATM for Cirrus, Visa, MasterCard, Maestro. There are also **Global Net** and **Red Unicard** ATMs that accept Visa, Plus and MasterCard, Maestro and Cirrus (the former makes a charge per transaction). ATMs usually give US$ if you don't request soles and

their use is widespread. Maximum allowed per transaction is US$140. It is safest to use ATMs during banking hours. At night and on Sun there is more chance of the transaction going wrong, or false money being in the machine. The compatibility of ATMs across Peru is increasing all the time. Your card has to be pretty obscure not to be able to obtain cash from an ATM, but availability decreases outside large towns. In smaller towns, take some cash.

Credit cards

Visa (by far the most widely accepted card in Peru), **MasterCard**, **Maestro**, **American Express** and **Diners Club** are all valid. There may be an 8-12% commission for all credit card charges. Often, it is cheaper to use your credit card to get money (dollars or soles) out of an ATM rather than to pay for your purchases. Of course, this depends on the interest rate for cash advances on your credit cards – ask your bank or card provider about this. Other options are to put extra money on your credit cards and use them as a bank card, or to take a prepaid currency card. There are many on offer, from, for example, **Caxton**, **FairFX**, **Travelex**, banks and other organizations. It pays to check their application fees and charges carefully.

Businesses

Businesses displaying credit card symbols are unlikely to take foreign cards. Make sure you carry the phone numbers that you need in order to report your card lost or stolen. In addition, some travellers have reported problems with their credit cards being 'frozen' by their bank as soon as a charge from a foreign country occurs. To avoid this problem, notify your bank that you will be making charges in Peru (and other countries).

Credit card companies

American Express, Travex SA, Av Santa Cruz 621, Miraflores, Lima, T01-710 3900, info@travex.com.pe. For ATM locations: www.americanexpress.com.

Diners Club, Canaval y Moreyra 535, San Isidro, T01-615 1111, www.dinersclub.com.pe.
MasterCard, Porta 111, p 6, Miraflores, T01-311 6000, T0800-307 7309, www.mastercard.com/pe/gateway.html. For ATM locations: www.mastercard.com.
Visa Travel Assistance, T0800-890 0623. For ATM locations: www.visalatam.com.

Exchange

All banks' exchange rates are considerably less favourable than *casas de cambio* (exchange houses). Long queues and paperwork may be involved. US$ and euro are the only currencies that should be brought into Peru from abroad (take some small bills). There are no restrictions on foreign exchange. Few banks change euro but *casas de cambio* will do so. Always count your money in the presence of the cashier. Street changers give much the same rates for changing small amounts of US$ or euro cash as *casas de cambio*, but avoiding paperwork and queuing. Take care: check your soles before handing over your US$, check their calculators, etc, and don't change money in crowded areas. If using their services think about taking a taxi after changing, to avoid being followed. Street changers congregate near an office where the exchange 'wholesaler' operates; the office will probably offer better rates than on the street.

Soles can be exchanged into dollars at the banks and exchange houses at Lima airport, and you can change soles for dollars with street changers and at any border. Dollars can also be bought at the borders.

American Express will sell traveller's cheques to cardholders only, but will not exchange cheques into cash. They are also very efficient in replacing stolen cheques, though a police report is needed. Travellers have reported great difficulty in cashing traveller's cheques in the jungle area, even Iquitos, and other remote areas. Always sign traveller's cheques in blue or black ink or ballpen.

Cost of living

Living costs in the provinces are 20-50% below those in Lima, although Cuzco is a little more expensive than other, less touristy provincial cities. For a lot of low-income Peruvians, many items are simply beyond their reach.

Cost of travelling

The approximate budget is US$35-50 per person per day for living comfortably, with transport, or US$15-20 a day for low-budget travel. Your budget will be higher the longer you stay in Lima and will depend on how many flights you take. Accommodation rates range from US$5 per person for the most basic *alojamiento* to US$15-30 for mid-range places, to over US$100 for top-of-the-range hotels in Lima and Cuzco). For meal prices, see box, page 35.

Opening hours

Banks See under Money, above. Outside Lima and Cuzco banks may close 1200-1500 for lunch. **Government offices** Jan-Mar Mon-Fri 0830-1130; Apr-Dec Mon-Fri 0900-1230, 1500-1700, but these hrs change frequently. **Offices** Mon-Fri 0900-1700. Most close on Sat. **Shops** 0900 or 1000-1230 and 1500 or 1600-2000. In the main cities, supermarkets do not close for lunch, some in Lima open 24 hrs. Some are closed on Sat and most on Sun.

Post

The postal system is **Serpost**. Correo Central on the Plaza de Armas in Lima is the best place for postage (open Mon-Fri 0800-1800). Sending packages out of Peru is incredibly expensive and is not really worth it but letters are much more reasonable; rates are US$2.30 to South America and US$2.50 to North and Central America, US$2.70 to Europe and US$3.12 to Australia. Postcards cost US$1.90.

You can also send letters registered at extra cost. Stamps, envelopes and cloth sacks (to send bigger parcels in) can all be bought at the central post office in Lima. Cuzco is also efficient for sending parcels. Don't put tape on envelopes or packages; wait until you get to the post office and use the glue they have. For emergency or important documents, use Serpost's own **EMS** service, or **DHL** and **Federal Express** in Lima and major cities.

To receive mail, letters can be sent to Poste Restante/General Delivery (*lista de correos*), your embassy, or, for cardholders, American Express office in Lima. Members of the **South American Explorers** can have post sent to them at either of the Peruvian offices. Try not to have articles sent by post to Peru – taxes can be 200% of the value.

Safety

The following notes on personal safety should not hide the fact that most Peruvians are hospitable and helpful. Peru is not a highly dangerous country to travel in, but it is by no means crime free. By being aware of the possible problems you may confront and by using a mixture of common sense and vigilance you can minimize the risks.

You need to take care everywhere but particularly in poor areas of cities, as this is where most theft takes place. While you should take local advice about being out at night, do not assume that daytime is safer than nighttime. If walking after dark, walk in the road, not on the pavement. You should also be on your guard during festivals, at markets and when streets are crowded. Care should be taken at all times and in most parts of Lima. Over the past couple of years there has been an alarming increase in aggressive assaults in centres along the gringo trail. Places like Cuzco have, at times, been plagued by waves of strangle muggings.

Check with **South American Explorers** for a current summary of the situation and how to keep safe. A friendly attitude on your part, smiling even when you've thwarted a thief's attempt, can help you out of trouble. Be especially careful when using ATMs and when arriving at or leaving from bus and train stations, when you have a lot of important belongings with you. Do not set your bag down without putting your foot on it, even just to double check your tickets. Be wary of accepting food, drink, sweets or cigarettes from unknown people on buses or trains; they may be drugged.

Keep all documents secure and hide your main cash supply in different places or under your clothes. Keep cameras in bags, take spare spectacles and don't wear wristwatches or jewellery. If you wear a shoulder-bag, carry it in front of you. Small personal alarms are a good idea. Backpacks can be covered with a sack (a plastic one will also keep out rain and dust) with maybe a layer of wire netting between. Make photocopies of important documents and give them to family or friends. Alternatively send yourself an email containing all important details, addresses, etc which you can access in an emergency. Where there is no safe or locker in your room, you should be able to leave valuables in the hotel's safe-deposit box. But keep a record of what you have deposited. If none of these options is available, lock everything in your pack and secure that in your room (some people take eyelet-screws for padlocking cupboards or drawers). If you lose your valuables, always report it to the police and note details of the report for insurance purposes. Double check that all reports written by the police actually state your complaint. The **tourist police** in Lima are excellent and, if you can, report any incidents to them (see page 41).

If someone spits, smears mustard, or sprays paint or shampoo on to your clothes, walk on to a safe, private place to clean yourself up. Similarly, ignore strangers' remarks like 'what's that on your shoulder?' or 'have you seen that dirt on your shoe?'. Furthermore, don't bend over to pick up money or other items in the street. These are all ploys intended to distract your attention and make it easy for an accomplice to rob you. If someone follows you while you're in the street, let him catch up with you and 'give him the eye'. Ruses involving 'plainclothes policemen' are infrequent, but it is worth knowing that the real police only have the right to see your passport (not your money, tickets or hotel room).

Until 2008 the activities of the terrorist groups Sendero Luminoso and MRTA had seemed to be a thing of the past, but neither organization was completely non-functional. Reports indicate that Sendero Luminoso was mobilizing again in the areas where its remants had gone to ground, the drug-growing zones of the Huallaga Valley and the jungle east of Ayacucho. In 2010 it was still safe to travel to all parts of Peru except those just mentioned, but it is important to inform yourself of the latest situation before going.

While in Lima or Cuzco, you can check in at **South American Explorers**, for the latest travel updates (Lima T01-444 2150, Cuzco T084-245484). Also check with the tourist police, your embassy or consulate.

Never offer a bribe unless you are fully conversant with local customs. Wait until the official makes the suggestion, or offer money in a form that is apparently not bribery, eg 'In our country we have a system of on-the-spot fines (*multas de inmediato*). Is there a similar system here?' Do not assume that an official who accepts a bribe is prepared to do anything else that is illegal. You bribe him to persuade him to do his job, or to persuade him not to do it, or to do it more quickly, or more slowly. You do not bribe him to do something which is against the law. If an official suggests that a bribe must be paid before you can proceed on your way, be patient and he may relent.

Many places in the Amazon and in Cuzco offer experiences with **Ayahuasca** or **San Pedro**, often in ceremonies with a shaman. These are legal, but always choose a reputable tour operator or shaman. Do not go with the first person who offers you a trip. Single women should not take part. There are plenty of websites for starting your research.

Students travellers

If you are in full-time education you will be entitled to an **International Student Identity Card**, which gives you special prices on all forms of transport (air, sea, rail, etc), and access to a variety of other concessions and services. If you need to find the location of your nearest ISIC office contact: **The ISIC Association**, www.isic.org.

Students can obtain very few reductions in Peru with an international student card, except in and around Cuzco, at museums and Ministerio de Cultura sites. To be any use in Peru, it must bear the owner's photograph. An ISIC card can be obtained in Lima from **Intej**, Av San Martín 240, Barranco, T01-247 3230, or Portal de Panes 123, of 304, Cuzco, T084-256367, www.intej.org.

Tax

General sales tax of 19% is automatically added to the bill. There is also a departure tax when flying, see page 22.

Telephone → *Country code +51.*

The main service provider is **Telefónica**, www.telefonica.com.pe (or **Telser** in Cuzco), which has offices in all large and medium-sized towns. **Telefónica** offices are usually administrative and phones are provided on the street outside. Local, national and international calls can be made from public phone boxes with prepaid phone cards that can be bought at **Telefónica** offices or the many private phone offices called *locutorios*. Also, there are cards for a number of other

carriers for long-distance calls. Their rates are very competitive and there are usually special offers. Collect calls are possible to almost anywhere by ringing the international operator (T108). This is also the number for directory enquiries and for international directorty options (they speak English). Your home telephone company can give you the number to call as well. **Net Phones** are popular; costs and service vary. SKYPE can also be used.

The numbering system for mobile/cellular phones is as follows: for Lima mobiles, add 9 before the number, for the departments of La Libertad 94, Arequipa 95, Piura 96, Lambayeque 97; for other departments, add 9 – if not already in the number – and the city code (for example, Cuzco numbers start 984). Note also that some towns are dominated by **Claró**, others by **Movistar** (the 2 main mobile companies). As it is expensive to call between the 2 you should check, if spending some time in 1 city and using a mobile, which is the best account to have.

Red Privada Movistar (RPM) and **Red Privada Claró (RPC)** are operated by the respective mobile phone companies. Mobile phone users who subscribe to these services obtain a 6-digit number in addition their 9-digit mobile phone number. Both the 6- and 9-digit numbers ring on the same physical phone. The RPM and RPC numbers can be called from anywhere in Peru without using an area code, you just dial the 6 digits, and the cost is about 20% of calling the 9-digit number. This 80% discount usually also applies when calling from *locutorios*. Many establishments including hotels, tour operators and transport companies have both RPM and RPC numbers.

Time → *Peru is 5 hrs behind GMT.*

Peruvians, as with most Latin Americans, have a fairly relaxed attitude towards time. They will think nothing of arriving an hour or so late on social occasions. If you expect to meet someone more or less at an exact time, you can tell them that you want to meet *en punto* or specify *la hora inglesa* (English time).

Tipping

In most of the better restaurants a 10% service charge is included in the bill, but you can give an extra 5% as a tip if the service is good. The most basic restaurants do not include a tip in the bill, and tips are not expected. Taxi drivers are not tipped – bargain the price down, then pay extra for good service if you get it. Tip cloakroom attendants and hairdressers (very high class only), US$0.50-1; railway or airport porters, US$0.50; car wash boys, US$0.30; car 'watch' boys, US$0.20. If going on a trek or tour it is customary to tip the guide, as well as the cook and porters.

Toilets

Most Peruvian toilets are adequate but the further you go from main population and tourist centres, the poorer the facilities, so you may require a strong stomach and the ability to hold your breath for a long time. Almost without exception used toilet paper or feminine hygiene products should not be flushed down the pan, but placed in the receptacle provided. This applies even in quite expensive hotels. Not doing so will block the pan or drain, which can be a considerable health risk. It is quite common for people to stand on the toilet seat, as they do in Asia.

Tour operators

UK and Ireland
The Adventure Company, Cross and Pillory House, Cross and Pillory Lane, Alton, Hampshire, GU34 1HL, T0845-450 5316, www.adventurecompany.co.uk.

Adventure Peru Motorcycling, Coldharbour Barn, Battle Rd, Dallington, near Heathfield, East Sussex TN21 9LQ, T01424-838618, www.perumotorcycling.com. In Peru based in Cajamarca, T0051-76-366630. Motorcycling adventure tours from 10 days to 4 weeks throughout the country, bikes provided, full back-up team, run by experienced bikers.
Amazing Peru, 9 Alma Rd, Manchester M19 2FG, T0800-520 0309, T1-800-216 0831 (Canada), T1-800-704 2915 or T1-800-704 2949 (USA), www.amazingperu.com. Professional and well-organized tours to Peru, with knowledgeable guides.
Amazing Voyages, 52 Brook St, London W1K 5DS, T020-7268 2053, www.amazing voyages.co.uk. Luxury travel specialist.
Andean Trails, The Clockhouse, Bonnington Mill Business Centre, 72 Newhaven Rd, Edinburgh EH6 5QG, T0131-467 7086, www.andeantrails.co.uk. For mountain biking, trekking and other adventure tours.
Andes, 37a St Andrews St, Castle Douglas, Kirkcudbrightshire DG7 1EN, Scotland, T01556-503929, www.andes.org.uk. For climbing trips in Peru and all South America.
Audley Latin America, New Mill, New Mill Lane, Witney, Oxfordshire, OX29 0SX, T01993-838000, www.audleytravel.com.
Austral Tours, 20 Upper Tachbrook St, London SW1V 1SH, T020-7233 5384, www.latinamerica.co.uk. Tailor-made tours, flights and accommodation in Latin America.
Chimu Adventures, www.chimuadventures. com. Web based company providing tours, treks, active adventures and accommodation throughout South America and the Antarctic.
Condor Journeys and Adventures, 2 Ferry Bank, Colintraive, Argyll PA22 3AR, T01700-841318, www.condorjourneys-adventures.com. Eco and adventure tourism with specially designed tours to suit your requirements.
Dragoman, Camp Green, Debenham, Suffolk IP14 6LA, T01728-861133, www.dragoman.com. Overland camping and/or hotel journeys throughout both South and Central America.

Exodus Travels, Grange Mills, 9 Weir Rd, London SW12 0NE, T020-8675 5550, www.exodus.co.uk. Experienced in adventure travel, including cultural tours and trekking and biking holidays.

Explore, Nelson House, 55 Victoria Rd, Farnborough, Hampshire GU14 7PA, T0845-0131537, www.explore.co.uk. Highly respected operator. They offer 2- to 5-week tours in more than 90 countries worldwide, including Peru. Small groups. Well executed.

Galapagos Classic Cruises in conjunction with **Classic Cruises** and **World Adventures**, 6 Keyes Rd, London NW2 3XA, T020-8933 0613, www.galapagoscruises.co.uk. Specialize in individual and group travel including cruises, scuba-diving and land-based tours to the Galapagos, Peru and Bolivia.

Guerba Expeditions, Wessex House, 40 Station Rd, Westbury, Wiltshire BA13 3JN, T01373-828303/T0203-147 7777, www.guerba.com. Adventure holidays, from trekking safaris to wilderness camping.

High Places, Globe Centre, Penistone Rd, Sheffield S6 3AE, T0845-257 7500, www.highplaces.co.uk. Trekking and mountaineering trips.

Journey Latin America, 12-13 Heathfield Terr, Chiswick, London W4 4JE, T020-8747 8315, www.journeylatinamerica.co.uk. The world's leading tailor-made specialist for Latin America, running escorted tours throughout the region; they also offer a wide range of flight options.

KE Adventure Travel, 32 Lake Rd, Keswick, Cumbria CA12 5DQ, T017687-73966, www.keadventure.com. Specialist in adventure tours, including 3-week cycling trips in and around Cuzco.

Kumuka Expeditions, 40 Earls Court Rd, London W8 6EJ, T0207-937 8855, www.kumuka.com. Overland tour operator for small groups, both escorted or truck-based. Offices in Ireland, Germany, USA, Canada, Australia, New Zealand, South Africa and UAE.

Last Frontiers, The Mill, Quainton Rd, Waddesdon, Bucks HP18 0LP, UK, T01296-653000, www.lastfrontiers.com.

South American specialists offering tailor-made itineraries plus family holidays, honeymoons, and Galápagos cruises.

Latin American Travel Association (LATA), 46 Melbourne Rd, London SW19 3BA, www.lata.org. For useful country information and listing of all UK tour operators specializing in Latin America.

Llama Travel, Oxford House, 49A Oxford Rd, London N4 3EY, T020-7263 3000, www.llama travel.com. Tours throughout Peru.

Naturetrek, Cheriton Mill, Cheriton, Alresford, Hampshire SO24 0NG, T01962-733051, www.naturetrek.co.uk. Birdwatching tours throughout the continent, also botany, natural history tours, treks and cruises.

Oasis Overland, The Marsh, Henstridge, Somerset BA8 0TF, T01963-363400, www.oasisoverland.co.uk. Small-group trips in Peru and overland trips across South America.

Reef and Rainforest Tours, Dart Marine Park, Steamer Quay, Totnes, Devon TQ9 5AL, T01803-866965, www.reefandrainforest. co.uk. Specialists in tailor-made and group wildlife tours.

Select Latin Amercia (incorporating Galapagos Adventure Tours), 3.51 Canterbury Court, 1-3 Brixton Rd, Kennington Park Business Centre, London SW9 6DE, T020-7407 1478, www.selectlatinamerica.co.uk. Quality tailor-made holidays and small-group tours.

South American Experience, Welby House, 96 Wilton Rd, Victoria, London SW1V 1DW, T0845-2773366, www.southamerican experience.com. Flights and accommodation bookings as well as tailor-made trips since 1987.

Steppes Latin America, 51 Castle St, Cirencester, Glos GL7 1QD, T01285-880980, www.steppestravel.co.uk. Tailor-made itineraries for destinations throughout Latin America.

Sunvil Latin America, Sunvil House, Upper Sq, Old Isleworth, Middlesex TW7 7BJ, T020-8568 4499, www.sunvil.co.uk. Small groups or individual tours.

Tribes Travel, 12 The Business Centre, Earl Soham, Woodbridge, Suffolk IP13 7SA, T01728-685971, www.tribes.co.uk. Has an associated charitable foundation that aims to relieve poverty in indigenous communities.
Trips Worldwide, 14 Frederick Pl, Clifton, Bristol BS8 1AS, T0800-840 0850, www.tripsworldwide.co.uk. Tailor-made tours to South America.
Tucan Travel, 316 Uxbridge Rd, Acton, London W3 9QP, T020-8896 1600; Av del Sol 616, oficina 202, AP 0637, Cuzco, T51-84-241123; and 217 Alison Rd, Randwick, NSW 2031, Sydney, T02-9326 6633, www.tucantravel.com.
Veloso Tours, ground floor, 34 Warple Way, London W3 0RG, T020-8762 0616, www.veloso.com.

Continental Europe
Nouveaux Mondes, Rte Suisse 7, CH-1295 Mies, Switzerland, T+41-22-950 9660, www.nouveauxmondes.com.
South American Tours, Stephanstrasse 13, D-60313, Frankfurt/M, Germany, T+49-69-405 8970, www.southamericantours.de. For holidays, business travel, or special packages. Has an office at C Bolognesi 381, Miraflores 18, Lima, T01-446 7799, and in New York, Tokyo, Montevideo, Quito, Rio de Janeiro, Santiago de Chile and Buenos Aires.

North America
Discover Latinamerica, 6205 Blue Lagoon Drive, suite 310, Miami, FL 33126, T305-266 5827, www.discoverlatinamerica.com.
eXito, 108 Rutgers St, Fort Collins, CO 80525, T1-800-655 4053, www.exito-travel.com.
GAP Adventures, 19 Charlotte St, Toronto, M5V 2H5, Canada, T1-800-708 7761 (in North America), 40 Star St, London W2 1QB, T0870 999 0144, T1-416-260 0999 (outside North America and UK), www.gapadventures.com.
Ladatco, 3006 Aviation, Suite 3A, Coconut Grove, FL 33133, USA, T1-800 327 6162, www.ladatco.com. 'Themed' explorer tours based around the Incas, mysticism, etc.
Myths and Mountains, 976 Tee Court, Incline Village, NV 89451, T775-832 5454, www.mythsandmountains.com.
Peru For Less, T1-877-269 0309 (USA toll free) T0203-002 0571 (UK), www.peruforless.com. Customized tours to Peru and Latin America, price and service guarantee. Based in Texas, offices in Lima and Cuzco.
Puchka Peru, www.puchkaperu.com. Specializes in textiles, folk art and market tours.
Tambo Tours, USA, T1-888-2-GO-PERU (246- 7378), www.2GOPERU.com. Long-established adventure and tour specialist with offices in Peru and the USA. Customized trips to the Amazon and archaeological sites of Peru, Bolivia and Ecuador.

Tropical Nature Travel, PO Box 5276, Gainesville, FL 326270 5276, T1-877-827 8350, www.tropicalnaturetravel.com. Ecotour company with itineraries to Peru.

Wildland Adventures, 3516 NE 155 St, Seattle, WA 98155-7412, USA, T206-365 0686, T800-345 4453, www.wildland.com. Specializes in cultural and natural history tours to the Andes and Amazon.

South America

For Lima- and Cuzco-based operators, see Activities and tours, pages 114 and page 299.
Aracari Travel Consulting, Schell 237 No 602, Miraflores, Lima, T01-651 2424, www.aracari.com. Regional tours in Peru.
Condor Travel, Armando Blondet 249, San Isidro, Lima 27, T01-615 3000, www.condortravel.com. In USA T1-877-236 7199. A full range of tours, including custom-made, and services in Bolivia, Ecuador and Peru (offices in each country), with a strong commitment to social responsibility.
Kolibri Expeditions, contact Gunnar Engblom, Lima, T01-273 7246, www.kolibriexpeditions.com. Birdwatching, trip reports, recent sightings, travel tips, travel partners, range extensions, identification help, also www.birding-peru.com. **Birding Peru** e-group: birdingperu-subscribe@yahoogroups.com.
SouthAmerica.travel, www.southamerica. travel. Internet-based tour operator with offices in Peru (Jr Elías Aguirre 141, of 313, Miraflores, Lima, T01-719 7792), Germany (Hauptstr 131, D-70563 Stuttgart, T+49-711-856 6972), USA (322 SE Park Hill Dr, Chehalis WA 98532, T1-800-747 4540) and in Rio de Janeiro and Buenos Aires. Covering every type of travel throughout South America.
Surtrek, Av Amazonas 897 y Wilson, Quito, Ecuador, T593-2-250 0530, www.surtrek.com. Customized private group and individual adventure tours throughout South America.

Rest of the world

Adventure World, Level 20, 141 Walker St, North Sydney NSW 2060, T02-8913 0755, and Level 9, 40 St Georges Terrace, Perth 6000, T08-9226 4524, www.adventureworld.com.au. Escorted group tours, locally escorted tours and packages to Peru and all of Latin America.

Tourist information

Tourism promotion and information is handled by **PromPerú**, Edif Mincetur, C Uno Oeste 50, p 13, urb Córpac, San Isidro, T01-224 3131, www.peru.info. They produce promotional material but offer no direct information service to individual tourists. The website does carry plenty of background and other information. PromPerú runs an information and assistance service, **i perú**, T01-574 8000 (24 hrs). Main office: Jorge Basadre 610, San Isidro, Lima, T01-421 1627, iperulima@promperu.gob.pe, Mon-Fri 0830-1830. Also a 24-hr office at Jorge Chávez airport; and throughout the country.

There are tourist offices in most towns, either run by the municipality, or independently. **Indecopi**, in Lima T01-224 7800, www.indecopi.gob.pe, is the government-run consumer protection and tourist complaint bureau. This body (with offices, kiosks and information stands in every town) will help with complaints regarding customs, airlines, travel agencies, accommodation, restaurants, public authorities or if you have lost, or had stolen, documents. For information on national parks and protected areas, see **El Servicio Nacional de Áreas Naturales Protegidas por el Estado** (SERNANP), C Diecisiete 355, Urb El Palomar, San Isidro, Lima, T01-717 7500, www.sernanp.gob.pe.

Outside Peru, tourist information can be obtained from Peruvian embassies and consulates, see page 44.

With regard to security, it is better to seek advice before you leave from your own consulate than from travel agencies. Also contact: **British Foreign and Commonwealth Office**, Travel Advice Unit, T0845-850 2829 (travel advice), T020-7008

1500 (consular assistance from abroad). Footprint is a partner in the Foreign and Commonwealth Office's **Know before you go** campaign, www.fco.gov.uk/en/travel-and-living-abroad/. **US State Department's Bureau of Consular Affairs**, Overseas Citizens Services, T1-888-407 4747 (from overseas: T202-501 4444), www.travel.state.gov. **Australian Department of Foreign Affairs**, T+61-2-6261 3305, www.smartraveller.gov.au/. **South American Explorers**, www.saexplorers.org, is a non-profit, educational organization that functions primarily as an information network for Peru and South America and is the most useful organization for travellers in the continent. They have offices in Lima, Cuzco, Quito, Buenos Aires and the USA. Full details are given in the Lima and Cuzco sections, see pages 66 and 272. For tourist organizations within Peru, see below.

Useful organizations

Agotur (Asociación de Guías Oficiales de Turismo), Av La Paz 678, Miraflores, Lima, www.agotur.com. With a full list of associated guides and access to the Ley de Guía.
Apavit (Asociación Peruana de Agencias de Viaje y Turismo), Antonio Roca 121, Santa Beatriz, Lima, T01-433 1111, www.apavitperu.org.
Apotur (Asociación Peruana de Operadores de Turismo), C San Fernando 287, Miraflores, Lima 18, T01-446 4076, www.apoturperu.org.
Aptae (Asociación Peruana de Operadores de Turismo de Aventura y Ecoturismo), Bolognesi 125, of 703, Miraflores, Lima 18, T01-447 8476, www.aptae.org.

Useful websites

www.aboutcusco.com, **www.cuscoon line.com** and **www.cusco.net** Among many websites about Cuzco, in Spanish, English and other languages.
www.adonde.com For general information.
www.andeantravelweb.com/peru Andean adventure travel, with advice, links and more (English and Spanish).
www.livinginperu.com Informative guide in English for people living in Peru.
www.machu-picchu.info All about Machu Picchu.
www.mcultura.gob.pe Website of the Ministerio de Cultura, which has replaced the Instituto Nacional de Cultura, www.inc.gob.pe (website still operational).
www.minam.gob.pe Ministerio del Ambiente (Spanish).
www.planeta.com Ron Mader's website containing masses of useful information on ecotourism, conservation, travel, news, links, language schools and articles.
www.rree.gob.pe Ministry of Foreign Affairs, for consular information, etc.
www.terra.com.pe Click on Turismo to get to the travel page (in Spanish).
www.traficoperu.com Online agent with lots of information (in Spanish and English).
www.yachay.com.pe Red Científica Peruana, click on Turismo.
www.leaplocal.org Recommends good-quality local guides, helping communities benefit from socially responsible tourism.

Visas and immigration

Tourist cards No visa is necessary for citizens of countries in the European Union, most Asian countries, North and South America and the Caribbean, or for citizens of Andorra, Belarus, Croatia, Iceland, Israel, Liechtenstein, Macedonia, Moldova, Norway, Russian Federation, Serbia and Montenegro, Switzerland, Ukraine, Australia, New Zealand and South Africa. A tourist card (**TAM** – Tarjeta Andina de Migración) is free on flights arriving in Peru, or at border crossings for visits of up to 183 days. The form is in duplicate, the original given up on arrival and the copy on departure. A new tourist card must be obtained for each re-entry. If your tourist card is stolen or lost, get a new one at **Migraciones**, Digemin, Av España 730, Breña, Lima, T01-417 6900/433 0731, www.digemin.gob.pe, Mon-Fri 0800-1300.

Tourist visas For citizens of countries not listed above, tourist visas cost £20.70 (about US$32.50) or equivalent, for which you require a valid passport, a departure ticket from Peru (or reservation showing arrival and departure dates), 1 colour passport photo, 1 application form, hotel reservation or package tour confirmation and proof of economic solvency.

Under Decree 1043 of Jun 2008, once in Peru tourists may not extend their tourist card or visa. It's therefore important to insist on getting the full number of days to cover your visit on arrival (it's at the discretion of the border official). If you exceed your card or visa, you'll pay a US$1-per-day fine.

All foreigners should be able to produce on demand some recognizable means of identification, preferably a passport. You must present your passport when reserving tickets for internal as well as international travel. An alternative is to photocopy the important pages of your passport – including the immigration stamp, and have it legalized by a 'notario público' (US$1.50). We have received no reports of travellers being asked for an onward ticket at the borders at Tacna, Aguas Verdes, La Tina, Yunguyo or Desaguadero. Travellers arriving by air are not asked for an onward flight ticket at Lima airport, but it is possible that you will not be allowed to board a plane in your home country without showing an onward ticket.

Business visas A visitor who is going to receive money from Peruvian sources must have a business visa: requirements are a valid passport, 1 colour passport photo, return ticket or reservation and a letter from an employer stating the nature of business, length of stay and guarantee that any Peruvian taxes will be paid and proof of solvency of the company. The visa costs £20.70 (about US$32.50) and allows the holder to stay 183 days in the country. On arrival business visitors must register with the **Dirección General de Contribuciones** for tax purposes.

Student visas To obtain a student visa you must enter the country as a tourist and then apply at **Migraciones** in Lima (address above). In addition to completing the general visa form you must have proof of adequate funds, affiliation to a Peruvian body, and a letter of consent from parents or tutors if you are a minor. The cost is US$20. Full details are on the Digemin website (in Spanish). See above.

Weights and measures

Metric.

Women travellers

Generally women travellers should find visiting Peru an enjoyable experience. However, machismo is alive and well here and you should be prepared for this and try not to overreact. When you set out, err on the side of caution until your instincts have adjusted to the customs of a new culture.

It is easier for men to take the friendliness of locals at face value; women may be subject to much unwanted attention. To minimize this, do not wear suggestive clothing and do not flirt. By wearing a wedding ring, carrying a photograph of your 'husband' and 'children', and saying that your 'husband' is close at hand, you may dissuade an aspiring suitor. If politeness fails, do not feel bad about showing offence and departing. When accepting a social invitation, make sure that someone knows the address and the time you left. Ask if you can bring a friend (even if you do not intend to do so).

If, as a single woman, you can befriend a local woman, you will learn much more about the country you are visiting as well as finding out how best to deal with the barrage of suggestive comments, whistles and hisses that will invariably come your way.

There is a very definite 'gringo trail' that you can join, or follow, if seeking company.

This can be helpful when looking for safe accommodation, especially if arriving after dark (which is best avoided).

Working and volunteering in Peru

Voluntourism

There are many opportunities for volunteer work in Peru (**South American Explorers** has an extensive database). Most volunteers do not need a visa for Peru, but you must check with a Peruvian consulate that this applies to you. The site www.trabajovoluntario.org helps volunteers and organizations to get in touch and browse for opporutnities. Likewise, www.volunteersouthamerica.net, a continent-wide directory of low-cost to zero-cost programmes, offers several opportunities in Peru. In Cuzco, **Hope Foundation** (at Marani Hotel, see page 97) and **Amauta Spanish School** (see page 125) accept volunteers. For information outside Peru on voluntary work and working abroad, try www.idealist.org for community organizations, volunteer opportunities and non-profit careers.

There is some overlap between volunteering and gap-year or career-break tourism as many people who make this type of trip are going to do some form of work. There is an increasing amount of help for students on a gap year and the career-break market is growing fast. www.gapyear.com, www.lattitude.org.uk, www.thecareerbreak site.com and www.yearoutgroup.org cater for that year away. For a range of other options, try www.i-to-i.com, www.hands upholidays.com for project vacations, www.madventurer.com, www.thepod site.co.uk (Personal Overseas Development) and www.visionsserviceadventures.com, www.projects-abroad.co.uk, for teaching-based projects and other activities. The website www.amerispan.com is principally concerned with language learning and teaching but also has a comprehensive list of volunteer opportunities.

Contents

Footprint features

Cuzco

Machu □
Picchu

Cuzco ■

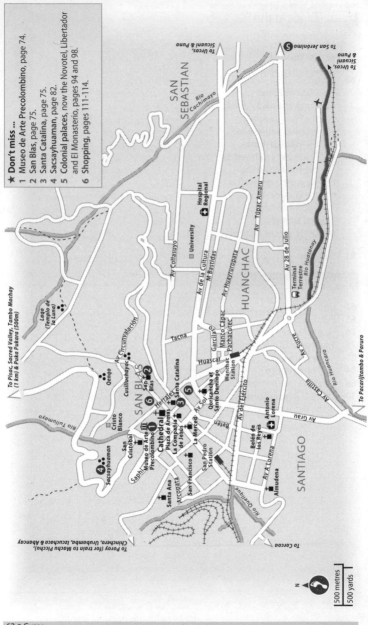

★ **Don't miss ...**
1 Museo de Arte Precolombino, page 74.
2 San Blas, page 75.
3 Santa Catalina, page 75.
4 Sacsayhuaman, page 82.
5 Colonial palaces, now the Novotel, Libertador and El Monasterio, pages 94 and 98.
6 Shopping, pages 111-114.

To Pisac, Sacred Valley, Tambo Machay (1 km) & Puka Pukara (500m)

To Urcos, Sicuani & Puno

To San Jerónimo

To Urcos, Sicuani & Puno

To Pacaritambo & Paruro

To Corcoa

To Poroy (for train to Machu Picchu), Chinchero, Urubamba, Izcuchaca & Abancay

SAN SEBASTIAN

SAN BLAS

HUANCHAC

SANTIAGO

Hospital Regional

Terminal Terrestre

University

Av Collasuyo

Av de la Cultura

M Bastidas

Av Huayruropata

Av Tupac Amaru

Av 28 de Julio

Río Cachimayo

Río Huatanay

Av Sucre

Av Huancaro

Av Castilla

Río Huancaro

Manco Cápac

García

Pachacutec

Huascar

Tacna

Cusilluchayoc

Av Circunvalación

Lago (Templo de la Luna)

Qengo

Cristo Blanco

Río Tullumayo

San Cristóbal

Sacsayhuaman

Museo de Arte Precolombino

Cathedral

La Compañía de Jesús

Plaza de Armas

San Pedro Station

Saphi

Arcopata

Santa Ana

San Francisco

La Merced

Belén

Av de Ejército

Av A Lorena

Río Chunquipuquio

Almudena

Belén de los Reyes

Antonio Lorena

Av Sol

Qoricancha at Santo Domingo

Wanchaq Station

Santa Catalina

Heladeros

San Blas

N

500 metres
500 yards

Cuzco stands at the head of the Sacred Valley of the Incas and is the jumping-off point for the Inca Trail and famous Inca city of Machu Picchu. Not surprising, then, that this is the prime destination for the vast majority of Peru's visitors. In fact, the ancient Inca capital is now the 'gringo' capital of the entire continent. And it's easy to see why. There are Inca ruins aplenty, as well as fabulous colonial architecture, stunning scenery, great trekking, river rafting and mountain biking, beautiful textiles and other traditional handicrafts – all within easy reach of the nearest cappuccino or comfy hotel room.

The history books describe the Incas' mythical beginnings, their rapid rise to power, their achievements and their equally rapid defeat by the Spaniards, who converted the pulse of the Inca Empire into a jewel of their own. Yet Cuzco today is not some dead monument. Its history breathes through the stones and the Quechua people bring the city to life with a combination of pre-Hispanic and Christian beliefs.

Getting there

By air Most travellers arriving from Lima will do so by air. No flights arrive in Cuzco at night. The airport is at Quispiquilla, near the bus terminal, 1.6 km southeast of the centre. For airport information T084-222611/601. You can book a hotel at the airport through a travel agency, but this is not really necessary. Many representatives of hotels and travel agencies operate in the baggage retrieval area, offering transport to the hotel with which they are associated. If you haven't booked in advance, take your time to choose your hotel, at the price you can afford. Also in baggage retrieval are mobile phone rentals, ATMs, **LAC Dollar** money exchange, an **Oxyshot** oxygen sales stand and an **iperú** office. There are phone booths, restaurant and cafeteria at the airport. There is also a Tourist Protection Bureau desk. Do not forget to pay the airport tax at the appropriate desk before departure. A taxi to and from the airport costs US$2-3.50 (US$7.25 from official taxi desk). Colectivos to the centre cost US$0.30 from outside the airport car park. ▶▶ *For flight information, see Getting there, page 22, and Getting around, page 25.*

By bus All long-distance buses arrive and leave from the Terminal Terrestre, Avenida Vallejo Santoni, block 2 (Prolongación Pachacútec), in Ttio district. A colectivo to/from the centre costs US$0.30; a taxi US$1. Platform tax US$0.35. Transport to your hotel is not a problem as bus company representatives are often on hand.

By train There is one train station in Cuzco, **Estación Wanchac** ⓘ *C Pachacútec, T084-581414*, for the **PerúRail** service to Juliaca and Puno. The office here offers direct information and ticket sales for all **PerúRail** services. When arriving in Cuzco, a tourist bus meets the train to take visitors to hotels. Machu Picchu trains do not leave from the city, but from **Poroy** (PerúRail), over the hill from Cuzco on the road to Urubamba, taxi US$9, or from Ollantaytambo (see page 144), **Inca Rail** ⓘ *Av Sol 613, T084-233030, www.inca rail.com.pe*, **Machu Picchu Train** ⓘ *Av Sol 576, T084-221199, www.machupicchutrain.com*, and **PerúRail** services. There is a sales office for **PerúRail** ⓘ *Plaza de Armas, Portal de Carnes 214, T084-260809, cuscoplaza@perurail.com.* ▶▶ *See Transport, page 124. For trains to Machu Picchu, see page 166.*

Getting around

The centre of Cuzco is small and is easily explored on foot. Bear in mind, however, that at this altitude walking up some of the city's steep cobbled streets may leave you out of breath, so you'll need to take your time. It is even possible to walk up to Sacsayhuaman, but a better idea is to take a combi (minivan) to Tambo Machay and walk back downhill to town via Qenqo and Sacsayhuaman. Combis are the main form of public transportation in the city; they are well organized, cheap and safe. Taxis in Cuzco are also cheap and recommended when arriving by air, train or bus, and at night. ▶▶ *For further details, see Transport page 122.*

If you wish to explore this area on your own, road map (*Hoja de ruta*) No 10 is an excellent guide. You can get it from the **Touring y Automóvil Club del Perú**, see page 124. They have other maps. There are, however, very few good maps of Cuzco available. Streets in Cuzco have multiple spellings (k and be substituted for q, for example) and street numbers can be out of order, with the 100s followed by 600s.

Permission to enter

A combined entry ticket to 16 of the main historical and cultural sites in and around Cuzco, called the **Boleto Turístico del Cusco** (**BTC**), costs US$45/ €33.50 (S/.130) and is valid for 10 days. It is payable in soles only. The 16 sites are: Municipal Exposición de Arte Contemporáneo, Museo Histórico Regional (Casa Garcilaso), Museo de Arte Popular, Museo de Sitio Qoricancha (but not Qoricancha itself), Centro Qosqo de Arte Nativo and Monumento Pachacútec in Cuzco city; the archaeological sites of Sacsayhuaman, Qenqo, Puka Pukara and Tambo Machay: the archaeological sites of Pisac, Ollantaytambo, Chinchero and Moray in the Sacred Valley; and the archaeological sites of Tipón and Piquillacta, southeast of Cuzco. A two-day ticket, costing US$24/€18 (S/.70), allows entry to Sacsayhuaman, Qenqo, Puka Pukara and Tambo Machay, or Pisac, Ollantaytambo, Chinchero and Moray. No individual tickets are available, except to Moray, Tipón and Piquillacta, which cost US$3.60 (S/.10) each. A two-day ticket, costing US$24/€18 (S/.70), allows entry to city museums included in the main ticket.

The BTC can be bought at the offices of **Cosituc**, which sells the ticket, at Av Sol 103, of 102, Galerías Turísticas, T084-261465, Monday-Saturday 0800-1800, Sunday 0800-1300, or

Yuracpunku 79-A (east of centre, go along Recoleta), www.boletinturistico cusco.com or www.cosituc.gob.pe, or at any of the sites included in the ticket. For students with an ISIC card, the BTC costs US$24 (S/.70), which is only available at the Cosituc office upon presentation of the student card. Take your ISIC card when visiting the sites, as some may ask to see it.

Entrance tickets for Museo Inka (Palacio del Almirante), Santo Domingo/ Qoricancha and La Merced are sold separately, while the cathedral (including the churches of El Triunfo and La Sagrada Familia), La Compañía, Templo de San Blas and the Museo de Arte Religioso del Arzobispado are included on a religious buildings ticket costing US$17.75 (S/.50), valid for 10 days. Each of these sites may be visited individually.

All sites are crowded on Sundays. Photography is not allowed in the churches and museums.

Machu Picchu ruins and Inca Trail entrance tickets are sold at the **Ministerio de Cultura Cusco** (ex-Dirección Regional de Cultura, DRC), Av de la Cultura 238, Condominio Huáscar, T084-236061, www.drc-cusco.gob.pe, Monday-Friday 0715-1600, or electronically at http://boletajevirtual.drc-cusco.gob.pe or www.machupicchu.gob.pe.

Tourist information

The official **tourist office** ⓘ *Portal Mantas 117-A, next to La Merced church, T084-263176, 0800-1830, closed Sun afternoon*, is supplemented by tourist information desks run by **iperú** ⓘ *at the airport, T084-237364, open when flights arrive and depart; also at Av del Sol 103, of 102, Galerías Turísticas, T084-252974, daily 0830-1930*. The **Dircetur** office is at ⓘ *Plaza Túpac Amaru Mz 1 Lte 2, Wanchac, T084-223761, Mon-Fri 0800-1300*. It has a good map of the city centre. See box above for the offices of Cosituc and Ministerio de Cultura for Machu Picchu.

South American Explorers ① *Atoqsaycuchi 670, San Blas, T084-245484, cuscoclub@ saexplorers.org, Mon-Fri 0930-1700, Sat 0930-1300; also in Lima (see page 272)*, is an excellent resource and haven for the traveller. It's worth making the climb up the steps to the large new clubhouse which has a garden. They provide great information on the Cuzco area including a comprehensive map of the city and area, an extensive English-language library, expedition reports, weekly events, local discounts and free internet for members, phone and mail service and equipment storage. They also have rooms for rent, practical advice on responsible tourism and a volunteer resource centre. The Club's recycling centre receives plastic and glass bottles for recycling and there's a water refill station to minimize purchase of plastic bottles. They have also been involved in establishing a pilot recycling project in San Blas, including composting of organic materials. Their leaflet *Enjoy Cusco Safely* is invaluable (for more advice see box, page 135).

Perú Verde ① *Ricaldo Palma J-1, Santa Mónica, T084-226392, www.peruverde.org*, provides information and free video shows about Manu National Park and Tambopata National Reserve. The staff are friendly and also have information on programmes and research in the jungle area of Madre de Dios, as well as distributing the beautiful but expensive book on the Manu National Park by Kim MacQuarrie and André Bartschi.

Safety

If you need a *denuncia* (a report for insurance purposes, available from the Banco de la Nación), the **tourist police** ① *C Saphi 510, T084-249665/221961*, will type it out. Always go to the police when robbed, even though it will take a bit of time. Police patrol the streets, trains and stations, but one should still be vigilant. On no account walk back to your hotel after dark from a bar or club, as muggings do occur. For safety's sake, pay the US$1 taxi fare, but not just any taxi. Ask the club's doorman to get a licensed taxi for you (see Taxis, page 124).

Other areas in which to take care include Santa Pedro market, the San Cristóbal area and at out-of-the-way ruins. **Indecopi (Consumer Protection Bureau)** ① *Av Manco Inca 209, Wanchac, T084-252987, mmarroquin@indecopi.gob.pe, toll free T0800-44040 (24-hr hotline, not available from pay phones)*, protects the consumer rights of all tourists and helps with any problems or complaints. They can be helpful in dealing with tour agencies, hotels or restaurants.

Background

The ancient Inca capital is said to have been founded around AD 1100. According to the central Inca creation myth, the Sun sent his son, Manco Cápac and the Moon sent her daughter, Mama Ocllo, to spread culture and enlightenment throughout the dark, barbaric lands. The Sun pitied the people of this savage region because they could not cultivate the land, clothe themselves, make houses, nor had they any religion. Manco and Mama Ocllo emerged from the icy depths of Lake Titicaca and began their journey in search of the place where they would found their kingdom. They were ordered to head north from the lake until a golden staff they carried could be plunged into the ground for its entire length. The soil of the altiplano was so thin that they had to travel as far as the valley of Cuzco where, on the mountain of Huanacauri, the staff fully disappeared and the soil was found to be suitably fertile. This was the sign they were looking for. They named this place Cuzco, meaning 'navel of the earth' according to popular legend (there is no linguistic basis for this). The local inhabitants, on seeing Manco Cápac and Mama Ocllo with their fine clothes and jewellery (including the adornments in their long, pierced ears, which became a symbol of the Incas) immediately worshipped them and followed their instructions, the men being taught by Manco Cápac, the women by Mama Ocllo. See also boxes on page 147 and page 309.

Thus the significance of Cuzco and the sacred Urubamba Valley was established for many centuries to come. As Peter Frost states in his *Exploring Cuzco*: "Cusco was more than just a capital city to the Incas and the millions of subjects in their realm. It was a Holy City, a place of pilgrimage with as much importance to the Quechuas as Mecca has to the Moslems. Every ranking citizen of the empire tried to visit Cusco once in his lifetime; to have done so increased his stature wherever he might travel."

Today, the city's beauty cannot be overstated. It is a fascinating mix of Inca and colonial Spanish architecture: colonial churches, monasteries and convents and pre-Columbian ruins are interspersed with hotels, bars and restaurants that have sprung up to cater for the tourists who flock here for the atmosphere. Almost every central street has remains of Inca walls, arches and doorways. Many streets are lined with perfect Inca stonework, now serving as the foundations for more modern dwellings. This stonework is tapered upwards (battered); every wall has a perfect line of inclination towards the centre, from bottom to top. The curved stonework of the Temple of the Sun, for example, is probably unequalled in the world.

Cuzco has developed into a major commercial centre of 326,000 inhabitants, a large proportion of whom are Quechua. Despite its growth, however, the city is still laid out much as it was in Inca times. The Incas conceived their capital in the shape of a puma and this can be seen from above, with the Río Tullumayo forming the spine, Sacsayhuaman the head and the main city centre the body. The best place for an overall view of the Cuzco Valley is from the puma's head – the top of the hill of Sacsayhuaman.

Sights

Not even the most ardent tourist would be able to visit all the sights in Cuzco city. For those with limited time, or for those who want a whistle-stop tour, a list of must-sees would comprise the combination of Inca and colonial architecture at Qoricancha; the huge Inca ceremonial centre of Sacsayhuaman; the paintings of the Last Supper and the 1650 earthquake in the cathedral; the main altar of La Compañía de Jesús; the pulpit of

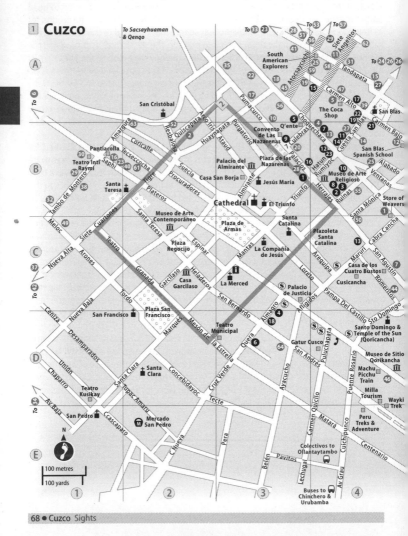

Cuzco

San Blas; the high choir at San Francisco; the monstrance at La Merced; and the view from San Cristóbal. If you have the energy, take a taxi up to the White Christ and watch the sunset as you look out upon one of the most fascinating cities in the world. And if you only visit one museum, make it the Museo Inka, which has the most comprehensive collection.

Unless your Spanish is up to scratch a good guide can really improve your visit, as most of the sights do not have any information or signs in English. Either arrange this before you set out or hire one of those hanging around the sight entrances. The latter is much easier to do in the low season; good guides are often booked up with tour agencies at

➡ **Cuzco maps**

Sleeping
1 Albergue Casa Campesina C4
2 Albergue Municipal B2
3 Andean South Inn B5
4 Andenes al Cielo B4
5 Andes de San Blas A4
6 Cahuide A1
7 Casa Andina Koricancha C4
8 Casa Andina Private Collection Cusco C5
9 Casa Andina San Blas B5
10 Casa Cartagena A3
11 Casa de la Gringa 1 A4
12 Casa de la Gringa 2 B4
13 Casa Elena B4
14 Casa San Blas & Tika Bistro Gourmet B4
15 Casona Les Pleiades A4
16 Cusco Plaza 2 B1
17 El Arqueólogo A3
18 El Balcón Colonial A3
19 El Grial A3
20 El Monasterio B3
21 Estrellita C5
22 Flying Dog Hostel A3
23 Goldie's Guest House B1
24 Hosp El Artesano de San Blas A4
25 Hosp Familiar Inti Quilla A4
26 Hosp Inka A5
27 Hostal Amaru B4
28 Hostal Casa de Campo A3
29 Hostal El Balcón B1
30 Hostal Familiar B1
31 Hostal Familiar Mirador del Inka A4
32 Hostal Killipata B1
33 Hostal Kuntur Wasi A3
34 Hostal Luzerna D1
35 Hostal María Esther A3
36 Hostal Pakcha Real A4
37 Hostal Qorichaska C1
38 Hostal Rickch'airy B1
39 Hostal Sambleño A4
40 Hostal San Isidro Labrador B2
41 Hostal Tika Wasi A3
42 Hostel Loki C1
43 La Casa de Fray Bartolomé & Panadería Qosqo Maki C5
44 Libertador Palacio del Inka C4
45 Los Apus Hotel y Mirador A3
46 Maison de la Jeunesse D4
47 Marani A4
48 Munay Wasi Inn C5
49 Niños Hotel C1
50 Novotel C4
51 Pensión Alemana A3
52 Piccola Locanda & L'Osteria Restaurant B2
53 Quinua Villa Boutique A3
54 Res Torre Dorada E6
55 Ruinas B4
56 Rumi Punku A3
57 Samay Wasi I A4
58 Samay Wasi II A4
59 Second Home Cusco A3
60 Sonesta Hotel Cusco E6
61 Suecia II B2
62 The Blue House A4
63 The Walk on Inn B2
64 Yamanyá Backpackers D3

Eating
1 A Mi Manera B3
2 Aldea Yanapay B4
3 Baco B3
4 Café El Ayllu D3
5 Café Punchay A3
6 Chifa Sipan D3
7 Chocolate A4
8 Cositas Café y Arte B4
9 Divina Comedia B3
10 El Encuentro B4
11 Granja Heidi B4
12 Inka...fé B4
13 Inkanato C4
14 Jack's Café B4
15 Juanito's Sandwich Bar A4
16 Justina B3
17 La Bodega A4
18 Los Toldos D3
19 Macondo A4
20 Manu Café E6
21 Pachapapa B4
22 Panadería El Buen Pastor A4
23 El Batán del Inka B4

Bars & clubs
23 Bar 7 A3
24 Caos Disco E6
25 Frogs Restaurant & Lounge B4
26 Hierba Buena Lounge A4
27 Km 0 (Arte y Tapas) A4
28 Marcelo Batata B3
29 Siete Angelitos A4

busy times of year. A tip is expected at the end of the tour; this gives you the chance to reward a good guide and get rid of a bad one! ▸ *For listings, see pages 91-127.*

Plaza de Armas

The heart of the city in Inca days was *Huacaypata* (the place of tears) and *Cusipata* (the place of happiness), divided by a channel of the Río Saphi. Today, Huacaypata is the Plaza de Armas and Cusipata is Plaza Regocijo. This was the great civic square of the Incas, flanked by their palaces, and was a place of solemn parades and great assemblies. Each territory conquered by the Incas had some of its soil taken to Cuzco to be mingled symbolically with the soil of the Huacaypata, as a token of its incorporation into the empire.

As well as the many great ceremonies, the plaza has also seen its share of executions, among them the last Inca Túpac Amaru, the rebel *conquistador* Diego de Almagro the Younger, and the 18th-century indigenous leader Túpac Amaru II.

Around the present-day Plaza de Armas are colonial arcades and four churches. In the mid-1990s the mayor insisted that all the native trees be pulled down as they interrupted views of the surrounding buildings. The trees were replaced with the flowerbeds you see today. You may be forgiven for thinking the graceful, imposing church on the southeast

2 Around Plaza de Armas

➡ Cuzco maps
1 Cuzco, page 68
2 Around Plaza de Armas, page 70

side of the plaza is the cathedral. However, this is **La Compañía de Jesús**. When the Jesuits started building, the other Catholics asked the Pope to intervene, complaining it was too ornate and overshadowed the presence of the cathedral. The Pope failed to act in time and La Compañía de Jesús was completed in all its splendour.

Cathedral

ⓘ *Entry US$9, students half price, or by religious buildings ticket; open daily 1000-1800, Quechua Mass at 0500-0600.*

The early 17th-century baroque cathedral (on the northeast side of the square) forms part of a three-church complex: the cathedral itself, Iglesia Jesús y María (1733) on the left as you look at it and El Triunfo (1533) on the right. There are two entrances; the cathedral doors are used during Mass but the tourist entrance is on the left-hand side through Iglesia Jesús y María.

Two interesting legends surround the western tower of the cathedral. According to the first, a captured Inca prince is bricked up in the tower. His only means of escape is for the tower to fall, at which point he will reclaim his people and land. Believers' hopes were raised when the tower was severely damaged in the 1950 earthquake, but it failed to fall before restoration started, incarcerating the prince until this very day.

Plateros detail

50 metres
50 yards

Sleeping 🛏
1 Aranwa Cusco Boutique *B1*
2 Andean Wings *A1*
3 Brituvian Inn *A3*
4 Casa Andina Catedral *C3*
5 Casa Andina Plaza *C2*
6 Cusco Plaza 1 *B3*
7 Del Prado Inn *B3*
8 EcoPackers *A1*
9 El Procurador del Cusco *A2*
10 Emperador Plaza *C3*
11 Hostal Corihuasi *A2*
12 Hostal Qosqo *C2*
13 Hostal Resbalosa *A3*
14 Hostal Royal Frankenstein *B1*
15 Hostal Turístico Plateros *Plateros detail*
16 La Casona Inkaterra *B3*
17 Loreto Boutique Hotel *C2*
18 Marqueses *B1*
19 Munay Wasi *A3*
20 Pariwana *C1*
21 Pirwa *B3*
22 Sonesta Posadas del Inca *B2*
23 The Point 21 *C1*

Eating 🍴
1 Al Grano *C3*
2 Amaru *Plateros detail*
3 Bembos *C2*
4 Bistrot 370 *C3*
5 Café El Ayllu *B3*
6 Café Halliy *Plateros detail*
7 Café Perla *C3*
8 Chez Maggy *B2*
9 Chicha, El Truco & Taberna del Truco *B1*
10 Cicciolina *C3*
11 Circus Restobar *A1*
12 Dolce Vita *C3*
13 El Encuentro *A2, C3*
14 El Fogón *Plateros detail*
15 Fallen Angel restaurant & Guesthouse *B3*
16 Fusiones & Night Sky Disco *C2*
17 Incanto & Greens Organic *C3*
18 Inka Grill *B2*
19 Kusikuy *B3*
20 La Bondiet *C1*
21 La Cosa Nostra *Plateros detail*
22 La Retama *B2*
23 La Tertulia *B2*
24 Limo *B3*
25 Los Candiles *Plateros detail*
26 Maikhana *C2*
27 MAP Café *B3*
28 Pachacútec Grill & Bar *B2*
29 Pisku'o *C3*
30 Pucará *Plateros detail*
31 Sara *C3*
32 The Real McCoy *Plateros detail*
33 Trotamundos *B2*
34 Tupananchis *C1*
35 Two Nations *A3*
36 Víctor Victoria *A2*
38 Yahuu Juice Bar *C1*
39 Yaku Mama *A2*

Bars & clubs 🍸
40 Cross Keys Pub *C3*
41 El Garabato Video Music Club *B2*
42 Extreme *B3*
43 Indigo *A2*
44 Kamikaze *B2*
45 La Chupitería Shots Bar *A2*
46 Los Perros *A2*
47 Lost City *A2*
48 Mama Africa *B2*
49 Mythology *B3*
50 Norton Rat's Tavern & Hostal Gocta Cusco *C3*
51 Paddy's Pub *C3*
52 Roots *A2*
53 Rosie O'Grady's *C3*
54 Ukuku's *Plateros detail*

The same tower holds the largest bell in the city, weighing 5980 kg. After two failed attempts at casting the bell, María Angola, an Afro-Peruvian woman, is said to have thrown a quantity of gold into the smelting pot on the third, successful attempt. The bell was then named after her. During the 1950 earthquake *María Angola* was damaged, so now her hoarse voice is only heard on special occasions.

The cathedral itself was built on the site of the Palace of Inca Wiracocha (*Kiswarcancha*). Stones from Sacsayhuaman were used in its construction after the architect, Juan Miguel de Veramendi, ordered the destruction of the Inca fortress. Although Spanish designers and architects supervised its construction, it took nearly 100 years of Quechuan blood, sweat and tears to build. The ground plan is in the shape of a Latin cross with the transept leading into the two side-churches.

Built on the site of *Suntur Huasi* (The Roundhouse), **El Triunfo** was the first Christian church in Cuzco. The name ('the Triumph') came from the Spanish victory over an indigenous rebellion in 1536. It was here that the Spaniards congregated, hiding from Manco Inca who had besieged the city, almost taking it from the invaders. The Spaniards claim to have witnessed two miracles here in their hour of need. First, they were visited by the Virgin of the Descent, who helped put out the flames devouring the thatched roofs, then came the equestrian saint, James the Greater, who helped kill many indigenous people. The two divinities are said to have led to the Spanish victory; not only was it the triumph of the Spaniards over the Incas, but also of the Catholic faith over the indigenous religion.

The gleaming, renovated gilded main altar of the **Iglesia Jesús y María** draws the eyes to the end of the church. However, take the time to look up at the colourful murals which have been partially restored. The two gaudy, mirror-encrusted altars towards the front of the church are also hard to miss. Walking through into the cathedral's transept, the oldest surviving painting in Cuzco can be seen. It depicts the 1650 earthquake. It also shows how, within only one century, the Spaniards had already divided the main plaza in two. *El Señor de los Temblores* (the Lord of the Earthquakes) can be seen being paraded around the Plaza de Armas while fire rages through the colonial buildings with their typical red-tiled roofs. Much of modern-day Cuzco was built after this event. The choir stalls, by a 17th-century Spanish priest, are a magnificent example of colonial baroque art (80 saints and virgins are exquisitely represented), as is the elaborate pulpit. On the left is the solid-silver high altar; the original *retablo* behind it is a masterpiece of native woodcarving by the famous Quechuan **Juan Tomás Tuyro Túpaq**. At the far right-hand end of the cathedral is an interesting local painting of the Last Supper. But this is the Last Supper with a difference, for Jesus is about to tuck into a plate of *cuy* (guinea pig), washed down with a glass of *chicha*. In the sacristy there is a good selection of artwork including portraits of all the bishops and archbishops of Cuzco, including Vicente de Valverde, the Dominican friar who accompanied Pizarro and who was instrumental in the death of Atahualpa. He was bishop of Cuzco until 1541, the year he died. The painting of the crucified Christ is strange because his body is rather effeminate. This is also noted in other paintings of Christ from the Cuzqueño school. This may be because the artists used female models, or could be simply how the Quechuan artists perceived him.

Many of the cathedral's treasures are hidden in a safe behind one of the carved doors. Much venerated is the crucifix of *El Señor de los Temblores*, the object of many pilgrimages and viewed all over Peru as a guardian against earthquakes. You may be forgiven for thinking he has a Quechuan complexion but this is actually due to many years' exposure to candle smoke! This is the most richly adorned Christ in the cathedral with his gold crown and his hands and feet pierced by solid gold, jewel-encrusted nails. The original wooden altar was destroyed by fire and dedicated locals are slowly covering the new plaster one with silver.

The chapel of **St James the Greater** contains a statue of the saint on horseback. The painting depicts him killing the local indigenous people as he appeared in the miracle.

Entering **El Triunfo** there is a stark contrast between the dark, heavy atmosphere of the cathedral and the light, simple structure of this serene church. The fine granite altar is a welcome relief from the usual gilding. Here the statue of the *Virgin of the Descent* resides and, above her, is a wooden cross known as the *Cross of Conquest*, said to be the first Christian cross on Inca land brought from Spain by Vicente de Valverde.

Going down into the **catacomb** (closed on Sundays), originally used to keep the bodies of important people, you will find a coffer containing half the ashes of the Cuzqueño chronicler Inca Garcilaso de la Vega, born of a Spanish father and Inca princess mother. The ashes were only sent back from Spain in 1978. The paintings of the parables, which used to hang on the central columns, have been moved to the Museo de Arte Religioso.

La Compañía de Jesús
① *Entry US$3.55, or by religious buildings ticket, open daily 0900-1750.*
On the southeast side of the plaza is the beautiful church of La Compañía de Jesús, built in the late 17th century on the site of the *Amarucancha* (Palace of the Serpents), residence of the Inca Huayna Cápac. First it was given to Pizarro after the Spanish conquest, then it was bought by a family who eventually donated it to the Jesuits after their arrival in 1571. The church was destroyed in the earthquake of 1650. The present-day building took 17 years to construct and was inaugurated in 1668. When the Jesuits were expelled from Peru most of the valuables were taken to Spain. The altarpiece is a dazzling work of art. Resplendent in its gold leaf, it stands 21 m high and 12 m wide. It is carved in the baroque style, but the indigenous artists felt that this was too simple to please the gods and added their own intricacies in an attempt to reach perfection. Gold leaf abounds in the many *retablos* and on the carved pulpit. The painting on the left-hand side of the door as you enter is historically interesting. It depicts the marriage of Beatriz Qoya, niece of Túpac Amaru, to Martín García de Loyola, the nephew of one of Túpac's captors. Thus, de Loyola joins the line of succession for the Inca king's inheritance. The cloister is also noteworthy, though it has been closed for restoration for many years.

North and northeast of the Plaza de Armas

Museo Inka
① *Cuesta del Almirante 103, T084-237380, Mon-Fri 0800-1900, Sat 0900-1600, US$3.*
The **Palacio del Almirante**, just north of the Plaza de Armas, is one of Cuzco's most impressive colonial houses. Note the pillar on the balcony over the door, showing a bearded man from inside and a naked woman from the outside. The palace houses the interesting Museo Inka, run by the Universidad San Antonio Abad, which exhibits the development of culture in the region from pre-Inca times to the present day. The museum has a good combination of textiles, ceramics, metalwork, jewellery, architecture, technology, photographs and 3-D displays. It has an excellent collection of miniature turquoise figures and other objects made as offerings to the gods. The display of skulls, deliberately deformed by trepanning, is fascinating, as is the full-size

tomb complete with mummies stuck in urns! The section on coca leaves gives a good insight into the sacred Inca leaf. Old photographs of Machu Picchu are good to see after a visit, for 'then and now' comparisons. The painting of the garrotting of Inca Atahualpa, watched over by Vicente de Valverde, is gory but informative. There are no explanations in English so a guide is a good investment. During the high season local Quechuan weavers can be seen working in the courtyard. The weavings are for sale, expensive but of very good quality.

Opposite, in a small square on Cuesta del Almirante, is the colonial house of **San Borja**, which was a Jesuit school for the children of upper-class mestizos.

Museo de Arte Religioso
ⓘ *Hatun Rumiyoc y Herrajes, 2 blocks northeast of Plaza de Armas, 0800-1800, included on the religious buildings ticket, or US$5.35.*
The **Palacio Arzobispal** was built on the site of the palace occupied in 1400 by the Inca Roca and was formerly the home of the Marqueses de Buena Vista. It contains the Museo de Arte Religioso which has a fine collection of colonial paintings, furniture and mirrors. The Spanish tiles are said to be over 100 years old and each carved wooden door has a different design. The collection includes the paintings of a 17th-century Corpus Christi procession by the indigenous master Diego Quispe Tito, which used to hang in the church of Santa Ana. They now hang in the two rooms at the back of the second smaller courtyard.

The first picture on the right-hand side in the first room is an example of a travelling picture. The canvas can be rolled up inside the cylindrical wooden box which becomes part of the picture when it is hanging. The stained-glass windows in the chapel were made in Italy. The one on the left-hand side depicts the Lord of the Earthquakes. The priest's vestments belonged to Vicente de Valverde; the black was used for funerals, white for weddings and red for ceremonial masses. There are many paintings of the Virgin of the Milk, in which the Virgin Mary is breastfeeding Jesus, a sight not seen in Western religious paintings. The throne in the old dining room is 300 years old and was taken up to Sacsayhuaman for the Pope to sit on when he visited in 1986. Visitors can also see a bed that Simón Bolívar slept in.

Museo de Arte Precolombino (MAP)
ⓘ *Plaza de las Nazarenas 231, www.map.org.pe, 0900-2200, US$7, US$3.50 with student card; under same auspices as the Larco Museum in Lima.*
In the Casa Cabrera, on the northwest side of the plaza, this beautiful two-floor museum, set around a spacious courtyard, opened in June 2003. It is dedicated to the work of the great artists of pre-Columbian Peru. Within the expertly lit and well-organized galleries are many superb examples of pottery, metalwork (largely in gold and silver) and woodcarvings from the Moche, Chimú, Paracas, Nazca and Inca empires. There are some vividly rendered animistic designs, giving an insight into the way Peru's ancient peoples viewed their world and the creatures that inhabited it. All the exhibits carry extensive explanations in English and Spanish, and there are some illuminating quotes regarding the influence of pre-Columbian art in Europe and beyond, for example in the work of Pablo Picasso and his contemporaries. The museum, which is highly recommended, has a restaurant/café (see Eating, page 103) and stores such as a branch of the **Center for Traditional Textiles of Cusco**. One of two such stores in town (see page 111), you can often see local villagers weaving the pieces that are on sale using techniques that haven't changed in centuries.

Convento de las Nazarenas

The Convento de las Nazarenas, on Plaza de las Nazarenas, is now an annexe of **El Monasterio** hotel. You can see the Inca-colonial doorway with a mermaid motif, but ask permission to view the lovely 18th-century frescos inside. **El Monasterio** itself is well worth a visit; ask at reception if you can have a wander around (see Sleeping, page 94). Built in 1595 on the site of an Inca palace, it was originally the **Seminary of San Antonio Abad** (a Peruvian National Historical Landmark). One of its most remarkable features is the baroque chapel, constructed after the 1650 earthquake. Look at the altar: to the right is a painting that slides to one side allowing access to a stairway, down which the statues of saints on high can be liberated for use in the Corpus Christi procession of June. Attempts have been made to restore the paintings outside in the cloister but, as can be seen in an alcove, the paint keeps peeling away and much is painted white. If you are not disturbing mealtimes, check out the dining room. This is where the monks used to sing. The masks on the walls represent the Spaniards when they arrived in Cuzco – the eyes are red with greed and the skin yellow from all the gold they took. Moving back to the second cloister, turn left at the restored painting in the alcove to see a small courtyard which used to be a farm; guests claim to have seen ghosts here. One last curiosity is *Samson's Martyrdom*, an 18th-century painting in the mestizo style, next to room 422. Look at the tray on the floor – those are Samson's eyes. Gruesome!

San Blas

The San Blas district, called Tococache in Inca times, has been put on the tourist map by the large number of shops and galleries which sell local carvings, ceramics and paintings (see page 111). Even though it's a bit of climb from the Plaza de Armas, it has also become a popular place to stay and eat, with lots of choice and nothing too expensive. The **Templo de San Blas** ① *Carmen Bajo, 0800-1800, on the religious buildings ticket, or US$5.35*, is a small and simple rectangular adobe building whose walls were reinforced with stone after the 1650 and 1950 earthquakes. It comes as some surprise to learn that it houses one of the most famous pieces of woodcarving found in the Americas, a beautiful mestizo pulpit carved from a single cedar trunk. Images of eight heretics are carved at the base of the pulpit; see if you can spot Henry VIII and Queen Elizabeth I of England among them. Above are carved the four Evangelists and, crowning the pulpit, supported by five archangels, is the statue of Saint Paul of Tarsus, although some believe it to be Jesus Christ. The skull is supposed to be that of the sculptor. There are many stories surrounding the artist. Some say he was an indigenous leper who dedicated his life to the carving after he was cleansed of the disease. The church was built and used by indigenous inhabitants and the Cuzco baroque altarpiece was designed to compete with any in the city.

East and southeast of the Plaza de Armas

Santa Catalina

① *Arequipa at Santa Catalina Angosta, Sat-Thu 0900-1200, 1300-1700, Fri 0900-1200, 1300-1600. There are guided tours by English-speaking students; a tip is expected. Church open daily 0700-0800.*

The church, convent and museum are magnificent. Santa Catalina was the founder of the female part of the Dominican Order, which also founded the beautiful convent of the same name in Arequipa. The Cuzco convent is ironically built upon the foundations of the *Acllahuasi* (House of the Chosen Women), the most important Inca building overlooking

Heart of stone

Just wandering around the streets of Cuzco gives you a sense of the incredible craftsmanship of the Inca stonemasons. Some of the best examples can be seen in the **Callejón Loreto**, running southeast past La Compañía de Jesús from the main plaza. The walls of the **Acllahuasi** (House of the Chosen Women) are on one side, and of the Amarucancha on the other. There are also Inca remains in **Calle San Agustín**, to the east of the plaza. The famous **Stone of 12 Angles** is in **Calle Hatun Rumiyoc**, halfway along its second block, on the right-hand side going away from the plaza. The finest stonework is in the celebrated curved wall beneath the west end of **Santo Domingo**. This was rebuilt after the 1950 earthquake, when a niche that once contained a shrine was found at the inner top of the wall. Excavations revealed Inca baths below here, and more Inca retaining walls. Another superb stretch of late-Inca stonework is in **Calle Ahuacpinta**, outside Qoricancha, to the east or left as you enter. True Inca stonework is wider at the base than at the top and features ever-smaller stones as the walls rise. Doorways and niches are trapezoidal. The Incas clearly learnt that the combination of these four techniques helped their structures to withstand earthquakes. This explains why, during the two huge earthquakes in 1650 and 1950, Inca walls stayed standing while colonial buildings tumbled down. The walls of Hotel Libertador, near Santo Domingo, show an Inca stonemason following a Spanish architect – the walls are vertical and the doorways square. However, the stones are still beautifully cut and pieced together.

the main plaza. The Quechuan women were chosen for their nobility, virtue and beauty to be prepared for ceremonial and domestic duties – some were chosen to bear the Inca king's children. No other man was allowed to set eyes on the Chosen Women and if he had any relationship with one, he, his family and livestock would all be killed.

Today the convent is a closed order where the nuns have no contact with the outside world. There is a room at the back of the church where the nuns can participate in Sunday Mass. It is separated from the church by a heavy metal grill so although they cannot be seen their voices can still be heard. In this room there is the only signed painting in the museum. The artist was, of course, Spanish, as local artists were either forbidden or unable to sign their work. The church has an ornate, gilded altarpiece and a beautifully carved pulpit. The altarpieces are all carved by different craftsmen.

The museum has a wonderful collection of Cuzqueño school paintings spanning the decades of Spanish rule; a good guide can point out how the style changes from the heavy European influence to the more indigenous style. One obvious difference can be seen in the paintings of the Lord of the Earthquakes in the corridor. Early paintings show Christ wearing a white loincloth typical of European art, but in others he is seen wearing a very light, almost transparent skirt. The beautifully coloured murals in the Scriptures Room show the difference between the devoted lives of the religious order in the upper section and the frivolity of the courtier's life. The floral designs covering the lower section and the archways are the indigenous artists' way of paying tribute to *Pachamama*, Mother Earth. This can also be seen in the upstairs room, which has many paintings of the Virgin. The dresses are triangular, in the shape of mountains, which were seen as gods by the indigenous people. Another addition can be seen in the painting of the Virgin of

Bethlehem. The baby Jesus is held at an awkward angle because he has been swaddled tightly from neck to feet in the manner of indigenous babies. The gold patterns are applied to these paintings by the use of a stamp. This is carried out by a separate artist once the painting has dried. Many of the works of art, bureaux and ornaments were given to the Order by the families of the joining novices.

Much original Inca stonework can be seen in the streets, particularly in the **Callejón Loreto**, running southeast past La Compañía de Jesús from the main plaza. The walls of the *Acllahuasi* are on one side, and of the *Amarucancha* on the other. There are also Inca remains in Calle San Agustín, east of the plaza. The famous **Stone of 12 Angles** is in Calle Hatun Rumiyoc, halfway along its second block, on the right-hand side going away from the plaza. The finest stonework is in the celebrated curved wall beneath the west end of Santo Domingo. This was rebuilt after the 1950 earthquake, when a niche that once contained a shrine was found at the inner top of the wall. Excavations have revealed Inca baths below here, and more Inca retaining walls. Another superb stretch of late-Inca stonework is in **Calle Ahuacpinta**, outside Qoricancha, to the east or left as you enter. True Inca stonework is wider at the base than at the top and features ever-smaller stones as the walls rise. Doorways and niches are trapezoidal. The Incas clearly learnt that the combination of these four techniques helped their structures to withstand earthquakes. This explains why, in two huge earthquakes (1650 and 1950), Inca walls stayed standing while colonial buildings tumbled down.

If you continue down Arequipa from Santa Catalina you come to Calle Maruri. Between this street at Santo Domingo is **Cusicancha** ① *Mon-Fri 0730-1600, sometimes open at weekends, US$1.75,* an open space showing the layout of the buildings as they would have been in Inca times. Recovered from what was a barracks are Inca walls and niches and a colonial arch. There is an exhibition space and alpacas and vicuñas wandering around the grassy areas.

Also worth a visit is the palace called **Casa de los Cuatro Bustos**, whose colonial doorway is at San Agustín 400. This palace is now the **Hotel Libertador**. The general public can enter the hotel from Plazoleta Santo Domingo, opposite the Temple of the Sun/Qoricancha.

Qoricancha at Santo Domingo
① *Mon-Sat 0830-1730, Sun 1400-1700 (except holidays), US$3.55, or joint ticket with Santa Catalina US$6 (not on the BTC visitor ticket). There are English-speaking guides outside who expect a tip of US$2-3.*
This is one of the most fascinating sights in Cuzco. Behind the walls of the Catholic church are remains of what was once the centre of the vast Inca society. The Golden Palace and Temple of the Sun was a complex filled with such fabulous treasures of gold and silver it took the Spanish three months to melt it all down. You will be able to see what was the Solar Garden – where life-sized gold sculptures of men, women, children, animals, insects and flowers were placed in homage to the Sun God – and marvel at near-complete temples with the best Inca stonework in Cuzco. On the walls were more than 700 gold sheets weighing about 2 kg each. The *conquistadores* sent these back intact to prove to the King of Spain how rich their discovery was.

The first Inca, Manco Cápac, is said to have built the temple when he left Lake Titicaca and founded Cuzco with Mama Ocllo. However, it was the ninth Inca, Pachacútec, who transformed it. When the Spaniards arrived, the complex was awarded to Juan Pizarro, the younger brother of Francisco. He in turn willed it to the Dominicans who ripped much of it down to build their church.

The festival of Inti Raymi

The sun was the principal object of Inca worship and at their winter solstice, in June, the Incas honoured the solar deity with a great celebration known as Inti Raymi, the sun festival. The Spanish suppressed the Inca religion, and the last royal Inti Raymi was celebrated in 1535.

However, in 1944 a group of Cuzco intellectuals, inspired by the contemporary 'indigenist' movement, revived the ceremony in the form of a pageant, putting it together from chronicles and historical documents. The event caught the public imagination, and it has been celebrated every year since then on 24 June, now a Cuzco public holiday. Hundreds of local men and women play the parts of Inca priests, nobles, chosen women, soldiers (played by the local army garrison), runners, and the like. The coveted part of the Inca emperor Pachacútec is won by audition, and the event is organized by the municipal authorities.

It begins around 1000 at the Qoricancha – the former sun temple of Cuzco – and winds its way up the main avenue into the Plaza de Armas, accompanied by songs, ringing declarations and the occasional drink of *chicha*. At the main plaza, Cuzco's presiding mayor is whisked back to Inca times, to receive Pachacútec's blessing and a stern lecture on good government. Climbing through Plaza Nazarenas and up Pumacurcu, at about 1400 the procession reaches the ruins of Sacsayhuaman, where tens of thousands of people are gathered on the ancient stones.

Before Pachacútec arrives, the *Sinchi* (Pachacútec's chief general) ushers in contingents from the four *Suyus* (regions) of the Inca empire. Much of the ceremony is based around alternating action between these four groups of players. A *Chaski* (messenger) enters to announce the imminent arrival of the Inca and his *Coya* (queen). Men sweep the ground before him and women scatter flowers. The Inca takes the stage alone, and has a dialogue with the sun. Then he receives reports from the governors of the four *Suyus*. This is followed by a drink of the sacred *chicha*, the re-lighting of the sacred fire of the empire, the sacrifice (faked) of a llama, and the reading of auguries in its entrails. Finally the ritual eating of *sankhu* (corn paste mixed with the victim's blood) ends the ceremonies. The Inca gives a last message to his assembled children and departs. The music and dancing continues until nightfall.

The temple complex Walk first into the courtyard then turn around to face the door you just passed through. Behind and to the left of the paintings (representing the life of Santo Domingo Guzmán) is Santo Domingo. This was where the Temple of the Sun stood, a massive structure 80 m wide, 20 m deep and 7 m in height. Only the curved wall of the western end still exists and will be seen (complete with a large crack from the 1950 earthquake) when you later walk left through to the lookout over the Solar Garden. The Temple of the Sun was completely covered with gold plates and there would have been a large solar disc in the shape of a round face with rays and flames. One story, with no historic basis to it, is that *conquistador* Mancio Sierra de Leguizamo was given this in the division of spoils but he lost it one night playing dice. Whether a *conquistador* lost it, or the Incas spirited it away, the solar disc has not been found.

Still in the baroque cloister, close by and facing the way you came in, turn left and cross to the remains of the **Temple of the Moon**, identifiable by a series of niches. The Moon, or

Mamakilla, was the Sun's wife. The walls were covered in silver plates and the dark horizontal stripe in the niches shows where they were attached. Have a look at the stonework. This is a fantastic example of polished joints so perfectly made it is impossible to slip even a playing card in between. In fact, all the walls of the temples around this courtyard are fine examples of Inca stonemasonry.

Further round the courtyard, anticlockwise, is a double door-jamb doorway. Beyond this is the so-called **Temple of Venus and the Stars**. Stars were special deities used to predict weather, wealth and crops. There's a window around which, on the inside, holes can be seen where the Spaniards prised out precious stones. The roofs of all these temples would have been thatched, but on the ceiling here was a beautiful representation of the Milky Way. The 25 niches would have held idols and offerings to the cult of the stars and the walls around them were plated in silver (notice again the dark stripes). In the **Temple of Lightning** on the other side of the courtyard is a stone. Stand on this and you will appreciate how good the Incas were as stonemasons: all three windows are in perfect alignment. The Lightning was the Sun's servant while the Rainbow, subject of the next and last temple, was also important because it came from the Sun. A rainbow was painted onto the gold plates which coated the walls.

The gold thread used in the vestments of Catholic priests (on display in the sacristy which you pass on your way to the Solar Garden) pales into insignificance when you consider the vast quantities of gold housed in this most special of Inca temple complexes. Yet, to the Incas, gold and silver had little monetary value, and were prized only for their religious significance. As you gaze over the grass lawn to the Avenida Sol, this may help you believe that there truly was once a garden here filled with flowers, insects, animals and people, all fashioned in gold and silver. What a sight that must have been!

Museo de Sitio Qoricancha

① *Mon-Sat 0900-1200, 1300-1700, Sun 0800-1400. Entrance by the BTC Visitor Ticket. The staff will give a guided tour in Spanish, but please give a tip.*

The former Museo Arqueológico is now housed in an underground site on Avenida Sol, in the gardens below Santo Domingo. It contains a limited collection of pre-Columbian artefacts, a few Spanish paintings of imitation Inca royalty dating from the 18th century, photos of the excavation of Qoricancha, and some miniature offerings to the gods. It's a good idea to visit Santo Domingo before the museum, in order to understand better the scant information given.

Other sights southeast of the centre

Between the centre and the airport on Alameda Pachacútec, the continuation of Avenida Sol, 20 minutes' walk from the Plaza de Armas, there is a statue of the **Inca Pachacútec** placed on top of a **Lookout Tower** ① *1000-2000, free*, from which there are excellent views of Cuzco. Inside are small galleries and a coffee shop.

Avenida La Cultura, which runs southeast out of the city and eventually becomes the road to Sicuani and Lake Titicaca, passes through **Urbanización Magisterio**, one of the favoured areas to live in the city. Many foreigners, including overseas students, stay here. This is the other, modern side of Cuzco, with up-to-date services and just a US$1 taxi ride to the centre. Over the five blocks you'll find restaurants, including fast-food places with games for kids, every type of shop, internet cabins and long-distance phone services, laundries, safe long-term car parking, hairdressers, drugstores, pharmacies and video and DVD rental.

South and southwest of the Plaza de Armas

La Merced

ⓘ *C Márquez, monastery and museum 1430-1700, church Mon-Fri 0800-1700, Sat 0900-1600, US$1.*

La Merced was originally built in 1534 by the religious order of Mercedarians (founded in 1223 by the French Saint Peter Nolasco), whose main aim was to redeem the natives. The church was razed in the 1650 earthquake and rebuilt by indigenous stonemasons in the late 17th century. The high altar is neoclassical with six gilded columns. There are a further 12 altars. Inside the church are buried Gonzalo Pizarro, half-brother of Francisco, and the two Almagros, father and son. Their tombs were discovered in 1946.

Attached is a very fine monastery. The first cloister is the most beautiful with its two floors, archways and pillars. The pictures on the first floor depict the saints of the order, but those on the second floor have been removed for restoration. The small museum can also be found here. This houses the order's valuables including the priceless monstrance (a vessel used to hold the consecrated host). It is 1.2 m high, weighs over 22 kg and is decorated with thousands of precious stones. Note the two huge pearls used for the body of a mermaid. There are many other precious religious objects including a small Christ carved in ivory, crowns and incense burners. The painting of the Holy Family is ascribed to Rubens. The superb choir stalls, reached from the upper floor of the cloister, can only be seen by male visitors and, then, only if you can persuade a Mercedarian friar to show them to you.

Around Plaza Regocijo

The **Museo Histórico Regional** ⓘ *Casa Garcilaso, C Garcilaso y Heladeros, daily 0730-1700; entrance with BTC tourist ticket (see box, page 65); a guide is recommended and is usually available at the ticket office; many of them speak English*, tries to show the evolution of the Cuzqueño school of painting. It also contains Inca agricultural implements, a mummy from Nazca complete with 1-m-long hair, colonial furniture and paintings, a small photographic exhibition of the 1950 earthquake and mementos of more recent times. Upstairs there is an exhibition room which holds temporary exhibits from photography to recently excavated finds. The museum is disjointed and even the Spanish explanations are minimal.

If you are walking up Garcilaso, the **Marqueses Hotel**, on the right, has one of the most unusual colonial courtyards. Attractive brick arches single this out from other patios in Cuzco as do the sculpted faces of the previous noble owners which stare out from above them. This house has been restored and converted from the old Hostal Los Marqueses into a hotel (see Sleeping, page 92).

Museo de Arte Contemporáneo ⓘ *Casa de Gobierno, Plaza Regocijo; free with BTC tourist ticket*, is only worth popping into if you are in the area and it is raining as it holds very few pieces.

Around Plaza San Francisco

San Francisco church ⓘ *Plaza San Francisco, 3 blocks southwest of the Plaza de Armas, daily 0600-0800, 1800-2000*, is an austere church reflecting many indigenous influences, but it has a wonderful monastery, cloister and choir. The monastery is under reconstruction, so if you wish to visit, approach the door to the left of the church, shake it and, if the administrator appears, ask if he will show you around. Agree on a price before you enter. If

Getting in a flap

Some love it, some hate it – but travel a couple of kilometres down the Avenida de la Cultura (the route to Paucartambo) and you won't miss it. Standing on a column six storeys high in the middle of the road is a massive condor, the Inca god called upon to protect the kingdom from the *conquistadores*. This modern-day marvel (or monstrosity, depending on your point of view) was built from the aluminium of a plane donated by the army. The artist (who died young) also created the monument of Pachacútec, the greatest Inca ruler of all, which visitors see on arrival at Cuzco airport (a second such sculpture is being built a short distance above the first). The condor's construction (which stands in sight of the poor barrios of San Sebastián) cost US$1.5 million and three people's lives in two accidents. The day of its inauguration, the massive bird caused a flap among the dignitaries below as an earth tremor started up and the wings began to move up and down! The beak is said to be gold, a sorry sight to the poor below who have no way of preying upon its treasure – the tower can be scaled only by locked stairs within.

he starts asking for money to take photographs and then a further tip at the end because of his good service ask him for a *boleta de venta* for the money you paid up front.

The cloister is the oldest in the city, built in the Renaissance style, but with diverse influences. The ground floor has several crypts containing human bones. Some of the bones have been used to write out phrases to remind the visitor of his or her mortality! The fabulous high choir contains 92 detailed carvings of martyrs and saints. The rotating lectern inlaid with ivory skulls (the Franciscan monks' symbol) was used to hold large books. Over the years the wooden ledge has been worn away by the continuous turning of pages.

On one of the stairways the largest painting in South America (12 m high, 9 m wide) can be seen. It records the 12 branches of the Franciscan Order – 683 people are present. Make sure you look up at the colourful, painted ceiling, restored after the 1950 earthquake.

Around Mercado Santa Ana

Heading towards Santa Ana market and San Pedro station from Plaza San Francisco, you pass Santa Clara arch and the nuns' church of **Santa Clara** ① *daily 0600-0700*. It is singular in South America for its decoration, which covers the whole of the interior. Its altars are set with thousands of mirrors.

San Pedro ① *in front of the Santa Ana market, Mon-Sat 1000-1200, 1400-1700*, built in 1688, has two towers made from stones brought from an Inca ruin. The most interesting aspect of this church is the walk to it through the Santa Clara arch early in the morning. If you have only seen the Plaza de Armas and surrounding area a walk here will show you another side of Cuzco life. The street stallholders will be setting up and the Santa Ana market is worth a visit.

Southern outskirts

The church of **Belén de los Reyes** ① *Mon, Tue, Wed, Thu and Sat 1000-1200, 1500-1700*, was built by an indigenous architect in the 17th century. It has a striking main altar with silver embellishments at the centre and gold-washed *retablos* at the sides.

West and northwest of the Plaza de Armas

Above Cuzco, on the road up to Sacsayhuaman, is **San Cristóbal**, built to his patron saint by Cristóbal Paullu Inca. The church's atrium has been restored and there is access to the Sacsayhuaman Archaeological Park. North of San Cristóbal, you can see the 11 doorway-sized niches of the great Inca wall of the **Palacio de Colcampata**, which was the residence of Manco Inca before he rebelled against the Spanish and fled to Vilcabamba. Above San Cristóbal church, to the left, is a private colonial mansion, **Quinta Colcampata**, once the home of the infamous explorer and murderer, Lope de Aguirre. It has also been home to many other important personages including Simón Bolívar and Hiram Bingham during the years of his excavation of Machu Picchu in 1915-1916. It has been restored but is not open to the public.

Cristo Blanco, arms outstretched and brilliantly illuminated at night, stands over the town and is clearly visible if you look north from the Plaza de Armas. He was given to the city as a mark of gratitude by Palestinian refugees in 1944. A quick glance in the local telephone directory reveals there is still a large Arab population in Cuzco.

Sacsayhuaman and around

Sacsayhuaman

① *30 mins' walk from the town centre (see below). Taxi US$1.50. Daily 0700-1730 (go earlier if you wish and definitely try to get there before midday when the tour groups arrive). Entry with BTC tourist ticket (see box, page 65). Free student guides available, but you should tip them. There are lights to illuminate the site at night.*

There are some magnificent Inca walls in the ruined ceremonial centre of Sacsayhuaman, on a hill in the northern outskirts. The Inca stonework is hugely impressive and the massive rocks, weighing up to 130 tons, are fitted together with absolute precision. Three walls run parallel for over 360 m and there are 21 bastions.

Sacsayhuaman was thought for centuries to be a fortress, but the layout and architecture suggest a great sanctuary and temple to the Sun, rising opposite the place previously believed to be the Inca's throne – which was probably an altar – carved out of the solid rock. Broad steps lead to the altar from either side. Zigzags in the boulders around the 'throne' are apparently '*chicha* grooves', channels down which maize beer flowed during festivals. Up the hill is an ancient quarry, the Rodadero, now used by children as a rock slide. Near it are many seats cut perfectly into the smooth rock.

The hieratic rather than the military hypothesis was supported by the discovery in 1982 of the graves of priests; it is unlikely that priests would have been buried in a fortress. The precise functions of the site, however, will probably continue to be a matter of dispute as very few clues remain, due to its steady destruction. The site survived the first years of the conquest. Pizarro's troops had entered Cuzco unopposed in 1533 and lived safely at Sacsayhuaman, until the rebellion of Manco Inca, in 1536, caught them off guard. The bitter struggle which ensued became the decisive military action of the conquest, for Manco's failure to hold Sacsayhuaman cost him the war and the empire. The destruction of the hilltop site began after the defeat of Manco's rebellion. The outer walls still stand, but the complex of towers and buildings was razed to the ground. From then until the 1930s Sacsayhuaman served as a kind of unofficial quarry of pre-cut stone for the inhabitants of Cuzco. As the site's tourism value has increased in recent years, so care and restoration have been given greater priority also.

From the city centre to Sacsayhuaman on foot You can walk to the paved perimeter road around the north side of Sacsayhuaman from the centre of Cuzco. From the Plaza de Armas go up Calle Suecia (straight up from the Portal de Carnes), or up Cuesta del Almirante to Plaza Nazarenas, then turn left onto Calle Pumacurco. Calle Saphi and any of the pedestrian streets to the right of this street (eg Resbalosa or Amargura staircase) will also take you there. From San Blas, take Tandapata heading east (away from the Plaza San Blas). A couple of blocks past Atoqsaycuchi you go down a set of steps and pass over the Sapatiana bridge; to your left there is a sort of waterfall and to the right the Huaca Sapatiana, one of the sacred Inca *huacas*. Looking further up towards the right beyond the Huaca, you will see a colonial aqueduct. Continue straight ahead (following the signs at Sapatiana) and you go back up a set of stairs and connect with Calle Pumacurco. Turn right and continue uphill; this street takes you directly to the entrance to Sacsayhuaman. For a closer look at the colonial aqueduct, take the next right and follow this pedestrian pathway; it ends at the aqueduct itself. Return to Pumacurco to continue up to Sacsayhuaman.

All of these will lead you to a small ticket booth just a few metres above San Cristóbal church. Leave the paved road at the booth to climb a wide set of stone steps on the left of a small stream. This leads up the steep but obvious valley between the Cristo Blanco statue and the ruins' walls that are visible even from the town centre. Head north and up to the Sacsayhuaman archaeological site.

Walks around Sacsayhuaman

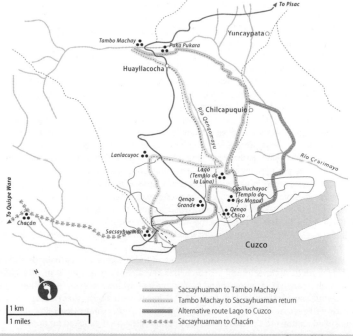

	Sacsayhuaman to Tambo Machay
	Tambo Machay to Sacsayhuaman return
	Alternative route Laqo to Cuzco
	Sacsayhuaman to Chacán

1 km
1 miles

Dog eared advice

The further you go into the country-side, the more likely you are to run into large bands of working farm dogs, some of which are sometimes inclined to defend their patch. As with most animals, the best solution is to keep calm, face the dogs and make an organized retreat. Pick up a stick or a couple of stones just in case. Usually the dogs' owner will turn up and all will end *tranquilo*. Whatever you do, panicking and running is the most likely to end in a nasty bite. It's not common, but it sometimes happens.

Sacsayhuaman to Tambo Machay

From Sacsayhuaman, the route leads east by northeast, part of the way along the modern paved highway, until reaching the turn-off for Qenqo, about 2 km away. First pass **Qenqo Chico**, then **Qenqo Grande** (see also page 89) and then following the exit road out of Qenqo – just before it joins the main paved highway running to the northeast, another smaller road feeds into it from the right. Follow this road which will soon curve left before reaching a large group of houses (Villa San Blas), about 200 m away, on the other side of a gully.

In the immediate vicinity of **Villa San Blas**, the paved road circles around a *huaca* (shrine) in the form of a small rock outcropping with finely cut and polished niches and little platforms. From that point, an older dirt track heads off in a northerly direction. Continue along this track for about 50 m, enough to steer comfortably clear of the houses, the children and the dogs, and then leave this secondary road altogether, striking off to the right, at right angles to it, and begin hiking east, skirting around fields and depressions (the remains of reservoirs), following any of several footpaths, but always maintaining a fairly straight course.

About 400 m away, there is a gentle descent into a shallow creek bed. After crossing it and walking on for almost 100 m, you will find some Inca stone walls. This marks the beginning of a semi-subterranean archaeological site similar to Qenqo. Because it does not protrude significantly above the level of the surrounding terrain, it is not easy to distinguish from many other rocky outcrops scattered throughout the area. It is, however, a conglomeration of large boulders with walkways and interconnecting galleries between them. The rocks are extensively sculpted with the usual array of niches and platforms and a great profusion of carvings, many of which represent monkeys and snakes, as well as what is thought to have been a large sculpted stone representing a toad. There are also remains of a liturgical fountain and a very battered, partially defaced, but still clearly perceptible stone sculpture of a large feline, possibly a puma, perhaps a jaguar (a plausible explanation given the presence of other examples of jungle fauna – the monkeys and snakes). This was once a *huaca* of great importance. The name given to this site is **Cusilluchayoc** ('place of the monkeys', from *kusillo*, monkey in Quechua). In Spanish this site is called Templo de los Monos and most guides and local directories refer to it as such. The original Inca name is unknown.

Also unknown is the reason why so many of these *huacas* are partially or almost totally buried. Archaeological research has revealed as much as 3 m of niches, pedestals, carvings and masonry below present ground level. Throughout the Sacsayhuaman Archaeological Park all the lower sections of the various *huacas* uncovered over the last 30 years are much lighter in colour, in many cases almost white, in marked contrast to the weathered grey patina of the parts exposed for hundreds of years. The lower levels retain the original luminosity of the polished limestone, traces of what must have been a dazzling landscape. Did the Incas themselves attempt to conceal their religious shrines from the *conquistadores*? Or was it the fanatic persecution of heathen idolatry undertaken by the Christians during and after the conquest, which entombed the native places of worship? Alternatively, the consistency of the landfill and the uniformity of the depth throughout the area could suggest a natural or geological cause. Landslides brought about by earthquake or flooding are possibilities. Although records from the last 500 years detail devastating earthquakes in the Cuzco region, as well as floods and similar natural disasters, there are no specific references to great displacements of earth having obliterated this area.

After walking through Cusilluchayoc, you reach a well-defined, straight dirt track, flanked by sections of adobe walls with cacti and agave growing on them. This is a section of the ancient **Inca road** from Cuzco to Pisac, still used by highland folk descending from the hills to Cuzco. Turn left on this road and head northeast (away from Cuzco) for about 300 m, towards a very prominent rock outcrop rising some 40 m above the surrounding fields. This is yet another important Inca *huaca*, currently known as **Laqo**, the **Temple of the Moon** (although the original Inca name is unknown). The Ministerio de Cultura is excavating the site, revealing the Inca complex. *Laqo* has more than one meaning in Quechua: it can be interpreted as 'confusing, misleading, enigmatic', but it is also the name of an algae found along Andean streams and marshes. And such a stream runs just below the site and so the place name would seem to derive from that. Still, it is also an enigmatic place. The name more commonly used by the local inhabitants is **Salonniyuc**, a hybrid Spanish-Quechua word roughly meaning 'place of the *salón* (hall or room)'. Another name is Salapunku or Salonpunku, with the same Spanish noun plus the Quechua *punku* (door, doorway). It is always Laqo on maps.

Laqo is a formation of grey, porous limestone, some 50 m high. A split, large enough to walk through, cuts into the rock. There are two large caves with remains of zoomorphic sculptures similar to those in Cusilluchayoc. Carved in the rock are niches and an altar upon which sunlight and moonlight fall at certain times of the year, filtered through the fissure above (hence the name Templo de la Luna – Temple of the Moon). The external surfaces also have carvings, sculptures, niches, stairways and the remains of a sundial, similar to the *intihuatanas* at Machu Picchu and Pisac.

Laqo has always been an observatory. Standing at the summit it is easy to appreciate why: it is the best single vantage point from which to view not only the Cuzco countryside, but also to see through the fabric of Andean time. To the southeast, about 100 km away as the crow flies, rises the great snowy peak of **Ausangate**, 'the one that pulls – or herds – the others', 6384 m above sea level, revered *apu* of the eastern Andes and grandfather of mountains. Some 70 km closer, in the same direction, loom the dark, jagged crags of **Pachatusan** 'pillar – or fulcrum – of the earth', at 4950 m, one of the children of Ausangate. And only 10 km away, aligned with father and grandfather, the young and green **Pikol**, one of the local *apus*, 4200 m high. Every mountain, every hill, is an *apu*, each possessing its individual identity and name. The *apus* are masculine and they all belong to a hierarchical order. At the same time, each *apu* is both offspring and consort of Mother Earth, *Pachamama*, source of all life, the indivisible and fundamental feminine element in nature.

Almost all the limestone outcrops scattered throughout the countryside are in effect *huacas*, all intricately carved and sculpted. There are also groves of eucalyptus trees, imported to Peru from Australia (via California) in the mid-19th century; adobe walls

Ceques – the cosmic dial

To understand the basis on which many Inca roads were laid out, one needs to know a little about the *ceque* system. This involves a complex series of lines and associated *huacas* (shrines) that radiated out from Cuzco and had astronomical, calendric and sacred connotations. The centre point of this giant dial is generally taken to be the Qoricancha, although some say a pillar and the tower of the Suntur Huasi on the Huacaypata (the Plaza de Armas) were the sighting points. Forty-one lines emanated from the hub, some hundreds of kilometres long. The lines were not necessarily marked on the ground, but ran dead straight towards the horizon. Four were the intercardinal roads to the four quarters of Tahuantinsuyo,

others aimed at the equinox and solstice points, others to the points where different stars and constellations rise. On or near these rays, about 328 *huacas* (shrines) and survey points were distributed. The lines served various purposes: they were used for tracking the movements of sun and stars; they helped predict the best time for planting crops; they were instrumental in irrigation (about a third pointed to springs and other water sources). Certain *ceques* and their *huacas* were under the jurisdiction of particular *panacas* (clans). As well as delineating *panaca* property, the lines helped to define the organization of land, water and work and the rituals and ceremonies which began and closed work cycles.

belonging to kilns and brickworks from colonial times; ancient irrigation canals contouring many kilometres of mountain slopes; fields of native amaranth, maize, beans and potatoes interspersed with other fields sown with cereals of European origin, such as wheat, barley and oats.

At the northern end of Laqo, there is a dirt road, about 10 m wide, running east to west. Beyond it lies a flat open field about 50 m long, which culminates on the side of a steep ravine with a shallow stream descending from the north. This runs through the many carved limestone outcrops, turns slightly to the southeast and flows on in the direction of Cuzco. The same Inca road followed from Cusilluchayoc to Laqo descends into this ravine, crosses the stream and continues its northeasterly course, gradually climbing and skirting around the southeastern flanks of the mountains, crossing into a small valley and then into a larger one, eventually reaching the village of **Chilcapuquio**, about 2 km from Laqo. The Ministerio de Cultura has new signs just past Laqo (Templo de la Luna) indicating this route, called 'Via Troncal Antisuyo'. The cliffs and rocky canyon walls along this section display many overhangs and cave-like openings, some at ground level and others many metres higher. These are the remains of burials dating back to Inca times. It is not uncommon to find remains of ceremonial offerings, such as bouquets of flowers, candles, coca leaves and tobacco, tributes by the people of today to the eternal spirits of the mountains.

Beyond Chilcapuquio, the main trail swerves to the right and gradually begins heading eastward, climbing about 100 m towards **Yuncaypata**, another, larger, community. Before the main trail reaches and crosses another stream, called the Ccorimayo on maps, it is best to strike away from it, following any of several smaller trails which will be found on the left heading north. These paths follow the course of the Ccorimayo, always on the left side of its ravine, gradually pulling away from it and climbing above it. About 2 km to the north of the point where one has struck off the main trail, and 200 m higher, poised atop a prominent rock buttress, lies the site of **Puka Pukara** and, a further kilometre beyond it, crossing the modern paved road from Cuzco to Pisac, are the ruins of **Tambo Machay** (see page 90) and the finishing point of this hike.

The return from Tambo Machay

You can return from Tambo Machay to Cuzco by simply following the main paved road. There is also (time permitting) an interesting off-road alternative. Begin by following the main paved road going back to Cuzco, retracing your steps past Puka Pukara. The road soon reaches the vicinity of the modern community of **Huayllacocha**. On the left side of the road, a small ravine can be seen, descending southward. This is the **Qenqomayu**, the zigzagging river, the same which eventually flows 50 m past the northern end of Laqo and which the trail from there to Chilcapuquio and Puka Pukara earlier crosses. Several footpaths, along either the left or right slopes of the gully, descend for about 3 km to reach the vicinity of Laqo.

About 500 m after starting the descent there is a notable feature on the right bank of the canyon: the western canyon walls become vertical cliffs, extensively pockmarked with open holes, most of them many metres above ground level. They are graves (all looted) dating back to Inca times and representing one of the largest cemeteries in the department of Cuzco. A similar one can be seen opposite the northern side of the ruins of Pisac. Facing the vertical necropolis in the Qenqomayu gully is an Inca wall, of fine masonry, running for about 100 m. Its function is not known but it may indicate a shrine buried in the hill behind it, or some kind of canalization of the Qenqomayu, channelling its course toward Cuzco.

You approach Laqo but, to avoid visiting the site again, gradually climb above and away from the Qenqomayu in a southwesterly direction, eventually to descend and meet the dirt road which runs from east to west in front of the northern end of Laqo. Once on this road, head west for about 1 km, until rejoining the main paved highway from Pisac to Cuzco, now heading south toward Cuzco. Cross the highway, turn left, and less than 50 m south there is a turn-off to the right (west). Directly above lies another limestone promontory, the site of another enigmatic *huaca*. The outer surface displays many carvings, though none as fine as the ones in Laqo or Cusilluchayoc. The inner part of the *huaca* is a labyrinth of passageways and narrow caves. The official name of this site is **Lanlacuyoc**, which roughly translates as 'that which has an evil (or mischievous) spirit'. Its more popular name is **Zona X**, no doubt bestowed upon it 25 years ago during Cuzco's hippy period (the Kathmandu of the West, as it was called), when this particular archaeological site acquired a keen degree of interest. At the time of writing, the evil aspect of the caves overshadowed the mysterious as assaults have occurred here. For safety reasons they were closed to visitors.

Leaving the recent and ancient past behind, follow the paved road for about 3 km, past the ruins of a colonial kiln, an Inca quarry, countless clumps of intricately carved limestone and occasional parked cars with romantic couples in pursuit of the timeless ritual. Soon after the first few turns, Sacsayhuaman comes into view. Any options for getting off the road, as long as they are on the left and head down towards Sacsayhuaman, are good.

Variations on the route

Both of these hiking routes can be undertaken in reverse. It is also possible to hike northward from Laqo, after coming there from Cusilluchayoc, following the course of the Qenqomayu upward for about 3 km eventually reaching Huayllacocha on the main paved Cuzco to Pisac highway, a few hundred metres before Puka Pukara. This avoids the longer roundabout way from Laqo to Chilcapuquio. The routes can be modified and combined according to time limitations and weather conditions. Likewise, it is possible to take motor transport to the furthest point, in this case Tambo Machay, and from there begin walking back in the direction of Sacsayhuaman and Cuzco.

An alternative route Laqo to Cuzco

After walking 1 km beyond Laqo, head northeast along the Inca road from Cusilluchayoc (which goes to Pisac) and follow it uphill to the right of the hill. The trail crosses from a narrow valley to a wider valley. After a grove of eucalyptus you will see well-preserved Inca terraces, to the right of which is **Inkiltambo**. Here is a vast area of carved niches, which housed the mummies of the ancestors of the Inca community that looked after the *huaca*. On the evening of the equinox, the sun is said to set precisely in the centre of one of the topmost niches.

From Inkiltambo you go down the *quebrada* (ravine) of **Choquequirau**, taking the trail on the right side of the stream. You pass colonial kilns and then take a trail that goes up the right side of the valley, leading to a superb view of the **Huatanay Valley** and **San Jerónimo** (see page 208). The outskirts of Cuzco are reached through a gap in the ridge. A dirt track crosses the hillside towards Cuzco to meet the paved road, which you follow to the right for about 100 m until you find the path again on the opposite side. This leads to **Titicaca** (or Tetekaka) *huaca*, which now has a cross and chapel. The shrine stands on the *ceque* (see page 86) of the winter solstice and Peter Frost (in his *Exploring Cuzco*) associates this fact with the alignment of the *huaca* with the legendary birthplace of the sun in Lake Titicaca. Above the shrine, the path splits; take the upper fork and continue to the *huaca* called **Mesa Redonda**, so called for its flat, table-like rock. Beyond, you go downhill into the city.

Sacsayhuaman to Chacán

Take any of the pedestrian routes to the Sacsayhuaman archaeological site described above. The simplest way to find the Chacán Trail from Sacsayhuaman's busy car park is to enter the site at the grassy flat esplanade. Ascending above the furthest wall from the city you'll find a gently sloping but clear trail, taking you up above the main body of the ruins and still further away from the city. As you walk away from Cuzco you'll pass a small ampitheatre-like structure on your left. A few minutes further on, just to your right is an oval rock several metres across and almost as tall. Its form has several carved steps cut into it, as do some other rocks in the area. Just above this point you hit the small paved road that cuts a wide arc above Sacsayhuaman. At this point it's significantly below its highest, but on the far side of the road is an obvious trail, that winds steeply up the hill in front of you.

A blue **Ministerio de Cultura** signboard reads: "Saqsaywaman – Patrimonio Cultural De La Nación", and "Sitio Arqueológico Hatun Chinkana". Below this there's a much smaller but clear sign pointing to the lefthand trail and Chacán. It reads: "Qhapaq Nan-Chakan-Nustha Pakana". Follow this trail uphill, heading generally northwards with the large river valley on your left and hill to your right. You will jog first right, then left, and pass through a small settlement of adobe huts with tiled roofs. This now brings you to an irrigation channel made of concrete heading left at a fork in the road. Do not miss this channel, as it leads directly to **Chacán**. Because of new buildings and low walls, it can be confusing to find the right trail, but if you faithfully follow the channel, you can´t go wrong. Locals are also friendly and will point out the way to Chacán, a well-known local landmark. A walking stick is handy here as you may run into farmers´ guard dogs or even bulls. Follow the channel upstream for 2 km, where it meets the Tica Tica Valley. Here a natural bridge (Chacán means 'bridge place') carries the channel across the gorge while the stream runs 25 to 30 m below. Above this exceptional barrier stands a large carved rock built between stone walls. This is another of Cuzco's sacred *huacas*. If you cross the bridge and go down to your right towards the edge of the cliff, you will reach a lookout point at the front of a cave, which has Inca carvings. Entering this cave, you come to a natural balcony, called El Balcón del Diablo (Devil´s Balcony). From here you can look down on the Río Tica Tica emerging from another cave, which runs beneath Chacán.

One kilometre upstream from Chacán are the ruins of **Ñustapacana**. The surroundings of this site are full of fine terraces, stone walls and another *huaca*.

Back at Chacán, go west at the crossroads just past the natural bridge (this is to your right if returning from Ñustapacana; to your left if you´ve just passed Chacán from the trail along the concrete canal). This will take you west on a high trail above and along the river which will be below, to your left. You will no longer be following the concrete channel, which continues straight on from Chacán uphill. Follow this high path for about a kilometre to a place where the ravine widens and there are high bluffs on either side. Look for a eucalyptus plantation (or its remains, if it has been cut down) on the opposite side of the river. Walk down to the river at this point and cross over. Along this path you will see rocks carved in the shape of pyramids and other Andean religious motifs. Most prominent is a rock, some 2.5 m in height, whose central symbol has been defaced. This is **Quispe Wara** (Crystal Loincloth). Associated with this shrine are high-quality Inca walls and aqueducts, which can be seen on the return to Cuzco. Stay on the left bank of the river at Quispe Wara and climb straight uphill until you reach a narrow road. A leisurely 2-km descent takes you through the Llaullipata ecological reserve, which houses the new Cuzco Planetarium as well as the **Inca Tambo Hotel**. After this, turn left for 100 m to get back to the paved road at the bend just below Sacsayhuaman.

With good navigational skills and plenty of time, it's also possible to hike directly cross country, between Zona X (Lanlacuyoc) and Chacán. This covers some beautiful rural valleys and Andean scenes a million miles from the tourist hustle and bustle of Cuzco: young boys guarding small herds of cattle; hardy Quechua folk ploughing the fields and taking mules and llamas to market in Cuzco's more rugged corners.

Other sites near Cuzco

Along the road from Sacsayhuaman to Pisac, past a radio station, at 3600 m, is the temple and amphitheatre of **Qenqo** ① *on the BTC visitor ticket*. These are not exactly ruins, but are some of the finest examples of Inca stone carving *in situ*, especially inside the large hollowed-out stone that houses an altar. The rock is criss-crossed by zigzag channels that give the place its name and which served to course *chicha*, or perhaps sacrificial blood, for purposes of divination. The open space that many refer to as the 'plaza' or 'amphitheatre' was used for ceremonies. The 19 trapezoidal niches, which are partially destroyed, held idols and mummies.

The Inca fortress of **Puka Pukara** ① *about 6 km from Qenqo, BTC visitor ticket* (whose name translates as Red Fort), was actually more likely to have been a *tambo*, a kind of post-house where travellers were lodged and goods and animals housed temporarily. It is worth seeing for the views alone.

A few hundred metres up the road is the spring shrine of **Tambo Machay** ① *also on the BTC visitor ticket*, still in excellent condition. There are many opinions as to what this place was used for. Some say it was a resting place for the Incas and others that it was used by Inca Yupanqui as a hunting place – the surrounding lands, even today, hide many wild animals including deer and foxes. As this Inca was a living god, Son of the Sun, his palace would also have been a sacred place. There are three ceremonial water fountains built on different levels. As water was considered a powerful deity, it is possible that the site was the centre of a water cult. Water still flows by a hidden channel out of the masonry wall, straight into a little rock pool traditionally known as the Inca's bath.

Taking a guide to the sites mentioned above is a good idea and you should visit in the morning for the best photographs. Carry your multi-site ticket as there are roving ticket inspectors. You can visit the sites on foot; it's a pleasant walk through the countryside requiring half a day or more, though remember to take water and sun protection, and watch out for dogs. An alternative is to take the Pisac bus up to Tambo Machay (which costs US$0.70) and walk back. Another excellent way to see the ruins is on horseback, arranged at travel agencies, or by bicycle. An organized riding tour (with guide) will go to all the sites for US$10-15 per person, not including entrance fees. Rent a bike for US$25 for a full day; it's a 45-minute to one-hour ride from the city. A taxi will charge US$30 for three people. Some of these ruins are included in the many city tours available. ▸▸ *For further details, see Activities and tours, page 114.*

◉ Sleeping

You should book more expensive hotels well in advance through the internet or a good travel agency, particularly for the week or so around **Inti Raymi** (page 78), when prices are much higher. Hotel prices, especially in the mid to upper categories, are often lower when booked on the internet. Always check for special offers as, when there are fewer tourists, hotels may drop their prices by as much as half. Be wary of unlicensed hotel agents for mid-priced hotels, who are often misleading about details; their local nickname is *jalagringos* (gringo pullers), or *piratas* (pirates). Taxis and tourist minibuses meet arriving trains and take you to the hotel of your choice for US$0.75-1, but be insistent. Many hotels and *hostales* can arrange tours: don't be pressured into buying, but compare services with outside agencies for best value.

It is cold at night in Cuzco and many hotels do not have heating. It is worth asking for an *estufa*, a heater, which some places will provide for an extra charge. When staying in the big, popular hotels, allow plenty of time to check out if you have a plane or train to catch; front desks can be very busy. Assume that hotels have free luggage storage and 24-hr hot water in pre-heated tanks, unless otherwise stated. The city can suffer from water shortages. Cuzco's low-power electric showers often do a poor job of heating the very cold water and their safety is sometimes questionable.

Plaza de Armas and around
p70, maps 68 and p70

LL Aranwa Cusco Boutique Hotel, San Juan de Dios 255, T084-4341452, www.aranwa hotels.com/cusco. New, luxury option near the centre, by the owners of the **Aranwa Sacred Valley**. Restored 16th century mansion with courtyard and flower-filled gardens, antiques and paintings from the Cuzco school. Luxury bathrooms, jacuzzis, underfloor heating, oxygenated rooms, spa, business centre, high-speed internet. Also **Mishti Gourmet Restaurant** and **Khasikay Bar**.

LL-L Andean Wings, Siete Cuartones 225, T084-243166, www.andeanwingshotel.com. In a restored 17th-century house, 5-star boutique hotel, each room, whether suite or standard, is of a good size and individually decorated with modern art and antiques, one with disabled access, some with jacuzzi, intimate and welcoming. Restaurant in covered patio, breakfast included, bar with tapas, Wi-Fi, laundry service. Artworks for sale and has a spa. In the same group as **Casas de la Gringa** and **Another Planet** (see below).

AL Brituvian Inn, Suecia 345, T084-245858, www.brituvianinn.com. Boutique hotel just off the main plaza in the former residence of Gonzalo Pizarro. Rooms have flat screen cable TV, heating, phone, minibar, safe, hair dryer, bathrobes and other treats, some even have the only water beds in Cuzco, with coffee shop and piano bar.

AL Del Prado Inn, Suecia 310, T084-224442, www.delpradoinn.com. A very smart hotel just off the plaza. 24-hr room service available, and closed-circuit TV in the public areas for additional security, Wi-Fi. Suites with jacuzzi.

AL Ruinas, Ruinas 472, T084-260644, www.hotelruinas.com. A comfortable hotel conveniently located close to the plaza, good facilities (TV, Wi-Fi, minibar, etc) and comfortable beds, helpful staff, price includes buffet breakfast. A new Marriott hotel is being built nearby.

AL Sonesta Posadas del Inca, Portal Espinar 108, T084-227061, www.sonesta.com. Price includes buffet breakfast. Warmly decorated rooms with heating, safe and cable TV. Some rooms on 3rd floor have view of the plaza. Very helpful staff who speak English, restaurant serves Andean food, excellent service, business centre available.

AL-A Casa Andina, T01-213 9739 (in Lima), www.casa-andina.com. There are 5 attractive hotels in this bright, cheerful chain, all recommended, each with heating, Wi-Fi, TV, restaurant, breakfast included. **Casa Andina Private Collection – Cusco**, Plazoleta de Limacpampa Chico 473, T084-232610. The most upmarket and comfortable in the group, in a 16th-century mansion with 4 courtyards, enriched oxygen available in the rooms, plus a gourmet restaurant serving local cuisine and a bar with an extensive *pisco* collection. **Casa Andina Classic - Cusco Plaza**, Portal Espinar 142, T084-231733. 1½ blocks from the Plaza de Armas facing Plaza Regocijo, elevator, ATM. **Casa Andina Classic – Cusco Koricancha**, San Agustín 371, T084-252633. A combination of 2 manor houses with 2 courtyards, by the Temple of the Sun. **Casa Andina Classic – Cusco Catedral**, Santa Catalina Angosta 149, T084-233661. Right by the cathedral with exposed Inca stone wall in the lobby. **Casa Andina Classic – Cusco San Blas**, Chihuampata 278, San Blas, T084-263694. 3 blocks from the plaza with views over the city, colonial courtyard with fountain.

A Emperador Plaza, Santa Catalina Ancha 377, T084-227412, www.emperadorplaza. com. Price includes buffet breakfast and airport transfer. A modern, light, airy hotel with friendly and helpful English-speaking staff. Cable TV, hairdryer, gas-heated showers and electric radiators.

A Hostal Gocta Cusco, Santa Catalina Angosta 116, nortonrats@yahoo.com. Reached through **Norton Rat's Tavern** (see page 107), with same owner. 6 rooms with good baths decorated with historic photographs, hot water, room service from the bar, cable TV, Wi-Fi. New in 2010.

A Loreto Boutique Hotel, Pasaje Loreto 115, Plaza de Armas, T084-226352, www.loreto boutiquehotel.com. Price includes buffet breakfast. Great location; 12 spacious rooms with original Inca walls, upgraded to "boutique" status. Laundry service, will help organize travel services including guides and taxis, free airport pick-up.

A-B Hostal Corihuasi, C Suecia 561, T084-232233, www.corihuasi.com. Price includes continental breakfast and airport pickup. A tough climb up from the northernmost corner of the Plaza de Armas, tranquil, popular with tour groups. Friendly, some rooms with good views (the best is from room No 1), cable TV, solar heating, Wi-Fi. Recommended.

A-C Marqueses, Garcilaso 256, T084-264249, marqueses@sastravelperu.com. Restored in Spanish colonial style, with 16th- and 17th-century-style religious paintings and 2 lovely courtyards. Rooms have heavy curtains and some are a little dark; luxury rooms have bath. Prices include buffet breakfast and discounts are available for guests booked on SAS Travel tours (see page 117).

B-C Hostal Qosqo, Portal Mantas 115, near the Plaza de Armas, T084-252513, www.suqosqohostal.com. Bargain hard for a discount. Price includes continental breakfast, a heater and cable TV. The state of decor and quality of mattress varies from room to room but most stay here for its proximity to the plaza. Clean, friendly and helpful.

C-D The Walk on Inn, Suecia 504, T084-235065, www.walkoninn.com. 2 blocks from Plaza de Armas, private or shared bathrooms, breakfast US$2, free internet and Wi-Fi, laundry, free airport and bus station pick-up.

D Hostal Turístico Plateros, Plateros 348, T084-236878, plateroshostal@hotmail.com. Price includes continental breakfast. Clean, good-value *hostal* in a great location, pleasant communal area with cable TV. The best rooms overlook the street.

D-E El Procurador del Cusco, Coricalle 440, Prolongación Procuradores, at the end of Procuradores, T084-243559, http://hostel procuradordelcusco.blogspot.com. **G** per person without bathroom, price includes use of the basic kitchen (no fridge) and laundry area. Basic rooms and the beds somewhat hard, but upstairs is better. Staff are very friendly and helpful, good value.

D-E Hostal Resbalosa, Resbalosa 494, T084-224839, www.hostalresbalosa.com.

Private or shared bath. Breakfast extra; laundry service, internet. Superb views of the Plaza de Armas from a sunny terrace. Owner Georgina is very hospitable. Best rooms have a view, others may be pokey. Most guests love this place; consequently it's often full.

D-E Hostal Royal Frankenstein, San Juan de Dios 260, 2 blocks from the Plaza de Armas, T084-236999, www.hostal-frankenstein.net. This unforgettable place, with its ghoulish theme, has good services: fully equipped kitchen, cable TV in the living room, safe, laundry facilities and service, Wi-Fi, good mattresses but few rooms have outside windows, heaters for hire. German owner. Recommended.

D-F pp Ecopackers, Santa Teresa 375, T084-231800, www.ecopackersperu.com. Ecologically friendly, well-regarded *hostal* in a colonial *casona* 1 block from the plaza, double rooms with en suite or dorm rooms for 4-18 people, communal kitchen, games room, bar, large-screen TV room, Wi-Fi, garage for bicycles or motorcycles.

D-F pp Pariwana, Mesón de la Estrella 136, T084-233751, www.pariwana-hostel.com. Variety of rooms in a converted colonial mansion with courtyard, from doubles with private bath to dorms sleeping 11+, also girls only dorm, restaurant, bar/lounge, with breakfast, kitchen, internet and Wi-Fi, lockers, English spoken, lots of activities.

E-F pp Pirwa Hostels, T084-244315, www.pirwahostelscusco.com. This chain of hostels offers a range of rooms from private doubles with bath to dorm rooms, in colonial buildings, breakfast included, internet, use of kitchen, 24-hr reception: **Pirwa Suecia**, Suecia 300, the bed-and-breakfast branch; **Pirwa Posada del Corregidor**, Portal de Panes 151 (Plaza de Armas); **Pirwa Backpackers San Blas**, Carmen Alto 283; and **Pirwa Backpackers Colonial**, Plaza San Francisco 360.

E-F pp **The Point**, Mesón de la Estrella 172, T084-252266, www.thepointhostels.com. Doubles or dormitories, includes breakfast, free internet and Wi-Fi, good beds, hot showers, clean, bar with good party atmosphere and nightly events. Has a travel centre which can arrange trips, see general note, page 91.

North and northeast of the Plaza de Armas *p73, maps p68 and p70*

LL Casa Cartagena, Pumacurco 336, T084-261171, www.casacartagena.com. In a converted monastery and national heritage building, super-deluxe facilities with Italian design, original Inca walls and colonial-era frescos. Large, luxurious suites with butler service all provide individual heating and cooling systems as well as an 'oxygen-enrichment' system, available for US$50. **La Chola** restaurant, extensive **Qoya** spa, business centre, Wi-Fi.

LL The Fallen Angel Guest House, Plaza Nazarenas 221, T084-258184, www.fallen angelincusco.com/theguesthouse. The owners of the well-known Fallen Angel restaurant, see page 103, have created a 4-room luxury hotel upstairs. Each suite is decorated in its own lavish style (with living room, dining room, bathroom with bath tub, memory foam pillows and mattresses, feather duvets, bio-ethanol heating) to create a distinct atmosphere, very comfortable and a far cry from the usual adaptation of colonial buildings elsewhere in the city. With all amenities, including Wi-Fi and use of the restaurant below. Excellent service and helpful staff.

LL Hotel El Monasterio, Palacio 136, Plazoleta Nazarenas, T084-604000, www.monasteriohotel.com. This 5-star beautifully restored Seminary of San Antonio Abad is central and one of the best hotels in town for historical interest; it is worth a visit even if you cannot afford to stay (see page 75). Soft Gregorian chants follow you as you wander through the baroque chapel, tranquil courtyards and charming cloisters, admiring the excellent collection of religious paintings. Spacious rooms and suites with all facilities, including cable TV. Many rooms offer an oxygen-enriched atmosphere to help clients acclimatize, for an additional fee. Staff, who all speak English, are very helpful and attentive. The price includes a great buffet breakfast (available to non-residents) which will fill you up for the rest of the day. The restaurant serves lunch and dinner à la carte.

LL La Casona Inkaterra, Plaza Las Nazarenas 113, T084-234010, www.inkaterra.com. Another hotel in a building with a long history, being in a converted 16th-century mansion, built on the site of Manco Cápac's palace. This 1st-class private, colonial-style boutique hotel has 11 exclusive suites, all facilities, concierge service with activities and excursions. Guests are given individual attention in the height of luxury. Breakfast is included, lunch and dinner are available, plus many other services including spa. In the **Relais & Chateaux** group.

LL Novotel, San Agustín 239, T084-581033, www.novotel.com/gb/hotel-3254-novotel-cusco/. 4-star, cheaper in modern section; price includes buffet breakfast. Converted from the home of *conquistador* Miguel Sánchez Ponce who accompanied Pizarro in the taking of Cajamarca, it was remodelled after the 1650 earthquake by General Pardo de Figueroa who built the lovely stone archways and commissioned paintings of the saints of his devotion on the grand stairway. Beautiful courtyard, roofed in glass, with sofas, coffee tables and pot plants around the central stone fountain. The modern 5-storey rear extension has excellent airy and bright rooms. All have sofas, cable TV, central heating and bathtubs. Those above the 2nd floor have views over Cuzco's red-tiled rooftops. Rooms in the colonial section are not much different but have high, beamed ceilings and huge beds. There are 2 restaurants and a French chef.

AL El Arqueólogo, Pumacurco 408, T084-232522, www.hotelarqueologo.com. Price includes buffet breakfast. Services include oxygen, a library and hot drinks. A colonial building on Inca foundations, this has rustic but stylish decor. Lovely sunny garden with comfy chairs and a small restaurant that serves interesting Peruvian food and fondue. French and English spoken. Recommended. Also has a bed and breakfast *hostal* at Carmen Alto 294, T084-232760, **A-B**, and Vida Tours, Ladrillo 425, T084-227750, www.vidatours. com. Traditional and adventure tourism.

AL Rumi Punku, Choquechaca 339, T084-221102, www.rumipunku.com. A genuine Inca doorway leads to a sunny, tranquil courtyard. 20 large, clean, comfortable rooms, helpful staff and safe. Highly recommended.

AL-A Piccola Locanda, Resbalosa 520, T084-252551, www.piccolalocanda.com. This colourful Peruvian/Italian-run B&B is a steep walk up from the Plaza de Armas. If you've just arrived in Cuzco and the altitude is taking its toll, ask a taxi driver to drop you at San Cristóbal church and then stroll down to the hotel. Rooftop terrace has 360-degree views. It boasts the excellent restaurant I 'Osteria, a TV/DVD room, pleasant courtyard. Rooms in individual style, some without bath. Associated with **Perú Etico** tour company and 2 children's projects, one in the village of Huaro, helping children with various physical and mental handicaps, and the other in Urubamba providing a home and learning centre for children facing parental abuse. Volunteers are sometimes required to aid these projects.

A-B Andenes al Cielo, Choquechaca 176, T084-222237, www.andenesalcielo.com. Boutique hotel short walk from the plaza at

tht foot of the San Blas art district. 15 rooms in renovated historic home, all with either balconies or patios as well as private baths, flat screen TVs, phones and heating. Buffet breakfast incuded, free airport pick up, Wi-Fi, luggage storage, gym. Recommended.

A-B Cusco Plaza 1, Plaza Nazarenas 181, T084-246161, www.cuscoplazahotels.com. Price includes continental breakfast. Situated on a lovely small plaza in the town centre, clean rooms all with cable TV. Room 303 has the best view.

C Casa Elena, Choquechaca 162, T084-241202, www.casaelenacusco.com. French/Peruvian hostel, very comfortable and friendly, breakfast included. Highly recommended.

C Flying Dog Hostel, Choquechaca 469, T084-253997, www.flyingdogperu.com. Shared and private rooms and family suites, kitchen facilities, bar, living room with TV and DVD, buffet breakfast included.

C Hostal María Esther, Pumacurco 516, T084-224382, http://hostalmariaesther. free.fr/. Price includes continental breakfast; heating extra. This very friendly, helpful place has a lovely garden, a lounge with sofas and a variety of rooms. There is also car parking. Recommended.

E El Balcón Colonial, Choquechaca 350, T084-238129, balconcolonial@hotmail.com. Accommodation for 11 people in this family house. Basic rooms with foam mattresses but hospitality is exceptional. Free airport pick-up. Continental breakfast and hot showers extra, use of the kitchen and laundry extra.

San Blas *p75, map p68*
Note that *hostales* on Calles Atocsaycuchi and Siete Angelitos and some of the streets above Plaza San Blas do not have vehicular access right to the door.

L-AL Casa San Blas, Tocuyeros 566, just off Cuesta San Blas, T084-237900, www.casasan blas.com. An international-standard boutique hotel with bright, airy rooms decorated with traditional textiles. Breakfast, served in the **Tika Bistro** downstairs, and Wi-Fi are included. Pleasant balcony with good views, very attentive service.

L-A Quinua Villa Boutique, Pasaje Santa Rosa 8, T084-242646, www.quinua.com.pe. Furnished boutique apartments, artistically designed, each with historic theme based on Inca history, modern, fully equipped bath and kitchens, flatscreen TV, DVD, stereo and phone, American breakfast and daily cleaning service included.

L-A Second Home Cusco, Atocsaycuchi 616, T084-235873, www.secondhomecusco.com. Individually designed 2-room suites with en suites, cable TV, Wi-Fi, phones, breakfast included, free pick-up from airport. Taxi service is not available to the door.

AL Los Apus Hotel y Mirador, Atocsaycuchi 515, corner with Choquechaca, T084-264243, www.losapushotel.com. Price includes buffet breakfast and airport pick-up; laundry US$1 per kg. Swiss-owned, very clean and smart with beamed bedrooms fitted with cable TV and real radiators! Tall travellers will love the 2.3-m-long beds. Disabled facilities.

A Casona Les Pleiades, Tandapata 116, T084-506430, www.casona-pleiades.com. Small guesthouse in renovated colonial house, cosy and warm, generous hosts, gas-heated water, buffet breakfast included, cable TV, Wi-Fi, roof terrace, video lounge and book exchange, café, free airport pick-up with reservation, lots of information for guests.

A-B Andean South Inn, Tandapata 635, T084-244353, www.andeansouth.com. Small boutique hotel tucked away in a corner of San Blas, no taxi service to the door as this part of the street (to the north of the Plaza San Blas) is pedestrian, also hard to locate as house numbers are a bit out of order. Restaurant and art gallery.

A-B Hostal Tika Wasi, Tandapata 491, T084-231609, www.tikawasi.com. Price includes breakfast and all rooms are heated. A family-run *hostal* with a lovely garden overlooking the city. Very stylish, softly lit rooms, great views. Comfortable beds and spotless bathrooms make this a good choice. Supports social projects.

B El Grial, Carmen Alto 112, T084-223012, www.hotelelgrial.com. Family-run, 2 star hostel, in a 17th-century building, all rooms with private bathroom, cable TV, coffee shop, internet, laundry service and free luggage storage.

B Hostal Casa de Campo, Tandapata 296-B (at the end of the street), T084-244404, www.hotelcasadecampo.com. Price (10% discount for Footprint readers on presentation of the book) includes continental breakfast and free airport/rail/bus transfer with reservations. Bedrooms have fabulous views but it's quite a climb to get to them! Safety deposit box, laundry, meals on request and a sun terrace. Dutch and English spoken; take a taxi there after dark. Soon to open new apartments for families and honeymooners at **Casa Valer**.

B Marani, Carmen Alto 194, T084-249462, www.hostalmarani.com. Breakfasts available. Book exchange and information on Andean

life and culture. Large rooms with heaps of character, set around a courtyard. The **Hope Foundation** (www.stichtinghope.org) is run from here: Walter Meekes and his wife, Tineke, have built 20 schools in poor mountain villages and barrios, established a programme to teach teachers and set up a 30-bed burns unit in Cuzco general hospital. Good value, a great cause and highly recommended.

B Pensión Alemana, Tandapata 260, T084-226861, www.cuzco.com.pe. Price includes American breakfast; laundry and heating extra. Car parking available. Swiss-owned, modern European decor with a comfy lounge area, free internet, lovely garden with patio furniture. Recommended.

B-C Hostal Amaru, Cuesta San Blas 541, T084-225933, www.amaruhostal.com. (**D** with shared bathroom). Price includes breakfast and airport/train/bus pick-up. Services include oxygen, kitchen for use in the evenings only, laundry and free book exchange. Rooms around a pretty colonial courtyard, good beds, pleasant, relaxing, some Inca walls. Rooms in the 1st courtyard are best. Recommended. Also has **B Hostal Amaru II**, Chihuampata 642, San Blas, www.amaruhostal2.com, and **Hostería de Anita**, Alabado 525-5, T084-225933, amaruhostal3@speedy.com.pe, with bath, safe, quiet, good breakfast. Also runs the **Amaru Valle Hotel** in Urubamba.

C Andes de San Blas, Carmen Alto 227, T084-242346, www.andesdesanblas.com. Very friendly, family-run hostel in an excellent location mid-way along Carmen Alto. Great views of Cuzco, Sacsayhuaman and Cristo Blanco from the small rooftop terrace and some rooms. Basic breakfast, living room with sofas and TV, internet access downstairs. The family can arrange tours; see general note, page 91. Rooms are clean and pleasant with basic decoration and comfy beds. Generally good.

C Hostal Kuntur Wasi, Tandapata 352-A, T084-227570, www.kunturws.com. Cheaper without bath, services include a safe, use of the kitchen and laundry (both extra), Wi-Fi.

Great views from the terrace where you can breakfast. Very welcoming, helpful owners; a very pleasant place to stay.

C-D Hostal Sambleño, Carmen Alto 114, T084-262979, www.barnmed.com/hostalsambleno/index.htm. A lovely jumble of staircases overlooks a central courtyard. Rooms of varying quality, all with bath and hot water, breakfast available, laundry service. Beds are comfy, showers are electric.

D Casa de la Gringa 1, corner of Tandapata and Pasñapacana 148 (also **Casa de la Gringa 2**, Carmen Bajo 226), T084-241168, www.casadelagringa.com. Relaxed and friendly, both locations in San Blas, with each room individually decorated, lots of art and colour, Wi-Fi, cable TV, DVD, CD player in the common areas, 24-hr hot water, heaters in the main lounges.

D Hostal Pakcha Real, Tandapata 300, T084-237484, www.hostalpakchareal.com. Price includes airport/train/bus pick-up; rooms with bath (**E** without); breakfast, heaters and use of kitchen extra. Family-run with the comforts of home. Laundry service, spotless rooms, friendly and relaxed, but confirm booking if arriving late.

D-E Hostal Familiar Mirador del Inka, Tandapata 160, off Plaza San Blas, T084-241804, www.miradordelinka.info. This *hostal* was redeveloped in a very stylish way, with its Inca foundations and white colonial walls. Bedrooms with bath are spacious and some have great views. Price includes breakfast. The owner's son Edwin runs trekking trips and has an agency on site.

E Hospedaje Inka, Suytuccato 848, T084-231995, http://hospedajeinka.weebly.com. Taxis leave you at Plaza San Blas, walk steeply uphill for 5-10 mins, or phone the *hostal*. Price includes bath (cheaper without) and breakfast. Wonderful views, spacious rooms, very helpful owner, Américo.

E Samay Wasi I, Atocsaycuchi 416, T084-253108, www.samaywasiperu.com. Clean, comfortable hostal in safe area with friendly staff, views of the city, hot water, Wi-Fi, breakfast included, cable TV, kitchen and laundry facilities, free airport pick-up. Also **Samay Wasi II** at Siete Angelitos 675, T084-236649.

F pp **The Blue House**, Kiskapata 291 (there are 2 Kiskapatas – this one runs parallel to and above Tandapata), T084-242407, www.aschisite02.activesbs.co.uk. Snug little *hostal*, excellent value, with reductions for longer stays, monthly rates around US$120. Breakfast is included, DVD room, shared kitchen and great views with a small park in front.

F Hospedaje El Artesano de San Blas, Suytucato 790, T084-2639689, manosand inas@yahoo.com. Many clean, bright and airy rooms. As with the **Hospedaje Inka**, you need to walk up from San Blas.

F Hospedaje Familiar Inti Quilla, Atocsaycuchi 281, T084-252659. Breakfast not included and no facilities for making food. Colourful rooms around a little court-yard, quiet (on pedestrian street so taxis cannot drop you at the door). Good value.

East and southeast of the Plaza de Armas *p75, map p68*
LL Libertador Palacio del Inka, in the Casa de los Cuatro Bustos (see page 77), at Plazoleta Santo Domingo 259, T084-231961, www.libertador.com.pe. Splendid 5-star, award-winning hotel built on Inca ruins (the walls can be seen in the restaurant and bar), set around courtyards. 254 well-appointed rooms; the attention to detail is so great there are even Nazca Lines drawn in the sand of the ashtrays! Enjoy Andean music and dance over dinner in the excellent **Inti Raymi** restaurant. Recommended.

AL Munay Wasi Inn, Av Tullumayo 418, T084-240283, www.munaywasi.com. In the restored Casa del Reloj, 4 blocks from the Plaza de Armas, price includes buffet breakfast, restaurant and bar. Also has a cheaper option, **F Munay Wasi**, Huaynapata 253, not far from the Plaza de Armas, T084-223661. Quiet, with basic, clean rooms, helpful.

D Hotel La Casa de Fray Bartolomé, Tullumayo 465, T084-233472, www.lacasa

defraybartolome.com. Run by the Casa Bartolomé de las Casas, a social development organization. 21 rooms with bath, ask for one overlooking the quiet atrium garden, not the street, inexpensive breakfast available, restaurant and bar. Next to the CBC library and bookstore and a nice bakery: **Panadería Qosqo Maki**.

F Albergue Casa Campesina, Av Tullumayo 274, T084-233466, reservas@apu.cbc.org.pe. Price includes breakfast, shared bathrooms only. A lovely place, set up to support the work of the **Casa Campesina** organization (www.cbc.org.pe/casacampesina/), which is linked to local *campesina* communities. On the same site is the **Store of the Weavers** (see Shopping, page 112). The money that people pay for accommodation goes to this good cause. 23% discount for **SAE** members.

F Estrellita, Av Tullumayo 445, parte Alta, T084-234134. Price includes breakfast and tea and coffee all day. TV, video and old stereo in the tiny communal sitting area, basic kitchen for guests. Rooms are multiples with shared bath, plus 2 with private bath. Basic but excellent value. It is about a 15-min walk from the centre. When you arrive ring the bell several times and wait; you will be given your own keys when you register. Safe parking for cars and bikes. Recommended.

South and southwest of the Plaza de Armas *p80, map 68*
AL-A Sonesta Hotel Cusco, Av Sol 954, T084-581200, www.sonesta.com/cusco/. Sonesta has refurbished the old Hotel Savoy, with modern, comfortable rooms, views of the city and surrounding mountains, cable TV, Wi-Fi, restaurant serving classic Peruvian cuisine and bar.

D Maison de la Jeunesse (affiliated to **Hostelling International**), Av Sol, Cuadra 5, Pasaje Grace, Edificio San Jorge (down a small side street opposite Qoricancha), T084-235617, www.hostellingcusco peru.com. Price is for a double room and includes bath and breakfast. A bed in a dorm with shared bath is **F**, breakfast included; HI discount. Very friendly hostel, TV and video room, internet, Wi-Fi, lockers, cooking facilities and very hot water.

D Yamanyá Backpackers, San Andrés 269, T084-224473, www.yamanya.com. New hostal with shared and private rooms, breakfast included, Wi-Fi, common areas with HD TV and DVD and – a rarity in Cuzco – a swimming pool.

West and northwest of the Plaza de Armas *p82, map p68*

AL-A Hostal El Balcón, Tambo de Montero 222, T084-236738, www.balconcusco.com. Price includes breakfast. Lovingly restored 1630 colonial house with rooms set around a beautiful garden, homely atmosphere. Ask for a TV if you want one. Restaurant and kitchen for guests, laundry service. Recommended.

A Cusco Plaza 2, Saphi 486, T084-263000, www.cuscoplazahotels.com. Under same management as the Cusco Plaza 1 (see page 95). The 24 nicely decorated rooms are set around 3 charming covered patios. Price includes American breakfast, and all rooms have cable TV and heating.

A-B Cahuide, Saphi 845, T084-222771, www.hotelcahuide-cusco.com. Price (negotiate for a discount, especially for longer stays) includes American breakfast. Cable TV in all rooms, ask for a heater. A modern hotel with 1970s furniture, plain white walls and comfy beds. Helpful staff.

B-C Hostal San Isidro Labrador, Saphi 440, T084-226241, labrador@qnet.com.pe Continental breakfast included in the price. Pleasant 3-star hostal with elegant but simple decor, colonial arches and lovely patios. Plenty of hot water and heating.

C Goldie's Guest House, Saphi 456, T511-242 5534, www.goldiesguesthouse.com. Self-contained accommodation (preferably long-term for a week or a month) in a pleasant and safe environment right in the centre of Cuzco (250 m from Plaza de Armas).

C Hostel Loki, Cuesta Santa Ana 601, T084-243705, www.lokihostel.com/en/cusco. (From **F** per person). Huge, ultra-funky hostel in a restored viceroy's residence on the super-steep Cuesta Santa Ana. Dorms and rooms are set around a beautiful courtyard, and the view alone makes the climb well worth the effort. The beds have comfortable duvets, there's plenty of hot water, free internet access and lots of chill-out areas. A great place to meet other travellers.

C Niños Hotel, Meloc 442, T084-231424, www.ninoshotel.com. Price does not include the excellent breakfast. Services include the cafeteria and laundry service, Dutch, English, German and French spoken. Spotless, beautiful rooms in a 17th-century colonial house funding a fantastic charity, *Niños Unidos Peruanos*, established by Jolanda van den Berg. Also has **Niños 2** (same price), on C Fierro, a little further from the centre, 20 nicely decorated, clean and airy rooms, surrounding the central courtyard, and apartments in the same price range, also on C Fierro. Also **AL-A** Niños Hacienda in the village of Huasao, with bungalows, rooms, pool, horse riding. Contact the main hotel for reservations or for weekend packages.

C-D Hostal Qorichaska, Nueva Alta 458, T084-228974, www.qorichaskaperu.com. Price includes breakfast, use of well-equipped kitchen, internet and safe. Also has dorms, mixed and women only, **F** per preson without breakfast. Laundry service. Rooms are clean and sunny; ask for the older rooms – they're bigger and have traditional balconies. Friendly and recommended.

F Hostal Familiar, Saphi 661, T084 239353. Popular *hostal* in a colonial house 3 blocks from the central plaza. Most beds are comfy, hot water all day. Luggage deposit costs US$2.85 a day for a big pack.

E Hostal Killipata, Killichapata 238, just off Tambo de Montero, T084-236668, www.cusco.net/killipata/. **F** per person in shared rooms. Very clean, family-run lodging with good showers, hot water and fully equipped kitchen. Breakfast is US$2 extra. Recommended.

E Hostal Rickch'airy, Tambo de Montero 219, T084-236606. **F** without bath.

Backpackers' haunt with views from the garden. Owner Leo has tourist information and will collect guests from the station. **E Suecia II**, Tecseccocha 465 (no bell – knock!), T084-239757, www.hostalsuecia2 cuzco.com (it is wise to book ahead). **F** without bath, breakfast extra from 0500. In a beautiful building, rooms are set around a glass-covered colonial courtyard and are warm. Beds have thick foam mattresses, water not always hot or bathrooms clean, can be noisy and the luggage store is closed at night, otherwise a good meeting place. **F Albergue Municipal**, Quiscapata 240, near San Cristóbal/Resbaloşa, T084-252506, albergue@municusco.gob.pe. Private rooms with double beds and dormitories in this very clean, helpful youth hostel. Nice communal area with cable TV and video. No rooms have bath. Great views, cafeteria and laundry facilities (laundry service US$0.75 per kg). Showers are electric, but there is no kitchen. **F Hostal Luzerna**, Av Baja 205, near San Pedro train station (take a taxi at night), T084-232762. Price includes breakfast. A nice family-run *hostal*, hot water, good beds, clean, safe to leave luggage. Recommended.

Away from the centre *map p68*
A Residencial Torre Dorada, C los Cipreses N–5, Residencial Huancaro, T084-241698, www.torredorada.com.pe. In a tranquil suburb to the west of the airport, this sparklingly clean modern hotel makes up in service for anything it might lose in location. Good size rooms with very comfortable beds, heating and plenty of hot water in the well-appointed en suite bathrooms. Buffet breakfast is included, as is free transportation to and from the airport/bus/train station, and daily to the historical centre of Cuzco. Internet access and Wi-Fi are also available. An excellent option for people looking to stay in a quieter part of town. Highly recommended.

🍴 Eating

Plaza de Armas and around
p70, maps p68 and p70
Procuradores and Plateros are 2 streets that lead off the northwest side of the Plaza de Armas. Procuradores, or **Gringo Alley** as the locals call it, is good for a value feed; its menus take the hungry backpacker from Mexico to Italy, Spain and Turkey. None is dreadful, many are very good indeed, especially for the price. Parallel with Gringo Alley, Plateros also has good-value places to eat. It is also lined with a great many tour operators, so you can wander up and down checking what deals are on offer.
A Mi Manera, Triunfo 393, T084-222219, www.amimaneraperu.com. Imaginative Novo Andino cuisine with open kitchen. Both great hospitality and a good atmosphere.
Bistrot 370, Triunfo 370, p 2, T084-224908. Lima chef Rafael Osterling's Cuzco restaurant. 'Fusion' cuisine, blending Peruvian classics with Oriental touches using ingredients from the Sacred Valley such as quinua, trout, ají and sauco (elderberries), smart and highly regarded, well-stocked bar and a good wine list, cosy seating areas. Service is variable.
Chicha, Plaza Regocijo 261, p 2 (above El Truco), T084-240520, www.chicha.com.pe. Daily 1200-2400. 1 of a group of 3 restaurants, the others in Arequipa and, yet to open, in Trujillo, which specialize in dishes of the region using recipes created by Chef Gastón Acurio (see under Lima, Eating). There are also light meals if you prefer or international favourites blended with local ingredients such as rocoto relleno pizza. The food here is of the highest standard in a renovated colonial house, at one time the royal mint, tastefully decorated, open-to-view kitchen, excellent selection of cocktails based on pisco, good service. Warmly recommended.
Cicciolina, Triunfo 393, 2nd floor, T084-239510, www.cicciolinacuzco.com. Sophisticated restaurant focusing largely on Italian/Mediterranean cuisine. It also has a

tapas bar and a boutique bakery; the kitchens are open to view. The impressive wine list draws from across the globe but the emphasis is on Latin American produce. Good atmosphere, fine decor and great for a treat. Ask about their **Catering** scheme: a gourmet picnic will be taken to the location of your choice, with chef, waiters and all the trimmings (best for groups).

ᵀᵀᵀ El Truco, Plaza Regocijo 261. Excellent local and international dishes, used a lot by tour groups, buffet lunch 1200-1500, nightly folk music at 2045, next door is **Taberna del Truco**, which is open 0900-0100.

ᵀᵀᵀ Fusiones, Av El Sol 106, Galería La Merced Int 208, T084-233341, www.fusiones-restaurant.com. Open 1100-2300. In the new commercial centre La Merced, 2nd floor, very close to Plaza de Armas. Novo Andino and international cuisine in a chic contemporary setting, fine wines. Accepts credit cards.

ᵀᵀᵀ Incanto, Santa Catalina Angosta 135, T084-254753, incanto@cuscorestaurants.com. Open daily 1100-2400. Under same ownership as **Inka Grill** and with the same standards, this new restaurant has Inca stone work and serves pastas, grilled meats, pizzas, desserts, accompanied by an extensive wine list. There is also a Peruvian delicatessen on the premises. Upstairs is **ᵀᵀ Greens Organic**, T084-243379, greens@cuscorestaurants.com, exclusively organic ingredients in fusion cuisine and a fresh daily buffet. There are a number of vegetarian dishes such as arúgula ravioli with goat's cheese as well as meat dishes.

ᵀᵀᵀ Inka Grill, Portal de Panes 115, T084-262992, www.inkagrillcusco.com. Daily 1100-2400. A long-standing reputation for top quality Novo Andino cuisine (the use of native ingredients and 'rescued' recipes) and innovative dishes, also home-made pastas, wide vegetarian selection, live music, excellent coffee and home-made pastries 'to go'. A good place to spoil yourself. Recommended.

ᵀᵀᵀ Kusikuy, Suecia 339, T084-292870. Mon-Sat 0800-2300. Some say this serves the best *cuy* (guinea pig, US$20) in town and the owners say if you give them an

hour's warning they will produce their absolute best. Many other typical Cuzco dishes on the menu. Set lunch is US$7. Also has live music.

ᵀᵀᵀ La Cosa Nostra, Plateros 358A, p 2, T084-232992, www.cosanostraristorante.com. Open 1200-2300. Sicilian/Peruvian owned Italian place with good food, a variety of pastas, authentic pesto, Bolognese and other sauces and many other traditional Italian specialities. Professional service and an extensive wine list.

ᵀᵀᵀ La Retama, Portal de Panes 123, 2nd floor, T084-226372. Excellent Novo Andino food and service. There's a balcony, an enthusiastic music and dance group and art exhibitions.

ᵀᵀᵀ Limo, Portal de Carnes 236, T084-240668, www.cuscorestaurants.com. On 2nd floor of a colonial mansion overlooking the Plaza de Armas, creative Peruvian cuisine with strong emphasis on fish and seafood, all prepared to the highest of standards. It has a pisco bar, good service and atmosphere. A good choice for a special occasion. Reservations required to secure a window seat.

ᵀᵀᵀ Pachacútec Grill and Bar, Portal de Panes 105, www.pachacuterestaurant.com. International cuisine including seafood and Italian specialities, also features folk music shows nightly.

ᵀᵀᵀ Pisku'o, Portal Belén 115, T084-231782. Entrance near the Gatos market on Plaza de Armas, on 2nd floor with great views from the balcony of the colonial churches, trendy new restaurant, nice selection of piqueos, wines and cocktails.

ᵀᵀᵀ Tunupa, Portal Confiturías 233, 2nd floor. One of the finest restaurants on the plaza (often used by tour groups). Also has the longest (glassed-in) balcony but this is narrow and best for couples only. Food is international, traditional and Novo Andino; wine list is limited. Also an excellent buffet that includes a pisco sour and a hot drink. In the evenings there is an excellent group playing 16th- and 17th-century-style Cuzqueñan music of their own composition, with dancers. Recommended.

❌❌❌ Tupananchis, Portal Mantas 180, T084-245159/976 4494, tupananchis_rest_cusco@hotmail.com. Tasty, beautifully presented Novo Andino and fusion cuisine in a smart, sophisticated atmosphere. Try the alpaca curry, river fish *ceviche* or stuffed chicken supreme. There is a café next door. Highly recommended.

❌❌ Al Grano, Santa Catalina Ancha 398, T084-228032. Mon-Sat 1000-2100. Lunchtime menu US$3 is a good option if you are fed up with other menus. Evening serves 5 authentic Asian dishes for US$6, menu changes daily. Without doubt some of the best coffee in town, vegetarian choices and breakfasts, including 'Full English'. Recommended.

❌❌ Maikhana, Av El Sol 106, T084-252044, www.maikhana.net. Authentic Indian restaurant in a mini-mall, serving filling curry, Indian breads, unlimited rice and lassies. Unlimited buffet at reasonable prices. Also has a coffee house and sports bar, free internet and phone.

❌❌ Pucará, Plateros 309. Mon-Sat 1230-2200. Peruvian and international food – no language skills required as a sample plate of their daily menu is placed in the window at lunchtime. Japanese owner does very good *aji de gallina* (garlic chicken) and cream of potato soup, pleasant atmosphere. Recommended.

❌❌ The Real McCoy, Plateros 326, p 2, T084-261111, http://www.bookingbox.org/realmccoy/index.html. A fabulous retreat for homesick Brits and Aussies. There's a good-value breakfast buffet, with PG Tips and Heinz Baked Beans, and a huge Full English. On offer for dinner are some English classics: fish and chips, meat pies, bangers and mash, to name but a few, followed by real puddings. Wi-Fi and comfy sofas and well-stocked book exchange, weekly pub quiz, special Sun roast beef dinner.

❌❌ Sara, Santa Catalina Ancha 370, T084-261691. Vegetarian-friendly organic café-bistro, stylish and modern setting, menu includes both traditional Peruvian dishes as well as pasta and other international dishes.

❌❌ Two Nations, Huaynapata 410 corner of Suecia, T084-240198. Friendly, comfortable restaurant with great food, run by an Australian/Peruvian couple. Fresh food, cooked to order using quality ingredients, from alpaca steaks to burgers or pizza, good value, large portions. Second location on Arequipa 265 has a courtyard open for lunch in the restored Túpac Inca Yupanqui Cultural Centre, which showcases local artists' contemporary art.

❌❌-❌ Circus Restobar, Santa Teresa 351, T084-222461, elio.cervera@gmail.com. Great food, tasty cocktails like mango mojitos, games and lots of 'toys': musical instruments, juggling, movies – even the bathrooms are fun! The most entertaining dining option in Cuzco, games for kids make this a great spot for families as well as couples.

❌ Bembos, Portal Comercio 153. Peru's answer to MacDonalds. Originally from San Isidro, Lima, Bembos has grown from sandwiches sold from the back of a bicycle to a chain in Lima and this one in Cuzco. Burgers and sandwiches are based on traditional Peruvian fare, such as *uchucuta* and *cecina con tacacho*. Very popular. Also has a coffee shop and internet on the 2nd floor.

❌ Chez Maggy, Procuradores 344, T084-234861. Popular place, mainly for wood-oven pizzas and beer, but also large menú including Peruvian specialities, burritos and pasta. Also on Plateros.

❌ El Encuentro, Santa Catalina Ancha 384, T084-247977, Choquechaca 136, T084-225496, and Tigre 130, www.restaurantelencuentro.blogspot.com. One of the best-value eateries, 3 courses of good healthy food and a drink will set you back US$2, very busy at lunchtime, especially at Santa Catalina.

❌ El Fogón, Plateros 365. Huge local *menú del día*, good solid food at reasonable prices. Very popular, recommended for lunch.

❌ Los Candiles, Plateros 323. Good set lunch.

❌ Víctor Victoria, Tecsecocha 466, T084-252854. Israeli and local dishes, highly recommended for breakfast, good value.

Cafés, delis and panaderías

Amaru, Plateros 325, 2nd floor, T084-246976. Limitless coffee, tea, great bread and juices served, even on non-buffet breakfasts. Colonial balcony; also a pub serving pizzas, etc. Recommended.

Café El Ayllu, Marqués 263, T084-255078, and Almagro 133, T084-232357, www.inkaworld.org/cafeayllu. The new locations of one of Cuzco's oldest cafés (it used to be on the Plaza de Armas). Fantastic breakfasts (try the special fruit salad, sandwiches, coffee and classical music as well as wonderful apple pastries. The *ponche con pisco* is an excellent way to end a cold evening. Superb service.

Café Halliy, Plateros 363. Popular meeting place, especially for breakfast, good for comments on guides, has good snacks and *copa Halliy* (fruit, muesli, yoghurt, honey and chocolate cake), also serves vegetarian dishes.

Café Perla, Santa Catalina Ancha 304, on the plazoleta, T084-774130. Extensive menu of light meals, sandwiches, desserts and coffee, including beans for sale roasted on the premises. Popular.

Dolce Vita, Santa Catalina Ancha 366 (with another branch on Márquez). 1000-2100. Delicious Italian ice cream, this *heladería* is an absolute must.

La Bondiet, Márquez y Heladeros and at Plateros 363. Clean, simple café with a huge selection of sweet and savoury pastries, empanadas, good sandwiches, juices and coffee, staff are young, friendly and efficient.

La Tertulia, Procuradores 44, p 2. Open until 2300. Breakfast served 0630-1300, includes muesli, bread, yoghurt, eggs, juice and coffee, all you can eat for US$3, superb value, vegetarian buffet daily 1800-2200, set dinner and salad bar for US$3.50, also fondue and gourmet meals, book exchange, newspapers, classical music.

Trotamundos, Portal Comercio 177, 2nd floor. Mon-Sat 0800-2400. One of the most pleasant cafés in the plaza if a bit pricey. Has a balcony overlooking the plaza and a warm atmosphere especially at night with its open

fire. Good coffees and cakes, safe salads, *brochetas*, sandwiches and pancakes as well as computers with internet access.

Yahuu Juice Bar, Marqués 200. Fresh inexpensive juices and smoothies as well as sandwiches, a the start of the pedestrian walkway on Marqués.

Yaku Mama, Procuradores 397. Good for breakfast; unlimited fruit and coffee. Service can be slow.

North and northeast of the Plaza de Armas *p73, maps p68 and p70*

TTT Baco, Ruinas 465, T084-242808, bacorestaurante@yahoo.com. Wine bar and bistro-style restaurant with same owner as **Cicciolina**. Specializes in *degustación* meals for groups, with barbecued and grilled meats, vegetarian dishes, interesting pizzas, and good wines. Unpretentious but comfortable, with a wide range of prices.

TTT Fallen Angel, Plazoleta Nazarenas 320, T084-258184, www.fallenangelincusco.com. Mon-Sat 1100 till whenever (bar closes at midnight, kitchen at 2300), Tue and Sun opens at 1500. Like nowhere else. This is the 2nd venture of Cuzco native Andrés Zúñiga (the other being **Macondo** – see below). The menu features steaks and some innovative pasta dishes. Cocktails are excellent. Live DJ at night. Regular parties/fashion shows are always events to remember. Free Wi-Fi. Always phone to reserve.

TTT MAP Café, Plaza de las Nazarenas 231, a glass structure in the Museo de Arte Precolombino, T084-242476. Operates as a café 1000-1830 and a restaurant 1830-2200. Serves excellent Peruvian-Andean cuisine and international food, with an innovative children's menu. It has a very good list of wines and piscos and the service is first class. After your museum visit, this is an ideal place for tea or coffee or a sophisticated meal.

TTT-TT Divina Comedia, Pumacurco 406, T084-437640, info@restaurantcusco.com. Daily 1230-1500, 1830-2300. An elegant restaurant just 1 block from the Monasterio hotel, diners are entertained by classical piano and singing. Friendly atmosphere with comfortable seating, perfect for a special night out, reasonable prices.

Justina, Palacios 110. Open Mon-Sat from 1800. Good value, good quality pizzería, with wine bar. It's at the back of a patio.

L'Osteria della Locanda, Quiskapata 215, T084-252551, riserve@osteriadellalocanda. com. Mon-Sat, evenings only; book in advance if possible. In the same group as Piccola Locanda and an Italian/Peruvian-run tour company. Excellent handmade Italian food, fresh pasta, pizza and lasagna created as you wait with imported olive oil and parmesan. US$0.50 per table goes towards 2 family-run children's projects in the area.

-Y Aldea Yanapay, Ruinas 415, p 2. Good café serving breakfast, lunch, dinner and Sun brunch. Run by a charity which supports children's homes (www.aldeayanapay.org). They welcome volunteers.

Cafés, delis and panaderías

Café Punchay, Choquechaca 229. German-owned café with speciality coffees, cocktails, pastas, sandwiches, cakes, garden and big screen for live sports broadcasts.

Chocolate, Choquechaca 162, T084-984 752172 (mob). Good for coffee and cakes but the real highlights are the fresh gourmet chocolates (up to European standards) and deliciously rich hot chocolate with marshmallows.

Cositas Café y Arte, Pasaje Inca Roca 108 and 110, T084-236410, info@cositascafe yarte.com. Inventive local cuisine, Peruvian tapas (*piqueos*) in a small, friendly, art-filled café round the corner from the famous 12-sided Inca rock. Profits support local social projects such as arts and crafts which are on sale in the café.

San Blas *p75, map p68*

Pachapapa, Plazoleta San Blas 120, opposite church of San Blas, T084-241318. Open 1130-2200. A beautiful patio restaurant in a wonderful old colonial house, with resident harp player. Under same ownership

as Inka Grill. Very good Cuzqueña dishes, including *pachamanca* (previous reservation required for 6 people). At night, diners can sit in their own private colonial dining room. Recommended.

El Batan del Inka, Hatun Rumiyoc 487, 2nd floor, T084-601304. Specializes in Peruvian food but also good international and vegetarian menu.

Granja Heidi, Cuesta San Blas 525, T084-238383. Offers 3- or 4-course *menú del día* in a clean and relaxed environment. There are usually vegetarian options; superb yoghurt, granola, ricotta cheese and honey and other breakfast choices.

Inka Panaka, Tandapata 140, T084-235034, www.bookingbox.org.uk/inkapanaka/. Artistic flair, gallery of local artists' work. Novo Andina cuisine, tasty innovative treats like ojitos de yucca (small yucca balls) stuffed with olives and chestnuts accompanied with a peanut satay sauce. Several other vegetarian options, also breakfast.

Jack's Café, on the corner of Choquechaca and San Blas. T084-806960. Opens at 0630 for great-value English breakfast. Excellent varied menu with generous portions, all in a light and relaxed atmosphere. Fabulous American-style pancakes and freshly ground local coffee. Lunchtime can be very busy, expect to queue outside in the high season.

La Bodega, Carmen Alto 146. Snug Dutch/Peruvian-owned café/restaurant serving hot chocolate by candlelight in the afternoons and with evening meals. Dishes come with a trip to the salad bar, American breakfast and a good-value lunch menu. Highly recommended.

Macondo, Cuesta San Blas 571, T084-229415. www.macondoincusco.com. A bit pricier than others in this range but fantastic. A casual, cosy, arty and comfortable restaurant that's been redecorated under a change of ownership. Serves an exotic menu with jungle and Novo Andino food. It also has an art gallery. Popular, and a steep 3-block walk from the plaza. Happy hour 1500-1800. Visa attracts a 10% surcharge. Recommended.

Ⅲ Tika Bistro Gourmet, Tocuyeros 566, T084-237900, www.casasanblas.com/tikabistro. A snug, beautifully decorated little eatery, underneath the **Casa San Blas**, offers an eating experience on par with London or Paris. Dishes range from filling and beautifully presented stuffed meats with spicy risottos, through to oriental plates of spicy beef wantons and spring rolls of various flavours, served with a variety of mouth-watering sauces. The wine list, largely Latin American, is excellent, as is the service.

Ⅰ Café Punchay, Choquechaca 229, T084-261504, www.cafe-punchay.de. Friendly, German-owned vegetarian restaurant, specialities include dumplings in mushroom sauce and a variety of pasta and potato dishes. There is a good range of wines and spirits and the best banana split in Cuzco. They have a very large projection screen on which they show international sports and you can bring a DVD for your own private movie showing.

Ⅰ Inka...fé, Choquechaca 131-A and Espaderos 142, T084-258073, www.inkafe.com.pe. Good coffee, set breakfasts and good-value lunch menus. Their signature dishes are Inka...fé chicken or risotto; excellent main meals at a good price. Range of sandwiches in French bread, hamburgers, salads and good desserts. English spoken. They have a delicatessen opposite at No 140.

Cafés, delis and panaderías
Juanito's Sandwich Café, Qanchipata 596. Cuzco's answer to a university greasy spoon burger bar. Great grilled veggie and meaty burgers and sandwiches with titles like 'La Cabaña' and the '4 x 4'. Coffee, tea and hot chocolate. Juanito himself is a great character, staff are friendly, and the café stays open late, a classic post-club/party retreat.

Panadería El Buen Pastor, Cuesta San Blas 579. Very good bread and pastries, excellent meat and chicken *empanadas*. The proceeds go to a charity for orphans and street children. Popular with backpackers. Recommended.

East and southeast of the Plaza de Armas *p75, map p68*
Ⅲ Inkanato, San Agustín 280, T084-222926, www.perou.net. Good food, staff dressed in Inca outfits and dishes made only with ingredients known in Inca times.

South and southwest of the Plaza de Armas *p80, map 68*
Ⅲ Los Toldos, Almagro 171 y San Andrés 219. If you're feeling peckish, on a budget and fancy being served by waiters in a bow tie, try their great chicken *brocheta*. Comes with fries, a trip to the salad bar and is enough for 2 people at just US$2.30. Also *trattoria* with home-made pasta and pizza, delivery T084-229829.

Ⅰ Chifa Sipan, Quera 251 (better than their other branch for tourists in Plateros). Owner Carlos may not sound Chinese but he is and joins in the cooking at this excellent

restaurant. There is no great ambience but it's busy at lunchtimes with locals, which speaks volumes. Skip to the back of the menu for better deals.

San Pedro market, to eat really cheaply, and if your stomach is acclimatized to South American food, head for the market 5 blocks southwest of the Plaza de Armas and eat at one of the many stalls. Food will cost no more than US$0.70 and 3-fruit juices are just US$0.45. Otherwise, look for the set *menús*, usually served 1200-1500, although they are no good for vegetarians.

Cafés, delis and panaderías
Manu Café, Av Pardo 1046. Good coffee and good food too in a jungle decor. It would be a sin to miss one of their liqueur coffees.

🎧 Bars and clubs

Bars
Bar 7, Tandapata 690, San Blas, T084-506472. Good food and drinks in a trendy bar specializing in local ingredients.
The Cross Keys, Triunfo 350 (upstairs), T084-229227, www.cross-keys-pub-cusco-peru.com. 1100-0130. English-style pub run by Barry Walker of **Manu Expeditions**, a Mancunian and ornithologist, this Cuzco institution moved from the Plaza de Armas in 2009 into its new, cosier location on Triunfo. Darts, cable sports, pool, bar meals, plus half-price specials Sun-Wed, great pisco sours, very popular, with a great atmosphere, loud and raucous in the evenings, quiet in the daytime, free Wi-Fi.

The Frogs Restaurant and Lounge, Huarankallqui 185, just off Ruinas, T084-221762. Roomy modern chic bar in historic building, with music, movies, pool table, football, a hookah room and good food as well.
Hierba Buena Lounge, Suytuccato 715-B, T084-260685. Restaurant and bar with live music, comfortable seats and hammocks on different levels with some private 'nooks', DVD library, cool ambience.
Indigo, Tecseccocha 2, p 2, T084-260271. Shows 3 films a day, also has a lounge and cocktail bar and serves Asian and local food. A log fire keeps out the night-time cold.
Km 0 (Arte y Tapas), Tandapata 100, San Blas. Lovely Mediterranean-themed bar tucked in behind San Blas. Good snacks and tapas (of course), affordable, and with live music every night (around 2200 – lots of acoustic guitar, etc).
La Chupitería Shots Bar, Tecseccocha 400. A fun bar with an amazing list of different shots and the widest variety of liquors in Cuzco, the place to try flaming shots, taste a 'brain damage' or sip a fine brandy or cognac. Cool music, lively atmosphere, a great evening.
Los Perros Bar, Tecseccocha 436, above Gringo Alley (Procuradores). Opens 1100 for coffee and pastries; kitchen opens at 1300; very good vegetarian lunch, closes 0100. A great place to chill on comfy couches listening to excellent music. There's a book exchange,

English and other magazines and board games. Occasionally hosts live music and special events. Opened a take-out only branch in 2009 at Suecia 368 which operates 2400-0600 for good-quality post-club food.

Lost City, Tecseccocha 429, T084-224349. Closed Mon. Sports bar showing international sports, from American football and baseball to soccer games on wide screen TVs. Super friendly, great pizzas, happy hour drink specials and free popcorn.

Marcelo Batata, Palacios 121, 3rd floor, T084-222424, www.cuzcodining.com. Bar/restaurant offering sandwiches and international food. The service is slow, but it's worth going to sit on the rooftop for the great 360° panorama and enjoy the Cuzco sunshine.

Norton Rat's Tavern, Santa Catalina Angosta 116, nortonrats@yahoo.com. Opens at 0700 for breakfast, and through the day till 0230. This pub has a fine, sunny balcony overlooking the corner of the Plaza de Armas. Pleasant, popular, with a pool table, dart boards and other games, cable TV and lots of flags and pictures of motorbikes. Owner Jeffrey Powers loves the machines and can provide information for bikers. Serves burgers, etc and a full Mexican menu, with a good selection of beers. See **Hostal Gocta Cusco**, page 92.

Paddy's Pub, C Triunfo 124, corner of the plaza. Open 1300-0100. An Irish theme pub, deservedly popular. Good seating and great food – the jacket potatoes, shepherd's pie and baguettes are all highly recommended.

Rosie O'Grady's, at Santa Catalina Ancha 360, T084-247935. Open 1100 till late (food served till midnight, happy hours 1300-1400, 1800-1900, 2300-2330). Has good music, tasty food. English and Russian spoken.

Clubs

Before your evening meal don't turn down flyers being handed out around the Plaza de Armas. Each coupon not only gives you free entry, it is worth a *cuba libre*. On the back of this tour you will be able to check out which club most suits your tastes. Sadly, the free entry-and-drink system doesn't appear to apply to Peruvians who are invariably asked to pay, even if their tourist companions get in for free. This discrimination should be discouraged. Also note that free drinks are made with the cheapest, least healthy alcohol; always watch your drink being made and obviously never leave it unattended. If you fancy learning a few Latin dance steps before hitting the dancefloor, many of the clubs offer free lessons. Ask at the door for details or look out for flyers.

Caos Disco, Av del Sol 948, T084-253564, www.caosdiversion.com. Active club with themed parties and events, music concerts, fashion parades.

El Garabato Video Music Club, Espaderos 132, 3rd floor. Daily 1600-0300. Dance area, lounge for chilling, bar with saddles for stools, tastefully decorated in a colonial setting, with live shows 2300-0300 (all sorts of styles) and a large screen showing music videos. Recommended.

Extreme, on Suecia, next door to **Magtas Bar**. An old Cuzco staple. Movies are shown late afternoon and early evening, but after midnight this place really gets going with an eclectic range of music, from 60s and 70s rock and pop to techno and trance. This place seems to give out more free drinks than most, so it's a good option for kicking off a big night on the town!

Kamikaze, Plaza Regocijo 274, T084-233865. Peña at 2200, good old traditional rock music, candle-lit cavern atmosphere, entry US$2.50 but usually you don't have to pay.

Mama Africa, Portal de Panes 190. Cool music and clubbers' spot. Serves good food from a varied menu, happy hour until 2300, good value.

Mythology, Portal de Carnes 298, p 2. Tucked in the corner of the plaza. A popular spot but don't expect cutting-edge tunes. It's more an early 80s and 90s combination of cheese, punk and classic. They also show movies in the afternoons. Food in served in the jungle themed **Lek Café**.

Corpus Christi in Cuzco

Corpus Christi is an annual festival celebrated on the Thursday after Trinity Sunday (generally in early June) by Roman Catholics everywhere. In Cuzco, Corpus is an exuberant and colourful pageant where profound faith and prayer share predominance with abundant eating and copious drinking.

All the Saints and Virgins are paraded through the city to the Plaza de Armas and, after being blessed, they are carried into the great cathedral to be placed in prearranged order, in two rows facing each other. The images are kept in the cathedral until the *octava* (the eighth day after their internment), when they are all escorted in procession back to their respective parishes and churches.

During these days and nights in each other's company, the Saints and Virgins, so the stories go, decide among themselves the future of the people for the forthcoming year. It is also said that they gamble at dice. Five hundred years ago, at the very same time of year and in this precise location, the mummified remains of the Incas were paraded in similar fashion and then laid in state. They consulted the Sun, the Moon, the Lightning and the Rains to learn what fate these elements were to bring in the course of the following year.

The Saints are the first to be paraded. The traditional race between San Jerónimo and San Sebastián is a joyous event. San Cristóbal, carved from a single tree trunk, is a heroic, elaborately painted figure, who leans upon a great staff. His powerful muscles and thick sinews forever shoulder the body of the infant Jesus as they ford a river. It is the heaviest statue of all and popular legend tells that underneath it lies a *huaca*, or sacred rock.

Santiago, the warrior saint and patron of Cuzco, enters astride his white horse, brandishing a sword. Trampled under the

---

Night Sky Disco, Av del Sol 106, Galería La Merced Int 208, p 3. One of the latest 'in' places to drink and dance.

Roots, Huaynapata 194 (just off Suecia). Plays mostly reggae, but there are other styles too, good atmosphere and popular.

Siete Angelitos, Siete Angelitos 638. Tiny hole-in-the-wall bar, just a couple of rooms really, but spectacular cocktails and good food (especially the pasta dishes and steaks), a friendly owner by the name of Walter and an awesome atmosphere when things get going. Often hosts guest DJs, ranging from Latin to trance.

Ukuku's, Plateros 316. US$1.35 entry or free with a pass. This is somewhat different to the other clubs as every night there is a live band that might play anything from rock to salsa. The DJ then plays a mixture of Peruvian and international music but the emphasis is on local. It has a good mix of Cuzqueños and

tourists. Videos are shown here at 1600 and 1800. Films are free with any purchase. Also has a good value restaurant at Carmen Alto 133.

⊙ Entertainment

There are plenty of places which show videos and DVDs. Some of the restaurants, bars and clubs which show films are listed in the text.

Centro Qosqo de Arte Nativo, Av Sol 604, T084-227901. There's a regular nightly folklore show here 1900-2030, entrance on the BTC visitor ticket.

Teatro Inti Raymi, Saphi 605. Music nightly at 1845, US$4.50 entry and well worth it.

Teatro Kusikay, Unión 117, T084-255414, www.kusikay.com (tickets from the theatre Mon-Sat 0900-2100 or, out of hours, **Inka Grill** or **Incanto** restaurants, or at the **Mayu Café** at hooves of his steed lies a vanquished demon in the likeness of a Moorish soldier. Santiago's name was the battle cry of the Spanish soldiers, but he soon came to represent Illapa, the Andean deity of thunder and lightning.

Next come the Virgins, dressed in pomp, some of them accompanied by archangels and cherubs. They are seen as the equivalent of the Mother Earth, *Pachamama*. The Virgin of Belén is always first, escorted by San José, who then stands to one side of the entrance of the cathedral, waiting for all the Virgins to be carried in. Santa Bárbara, the pregnant virgin, is the last.

Corpus is perhaps the city's greatest event. All the streets and the huge expanse of the Plaza de Armas are thronged with enormous crowds. The revered images, each several hundred years old and from a distinct parish of the city, command a host of fervent followers, including a band of musicians and troupe of dancers. Most important and conspicuous are the bearers, whose strenuous efforts are relieved at resting points, known as *descansos*. The bier carrying the image is placed on top of a scaffold and the bearers and followers are all given a round of *chicha*, and/or beer while the band plays on and *Ave Marias* are prayed one after the other, like a mantra. The respite over, one final toast is made to the statue, also to *Pachamama* and to the surrounding mountain summits, *los apus*. In many cases this is accompanied by fresh coca leaves and lime. Then the parade resumes its journey. As the processions converge upon the centre, they merge together into a larger procession, which becomes engulfed by the multitudes in the Plaza de Armas. The images as they are carried along seem to become swaying vessels navigating a sea of humanity, riding its waves.

Ollantaytambo train station). Mon-Sat 1930. US$35, thrilling show with spectacular dances based on the Mamacha Carmen festival of Paucartambo, with lavish costumes, special effects and a troupe of 30.

Teatro Municipal, C Mesón de la Estrella 149 (T084-227321 for information 0900-1300 and 1500-1900). This is a venue for plays, dancing and shows, mostly Thu-Sun. Ask for their programmes. They also run classes in music and dancing Jan-Mar that are great value.

⊛ Festivals and events

20 Jan Procession of saints in the San Sebastián district of Cuzco.

Feb/Mar Carnival in Cuzco is a messy affair with flour, water, cacti, bad fruit and animal manure thrown about in the streets. Be prepared.

Mar/Apr Easter Mon sees the procession of **El Señor de los Temblores** (Lord of the Earthquakes), starting at 1600 outside the cathedral. A large crucifix is paraded through the streets, returning to the Plaza de Armas around 2000 to bless the tens of thousands of people who have assembled there.

2-3 May Vigil of the Cross, a boisterous affair, takes place at all mountain tops with crosses on them.

Jun Qoyllur Rit'i (Snow Star Festival, see box, page 110), held at a 4700-m glacier north of Ausangate, 150 km southeast of Cuzco. It has its final day 58 days after Easter Sun.

Jun Corpus Christi, on the Thu after Trinity Sun, when all the statues of the Virgin and of saints from Cuzco's churches are paraded through the streets to the cathedral. This is a colourful event. The Plaza de Armas is surrounded by tables with women selling *cuy* (guinea pig), a mixed grill called *chiriuchu*

It's no fun at the snow festival

Qoyllur Rit'i is not a festival for the uninitiated or the faint-hearted. It can be very confusing for those who don't understand the significance of this ancient ritual. To get there involves a two-hour walk up from the nearest road at Mawayani, beyond Ocongate, then it's a further exhausting climb up to the glacier. It's a good idea to take a tent, food and plenty of warm clothing. Many trucks leave Cuzco, from Limacpampa, in the days prior to the full moon in mid-June. This is a very rough and dusty overnight journey lasting 14 hours, needing warm clothing and coca leaves to fend off cold and exhaustion. Several agencies offer tours.

Peter Frost writes: "The pilgrimage clearly has its origins in Inca or pre-Inca times, although the historical record dates it only from a miraculous apparition of Christ on the mountain, around 1780. It is a complex and chaotic spectacle, attended by hundreds of dance groups, and dominated by the character of the *ukuku*, the bear dancer, whose night vigil on the surrounding glaciers is the festival's best-known feature. The journey there is lengthy, gruelling and dusty, the altitude (4600 m at the sanctuary) is extremely taxing, the place is brutally cold, unbelievably noisy around the clock (sleep is impossible), and the sanitary conditions are indescribable."

(*cuy*, chicken, tortillas, fish eggs, waterweeds, maize, cheese and sausage) and lots of Cuzqueña beer.

24 Jun Inti Raymi, the Inca festival of the winter solstice (see page 78), at which locals outnumber tourists, is enacted at the fortress of Sacsayhuaman. The spectacle starts at 1000 at the Qoricancha (crowds line the streets and jostle for space to watch), then proceeds to the Plaza de Armas. From there performers and spectators go to Sacsayhuaman for the main event, which starts at 1300. It lasts 2½ hrs and is in Quechua. Locals make a great day of it, watching the ritual from the hillsides and cooking potatoes in pits in the ground. Tickets for the stands can be bought in advance from the **Emufec** office, Santa Catalina Ancha 333, T084-226711, www.emufec.gob.pe, and cost US$80 in June, less March-May. Standing places on the ruins are free but get there at about 1030 as even so-called reserved seats fill up quickly, and defend your space. Travel agents can arrange the whole day for you, with meeting points, transport, reserved seats and packed lunch. Don't believe anyone who

tries to persuade you to buy a ticket for the right to film or take photos. On the night before **Inti Raymi**, the Plaza de Armas is crowded with processions and foodstalls. Try to arrive in Cuzco 15 days before Inti Raymi. The atmosphere in the town during the build up is fantastic and something is always going on (festivals, parades, etc).

Aug On the last Sun in Aug is the **Huarachicoy Festival** at Sacsayhuaman, a spectacular re-enactment of the Inca manhood rite, performed in dazzling costumes by boys of a local school.

8 Sep **Day of the Virgin**, is the occasion for a colourful procession of masked dancers from the church of Almudena, at the southwest edge of Cuzco, near Belén, to the Plaza de San Francisco. There is also a fair at Almudena, and a bullfight on the following day.

8 Dec **Cuzco Day**, when churches and museums close at 1200.

24 Dec **Santuranticuy**, 'the buying of saints' is a huge celebration of Christmas shopping with a big crafts market in the Plaza de Armas, which is very noisy. It lasts until the early hours of the 25th.

O Shopping

Arts and crafts

Cuzco has some of the best craft shopping in all Peru. In the Plaza San Blas and the surrounding area, authentic Cuzco crafts still survive and woodworkers can be seen in almost any street. A market is held on Sat. The main market for artisans' stalls is at the bottom of Av Sol. There are also small markets of 10 or so permament stalls dotted around the city that offer goods made from alpaca as well as modern materials.

Cuzco is also the weaving centre of Peru and excellent textiles can be found at good value; but watch out for sharp practices when buying gold and silver objects and jewellery. Note that much of the wood used for picture frames, etc, is *cedro*, a rare timber not extracted by sustainable means.

Craft shops

Agua y Tierra, Plazoleta Nazarenas 167, and also at Cuesta San Blas 595, T084-226951. Excellent quality crafts from lowland rainforest communities, largely the Shipibo and Ashaninka tribes from the Selva Central whose work is considered to be among the finest in the Amazon Basin.

Apacheta, Santa Catalina 313, T084-238210, www.apachetaperu.com. Replicas of pre-Inca and Inca textiles, ceramics, alpaca goods, contemporary art gallery, and books on Andean culture.

Inkantations, Choquechaca 200. Radical baskets made from natural materials in all sorts of weird and wonderful shapes. Also ceramics and Andean weavings. Interesting and original.

La Pérez, Urb Mateo Pumacahua 598, Wanchac, T084-232186. A big co-operative with a good selection; they will arrange a free pick-up from your hotel.

Maky Artesanías, Carmen Alto 101, T084-653643. A great place to buy individually designed ceramics. Ask for discounts if buying several pieces.

Pedazo de Arte, Plateros 334B. A tasteful collection of Andean handicrafts, many designed by Japanese owner Miki Suzuki.

Primitiva, Hatun Rumiyoc 495, T084-260152, San Blas, www.coscio.com. Excellent Peruvian contemporary art gallery, largely featuring the work of Federico Coscio.

Seminario, Portal de Carnes 244, Plaza de Armas. Sells the ceramics of Seminario-Behar (see page 141), plus cotton, basketry, jewellery, etc. A visit is highly recommended for those who cannot get to their studio in Urubamba.

Fabric and clothing

Alpaca 3, Ruinas 472. Quality alpaca items.
Alpaca Golden, Portal de Panes 151, T084-251724, alpaca.golden@terra.com.pe. Also at Plazoleta Nazarenas 175. Designer, producer and retailer of fine alpaca clothing.

Arte Vivo del Cusco al Mundo, on the right-hand side in Capilla San Ignacio, Plaza de Armas. Open 1030-1300, 1530-2100. The outlet for 2 cooperatives of weavers.

Center for Traditional Textiles of Cusco, Av Sol 603, T084-228117, www.textilescusco.org. A non-profit organization that seeks to promote, refine and rediscover the weaving traditions of the area. Tours of workshops in Chinchero and beyond can de arranged, also weaving classes. In the Cuzco outlet you can watch weavers at work. The textiles are of excellent quality and the price reflects the fact that over 50% goes direct to the weaver. Recommended.

Hilo, Carmen Alto 260, T084-254536. Fashion gear for ladies and gents. Each item in this tiny little shop is designed separately and hand made on site. Influences seem to range from Inca to Heidi and back to Madonna's finest hour. Run by patrons Run by Eibhlin Cassidy who can adjust and tailor designs, and sometimes offers "The best Chai this side of Mumbai" to customers.

Josefina Olivera, Portal Comercio 173, Plaza de Armas. Open daily 1100-2100. She sells old ponchos and antique *mantas* (shawls), without the usual haggling. Her prices are high, but it is worth it to save pieces being cut up to make other items.

Kuna by Alpaca 111, Plaza Regocijo 202, T084-243233. High-quality alpaca clothing, with shops also in hotels **Monasterio**, **Libertador** and **Machu Picchu Sanctuary Lodge**, and at the airport.

Store of the Weavers (Asociación Central de Artesanos y Artesanas del Sur Andino Inkakunaq Ruwaynin), Av Tullumayo 274, T084-233466, www.cbc.org.pe/ tejidosandinos. A store administered by 6 local weaving communities, some of whose residents you can see working on site. All profits go to the weavers themselves. Most of the work utilizes traditional dyes and the fine quality of the *mantas* and other textiles on sale makes this store well worth a visit.

Jewellery

Calas, Siete Angelitos 619-B, San Blas. Handmade silver jewellery in interesting designs and alpaca goods from the community of Pitumarca.

Ilaria, Portal Carrizos 258, T084-246253, in hotels **Monasterio** and **Libertador** and at the airport. The Cuzco branches of a highly regarded Lima silver and jewellery store.

Inka Treasure, Triunfo 375, T084-227470, www.inkatreasure.com.pe. With branches at Av Pardo 1080, Plazoleta Nazarenas 159 and Portal de Panes 163. Also at the airport and the airport in Juliaca. Fine jewellery including goldwork, mostly with pre-Columbian designs, and silver with the owner's designs. Tours of workshops at Av Circunvalación, near Cristo Blanco. The stores also incorporte the work of famed jeweller Carlos Chakiras.

Mullu, Triunfo 120, T084-229831. Mon-Sat 1000-2100. Contemporary silver jewellery with semi- precious stones and cotton clothing with interesting designs.

Spondylus, Cuesta San Blas 505 y Plazoleta San Blas 617, T084-226929, spondyluscusco@mixmail.com. Interesting jewellery in gold and silver, also using semi-precious stones and shells. They will make your own design for you for a reasonable fee. They sell some nice T-shirts with Inca and pre-Inca designs.

Musical instruments

Taki Museo de Música de los Andes, Hatunrumiyoc 487-5. Shop and workshop selling and displaying musical instruments, knowledgeable owner, who is an ethno-musicologist. Recommended for anyone interested in Andean music.

Bookshops

Centro de Estudios Regionales Andinos Bartolomé de las Casas, Av Tullumayo 465, T084-233472, www.cbc.org.pe. Mon-Sat 1100-1400, 1600-1900. Good books on Peruvian history, archaeology, etc.

Jerusalem, Heladeros 143, T084-235408. English books, guidebooks, music, postcards, expensive book exchange.

Puro Perú, Heladeros 167. For new books, book exchange and music.

SBS (Special Book Services), Av Sol 781-A, opposite the post office, T084-248106. Mon-Fri 0830-1330, 1530-1930, Sat 0830-1300.

The Sun, Plazoleta Limacpampa Chico 471. This café/restaurant has the best book exchange, 1 for 1, maintained by an Australian.

Camping equipment

There are several places on Plateros which rent out equipment but check it carefully as it is common for parts to be missing. A deposit of US$100 is required, plus credit card, passport or plane ticket. Wherever you hire equipment, check the stoves carefully. White gas (*bencina*) costs US$1.50 per litre and can be bought at hardware stores, but check the purity. Stove spirit (*alcohol para quemar*) is available at pharmacies. Blue gas canisters, costing US$5, can be found at some hardware stores and at shops which rent gear. You can also rent equipment through travel agencies.

Cordillera Cusco, Garcilaso 210, T084-244133, www.cordillerastore.com. Boutique camping store. Footwear, clothing and accessories from top outdoor brands.
Edson Zuñiga Huillca, Mercado Rosaspata, Jr Abel Landeo P-1, T084-802831, T084-984 937243 (mob). 3 mins from Plaza de Armas, for repair of camping equipment and footwear, also equipment rental, open 24 hrs a day, 7 days a week, English and Italian spoken.
Tatoo Adventure Gear, C del Medio 130, T084-254211, www.tatoo.ws. Adventure gear, high-quality hiking, climbing and camping gear, big brand names: Colombia, Gore-Tex, Polartec, etc. The house brand, Tatoo, produces good trousers, thermals, fleeces and jackets. Imported hiking boots. Tatoo also has branches in Lima and Huaraz.

Food and natural products
Casa Ecológica Cusco, Triunfo 393, www.casaecologicacusco.com. Organic foods, wild honey, coffee, granola. Also natural medicines, indigenous art and weavings. They claim to pay fair prices when dealing with local suppliers.
The Coca Shop, Carmen Alto 115, San Blas, T084-260774, www.thecocashop.com. A tiny shop selling an interesteing selection of sweets and chocolates made using coca leaf flour. There is also plenty of information about the nutritional values of coca leaves.
La Cholita, Portal Espinar 142-B and at airport. Extra-special chocolates made with local ingredients.

Tik'a, www.tikasoapperu.com. Eco-friendly soaps, oils and beauty products made from local ingredients by Fiona Cameron and Carmen Pedraza.

Markets
San Jerónimo, just out of town (see page 208), is the location of the wholesale Sat morning fruit and vegetable market. Porters struggle past carrying heavy loads and there is a huge array of colourful fruit and vegetables, as well as *campesinos* in for the day to sell their produce and wares. Get there for 0800, but be aware that 'gringos' stick out like a sore thumb so take no valuables.

Food that's just as good, washed and not much more expensive can be bought at the markets in **Wanchac**, Av Garcilaso (not to be confused with C Garcilaso), or **San Pedro**, opposite Estación San Pedro, which sells a variety of goods. The best prices are at closing time or in the rain. Take care after dark. Sacks to cover rucksacks are available in the market for US$0.75. Both Wanchac and San Pedro are open every day from 0700.

El Molino, under the Puente Grau, sells contraband imported goods brought in without duty or tax being paid, but it is tolerated by the authorities. Everything from computers to personal stereos to trekking boots, pirated CDs and DVDs, cheap camera film and wine can be bought here (take a taxi for US$0.60). It is clean and safe (but take the usual precautions about valuables) and is open daily 0600-2030.

Supermarkets

D'Dinos Market, Av La Cultura 2003, T084-252656 for home delivery. Open 24 hrs, well supplied, takes credit cards.
Gato's Market, Portal Belén 115.
La Canasta, Av La Cultura 2000 block. Very well stocked, accepts credit cards, ATM outside.
Mega Market, Matará 271, Av Garcilaso at Plaza Tupac Amaru and Av La Cultura in Magisterio. Daily 0700-2200, credit cards accepted. US-style market.

▲ Activities and tours

There are a million and one tour operators in Cuzco. The sheer number and variety of tours on offer is bewildering and prices for the same tour can vary dramatically. You should only deal directly with the agencies and seek advice from visitors returning from trips. Agencies listed below are included under the field in which they are best known. City tours cost about between US$7-15 and last 4 hrs; check what sites are included (either too few or too rushed) and that the guide is experienced. 1-day Sacred Valley tours cost from US$20. Beware of tours that stop for long lunches at pricey hotels. Check if there are cancellation fees. Students will normally receive a discount on production of an ISIC card.

You could also consider hiring a private guide. As most of the sights do not have any information or signs in English, this can really improve your visit. Either arrange this before you set out or grab one of those hanging around the sights' entrances (this is much easier to do in the low season). A tip is expected at the end of the tour. Set prices: tours of the city or Sacred Valley cost US$50 for half-day, US$65 full day; a guide to Machu Picchu charges US$80 per day. A list of official guides is held by **Agotur Cusco**, C Heladeros 157, of 34-F, p 3, T084-233457, www.agoturcusco.org.pe. **Leap Local**, www.leaplocal.org, is a website that recommends good quality local guides.

Inca Trail and general tours

Only a restricted number of agencies are licensed to operate Inca Trail trips. **SERNANP**, Av José Gabriel Cosio 408, Urb Magisterial, 1 etapa, T084-229297, www.sernanp.gob.pe, verifies operating permits. Other agencies will sell Inca Trail trips, but pass clients on to the operating agency in a pooling system. This can cause confusion and booking problems at busy times.

Inclusion in our list does not guarantee that the company is licensed to operate the Inca Trail (2011). All those listed below have been recommended for their services (except for any reservations noted). Many agencies, and the alternatives they offer, plus a list and contact details for recommended local guides, can be found in the trip reports of **South America Explorers**, Atocsaycuchi 670, www.saexplorers.org (for members only).

Note that many companies offer treks as alternatives to the Inca Trail and its variations to Machu Picchu. Unlike the Inca Trail, these treks are unregulated. You should check that the trekking company does not employ the sort of practices (such as overloading porters, not clearing up rubbish) which are now outlawed on the trails to Machu Picchu.
Amazing Peru, C Yepez Miranda C-6, Magisterio, www.amazing peru.com. Professional and well-organized, recommended as providing the "perfect tour", knowledgeable guides.
Amazon Trails Peru, Tandapata 660, Cuzco, T084-437374, T084-984 714148 (mob), www.amazontrailsperu.com. Trekking tours around the area, including the Inca Trail, Salkantay and Choquequirao. Also trips to Manu.
Andean Treks, Av Pardo 705, T084-225701, www.andeantreks.com. Mon-Fri 0900-1300, 1500-1800, Sat 0900-1300. Manager Tom Hendrickson uses high-quality equipment and satellite phones. The company organizes interesting itineraries, from 2 to 15 days, with a wide variety of activities in this area and further afield.

Andina Travel, Treks and Eco-Adventures, Plazoleta Santa Catalina 219, T084-251892, www.andinatravel.com. Eco-agency with more than 10 years operating all local treks. Has a reputation in Cuzco for local expertise and community projects.

Big Foot, Triunfo 392 (of 213), T084-238568, www.bigfootcusco.com. Specialists in tailor-made hiking trips, especially in the remote corners of the Vilcabamba and Vilcanota mountains. Also the more conventional Inca Trail routes.

Breast Cancer Care, T0845-092 0805 (UK), www.breastcancercare.org.uk/events. Machu Picchu treks to raise money to support people with breast cancer. Treks leave 29 Apr 2011, 16 Sep 2011, 13 Apr 2012 and 7 Sep 2012.

Ch'aska, C Garcilaso 265, p 2 of 6, T084-240474, www.chaskatours.com. Dutch/Peruvian company that has quickly acquired a solid reputation offering cultural, adventure, nature and esoteric tours. They specialize in the Inca Trail, but also llama treks to Lares and recommended trips to Choquequirao.

Crillon Tours, PO Box 4785, Camacho Av 1223, La Paz, T(591-2)233 7533, www.titicaca.com. A company with over 50 years experience of tourism in Bolivia. Their hydrofoil trips on Lake Titicaca can link Cuzco and Machu Picchu with the Isla del Sol and Copacabana. Other joint scheduled tours with Peru arranged. Excellent bilingual guides and recommended in all ways.

Culturas Peru, Tandapata 345A, T084-243629, www.culturasperu.com. A Swiss/Peruvian company offering

adventure, cultural, ecological and spiritual tours. They specialize in alternative Inca trails.

Destinos Turísticos, Portal de Panes 123, of 101-102, Plaza de Armas, T084-228168, www.destinosturisticosperu.com. The owner speaks Spanish, English, Dutch and Portuguese and specializes in package tours from economy to 5-star budgets. Individuals are welcome to come in for advice on booking jungle trips to renting mountain bikes. Ask in advance if you require guides with specific languages. Informative and helpful.

EcotrailPeru, Av El Sol 106, p 2, No 205, T084-233357, www.ecotrailperu.com. Operates treks, tours and adventure trips throughout Peru for all fitness levels. Committed to sustainable travel.

Enigma Adventure, Jr Clorinda Matto de Turner 100, Magisterio 1a etapa, T084-222155, www.enigmaperu.com. Adventure tour agency run by Spaniard Silvia Rico Coll. Has an excellent reputation for well-organized and innovative trekking expeditions. In addition to the regular Inca Trail, she offers, for example, a 7-day programme to the remote and beautiful Laguna Sibinacocha, in the Vilcanota Mountains, or a 3-night trek into the Lares Valley. Set departures and fixed prices on some routes, but on the more remote excursions prices depend on group numbers. Also cultural tours to traditional weaving communities, Ayahuasca therapy and can arrange climbing and biking itineraries on demand. Enigma also offers a luxury trekking service.

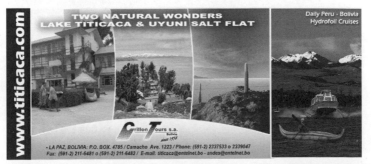

Explorandes, Av Garcilaso 316-A (not to be confused with C Garcilaso in the centre), T084-238380, www.explorandes.com. Experienced high-end adventure company. Their main office is in Lima, but trips can be arranged from Cuzco. Vast range of trips available in both Peru and Ecuador, easily booked through their well-organized website. Also arranges tours across Peru for lovers of orchids, ceramics or textiles. Award-winning environmental practices.

Fertur, C San Agustín 317, T084-221304, www.fertur-travel.com. Mon-Fri 0900-1900, Sat 0900-1200. Cuzco branch of the Lima tour operator.

Gatur Cusco, Puluchapata 140 (a small street off Av Sol 3rd block), T084-223496, www.gaturcusco.com. Esoteric, ecotourism, and general tours. Owner Dr José (Pepe) Altamirano is knowledgeable in Andean folk traditions. Excellent conventional tours, bilingual guides and transportation, helpful. Guides speak English, French, Spanish and German. They can also book internal flights.

Hiking Peru, Portal de Panes 109, of 6, T084-247942/ T084-984 651414 (mob), www.hiking peru.com. Concentrates on the less-beaten paths, eg 8-day treks to Espíritu Pampa, 7 days/6 nights around Ausangate, 4 days/3 nights Lares Valley Trek.

Inca Explorers, Ruinas 427, T084-241070, www.incaexplorers.com. Specialist trekking agency with a good reputation for small group expeditions executed in socially and environmentally responsible manner. More demanding, adventurous trips include a 2-week hike in the Cordillera Vilcanota (passing Nevado Ausangate), and Choquequirao to Espíritu Pampa, again for 2 weeks.

InkaNatura Travel, Ricardo Palma J1, T084-255255, www.inkanatura.com. Offers tours with special emphasis on sustainable tourism and conservation. Knowledgeable guides.

Liz's Explorer, Medio 114B, T084-246619, www.lizexplorer.com. For the Inca Trail and other trips. Inca Trail 4-day/3-night (minimum group size 10, maximum 16), other length of trips available. Liz gives a clearly laid out list of what is and what is not included. Down and fibre sleeping bags can be hired. If you need a guide who speaks a language other than English let her know in advance. Also city tours and the Sacred Valley. Feedback on trip is good, less so for the office.

Llama Path, San Juan de Dios 250, T084-240822, www.llamapath.com. A wide variety of local tours, specializing in Inca Trail and alternative treks, the company is involved in environmental campaigns and porter welfare. Many good reports received.

Machete Tours, Nueva Alta 432, int B, T084-224829, T084-984 631662 (mob), www.machetetours.com. Founded by born-and-bred jungle hand Ronaldo and his Danish partner Tina, **Machete** offer many innovative trekking trips, for example a 9-day traverse of the Cordillera Vilcabamba from the Apurímac Canyon and Choquequirao across the range to Machu Picchu itself. They also offer expeditions to Espíritu Pampa,

Ausangate and the Inca Trail. They have a new rainforest lodge on the remote Río Blanco, south of the Manu Biosphere Reserve and have set up camps deep in the forest. These jungle trips are focused more on hiking and rustic 'adventure' than those of the classic Manu operators. All the staff speak English. Eric is a recommended guide for Choquequirao.

Manu Nature Tours, Av Pardo 1046, T084-252721, www.manuperu.com. Trips to Manu Biosphere Reserve. Owned by Boris Gómez Luna, English spoken.

Perú Planet, Suecia 318, T084-251145, www.peru-planet.net. Peruvian/Belgian-owned agency offering tours of the Inca Trail, other treks around Cuzco and packages within Peru. Also to Bolivia and Patagonia.

Peru Treks and Adventure, Av Pardo 540, T084-222722, www.perutreks.com. Trekking agency set up by Englishman Mike Weston and his wife Koqui González. They pride themselves on good treatment of porters and support staff and have been consistently recommended for their professionalism and customer care. A portion of profits goes to community projects (school supplies and clothing accepted at office) and they have a homestay programme. Treks include Salkantay, the Lares Valley and Vilcabamba Vieja.

Q'ente, Choquechaca 229, p 2, T084-222535, www.qente.com. Their Inca Trail service is recommended and they offer a great variety of treks in the Cuzco area. They also offer traditional tours and longer packages. Prices depend on group size. Very good, especially with children.

SAS Travel, Garcilaso 270, Plaza San Francisco, T084-249194, www.sastravel peru.com. Discount for students. Inca Trail 4-day/3-night US$540 (can rent down bags for US$20). SAS offers a variety of alternatives to the classic Inca Trail. Before setting off you are told everything that is included and given advice on what personal items should be taken. Also Manu, family tours, mountain bike, horse riding and rafting trips can be organized. All guides speak English (some better than others). They can book internal flights at much cheaper rates than booking from overseas.

Sky Travel, Santa Catalina Ancha 366, interior 3-C (down alleyway near **Rosie O'Grady's** pub), T084-261818, www.skyperu.com. Open Mon-Sat. English spoken. General tours around city and Sacred Valley. 4-day/3-night Inca Trail in good-sized double tents and a dinner tent. The group is asked what it would like on the menu 2 days before departure. Other trips include Vilcabamba and Ausangate (trekking only), Colca and Misti (Arequipa) and Titicaca.

Tambo Tours, 4405 Spring Cypress Rd, Suite 210, Spring, TX 77388, USA, T1-888-2-GO-PERU (246-7378), T001-281 528 9448, www.2GOPERU.com. Long-established adventure and tour specialist with 20 years' experience in Peru. Offices in Peru and USA. Customized trips for families, individuals and groups to the Amazon and archaeological sites of Peru, Bolivia and Ecuador, including Machu Picchu.

Trekperu, Av República de Chile B-15, Parque Industrial, Wanchac, T084-261501, www.trekperu.com. Experienced trek operator as well as other adventure sports and mountain biking. Offers 'culturally sensitive' tours. 5-day/4-night Cuzco Biking Adventure visits Tipón ruins, Huacarpay Lake, Huanca, Pisac, Urubamba and Moray. Includes support vehicle and good camping gear. Sleeping bag required.

Tucan Travel, T084-241123, cuzco@tucan travel.com. Offer adventure tours and overland expeditions.

United Mice, Plateros 351, T084-221139, www.unitedmice.com. Offer a well-established and highly reputable service for the Inca Trail and alternatives via Salkantay and Santa Teresa. Good guides who speak languages other than Spanish. Discount with student card, good food and equipment. Also city tours in Spanish and English, Sacred Valley Tours in Spanish and English. They offer treks to Choquequirao for 5 days/4 nights.

Wayki Trek, Av Pardo 510, T084-224092, www.waykitrek.net. Budget travel agency, recommended for their Inca Trail service. Owner Leo grew up in the countryside near Ollantaytambo and knows the area very well. They run treks to several little-known Inca sites. Leo offers many interesting variations on the 'classic' Inca Trail and runs a programme where clients can visit porters communities before starting treks. Wayki also run treks to Ausangate, Salkantay and Choquequirao.

X-Treme Tourbulencia, Plateros 358, T084-222405, www.x-tremetourbulencia. com. They run the 'Classic Inka Trail' and alternative Inka treks, Ausangate, city tours and jungle trips.

Cultural and shamanic tours

Among the many forms of spiritual tourism offered in the Cuzco region, one that attracts much attention is shamanic and drug experiences. (The following list is not restricted to this type of tourism.) San Pedro and Ayahuasca have been used since before Inca times, mostly as a sacred healing experience. The plants are prepared with special treatments for curative purposes; they have never been considered a drug. If you choose to experience these incredible healing/teaching plants, only do so under the guidance of a reputable agency or shaman and always have a friend with you who is not partaking. If the medicine is not prepared correctly, it can be highly toxic and, in rare cases, severely dangerous. Never buy tours off the streets, never buy from someone who is not recommended and never try to prepare the plants yourself.

Another Planet, Tandapata y Pasñapacana 148, San Blas, T084-241168, or T084-974 790411 (mob), www.anotherplanetperu.net. Run by Lesley Myburgh, who operates mystical and adventure tours in and around Cuzco, and is an expert in San Pedro cactus preparation. She arranges San Pedro sessions for healing at physical, emotional and spiritual levels in the beautiful garden of her house outside Cuzco.

Tours meet at La Casa de la Gringa, see Sleeping, above. This a good place to stay if you are looking for this kind of experience. **Eleana Molina**, T084-984 751791 (mob), misticanativa@yahoo.com. For Ayahuasca ceremonies.

Milla Tourism, Av Pardo 689, T084-231710, www.millaturismo.com. Mon-Fri 0800-1300, 1500-1900, Sat 0800-1300. A wide variety of tours, including traditional, historical, educational and cultural. Also private tours arranged to Moray agricultural terracing and Maras salt mines in Sacred Valley. Guide speaks only basic English. They also arrange cultural and environmental lectures and courses.

Mountain biking

Cuzco offers a multitude of rides to suit all abilities. All ideally require a guide as its very easy to get lost in the Andes. Some options are: a half-day tour of nearby **Inca ruins** (Tambo Machay, Qenqo and Sacsayhuaman) exploring the very best of the single-track options. Each trip is customized to individual abilities. Don't forget your combined entrance ticket. **Chinchero–Moray–Maras–Las Salinas– Urubamba**: one of the finest 1-day trips in Peru, best done with a guide and support vehicle. It includes almost 1000 m of descent on a mix of dirt trails and donkey tracks as well as the Moray circular terraces and an amazing downhill through the spectacular saltpans. The **Lares Valley** offers some incredible downhill and uphill options on 2- to 3-day circuits including a relaxing soak in the beautiful Lares hot springs. Various descents from the sierra to the jungle: **Abra Málaga**: from 4200 m, an 80-km descent to the jungle, now know as part of the 'Inca Jungle Trail' (see page 184); **Tres Cruces to Manu**, a 250-km, beautiful dirt road ride offering big climbs and an even bigger (2-day) descent; and **Cuzco–Puerto Maldonado**, formerly a great Trans-Andean Challenge on a bike, now almost all tarmac. With a support vehicle this can be done in a 2-3 days of mainly downhill cycling, a good way to get to the jungle town of Puerto Maldonado from where jungle tours to lodges can be organized.

A wonderful new route takes cross-country riders from the shores of Lake Titicaca, through Juliaca, Lampa, Tinajani canyon and on dirt roads through the Andes to Cuzco in 8 days of tough but incredibly beautiful riding. Overnight riders camp and stay with local families and at an experimental alpaca farm. See **KE Adventure**, www.keadventure.com (page 54) for details.

There is a growing downhill mountain biking community in and around Cuzco and competitions are run most months on a series of world-class courses. To find out about and experience these rides, talk to the experts and rent a bike and guide for the day for a truly unforgettable day out. See Sports tour operators, page 120 for mountain biking companies.
Team Bike, Tullumayo 438, T084-224354, is a shop selling good quality parts and boxes for shipping.

Paragliding and ballooning

Magnificent scenery, soaring close to snow-capped mountains makes this an awesome experience. 45 km from Cuzco is **Cerro Sacro** (3797 m) on the Pampa de Chincheros with 550 m clearance at take-off. It is the launch site for cross-country flights over the Sacred Valley, Sacsayhuaman and Cuzco. Particularly good for parapenting is the **Mirador de Urubamba**, 38 km from Cuzco, at 3650 m, with 800-m clearance and views over Pisac. Note that the Sacred Valley offers exciting but challenging paragliding so if wind conditions are bad, flights may be delayed till the following day. Beware pilots offering suspiciously cheap flights; their experience and equipment is unlikely to be appropriate for the Sacred Valley's conditions.
Globos de los Andes, Aero Sports Club of the Sacred Valley, www.globosperu.com. Hot-air ballooning in the Sacred Valley and expeditions with balloons and 4WD lasting several days.

Rafting

The Cuzco region is probably the rafting capital of Peru, with more whitewater runs on offer than anywhere else in the country. When looking for an operator please consider more than just the price of your tour. Competition between companies in Cuzco is intense and price wars can lead to compromises in safety as corners are cut or less experienced (and therefore cheaper) guides are hired. Bargaining the price down will have the same effect. A 1-day rafting trip on the Vilcanota river will cost US$40 for a cheap trip, pooled by various agencies, with up to 30 other tourists. Expect to pay US$75-100 per person for a small group of, on average, 4 people with experienced guides, quality equipment, a safety kayaker and good food. A 3-day Apurímac rafting trip will cost US$200 for a pooled tour with 25-35 participants and no guarantee on equipment, guides, or safety record. Pay around US$450-600 for a safe, high-quality, environmentally friendly small-group trip. On a large and potentially dangerous river like the Apurímac, and when any of the rivers are high, this can make all the difference (fatalities occur, most recently in 2010 on the Río Urubamba). See Rafting, page 18, for more advice.

Urubamba Perhaps the most popular day run in the whole country, but try to avoid the sections heavily affected by pollution below Cuzco and from the towns of the Sacred Valley, especially around Ollantaytambo, as the waters contain raw sewage and have only average-quality rapids. Clean-up campaigns are organized periodically, but they just touch the surface of the problem. Further upriver from Cuzco, on the Chuquicahuana and Cusipata sections, the river is generally cleaner and the rapids are more fun. There is also a beautiful section called Piñipampa, just 45 mins' drive from Cuzco, where inflatable kayaking (or 'duckies' as they are called locally) is practised. Paddling your canoe through some fun, but not-too-frantic rapids in a beautiful canyon for half, or a whole day is suitable for anyone looking to try the next thing after rafting. This trip can be combined with a trip to visit Pisac market, or the ruins of Tipón and Pikillacta. There are various stretches of rafting on the river, from Grade I to Grade V+. Some are available all year, others depend on the season. Grade I, II and III rafting with children can also be organized, but check the operator has equipment (wetsuits, booties, life-jackets, etc) suitable for children and that they have experience in dealing with such groups. Ask a reputable operator for recommendations to suit your ability and always heed advice if the river is running high.

Apurímac Technically the true source of the Amazon, the Apurímac cuts a 2000-m-deep gorge through incredible desert scenery and offers probably some of the finest whitewater rafting sections on the planet. Some are rarely run, such as **The Abyss** or **Choquequirao** (consult an agency which caters for experts), but most popular for a multi-day trip is **Puente Hualpachaca-Puente Cunyac** (May-Nov, Grade IV-V): 3 days (better in 4) of non-stop whitewater through an awesome gorge just 5 hrs' drive from Cuzco. Wildlife includes condors, otters, foxes, deer and, if you are very lucky, pampas cats and pumas. Again, book with the experts to get you through rapids with names like *U-first*, *Toothache* and *Last laugh*. A new section of the Río Apurimac for rafting is called the **Black Canyon**. A spectacular 4-hr drive from Cuzco takes you to the village of Naihua from where it is 4 days of fairly relaxed, wilderness rafting with Grade III-IV+ rapids and a couple of portages around the trickiest rapids. There are hikes to waterfalls, pristine beaches for camping and the sense of being in the middle of nowhere for 3-4 days. The return from Hualpachaca to Cuzco takes approximately 4 hrs. See below for rafting companies. Cuzco rafting companies usually organize trips further afield. These include the **Río Tambopata**, slicing its way through the

Bahuaje-Sonene National Park all the way to Puerto Maldonado. After a 4WD drive from Lake Titicaca, this 9-day adventure includes Grade III-IV+ rapids and some of the best wildlife viewing in the Amazon Basin. Possibly the very best run in Peru is on the **Río Cotahuasi**, reached from Arequipa: over 8 days/120 km of world-class Grade IV and V whitewater rapids, in the deepest canyon. Every night camp is set up on beaches beside Inca ruins. It is best run May-Jun only. Both trips are made infrequently, so book in advance.

Sports tour operators
The following operators offer a range of adventure sports and activities.
Amazonas Explorer, Av Collasuyo 910, Miravalle, PO Box 722, T084-252846, www.amazonas-explorer.com. Experts in rafting, inflatable canoeing, mountain biking, horse riding and hiking; used by BBC. English owner Paul Cripps has great experience, but takes most bookings from overseas (in UK, T01874-658125, Jan-Mar; T01437-891743, Apr-Dec). However, he may be able to arrange a trip for travellers in Cuzco preferably with advanced notice. Rafting and inflatable canoeing includes Río Urubamba (1 day), Río Apurímac (3-4 days), Río Tambopata (14 days including Lake Titicaca), Cotahuasi (14 days out of Arequipa). Specialist kayaking trips can be organized on request. Also 5-day/4-night Inca Trail trip of the highest quality, and alternatives to the Inca Trail and Choquequirao to Machu Picchu. Amazonas offer an excellent variation of the Ausangate Circuit, featuring an extension to the little-visited Laguna Singrenacocha and an opportunity for ice-climbers to tackle the remote Campa Peak with experienced guides. New for 2011 is a trek to Espíritu Pampa, the last city of the Incas. Multi-activity and family trips are a speciality, catering for all ages, but juniors in particular. Mountain biking trips all use state-of-the-art, full-suspension Kona mountain bikes, expert guides and support vehicles where

appropriate. All options are at the higher end of the market and are highly recommended. Amazonas Explorer are also the first company to join www.onepercentfortheplanet.org, donating 1% of their turnover to a tree-planting project in the Lares watershed.

Apumayo, Jr Ricardo Palma N-5, Santa Mónica, Wanchaq, T084-246018, www.apumayo.com. Mon-Sat 0900-1300, 1600-2000. Urubamba and Apurímac rafting; Inca Trail trekking. Also mountain biking, eq Maras and Moray in Sacred Valley, or 5-day epic biking from Cuzco to Quillabamba, horse riding, multi-activity and cultural tours. This company also offers tours for disabled people, including rafting.

Apus Peru, Cuichipunco 366, T084-232691, www.apus-peru.com. Conducts most business by internet and specializes in alternatives to the Inca Trail. It has a strong commitment to sustainability and runs well-organized adventure trips. The agency is associated with **Threads of Peru**, www.threadsofperu.com, an NGO which helps weavers in the Lares Valley. Visits can be arranged through Apus Peru.

Camp Expeditions, Triunfo 392, of 202, T084-431468, www.campexpedition.net. All sorts of adventure tours, but specialists in climbing, for which they are recommended as most reliable, and trekking.

Cusco Adventure Team, Santa Catalina Ancha 398 (under Al Grano), T084-228032, www.cuscoadventureteam.com. Utilizing the experience of **Amazonas Explorers**, CAT offer half-day to 3-day bike rides and rafting and canoe trips for small groups or individuals, state of the art equipment, adventurous, safe and environmentally aware. Part of **Grupo Inca**, www.grupo inca.com (see **Amazonas Explorer**, above).

Eric Adventures, Urb Santa María A1-6, San Sebastián, T084-272862, www.eric adventures.com. Specialize in many adventure activities. They clearly explain what equipment is included in their prices

and what you will need to bring. They also rent motorcross bikes (US$70-90 per day), mountain bikes and cars and 4WDs. Prices are more expensive if you book by email, you can get huge discounts if you book in the office. A popular company.

Instinct, Av de la Cultura 1318, Wanchaq, T084-233451, www.instinct-travel.com. Run by the very experienced Juan and Benjamín Muñiz, this company now largely operates through web-based bookings, arranging both multi-week expeditions and shorter adventures for those already in the Cuzco area. **Instinct** offers activities as diverse as surf safaris on Peru's north coast to multi-day horseriding tours in the Sacred Valley.

Manu Expeditions, C Clorinda Matto de Turner 330, Urb Magisterial, primera etapa, T084-225990, www.manuexpeditions.com. As well as Manu trips (see page 263), also runs tailor-made bird trips in cloud- and rainforest around Cuzco and Peru, as well as butterfly watching, and has horse riding and a 9-day/8-night trip to Machu Picchu along a different route from the Inca Trail, rejoining at the Sun Gate. Barry Walker runs horse-supported treks to Choquequirao, starting from Huancacalle. Highly recommended.

The Medina Brothers, contact Christian or Alain Medina on T084-225163 or T084-984 653485/984 691670 (mob). Friendly family-run rafting company with good equipment and plenty of experience. They usually focus on day rafting trips in the Sacred Valley, but services are tailored to the needs of the client. Reasonable prices dependent on client numbers. Recommended.

Pachatusan Trek, Psje Esmeralda 160, Santiago, T084-231817, www.pachatusan trek.com. Offer a wide variety to treks, as alternatives to the Inca Trail, professional and caring staff.

River Explorers, C Garcilaso 210, int 128, T084-260926 or T084-984 909249, www.riverexplorers.com. An adventure company offering mountain biking, trekking and rafting trips (on the Apurímac, Urubamba and Tambopata). Experienced and qualified guides with environmental awareness. Apurímac rafting trips from US$385.

Terra Explorer Peru, T084-237352, www.terraexplorerperu.com. Offers a wide range of trips from high-end rafting in the Sacred Valley and expeditions to the Colca and Cotahuasi canyons, trekking the Inca Trail and others, mountain biking, kayaking (including on Lake Titicaca) and jungle trips. All guides are bilingual.

⊖ Transport

Air

See also Getting around, page 25, and Lima transport, page 301.

To **Lima**, 55 mins, daily flights with TACA, Star Perú, Peruvian Airlines and LAN. Flights are heavily booked in school holidays (May, Jul, Oct and Dec-Mar) and national holidays. To **Arequipa** and to **Puerto Maldonado**,

30 mins each daily with **LAN**. **Star Perú** also flies to Puerto Maldonado. To/from **La Paz** with **Aero Sur**, 3 times a week.

Airline offices

Aero Sur, Av Sol 948, CC Cusco Sol Plaza, of 120, T084-254691, www.aerosur.com. **LAN**, Av Sol 627-B, T084-225552. **Peruvian Airlines**, Del Medio 117, T084-254890. **Star Perú**, Av Sol 679, of 1, T084-262768. **TACA**, Av Sol 602, T084-249921, good service.

Bus
Local

Combis run 0500-2200 or 2300, US$0.30, to all parts of the city, including the bus and train stations and the airport, but are not allowed within 2 blocks of the Plaza de Armas. Stops are signed and the driver's assistant calls out the names of stops. By law all passengers are insured. After 2200 combis may not run their full route; demand to be taken to your stop, or better still, use a taxi late at night.

El Tranvía de Cusco is actually a motor coach that runs on the route of the original Cuzco tramway system. The route starts in the Plaza de Armas (except Sun morning) and ends at the Sacsayhuaman Archaeological Park. There is a 10-min stop at the mirador by the Cristo Blanco before descending to the Plaza de Armas. Departures start at 1000 daily, 1 hr 20 mins, with explanations of the city's history, architecture, customs, etc; US$2, US$1.40 for students with ID. For group reservations, call T084-740640.

Long distance

The bus terminal, **Terminal Terrestre**, is on Prolongación Pachacútec. Almost all direct buses to **Lima** (18-20 hrs) go via **Abancay**, 195 km, 5 hrs (longer in the rainy season), and **Nazca**, on the Panamerican Highway. This route is paved, but floods in the wet season can damage sections of the highway. If prone to car sickness, be prepared on the road to Abancay, there are many, many curves, but the scenery is magnificent (it also happens to be a great route for cycling). At Abancay, the road forks, the other branch going to **Andahuaylas**, a further 138 km, 10-11 hrs from Cuzco, and **Ayacucho** in the Central Highlands, another 261 km, 20 hrs from Cuzco. On both routes at night, take a blanket or sleeping bag to ward off the cold.

Molina, who also have an office on Av Pachacútec, just past the railway station, has buses on both routes. They run 3 services a day to **Lima** via **Abancay** and **Nazca**, and 1, at 1900, to **Abancay** and **Andahuaylas**. **Cruz del Sur**'s service leaves for **Lima** via Abancay at 0730 and 1400, while their more comfortable services depart at 1500 and 1600. **Turismo Ampay** and **Turismo Abancay** go 3 times a day to Abancay, and **Expreso Huamanga** once. **Bredde** has 5 buses a day to Abancay. Fares to **Abancay** US$10, **Nazca** up to US$28.50-46, **Lima** also US$28.50-46 for a reliable service; eg **Flores** or **Cromotex** (T084-249573, www.cromotex.com.pe). **Cruz del Sur** charges US$49-57 (*Cruzero* and *VIP* classes; same fares to Nazca and Ica).

Ormeño has a service from Cuzco to Lima via Arequipa which takes longer than the Abancay route (22 hrs), but is a more comfortable journey.

To **Lake Titicaca and Bolivia**: to **Juliaca**, 344 km, 6 hrs, US$5-12. The road is fully paved, but after heavy rain buses may not run. To **Puno**, via Juliaca, US$5-12; direct US$8.50 (*bus cama* US$12) 6 hrs. **First Class** and **Inka Express**, Av La Paz C-32, Urb El Ovalo, Wanchac, T084-247887, www.inkaexpress.com, have a service calling at Andahuaylillas church, Raqchi, La Raya, Sicuani and Pucará en route (lunch, but not entrance tickets, is included), US$30. Travel agencies sell this ticket. **Note** It is safest to travel by day on the Cuzco–Juliaca–Puno route.

To **Puerto Maldonado**, **Móvil** (Terminal Terrestre, T084-238223) at 1800, 1945, 8-10 hrs, US$16.

For bus services to other destinations, see the Transport section of the relevant chapter.

Car

Touring y Automóvil Club del Perú, Av Sol 349, T084-224561, cusco@touringperu. com.pe. A good source of information on motoring, car hire and mechanics (membership is US$45 per year).

Taxi

Taxis have fixed prices and should cost no more than US$1.20 in town (50% more after 2100 or 2200); and to the airport up to US$3.50 (touts at the airport and train station will always ask much higher fares). It is always best to have the exact fare if possible to avoid the taxi drivers who have no change. In town it is advisable to take municipality-authorized taxis that have a sticker with a number on the window and a chequerboard pattern on the side. Safer still are licensed taxis, which have a sign with the company's name on the roof, not just a sticker in the window. These taxis are summoned by phone and are more expensive (**Aló Cusco** T084-222222, **Ocarina** T084-247080).

Taxi trips to **Sacsayhuaman** cost US$10; to the ruins of **Tambo Machay** US$15-20 (3-4 people); a whole-day trip costs US$50-85, depending on how many sites around Cuzco and the Sacred Valley you visit.

Train

Details of the train services out of Cuzco can be found on www.perurail.com. For details of trains to Aguas Calientes for Machu Picchu, see box, page 166.

The train to **Puno** leaves at 0800, on Mon, Wed, Fri and Sat, arriving in Puno at 1800 (sit on the left for the best views). The train makes a stop to view the scenery at La Raya. Between Nov-Mar there is no train on Fri. There is only 1 class, *Andean Explorer*, US$220, includes lunch, afternoon tea, and luxury seating. Tickets can be bought in advance. The ticket office at Wanchac station is open Mon-Fri 0700-1700, Sat, Sun and holidays 0700-1200. The PerúRail office at Portal de Carnes 214 is open Mon-Fri 1000-2200, Sat, Sun and holidays 1400-2300. You can buy tickets on www.perurail.com, or through a travel agent.

❶ Directory

Banks and money exchange
Banks

All the banks along Av Sol have ATMs from which you can withdraw dollars or soles at any hour. Whether you use the counter or an ATM, choose your time carefully as there can be long queues at both. Most banks are closed between 1300 and 1600. All branches offer the same services as elsewhere in the country. **BCP**, Av Sol 189. **Banco de la Nación**, Av Sol y Almagro. **Interbank**, Av Sol y Puluchapata. Next door is **Banco Continental**, Av Sol 459. **Scotiabank**, Maruri y Arequipa.

ATMs

As well as the ATMs in banks (most of which have 24-hr police protection), there are others, accepting a wide range of international cards (the symbols of which are clearly displayed), around the Plaza de Armas, in San Blas and on Av La Cultura.

Casas de cambio

Many travel agencies and *casas de cambio* change dollars. Some of them change traveller's cheques as well, and some charge 4-5% commission. There are many *cambios* on the west side of the Plaza de Armas and on the west side of Av Sol, most change TCs. **LAC Dólar**, Av Sol 150, T084-257762, Mon-Sat 0900-2000, with delivery service to central hotels, cash and TCs, is recommended. The street changers hang around Av Sol, blocks 2-3, every day. Some of them will also change TCs. Whether in banks or on the street, check the notes carefully.

Embassies and consulates

Belgium, Av Sol 954, T084-224322. Mon-Fri 0900-1300, 1500-1700. **France**, Jorge Escobar, C Micaela Bastidas 101, 4th floor, T084-

233610. **Germany**, Sra Maria-Sophia Júrgens de Hermoza, San Agustín 307, T084-235459, acupari@terra.com.pe. Mon-Fri 1000-1200, appointments may be made by phone, it also has a book exchange. **Ireland**, Charlie Donovan, Santa Catalina Ancha 360 (Rosie O'Grady's), T084-243514. **Italy**, Sr Fedos Rubatto, Av Garcilaso 700, T084-224398. Mon-Fri 0900-1200, 1500-1700. **Netherlands**, Sra Marcela Alarco, Av Pardo 827, T084-241897, marcela_alarco@yahoo.com. Mon-Fri 0900-1500. **Spain**, Sra Juana María Lambarri, Av Pardo (Paseo de los Héroes) 1041, T084-984 650106. **Switzerland**, Av Regional 222, T084-243533. **UK**, Barry Walker, Av Pardo 895, T084-239974, bwalker@amauta. rcp.net.pe. **US Agent**, Dra Olga Villagarcía, Av Pardo 845, T084-231474, coreses@state.gov.

Immigration
Av Sol, Local Prefectural, p 1, T084-222741. Mon-Fri 0800-1300. Reported as not helpful.

Internet
You can't walk for 2 mins in Cuzco without running into an internet café, and new places are opening all the time. Most have similar rates, around US$0.50 per hr. The better places have scanners, webcams and CD burners, among other gadgets, and staff in these establishments can be very knowledgeable. The best cafés are usually those who have most recently updated their equipment, a constantly changing situation, so trial and error is the rule of the day. Many cafés now offer international telephone calls at very reasonable rates.

Language classes
Academia Latinoamericana de Español, Plaza Limacpampa 565, T084-243364, www.latinoschools.com. The same company also has schools in Ecuador (Quito) and in Bolivia (Sucre). They can arrange courses that include any combination of these locations using identical teaching methods and materials. Professionally run with experienced staff. Many activities per week, including dance lessons and excursions to sites of historical and cultural interest. Good homestays. Private classes US$170 for 20 hrs, groups, with a maximum of 4 students US$125, again for 20 hrs.
Acupari, San Agustín 307, T084-242970, www.acupari.com. The German-Peruvian Cultural Association offers Spanish classes.
Amauta Spanish School, C Suecia 480, T084-262345, www.amautaspanish.com. Spanish classes, 1-to-1 or in small groups, also volunteer work, Quechua classes and workshops on Peruvian culture, US$11.50 per hr 1-to-1, but cheaper and possibly better value for group tuition (2-6 people), US$114 for 20 hrs. They have pleasant accommodation on site, as well as a free internet café for students, and can arrange excursions and can help find voluntary work. They also have a school in Urubamba and can arrange courses in the Manu rainforest, in conjunction with Pantiacolla Tours SRL.

Amigos Spanish School, Zaguán del Cielo B-23, T084-242292, www.spanishcusco.com. Certified, experienced teachers, friendly atmosphere. All profits support a foundation for disadvantaged children. Private lessons for US$8 per hr, US$108 for 20 hrs of classes in a small group. Comfortable homestays and free activities available, including a 'real city tour' through Cuzco's poor areas.

Cusco Spanish School, Garcilaso 265, of 6 (2nd floor), T084-226928, www.cuscospanish school.com. US$175 for 20 hrs' private classes, cheaper in groups. School offers homestays, optional activities including dance and music classes, cookery courses, ceramics, Quechua, hiking and volunteer programmes. They also offer courses on an hacienda at Cusipata in the Vilcanota Valley, east of Cuzco.

Excel, Cruz Verde 336, T084-235298, www.excel-spanishlanguageprograms-peru.org. Very professional, US$7 per hr for private 1-to-1 lessons. US$229 for 20 hrs with 2 people, or US$277 with homestay, 1-to-1 for 20 hrs.

Fairplay Spanish School, Pasaje Zavaleta C-5, Wanchac, T084-984 789252, www.fairplay-peru.org. This relatively new NGO teaches Peruvians who wouldn't normally have the opportunity (Peruvian single mothers, for example) to become Spanish teachers themselves over several months of training. The agency then acts as an agent, allowing these same teachers to find work with visiting students. Classes with these teachers cost US$4.50 or US$6 per hr, of which 33% is reinvested in the NGO, the rest going direct to the teachers. Can also arrange volunteer work and homestay programmes.

La Casona de la Esquina, Purgatorio 395, corner with Huaynapata, T084-235830. US$5 per hr for 1-to-1 classes. Recommended.

Mundo Verde, Coviduc H-14, San Sebastián, T084-274574, www.mundoverdespanish. com. Spanish lessons with the option to study in the rainforest and the possibility of working on environmental and social projects while studying. Some of your money goes towards developing sustainable farming

practices in the area. US$250 for 20 hrs' tuition with homestay.

San Blas Spanish School, Carmen Bajo 224, T084-247898, www.spanishschoolperu.com. Groups, with 4 clients maximum, US$90 for 20 hrs' tuition (US$130 1-to-1).

Laundry

There are several cheap laundries on Procuradores, Suecia and Tecseccocha. **Adonai**, Choquechaca 216-A, San Blas. Good hole-in-the-wall laundry, US$0.60 per kg for wash and dry, friendly and usually reliable, small book exchange. **Dana's Laundry**, Nueva Baja y Unión. US$2.10 per kg, takes about 6 hrs. **Lavandería**, Saphi 578. Mon-Sat 0800-2000, Sun 0800-1300. Good, fast service, US$1 per kg. String markers will be attached to clothes if they have no label. **Lavandería Louis**, Choquechaca 264, San Blas. US$0.85 per kg, fresh, clean, good value. **Lavandería T'aqsana Wasi**, Santa Catalina Ancha 345. Same-day service, they also iron clothes, US$2 per kg, good service, speak English, German, Italian and French, Mon-Fri 0900-2030, Sat 0900-1900. **Splendid Laundry Service**, Carmen Alto 195. Very good, US$0.75 per kg, laundry sometimes available after only 3-4 hrs.

Medical services
Clinics and doctors

Clínica Panamericana, Urb Larapa Grande C-17, T084-270000, T084-984 785303 (mob), www.cuscohealth.com. 24-hr emergency and medical attention. Good. **Clínica Pardo**, Av de la Cultura 710, T084-240387, www.clinicapardo.com. 24-hr emergency and hospitalization/medical attention, international department, trained bilingual personnel, handles complete medical assistance coverage with international insurance companies, free ambulance service, visit to hotel, discount in pharmacy, dental service, X-rays, laboratory, full medical specialization. The most highly recommended clinic in Cuzco. **Hampi Land Clínica del Viajero**, Av Huáscar 105 A-26,

T084-240768, www.hampiland.com. Professional medical care for tourists, with pharmacy, vaccinations, diagnostics, etc, also has ambulance and evacuation service. **Hospital Regional**, Av de la Cultura, T084-227661, emergencies T084-223691. **Dr Ilya Gomon**, Pasaje Santa Cruz de Peñalva 288 (Huayna Ccapac), Wanchac, T084-965 1906, www.perucuzco.com/chiropractic_cusco/. Canadian chiropractor, good, reasonable prices, available for hotel or home visits. **Dr Gilbert Espejo** and **Dr Boris Espejo Muñoz**, both in the Centro Comercial Cusco, of 7, T084-228074 and T084-231918 respectively. If you need a yellow fever vaccination (for the jungle lowlands, or for travel to Bolivia or Brazil where it is required), it is available at the paediatric department of the **Hospital Antonio Lorena**, Plazoleta Belén 1358, T084-226511, from 0830 on Mon, Wed and Fri; they are free and include the international vaccination certificate.

Dentists
Dr Eduardo Franco, Av de la Cultura, Edif Santa Fe, oficina 310, T084-242207, T084-984 650179 (mob). 24-hr.

Massage and therapies
Casa de la Serenidad, Santa María P-8, San Sebastián, T084-792224, T084-948 671867 (mob), www.shamanspirit.net. A shamanic therapy centre run by Lilo Ccoyllor, a healer and Reiki Master who uses medicinal 'power' plants. It also has bed and breakfast and has received very good reports. **Healing Hands**, based at Loki Hostel. Angela is a reiki, shiatsu and craniosacral therapist. Very relaxing and recommended, track Angela down at Loki or drop her line at faeryamanita@hotmail.com. **Sebastián Style**, Av Sol 948, CC Cusco Sol Plaza, T084-240883, sebastianstyle@yahoo.com.ar. Salon for hairdressing and beauty treatments, massages and other therapies; personal service and will visit your hotel. If you want a more professional massage than what is offered on the street, but at the same time less costly than the services offered in big hotels, try this salon. Also look for yoga, massages etc advertised in respected cafés and restaurants.

Post offices
Central office, Av Sol at the bottom end of block 5, T084-225232. Mon-Sat 0730-2000, 0800-1400 Sun and holidays. Poste restante is free and helpful. Sending packages is not cheap. **DHL**, Av Sol 627, T084-244167. For sending packages or money overseas.

Telephone
There are independent phone offices in the centre. **Telefónica**, Av del Sol 386, T084-241111. For telephone and fax, Mon-Sat 0700-2300, 0700-1200 Sun and holidays.

Contents

Footprint features

Machu
Picchu

Cuzco

Sacred Valley

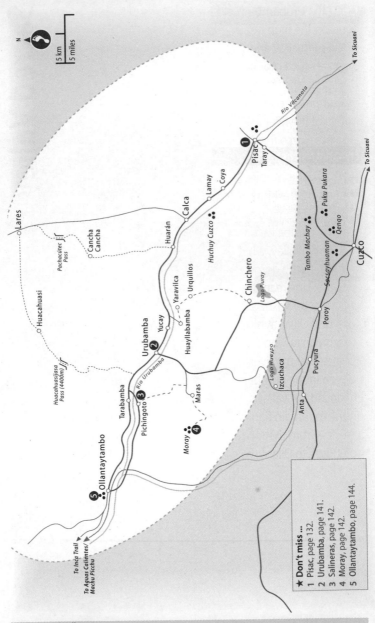

N

5 km
5 miles

To Sicuani

Rio Vilcanota

To Sicuani

Lares

Pachacutec
Pass

Cancha
Cancha

Huacahuasi

Huacahuasijasa
Pass (4400m)

Ollantaytambo

Tarabamba

Pichingoto

Rio Urubamba

Urubamba

Yucay

Yaravilca

Urquillos

Huayllabamba

Maras

Moray

Izcuchaca

Lago Huaypo

Chinchero

Lago Piuray

Poroy

Pucyura

Anta

Huarán

Calca

Lamay

Coya

Huchuy Cuzco

Taray

Pisac

Tambo Machay

Sacsayhuaman

Qenqo

Puku Pukara

Cuzco

To Aguas Calientes/
Machu Picchu

To Inca Trail

★ **Don't miss ...**
1 Pisac, page 132.
2 Urubamba, page 141.
3 Salineras, page 142.
4 Moray, page 142.
5 Ollantaytambo, page 144.

The Río Urubamba cuts its way through fields and rocky gorges beneath the high peaks of the Cordillera. The presence of giants such as Pitusiray and La Verónica is a constant reminder that to the Incas such mountains were *apus* (beings to be worshipped). The landscape is forever changing as shafts of sunlight fall upon plantations of corn, precipitous Inca terraces, tiled roofs, or the waters of the river itself. Brown hills, covered in wheat fields, separate Cuzco from this beautiful high valley. Major Inca ruins command the heights – Pisac, Huchuy Cuzco and Ollantaytambo are the best examples – and traditional villages guard the bridges or stand on the highlands.

The road from Cuzco climbs up to a pass, then continues over the pampa before descending into the densely populated Urubamba Valley, which stretches from Sicuani (on the railway to Puno) to the gorge of Torontoi, 600 m lower, to the northwest of Cuzco. Upstream from Pisac, the river is usually called the Vilcanota, downstream it is the Urubamba.

Beyond Ollantaytambo, the river begins its descent to the Amazonian lowlands, becoming wilder as it leaves the valley behind. That the river was of great significance to the Incas can be seen in the number of strategic sites they built above it. They enhanced the valley's fertility by building vast stretches of terraces on the mountain flanks and the Inca rulers had their royal estates here. It is from the Incas' own name for the river that the section from Pisac to Ollantaytambo is called 'Sacred' today.

Ins and outs

For the visitor, paved roads, plentiful transport and a good selection of hotels and eating places make this a straightforward place to explore. You can choose either a quick visit from the city or, better still, linger for a few days, savouring the sights and atmosphere. The valley itself is great for cycling and there are plenty of walking trails for one-day or longer excursions. Horse riding and rafting are also popular in this most visitor-friendly of tourist destinations. Furthermore, if the altitude of Cuzco itself is too much, you can hop on a minibus down to the valley – the 500-m difference can do wonders for your health. The best time to visit this area is April to May or October to November. The high season is from June to September, but the rainy season, from December to March, is cheaper and pleasant enough. ▶ *For listings, see pages 152-160.*

Getting there and around

From Cuzco you can get to the Sacred Valley by bus, car, taxi or as part of an organized tour. The road from Cuzco which runs past Sacsayhuaman and on to Tambo Machay (see page 82), climbs up to a pass, then continues over the pampa before descending into the densely populated Urubamba Valley. As the road drops from the heights above Cuzco, there are two viewpoints, Mirador C'orao and Mirador Taray, looking over the plain around Pisac and, beyond, the Pitusiray and Sawasiray mountains. This road then crosses the Río Urubamba by a bridge at Pisac and follows the north bank to the end of the paved road at Ollantaytambo. It passes through Calca, Yucay and Urubamba. Urubamba can also be reached from Cuzco by the beautiful, direct road through Chinchero (see page 141).

An organized tour to Pisac, Urubamba, Ollantaytambo and Chinchero, as the main places of interest in the Sacred Valley, can be fixed up anytime with a travel agent for about US$20 per person. These tours last only one-day and may be too brief. A taxi costs about US$85 for the round trip of the main sites of the valley and back to Cuzco. Taxis may also be hired to the individual towns, eg US$20 round-trip to Pisac. For a less hurried visit, explore the valley on foot, by bike or on horseback. Using public transport and staying overnight in Urubamba, Ollantaytambo or Pisac allows much more time to see the ruins and markets. ▶ *For further details, see Tour operators, page 114, and Transport, page 159.*

Pisac → *For listings, see pages 152-160. Colour map 2, B3. Phone code: 084.*

Only 30 km north of Cuzco is the village of Pisac, which is well worth a visit for its superb Inca ruins, perched precariously on the mountain, above the town. Pisac is usually visited as part of a tour from Cuzco but this often allows only 1½ hours here, not enough time to take in the ruins and splendid scenery.

Pisac village and market

The ruins are considered to be amongst the very finest in the valley. Strangely, however, most visitors don't come to Pisac for the ruins. Instead, they come in droves for its Sunday morning market, which is described variously as colourful and interesting, or touristy and expensive. This is, in part, explained by the fact that it contains sections for both the tourist and the local community. Traditionally, Sunday is the day when the people of the highlands come down to sell their produce (potatoes, corn, beans, vegetables, weavings, pottery, etc). These are traded for essentials such as salt, sugar, rice, noodles, fruit, medicines, plastic goods and tools. The market comes to life after the arrival of tourist

A market for beads

A major feature of Pisac's popular market is the huge and varied collection of multicoloured beads on sale. Although they are commonly called Inca beads, this is, in fact, something of a misnomer. The Incas were highly talented potters and decorated their ware with detailed geometric motifs, but they are not known to have made ceramic beads.

These attractive items have become popular relatively recently.

They used to be rolled individually by hand and were very time-consuming to produce. Now, in a major concession to consumerism, they are machine-made and produced in quantity, then hand-painted and glazed.

Today, the clay beads are produced in countless, often family-run, workshops in Cuzco and Pisac. Some are made into earrings, necklaces and bracelets, but many thousands are sold loose.

buses around 1000, and is usually over by 1500. However, there is also an important ceremony every Sunday at 1100 sharp, in which the *Varayocs* (village mayors) from the surrounding and highland villages participate in a Quechua Catholic Mass in **Pisac church**. It is a good example of the merging of, and respect for, different religious cultures. Pisac has other somewhat less crowded, less expensive markets on Tuesday and Thursday morning; it's best to get there before 0900.

On the plaza, which has several large *pisonay* trees, are the church and a small interesting **Museo Folklórico**. The town, with its narrow streets, is worth strolling around and, while you're doing so, look for the fine facade at Grau 485. The **Museo Comunitario Pisac** ① *Av Amazonas y Retamayoc K'asa, museopisac@gmail.com, daily 1000-1700, free but donations welcome*, was opened in 2009, with a display of village life, created by the people of Pisac. There are many souvenir shops on Bolognesi.

Inca ruins

① *Daily 0700-1730. If you go early (before 1000) you'll have the ruins to yourself. Entry with BTC visitor ticket (see box, page 65). Guides US$5, but the wardens on site are very helpful and don't charge anything to give out information.*

The ruins of Inca Pisac stand on a spur between the Río Urubamba to the south and the smaller Chongo to the east. It is not difficult to imagine why this stunning

Pisac

Not to scale

Sleeping 🛏
1 Hostal Varayoc
2 Paz y Luz
3 Pisac Inn
4 Residencial Beho
5 Royal Inka

Eating 🍴
1 Bakery
2 Blue Llama Café
3 Cuchara de Palo
4 Doña Clorinda
5 Miski Mijuna Wasi
6 Mullu
7 Ulrike's Café
8 Valle Sargado

location was chosen, as it provides an ideal vantage point over the flat plain of the Urubamba, the terraces below and the terraced hillsides across the eastern valley. In *The Conquest of the Incas*, John Hemming describes Pisac as one of the Incas' 'pleasure houses' in the Yucay Valley (another name for this stretch of the Urubamba). If it were merely that, it would have been some country estate. There were, however, many other facets to the site – defensive, religious and agricultural – all contributing to one of the largest Inca ruins in the vicinity of Cuzco. The buildings that can be seen today have been dated to the reign of Pachacútec (see page 308), to whom, it is said, the estate belonged.

To appreciate the site fully, allow five or six hours on foot. Even if going by car, do not rush as there is a lot to see and a lot of walking to do. Walking up, although tiring, is recommended for the views and location. It's at least one hour uphill all the way, but the descent takes 30 minutes. Horses are available for US$5 per person. Road transport approaches from the Kanchiracay end. The drive up from town takes about 20 minutes. Combis charge US$0.75 per person and taxis US$4 one way up to the ruins from near the bridge. Then you can walk back down (if you want the taxi to take you back down negotiate a fare and pick-up time). Overnight parking is allowed in the car park.

The walk up to the ruins begins from the town plaza, passing the Centro de Salud and a control post. The path goes through working terraces, giving the ruins a context. The first group of buildings is **Pisaqa**, with a fine curving wall. Climb up to the central part of the ruins, the **Intihuatana** group of temples and rock outcrops in the most magnificent Inca masonry. Here are the **Reloj Solar** (Hitching Post of the Sun) – now closed because thieves stole a piece from it – palaces of the moon and stars, solstice markers, baths and water channels. From Intihuatana, a path leads around the hillside through a tunnel to **Q'Allaqasa** (military area). Across the valley at this point, a large area of Inca tombs in holes in the hillside can be seen. The end of the site is **Kanchiracay**, where the agricultural workers were housed. At dusk you will hear, if not see, the *pisaca* (partridges), after which the place is named, and you may see deer too.

Pisac to Urubamba → For listings, see pages 152-160. Colour map 2, B2/3.

Calca and around
The first villages on the road from Pisac towards Urubamba are **Coya** and **Lamay** and the nearby warm springs, which are highly regarded locally for their medicinal properties. **Calca**, 18 km beyond Pisac at 2900 m, was the headquarters of Manco Inca at the beginning of his uprising against the Spaniards in 1536. Today it is a busy hub in the valley, with a plaza which is divided into two parts. Urubamba buses stop on one side, and Cuzco and Pisac buses on the other side of the dividing strip. Look out for the *api* sellers with their bicycles loaded with a steaming kettle and an assortment of bottles, glasses and tubs.

It is a two-day hike from Cuzco to Calca, via Sacsayhuaman, Qenqo, Puka Pukara, Tambo Machay and Huchuy Cuzco with excellent views of the eastern cordilleras, past small villages and along beautifully built Inca paths. There are many places to camp, but take water.

There are mineral baths at **Machacancha**, 8 km east of Calca. These springs are indoors, pleasantly warm and will open at night for groups. They are half an hour by taxi from town. About 3 km beyond Machacancha are the Inca ruins of **Arquasmarca**.

Rivers of rubbish

Every year on 15-16 September hundreds of students, *campesinos*, gringos, local companies and other volunteers board a bus in Cuzco with rubber gloves and rubbish bags in their hands. What are they doing? Saving the Río Urubamba.

The Urubamba, sacred river of the Incas, is a Peruvian national treasure. This historic waterway, however, is being polluted. El Río Willkamayu (as it is known in Quechua) is a danger to the health of the local people as it is seriously contaminated by plastic, oil, petrol and any number of other non-biodegradable products. The scale of the problem was revealed in the 2002 clean-up: nappies, clothing and labels that have been out of production for more than 10 years were found.

The Día del Río (Day of the River) is used as a celebration of ecology and education. The idea is to enlighten the young people of Peru through teaching and by example. South American Explorers leads the clean-up effort in partnership with many other companies. Meetings are held roughly once a month at the **South American Explorers** clubhouse at Atoqsaycuchi 670, San Blas, Cuzco, T084-245484, and have generated lots of ideas concerning cleaning the river in particular and recycling in general.

Cuzco is becoming more progressive on all ecological subjects. A new recycling plant has been opened to deal with the inorganic rubbish. It will take time but it is hoped that, in a few years, all households in Cuzco will be separating their refuse.

What you can do:
→ Bring a water bottle and fill it in designated areas.
→ Always leave plastic bottles in recycling bins.
→ Bring or buy biodegradable soap.
→ Say no to plastic bags in shops.
→ Carry a backpack.
→ Join the next Día del Río.

Huchuy Cuzco

The ruins of a small Inca town, Huchuy Cuzco (US$7.15 for trek and entry), are reached across the Río Urubamba and after a stiff three- to four-hour climb. Huchuy Cuzco (also spelt Qosqo), which in Quechua means 'Little Cuzco', was the name given to this impressive Inca site sometime in the 20th century. Its original name was Kakya Qawani, which translates as 'from where the lightning can be seen'. According to the Spanish chronicler Pedro de Cieza de León, the palaces and temples at Huchuy Cuzco were built by the eighth Inca, Viracocha, who conquered the area by defeating the ethnic groups settled there.

Huchuy Cuzco is dramatically located on a flat esplanade almost 600 m above Lamay and Calca in the Sacred Valley. The views from the site are magnificent, with the Río Urubamba far below meandering through fertile fields, and the sombre Pitusiray massif opposite, surrounded by other snowy peaks.

The ruins themselves consist of extensive agricultural terraces with high retaining walls. There are several buildings made from both the finely wrought stonework the Incas reserved for their most important constructions, and adobe mud bricks.

There are several ways to reach Huchuy Cuzco. A road has been built to the ruins from Calca. Alternatively, a steep trail goes to the site from behind the village of Lamay, which is reached by crossing the bridge over the river. Another longer route leads to Huchuy Cuzco from Tambo Machay near Cuzco, a magnificent one- or two-day trek along the route once taken by the Inca from his capital to his country estate at Huchuy Cuzco; some sections of the original Inca highway remain intact.

Yucay

A few kilometres east of Urubamba, Yucay has two large grassy plazas divided by the restored colonial church of **Santiago Apóstol**, with its oil paintings and fine altars. On the opposite side from Plaza Manco II is the **adobe palace** built for Sayri Túpac (Manco's son) when he emerged from Vilcabamba in 1558.

Back along the road towards Calca a bridge crosses the river to the village of **Huayllabamba** (see page 141). If you are not dashing along the road at the speed of a local minibus, it is pleasant to cross the river and amble along the quieter bank, through farmland and small communities.

Valle de Lares → *For listings, see pages 152-160.*

To the north of Urubamba and Calca, beyond the great peaks that tower above the Sacred Valley, lies the valley of **Lares**, an area famed for its traditional Quechua communities and strong weaving traditions. The mountainous territory that lies between these two valleys offers a great deal to the ambitious trekker. The entire Cordillera Urubamba is threaded with tracks and the remains of ancient Inca trails and, as you might expect, the variety of trekking routes is almost endless. Many of the locals may offer to sell weavings or *mantas* along the route, at prices a fraction of those in Cuzco. Remember, if you bargain, that many of these items take weeks, perhaps a month or more, to complete, so always give a fair price – at least here all the money goes to the weavers themselves!

Lares is also a perfect example of Peru's fabulous biking opportunities and it has something for everyone, suiting all levels of daring and technical ability. In two days you can freewheel from chilly mountain passes, past llamas and traditional Quechua communities, on unpaved but drivable roads, or follow old Inca trails down technical single tracks and through precipitous canyons alongside rushing mountain torrents. The area is firmly established with Cuzco agencies for trekking and cycling tours, often as an alternative, or add-on to the Inca Trail. **→** *See Cuzco Activities and tours, page 114.*

Lares trek: Huarán to Yanahuara → *4 days.*

The trek from Huarán to Yanahuara via Lares takes you through ancient native forests, past some of the Cordillera Urubamba's greatest snow peaks, their waters feeding jewelled lakes and cascades below, and provides an insight into the communities that inhabit this rugged and challenging land. Enjoy the trek and have a good soak in the hot springs in Lares.

Day one The trek begins in the small community of **Huarán**, 6 km to the west of Calca, just off the main highway heading for Urubamba. Public transport along the highway, in the form of combis and buses, is cheap and plentiful. The first day's hike is around four hours of actual walking time up a very steep, exceptionally beautiful and surprisingly wild valley directly to the north of, and above, Huarán. The path stays close to the sparkling water of the **Quebrada Cancha Cancha**, which runs in the valley's centre and is crossed by traditional wood/adobe bridges. It's hard to get lost as you are hemmed in by the steep valley walls: just keep heading north and up.

The lower section of the valley is heavily cultivated, but quite soon enters areas of ancient (highly endangered), red-barked *Polylepis* (*quenoal*) forest, then cloudforest full of bromeliads, cacti and more. The smooth rocks and boulders, rich vegetation and rushing stream conjure up an image of a Japanese garden, but on a vast scale, and all presided over by the turrets and battlements of the valley's sheer rock faces.

The village of **Cancha Cancha** is friendly and very scenic, nestled beneath impressive snow peaks. The small houses are reminiscent of the hobbits' village in *Lord of the Rings*. The mountain up to the left of the pass is **Sirihuani** (5399 m) and you can also see the back of **Chicón/Pico San Juan** to the west. A good campsite for the night is the grassy area just beyond the village.

Day two This is a long day's hiking – eight hours of walking plus breaks – but there are hot springs at the end. Cancha Cancha lies at the confluence of two valleys. Your route lies up the right-hand valley and high on its right flank. From Cancha Cancha you can see the Patchacútec Pass on a bearing of 40° from your position. You pass through a heavily cultivated area: traditional grass roofed houses, dry stone walls and potato fields. The following timings until the Pachacútec Pass are taken from Cancha Cancha.

After about 50 minutes a beautiful steep peak comes into view on the left. This is Sirihuani, visible earlier from Cancha Cancha up the left hand valley, which becomes increasingly Matterhorn-like as you head towards the pass. One hour 20 minutes: it's very

Lares trek

important to stay high on the valley's shoulder to get above the vast cliffs dominating the head of the valley. One hour 30 minutes: you're now high above the cliffs. Two clear lakes come into view; a third is just visible higher up the mountain. One hour 40 minutes: the three lakes are in line; Sirihuani, at a bearing of 300° behind the lakes, is now a sheer pyramid. One hour 50 minutes: turn a corner and the great peaks of **Pitusiray** and **Sawasiray** loom into view, their flanks coated with vast glaciers. Sawasiray (sometimes spelt Sahuasiray) has an estimated altitude of around 5770 m, making it possibly the highest peak in the Urubamba range, contested only by Verónica. One local legend recounts how Pitusiray and Sawasiray were once Inca lovers, bound together in death by an icy embrace. If using the IGN 1:100,000 map of the area, Sawasiray lies just to the east of the Urubamba sheet (27-R) on the Calca Map (27-S), and is referred to as Colquecruz.

The pass now lies between two black hills/mountains to the north. Three rocky fingers just to the right of the pass are visible from a great distance, even from Cancha Cancha on a clear day. After two hours 40 minutes you reach a hill just before the pass. This one actually has better 360° views than the pass itself: get your photos here! Dropping into a small dip, climb up the rounded hill and continue north around the base of the small rocky peak of **Cerro Azulorjo** (4958 m). Three hours after leaving Cancha Cancha you reach the summit of the **Pachacútec Pass**. There's a small lake below but it's not visible from the pass itself – have a look just before. Don't forget to build up the *apachetas* (pyramids of standing stones to honour the *apus*, or mountain spirits). Missionary groups have destroyed those on the pass.

Head north off Pachacútec; 20 minutes beyond the pass a huge valley, flat like a landing strip, opens up to the right, beneath you. Don't descend into the valley, stay high on its left flank. Your route lies left, branching off to the northwest just before the black rocky peak in front of you. Forty minutes beyond the pass you enter a new valley. The mountains in the distance lying at 320° are those of the **Terjuay Massif**, rising to 5330 m. This is considered a separate and distinct range, lying north of and parallel to the Cordillera Urubamba. Heading northwest descend a slippery shale/scree slope towards two lakes. The nearer lake has dried out considerably in the last few years; the further one is the larger. Still heading northwest, transfer in the saddle between the lakes from the left to the right side of the valley. There is a clear trail on the right side of the second, larger lake, and this curves to the left around its circumference. This route leads to the lake's exit stream at its western end. The trail follows the stream away from the lake, turning sharply to the north and descending beside a beautiful waterfall, known locally as the **Patsi** waterfall, whose multiple streams tumble 20 m or more over the cliff. You're now 1½ hours from the pass. Thirty minutes beyond the falls you reach the settlement of **Quisuarani** on the left side of the river. You've been walking on the right until this point. It's possible to camp here. Five minutes beyond the settlement cross back to the right side. Shortly after the village the path becomes a motorable track, which you can follow or cut off the curves using the many linked walking trails. After another 50 minutes you turn left onto the main Calca to Lares road.

About 1½ hours after joining the road you'll reach the main square of **Lares**, a sleepy town with a couple of basic hostels and shops. Beyond the town centre and up a small river valley are hot springs where you can bathe. To reach them, leave the square from its far corner and take the second left once on the street. An extra 15 minutes walking up the valley to the left of the river brings you to the pools. Ask for directions if unsure. The pools underwent renovations a few years ago, unfortunately incorporating the typical Peruvian love of concrete, but they are still excellent spots to unwind, especially at night, staring up at the star-studded night sky. Entry to the springs costs US$1.25 and space to pitch a tent a further US$1.50. Some very basic accommodation is also available with negotiation. There's a small shop selling drinks and snacks.

Day three A nice easy day, in terms of both navigation and length (just 3½ hours of hiking), with plenty of time to relax at the springs or explore Lares town (not a very daunting task!). Head west up the valley above the springs on the trail/road. After one hour the road crosses the stream to the right hand side. A log bridge aided the crossing at the time of writing. At this point the valley splits in two: take the larger right hand (western) valley. Your trail runs at 300° between ancient stone walls. After around one hour 20 minutes from the springs, original sections of Inca trail begin to appear. The path is on the left of the river, the valley a steep 'V', your course more southwest at this point. You're basically following the road, but it's far more pleasant to use the sections of Inca trail, which sometimes cut off the corners, where possible. As you continue, you gradually ascend higher on the side of the valley; the Inca trails now have marked drainage channels, a feature typical of ancient trails in this region. Two and a half hours after leaving Lares you reach the large community of **Huacahuasi**. **Nevado Pumahuanja** is visible to the southwest. Walk through the village towards the head of the valley. Passing the church bear slightly right and pick up the trail behind the small houses. The route climbs gently out of the village, continuing up the valley on its right side. After some time you will see waterfalls on the far (south) side of the valley. Forty-five minutes beyond Huacahuasi the valley splits and your trail curves to the right following into the near valley and heading away from the waterfalls. About 30 minutes further on are some flat grassy areas good for camping and for the assault on the final pass tomorrow.

Day four Six to seven hours' walking time, plus breaks. Head southwest above camp on the track towards the head of the valley. The pass soon becomes visible at 240° between the mountains, the trail clear at this point. It takes just under two hours to reach the top of the pass, the **Abra Huacahuasijasa** at an altitude of approximately 4400 m. Above you and to the left towers the snow peak of **Pumahuanja**, rising to 5330 m. A beautiful lake can now be seen to the southwest. Descending into this valley, leave the lake to your right and continue out of the lake basin into the valley proper, which now runs south towards the Sacred Valley and **Yanahuara**, your final destination. About an hour beyond the Abra Huacahuasijasa you continue past a second lake, this time passing it to your left. Now transfer back to the left side of the Quebrada. The valley takes its name from Aruravcocha, a higher and larger lake, and still boasts extensive stands of ancient *qenoal* trees: however, severe deforestation is taking place and it is feared that these woods may disappear entirely over the next few years. Beyond the second lake the valley drops away steeply, passing huge boulders of the glacial moraine, a remnant of the last ice age, and vast glaciers that once carved the Urubamba range. Now a couple of hours beyond the pass you come to the village of Mantanay. Just keep heading south, through another section of deep forest. Cactuses and bromeliads begin to make an appearance again as you head for the warmer climate of the Sacred Valley. A further two hours, through increasingly settled and cultivated land, brings you to the village of **Yanahuara**.

From Yanahuara infrequent combis and trucks leave for Urubamba: ask around in the village for the latest intelligence. If you find yourself marooned for the night, a further 30 minutes' slog down the rough road will bring you to the highway, with plentiful transport to Urubamba, Ollantaytambo and beyond.

Cycling route: Valle de Lares → *2 days.*

Several agencies in Cuzco can offer biking in this area and it's a good idea to take advantage of their services because, unless you're super fit, or a masochist, you're going to need some transport to get you to the top of the Abra de Lares twice, for the start of each day's ride. By the same token, a professional biking guide will be able to show you interesting sections of single track, provide technical advice and mechanical support. If you want to go it alone, local buses running between Calca and Lares will carry bikes on the roof; just make sure they're well tied on. And don't forget that you can spend the first night soaking away your bumps and bruises in the thermal springs at Lares (see page 138). ▸▸ *For further information, see Cuzco Tour operators, page 114.*

Day one: Abra de Lares to Lares The bus ride itself from Calca up to the pass is spectacular and provides an insight into the second day's biking. Reaching the pass at 4400 m you have a spectacular view in both directions: down the valley to Lares, back to Calca and also above to the glaciers of the Urubamba range – not a bad spot to start the day. In clear weather, the northward skyline beyond Lares is dominated by the Nevados of Quilloc and Terijuay, isolated peaks rising to more than 5300 m.

After the first 15-20 minutes of downhill on the road, you reach a left-hand turn-off leading you to a faint Inca trail running close to the stream for perhaps 40 minutes. The terrain varies from smooth grassy runs to some serious rocky sections requiring a fair amount of skill, but you can walk them if you're not sure. Just before rejoining the main road you pass the tiny rural community of **Charalpampa**, its small grass-roofed huts backed by the imposing glacier of Sawasiray (5770 m), one of greatest peaks of the Urubamba range. After rejoining the road another hour's biking will take you to a lush meadow beside the river, ideal for lunch. Ambitious bikers can take several short cuts, avoiding the bends, to reach this point. Beyond the meadow the valley drops away steeply, the river carving a deep whitewater canyon to the right of the road. It's not long before you reach Lares (see page 138).

Day two: Abra de Lares to Calca The second day sees you return to the dizzy heights of the *abra* before hurling yourself downhill once more, this time towards the Sacred Valley. From the heights of the pass a distinct Inca Trail is visible running along the right side of the valley, above the stream which lies at its centre. Like the previous day, a short downhill section on the road leads to a turn-off onto single track. This time the route diverges from the road for several hours. The trail kicks off through rolling farmland and pasture, fields of potatoes and flocks of sheep and alpacas. Despite its great age, the trail is clear, with some small sections of paving still visible, along with many drainage channels cutting across the route. These provide plenty of biking challenges. All the time, the main road to Calca is visible on the far side of the valley, rising high on its left shoulder.

Beyond the gentle valley the route becomes more technically challenging, with some sections providing thrills even for hardened biking addicts. Running close to the river the path enters a sheer canyon and a series of steep rocky descents. There are original sets of Inca stairs to be negotiated and several river crossings on traditional wood and adobe bridges – be as daring as you wish, or walk the tough bits! Emerging from the gorge you ride through the village of Tortora and out onto the main road. From Tortora onwards it's a long but straightforward descent on the road to Calca. There are plenty of short cuts eliminating the curves for those looking for a little excitement, otherwise look out for the traffic and enjoy the views on the way down. Calca itself is a pleasant town (see page 134), with a couple of decent cafés on the main square and good transport links to Cuzco and the rest of the Sacred Valley. Alternatively you can just keep on riding!

Urubamba and around → *For listings, see pages 152-160. Colour map 2, B2. Phone code: 084. Altitude: 2863 m.*

Like many places along the valley, Urubamba has a fine setting, with views of the Chicón snow-capped peaks and glaciers, and enjoys a mild climate. The main plaza, with a fountain capped by a maize cob, is surrounded by blue-painted buildings. Calle Berriózabal, on the west edge of town, is lined with *pisonay* trees. The large market square is one block west of the main plaza. Market days are Wednesday and Friday. The main road skirts the town and the bridge for the road to Chinchero is just to the east of town.

Sights

Seminario-Behar Ceramic Studio ① *C Berriózabal 405, a right turning off the main road to Ollantaytambo, T084-201002, www.ceramicaseminario.com, open daily (just ring the bell)*, was founded in 1979. Pablo Seminario has investigated the techniques and designs of pre-Columbian Peruvian cultures and has created a style with strong links to the past. Each piece, both utilitarian and artisitic, is handmade and painted, using ancient glazes and minerals, before firing. The resulting pieces are very attractive and Seminario has exhibited in US museums. Visitors may purchase items, tour the workshops to see the different techniques and watch a video (also on YouTube). Tours are given in Englsih and Spanish. As well as the Centro de Arte and shop, there is a small collection of Andean animals. Seminario-Behar also has a shop on the Plaza de Armas in Cuzco.

Chinchero → *Phone code: 084. Colour map 2, B3. Altitude: 3762 m.*
① *Site open daily 0700-1730. Entry by BTC visitor ticket (see page 65).*
Chinchero is northwest from Cuzco, high on the pampa just off a direct road to Urubamba. The streets of the village wind up from the lower sections, where transport stops, to the **plaza**, which is reached through an archway. The great square appears to be stepped, with a magnificent Inca wall separating the two levels. Let into the wall is a row of trapezoidal niches, each much taller than a man. From the paved lower section another arch leads to an upper terrace, upon which the Spaniards built an attractive **church**. It is open on Sunday for mass and at festivals but ask in the tourist office in Cuzco if it is open at other times, as it is worth spending a quiet moment or two inside to admire the ceiling, beams and walls, which are covered in beautiful floral and religious designs. The altar, too, is fine. From the upper earth- and grass-covered plaza, there are superb views over the mountain ranges. Opposite the church is a small local **museum**. Excavations have revealed many Inca walls, terraces and various other features.

The local produce **market** on Sunday morning is fascinating and very colourful, and best before the tour groups arrive. It's on your left as you come into town. There's also a small handicraft market, also on Sunday, up by the church. Chinchero attracts few tourists, except on Sunday. On the main road, a new Municipio and park were built in 2010. The town celebrates the **Day of the Virgin**, on 8 September. ▶▶ *For Festivals, see page 157.*

Chinchero to Huayllabamba → *3-4 hrs.*
There is a scenic path from Chinchero to Huayllabamba, the village on the opposite side of the Río Urubamba from the main road, between Yucay and Calca (see page 136). The hike is

quite beautiful, with fine views of the peaks of the Urubamba Range. The trail starts on the hill across the valley from the Chinchero ruins and leads down to the village of Urquillos. From here it's a short distance to Huayllabamba. The end of the hike is about 10 km before the town of Urubamba. You can either go on to Urubamba or back to Cuzco by looking for transport on the main road. Another trail follows the old Chinchero–Urubamba dirt road, to the left of the new paved road. Ask the locals if you are not sure. It runs over the pampa, with a good view of Chinchero, then drops down to the Urubamba Valley.

An alternative hike from Chinchero follows the spectacular Maras–Moray–Pichingoto salt mines route (see below). This brings you to the main Urubamba valley road, 10-12 km beyond the town of Urubamba. You could also take the more direct main road from Chinchero to Urubamba, with occasional short cuts, but this route is a lot less interesting.

Salineras
Five kilometres west of Urubamba is the village of **Tarabamba**, where a bridge crosses the Río Urubamba. If you turn right after crossing the bridge you'll come to **Pichingoto**, a tumble-down village built under an overhanging cliff. Also, just over the bridge and before the town, to the left of a small walled cemetery, is a salt stream. Follow the footpath beside the stream and you'll come to **Salinas**, a small village below which are a mass of terraced pre-Inca *salineras* (**salt pans**) ① *entry US$1.80, payable at whichever point you enter, top or bottom* , still in production after thousands of years. There are 3200 pools and 480 cooperative members. They only work the pans from May to October, during the dry season. These are now a fixture on the tourist circuit and can become congested with buses.

It's a 45-minute walk from Urubamba to the salt pans. The climb up from the bridge, on the right side of the valley, is fairly steep but easy, with great views of Nevado Chicón. The path passes by the cascade of rectangular salt pans, taking up to 1½ hours to the top. Take water as it can be very hot and dry here. From the summit of the cliff above the *salineras*, walk to **Maras**, about 45 minutes. Focus on the white, **colonial church** ① *US$1.50*, and visit it when you get there; it has been beautifully renovated. After Maras, there is a blue sign with two options for Moray, 9 km by the road, or 5 km through the fields, signed by blue arrows.

Moray
① *9 km west of Maras by road. Entry with the BTC visitor ticket (see box, page 65), or US$3.60; allow an hour for a full visit. A paved road leads from the main Chinchero-Urubamba road to Maras, from where an unpaved road in good condition leads to Moray. If you cannot get transport to Maras from Urubamba, take any combi between Urubamba and Chinchero, get out at the junction for Maras and walk from there.* ▸▸ *For further details, see Transport, page 159.*
This remote but beautiful site lies near the little town of **Maras** and is well worth a visit. There are three 'colosseums', used by the Incas, according to some theories, as a sort of open-air crop nursery, known locally as the laboratory of the Incas. The great depressions do not contain ruined buildings, but are lined with fine terracing. Each level is said to have its own microclimate. Moray is a very atmospheric place, which, many people claim, has mystical powers. The scenery around here is absolutely stunning. As you leave Maras, look back to the village with its church, tiled roofs and adobe walls framed by snowy mountains. All around are fields of wheat and other crops, such as *kiwicha*, whose tall, thin, violet-coloured flowers produce a protein-rich grain. At harvest-time the whole area turns from rich green to every shade of gold and

brown imaginable. To the northwest stands the majestic white peak of La Verónica. The light is wonderful in the late afternoon, but for photography it's best to arrive in the morning. The road eventually arrives at the guardian's hut, but there is little indication of the scale of the colosseums until you reach the rim.

The most interesting ways to get to Moray are on foot from Urubamba via the *salineras* (see above), or a day-long cycle trip, starting in Chinchero (see above) and ending at the foot of the *salineras* (a challenging descent; go with a specialist agency or guide). To return from Moray to the main road takes about three hours: 1½ hours to Maras, 45 minutes to the *salineras* and 45 minutes down to the road (much quicker than going up!). Hitching back to Urubamba is quite easy, but take care not to be stranded. One option is to hire a taxi which will take you to Moray, wait an hour, then take you to the Salineras, from where you can walk down to rejoin the main road between Urubamba and Ollantaytambo, US$20.

Cycling route: Chinchero to Urubamba → *1 day; 40 km.*
This day trip is one of the best you can do from Cuzco, taking in fabulous mountain scenery, mysterious archaeology (Moray), and giving an insight into the living culture of the Andes. You pass rich farmlands and finally take on a wild descent past the fascinating *salineras* (salt pans) beneath the picturesque town of Maras. All in all this biking odyssey covers around 40 km on two wheels, ranging from mellow peddles on relatively flat and well-surfaced roads to the truly demanding descent on narrow single track past the *salineras* themselves.

Don't underestimate this trip: you should be in relatively good shape and, remember, if you're not sure of a section, getting off and pushing is better than an impromptu flying lesson! This is a long day, so make sure you bring food and plenty of water. A good biking helmet, sunblock, sunglasses and a warm fleece are also advised. The IGN 1:100,000 topographic sheet covering the Urubamba area (available through the SAE in Cuzco) is of relatively little use here, as information on roads and tracks is seriously outdated. This fact, combined with difficulties of navigating over the relatively featureless agricultural landscape at the start of the ride, means that we recommend using a professional guide or specialist agency for this trip.

Guides with local knowledge will also find exciting off-road sections for ambitious clients. Many agencies hire private transport to get you and the bikes to Chinchero and back to Cuzco. If you're on a tight budget it's quite possible to use public buses, loading the bikes onto the roof rack; most guides and agencies won't have a problem with this, but watch those bikes carefully. ⏭ *For further details, see Activities and tours, page 118.*

The day's adventure usually starts at Chinchero, from where you head west on a good track, across expansive open farming country to the north of Laguna Huaypo. This is mostly easy riding over gently undulating land, with occasional diversions on single track. Views on clear days are spectacular, with the entire Cordillera Urubamba from Chicón/Pico San Juan to the impressive ice pyramid of Verónica laid out before you. Prior to arriving at Moray you join the main surfaced road. Moray is a good lunch spot, with drinks and snacks often available.

Heading out of Moray you ride east, taking in some good off-road sections before reaching the historic colonial town of Maras. From here it's all downhill as you race north towards the Sacred Valley. The day's most challenging riding is ahead! Have US$1.80 ready to gain entry to the *salineras* road. The trail is narrow, steep, with precipitous drops to the right, and has some treacherously sharp turns, so be careful; it's exciting, awesome fun though! The terraced salt pans, worked as they have been for centuries, are a great backdrop to a true biking adventure.

Reaching the Sacred Valley, cross the bridge to the north side of the Río Urubamba and on to the highway. Turn right for Urubamba 5 km away, and watch out for crazy drivers.

Ollantaytambo and around → *For listings, see pages 152-160. Colour map 2, A2.*
Phone code: 084. Altitude: 2800 m.

A trip to Ollantaytambo is a journey into the past, to a world governed by a concept of time very different to the one which holds sway nowadays. Today, the descendants of the people who founded Ollantaytambo continue to live there, watched over still by the sacred mountains of Verónica and Alankoma. They work the land as they have always done, with the same patience and skill that their ancestors employed to shape and then move the huge blocks of stone with which they built both their homes and the temples in which they worshipped. The attractive little town at the foot of some spectacular Inca ruins and terraces, is built directly on top of the original Inca town, or Llacta. Tourist facilities are growing now that most Machu Picchu trains terminate here.

Ins and outs
Getting there Ollantaytambo can be reached by bus from Cuzco, Urubamba and Chinchero. It is also one of the principal stations for catching the train to Machu Picchu; see page 166 for details. ▸▸ *For further details, see Transport, page 159.*

Getting around Ollantaytambo is small enough to walk around. The station is 15 minutes downhill from the plaza. There are *hostales*, restaurants and shops everywhere, including in the original part of town.

Tourist information The **Municipalidad** on the Plaza de Armas has a tourist office with leaflets and booklet (US$1.80), www.muniollantaytambo.gob.pe.

History
The Tambo Valley, as the Spanish chroniclers called it, is a fertile stretch of land sown with fields of maize which hug the banks of the Río Urubamba (Vilcanota) from Ollantaytambo to Machu Picchu. Long before the arrival of the Incas, the valley was inhabited by the Ayarmaca, who had migrated from Lake Titicaca, far to the southeast. On their long journey, this race of farmers followed the course of the Vilcanota, abandoning the harsh *altiplano* in search of a better climate for their agricultural activities. The Ayarmacas, known in the Spanish chronicles as Tampus, came from the same ethnic stock as the Incas of Cuzco, and maintained with them many cultural, linguistic and family ties which would ensure them, at least for a while, a degree of regional autonomy during the period of Inca imperial expansion. When Inca Pachacútec did begin to take control of neighbouring areas (see History, page 308), one of his first conquests was the Tambo Valley. The chronicles tell of two *curacas* (local chieftains), Paucar Ancho and Tokori Tupa, who led the resistance against the Inca, only to be defeated in the mid-15th century. Pachacútec sacked their town, subjugated its people and made their lands his royal estate.

On the death of Pachacútec in 1471, his properties were passed to the members of his *panaca* (royal household), the Hatun Ayllu (Great Clan). This was the Inca's extended family and formed the social, political and religious elite from whose ranks the new Inca would emerge. The Hatun Ayllu set about converting Ollantaytambo into a great agricultural complex by extending its terraces beyond the town. To reclaim still more land for cultivation, they straightened a 3-km stretch of the river, as well as building canals and irrigation channels to bring fresh water from the area's snow-capped peaks and highland lakes. They ordered the construction of *qolqas* (barns) to store the harvest, as well as establishing checkpoints to control access to the centre known today as Ollantaytambo. To link Ollantaytambo to the rest of their empire via the Royal Inca Highway (*Capac Ñan*), the Incas built a tremendous suspension bridge across the river. Still standing after more than five centuries, the single central buttress of that ancient bridge now supports a modern metal structure.

When Manco Inca decided to rebel against the Spaniards in 1536, he fell back to Ollantaytambo from Calca to stage one of the greatest acts of resistance to the *conquistadores*. Hernando Pizarro led his troops to the foot of the Inca's stronghold, which Hernando's brother Pedro later described as "so well fortified that it was a thing of horror". Under fierce fire, Pizarro's men failed to capture Manco and retreated to Cuzco, but Manco could not press home any advantage. The Inca siege of the Spaniards in Cuzco turned into stalemate and Manco was unable to capitalize on the arrival of Diego de Almagro's army from Chile to threaten the Pizarro brothers' hold on Cuzco. In

Ollantaytambo

To Patacancha & Lares

To Pinkullana

Calle de las Rosas

Kiswar Calle

Baño de la Ñusta

Chachacomayoc

Ruins

Museo Catcco

Río Patacancha

Orcobamba

Plaza Araccama

Entrance

Awamaki shop

Ventiderio

Plaza de Armas

Calle Principal

Wall of 100 Niches

Centro de Salud

Municipalidad

Minibuses to Urubamba & Cuzco

La Convención

KB Tours

Bio Museo

To Machu Picchu & Quillabamba

Aló K'antuyoc taxis & hostel

To Urubamba

To Paroy

Perú Rail & Inca Rail

N

500 metres
500 yards

1537, feeling vulnerable to further attacks, Manco left Ollantaytambo for Vilcabamba (see box, page 199).

It is easy to see, even today, how daunting an assault on the Inca's defences must have seemed to Pizarro. Great walled terraces of fine masonry climb the hillside, at the top of which is an unassailable sanctuary. The entire construction is superb, including the curving terraces, which follow the contours of the rocks overlooking the Urubamba. It was these terraces which were successfully defended by Manco Inca's warriors. Manco built the defensive wall above the site and another wall closing the Yucay Valley against attack from Cuzco. These are still visible on either side of the valley. Walking up the terraces is taxing enough, but imagine how impossible it must have been for armed *conquistadores* trying to scale the hill under a hail of missiles.

The Fortress

ⓘ *Daily 0700-1730; if possible, arrive very early, 0700, before the crowds, and avoid Sun afternoons, when tour groups from Pisac descend in their hundreds. Entry by BTC visitor ticket (see box, page 65), which can be bought at the site; guides at the entrance. Allow 2-3 hrs to explore the ruins fully.*

The ruins, known as the 'Fortress', were, in fact, a religious complex, with temples dedicated to the many divinities which comprised the Inca pantheon. The gods the Incas worshipped represented the forces of nature, and were seen, therefore, to control the agricultural life of the community. At the Fortress, we find the Temple of Viracocha, the creator god, as well as those devoted to the sun, water, earth and lightning. The magnificent terraces which lead up to the temple site were almost certainly used by astronomer-priests for the cultivation of corn for ceremonial purposes; the maize they grew there would mark the seasons for planting and harvesting for the rest of the community.

When you visit Ollantaytambo you will be confronted by a series of 16 massive stepped terraces of the very finest stonework, after crossing the great high-walled trapezoidal esplanade known as *Mañariki*. Beyond these imposing terraces lies the so-called Temple of Ten Niches, a funeral chamber once dedicated to the worship of the Pachacútec *panaca* (royal household). Immediately above this is the site popularly known as the Temple of the Sun, although it is not known for certain whether it was ever intended for that purpose. The remains of this temple consist of six monolithic upright blocks of rose-coloured rhyolite, forming a wall which, in common with other Inca temples, runs from east to west. A narrow, vertical course, like stone beading, separates the giant monoliths, on which traces of relief carving can be seen. Typical Andean motifs such as the *chakana* (Andean cross) are just visible, as well as other zoomorphic figures. These designs were defaced by the Spanish shortly after the conquest, as part of a systematic campaign by the victors physically to erase the indigenous religion. They have also suffered from erosion, however; sketches by the American traveller Ephrain George Squier, who visited Ollantaytambo in the 1870s, show that the figures were much more complete then. Below the Temple of the Sun, the dark grey stone is embellished today with bright orange lichen. Note how most of the stones have one or two protrusions at the bottom edge, a feature you will not see in Cuzco or Pisac.

You can either descend by the route you came up, or follow the terracing round to the left (as you face the town) and work your way down to the Valley of the Patacancha. On this route there are more Inca ruins in the small area between the town and the temple fortress, behind the church. Most impressive is the **Baño de la Ñusta** (Bath of the Princess), a grey granite rock, about waist high, beneath which is the bath itself. It is delicately finished with a

The Inn of Origin

One of the Incas' three creation stories is the *Inn of Origin*. This legend tells of Pacaritambo (the Inn, or House of Origin), which is also associated with another name, Tambotocco (the Place of the Hole). Like the *Children of the Sun* story, (see page 309), there are variations on the basic theme, which relates that four brothers and four sisters (three of each in some versions) emerged from the central cave of three in a cliff. The names of the brothers and sisters vary, but usually the men were called Ayar Cachi, Ayar Manco, Ayar Uchu and Ayar Sauca, and the women Mama Huaco, Mama Ocllo, Mama Coya and Mama Rahua. The brothers and sisters set out in search of good land on which to settle and on the way fell out with Ayar Cachi, who was much stronger, more violent and more arrogant than the others. They lured him back to the cave and walled him up inside before recommencing their journey. Soon, though, Ayar Cachi miraculously reappeared, telling them to move on to the valley of Cuzco and found the city. He then went to the mountain of Huanacauri where his spirit remained, becoming a place of veneration for the Incas. In return for their worship of him on the mountain, Ayar Cachi would intercede with the gods on their behalf to ensure prosperity and success in war. Ayar Manco then proceeded with his sisters to Cuzco, where, according to some versions, he built Qoricancha as his first house and

quickly earned the respect of the local people. A bloody twist to this story recounts how one of the sisters, on the lookout for the ideal land, came to Cuzco and petrified the inhabitants by killing one of them, ripping out his lungs and inflating them as she entered the village.

This myth has several elements in common with the *Children of the Sun*: siblings teaching the unenlightened people and founding Cuzco and the Inca dynasty; the discovery of fertile land on which to base the kingdom; the role of Huanacauri Mountain. Whereas the *Children of the Sun* borrows from the Lake Titicaca creation myth, the *Inn of Origin* borrows from another major American tradition; ancestors, especially brothers, coming out of rocks or the ground.

For the sake of completeness, the third main creation story concerns a shining mantle, the brightness of which as it reflected the sun's rays so dazzled the people that the wearer deceived them into believing that he descended from the Sun. Some versions say that Ayar Manco was the instigator of this trickery after he and his brothers emerged from Pacaritambo. He used sheets of silver strapped to his body to flash in the sun as he strode along a hilltop. An alternative version says that it was Sinchi Roca, Manco's successor, who was dressed in this magnificent robe by his mother. She thus led the people to believe that the boy was a ruler sent by the Sun.

three-dimensional *chakana* motif. The water falls over the relief arch into the pool, which was probably used for the worship of water in the form of ritual bathing. Some 200 m behind the Baño de la Ñusta along the face of the mountain are some small ruins known as **Inca Misanca**, believed to have been a small temple or observatory. A series of steps, seats and niches have been carved out of the cliff. There is a complete irrigation system, including a canal some 15 cm deep cut out of the sheer rock face at shoulder level.

Recently a two-dimensional '**pyramid**' has been identified on the west side of the main ruins of Ollantaytambo. Its discoverers, Fernando and Edgar Elorietta, claim it is the real

Pacaritambo, from where the four original Inca brothers emerged to found their empire (see box, page 147). Whether or not this is the case, it is still a first-class piece of engineering with great terraced fields and a fine 750-m wall creating the optical illusion of a pyramid. The wall is aligned with the sun's rays at the winter solstice, on 21 June. People gather at midwinter dawn to watch this event.

The mysterious 'pyramid', which covers 50-60 ha, can best be seen from the other side of the river. This is a pleasant, easy one-hour walk west from the Puente Inca, just outside the town. You'll also be rewarded with great views of the Sacred Valley and the river, with the snowy peaks of the Verónica massif as a backdrop.

The town

Entering Ollantaytambo from Urubamba, the road is built along the long **Wall of 100 Niches**. Note the inclination of the wall towards the road. Since it was the Incas' practice to build with the walls leaning towards the interiors of the buildings, it has been deduced that the road, much narrower then, was built inside a succession of buildings. The road leads into the Plaza de Armas (under repair in 2010). The road from the northwest corner of the plaza looks up to the Inca temple, but to get there you have to cross the bridge over the river and go down to the colonial church of Santiago Apóstol with its *recinto* (enclosure). The original colonial bridge was washed away in 2010; a temporary bridge spans the river. Beyond is a grand plaza, Araccama, full of handicraft stalls and soft drinks sellers, and the entrance to the archaeological site.

The original Inca town is behind the north side of the Plaza de Armas. The *canchas* (blocks of houses) are almost entirely intact and can be clearly seen. It's an impressive sight and it is worth wandering through the narrow alleys and streets to get a glimpse of the interiors of the blocks. All the streets have canals running down them which used to be used in the houses. Unlike modern cities, *llaqtas* (Inca towns) were not designed to house large populations. Inca society was essentially agrarian and, among the common people, almost everyone worked and lived on the land. The towns and cities that the Incas did build were meant to serve as residential areas for the state's administrative and religious elite.

Throughout the Inca Empire of Tawantinsuyo, the *llaqtas* were divided into two zones, along blood lines, between the two principal *ayllus* (clans), of Hanan and Urin. In Ollantaytambo, the Urin occupied the area which corresponds to the present-day village. Called *Qosqo Ayllu*, it was both an administrative centre and the home of the Pachacútec *panaca*. The streets were laid out in a simple grid pattern, with the whole forming the Inca trapezoid (see page 313). These streets, whose corners are marked with huge stone blocks, surround *canchas* (communal enclosures which house many families). Each *cancha* occupies half a block, with just one entrance on those streets which run parallel to the Río Patacancha. It is clear, from the elaborate double-jamb porticos which form their entrances, that these *canchas* were built for members of the Incas' social and religious elite. The Inca nobility did not work on the land: their *yanaconas* (servants) did it for them, and the remains of the homes of this servant class, built from much simpler materials, have been found in the northern part of the town.

At the junction of K'uychipunku and Calle La Convención is the **Bio Museo** ① *T084-204181, T084-984 962607 (mob), www.biomuseo.org, Tue-Sun 0930-2030, US$1.80 requested as a donation*, created by Maribel Torres León. It houses a comprehensive collection of native herbs, potatoes and grains. Working with a network of communities (**Inkaq Kusi Kausaynin**, www.tourrural.net) to preserve local foods and traditions, the museum not only shows the plants but offers essential oils, teas, etc for sale and demonstrates how plants are used as dyes. There are weaving, sculpture and medicinal workshops three days a week. Visitors can learn how to make *chicha*, grind and brew coffee in a traditional kitchen and, in the evening, there are storytelling sessions with music (at 1930, one hour, US$3.60).

El Museo CATCCO (Centro Andino de Tecnología Tradicional y Cultural de las Comunidades de Ollantaytambo) ⓘ *Casa Horno, Patacalle, 1 block from plaza, T084-204024, open intermittently in 2010,* was started with help from the British Embassy and run by Sr Joaquín Randall. It houses a fine ethnographical collection. Outside the museum, Catcco runs non-profit making cultural programmes, temporary exhibitions, concerts, lectures and guided walks to ruins.

An Ollantaytambo-based, non-profit organization, **Awamaki** ⓘ *Urb Pillcohuasi D-4, shop just before Plaza Araccama, T084-204149, www.awamaki.org,* runs trips to communities in the **Patacancha Valley** to visit the weavers. Trips include transport, a weaving demonstration and the chance to buy items direct from the makers. This is an initiative to revitalise the weaving tradition in the area and empower the women weavers. Weavings are also sold in the shop, where you can obtain all information and ask about volunteering opportunities.

Inca quarries at Cachiccata

It takes about a day to walk to the Inca quarries on the opposite side of the river and return to Ollantaytambo. The stone quarries of Cachiccata are located on the lands of the hacienda of the same name, some 9 km from Ollantaytambo. There are three quarries at the site: **Molle Puqro**, which the Incas were gradually abandoning at the time of the conquest; **Sirkusirkuyoc** and the smaller **Cachiccata**, which both seem to have been fully operational. The stone at Cachiccata, rose-coloured rhyolite, is just one of many types of stone used in the construction of Ollantaytambo, and it is still not known where the others came from. It would seem that all the quarries were abandoned when Manco Inca retreated from Ollantaytambo after confronting Hernando Pizarro's cavalry there in 1537.

Standing to the left of the six monolithic blocks which form the so-called Temple of the Sun at Ollantaytambo, you can see, looking west-southwest across the valley, the quarries of Cachiccata, below a mountain called Yana Urco. From here, you can appreciate the Herculean nature of the task that the builders of Ollantaytambo's magnificent temples set themselves.

Several generations of stonemasons and labourers must have worked in their thousands to quarry the huge blocks that the Incas used in the construction of the Temple of the Sun and the Royal House of the Sun. Once extracted, the stones would have been roughly shaped before being transported to the building site. Possibly using rollers, or more probably using the simple brute force of the thousands of men that the Incas' highly organized society would have been able to dedicate to the task, the blocks were then dragged for more than 6 km across open country.

The Incas would only have been able to cross the Río Urubamba in winter, when its waters are at their lowest ebb, and even then they could probably only have done so by diverting the river's course. It is thought that they dug two channels; the stones would then have been dragged across the dry left-hand channel while the river was being diverted through the right-hand one. This right-hand channel would then be drained in its turn to allow the stones to continue their painstaking progress.

The next task was to raise the rhyolite blocks from the valley floor up to the site known as the Fortress and, to accomplish this, the Incas' engineers built a great ramp. Looking down from the Temple of the Sun, to the left of the six monoliths, the remains of this ramp can still be seen, and they are even more clearly visible when you look up at the ruins from the valley floor. It is difficult to appreciate from today's highly mechanized perspective just how hard the Incas laboured to build Ollantaytambo, employing as they did a patience and skill born of a concept of time very different to our own. The stones were found near the summit of a mountain on the other side of the river valley after a prolonged search. They then had to be quarried, hewn into a rough shape, and hauled across the valley floor and up to the temple. Once there, they were sculpted by the master masons to fit together perfectly, to the design of an architect, or architects, of consummate skill.

Between the ruins and the quarries of Cachiccata, more than 50 enormous stones that never reached their destination lie abandoned. The inhabitants of the area call them **Las Piedras Cansadas** (the tired stones). It is still not known whether work on the temples ceased when the Spanish arrived, or whether it stopped during the civil war between Atahualpa and Huascar. The thousands of workers who were involved in the construction of Ollantaytambo, over a period of generations, almost certainly worked under the *mit'a* system (see page 310). For several months of each year they would have to leave their work to tend their crops and, in times of war, construction would have been abandoned and the workers integrated into the enormous conscripted armies upon which the Inca state depended. Another suggestion is that Colla workers from Lake Titicaca were employed in the construction of the site. This conclusion has been drawn from the similarities between the monoliths facing the central platform and the Tiahuanaco remains. According to this theory, the Colla are believed to have deserted halfway through the work, leaving behind all the unfinished blocks visible today. While most experts agree that the work on Ollantaytambo was begun under Pachacútec, it will probably never be known for certain exactly when Cachiccata's great stones first began to tire.

Pinkuylluna

Pinkuylluna Hill, on the western edge of Ollantaytambo, is home to the Sacred Valley's most impressive collection of *qolqas* (storehouses), structures which have often (and erroneously) been called prisons by local guides. The reason why these granaries were built so high up on the hillside is given by the 17th-century Spanish chronicler Bernabé Cobo: "[the Incas] built their storehouses outside their towns, in the high places that were fresh and well-ventilated ...". It is impossible to know with any certainty what kinds of produce were stored at Pinkuylluna, but the main harvest was certainly maize, which was probably stored alongside other crops. When viewed from the bridge in front of the ruins, a gigantic image, known locally as the Tunupa, can be seen on the hillside; it is thought by many observers to be a carved likeness of the Inca creator god, Viracocha.

Pinkuylluna can be climbed with no mountaineering experience, although there are some difficult stretches – allow two or three hours going up. The path is difficult to make out, so it's best not to go on your own. Walk up the valley to the left of the mountain, which is very beautiful and impressive, with Inca terraces after 4 km.

Pumamarca

Hidden away in the hills beyond the historic town, Pumamarca lies about two hours on foot from Ollantaytambo through fertile countryside sculpted long ago into a series of agricultural terraces which to this day are sown with corn and *kiwicha*. Pumamarca is a small, well-preserved Inca citadel 7 km north of, and 800 m above, Ollantaytambo. It lies at the confluence of the Río Patacancha and its tributary, the Yuracmayo (or White River). From there it dominates a strategic point, commanding a privileged view of both valleys, and would once have controlled access to Ollantaytambo from that direction, as well as guarding the canal which bears its name.

The ruins' high surrounding wall with its numerous zigzags suggests that the site was a fortress, although (as at Ollantaytambo) all the *qolqas* (storehouses) were built outside the main complex. Nobody knows for sure exactly when this citadel was built. Some researchers believe that it may have been another checkpoint, designed to limit access to Ollantaytambo from Antisuyo, the eastern *suyo* (quarter) of the Inca Empire. But the impressive nature of Pumamarca, built in classic Inca style, leads many scholars to conclude that it may have been one of the first Inca settlements in the area, and not just a simple outpost of Ollantaytambo.

The path to Pumamarca passes through the village of Munaypata and follows the Río Patacancha. At Pallata, 6 km from Ollantaytambo and 30 minutes before Pumamarca, the Miranda family will look after bicycles and other gear. They live in the first house in the village; the path from the road to the footbridge over the river passes their front door. Up the same valley are the indigenous villages of Marcacocha, Huilloc and Patacancha.

Cusichaca Valley

A major excavation project has been carried out since 1977 under the direction of Ann Kendall in the Cusichaca Valley, 26 km from Ollantaytambo, at the intersection of the Inca route (see www.cusichaca.org). Only 9 km of this road are passable by ordinary car. The Inca fort, **Huillca Raccay**, was excavated in 1978-1980, and work is now concentrated on **Llactapata**, a site of domestic buildings. Ann Kendall is now working in the Patacancha Valley northeast of Ollantaytambo. Excavations are being carried out in parallel with the restoration of Inca canals to bring fresh clean water to the settlements in the valley.

For Sleeping and Eating price codes and other relevant information, see pages 30-36.

● Sleeping

Pisac p132, map p133

A Royal Inka Pisac, Carretera Ruinas Km 1.5, T084-267236, www.royalinkahotel.com/ hpisac.html. In the same chain as the **Royal Inkas I** and **II** in Cuzco, this hotel can be reached by the hotels' own bus service. It is a short distance out of town, on the road that goes up to the ruins, a taxi ride after dark. Price includes taxes and breakfast. Camping is available for US$5 per person. A guide for the ruins can be provided. The rooms are comfortable, in a number of blocks in the grounds of a converted hacienda. There is an olympic-sized pool (day use US$3.50), sauna and jacuzzi (guest use only), tennis court, horse riding and bicycle rental. The restaurant is good and there is a bar. The hotel is popular with day-trippers from Cuzco. Staff are very helpful and accommodating.

B Paz y Luz, T084-203204, www.pazyluz peru.com. 10-15 mins' walk from Pisac Plaza, close to the river. American expat Diane Dunn owns this hotel with a pleasant garden, nicely designed rooms, all with private bath and breakfast included in the price. Good place to chill and admire the rural surroundings and impressive mountain landscapes that rise dramatically above Pisac. Diane also offers healing from many traditions (including Andean), sacred tours, workshops and gatherings. Recommended.

B Pisac Inn, at the corner of Pardo on the plaza, T084-203062, www.pisacinn.com. Bright and charming local decor and a pleasant atmosphere, clean and friendly, all rooms with private bath and hot water, around a flower-filled patio. Massage can be arranged, laundry service. Good breakfast, afternoon tea. See restaurant, **Cuchara de Palo**, below, also has a sidewalk café. The **Inn**

supports the Kusi Kawsay school initiative, www.kusikawsay.org.

C Hostal Varayoc, Mariscal Castilla 380, T084-223638, luzpaz3@hotmail.com. Renovated hotel around a colonial courtyard with working bread oven. Decor is smart and bathrooms are modern.

F Residencial Beho, Intihuatana 642, 50 m up the hill from the plaza, T/F084-203001. Ask for a room in the main building. They serve a good breakfast for US$1. The *hostal* has a shop selling local handicrafts including masks. The owner's son will act as a guide to the ruins at the weekend.

Pisac to Urubamba p134

LL Aranwa, between Calca and Urubamba (office Av Manuel Olguin 901, Monterrico-Surco, Lima 33, T01-434 1452), www.aranwa hotels.com. First of a new chain of spa hotels in Peru, 5-star, luxury accommodation with a full range of facilities and treatments at the Hacienda Yaravilca near Huayllabamba.

L-AL Sonesta Posadas del Inca, Plaza Manco II de Yucay 123, Yucay, T084-201107, www.sonesta.com. A converted 300-year-old monastery is now a hotel that is like a little village with plazas, lovely gardens, a chapel and 69 comfortable, heated rooms. The price includes buffet breakfast, but not taxes. **Inkafe** restaurant is open to all, serving Peruvian, fusion and traditional cuisine with a US$15 buffet. Lots of activities can be arranged – canoeing, horse riding, mountain biking, etc. There is a conference centre. Highly recommended. Also have hotels in Lima, Cuzco, Puno and Arequipa.

L-AL Urubamba Villas, in the hamlet of Higuspurco, between Urubamba and Yukay, T01-221 6691, www.urubamba-villas.com. Price is per person in 1 of 2 self-contained villas in spacious gardens, fully equipped, breakfast and dinner included, lunch optional, courtesy bottle of wine. Has a bar, access to excursions and activities with car and driver available.

AL La Casona de Yucay, Plaza Manco II 104, Yucay, T084-201116, www.hotelcasona yucay.com. Colonial house where Simón Bolívar stayed during his liberation campaign in 1824. The price includes taxes and breakfast. The rooms have heating and, outside, there are 2 patios and gardens. **Don Manuel** restaurant is good, also has bar. Helpful staff.

B The Green House, Km 60.2 Huarán, T084-984 770130 (mob), www.thegreenhouse peru.com. A charming retreat, only 4 rooms (1 with 4 beds), plenty of common areas with a comfy lounge with fireplace and dining room, beautiful garden. No TV in rooms, but there are DVDs to watch, restricted internet and no Wi-Fi, quiet area for meditation, small kitchen for guests' use. Dinner is available for US$13. Owners Gabriel and Bryan can provide information about independent walks and day trips in the area. Warmly recommended.

C Hostal Y'Llary, Plaza Manco II 107, Yucay, T084-201112, www.hostalyllary.com. A hostal in a remodelled building fronting the plaza, with gardens. Price includes bathroom and breakfast, nice garden.

Valle de Lares *p136, map p137*

L-AL Urubamba Boutique Lodge, Huarán, Calca, T084-251563, www.urubamba boutiquelodge.com, or www.pebhl.com. Brand new hotel in the same group as the Casa San Blas in the city. All rooms with bath and balconies, **Mayu Cocina Fuzion** restaurant, travel and medical assistance.

Urubamba and around *p141*

LL Río Sagrado (Orient Express), Km 76 Carretera Cuzco–Ollantaytambo, T084-201631, www.riosagrado.com. 4 km from Urubamba, set in beautiful gardens overlooking the river with views of surrounding mountains. Rooms and villas, Mayu Wilka spa, restaurant and bar, offfers various packages including *Hiram Bingham* train to Machu Picchu.

LL Sol y Luna, west of town, T084-201620, www.hotelsolyluna.com. Attractive bungalows and brand-new suites set off the main road in lovely gardens, pool, excellent buffet in restaurant, has an on-site spa and a varied wine cellar (wine tasting sessions can be arranged). French/Swiss-owned. Also arranges adventure and cultural activities and traditional tours.

LL Tambo del Inka, Av Ferrocarril s/n, T084-581777, www.luxurycollection.com/vallesagrado. A Luxury Collection resort and spa on the edge of town, in gardens by the river. Completely remodelled with a variety of rooms and suites, fitness centre, swimming pools, **Hawa** restaurant, bar, business facilities and lots of activities arranged.

LL-AL Casa Andina Private Collection Sacred Valley, 5º paradero, Yanahuara, between Urubamba and Ollantaytambo, T084-984 765501 (mob), www.casa-andina.com. In its own 3-ha estate, with all the facilities associated with this chain, plus a gym, organic garden and restaurant with Novo Andino cuisine. Adventure activities can be arranged here. It also has a spa offering a range of massages and treatments and a planetarium and observatory, showing the Inca view of the night sky.

L K'uychi Rumi, Km 73.5 on the road to Ollantaytambo, 3 km from town, T084-201169, www.urubamba.com. 6 cottages for rent with 2 bedrooms, fully equipped, fireplace, terrace and balcony, surrounded by gardens. Price is for 1-2 people, each house can accommodate 6. Book in advance.

L San Agustín Monasterio de la Recoleta, Jr Recoleta s/n, T084-201004, www.hoteles sanagustin.com.pe. In a converted monastery (the earliest in Cuzco) east of town, this hotel has suites and standard rooms with heating and all facilities, **San Isidro** restaurant. From the main road take Jr Hortencia Lorena from the Primax service station, otherwise 9 de Noviembre and C Recoleta from town centre.

A San Agustín Urubamba, Carretera Cuzco–Pisac Km 69, T084-201444, www.hotelessan agustin.com.pe. An upgraded hotel in a lovely setting just out of Urubamba, with suites and standard rooms, pool, sauna, massage and jacuzzi, **Naranjachayoc's** restaurant and bar.

B Posada Las Tres Marías, Zavala 307, T084-201006, www.posadatresmarias.com. A little way from the centre, quiet. Comfortable rooms with hot water and no TV, lovely garden and shady terrace, breakfast included (can be early), laundry service, welcoming hosts. Recommended.

D Hospedaje Los Jardines, Jr Convención 459, T084-201331, www.hospedajelos jardines.blogspot.com. An attractive guesthouse with comfortable rooms with bath and hot water, non-smoking, delicious breakfast US$3.25 extra (vegans catered for), safe, lovely garden, laundry. Discounts for long stays. **Sacred Valley Mountain Bike Tours** also based here.

D pp Las Chullpas, 3 km west of town in the Pumahuanca Valley, T084-201568, www.uhupi.com/chullpas. Very peaceful, includes excellent breakfast, vegetarian meals, English and German spoken, Spanish classes, natural medicine, treks, horse riding, mountain biking, camping US$3 with hot shower. Mototaxi from town US$0.85, taxi (ask for Querocancha) US$2.

E Hostal Buganvilla, Jr Convención 280, T084-205102, T084-984 618900 (mob). Sizable rooms with bath, hot water, TV, breakfast on request, quiet, clean.

E Hostal Indigo, Jr Roca Fuerte 1, T084-509716, www.cusco-peru.de. On the edge of town on the road to Yucay, modern hostal, with bath, hot water, breakfast, garden, family-run.

E Hostal Urubamba, Bolognesi 605, T084-201062. Basic but clean, pleasant rooms with bath and cold water, TV, cheaper without bath, no breakfast.

Chinchero *p141*

C La Casa de Barro, T084-306031 www.lacasadebarro.com. New modern hotel, price includes American breakfast, with bath, hot water, bar, restaurant, tours arranged.

Ollantaytambo and around
p144, map p145

Hospedajes and *hostales* are opening up all over town, including in the Inca town and on Av Ferrocarril (eg from the new **B Tunupa Lodge**, No 50, T084-204025, tunupalodgehtl@hotmail.com, to **Wayra's**, 50 m from the station, T084-204019, and **El Bosque**, T084-204148, with restaurant and internet, both **D**). There are other places to stay along the Calle de las Cien Ventanas/C Principal, leading into town. Closest to the centre is **Las Portadas**, T084-204008, hsjlasportadas05@yahoo.es.

AL Pakaritampu, C Ferrocarril s/n, T084-204020, www.pakaritampu.com. The price includes breakfast and taxes. This modern, 3-star hotel has 37 rooms with bath and views. It is owned by a former Peruvian women's volleyball star. There is a TV room, restaurant and bar, internet and Wi-Fi for guests, laundry, safe and room service, all set in beautiful gardens. Adventure sports and tours can be arranged. Buffet lunch and dinner are extra. Excellent quality and service.

A Hostal Sauce, C Ventiderio 248, T084-204044, www. hostalsauce.com.pe. Modern hotel in the centre. Smart, simple decor and views of the ruins from some rooms.

A Ñustayoc Mountain Lodge and Resort, 5 km west of Ollantaytambo, just before Chillca and the start of the Inca Trail, T01-275 0706 (Lima), www.nustayoclodge.com. Large and somewhat rambling lodge in a wonderful location with great views of the snowy Verónica massif and other peaks. There's a lovely flower-filled garden and grounds. Nicely decorated, spacious rooms, all with private bath. Price includes continental breakfast served in the large restaurant area.

A-B Apu Lodge, C Lari, T084-797162, www.apu lodge.com. On the edge of the old Inca town, great views of the ruins and surrounding mountains. Run by Scot Louise Norton and husband Arturo, good service, can help organize tours and treks. They work with **Leap Local** (www.leap local.org) guides project.

A-B El Albergue, within the railway station gates, T084-204014, www.elalbergue.com. Owned by North American artist Wendy Weeks, the *albergue* has 16 rooms with bath, Wi-Fi, some with safe. Price includes breakfast; also has **Café Mayu** on the station and a good open-plan restaurant and kitchen for lunch and dinner. The rooms are full of character and are set in buildings around a courtyard and lovely gardens. Great showers and a eucalyptus steam sauna. The whole place is charming, relaxing and homely. Books for sale and exchange, also handicrafts and **Matacuy** digestif. It's very convenient for the Machu Picchu train and a good place for information. Private transport can be arranged to nearby attractions, also mountain-biking, rafting and taxi transfers to the airport. Highly recommended.

C Hostal Iskay II, Patacalle s/n, T084-204004, www.hostaliskay.com. In the Inca town, overlooking the Fortress from the garden and terrace. Car access is difficult. Only 6 rooms, price includes buffet breakfast, bath, hot water, internet and Wi-Fi. There is a video and music room, free tea and coffee, use of kitchen. A pleasant place with good reports.

C Hostal K'uychipunku, K'uychipunku 6, T084-204175, www.kuychipunku.com. Very close to Plaza Araccama, rooms with bath and hot water, breakfast included, modern, some with view, courtyard, internet and Wi-Fi, new in 2009.

C Hostal Munay T'ika, Av Ferrocarril 118, T084-204111, www.munaytika.com. Price includes breakfast and bath. Dinner is served by arrangement. Sauna costs US$5 with prior notice. Also has a nice garden, internet and Wi-Fi. Recommended. Also owns the **Tawa Chaki** restaurant/pizzería on the corner of Plaza Araccama, with *menú turístico* and à la carte, indoors and garden dining.

C Sol Ollantay, C Ventiderio s/n by the bridge between the 2 plazas, T084-204130, www.sol-ollantay.com. Tastefully renovated in 2009 with new bathrooms, hot water. Price includes breakfast, no other, meals. Good views from most rooms.

C-D Don Ascencio B&B, Av Ferrocarril s/n, T084-204178, garitho@hotmail.com. New in 2010, with bath and breakfast, TV, heaters if needed. Beside it is **Orishas** bar/restaurant, ₩₩-₩, with Wi-Fi, serving the popular tourist selection (see below), but a bit more upmarket and with a good café.

C-D Las Orquídeas, at the top of Av Ferrocarril, T084-204032, www.hostallas orquideasollantaytambo.com. A good choice. Price includes breakfast, hot water, Wi-Fi, fairly small but nice rooms, flower-filled patio. May be used by tour groups.

C-E pp **Hostal KB Tambo**, C Ventiderio between the main plaza and the ruins, T084-204091, www.kbtambo.com. Spacious, comfortable rooms, suites, garden view or standard, hot water, Wi-Fi, flower-filled garden, very good restaurant (₩), breakfast extra. Reserve in advance. Also offers adventure tours.

F pp **Hostal Chaska Wasi**, C del Medio s/n, T084-204045, www.hostalchaskawasi. com. Cheaper with shared bath, with continental breakfast, rooms for up to 4 sharing. For a private room reserve in advance. A B&B snuggled away in the small alleys behind the plaza, bar and terrace, lunch and dinner on request, clean, simple, use of small kitchen, internet, laundry service. Owner Katy is very friendly.

F Hostal Ollanta, on the south side of the plaza, T084-204116. Basic and clean, but with a great location. All rooms with shared bath.

F pp **Hostal Tambo**, C Horno, north of the plaza, T084-773262 or T084-984 489094, paula1_79@hotmail.com. Cheaper for groups, breakfast extra. Once past the brown door you emerge into a garden full of fruit trees and flowers. Small, rooms for up to 3 people, basic, shared bath, hot water. Paula is very friendly.

Camping

Restaurant Huatucay, at the edge of the Inca town, between Patacalle and the road to Patacancha, has camping for US$3.60 per person. There are toilets, a minimarket and the restaurant serves typical food.

🍴 Eating

Pisac p132, map p133

¶¶¶-¶¶ Cuchara de Palo, in Pisac Inn, on the Plaza. "Gourmet Andean cuisine". Serves meals using fresh, local ingredients as well as pizza on Sun market day. It also has a bar with various styles of pisco sour, cocktail hour, charming atmosphere.
¶¶-¶ Miski Mijuna Wasi, on the Plaza de Armas, T084-203266. Serves very tasty local food, typical Novo Andino and international dishes. Also has a *pastelería*.
¶¶-¶ Mullu, Plaza de Armas 352 and Mcal Castilla 375, T084-208182. Tue-Sun 0900-1900. Café/restaurant related to the Mullu store in Cuzco, also has a gallery promoting local artists, www.mullu.com.pe.
¶ Doña Clorinda, on the plaza opposite the church. A very friendly place. It doesn't look very inviting but cooks tasty food, including vegetarian options.
¶ Valle Sagrado, Av Amazonas 116 (the main street where buses go towards Urubamba). Good quality, generous portions and a lunchtime buffet that includes vegetarian options. Go early before the tour groups arrive. **Valle Sagrado II** was not yet open at the time of writing.

Cafés

Bakery, Av Mcal Castilla 372, sells excellent cheese and onion *empanadas* for US$0.25, suitable for vegetarians, and good wholemeal bread. The oven is tremendous.
Blue Llama Café, corner of the plaza opposite **Pisac Inn**, T084-203135, www.bluellamacafe.com. A cute, colourful café with a huge range of teas, good coffee, breakfasts and daily menus.
Ulrike's Café, Plaza de Armas 828, T084-203195, ulrikescafe@terra.com.pe. This comfortable café is renowned for its apple crumble with ice cream, to say nothing of great coffee, smoothies and a wide range of international cuisine. Also serves a good value, 3-course daily *menú*. A good place to chill after a hard day exploring the market and ruins.

Calca and around p134

There are some basic restaurants around the plaza in Calca.

Urubamba and around p141

¶¶¶ Tunupa, Km 77, on left side of the road on the riverbank, in a renovated colonial hacienda (same ownership as **Tunupa** in Cuzco), zappa@terra.com.pe. Andino cuisine; buffet lunch 1200-1500. Dinner (1800-2030) is à la carte. Excellent food served indoors or outdoors, bar, lounge, library, chapel, gardens, stables and an alpaca-jewellery shop. Outstanding exhibition of pre-Columbian objects and colonial paintings. **Seminario**'s ceramics feature in the decor. People on valley tours are served a varied buffet including Novo.
¶¶¶-¶¶ El Huacatay, Arica 620, T084-201790, http://elhuacatay.com. Open Mon-Sat. A small restaurant with a reputation for fine, creative fusion cuisine (local, Mediterranean, Asian).
¶¶ El Fogón, Parque Pintacha, T084-201534. Traditional Peruvian food, large servings, nice atmosphere. Recommended.
¶¶ El Maizal, on the road before the bridge, T084-201454. Country-style restaurant with a good reputation, buffet service with a variety of typical Novo Andino dishes, plus international choices, beautiful gardens with native flowers and fruit trees. Recommended. They also have a hotel of the same name.
¶¶ Quinta los Geranios, on the main road before the bridge, T084-201043. Regional dishes, excellent lunch with more than enough food.
¶ La Chepita, Av 1 de Mayo, M6, in a small plaza. The place to go on Sun for regional food in the biggest portions you have ever seen. Get 1 plate between 2.
¶ Pizza Wasi, Av Mcal Castilla 857, T084-434751 for delivery. Good pizzas and pastas. Mulled wine served in a small restaurant with nice decor, also has eating upstairs. Clean, good value. Recommended. Has another branch on Plaza Araccama in Ollantaytambo.

Cafés

Café Plaza, Bolívar 440, on the plaza. Serves breakfasts, meals, desserts, teas and coffee and has a pottery shop next door.

Misky Sonq'o, Comercio 337. For coffee, breakfast, juices, burgers, toasties and snacks.

Ollantaytambo and around
p144, map p145

There are restaurants all over town offering *menú turístico*, pizzas, pastas, snacks, juices and hot drinks, just the stuff before boarding the train to Machu Picchu. Several can be found on the Plaza de Armas, others on Av Ferrocarril.

ᵀᵀᵀ-ᵀᵀ Panaka, Plaza de Armas corner of Chaupi Calle, T084-204047, www.panakagrill.com. More upmarket place for Peruvian dishes, *parrillas*, pizza and pasta. The bar has a wide range of drinks. Also has a daily *menú* for US$9.

ᵀᵀ Blue Puppy, C Horno at the plaza, T084-630464, www.cuzcodining.com. Restaurant and lounge in the same group as **Marcelo Batata** in Cuzco. Open for breakfast, lunch and dinner, serving Tex-Mex, local dishes, pizzas, soups, salads and desserts. Also has a bar, sports and DVDs on the screen, new in 2010.

ᵀᵀ El Chasqui, C Ventiderio y Av Ferrocarril, T084-204143. Peruvian dishes and the popular fare mentioned above. 3 eating areas, OK. Also has a shop and a **Hostal**, hostalchasqui@hotmail.com, rooms with bath and hot water.

ᵀᵀ Heart's Café, on Plaza de Armas, T084-204078, www.livingheartperu.org. Open 0700-2100. Mainly wholefood restaurant serving international and Peruvian dishes, including vegetarian, box lunch and take-away available, good coffee. Owned by Sonia Newhouse, who directs all profits to education and self-help projects in the Sacred Valley. Bright and run by villagers. Deservedly popular and recommended.

ᵀᵀ Il Cappuccino and **Kusicoyllor**, Plaza Araccama. Offers the best cappuccino in town, in fact great coffee generally. Good continental and American breakfasts. Also

serves *menú turístico*, lunch and dinner, desserts, juices and light meals.

ᵀᵀ Mayupata, Jr Convención s/n, across the bridge on the way to the ruins, on the left, T084-204083. It opens at 0600 for breakfast, and serves lunch and dinner. Serving international choices and a selection of Peruvian dishes, pizzas, desserts, sandwiches and coffee. The bar has a fireplace; river view, relaxing atmosphere.

ᵀᵀ-ᵀ Alcázar Café, Chaupi Calle (C del Medio s/n), 50 m from the plaza, T084-204034, alcazar@ollantaytambo.org. Mostly vegetarian restaurant, also offering fish and meat dishes, pasta specialities. Offers excursions to traditional Andean communities.

ᵀᵀ-ᵀ La Ñusta, Plaza de Armas corner of Chaupi Calle, ask here about their *hospedaje*. Popular, good food, snacks, soups, salads and juices available.

Cafés

Calicanto, on the righthand side just before the bridge leading to Plaza Araccama. For coffees and light meals, etc, overlooking the river that divides the town.

Inca Bucks, Plaza Araccama. Serves a wide variety of coffees and teas, also iced varieties, milkshakes and cold drinks.

Inka's Park, Plaza de Armas. Friendly, central café which also has *hospedaje* in the **E** range (with bath and hot water). Meals are not included in the lodging price.

Ripoka, K'uychipunku y La Convención. Tucked away opposite the Bio Museo, small café that also sells handicrafts from the rainforest.

⊛ Festivals and events

Pisac *p132, map p133*
15 Jul A local fiesta is held.

Pisac to Urubamba *p134*
15-16 Aug Fiesta de la Virgen Asunta is held in Coya. Lamay hosts a festival on 15th.

Urubamba and around *p141*

May-Jun These are the harvest months, with many processions following mysterious ancient schedules. Urubamba's main festival, **El Señor de Torrechayoc**, takes place during the first week of Jun.

8 Sep Chinchero celebrates the Day of the Virgin.

Ollantaytambo and around
p144, map p145

5-8 Jan Celebration of the **Bajada de Reyes Magos** (the Magi), when people from the highland communities bring down to Ollantaytambo the Niño Jesús, dressed in a poncho, etc. There is some traditional dancing, a bull fight, local food and a fair.

17 Feb **Chutanacuy**, a tug-of-war between groups from the 2 halves of town, with dancing also.

Mar-Apr The **Fiesta de Compadres**, a moveable feast 10 days before Carnavales and 13 days before Ash Wednesday, is celebrated in the small, indigenous village of **Marcacocha**, close to Ollantaytambo by local transport or on foot. There is a delightful chapel on an Inca site, the dance of the *huayllata* (Andean goose), a mass and a bullfight in the smallest bullring imaginable, all in beautiful surroundings.

As elsewhere, **Semana Santa**, the week before **Easter**, is a lovely time of year. **Jun** Pentecost, 50 days after Easter, is celebrated by the **Fiesta del Señor de Choquekillca**, patron saint of Ollantaytambo. There are several days of dancing, weddings, processions, Masses, feasting and drinking (the last opportunity to see traditional Cuzqueño dancing).

29 Jun Following Inti Raymi in Cuzco, there is a colourful festival, the **Ollanta-Raymi**, at which the Quechua drama, *Ollantay*, is re-enacted.

29 Oct is the **Aniversario de Ollantaytambo**, a festival with dancing in traditional costume and many local delicacies for sale.

▲ Activities and tours

Pisac to Urubamba *p134*
Munaycha, Km 60.2 Carretera Pisac-Urubamba, Huarán, T084-984 770108, www.munaycha.com. Near **The Green House**. Duilio and Andrea Vellutino, specialists in kayaking, mountain biking, trekking and other sports, half- and 1-day trips as well as longer adventures. Also traditional tours in the Sacred Valley.

Urubamba and around *p141*
Agrotourism
Chichubamba, Casa de ProPerú, Jr Rejachayoc, Urubamba, T084-201562, www.agrotourismsacredvalley.com. A community tourism project which lets visitors take part in a number of traditional activities (culinary, horticulture, textiles, ceramics, beekeeping, etc, US$3 pp, cheaper for groups), hiking US$10, lodging **E** per person and local meals. It's about 10 mins' walk from Urubamba; follow the signs.

Horse riding
Perol Chico, 5 km from Urubamba at Km 77, T084-974 798890/974 780020 (mob), www.perolchico.com. Owned and operated by Eduard van Brunschot Vega (Dutch/Peruvian), 1- to 14-day trips from Urubamba, good horses, riding is Peruvian Paso style; 1-day trip to Moray and the salt pans costs US$110 (minimum 2 people, starting in Cuzco). Recommended.

Trekking
Haku Trek, contact Javier Saldívar or Yeral Quillahuman, T084-961 3001 (mob). A cooperative tourism project in the Chicón Valley (the mountain valley above Urubamba), run by residents of the community. 3 different hiking trips are offered: two 1-day hiking options (US$20 per person including food and accommodation) and a third, 2-day hike up to the Chicón Glacier itself (US$45 all inclusive). Hikes are based at a simple, but beautifully located

eco-lodge in the valley and profits are used to fund reforestation of native forest in the area. **Peru Alive**, Av Convención 210, Urubamba, T084-401395, T084-984 698232 (mob), www.perualive.com. Agency run by the group **Ayni Kallpa** for treks such as Choquequirao, small, good value, all proceeds go to local people.

Ollantaytambo and around
p144, map p145

On the south side of the Plaza de Armas trips to local sites, horse riding and more are offered by various tour operators, including **KB Tours**, T084-204133 (separate from **Hostal KB Tambo**, above). These, and other agencies on Av Ferrocarril offer 'free tourist information'.

⊖ Transport

To organize your own Sacred Valley transport, try one of the taxi drivers listed on page 124.

Pisac *p132, map p133*
Bus

To **Cuzco**, buses leave from C Puputi on the outskirts of Cuzco, near the Clorindo Matto de Turner school and Av de la Cultura. 32 km, 1 hr, US$0.85. Colectivos, minibuses and buses leave when full, between 0600 and 1600; also trucks and pickups. Buses returning from Pisac are often full. The last one back leaves around 2000. Taxis charge about US$20 for the round trip.

To **Pisac**, **Calca** (18 km beyond Pisac) and **Urubamba**, buses leave from Av Tullumayo 800 block, Huanchac, US$1.

Urubamba and around *p141*
Bus

The bus and combi terminal is just west of town on the main road. To **Calca**, **Pisac** (US$1, 1 hr) and **Cuzco** (2 hrs, US$1.80), from 0530 onwards. Also buses to Cuzco via **Chinchero**, same fare.

Colectivos to **Cuzco** can be caught outside the terminal and on the main road,

US$1.80. Combis run to **Ollantaytambo**, 45 mins, US$0.50. There are also buses from here to **Quillabamba**.

Chinchero *p141*
Bus

In **Cuzco**, combis and colectivos for Chinchero leave from 300 block of Av Grau, 1 block before crossing the bridge. 23 km, 45 mins, US$0.75; and for **Urubamba** a further 25 km, 45 mins, US$0.75.

To **Maras**, there is a paved road from the main road between Chinchero and Urubamba to the village of Maras, 4 km, and from there an unmade road in good condition leads to Moray, 9 km. Ask in Maras for the best route to walk, other than on the main road. Any bus between Urubamba and Cuzco via Chinchero passes the clearly marked turning to Maras, 20 mins from Chinchero. From the junction taxi colectivos charge US$1.50 per person to Maras, or you can walk (30 mins). There is public transport from Chinchero to Maras and regular pickup trucks that carry people and produce in and out. Transport stops running between 1700 and 1800; it costs between US$0.60 and US$1. Hitching back to **Urubamba** is quite easy, but there are no hotels at all in the area, so take care not to be stranded.

Taxis

Taxis wait at the Maras/Moray junction on the Urubamba/Chinchero road. They charge US$20 to go to **Salinas** and then on to **Moray**, with a 1-hr wait at each. Radio taxi: **Aló Urubamba**, T084-201010, reliable, will pick up anywhere, supposedly 24 hrs, US$20-25 to **Cuzco**.

Ollantaytambo and around
p144, map p145
Bus

The main colectivo stop is outside the market, near the Plaza de Armas. There is a direct bus service to Ollantaytambo from Av Grau, **Cuzco**, at 0745 and 1945 direct (or catch a bus to Urubamba from Av Grau). From

Ollantaytambo to Cuzco at 0715 and 1945; the fare is US$2.85. Direct taxi colectivo service from C Pavitos, Cuzco, leaves when full US$3.60 to Ollantaytambo. Minibuses and taxis leave the small Terminal de Transportes just up from Ollantaytambo station at train times for **Urubamba** and **Cuzco**, US$3.60 shared to either place, but they may try to charge US$24 as a private service only. Say you'll go to the colectivo terminal and they may reduce the price. Transfers and tours with **Aló K'antuyoc**, at the hostel of that name on Av Ferrocarril, T084-204147, kantuyoc@hotmail.com.

Train

See page 166. The station is 15 mins' walk from the plaza down Av Ferrocarril (turn left just before the bridge that leads to the ruins). There are colectivos and mototaxis at the Plaza for the station when trains are due. You won't be allowed on the station unless you have previously bought a ticket for the train (unless you are staying at **El Albergue**); the gates are locked and only those with tickets can enter. Trains pull in and out from about 0530 until after 2200 and things get pretty chaotic at the station and on Av Ferrocarril at arrival and departure times.

Perú Rail and Inca Rail have parking lots and ticket offices on Av Ferrocarril. **Inca Rail** office open 0545-0745, 0945-1245, 1445-1745. Between their offices and the station are several café/restaurants (**Tawa's, Miski Unu, Café Perla, Café d'Paris** – the last 2 serve real coffee), a cambio, internet, toilets, minimarket and grocery stalls.

⦿ Directory

Pisac *p132, map p133*
Banks Money exchange at the **Blue Llama** Café on the plaza. There is an ATM on the plaza next to **Ulrike's Café** (sometimes hard to find behind the market stalls!). **Internet and telephone** On the same side of the plaza as the museum is the municipal building with a computer centre (internet for US$0.75 per hr, closed Sun morning); also a public phone booth.

Pisac to Urubamba *p134*
Internet In Calca, the municipal library has internet connection. In **Yucay**, there are several places.

Urubamba and around *p141*
Banks Banks in the town centre on Comercio. ATM on the plaza at **Caja Municipal Arequipa**, Visa and MasterCard. Also **GlobalNet** on main road at the **Pecsa** service station, junction of M Castilla. **Internet and telephone** There are **locutorios** around the centre, not many and sometimes not well-signed. **Medical services** Casa del Bienestar, Plaza Manco Capac II s/n, Yucay, T084-201446 or T084-984 273539 (mob), Mario Orihuela. Recommended for massage and other treatments. **Post** Serpost, post office, Plaza de Armas.

Ollantaytambo and around
p144, map p145
Banks BCP ATM at C Ventiderio 248, between the Plaza and Av Ferrocarril, in Hotel Sauce. **Globalnet** on north side of Plaza. **Internet** Several places in town, many with call centres. **Medical services** Hampi Land Traveller's Clinic C Cien Ventanas s/n, T084-797164, and on the Plaza de Armas, T084-797164, www.hampiland.com. Medical centre, with ambulance and evacuation service and professional medical care.

Contents

Footprint features

Machu
Picchu

Cuzco

Machu Picchu

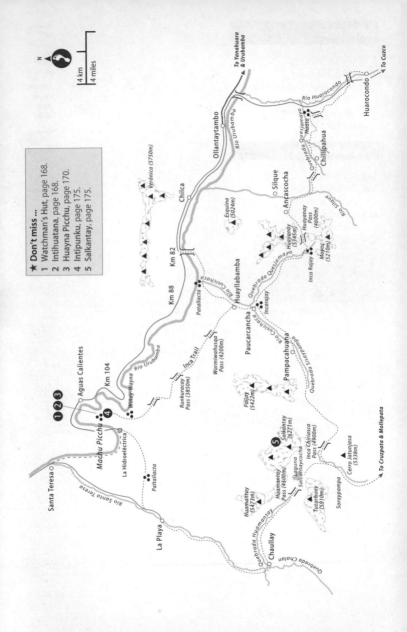

★ Don't miss ...

1 Watchman's Hut, page 168.
2 Intihuatana, page 168.
3 Huayna Picchu, page 170.
4 Intipunku, page 175.
5 Salkantay, page 175.

If you're looking for a picture that sums up South America, Machu Picchu is usually what first springs to mind. On the television, in brochures, on packets of coffee, you name it, Machu Picchu has become a kind of shorthand for lost civilizations, the thrill of discovery, exotic travel and, above all, the mystery that can still be found in an increasingly technological world. In 2011, of course, it will be more in evidence than ever as the 100th anniversary of Hiram Bingham's arrival is celebrated. At the same time it is accessible; hundreds of thousands of tourists visit it each year. And yet it transcends the many roles that it has acquired – photogenic image, tourist magnet, centre of controversy – through the strength of its stones, the way it is intimately tied to its surroundings, its enigmas and its beauty. The wonder of Machu Picchu has been well documented over the years. Equally impressive is the centuries-old Inca Trail that winds its way from the Sacred Valley near Ollantaytambo and is encompassed by the 325-sq-km Machu Picchu Historical Sanctuary. Machu Picchu itself cannot be understood without the Inca Trail. Its principal sites are ceremonial in character, apparently in ascending hierarchical order. The trail is essentially a work of spiritual art, like a Gothic cathedral, and walking it was formerly an act of devotion. It is unfortunate that the number of tourists who have committed themselves to repeating this Inca devotion, or at least undergoing the necessary penance of four exhausting days, has exceeded the tolerance of the trail itself, leading to severe damage. In addition, the Inca Trail has become, in many tourists' minds, the only Inca trail, when in fact there are many others which lead to Machu Picchu, perhaps without the same ceremonial meaning but with just as much great trekking through fine landscapes. These are now being sold as Inca Trail alternatives, avoiding, it is hoped, the risk of over-exploitation.

Ins and outs

Getting there

There are two ways to get to Machu Picchu. The easy way is by **train** from Poroy (over the hill from Cuzco), or Ollantaytambo, with a bus ride for the final climb from the rail terminus at Aguas Calientes to the ruins (see Transport, page 189, for the times). The walk up from Aguas Calientes takes 1½ to two hours, following the Inca path. Walking down to Aguas Calientes, if staying the night there, takes between 30 minutes and one hour. The ruins are quieter after 1530, but don't forget that the last bus down from the ruins leaves at 1730. The strenuous, but most rewarding way to Machu Picchu is to hike one of the Inca trails, the 'classic' example of which is described in its own section (see page 171). ▶▶ For further details, see box, page 166 and Transport, page 189.

Visitor information Tickets for Machu Picchu must be purchased in advance from the **Ministerio de Cultura** ① *Av Pachacútec cuadra 1, Aguas Calientes, 0500-2200, in Cuzco, www.drc-cusco.gob.pe, or online from http://boletajevirtual.drc-cusco.gob.pe or www.machu picchu.gob.pe.* The agency officially responsible for the site is **Unidad Gestión de Machu Picchu** ① *C Garcilaso 223, Cuzco; T084-242103.* It is an excellent source of information on Machu Picchu and this is the place to which any complaints or observations should be directed. **iperú** ① *in the Ministerio de Cultura office, as above, of 4, T084-211104, iperumachupicchu@promperu.gob.pe, daily 0900-1300 and 1400-2000,* can provide general information. ▶▶ For listings, see pages 186-189.

Making the most of Machu Picchu

→ Allow at least a day to appreciate the ruins and their surroundings fully. Although there is still a thriving business in one- or two-day trips, a quick visit hardly gives you time to recover from the initial sense of awe.

→ Avoid Monday and Friday when there is usually a crowd of guided tours en route to or from Pisac's Sunday market, all wanting lunch at the same time.

→ Visit early or late. The ruins are at their busiest in the morning after 0830. The site is quieter after 1530 although a lot of people do stay on to see the sun setting behind the mountains.

→ Try to be there for dawn or dusk to enjoy the changing of the light. A good time to visit is before 0830, when the views are at their best.

→ Find time to peer into corners, investigate the angles of stones, the weight of lintels, the outlook of windows. See how rocks and openings align themselves with peaks across the valley.

→ Take your own food and plenty of drinking water. The Machu Picchu Sanctuary Lodge (see Sleeping, page 186) has a restaurant serving buffet lunch and there's a snack bar beside the entrance but neither place is cheap. Note, too, that food is not officially allowed into the site.

→ In the dry season sandflies can be a problem, so take insect repellent and wear trousers and long-sleeved shirts.

Background

For centuries Machu Picchu was buried in jungle, until Hiram Bingham stumbled upon it in July 1911. It was then explored by an archaeological expedition sent by Yale University. Machu Picchu was a stunning find. The only major Inca site to escape 400 years of looting and destruction, it was remarkably well preserved. And it was no ordinary Inca settlement. It sat in an inaccessible location above the Urubamba Gorge, and contained so many fine buildings that people have puzzled over its meaning ever since.

Bingham claimed he had discovered the lost city of Vilcabamba, and for 50 years everyone believed him. But he was proved wrong, and the mystery deepened. Later discoveries revealed that Machu Picchu was the centre of an extensive Inca province. Many finely preserved satellite sites and highways also survive. This is craggy terrain and the value of a province with no mines and little agricultural land – it was not even self-sufficient – is hard to determine. Bingham postulated it was a defensive citadel on the fringes of the Amazon. But the architecture fails to convince us, and in any case, defence against whom?

The Incas were the first to build permanent structures in this region, which was unusual because they arrived at the tail end of 4000 years of Andean civilization. Sixteenth-century land titles discovered in the 1980s revealed that Machu Picchu was built by the Inca Pachacútec, founding father of the Inca Empire. But they do not tell us why he built it. One reasonable speculation is that this area provided access to coca plantations in the lower Urubamba Valley. However, the fine architecture of Machu Picchu cannot be explained away simply as a coca-collecting station.

Travelling by train to Machu Picchu

Three companies operate along this route: **PerúRail** (Avenida Pachacútec, Wanchac Station, T084-581414, www.perurail.com) runs to Machu Picchu from Poroy, near Cuzco, and from Ollantaytambo. **Inca Rail** (Avenida El Sol 611, Cuzco, T084-233030, or Lima T01-613 5288, www.incarail.com.pe) runs from Ollantaytambo to Machu Picchu. **Machu Picchu Train** (Avenida Sol 576, T084-221199, www.machupicchutrain.com) also runs from Ollantaytambo. All trains run to **Aguas Calientes** (the official name of this station is 'Machu Picchu'). PerúRail and Inca Rail also have ticket offices near the station in Ollantaytambo. The station for the tourist trains at Aguas Calientes is on the outskirts of town, 200 m from the Pueblo Hotel and 50 m from where buses leave for Machu Picchu ruins. There is a paved road in poor condition between Aguas Calientes and the start of the road up to the ruins.

There are four classes of PerúRail tourist train. Note that timetables and prices are subject to frequent change. Tickets for all trains may be bought at Wanchac station and the sales office on Portal de Carnes, Plaza de Armas, in Cuzco, at travel agencies, or via PerúRail's website, www.perurail.com.

Vistadome (US$71 one way) departs from Poroy daily at 0653, arriving at Aguas Calientes (Machu Picchu) at 1038. It returns from Machu Picchu at 1600, reaching Poroy at 1942.
Expedition (US$48 one way) departs Poroy daily at 0742, reaching Aguas Calientes at 1151. It returns at 1703, getting back to Poroy at 2101.
Hiram Bingham (US$334 one way) is a super-luxury train with dining car and bar. It leaves Poroy Monday to Saturday at 0910 with brunch on board, reaching Aguas Calientes at 1309. It leaves Aguas Calientes at 1807, cocktails, dinner and live entertainment on board, arriving in Poroy at 2159 with a bus service back to Cuzco hotels. The cost includes all meals, buses and entry to the ruins.
Ollantaytambo Vistadome (US$43, US$53 and US$60 one way: the more expensive trains arrive at Machu Picchu at peak times) leaves Ollantaytambo five times a day from 0659 to 1615, returning from Aguas Calientes at 1322 to 2020; journey time is about two hours. Tickets include food in the price. These trains have toilets, video, snacks and drinks for sale.

Recent studies have shown that the Temple of the Sun, or Torreón, was an observatory for the solstice sunrise, and that the Intihuatana stela is the centre point between cardinal alignments of nearby sacred peaks. The Incas worshipped nature: the celestial bodies, mountains, lightning, rainbows, rocks – anything, in fact, that was imbued with spiritual power.

This spiritual component is the key to understanding Machu Picchu. The Bingham expedition identified 75% of the human remains as female, and a common belief is that Machu Picchu was a refuge of the Inca 'Virgins of the Sun'. However, the skeletons were re-examined in the 1980s using modern technology, and the latest conclusion is that the gender split was roughly 50/50.

Machu Picchu was deliberately abandoned by its inhabitants – when, we do not know. This may have happened even before the Spanish conquest, perhaps as a result of the Inca civil wars, or the epidemics of European diseases which ran like brushfires ahead of

Ollantaytambo Backpacker (US$31 and US$34 one way) departs four times a day from 0602-2312, returning from Aguas Calientes 0505-2230. Seats can be reserved even if you're not returning the same day.

Ollantaytambo Expedition (US$43 one way) leaves at 0910, arriving at Aguas Calientes at 1118, returning at 1924, reaching Ollantaytambo at 2115. An *autovagón* service from Ollantaytambo at 0815 has a connecting bus from Wanchac station in Cuzco (US$60). It returns from Aguas Calientes at 1845.

Inca Rail has three trains a day Ollantayambo–Machu Picchu (*Yllari* at sunrise, *Waala* in the morning and *Tutayay* at sunset), with fares at US$50 one way executive class, US$75 one way 1st class. Coaches have a/c and heating, snacks are available.

Machu Picchu Train also has three trains a day Ollantayambo–Machu Picchu (*The Lost City Traveller* at 0720, returning 1612, *Cusco Imperial* and *Sunrise* – at the time of writing the last two were awaiting schedules). *The Lost City Traveller* fare is US$59. Journey time is 1 hour 25 minutes. Coaches have been specially designed for the service.

Local trains

Tourists are not permitted to travel on the local train from Cuzco to Machu Picchu, but you can avoid the train services altogether. Take a bus from Cuzco towards Quillabamba at 1900, US$6 (other buses in the day may not connect with onward transport). Get out at **Santa María** (about seven hours) where minibuses wait to go to **Santa Teresa**, two hours, US$2.10. You'll reach Santa Teresa by sunrise in time to buy breakfast. From Santa Teresa you have to cross the Río Urubamba by the new bridge and walk 6 km to the Central Hidroeléctrica, a nice, flat road, or take a combi, US$10-15. From the Hidroeléctrica train station it's 40 minutes on the local train to Aguas Calientes at 1520, US$8 for tourists, or you can walk along the railway in two-three hours (at Km 114.5 is **F** per person **Hospedaje Mandor**, about 2 km from bridge to Machu Picchu). To return, at 0600 walk from Aguas Calientes to Santa Teresa to catch a bus at 1000 to Santa María, arrive at 1200. At 1300 take a bus back to Cuzco, arriving between 1900-2000. Or take the local train from Aguas Calientes to Santa Teresa at 1210, stay in a hostal, then take the 1000 bus to Santa María. If using this route, don't forget to buy your ticket for Machu Picchu in Cuzco, unless you want to buy it in Aguas Calientes.

the Spanish in the New World. One theory proposes that the city ran dry in a period of drought; another suggests a devastating fire. Or the city may have been evacuated during the period of Inca resistance to the Spanish, which lasted nearly 40 years and was concentrated not far west of Machu Picchu.

Visiting Machu Picchu → *For listings, see pages 186-189. Colour map 2, A2.*

ⓘ *Daily 0600-1730. Entrance fee is US$44.55 (S/.126), to be purchased in advance from the Ministerio de Cultura, see page 164. Students with a valid ISIC card pay US$22.30. It is only possible to pay in soles. You cannot take backpacks into Machu Picchu; leave them at the entrance for US$1. Guides are available at the site, they are often very knowledgeable and worthwhile. The official price for a guide is US$80 for a full tour for 1-10 people.*

There is a tremendous feeling of awe on first witnessing this incredible sight. The ancient citadel of Machu Picchu, 42 km from Ollantaytambo by rail, straddles the saddle of a high mountain at 2380 m, with steep terraced slopes falling away to the fast-flowing Río Urubamba snaking its hairpin course far below in the valley floor. Towering overhead is Huayna Picchu, and green jungle peaks provide the backdrop for the whole majestic scene. In comparison with many archaeological ruins, there are so many standing buildings that it requires no stretch of the imagination to work out what the city looked like. What function some of those buildings had and the meaning of their enigmatic symbols is harder to guess at, but this adds to the allure of the site.

Once you have passed through the ticket gate you follow a path to a small complex of buildings which now acts as the **main entrance (1)** to the ruins. It is set at the eastern end of the extensive **terracing (2)** which must have supplied the crops for the city. Above this point, turning back the way you have come, is the final stretch of the Inca Trail leading down from **Intipunku** (Sun Gate), see page 175. From a promontory here, on which stands the building called the **Watchman's Hut (3)**, you get *the* perfect view of the city (the one you've seen on all the postcards), laid out before you with Huayna Picchu rising above the furthest extremity. Go round the promontory and head south for the **Intipata** (Inca bridge), see page 170.

The main path into the ruins comes to a **dry moat (4)** that cuts right across the site. At the moat you can either climb the long staircase which goes to the upper reaches of the city, or you can enter the city by the baths and Temple of the Sun.

The more strenuous way into the city is by the former route, which takes you past quarries on your left as you look down to the Urubamba on the west flank of the mountain. To your right are roofless buildings where you can see in close-up the general construction methods used in the city. Proceeding along this level, above the main plazas, you reach the **Temple of the Three Windows (5)** and the **Principal Temple (6)**, which has a smaller building called the **Sacristy (7)**. The two main buildings are three-sided and were clearly of great importance, given the fine stonework involved. The wall with the three windows is built onto a single rock, one of the many instances in the city where the architects did not merely put their construction on a convenient piece of land. They used and fashioned its features to suit their concept of how the city should be tied to the mountain and its forces, and the alignment of its stones should relate to the surrounding peaks. In the Principal Temple, a diamond-shaped stone in the floor is said to depict the constellation of the Southern Cross.

Continue on the path behind the Sacristy to reach the **Intihuatana (8)**, the 'hitching-post of the sun'. The name comes from the theory that such carved rocks (*gnomons*), found at all major Inca sites, were the point to which the sun was symbolically 'tied' at the winter solstice, before being freed to rise again on its annual ascent towards the summer solstice. The steps, angles and planes of this sculpted block appear to indicate a purpose beyond simple decoration, and researchers, such as Johan Reinhard in *The Sacred Center*, have sought to explain the trajectory of each alignment. Whatever the motivation behind this magnificent carving, it is undoubtedly one of the highlights of Machu Picchu.

Climb down from the Intihuatana's mound to the **Main Plaza (9)**. Beyond its northern end is a small plaza with open-sided buildings on two sides and on the third, the **Sacred Rock (10)**. The outline of this gigantic, flat stone echoes that of the mountains behind it. From here you can proceed to the start of the trail to Huayna Picchu (see page 170). Returning to the Main Plaza and heading southeast you pass, on your left, several groups of closely packed buildings which are thought to have been **living quarters** and

Machu Picchu

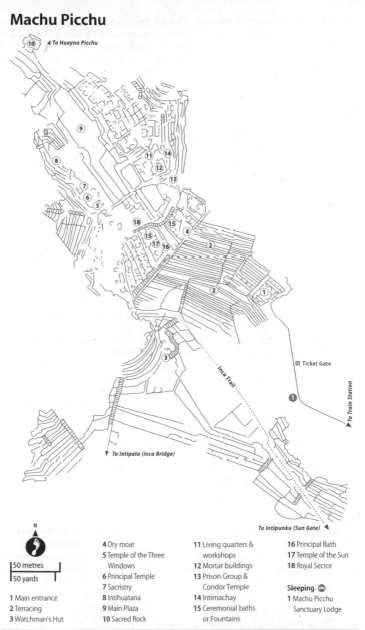

To Huayna Picchu

To Intipata (Inca Bridge)

Inca Trail

Ticket Gate

To Train Station

To Intipunku (Sun Gate)

N

50 metres
50 yards

1 Main entrance
2 Terracing
3 Watchman's Hut

4 Dry moat
5 Temple of the Three
   Windows
6 Principal Temple
7 Sacristry
8 Intihuatana
9 Main Plaza
10 Sacred Rock

11 Living quarters &
   workshops
12 Mortar buildings
13 Prison Group &
   Condor Temple
14 Intimachay
15 Ceremonial baths
   or Fountains

16 Principal Bath
17 Temple of the Sun
18 Royal Sector

Sleeping
1 Machu Picchu
   Sanctuary Lodge

workshops (11), **mortar buildings (12)** – look for the house with two discs let into the floor – and the **Prison Group (13)**, one of whose constructions is known as the **Condor Temple**. Also in this area of the site is a cave called **Intimachay (14)**.

A short distance from the Condor Temple is the lower end of a series of **ceremonial baths (15)** or fountains. They were probably used for ritual bathing and the water still flows down them today. The uppermost, **Principal Bath (16)**, is the most elaborate. Next to it is the **Temple of the Sun (17)**, or Torreón. This singular building has one straight wall from which another wall curves around and back to meet the straight one, but for the doorway. From above, it looks like an incomplete letter P. It is another example of the architecture being at one with its environment as the interior is taken up by the partly worked summit of the outcrop on which the building is constructed. All indications are that this temple was used for astronomical purposes. Underneath the Torreón a cave-like opening has been formed by an oblique gash in the rock. Fine masonry has been added to the opposing wall, making a second side of a triangle, which contrasts with the rough edge of the split rock. The blocks of masonry appear to have been slotted behind another sculpted piece of natural stone, which has been cut into a four-stepped buttress. Immediately behind this is a two-stepped buttress. This strange combination of the natural and the man-made has been called the Tomb or Palace of the Princess. Across the stairway from the complex which includes the Torreón is the group of buildings known as the **Royal Sector (18)**.

Huayna Picchu

ⓘ *Visitors are allowed access twice daily, 0700 and 1000, latest return time 1500. Maximum 200 people on the mountain at any time. Check with the Ministerio de Cultura in Aguas Calientes or Cuzco for current access times and to sign up for a spot.*

Synonymous with the ruins themselves is Huayna Picchu, the verdant mountain overlooking the site. There are also ruins on the mountain itself, and steps to the top for a superlative view of the whole magnificent scene, but this is not for those with vertigo. The climb takes up to 90 minutes but the steps are dangerous after bad weather and you shouldn't leave the path. You must register at a hut at the beginning of the trail. The other trail to Huayna Picchu, down near the Urubamba, is via the Temple of the Moon: two caves, one above the other, with superb Inca niches inside, sadly blemished by graffiti. To reach the **Temple of the Moon** from the path to Huayna Picchu, take the marked trail to the left; it is in good shape. It descends further than you think it should. After the Temple you may proceed to Huayna Picchu, but this path is overgrown, slippery when wet and has a crooked ladder on an exposed part about 10 minutes before the top (not for the faint-hearted). It is safer to return to the main trail to Huayna Picchu, but this adds about 30 minutes to the climb. The round trip takes about four hours.

Intipata

The famous Inca bridge – **Intipata** – is about 30 minutes along a well-marked trail south of the Royal Sector. The bridge, which is actually a couple of logs, is spectacularly sited, carved into a vertiginous cliff-face. The walk is well worth it for the fine views, but the bridge itself is closed to visitors. Not only is it in a poor state of repair, but the path before it has collapsed.

The classic Inca Trail is a three- to four-day route to Machu Picchu, starting from the Sacred Valley near Ollantaytambo. What makes this hike so special is the stunning combination of Inca ruins, unforgettable views, magnificent mountains, exotic vegetation and extraordinary ecological variety. The government acknowledged all this in 1981 by including the trail in a 325-sq-km national park, the Machu Picchu Historical Sanctuary. Machu Picchu itself cannot be understood without the Inca Trail. Its principal sites are ceremonial in character, apparently in ascending hierarchical order. This Inca province was a unique area of elite access. The trail is essentially a work of spiritual art, like a Gothic cathedral, and walking it was formerly an act of devotion. ⇥ *For alternative Inca routes, see page 184.*

Ins and outs

Entrance tickets and tours   An entrance ticket for the trail or its variations must be bought at the **Ministerio de Cultura** office in Cuzco; no tickets are sold at the entrance gates. Furthermore, tickets are only sold on presentation of a letter from a licensed tour operator on behalf of the visitor, with full passport details. Tickets are non-refundable and cannot be changed so make sure you provide accurate passport details to your tour operator. There is a 50% discount for students, but note that officials are very strict, only an ISIC card will be accepted as proof of status. Tickets are checked at Km 82, Huayllabamba and Wiñay-Wayna.

On all hiking trails (Km 82 or Km 88 to Machu Picchu, Salkantay to Machu Picchu, and Km 82 or Km 88 to Machu Picchu via Km 104) adults must pay US$86, students and children under 15 US$43. On the **Camino Real de los Inkas** from Km 104 to Wiñay-Wayna and Machu Picchu (see page 175) the fee is US$51 per adult, US$28 for students and children; Salkantay to Huayllabamba and Km 88 is US$51. The **Salkantay trek** (see page 175) is subject to a US$45 trekking fee.

Travel agencies in Cuzco arrange transport to the start, equipment, food, etc, for an all-in price. Prices vary from about US$450 to US$540 per person for a responsible four-day, three-night trek (similar prices are charged for the Salkantay trek). Remember that you get what you pay for and bear in mind that prices lower than those above suggest that corners are being cut, with less attention paid to the environment and the porters. This respect is, after all, the goal of the 2001 legislation.

There is a quota for agencies and groups to use the trail, but some agencies make block bookings way in advance of departure dates. This makes it much harder for other agencies to guarantee their clients places on the Trail. Consequently, current advice is to book your preferred dates as early as possible, between two months and a year in advance depending on the season you want to go, then confirm nearer the time. There have been many instances of disappointed trekkers whose bookings did not materialize: don't wait till the last minute and always check your operator's cancellation charges.

You can save a bit of money by arranging your own transport back to Ollantaytambo in advance, either for the last day of your tour, or by staying an extra night in Aguas Calientes and taking the early morning train, then a bus back to Cuzco. If you take your own tent and sleeping gear, some agencies give a discount. Make sure your return ticket for the tourist train to Cuzco has your name on it, otherwise you have to pay for any changes.

Advice and information Although security has improved in recent years, it's still best to leave all your valuables in Cuzco and keep everything else inside your tent, even your shoes. Avoid the July/August high season and the rainy season from November to April (note that this can change, so check in advance). In the wet it is cloudy and the paths are very muddy and difficult. Also watch out for coral snakes in this area (black, red, yellow bands). Please remove all your rubbish, including toilet paper, or use the pits provided. Do not light open fires as they can get out of control. The **Annual Inca Trail Clean-up** takes place usually in September. Many agencies and organizations are involved and volunteers should contact **South American Explorers** in Cuzco (see page 66) for full details of ways to help.

If you feel that your porters have been neglected or abused on the trek, express this to your agency, inform the **South American Explorers** and please also drop us a line at

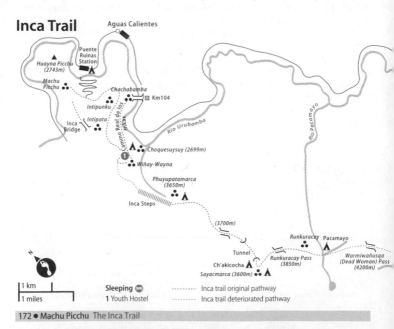

Inca Trail

Footprint (go to www.footprinttravelguides.com or send us a letter to our Bath address in the UK). We read all your letters and agencies who repeatedly mistreat their porters will be removed from our publications.

Equipment It is cold at night and weather conditions change rapidly, so it is important to take strong footwear, rain gear and warm clothing (this includes long johns if you want to sleep rather than freeze at night): dress in layers. Also take food, water, water purification tablets, insect repellent, sunscreen, a hat and sunglasses, a supply of plastic bags, coverings (blankets, ponchos, etc), a good sleeping bag, a torch and a stove for preparing hot food and drink to ward off the cold at night. It is worth paying extra to hire a down sleeping bag if you haven't brought your own. A paraffin (kerosene) stove is preferable, as fuel can be bought in small quantities in markets.

A tent is essential, but if you're hiring one in Cuzco, check carefully for leaks. Caves marked on some maps are little better than overhangs and are not sufficient shelter to sleep in. You could also take a first-aid kit; if you don't need it, the porters probably will, given their rather basic footwear. It is forbidden to use trekking poles because the metal tips are damaging the trail. Instead, buy a carved wooden stick on sale in the main plaza in Ollantaytambo or at the trail head. Many will need this for the steep descents on the path.

All the necessary equipment can be rented in Cuzco, see page 112. Good maps of the trail and area can be bought from **South American Explorers** in Lima or Cuzco, see pages 66 and 272. If you have any doubts about carrying your own pack, porters/guides are available through Cuzco agencies. Always carry a day-pack, though, with water and snacks, in case you walk at a faster or slower pace than the porters. Take enough cash to ensure that your group tips a minimum of US$10 per porter, plus the tips for the guides and cook, and for your purchases at the end of the trail.

The trek → 3½ days.

Day one The trek to the sacred site begins either at Km 82, **Piscacucho**, or at Km 88, **Qorihuayrachina**, at 2600 m. In order to reach Km 82, hikers are transported by their tour operator (see above) in a minibus on the road that goes to Quillabamba. From Piri onward the road follows the riverbank and ends at Km 82, where there is a bridge. You can depart as early as you like and arrive at Km 82 faster than going by train. The Inca Trail equipment, food, fuel and personnel reach Km 82 (depending on the operator's logistics) for the Inrena staff to weigh each bundle before the group arrives. When several groups are leaving on the same day, it is more convenient to arrive early.

Km 88 can only be reached by train, subject to schedule and baggage limitations. The train goes slower than a bus but you start your walk nearer to Patallacta (also known as Llaqtapata) and Huayllabamba.

Inca Trail regulations

The year 2001 signalled the beginning of strict new rules on the Inca Trail; tourists should be aware of the following regulations:

→ All agencies must have a licence to work in the area.

→ Groups of up to seven independent travellers who do not wish to use a tour operator are allowed to hike the trail accompanied by an independent, licensed guide, as long as they do not employ any other support staff, such as porters or cooks.

→ A maximum of 500 visitors and support staff per day are allowed on the trail.

→ Operators pay US$12 for each porter and other trail staff to use the Trail. A porter's wage should be US$50 (S/.165.60). Porters are not permitted to carry more than 20 kg (less scrupulous agencies find ways to circumvent these requirements).

→ Littering is banned. Plastic water bottles may not be carried on the trail; only canteens are permitted.

→ Pets and pack animals are prohibited, although llamas are allowed as far as the first pass.

→ Groups have to use approved campsites; on the routes from Km 82, Km 88 and Salkantay, the campsites may be changed with prior authorization.

→ The Inca Trail is closed each February for maintenance.

The first ruin is **Patallacta**, near Km 88, the utilitarian centre of a large settlement of farming terraces which probably supplied the other Inca Trail sites. From here, it is a relatively easy three-hour walk to the village of **Huayllabamba**. Note that the route from Km 82 goes via **Cusichaca**, the valley in which Ann Kendall worked (see page 151), rather than Patallacta.

A series of gentle climbs and descents leads along the Río Cusichaca, the ideal introduction to the trail. Huayllabamba is a popular camping spot for tour groups, so it's a better idea to continue for about an hour up to the next site, **Llulluchayoc** (Three White Stones), which is a patch of green beside a fast-flowing stream. It's a steep climb but you're pretty much guaranteed a decent pitch for the night. If you're feeling really energetic, you can go on to the next camping spot, a perfectly flat meadow, called **Llulluchapampa**. This means a punishing ascent for one hour 30 minutes through cloudforest, but it does leave you with a much easier second day. There's also the advantage of relative isolation and a magnificent view back down the valley.

Day two For most people the second day is by far the toughest. It's a steep climb to the meadow, followed by an exhausting 2½-hour haul up to the first pass – aptly named **Warmiwañusqa** (Dead Woman's Pass) – at 4200 m. The feeling of relief on reaching the top is immense. After a well-earned break it's a sharp descent on a treacherous path down to the Pacamayo Valley, where there are a few flat camping spots near a stream if you're too weary to continue.

Day two/three If you're feeling energetic, you can proceed to the second pass. Halfway up comes the ruin of **Runkuracay**, which was probably an Inca *tambo* (post-house). Camping is no longer permitted here. A steep climb up an Inca staircase leads to the next pass, at 3850 m, with spectacular views of Pumasillo (6246 m) and the Vilcabamba range. The trail descends to **Sayacmarca** (Inaccessible town), a spectacular site over the Aobamba Valley, where it's possible to camp. Just below Sayacmarca lies **Conchamarca** (Shell Town), a small group of buildings standing on rounded terraces.

Day three A blissfully gentle two-hour climb on a stone highway, leads through an Inca tunnel and along the enchanted fringes of the cloudforest, to the third pass. This is the most rewarding part of the trail, with spectacular views of the entire Vilcabamba range, and it's worth taking the time to dwell on the wonders of nature. Then it's down to the extensive ruins of **Phuyupatamarca** (Cloud-level Town), at 3650 m, where Inca observation platforms offer awesome views of nearby Salkantay and surrounding peaks. There is a 'tourist bathroom' here, where water can be collected, but purify it before drinking.

From here an Inca stairway of white granite plunges more than 1000 m to the spectacularly sited and impressive ruins of **Wiñay-Wayna** (Forever Young) ① *entry US$5.75*, offering views of recently uncovered agricultural terraces at **Intipata** (Sun Place). A trail, not easily visible, goes from Wiñay-Wayna to the terracing. There is a youth hostel at Wiñay-Wayna (see Sleeping, page 186) and there are spaces for a few tents, but they get snapped up quickly. After Wiñay-Wayna there is no water, and no place to camp, until Machu Picchu. A gate by Wiñay-Wayna is locked between 1530 and 0500, preventing access to the path to Machu Picchu at night.

Day four From Wiñay-Wayna it is a gentle hour's walk through a forest of trees and giant ferns to a steep Inca staircase, which leads up to **Intipunku** (Sun Gate), where you look down, at last, upon Machu Picchu, basking in all her glory. Your aching muscles will be quickly forgotten and even the presence of the functional hotel building cannot detract from one of the most magical sights in all the Americas.

Camino Real de los Inkas → *4-5 hrs.*
The Inca Trail from Km 104 This short Inca Trail is used by those who don't want to endure the full hike. It starts at Km 104, where a footbridge gives access to the ruins of **Chachabamba** and the trail ascends to the main trail at Wiñay-Wayna. Halfway up is a good view of the ruins of **Choquesuysuy**. The first part is a steady, continuous three-hour ascent (take water) and the trail is narrow and exposed in parts. About 15 minutes before Wiñay-Wayna is a waterfall where fresh water can be obtained (best to purify it before drinking).

Salkantay treks
Four hours' drive west of Cuzco is **Mollepata**, starting point for two major alternatives to the 'classic' Inca Trail. Both treks pass beneath the magnificent glacial bulk of **Salkantay**, at 6271 m the loftiest peak of the Vilcabamba range. The first trek (see page 177) takes the northwestern pass under Salkantay, leading into the high jungles of the Santa Teresa valley and eventually down to the town of Santa Teresa itself at the confluence with the Río Urubamba, from where Aguas Calientes and Machu Picchu are accessible.

The second trek (see page 179) often referred to as the **High Inca Trail**, follows the same route up to the base of Salkantay before turning east across the Inca Chiriasca Pass at approximately 4900 m. This route then descends via Sisaypampa, from where you trek to Pampacahuana, an outstanding Inca ruin. The remains of an Inca road then go down to the singular Inca ruins of Paucarcancha, also known as Incarajay. Paucarcancha is also an important camping site on the Ancascocha trek (see page 180).

On the third day you join the classic Inca Trail at Huayllabamba, before continuing to Machu Picchu. Because the route follows the Km 88 trail in its second half, permits are required and thus booking in advance is highly recommended. Due to regulations it is not possible to trek this route without a registered Peruvian guide. There is an obligatory change from animals to porters before you reach Huayllabamba.

The initial road journey to Mollepata is in itself quite spectacular, passing through lush agricultural land and winding through and above steep-sided river canyons. The rivers here run from the peaks of the Vilcabamba mountains and into the mighty Río Apurímac gorge just to the south of the road. Keep your eyes peeled to the right and, weather permitting, you can catch glimpses of La Verónica (5750 m) at the western end of the Urubamba range, and Salkantay itself, protruding like a bleached shark's tooth above the lower ridges of the Cordillera Vilcabamba. The road is good-quality tarmac until the turn-off just beyond Limatambo, in the Río Colorado valley floor. A dirt road then winds steeply up to Mollepata, a relaxed and picturesque rural community. Improvements in the road now mean most supported treks begin at **Cruzpata**, a little further up the track to the north of Mollepata. This cuts out a few hours' walk and makes the first day's trek to Soraypampa more relaxed.

Salkantay treks

Sleeping 🛌	
1 Colpa Lodge	3 Salkantay Lodge & Adventure Resort
2 Lucma Lodge	4 Wayra Lodge

Santa Teresa trek: Cruzpata to Santa Teresa → *4 days.*

The restrictions on the Inca Trail quickly turned the Santa Teresa Trek into the most popular alternative to the 'classic' Trail, but the authorities have ruled that this trek may only be done with an agency and trekkers are charged US$89 when they pass through Soraypampa.

Day one Start the trek from Cruzpata at 3100 m, or walk up to this point following the road from Mollepata. Trek north-northwest on the left side of valley, following the clear trail/road on a very gentle climb into the mountains. Your route takes you inexorably closer to the great peak of **Tucarhuay** (5910 m) which stands above Soraypampa, your destination for today's hike. You'll pass small mountain settlements and areas of montane forest rich in Andean flowers. Look out for mountain caracaras and hummingbirds. After four to five hours' hiking, streams begin to cross the trail with increasing regularity. The vegetation begins to thin out and about 30 minutes before reaching Soraypampa the awesome silhouette of Salkantay starts to reveal itself to your right.

    Soraypampa, the grassy plain cradled beneath the peaks, is divided by a large stream running through its centre. Make sure you camp on the better-drained land above the stream. The air is wonderfully clear, with luminous stars at night. If you're feeling energetic, or want to cut down walking time over the pass tomorrow, it's possible to camp further up the valley towards Salkantay (see next paragraph).

Day two One hour's walking on the left side of the valley heading northeast brings you to **Salkantay Pampa**, below the mountain's glacial moraines. There's a nice rest spot just after a wall and before a stream. Over the next 1½ hours you will climb steeply up the left side of the valley on switchbacks above the pampa. The trail now begins to swing to the left, taking you northwest to west-northwest between the bulk of Tucarhuay and Salkantay. The latter's glaciers tower almost two vertical kilometres above you, a sight that draws your gaze again and again. You now pass a small lake filled with green algae on your right. This is referred to as **Salcantaycocha** on the IGN sheet.

    Thirty minutes above the lake you reach the pass at approximately 4500 m. (There is some confusion over the name of this pass; we call it the Huamantay Pass for ease of reference.) Views are stunning with Salkantay to the north and east, Tucarhuay to the south and, running to the northwest, **Huamantay**, Salkantay's smaller extension, nonetheless impressive with two jagged, glaciated peaks rising to over 5400 m. Visible far away down the valley to the northwest lies the vast bulk of the **Pumasillo/Sacsarayoc** massif, another of Vilcabamba's little-known giants. Standing stones cover the highest points of the pass, built and balanced to honour Pachamama and the *apus* of the mountains.

    On the far side of the pass the path descends steeply, twisting down into the valley of the **Quebrada Huamantay** (according to the IGN sheet once again – local names may vary). After an hour or so the trail crosses a stream and the valley begins to flatten out into an area of rugged *puna* grasses and pastures. The route generally follows the left-hand side of the valley and, after a further two hours, reaches a wide pampa, **Wayraqpunku**, to the left of the Quebrada. If you're tired, or want to add an extra day to the trek, many areas along this section of the valley would make fine camping spots with magnificent sunrise views of the mountains behind. Another 25 minutes and the pampa drops away suddenly into a steep-sided canyon. Your route still on the left side of the valley, you leave the *puna* behind and enter the realm of the forest. The vegetation is stunted at first, known as dwarf or elfin forest, the trees gradually gaining height as you descend and finally becoming true cloudforest a few hundred metres above **Chaullay**. Bamboo also becomes more prevalent as you descend and the trail sometimes steeper with sharp drops on the right. Half an hour before arriving at Chaullay, the destination for the day's hike, there are two small, earthen cliffs on the far side of the valley. These are clay licks, or *collpas*, used by parakeets to supplement their diets with minerals and to help them cleanse their systems of toxins sometimes found in unripe fruit. Chaullay is a small community with plenty of space for camping and a few stores from which basic supplies are sometimes available. Keep all valuables, including hiking boots, inside your tent at night.

Day three On leaving Chaullay you cross a bridge over the **Quebrada Chalán** almost immediately. From this point on, the route takes a roughly north or north-northeast direction (always downstream) in the Santa Teresa valley until its confluence with the Urubamba tomorrow. Thirty minutes later you reach a second village, **Colcanpampa**, and its surrounding fields, which is a possible alternative campsite. Ten minutes after the field the track branches: take the right, more heavily used track. After a further five minutes go straight on at the junction. This entire area is dense high-altitude rainforest clinging to steep slopes, utterly wild apart from the occasional clearing in the valley bottoms. The trail itself is not for those with vertigo problems, as it is often narrow, steep and has sheer drops on one side. A second river crossing is reached after 10 minutes. You're crossing the **Río Totora** where it merges with the Quebrada Chalán, the result of which is **Río Santa Teresa**. On the far side of the bridge is a grassy area ideal for a quick break, and just a few metres up the Totora, on the far side, is a hot sulphur spring, although it's far from easy and possibly dangerous to reach.

Thirty minutes more and you pass a small farm, but you're still enveloped in the forest. Butterflies abound, the sound of cicadas fills the air, along with the roar of water rushing towards the vastness of the Amazon. Everywhere you look is thick with living forms, and the contrast to the sterile glacial world above is quite mind-blowing. Ten minutes more and you cross a big stream flowing down from the left. Climb 20 m up the streambed and you'll see the trail continuing on the far side. Twelve minutes beyond, you reach a lovely three-tiered waterfall, great for a refreshing dip, but be careful of sharp stones and other refuse in the churning pool below. Some 45 minutes beyond this the trail emerges briefly onto a stony beach, possibly flooded in times of very high water. Another stream is crossed, and after a further 45 minutes you reach **Uscamayuc**, a clearing with huts and running water, a good lunch stop and possible campsite. Sometimes fruits from the local *chakras* (smallholdings) are available.

From this point onwards the trail begins to flatten out and the land is increasingly utilized for agriculture. Over the next one to two hours you cross three small bridges until reaching a sandy beach. This is a good place for a wash and rest, and if you want to camp a little away from civilization this could be a good option, as **La Playa** lies only 10 minutes or so down the track. Compared with other settlements on the route so far, this is a sprawling metropolis, with lots of houses, a large school and a drivable road connecting it to the outside world across the bridge. The football field just before the bridge makes a decent campsite for those who prefer company and easy access to beer and other luxuries. Make sure all valuables are locked away safely in your tent.

Day four If you don't fancy walking down the valley to Santa Teresa town, it may be possible to hitch a ride on one of the trucks that work this road. If you want to walk, keep reading the description below. Cross the bridge to the right or eastern side of the Santa Teresa. The road runs high above the river, passing through coffee and banana plantations. Thirty minutes' walk from the bridge you have the option to hike on a restored Inca trail, up the steep mountain to the right (east), towards the recently discovered ruins of **Patallacta**, and on to the hydroelectric station just below Aguas Calientes. For a full description of this route see Day 7 of the Vilcabamba Traverse Trek (see page 238).

The second option, not as spectacular but easier on weary muscles, is to continue down the road to Santa Teresa. A couple of hours after leaving La Playa you once again cross the river back to the left-hand bank. After just over three hours' walking in total you reach another bridge crossing the **Río Sacsara**, just above its confluence with the Santa Teresa. You're now in the ghost town of Santa Teresa Vieja with its pretty church, abandoned after a devastating flood several years ago. Hundreds of people died as flood waters rushed off the heavily deforested and eroded mountains above. The new village, located on a hill just above the old town, was also damaged by flooding in 2010. Thirty minutes more and you cross another bridge, this one just below the Santa Teresa's confluence with the Sacsara. A few minutes more and you arrive at a new bridge crossing the Río Urubamba. Over the bridge, walk 6 km or take a *combi* costing US$10-15 to **La Hidroeléctrica**, from where you can catch the local train, US$8 for tourists, to Aguas Calientes at 1520. Alternatively, walk along the railway tracks to Aguas Calientes, a further two to three hours through subtropical forest (at Km 114.5 is **F** per person, **Hospedaje Mandor**). Take yourself to the hot springs and soothe those aches away!

High Inca Trail: Cruzpata to Huayllabamba → *3 days.*
Day one This trail uses the same route as the Santa Teresa trek (see page 177) until reaching Salkantay Pampa, just underneath the glacial moraines. It's a good idea to camp as far up the valley as possible, due to the demanding nature of the pass on the following day.

Day two Today's trek takes you over the **Inca Chiriasca Pass**. Not to be underestimated, the pass lies at 4900 m (some estimates state over 5000 m) making proper acclimatization to altitude essential. You should also be prepared for severe weather conditions, including the possibility of snow, at any time of year. At the foot of the glacial moraines turn right, crossing the stream and beginning your climb steeply up the valley's flank. The pass lies to the west of your position, just underneath and to the south of Salkantay's southernmost glaciers and snowfields. Following the fairly clear path you've got three or four hours' tough slog ahead of you, battling up steep trails and loose scree slopes. All the time the vast bulk of **Salkantay** looms above you, drawing increasingly close and entirely dominating the vista to the north. The pass itself lies just underneath a steep rocky spire, and there's precious little room to manoeuvre once up there. The rocky peak of **Cerro Jatunjasa** further hems you in to the south. Salkantay's glaciers seem close enough to touch. Beyond Inca Chiriasca you descend roughly to the southeast, zigzagging down a steep scree slope: be careful, as it's easy to loose your footing, especially if there's some snow cover. You're heading into the valley of the **Quebrada Sisaypampa**, which quickly shifts its course 90° and continues its descent to the northeast. About 2½ hours beyond the pass you reach some areas flat enough for camping. Take a break, you deserve it after a long day (eight hours in all).

Day three A short day today, 3½ hours following the stream down into the valley. You pass the friendly village of **Pampacahuana** and the village school on the left of the stream. The local teacher enjoys visitors and can always use extra materials (pens, books, etc) if you have them spare. Beyond the community, the trail shifts to the right-hand side of the Quebrada and you arrive at your destination, the village of **Paucarcancha** and its ruins, also known as **Incarajay**. You can camp below the ruins or near the small shop on the far side of the bridge.

From this point onwards you have three options, the first being to descend to **Huayllabamba** on the left side of the river and from there to join the Inca Trail (see page 174 for details). The second option is to continue beyond Huayllabamba and exit the trail at Km 82 near Ollantaytambo, where you can obtain transport back to Cuzco. The third option is to head up the valley of the **Quebrada Quesjamayo** to the southeast, a reverse of the multi-day Ancascocha trek. The second and third options are detailed in the description of the Ancascocha route, see below.

Ancascocha trek: Huarocondo to Km 82 → *4 days.*
Named after a diminutive but beautifully situated community in the Cordillera Vilcabamba's remote eastern fringe, this is a little-known, but worthy addition to the growing list of alternative Inca trails. Crossing three fairly steep passes, it offers fabulous views of some of the region's best-known snow peaks, Salkantay and La Verónica foremost among them. Unsung attractions such as the impressive Nevado Huayanay, which towers above a landscape laced with icy lakes and cascades, are an added bonus. Along with the natural attractions you'll pass interesting ruins, fragmented sections of Inca trail and friendly pastoral communities. Ancascocha can easily be combined with the classic Inca Trail (given the timely reservation of permits), or longer routes into the heart of the Vilcabamba range. For those with more limited time, transport direct to either Aguas Calientes or Cuzco can be obtained from the trail's end.

Day one   Huarocondo, a pretty, untouristy town is the launching point for the trek. The main plaza is worth a look, with its elegant colonial church framed by rugged mountains behind. The town's famed roast pig, *lechón*, is a greasy but tasty treat. Unsurprisingly, the best place to experience this is the **Casa de Lechón** on the north side of the plaza. The start of the trail itself lies to the northwest, about 4 km down the fertile river valley of the **Río Huarocondo**. With wheeled transport it will take you 10 minutes to reach, otherwise bet on an hour's walk to the trailhead, a small footbridge to the left of the road. A yellow sign beneath the bridge states the completion date of 1998, during the service of Alcalde Prof Daniel Vargas. The bridge's location more or less corresponds to **Paropiso** marked on the IGN Urubamba map.

Cross the bridge and the railway tracks immediately after (this is the Cuzco to Aguas Calientes line) and continue straight on, on a bearing of 300°. The trail gently climbs above the tracks, heading through dry, scrubby country, and is now easily followed. After 30 minutes you pass a rustic shelter with fine views, built for trekkers and local mule drivers. On a bearing of 320° you can see your immediate objective, the **Abra Watuq'asa** in a saddle at 3800 m. Above it lies the Inca ruin of **Huata**. An Inca wall running down the ridge, just to the right of the pass, is visible from a great distance. Two hours from the bridge you should reach the pass; there's very little water on this section of trail in the dry season. The ruins of Huata are impressive, with tall lower walls and square bastions resembling a medieval European castle. A short hike up to a second set of walls and fortifications that wrap themselves around the hill's summit rewards you with views of Chicón, Halancoma and La Verónica.

Your route now lies down the impressive valley to the west. From the pass it's a 30- to 40-minute decent to a small glade above the village of **Pomatales**. This might be a good lunch spot. The lower section of the valley boasts significant stands of native Andean woodland. Passing the glade, the trail leads to the far side of the valley and turns back on itself, climbing and heading north for a short distance, initially passing through a quarried defile. Keeping to the main trail, the route follows the contours of the hill, after 15 minutes turning west out of the Pomatales Valley and into that of **Chillipahua**. Strange parallel rock formations on the far side of the valley, possibly limestone, lance vertically down towards the river below. Thirty minutes from the glade the trail flattens out, running high on the valley's left shoulder. A further 10 minutes and the way splits: take the lower trail. The valley now turns southwest and tonight's campsite comes into view, the small community of **Chillipahua**. Beyond the school is a football field close to a stream running through the valley's centre, and this is as good a place to pitch your tent as any. Four to five hours in total at a steady pace.

Day two Head up the valley from camp. After five minutes cross to the right side of the river just before reaching a wall on the waterway's left bank. Follow the river on its right bank and after about 25 minutes on the trail you'll reach a T-junction: take the left-hand fork, staying close to the river. After a further 20 minutes, turn into the right-hand valley, following the small *quebrada* (stream). You're heading west now, through high *puna*, thick with tough *ichu* grass. If you hike in June or July you might find locals harvesting and drying their annual potato crop. One and a half hours from leaving camp, still climbing up the left-hand side of the valley, a stream crosses the route; don't forget to look behind you for good views of Chicón. The pass, locally known as the **Abra Chillipahua** or **Chochoccasa**, lies slightly to the left of a jagged rocky mountain, the 4500-m **Cerro Chachicata**. Heavy use from both man and beast has led to significant erosion, making the pass easy to identify. Two hours from

Ancascocha trek

camp brings you to the pass's summit at 4525 m. A precipitous view greets you on the far side, the vista dropping sharply down below you to the valley of the **Río Silque**, and northwest across the valley to the rugged and magnificent 5345-m **Nevado Huayanay**.

Descend on the steep western path straight over the pass and into the valley. After 20 minutes of descent into the *quebrada* you pass the tiny house of local herders. Ten minutes more and you come to the Río Silque valley floor. Cross the river and follow the trail right/north/downstream on the far (left) side. After a few minutes you pass a house with a walled *chakra* where a stream enters from the left-hand valley with a steep cliff rising above. Don't follow this *quebrada*; keep following the Río Silque. Views of Verónica become increasingly impressive, perfectly framed by the valley's dark walls.

One and a quarter hours after leaving the *abra* you cross a significant landslide, and a further 25 minutes beyond this, a wide *quebrada* enters from the west. The small, fairly traditional community spread out across the valley floor is **Ancascocha**, with the rectangular schoolhouse visible from the trail. Head down into the Ancascocha valley. You'll find the locals welcoming and it's possible to camp on the school football pitch or further up the valley with the residents' permission. The river running through the valley is marked as the **Quebrada Huayanay** on the IGN Urubamba sheet. It'll take four or five hours at a steady pace.

With its spectacular location at the foot of snow-capped Huayanay, it would easily be possible to spend a second day exploring the valley and its surroundings. A nice walk takes you up to a waterfall at the right-hand side of the valley's head, above a marshy area rich in birdlife (Andean geese, caracaras, etc); this takes an hour return. With a spare day you can hike high above the village to the little-visited source of this cascade, an isolated glacial lake. Ask the villagers for directions.

Day three Continue up the valley above Ancascocha and then take the southwest/left-hand branch under the bulk of Huayanay, keeping to the left-hand side of this *quebrada* as you steadily ascend. You're heading towards to the black triangular rock peak, the non-glaciated face of **Nevado Moyoc** that comes into view a short distance up the trail. Maintain a heading following trails of around 240°, and after just over an hour a beautiful emerald lagoon comes into view beneath you and to the right. A waterfall feeds the lake from its far end. The Huayanay Pass, the highest on the trek at 4600 m, lies at 240° between the peak of Moyoc and vast mass of Huayanay's glaciers above you. The easiest route to the pass starts from the left-hand corner of the lake, and rises on a clear diagonal, running high above both lagoon and falls. A second, very steep route leads up a trail to the right of the falls – this one looks impossible for pack animals.

Two hours after leaving camp you pass some interesting sections of ancient Inca wall on the way to the high *abra* and soon after this the trail flattens into a high-altitude grassy valley, only slowly gaining height. You pass a chain of jewel-like lakes framed by the snows behind. The lakes are surprisingly rich in water plants and aquatic insects. The surrounding area is rich pasture, used by locals to graze sheep, horses and alpacas. A final steep push leads you to the pass, marked by an *apucheta* (a group of standing stones built to honour the spirits of the mountains), almost three hours after leaving Ancascocha. Spectacular views surround and you get a peek at the almost-vanished Moyoc glacier.

After the pass the trail turns to the west/right. On a clear day the razor peak of Salkantay is an awe-inspiring reference point in front of you. Maintaining a roughly westward heading, you descend into the northward-running valley below the pass. This should take about 20 minutes. Cross the stream to the left-hand side of the *quebrada*, referred to as **Pucamayo** on the IGN sheet. Just above the stream lies the ancient Inca ruin of **Inca Rajay**, its low walls studded with flowers and mosses. At this point you turn northwest heading down the Pucamayo Valley. To the right lie the vast ramparts of **Huayantay**, this time its rear or western aspect. As you continue down the valley, the stream quickly drops away below you, running deep in a ravine to your right. Twenty minutes from Inca Rajay you cross a stream entering from the left, and 10 minutes after this you pass a steep cliff to your right, braided by two elegant waterfalls. After a further 20 minutes you cross a stream and enter the now-much-flatter valley floor, shortly afterwards passing the small settlement of **Muya Muya**. Beyond the village the valley drops steeply, turning to the left, now running more to the west. For the first time bushes and trees appear en masse. The trail crosses and re-crosses a dried out streambed before arriving at **Questa** (pronounced Keska), a settlement lying at 3700 m, some two hours after passing Inca Rajay. It's usually possible to camp next to the school.

Day four On leaving the village, the valley once again heading northwest, cross a wood and adobe bridge to the left-hand side of river. Below Questa the pastoral landscape seems timeless and tranquil, untouched by the modern world. Stick to the high left-hand side of the valley to avoid a small canyon 25 minutes' walk beyond your camp. The trail continues a further 45 minutes before skirting above the extensive ruins of **Paucarcancha** (also referred to as Incarajay), the site dominating a village of the same name. At this point the **Río Quesjamayo** flows into the **Río Cusichaca**. Cross a bridge to the far (west) bank of the Cusichaca. A small house here doubles as a shop, with basic supplies – rice, pasta, tomato sauce and, of course, Coca Cola. The terraces are a good place to camp if you fancy walking beyond Questa on Day three.

You can extend this trek into the Vilcabamba range, for example either to on the traverse trek to Choquequirao (see page 234) or the valley of Santa Teresa (see page 177) by turning south up the Cusichaca Valley towards Salkantay and the Inca Chiriasca Pass, a substantial undertaking at 4900 m.

Otherwise, after leaving the shop, head downriver, following the path through increasingly lush vegetation. Bamboo and bromeliads make an appearance for the first time, perhaps the remnants of a section of cloudforest before cultivation. You reach a junction after 15 minutes: take the right, more heavily used trail. Another five minutes and you arrive at **Huayllabamba**, one of the camps on the classic Inca Trail to Machu Picchu. If you have obtained Inca Trail permits (booking months in advance essential) and have a licensed guide, a left turn on the far side of Huayllabamba will start you on the route to Dead Woman's Pass (see page 174).

If concluding the trek at either Km 88 (for train transport to Aguas Calientes) or Km 82 (for bus transport to the Sacred Valley or Cuzco) keep heading north down the valley on what would normally be the first day of the Inca Trail. If you're hiking later in the day you will encounter a great number of porters and tourists heading for Huayllabamba. After about 1½ hours you reach a junction above the ruins of Patallacta. Turn right, initially up a hill, for Km 82, or left, then left again for Km 88, which lies just beyond the ruins. It takes another 2½ hours to reach the bridge crossing the Río Urubamba and Km 82. Early in the morning buses dropping tourists onto the 'trail' will take hikers back to Cuzco for a small fee. Make sure you get to Km 82 before midday to maximize chances of finding transport. If catching the train from Km 88, make sure you've pre-booked tickets and confirmed times in Cuzco, and that the train has clear instructions to stop at the station.

Other routes

There are other routes which approach the Inca Trails to Machu Picchu, such as the access through the Millpo Valley in the Salkantay area. A three-night trek goes from Km 82 to Km 88, then along the Río Urubamba to Pacaymayo Bajo and Km 104, from where you take the Camino Real described on page 175 to Wiñay-Wayna and Machu Picchu. Good day hiking trails have also been opened along the left bank of the Urubamba river, starting from Aguas Calientes and crossing the bridge of the hydroelectric plant to Choquesuysuy. You can use the trail along the Urubamba river as an alternative route when leaving Machu Picchu: it is 27 km from Aguas Calientes to Km 82, from where you can catch a bus to Ollantaytambo or Cuzco. Allow at least 5½ hours to get to Km 82 on the rough track. Food and drinks are sold at Km 88, but there is nowhere to stay en route.

Inca Jungle Trail

This is offered by several tour operators in Cuzco: on the first day you cycle downhill from Abra Málaga to Santa María, 80 km of mainly downhill riding through changing scenery which includes Inca ruins, coffee plantations and lush high jungle and cloud forest. Be aware, though, that this is the main Quillabamba–Cuzco highway with speeding vehicles inattentive to cyclists on the road. As ever, you get what you pay for and cheap tours will have bikes with poor or no brakes or gears, no safety or luggage-carrying backup. The second day is a hard seven-hour trek from Santa María to Santa Teresa. It involves crossing three adventurous bridges and bathing in the hot springs at Santa Teresa (US$1.65 entry – refurbishment underway after 2010 floods). The third day is a six-hour trek from Santa Teresa to Aguas Calientes and the final day is a guided tour of Machu Picchu. Find out what equipment, support and standards are offered by tour operators before paying.

Aguas Calientes → *For listings, see pages 186-189. Colour map 2, A2. See also map, page 185. Phone code: 084.*

Only 1.5 km back along the railway from Puente Ruinas, this is a popular resting place for those recovering from the rigours of the Inca Trail. It is named Aguas Calientes (or just Aguas) after the hot springs above the town. It is also called the town of Machu Picchu. Most activity is centred around the old railway station, on the plaza, or on Avenida Pachacútec, which leads from the plaza to the **thermal baths** ① *daily 0500-2030, US$3.15.* They consist of a communal pool, which smells a bit sulphurous, 10 minutes' walk from the town by the banks of the river amid rich cloud forest vegetation. You can rent towels and bathing costumes for US$3 at several places on the road to the baths, or buy them if you prefer. There are basic toilets, changing facilities and showers. Take soap and shampoo and keep an eye on your valuables. The new **Museo Manuel Chávez Ballon** ① *Carretera Hiram Bingham, Wed-Sun 0900-1600, US$6,* displays objects found at Machu Picchu.

Putucusi

An interesting day hike out of Aguas Calientes ascends Putucusi Mountain. Local people consider Putucusi to be a protector mountain for the area and it gives stupendous views of Machu Picchu and its surroundings. Follow the railway line out of town towards Machu Picchu and look for some stone stairs and a trail on your right (there is a blue sign). The climb to the top takes up to two hours, is very steep and involves several ladder sections, so it's not for the faint-hearted.

Aguas Calientes

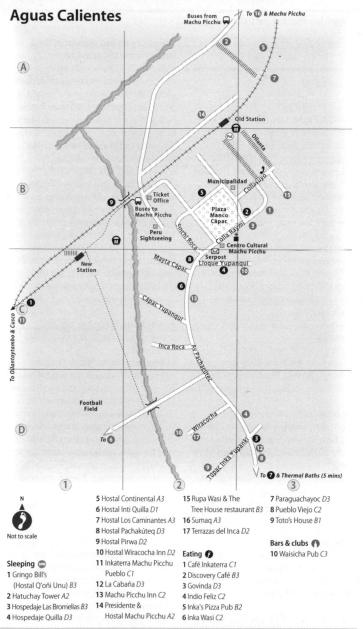

Buses from Machu Picchu 🚌

To 16 & Machu Picchu

Old Station

Ollanta

Municipalidad

Ticket Office

Buses to Machu Picchu

Peru Sightseeing

Plaza Manco Cápac

Sinchi Roca

Colla Raymi

Collasuyo

Centro Cultural Machu Picchu

Serpost

Lloque Yupanqui

Mayta Cápac

Cápac Yupanqui

Inca Roca

N. Pachacútec

New Station

To Ollantaytambo & Cusco

Football Field

Wiracocha

Tupac Inka Yupanki

To 6

To 7 & Thermal Baths (5 mins)

N
Not to scale

Sleeping 🛏

1 Gringo Bill's
   (Hostal Q'oñi Unu) *B3*
2 Hatuchay Tower *A2*
3 Hospedaje Las Bromelias *B3*
4 Hospedaje Quilla *D3*

5 Hostal Continental *A3*
6 Hostal Inti Quilla *D1*
7 Hostal Los Caminantes *A3*
8 Hostal Pachakúteq *D3*
9 Hostal Pirwa *D2*
10 Hostal Wiracocha Inn *D2*
11 Inkaterra Machu Picchu
    Pueblo *C1*
12 La Cabaña *D3*
13 Machu Picchu Inn *C2*
14 Presidente &
    Hostal Machu Picchu *A2*

15 Rupa Wasi & The
   Tree House restaurant *B3*
16 Sumaq *A3*
17 Terrazas del Inca *D2*

Eating 🍴

1 Café Inkaterra *C1*
2 Discovery Café *B3*
3 Govinda *D3*
4 Indio Feliz *C2*
5 Inka's Pizza Pub *B2*
6 Inka Wasi *C2*

7 Paraguachayoc *D3*
8 Pueblo Viejo *C2*
9 Toto's House *B1*

Bars & clubs 🍸

10 Waisicha Pub *C3*

⊙ Machu Picchu listings

For Sleeping and Eating price codes and other relevant information, see pages 30-36.

⊜ Sleeping

Machu Picchu *p167, map p169*
LL Machu Picchu Sanctuary Lodge, Carretera Hiram Bingham Km 7.5, under the same management as the **Hotel Monasterio** in Cuzco, T084-984 816956 (mob), www.sanctuary lodge.net. This hotel, at the entrance to the ruins, has some environmentally friendly features. The rooms are comfortable, the service is good and the staff helpful. Electricity and water available 24 hrs a day. Food in the restaurant is well cooked; the restaurant is for residents only in the evening, but the buffet lunch is open to all. The hotel is usually fully booked well in advance; if struggling for a booking try Sun night as other tourists find Pisac market a greater attraction.

Camping
Camping is not allowed at Intipunku, nor anywhere else at the site; guards may confiscate your tent. There is a free campsite beside the rail tracks at Puente Ruinas station.

The Inca Trail *p171, map p172*
G pp Youth Hostel, Wiñay-Wayna. With bunk beds, showers and a small restaurant. It is often fully booked. You can sleep on the floor of the restaurant more cheaply, but it is open for diners until 2300. There are also spaces for a few tents, but they get snapped up quickly too. The hostel's door is closed at 1730.

Camping
The approved campsites are currently at **Huayllabamba**, **Llulluchayoc**, **Llulluchapampa**, **Pacaymayo Valley**, **Runkuracay** and **Phuyupatamarca**.

Salkantay treks *p175, map p176*
Machu Picchu Lodge to Lodge, T084-243636 (Lima T01-421 6952), www.mountainlodgesofperu.com. **Mountain Lodges of Peru** have set up a series of lodges on the Santa Teresa trek to Machu Picchu. Fully guided tours take 7 days, going from lodge to lodge, which are at Soraypampa (**Salkantay Lodge and Adventure Resort**), Huayraccmachay (**Wayra Lodge**), Collpapampa (**Colpa Lodge**) and Lucmabamba (**Lucma Lodge**). Contact **Mountain Lodges of Peru** for rates, departure dates as well as all other details.
F pp Hospedaje Mollepata, Mollepata, T084-832103, or Cuzco T084-245449. Just above the plaza, behind the solid, elegant church. Hot-water electric shower, nice courtyard with café and ÑanTika restaurant attached. Swings in the courtyard are a real bonus!

Aguas Calientes *p184, map p185*
It is advisable to book a hotel in advance from Cuzco.
LL Inkaterra Machu Picchu Pueblo. Reservations: Andalucía 174, San Isidro, Lima, T01-610 0400; in Cuzco at Plaza las Nazarenas 167, T084-234010, www.inkaterra.com. Beautiful colonial-style bungalows have been built in a village compound surrounded by cloudforest 5 mins' walk along the railway from the town. The hotel has lovely gardens in which there are many species of birds, butterflies and orchids. There is a pool, spa and an expensive restaurant. It offers tours to Machu Picchu, several guided walks on the property and to local beauty spots. The buffet breakfasts are great. It also has the **Café Inkaterra** by the railway line. The hotel is involved in a project to rehabilitate spectacled bears and release them back into the wild. Recommended, but there are a lot of steps between the public areas and rooms.
LL Sumaq, Av Hermanos Ayar Mz 1, Lte 3, T084-211059, www.sumaqhotelperu.com.

An impressive 5-star hotel near the Urumba river with on-site spa, bar and restaurant.

LL-L Hatuchay Tower, Carretera Puente Ruinas block 4, T084-211201, www.hatuchay tower. com. This smart, modern hotel is below the old station. Buffet breakfast and all taxes are included. There are standard rooms and luxury suites with hot water.

AL La Cabaña, Av Pachacútec M20-3, T084-211048, www.lacabanamachupicchu.com. Price includes bathroom and continental breakfast. Rooms have hot water. There is a café, laundry service and a DVD player and TV (with a good selection of movies) for clients in the lounge. The staff are helpful and can provide information on interesting local walks. The hotel is popular with groups.

AL Machu Picchu Inn, Av Pachacútec 101, T084-211057, mapiinn@peruhotel.com.pe. The price includes bathroom and breakfast. A modern hotel, with a functional atmosphere.

AL-A Gringo Bill's (Hostal Q'oñi Unu), Colla Raymi 104, T084-211046 (Cuzco office Av El Sol 520, T084-223663), www.gringobills.com. From deluxe to standard rooms, price includes bathroom and continental breakfast. An Aguas Calientes institution, it's friendly, relaxed, with a lot of coming and going, hot water, good beds, luggage store, laundry and money exchange. Good but expensive meals are served in the restaurant; breakfast starts at 0530 and they offer a packed lunch to take up to the ruins. Sadly for Gringo Bill's the monstrous new municipal building has been plonked right in front of the hotel and obscures the views from rooms which once looked out over the plaza.

AL-A Rupa Wasi, C Huanacaure 180, T084-211101, www.rupawasi.net. Rustic 'eco-lodge', located up a small alley off Collasuyo. The lodge and its owners have a very laid-back, comfortable style, there are great views from the balconies of the 1st-floor rooms and purified water (so you don't have to buy more plastic). Birdwatching and other treks available. Breakfast is included and half-board is available: gourmet cuisine

in the recommended restaurant. Cookery classes are offered, too.

A Presidente, at the old station, T084-211034 (Cuzco T084-244598), www.hostal presidente.com. Next to Hostal Machu Picchu, see below, this is the more upmarket half of the establishment. Rooms without river view are cheaper, but the price includes breakfast and taxes. There seems to be only minimal difference between this and **Machu Picchu**, which represents much better value for money.

B Hostal Continental, Av Imperio de los incas 127, near the old train station, T084-211065, http://hostalcontinentalperu.com. Very clean rooms with good beds, hot showers. This renovated *hostal* is in the same group as the **Presidente** and **Hostal Machu Picchu**.

C Hostal Machu Picchu, at the old station, T084-211065, sierrandina@gmail.com. Price includes breakfast and taxes. A clean, functional establishment, which is quiet and friendly (especially Wilber, the owner's son). There is hot water, a nice balcony over the Urumba, a grocery store and travel information is available. Recommended.

C Hostal Pachakúteq, up the hill beyond Hostal La Cabaña, T084-211061. Rooms with bathroom and 24-hr hot water. Breakfast is included, quiet, family-run. Recommended.

C Hostal Wiracocha Inn, C Wiracocha, T084-211088, www.wiracochainn.com. Rooms with bath and hot water. Breakfast included. There is a small garden at this very friendly and helpful *hostal*. Some rooms have been converted into suites and are offered at a higher price. It's popular particularly with European groups.

D Hospedaje Las Bromelias, Colla Raymi, T084-211145. Just off the plaza before **Gringo Bill's**, this is a small place that has rooms with bath and hot water. Accommodation is cheaper without bath.

D Hospedaje Quilla, Av Pachacútec, T084-211009, between Wiracocha and Túpac Inka Yupanki. Price includes breakfast, bath and hot water. Rents bathing gear for the hot springs if you arrive without it.

E Hostal Inti Quilla, C Aymuraypa Tikan s/n, Urb Las Orquídeas, T084-211096, hostalintiquillamapi@hotmail.com. On the other side of the river fom most hotels. Private bath and hot water, laundry, friendly, clean, good value.

E Hostal Los Caminantes, Av Imperio de los Incas 140, by the railway just beyond the old station, T084-211083. Price per person for a room with bathroom. Hot water but breakfast extra. Basic but friendly and clean.

E Hostal Pirwa, C Túpac Inka Yupanki, www.pirwahostelscusco.com. With breakfast, TV, bath and luggage store, this hostel is in the same group as in Cuzco, Lima and elsewhere.

E Terrazas del Inca, C Wiracocha s/n, T084-211113, www.terrazasdelinca.com. Safety deposit box, rooms with private bath, continental breakfast included, use of kitchen. Friendly and helpful staff. Recommended.

Camping

The only official campsite is in a field by the river, just below Puente Ruinas station, it has toilets and showers, US$3.50 per person. Do not leave your tent and belongings unattended.

🍴 Eating

Machu Picchu *p167, map p169*
Machu Picchu Sanctuary Lodge (see Sleeping, page 186) has a restaurant serving buffet lunch. There's also a snack bar beside the entrance but you're advised to take your own food and drink.

Aguas Calientes *p184, map p185*
Pizza seems to be the most common dish in town, but many of the pizzerias serve other types of food as well. The old station and Av Pachútec are lined with eating places. Check if tax is included as Aguas Calientes is the only place in Peru where it is often added to the published price.

₩₩₩ Café Inkaterra, on the railway, just below Inkaterra Machu Picchu. US$15 for a great lunch buffet with scenic views of the river.

₩₩ Indio Feliz, C Lloque Yupanqui, T084-211090, www.indiofeliz.com. Great French cuisine, excellent value and service, set 3-course meal for US$10, good pisco sours. Expanded to include a bar area with elaborate decor and great atmosphere. Highly recommended.

₩₩ Inka's Pizza Pub, on the plaza. Good pizzas, changes money and accepts TCs.

₩₩ Inka Wasi, Av Pachacútec, www.inkawasi restaurant.com. A very good place to eat. Atmospheric and warm because of the open fire in the centre. Full Peruvian and international menu including pizza and pasta.

₩₩ Pueblo Viejo, Av Pachacútec, near the plaza. Good food in a spacious but warm environment. Price includes salad bar.

₩₩ Toto's House, Av Imperio de los Incas, on the railway line. Same owners as **Pueblo Viejo**. Good value and quality *menú*. Also serves a buffet from 1130 to 1500 every day.

₩ Discovery Café, Plaza de Armas, T084-211355. Without a doubt both the best internet connection and coffee in Aguas Calientes. Several computers and Wi-Fi.

₩ Govinda, Av Pachacútec y Túpac Inka Yupanki. Vegetarian restaurant with a cheap set lunch. Recommended.

₩ Paraguachayoc, Av Pachacútec, at the top near the baths. Charming little restaurant with trout farm where you can catch your own dinner. US$5 for a whole trout with chips and drink.

₩ The Tree House, Jr Huancarane (at **Rupa Wasi Eco-Lodge**) T084-211101. Restaurant serving gourmet organic food.

🍷 Bars and clubs

Aguas Calientes *p184, map p185*
Waisicha Pub, C Lloque Yupanqui. For good music and atmosphere.

▲▲ Activities and tours

Aguas Calientes *p184, map p185*
For details of specialist operators in Cuzco, see Activities and tours, page 114.
Peru Sightseeing, www.perusightseeing. com. The only agency in Aguas Calientes, they offer guided trips to Machu Picchu with audio tours as well as a local guide. You can book a whole 2 or 3 day package in advance, or just the Machu Picchu tour. Also half-day tours in the area to Mandor and the Machu Picchu musuem. Can make onward travel arrangements.

⊖ Transport

Aguas Calientes *p184, map p185*
Bus
To **Machu Picchu** every 30 mins from 0630 to 1300, US$14 return, US$7 single, valid for 48 hrs. Buses return from the ruins 1200-1730. It is also possible to take a bus down 0700-0900. The ticket office is opposite the bus stop, which is 50 m from the railway station. Tickets can also be bought in advance at **Consetur**, Santa Catalina Ancha, Cuzco, to save queuing when you arrive in Aguas Calientes.

Train
For details of travelling by rail to Machu Picchu, see box, page 166.

❶ Directory

Aguas Calientes *p184, map p185*
Banks There are several ATMs in town and a branch of BCP for changing TCs, which also has an ATM. It is not uncommon for ATMs to run out of cash at weekend. **Internet** Many internet shops, average price US$1 per hr; slow connection. **Discovery Café** (see Eating, above) has the best connection. **Medical services** Hampi Land, C Hermanos Ayar, Lote 6 Mz 10, T084-782641, www.hampiland.com. Professional, 24-hr medical care for tourists, with emergency rescue and ambulance services, pharmacy, oxygen. **Urgent Medical Center**, Av de Los Incas 119, T084-211005, T084-984 761314 (mob). Good care at affordable prices. **Post** Serpost agencies, just off the plaza, between the Centro Cultural Machu Picchu and Galería de Arte Tunupa, and on the railway line. **Telephone** Oficina on C Collasuyo, and there are plenty of phone booths around town.

Contents

Footprint features

Beyond Machu Picchu

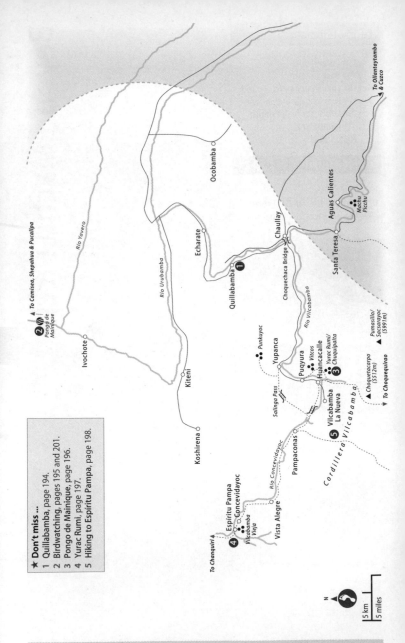

★ **Don't miss...**

1 Quillabamba, page 194.
2 Birdwatching, pages 195 and 201.
3 Pongo de Mainique, page 196.
4 Yurac Rumi, page 197.
5 Hiking to Espíritu Pampa, page 198.

The lower reaches of the Río Urubamba beyond Machu Picchu are the gateway to regions that are very different from the highlands of Cuzco, yet intimately linked to it by history. Peru's rugged and largely unexplored Vilcabamba Mountains lie to the north and east of the main Andean chain, situated between the canyons of the mighty Apurímac and Urubamba rivers. Extending a mountainous limb into the Amazon Basin, they rise from tropical rainforest to the freezing glaciers of Nevado Salkantay at 6271 m, an area of around 30,000 sq km.

The most important town in this area is Quillabamba, where, they say, it is summer all year round. From here you head north to the end of the Andes and the beginning of the vast jungle. The limit between the two is marked by the waterfalls and canyon of the Pongo de Mainique, frequently described as one of the most beautiful places on earth. East of Quillabamba is Vilcabamba Vieja, the mysterious last stronghold of the Incas, where Manco Inca and his followers maintained Inca traditions, religion and government outside the reach of the Spanish authorities. Long sought by *conquistadores* and archaeologists, Vilcabamba Vieja is now the destination of one of Peru's hardest treks.

Ins and outs

As no passenger trains for tourists run beyond Aguas Calientes, the only route to Quillabamba is by road from Cuzco via Ollantaytambo. Beyond Quillabamba, road transport continues to Ivochote, for boats to the Pongo de Mainique, and to Huancacalle for treks to Espíritu Pampa. ►► *For further details see Transport, page 204.*

Background

In 1536, three years after the fall of the Inca Empire to the Spanish *conquistadores*, Manco Inca led a rebellion against the conquerors (see box, page 199). Retiring from Cuzco when Spanish reinforcements arrived, Manco and his followers fell back to the remote triangle of Vilcabamba and established a centre at Espíritu Pampa. Centuries after the eventual Spanish crushing of Inca resistance, the location of the neo-Inca capital of Vilcabamba was forgotten; the search for it provoked Hiram Bingham's expeditions and his discovery of Machu Picchu. Bingham also discovered Vilcabamba Vieja, without realizing it, but its true location at Espíritu Pampa was only pinpointed by Gene Savoy in the 1960s, and was not confirmed irrefutably until the work of Vincent Lee in the 1980s.

Vilcabamba lies in a region of immense biological diversity known as the Tropical Andes Eco-region, the meeting of the Andes and the Amazon, which supports the greatest range of animal and plant life on the planet. This diversity is the result of massive variations in altitude, climate and habitat within a relatively small area. Vilcabamba's isolation has also meant that many high-altitude species have been cut off from other populations for thousands, perhaps millions of years, developing separate characteristics and eventually becoming new species, endemic to the region.

In the face of growing threats from oil and gas companies and settlement from the more densely populated mountain regions of Peru, Conservation International and the Smithsonian Institute conducted a 'rapid assessment programme' finding, among others, 12 previously unknown species of amphibian and reptile, plus a very large rodent. These studies aided the recent creation of the Otishi National Park in some of the range's most remote recesses.

In the foothills and surrounding river valleys live four indigenous groups: the Nahua, Nanti, Kirineri and Machiguenga. Some of these people live in voluntary isolation from the outside world. Sadly, both the people and wilderness are under threat; it's an all-too-familiar story. Shell explored the area in the early 1980s and its encounters with uncontacted tribes led to the deaths of at least 42% of the Nahua population, largely through introduced diseases to which these people had little or no immunity. Despite improving its social and environmental practices, Shell pulled out of the region in the late 1990s, but the gas field it discovered, Camisea, is still under development.

Quillabamba and around → *For listings, see pages 203-204. Colour map 2, A2. Phone code: 084.*

'La Ciudad de Eterno Verano' (The City of Eternal Summer), as it is known, was once a prosperous town from the sale of coffee. It has now become the overnighting spot for people going to Vilcabamba, Espíritu Pampa and the magnificent Pongo de Mainique, the region's gateway to the Amazon. This delightful market town now survives on the export of fruit, coffee, honey and other produce to Cuzco. There is a Dominican mission here. The tourist season is from June to July, when Peruvian holidaymakers descend on

Camisea Natural Gas Project

Since 2003, almost all of Peru's Amazonian lowlands have been open, by government decree, to oil and gas exploration. This includes the the Nahua Kugakapori Reserve (for uncontacted or little-contacted tribal groups), in which the Camisea gas field is located. Construction of two pipelines taking gas from Camisea to Lima cut a swathe of destruction across the Reserve and the Vilcabamba range. The destination for the gas is an export terminal and liquefaction plant on the Pacific coast. This is in the buffer zone of the Paracas National Reserve, which has some of the most significant bird and marine mammal populations on the entire Pacific coast of South America. Serious environmental and social risks scared off a number of investors, but in September 2003 the Camisea Consortium received funding worth US$135 million from the Interamerican Development Bank. Initially the bank refused to disburse final instalments until social and environmental conditions were met, but subsequently endorsed the loan despite outside criticism of the shortcomings of its own report.

By 2005 pressure was being exerted to begin development of 'block 56', 56,680 ha within Nahua territory. This project is now known as Camisea 2.

Major liquid-gas spills from pipe ruptures occurred in the first 18 months of the pipeline's operation, and this, together with diesel spills totalling several thousand gallons, increased indigenous opposition to Camisea 1 and 2. Local tribal groups state that both fish and wildlife populations have decreased significantly since the initiation of the project. There have also been large increases in infectious diseases and reports of forced relocation of tribes within the Nahua Kugakapori Reserve.

Deforestation of the Vilcabamba range's western slope began in Inca times, but the east has remained unaffected by population pressure and cultivation. Indigenous people, conservationists and ecotourism interests are fighting to preserve its treasures. Similar opposition to hydrocarbon exploration and the colonisation it brings in Amazonas department in northern Peru in 2010 led to violent clashes between locals and the police. Whether such clashes between the people of the forest and the oil and gas industry will become more common remains to be seen.

See also Robert Goodland's *Peru: Camisea Natural Gas Project. Independent Assessment of the Environmental and Social Priorities*. Another source is www.amazonwatch.org.

---

the town to absorb its wonderful warm and sunny climate and relaxed atmosphere. Although Quillabamba has plenty to offer, it's normally overlooked by foreign tourists because of the incredibly bumpy but beautiful ride to get there.

The road to Quillabamba

After leaving Ollantaytambo, the road passes through **Peña**, a place of great beauty. Once out of Peña, the paved road climbs on endless zigzags, offering breathtaking views, to reach the **Abra Málaga Pass**, just below the beautiful glaciated peak of Verónica. Here, where the paving ends, at 4000-4300 m, are some patches of *polylepis* woodland, which contain a number of endangered birds. These include the white-browed tit spinetail, the ash-breast tit tyrant and the royal cinclodes. Since it is so accessible, this has become a prime site for birdwatchers, and conservationists are working hard to protect the area. At Chaullay the road meets the old Machu Picchu to Quillabamba railway and continues parallel to the Río Urubamba to Quillabamba.

Around Quillabamba

For the weary traveller one of the biggest attractions, about 1.5 km from Quillabamba, is **Sambaray** ① *US$0.20; combi US$0.30, taxi US$1*, a recreation area with an outdoor swimming pool, restaurant, volleyball and football field. As Sambaray is situated on the Río Alto Urubamba, you can also swim in the river, or, if you're feeling brave, tube down it. Ask locals for the best place to start, as the river can be quite rapid. **Siete Tinajas** (Seven Small Baths) is a beautiful waterfall some 45 minutes by combi from town (take the bus from Paradero El Grifo, US$1). It is well worth the trip for the photos alone, although be careful when climbing to the top, as it can be very slippery.

Pongo de Mainique and the Amazon Basin

Before the Río Urubamba enters the vast plain of the Amazon Basin it carves its way through one last wall of foothills and the result is spectacular. The Pongo de Mainique is a sheer rainforest canyon, hundreds of metres deep with the Urubamba surging through its centre and many small waterfalls tumbling in on either side. The Machiguenga people who live in the area believe this to be a portal to the afterlife and it's easy to see why. It is an awe-inspiring journey. The Machiguengas, however, are very private people and do not take kindly to uninvited strangers; if you wish to visit them on their reserve take someone who has contact with them. The jungle surrounding the canyon is home to much wildlife, including many species of macaw.

To get to the Pongo de Mainique, take a bus from Quillabamba's northern bus 'terminal' (a dusty outdoor affair with many foodstalls and the occasional ticket booth) to **Ivochote**, via a new road into the jungle (see Transport, page 204). The road can be in terrible condition in places. En route you'll pass **Kiteni**, a rapidly expanding jungle town. Ivochote is the end of the road, literally, but it develops a party atmosphere on Saturdays, market day in the jungle. Due to the Camisea Natural Gas Project (see box, page 195), downriver boat traffic is fairly intense. *Lanchas* (boats) head downstream early in the morning on most days during the dry season. In the wet season (roughly December to April) the river may be too dangerous to navigate, especially the rapids in the Pongo itself. When the river is high you rocket through in about five minutes; in the dry season, it's a more leisurely drift through the Pongo. Depending on your bargaining ability, passage downriver to the Pongo or to the **Casa de los Ugarte** (see Sleeping, page 203) will set you back about US$10, providing the captain has trading business downstream. Hiring a boat independently will cost a lot more. To return upstream prices are roughly one-third higher, owing to the increased amount of fuel required to motor against the current. Two to three hours downstream from the Casa de los Ugarte, on the right-hand bank of the river, you pass the Machiguenga community of **Timpía**. Here is the community-run **Sabeti Lodge** (see Sleeping, page 203), which has a number of activities and excursions in the region, including trips to the Pongo and visits to two of the best *colpas*, clay-licks, in Peru.

Beyond the Pongo a day's boat travel will bring you to **Malvinas**, centre of the hugely controversial Camisea Natural Gas Project, and on to **Camisea** itself. If you wish to stay here, you must ask the *presidente* of the community first. Another day downriver and you'll reach **Sepahua**, a largely indigenous village on the edge of the Alto Purús region. It has a few *hostales* and you can buy pretty much anything you need. Those with time and an adventurous spirit can continue downriver to **Pucallpa** via Atalaya (several *hostales*, market and a tourist office on the plaza which will help with day trips). To go all the way to **Iquitos** in the north means, overall, a journey of 2500 km by boat, an incredible opportunity to see the Peruvian jungle.

Huancacalle and around → *For listings, see pages 203-204.*

At **Chaullay**, the historic **Choquechaca Bridge**, built on Inca foundations, permits drivers to cross the river to the village of Huancacalle, a two-street village (no restaurants but a few shops) between four and seven hours from Quillabamba. Huancacalle is the best base for exploring the nearby Inca ruins of Vitcos and the starting point for the trek to Espíritu Pampa. You can also hike up to **Vilcabamba La Nueva** from Huancacalle. It's a three-hour walk through beautiful countryside with Inca ruins dotted around. There is a mission run by Italians, with electricity and running water, where you may be able to spend the night.

Walking tour of Vitcos and Yurac Rumi → *3-4 hrs.*
The Inca sites of Vitcos and Yurac Rumi lie behind the hill that rises immediately on the far side of the river from Huancacalle. Both sites are easily accessible and well worth the effort of a visit. Allow plenty of time for hiking to and visiting the ruins, although three hours is sufficient for a whirlwind tour. Guides can be hired in Huancacalle for a small fee.

Just past the **Hospedaje Sixpac Manco**, cross the bridge on your left. On the far side of the river the trail splits – take the left-hand fork. The right-hand trail leads to the Choquetacarpo pass and, eventually, to **Choquequirao**, a magnificent Inca citadel (see page 232). The left-hand track leads up an impressive restored Inca stairway to a small field. It's a steep climb. Follow the incline of the field and another small restored section of Inca Trail. From this point you will see the beautifully sculpted **Yurac Rumi**, the **White Rock** of the Incas (also referred to as **Chuquipalta**), once the most sacred site in South America. The rock is very large (8 m high and 20 m wide), with intricate and elaborate carvings, now covered in lichen. The rock has an intricate system of water channels surrounding it and these run into a finely carved Inca bath, in excellent condition. Underneath the White Rock on the right-hand side lies a series of 'seats'; local guides claim these were used by the Inca's chosen virgins during ceremonies held at the site. Shadows and light play strangely on the rock's finely carved features; take the time if you can to return later in the day and have another look.

From the White Rock continue downhill, following the contour of the hill to the left. As you walk down the valley, **Ñustahispanan** comes into view – agricultural terraces, another sacred rock and a stone mimicking the shape of the mountains down the valley.

Following the trail on the left-hand side of the valley climbs to **Vitcos** ① *entry US$11*, with mountains silhouetted behind. At Vitcos you will find **Manco Inca's Palace**, a beautiful multi-doored building with excellent stonework. It was the palace of the last four Inca rulers from 1536 to 1572 and was discovered by Hiram Bingham in 1911, the same year he discovered Machu Picchu. Unlike that more famous site, Vitcos has documented historical associations which make a visit particularly interesting and rewarding. Above the palace is a flat area, perhaps originally used for ceremonial purposes, with fantastic 360° views, from the snowy peaks of the Vilcabamba range to the verdant valleys below. The entire site is highly defensible, surrounded on three sides by steep drops and accessed by a thin bridge of land on the fourth. To return to Huancacalle, retrace your steps or descend to the road on the far side of the river.

The trek to Espíritu Pampa from Huancacalle takes three days, but would be a more comfortable undertaking in four. Vilcabamba Vieja itself is quite a large site, and further groups of buildings may still be awaiting discovery in the densely forested mountains surrounding the valley. Give yourself at least a day at the site to soak up the atmosphere before continuing a further six hours to Chanquiri, the starting point for transport to Kiteni and Quillabamba.

Ins and outs

ⓘ *The Ministerio de Cultura charge for this trek is US$38.20 (students US$19), not including entry to the archaeological site, US$11.*

Guides and supplies An excellent guide is Jesús Castillo Alveres who can be contacted through the **Hospedaje Sixpac Manco** in Huancacalle (see page 203). Many members of the Cobos family (see page 201) are guides; Juvenal Cobos has guided for BBC documentary teams among others. A good rate of pay for guides/mule drivers is US$8 per day, plus expenses, and US$6 per mule or horse used (in some seasons, the trail is unsuitable for horses). Before you leave be very clear about your exact itinerary and expectations; some guides have been known to leave clients in Espíritu Pampa, half a day's hike from the roadhead in Chanquiri. Always ask if you have to provide sufficient food and a waterproof tent by way of accommodation for your guide on the trail. If you enjoy your trip give your guide a tip; it will be appreciated. Remember, *arrieros* (mule drivers) based in Huancacalle have to walk all the way back along the route, a journey of at least two and a half days, and for this they don't charge. Always take all plastic and non-biodegradable rubbish back to Cuzco for more efficient disposal. All supplies must be brought from Huancacalle as even basic items are scarce on the trail.

Best time to visit The best time of year is from May to November, possibly December. Outside this period it is very dangerous as the trails are extremely narrow and can be thick with mud and very slippery. Insect repellent is essential; there are millions of mosquitoes. Also take along painkillers and other basic medicines, which will be much appreciated by the local people should you need to take advantage of their hospitality.

Day one: Huancacalle to Río Chalcha → *6-7 hrs' walking.*

From **Hospedaje Sixpac Manco** follow the course of the Río Vilcabamba upstream, staying on the right side. Your compass bearing is roughly west and you'll maintain this direction for most of the first day and, indeed, the trek to Espíritu Pampa itself. You're heading towards the Abra Colpapasa (Colpapasa Pass), which lies to the right of the jagged peaks in front of you. Climb up the right bank until you reach the road heading for Vilcabamba La Nueva. Near a slightly Swiss-looking house with a diamond-shaped image of Christ, turn right up the hill. After 70 m or so, turn left off the road up the dirt track. The trail starts edging towards the peaks, beginning to leave the river's course behind. This whole area is a picturesque mix of cloudforest remnants and farmland. Just before another crucifix and where the stream crosses the trail (you're back on the road again!) turn right and traverse the small concrete bridge. On the far side head up this valley, keeping on the left of the stream. After a short time you rejoin the road once more. Turn right and keep ascending the valley. From here to Vilcabamba La Nueva you can essentially follow the road, electricity cables and river up the valley. Look out for short cuts to avoid the bends. As you approach

The last Incas of Vilcabamba

After Pizarro killed Atahualpa in 1532 the Inca Empire disintegrated rapidly, and it is often thought that native resistance ended there. But in fact it continued for 40 more years, beginning with Manco, a teenage half-brother of Atahualpa.

In 1536, Manco escaped from the Spanish and returned to lead a massive army against them. He besieged Cuzco and Lima simultaneously, and came close to dislodging the Spaniards from Peru. Spanish reinforcements arrived and Manco fled to Vilcabamba, a mountainous forest region west of Cuzco that was remote, but still fairly close to the Inca capital, which he always dreamed of recapturing.

The Spanish chased Manco deep into Vilcabamba but he managed to elude them and continued his guerrilla war, raiding Spanish commerce on the Lima highway, and keeping alive the Inca flame. Then, in 1544, Spanish outlaws to whom he had given refuge murdered him, ending the most active period of Inca resistance.

The Inca line passed to his sons. The first, a child too young to rule named Sayri Túpac, eventually yielded to Spanish enticements and emerged from Vilcabamba, taking up residence in Yucay, near Urubamba in 1558. He died mysteriously – possibly poisoned – three years later.

His brother Titu Cusi, who was still in Vilcabamba, now took up the Inca mantle. Astute and determined, he resumed raiding and fomenting rebellion against the Spanish. But in 1570, Titu Cusi fell ill and died suddenly. A Spanish priest was accused of murdering him. Anti-Spanish resentment erupted, and the priest and a Spanish viceregal envoy were killed. The Spanish Viceroy reacted immediately, and the Spanish invaded Vilcabamba for the third and last time in 1572.

A third brother, Túpac Amaru was now in charge. He lacked his brother's experience and acuity, and his destiny was to be the sacrificial last Inca. The Spanish overran the Inca's jungle capital, and dragged him back to Cuzco in chains. There, Túpac Amaru, the last Inca, was publicly executed in Cuzco's main plaza.

The location of the neo-Inca capital of Vilcabamba was forgotten over the centuries, and the search for it provoked Hiram Bingham's expeditions and his discovery of Machu Picchu. Bingham also discovered Vilcabama the Old, without realizing it, but the true location at Espíritu Pampa was only pinpointed by Gene Savoy in the 1960s, and wasn't confirmed irrefutably until the work of Vincent Lee in the 1980s.

Vilcabamba La Nueva the valley floor begins to flatten out into agricultural and grazing land. An Italian-sponsored programme is supporting a carpentry project here, hence the impressive buildings in parts of the village.

When you enter Vilcabamba take the first right at the junction. You want to head up the large valley to the right, not the smaller valley rising above the town to your left. You're heading roughly north-northwest at this point. Cross the stream at the bottom of the smaller valley, following the road along the left-hand side of the larger westerly valley. Holding your course up the river, you reach the **Abra Colpapasa** at over 4000 m. Here there's a sign announcing government plans to improve the route to Espíritu Pampa. From the pass, given clear weather (which the author didn't have!) you can see many of the great snow peaks in the Vilcabamba range, including Salkantay and Pumasillo (also marked as Sacsarayoc on many Peruvian maps). Once through, follow the left side of the pass, descending gently. There's a 'road' – possibly work in progress – that follows a high line in early sections of the valley, and several short-cut paths cutting off the bends beneath. You're still heading west. After one hour there's a magnificent set of Inca steps dropping steeply towards the river and the valley floor. The trail turns to the left slightly, crossing another stream entering the main flow from the left by a nicely constructed wooden bridge, the **Puente Malcachaca**. Before crossing the bridge two trails come into view on the far side. The higher one leads to the village of Pampaconas and on to Espíritu Pampa. The lower trail (described below) circumvents the village, following the river directly to Espíritu Pampa. This route also leads to several beautiful potential campsites by the river, the best of which are another 15 to 20 minutes' walk from the bridge. If you still feel energetic, you could continue to the Pampas just below the tiny settlement of Ututu (see Day two, below). The river here carries the local name of the **Río Chalcha**. It is generally marked on maps as the **Río Concevidayoc**, but carries local names in several sections.

Day two: Río Chalcha to Vista Alegre → *A total of 6½-7 hrs' walking.*
From the campsites near the Chalcha, carry on descending further into the valley – and the Amazon Basin. As you advance the vegetation becomes wilder and less disturbed. The hills on the far side of the river are dominated by stands of virgin cloudforest. With the continuing loss in elevation the trees become studded with epiphytes, plants that make their home on the branches of large trees. They lack root systems so obtain all nutrients and moisture directly from the humid atmosphere and thus are indicators of cloudforest and rainforest environments. The path follows the river closely, passing through a patchwork of fields and natural vegetation. You can feel the air become stickier and more humid as you descend. The tiny and idyllic settlement of **Ututu** is reached 1½ hours after the camp. Perhaps only 10 or 20 people call Ututu home and their lifestyle seems little influenced by the modern world. Just beyond, through picturesque *pampa*, you cross an orange suspension bridge across the Chalcha to its right bank. The path now enters a spectacular stretch of ancient cloudforest, choked with mosses and vines. In many sections the route follows wonderful sections of Inca trail, stairs, etc. All the time the river roars on your left, gathering strength from the many small creeks that join it. This section lasts between one and 1½ hours, but serious birdwatchers with a day to spare would be well rewarded. The area abounds in birdlife, with many colourful species of tanager, among others. Throughout this section of the trail you're heading more or less northeast.

You now come to a second orange suspension bridge, crossing back to the left- hand side of the valley. A brief climb offers splendid views of the densely forested peaks in the Vilcabamba range, especially on the right side of the river. Sadly, much of the forest on the trail side in this section has been cut or burned to create small farming plots or *chacras*. Walking close to the ridgeline, the river far below, you pass lush secondary forest and scrub before descending to **Vista Alegre** through a more heavily populated area. The Concevidayoc now carries the local name of Río Vista Alegre. Before you reach camp, located in a convenient football field, you cross three bridges. The first is a fragile construction of dubious safety, made with rough-hewn logs balanced against each other in the centre. In the dry season it's possible to wade across the river and this could be a better option. The second bridge, Cedrochaka, is a simple log affair, but secure. The third, Puente Vista Alegre, just before the field, is adequate for most walkers.

Day three: Vista Alegre to Espíritu Pampa → *About 7 hrs' walking.*

Carry on downstream. After a couple of minutes you'll cross a stony riverbed – a stream entering the Río Vista Alegre. A few logs form a rough bridge which may be impassable in heavy rain. The path continues on the far side towards a junction – take the right-hand path. The trail follows the river's left bank, largely surrounded by forest, heading roughly north-northeast. After an initial alternation between forest and stony beaches the track enters the largest stretch of primary forest on the route. For the next four or five hours, it is broken only by the tiny dwellings of five or six families who live in the area. The route ascends and descends many times between feeder streams entering the main river. You've now returned to your northwesterly course. There are great views of the jungle from various viewpoints on the route.

Again, this is a great area for birding, this time in the transition zone between the cloudforest and the lowland tropical forest. The area seems especially rich in examples of the trogon family, with quetzals very much in evidence. As the trail continues the river drops further and further beneath you. You're walking high on the left slope of the valley. After two hours you reach the tiny settlement of **Urpipata**, set on a hilltop. The **Río Tunqimayo**, 15 minutes further on, is crossed by a spectacular wooden bridge. There are crystal-clear pools in the river, ideal for a refreshing dip. This could be a good campsite if you have time, though space for tents is very limited. A second bridge, 1½ hours further on, crosses the **Río Yuquemayo**.

The dispersed settlement of **Concevidayoc** comes into view 5½ hours from the start of the day's trek. The river below now carries the same name. After another hour you come to the **Puente Pumachaca**, crossing another of the Concevidayoc's tributaries. Around Concevidayoc there are many small side trails leading to houses and fields, but the main trail is obvious. You pass the small ruin of the house of Don Cobos on the left-hand side. If you don't want to proceed further this would be a good camping spot. The Cobos family has been instrumental in the most significant explorations of the Espíritu Pampa area and still guide today, based at the **Hospedaje Sixpac Manco** in Huancacalle.

Shortly after the Cobos' house the trail splits, but a blue arrow indicates the higher trail and route to Espíritu Pampa. Finally you reach the **Abra Tucuiricco** and the foundations of a small but well-constructed Inca house, perhaps built as a lookout to warn of approaching enemies. From here you can look down on Espíritu Pampa and Manco's Vilcabamba Vieja. A flight of restored Inca stairs leads downhill and 20 minutes later you come to the small settlement of **Espíritu Pampa**. A large sign announces the restoration of Espíritu Pampa and Vilcabamba. There's a modest shop in the village run by the wife of Américo, Vilcabamba's caretaker. The shop has a pretty limited selection of goods, but sells biscuits, rice, eggs and, of course, Coca Cola. In front of the houses themselves is a small field which is perfect for camping.

Day four: Vilcabamba Vieja

A trail leads up behind the houses to the ruins of Vilcabamba Vieja, a mere 10 minutes' walk away. Some of the lower ruins are being restored but the ruins on higher ground are still romantically consumed by the jungle, with vines and the huge root systems of forest giants wrapped around the remains of finely built houses. What is also apparent is how different this city is, compared with others in the Inca Empire, set as it is in a low valley on the edge of the Amazon Basin. This is a city and a civilization out of its element, the Incas far from their beloved mountains, forced to the very edge of their empire by the European invaders. For birdwatchers there are several leks (display grounds) of the Andean cock-of-the-rock, Peru's national bird. Its strange calls echo throughout the ruins.

Day five: Espíritu Pampa to Chanquiri → *About 5 hrs' walking.*

To leave Espíritu Pampa, follow the path that crosses directly in front of the houses, leaving from the north side of the field. The path then crosses the **Río Santa Isabel** after 10 to 15 minutes on a suspension bridge carrying the same name. You are now heading east-northeast, swinging more to the north as you continue. You're on the left bank of the Santa Isabel, following the river downstream towards its confluence with the Río Concevidayoc. The valley is quite densely populated here, with much slash and burn agriculture and consequent forest clearance. After an hour or so you pass **Chuntabamba**, a small settlement with a school, small shop, etc. There are many little side trails leading to fields and houses in this area, but the main trail is always obvious. You're still heading north at this point. The Santa Isabel merges with the Río Concevidayoc after about 2½ hours and enters a steep forested canyon. You follow the trail to the left in a picturesque valley of a tributary entering from the west, crossing the **Puente Santa Victoria**, before returning to the course of the main river. You now descend steeply to the river and cross the **Azulmayo** (or Asolmayo) suspension bridge.

The route begins to climb steeply on the far side. At a split in the trail turn left (north) – if you've taken the correct turn you'll come to a small concrete bridge over a stream five minutes later. It's a very tough, steep climb for up to 1½ hours. **Chanquiri** comes into view in the valley below from the highest point of the climb, high on the side of the hill (but below the summit). This small town lies on the right-hand side of the valley that joins the Santa Isabel, just below the confluence of the two. The valley is that of the **Río San Miguel**. Following the hill into the San Miguel Valley, cross the sturdy **Puente La Resistencia**. Head up the opposite bank until it meets with a road. The road is impassable for vehicles in the higher section, because of many landslides. Some 30 minutes later you arrive in Chanquiri.

⊚ Beyond Machu Picchu listings

For Sleeping and Eating price codes and other relevant information, see pages 30-36.

⊜ Sleeping

Quillabamba *p194*

C Hostal Quillabamba, Prolongación M Grau 590, just behind the main market, T084-281369, http://hostalquillabamba.com. Highly kitsch design, one of the largest hostels in Quillabamba, all rooms have private bath, TV (local channels only) and telephone, swimming pool (which occasionally has water in it), restaurant, parking. Less appealing is the small zoo. They also have a cockfighting school for the championship, which is held every year in late Jul.

C-D Hostal Don Carlos, Jr Libertad 566, T084-281150, www.hostaldoncarlosquilla bamba.com. Clean and simple, all rooms have private shower with generally hot water. There is a bar and restaurant.

D-E Hostal Alto Urubamba, Jr 2 de Mayo 333, T084-281131, altourub@ec-red.com. Rooms with shared bath cheaper. Spotlessly clean, pleasant hotel, 1 block from the Plaza de Armas. Staff are friendly and knowledge-able. Small local restaurant attached and there are great views over the town from the roof. Highly recommended.

Pongo de Mainique and the Amazon Basin *p196*

F Hostal La Casa de los Ugarte, just beyond the Pongo, on the left bank of the river (if heading downstream). The small hacienda of Ida and Abel Ugarte. They are very helpful and will let you camp on their land for a small fee. They have a modest general store and basic supplies, fruit and very fresh eggs are available. The forest behind the hacienda is rich in wildlife and the family may be able to arrange expeditions in the jungle, given time to make the arrangements.

F Hostal Pongo de Mainique, Ivochote, just behind **F Señor de Huanca**, Ivochote, on the right once over the footbridge. The former is the nicer of the 2, although both are basic.

F Hostal Vanessa, Sepahua. On the main street close to the port, very pleasant.

Sabeti Lodge, Timpía, www.sabetilodge.com, or contact the Centro para el Desarrollo del Indígena Amazónico (CEDIA), T01-420 4340. The lodge founded by the Machiguenga community, CEDIA and Perú Verde. Offers 4- and 5-night packages for eco and eco-mystical tourism with guided tours (contact them directly for prices). With restaurant and bar.

Huancacalle *p197*

Villagers will accept travellers in their very basic homes (take a sleeping bag).

F Hospedaje Sixpac Manco, managed by the Cobos family, this hostel is fairly comfortable and has good beds.

Huancacalle to Espíritu Pampa *p198*

Chanquiri has no hostel, but you can sleep on someone's floor, perhaps at the small restaurant/shop on the west side of the plaza. If they like you and you buy a meal and a couple of drinks they may not charge for accommodation. The main plaza isn't ideal for camping.

❷ Eating

Quillabamba *p194*

Quillabamba is a great place for freshly squeezed fruit juices – head for the 2nd floor in the main market. **Gabbi's Juice Stall**, on the far right-hand side, is especially good.

❡ El Gordito, on Espinar. A good place for chicken.

❡ Pizzería Venecia, Jr Libertad 461, on the Plaza de Armas, T084-281582. Decent pizza, delivery available.

❡ Pub Don Sebas, Jr Espinar 235 on Plaza de Armas. Great sandwiches, run by Karen Molero who is very friendly and always ready for a chat.

Ø Transport

Quillabamba *p194*

Most buses leave **Cuzco** for Quillabamba from the Terminal Terrestre de Santiago between 1800 and 2000. Journey time is about 8 hrs, although expect 14 hrs or more in the rainy season, because of landslides. 4 bus companies on this route are: **Valle de los Incas**, T084-244787, **Ben Hur**, T084-229193, **Ampay**, T084-245734, and **Selva Sur**, T084-247975. **Selva Sur** has 2 buses on the route, one of which is quite comfortable, with good reclining seats, perhaps the best bus for the journey. Buy tickets in advance, US$6. **Ampay** also runs from **Ollantaytambo** to Quillabamba. The bus station in Quillabamba is on Av 28 de Julio and buses depart for **Cuzco** daily, with buses leaving in the morning around 0700 and evening. There are extra services at weekends. Taxi colectivos provide a faster service to Quillabamba from outside the Almudena cemetary in Cuzco, they leave when full and make the journey in 6 hrs.

From **Quillabamba** buses take 10 hrs to reach **Ivochote** and cost around US$4. Ask locals for their opinions on the best companies for this route. Buses (combis) leave Quillabamba for **Huancacalle** daily from Jr San Martín, near Plaza Grau, at 0900 and 1200, US$3.30. The journey takes 4-7 hrs. On Fri they go all the way to **Vilcabamba La Nueva**.

Pongo de Mainique and the Amazon Basin *p196*

Boat

For boats beyond Ivochote, you may have to wait a few days for a boat downstream, but try to get as far as Bajo Pongo or **Timpia**, 4 hrs, US$10. It's a further 4 hrs, US$10 to **Camisea**. After **Sepahua** boats are larger, boats more frequent and distances greater. To **Atalaya** you can take an express, 10 hrs, US$15, or a delivery boat, up to 2 days. From here boats go to **Pucallpa**.

Huancacalle to Espíritu Pampa *p198*

Bus From **Chanquiri**, at the end of the Espíritu Pampa trail, trucks and buses leave for **Kiteni** and **Quillabamba** on Wed and Sun. It's an 8- to 12-hr ride, US$2.50. Finding transport at other times of the week can be problematic.

❶ Directory

Quillabamba *p194*

Banks BCP, Jr Libertad, is good for TCs. Banco Continental, Av F Bolognesi, accepts Visa and Cirrus. **Internet** Ciber Master, Jr Espinar, on the plaza.

Contents

Footprint features

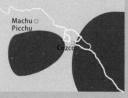

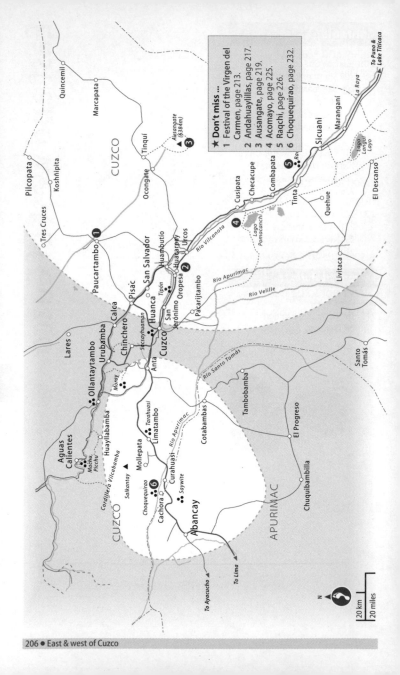

Don't miss ...

1 Festival of the Virgen del Carmen, page 213.
2 Andahuaylillas, page 217.
3 Ausangate, page 219.
4 Acomayo, page 225.
5 Raqchi, page 226.
6 Choquequirao, page 232.

Most visitors to Cuzco, after seeing the city, head for the Sacred Valley and Machu Picchu, but to the east and west are many equally tempting propositions. This part of the country is singularly off the beaten track in relation to the rest of the region. It's an area of myths, reputed to be where the founders of the Inca dynasty emerged into the world.

Along or near the main road from Cuzco to Lake Titicaca are a number of archaeological sites, the most prominent of which are Tipón and Raqchi, while the colonial churches at Andahuaylillas and Huaro are among the most fascinating in the whole region. There are beautiful lakes, too; four of them are near the village of Acomayo, while Huacarpay is an excellent place for walking and birdwatching. Also accessible from this road is the majestic Ausangate massif, where you can do some serious high-altitude trekking.

And not to be outdone, the western part of the region also boasts its own 'lost city', at Choquequirao. As impressive as Machu Picchu but, in comparison, much less visited, this is a tremendous site, and getting there requires an expedition of four days or more.

East of Cuzco

A paved road runs southeast from Cuzco to Sicuani, at the southeastern edge of the Department of Cuzco. It follows the valley of the Río Vilcanota (the upper stretch of the Urubamba) as it cuts through the altiplano. Ruins dot the hillsides, demonstrating the spread of the Incas' influence towards their spiritual home at Lake Titicaca, which is also the road's destination at Puno. A smattering of distinctive colonial churches can be found along the route. Northeast of the Vilcanota is the mountain range of the same name, crowned by the snowy summit of Ausangate, one of the Incas' great apus. Its glaciers and lakes are the backdrop to one of the region's finest treks. At the other extreme, the deep canyons of the Río Apurímac are a side trip away.
▶▶ For listings, see pages 228-230.

Ins and outs
Combis run every 15-20 minutes between Cuzco and Sicuani, and more frequently to the villages and towns in between. To visit the beautiful mountain lakes and Inca bridge west of the main road, consider renting a 4WD for two days. ▶▶ For further details, see Transport, page 229.

South to Pacarijtambo

Pacarijtambo is a good starting point for the three to four hours' walk to the ruins of **Maukallaqta**, which contain good examples of Inca stonework. From there, you can walk to **Pumaorca**, a high rock carved with steps, seats and a small puma in relief on top. Below this are more Inca ruins.

From Cuzco there are buses and trucks to Pacarijtambo, US$3. You can find lodging for the night at the house of the Villacorta family and leave for Cuzco by truck the next morning. On the way back, you'll pass the caves of **Tambo Toco**, where a legend says that the four original Inca brothers emerged into the world, thus contradicting the story that the brothers emerged at Ollantaytambo (see box, page 147).

San Jerónimo to Huanca trek → For listings, see pages 228-230.

Leaving Cuzco, you will soon pass the condor monument (see box, page 81) of San Sebastián then enter the old colonial town of **San Jerónimo**, which has become almost a suburb of the sprawling city and is now home to Cuzco's wholesale Saturday morning food market (see page 113). San Jerónimo is the starting point for an excellent trek to Huanca.

San Jerónimo to Huaccoto → 4-5 hrs.
From San Jerónimo, head north along Calle Clorinda Matto de Turner (past the main produce market on the left and the **Andenes de Andrea** restaurant). Further along is the cemetery. The street becomes an unpaved road, swings to the right (east) for 500 m and then left (north) again on its definite course up the mountain. There is a 4WD road which connects San Jerónimo with Huaccoto, laboriously winding its way for 15 km from 3200 m up to 4000 m. Much more interesting and worthwhile, is to follow the old Inca and Spanish colonial track, which ascends the *quebrada* (ravine) of the Huaccotomayu and is only about half as long and more direct, but also steep in places. This road is wide, very clearly marked and widely travelled. Heading north by northwest, the pedestrian road

leaves the narrow streets of the town. On the way out, the road winds past the remains of once great colonial *estancias*.

The most striking feature of the landscape is the thousands of eucalyptus trees covering the slopes of all the surrounding hillsides. Few truly old trees remain (the eucalyptus was first introduced to this region in the 1870s and 1880s). There are large groves of 20- to 40-year-old trees growing out of older and thicker stumps, harvested in the mid-20th century, interspersed with extensive patches of much younger trees. The air is dense with that most invigorating and promising aroma of menthol.

Below you can see the red-tiled roofs of San Jerónimo and the broader expanse of the valley of the Río Huatanay, gradually making its way southeast towards its confluence with the Río Urubamba – only 20 km away – whose waters will eventually flow into the Amazon region and on to the Atlantic Ocean.

The broad trail climbs the mountainside, intersecting the many turns and twists of the little-used track. The walking trail pretty much follows the course of a fast-flowing *acequia* (irrigation channel), no doubt originally constructed by the Incas or their predecessors, the Huari-Tiahuanacos, who built Piquillacta (see page 214). There are other canals and aqueducts, which distribute the water from the numerous *puquios* (natural springs) that sprout from the slopes and gullies of **Cerro Pachatusan** (the pillar, or pivot of the world), which, although its main peak and summit are not yet visible, we have been ascending since San Jerónimo.

As the eucalyptus groves begin to thin out, the ridge line and highlands finally become visible. Due north is the prominent, pyramidal summit of **Pikol**, a minor *apu* (mountain) but an important landmark. Its name is clearly carved on its slopes. To the right of it, at roughly two o'clock, a short segment of jagged dark grey boulders and rocks can clearly be seen. This is the first hint of the **Huaccoto** quarries and the principal reference point to head for. In Inca times and throughout the colonial and republican periods, Huaccoto was the site of an important stone quarry and a principal source of building materials for the Inca temples and Spanish colonial mansions of Cuzco. To the immediate right is the gully formed by the

San Jerónimo to Huanca trek

Río Huaccotomayu, which will somehow vanish into the mountain slope a few hundred metres beyond and above.

The treeline is at about 3700-3800 m. You emerge from it into an altogether different world. The panorama is wide and very luminous (assuming, of course, that the weather is fine). The landscape is composed of rolling hills, dotted with tarns that can swell into flooding lakes during the rainy season. Although the ever-growing African *kikuyo* grass (introduced to the area in the early 20th century) has already made headway into this last pocket of native highland flora, it is the native grasses – the *ichu* and its nearest relatives – which predominate, but only briefly. Soon you reach a landscape devoid of trees, with cushion plants growing low to preserve heat and moisture. The most common is the *yareta*, a bright green bubble-like growth, reminiscent of coral and often, incorrectly, referred to as tundra. Beyond the foreground of rolling hills of *yareta*, scattered with tarns, are several chains of great mountain peaks.

Huaccoto to Huanca

From Huaccoto it is possible for experienced climbers to make a detour to the summit of **Pachatusan**, heading for the first of its many false summits (east, then south along the slope of the mountain). Alternatively, continue on the same well-worn path that brought you to this point. A gentle climb of a few more metres over the next 1 km, veering slightly east by northeast, sets course towards an obvious breach between Pachatusan and its northwestern extension, known as **Cerro Quellomina**. This pass and a winding trail descend through a maze of impregnable crags, all the way down to the green valley of the Urubamba, which makes its way from southeast to northwest, splaying out into various branches and channels, creating islets and sandbanks which disappear in the rainy season.

Along the crest, close to the pass, are numerous wooden crosses draped in long, flowing, veil-like cloths, many of them well over 3 m tall. These have been erected by pilgrims and devotees and each year they are clad in fresh garments. A few hundred metres along the pass, on the left, is the entrance to what were once the famous **Yanantín** gold mines, belonging to the Marqués de Valleumbroso, which now yield only copper. The entire area was once known as the Marquesado de Oropeza. The trail, very wide and easily recognizable, twists down through the rock spires. Another 200 m beyond is a small Inca fortress perched on one of the buttresses. Closer inspection reveals the remains of other observation points and Inca constructions among the rock towers. Just below this point, another major trail branches off to the left (northwest), climbing up to a well-marked pass. This is an original Inca road, leading back up to Ccoricocha and eventually Huchuy Cuzco and on to Chinchero.

Soon, although still far below your present position, a large, relatively flat area comes into view, with many buildings, cereal cultivation and groves of very tall, old eucalyptus trees. This green belt of fertility amid the seemingly relentless precipices of Pachatusan's northeastern face is **Huanca**, site of the famous sanctuary, one of the great religious shrines of the Andes. Its fame spreads far beyond its immediate vicinity. Devotees, belonging to branches and brotherhoods, come from as far as Ecuador and Bolivia.

Sanctuary of El Señor de Huanca

The Sanctuary of El Señor de Huanca stands above the clouds, surrounded by flower-filled gardens and trees of many kinds. It is a great gathering place of so many hopes and wishes for goodness, protected by the great misty crag, Pachatusan. From Huaccoto, three hours' hiking, not counting the unavoidable stops to appreciate the scenery, should bring you to the grounds of the sanctuary. The Mercedarian fathers, though fewer than in the past, are still there to greet visitors. The father in charge, whose title is Comendador Capellán, requests that all hikers descending from Huaccoto past the springs pick up all the garbage they can, as a contribution to the conservation of the sanctuary grounds. Lodging and meals are available for pilgrims and hikers (see Sleeping, page 228). There is also a public telephone. Note that there is always a ride available from the sanctuary, as the priests are more than willing to help the faithful who need transport; ring the bell of the private quarters and the resident priest will assist. Of course, a contribution to the sanctuary will be appreciated. ▶▶ *For details of how to reach the sanctuary by road, see Transport, page 229.*

History of the sanctuary We know from Spanish chroniclers of the mid-16th century, such as Pedro de Cieza de León and Juan Polo de Ondegardo, that the Apu Pachatusan was a major *huaca* (shrine) long before the conquest. It was the origin of the ashlars and stone used for building Imperial Cuzco of Pachacútec. It had numerous springs on both its western and eastern slopes. Last but not least, as the later exploitation of the rich mines of the Marqués de Valleumbroso confirmed, it was a source of gold, silver and copper, all of great importance in pre-Columbian Peru, but of much greater value to the piratical economy of 16th-century Europe. (The gold was weighed in the aptly named town of Oropesa, some 10 km beyond San Jerónimo and close to Piquillacta, which was founded by the Spaniards in the boom years of the late 16th century.) Even before the Incas and Spaniards (as well as the Huari-Tiahuanacos of Piquillacta), two fundamental elements characterized the mountain: the abundance of fresh water springs and a large population of puma. Today the puma have disappeared, but the deer that must have constituted their prey can still be seen in groups in more isolated parts of the mountain.

Instead of succumbing to the zeal of the early crusading *conquistadores*, Pachatusan's sacredness was absorbed and adapted in the more enlightened approach of religious syncretism that prevailed in the mid-17th to late 18th century. How else was the Marqués de Valleumbroso going to get the locals to work the mines? At Huanca, the necessary Christian miracle took place in 1675, 25 years after the great earthquake of 1650. It was a time when miracles, no matter their provenance, were universally required.

In May that year, one Diego Quispe, a native of Chincheros working in the Yanantín mines, committed some grave disciplinary error for which he was to be dealt severe punishment the next day. He fled into the crags and gullies of Apu Pachatusan, trusting more in the justice of the earth than that of his overlords. He crept into the furthest depths of an overhang and began to pray. As night fell and Quispe prepared to resume his flight to freedom, the miracle took place. Jesus appeared to him, wearing the crown of thorns and bleeding from the lashes on his back. He spoke the words: "Diego, I have chosen this site to be a volcano of love and a pure spring of regeneration and forgiveness. Go to your home and let the local priest and all your people know. I shall await you here." Diego took a silver chain from his neck and laid it at the base of the rock where the apparition occurred (the first of many centuries of gifts and tributes to El Señor de Huanca).

Diego's life was spared, and more miracles followed. In the course of the next two generations, the boulder acquired a painting of Christ being whipped by a stylized, Moorish-looking ruffian (an ironic echo of the treatment inflicted upon the mineworkers by the Marqués de Valleumbroso). In time, ownership of the land passed to the religious order of La Merced of Cuzco (Mercedarios). A large sanctuary was built over the original boulder and among the devotees whose generosity contributed to its construction are various South American presidents, the elder Alessandri of Chile prominent among them.

Today, the boulder and traces of the painting are partially visible through glass. Nearly 400 years' accumulation of plaques, icons and messages are everywhere. People come on foot, on horseback and by car to fill empty coke bottles and glass jars with the magic water that flows out of Apu Pachatusan just above the sanctuary.

Towards Paucartambo → *For listings, see pages 228-230.*

Saylla to Oropesa

Southeast from San Jerónimo the valley begins to narrow as you reach **Saylla**, famous for its *chicharrones* – deep-fried pieces of pork. Between here and Oropesa are the extensive ruins of **Tipón** ① *entry US$3.60, or BTC ticket, see box, page 65, 1 hr on foot from Tipón village (taxis available).* They include baths, terraces, irrigation systems and a temple complex, accessible by a path leading from just above the last terrace, all in a fine setting. If you head to the left at the back of the site, there is a small pathway. Follow the trail round to where you will see more small ruins. From there you will find an amazing Inca road with a deep irrigation channel, which can be followed to reach **Cerro Pachatusan** in two to three days (see also San Jerónimo to Huanca trek, page 208).

Further on is **Oropesa**, which has been known as Cuzco's breadbasket since colonial times and is the national capital of this staple foodstuff. Try the delicious large, sweet circular loaves known as *chutas*. Most buses will slow down when passing through so that people can buy through the windows. The church has a fine ornately carved pulpit. Next comes the village of **Huacarpay**, near the shores of Laguna de Huacarpay, in the **Piquillacta Archaeological Park**. For details of Inca ruins and walks around this area, see page 214.

Huambutío to Pisac

About 3 km beyond Oropesa, just past Huacarpay, is a turning left to **Huambutío**. Here the road divides. The higher road, called Carretera Carmen Bonita, goes north to Paucartambo, on the eastern slope of the Andes (see below), and on to Manu. The other road heads northwest, following the river bank past Huambutío, Vilcabamba and San Salvador (for access to the sanctuary at Huanca, see page 210) and on to Pisac (see page 132). At Pisac the road connects with the road to the Sacred Valley of the Urubamba, as well as the road back to Cuzco via Sacsayhuaman.

Huambutío and its surroundings were badly damaged by floods in 2010. The road from Huambutío northwest to Pisac (about 20 km) is unpaved and poor. This is an access road for the first river-rafting section on the Río Urubamba, which also connects with another rafting route from Piñipampa. In the rainy season, and for less experienced rafters, the Huambutío (Piñipampa) to Pisac river section is safer to run. The rapids are Class II to III. The rafting trip is 30-35 km long with spectacular views of the Urubamba valley that are not seen on a conventional valley tour. This part of the river offers views of the Sanctuary of El Señor de Huanca. ▸▸ *For Cuzco operators offering rafting trips, see Activities and tours, page 119. See also Rafting, page 18.*

Paucartambo and around

This once remote town, 80 km east of Cuzco, is on the road to Pilcopata, Atalaya and Shintuya and is now the overland route used by tour companies from Cuzco into Manu Biosphere Reserve (see page 250). Consequently, it has become a popular tourist destination.

The fiesta of the Virgen del Carmen

In the village of Paucartambo, 80 km east of Cuzco, a pagan-Christian festival celebrates the Virgen del Carmen annually on 15-17 July. Her feast days are in the Quechua month of Earthly Purification. There are two popular myths surrounding the history of the Virgen del Carmen.

The first tells how the Virgin appeared in Paucartambo. The story goes that a rich Ccolla woman called Felipa Begolla came to Paucartambo to trade goods. One day she was unloading her wares, when, in one of her earthenware pots, the head of a beautiful woman appeared and a sweet voice spoke to her: "Do not be afraid, my dear, my name is Carmen". The head shone like the rays of the sun. Felipa contracted a great cabinetmaker in the town to carve a body made of fine wood on which to place the beautiful head. She brought the statue of the Virgin into the town's church and all the Ccolla people celebrated because the Virgin had arrived in a pot from Ccollao, an area beginning 150 km southeast of Cuzco, beyond the Ausangate massif, covering the enormous highland plateau that includes Titicaca and stretching as far as northern Argentina. The Ccolla swore to come to Paucartambo every year on 16 July so that the Virgin would not feel sad at being away from her own land. The Virgen del Carmen festival became popular and so, each year, dancing groups dressed in colourful costumes with decorated masks came to re-enact the old folk tales. (Sra Betty Yabar, *Testimonio de Cheqec*, 1971)

In the other popular myth, the Chontakirus, a tribe from the jungle, tell that the Ch'unchos, who in history and fables embody profanity and contempt for sacred things, stole the statue of the Virgin from the Ccollas of Puno who were taking it to Paucartambo for the Corpus Christi celebrations. During the confrontation the Ch'unchos killed the Ccollas and threw the statue into the Río Amaru (river of the serpent). From that day, the river was renamed the Madre de Dios, after the Mother of God. The statue was rescued from the waters and taken to the church in Paucartambo, where she remains. Scars from the arrows in her chest can still be seen (Sra Alfonsina Barrionuevo, *Cuzco Mágico*, 1968).

For the festival, the church is decorated, with the Mamacha Carmen dressed in fine clothes, and she is visited by the dancing Comparsas. Some travel from far away, such as the Negritos who, in colonial times, came to dance for the Virgin, praying for their freedom. The Ch'unchos, her captors, are her main dancers and they guard her along the route of the procession. The party continues for the next two days with lots of dancing and music. Each dancing group has its own station in town and every year important people are named as Carguyocs, who are in charge of a particular dancing group at every ceremony. The Carguyocs cover all the costs of the festivity for the dancers and for all the people who visit. They provide lodging, food and drink.

The Mamacha Carmen is taken out on her final procession to the colonial stone bridge (built by King Carlos III of Spain in the 18th century). She then blesses the four Suyos, or cardinal points. The Saqras (demons) scurry over the rooftops trying to tempt her, but the Virgin with her kindness makes them repent. In the afternoon, a re-enactment of the battle between the Ccollas and the Ch'unchos, called the Guerrilla, takes place. The whole town gets involved and the music, dancing and drinking continue.

On 15-17 July, the **Fiesta of the Virgen del Carmen** is a major attraction and well worth seeing. Masked dancers enact rituals and folk tales in the streets (see page 213).

Since colonial times Paucartambo was on the route for produce brought from the jungle to the sierra and thence to the coast. King Carlos III of Spain had a stone bridge built across the river here in the 18th century to replace the previous rope bridge. The locals claimed that the reason the king lost such a large proportion of the *diezmos reales* (tithes, or one-tenth tax on annual produce) due to him from the area was that the mule loads were too heavy for the original bridge. The stone bridge may have solved his tax problem, but it also furthered his aim of promoting the development of Paucartambo and encouraging scientific and exploratory expeditions in the region.

You can walk from Paucartambo to the *chullpas* of **Machu Cruz** in about an hour, or to the *chullpas* of **Pijchu** (take a guide). You can also visit the Inca fortress of **Huatojto**, which has fine doorways and stonework. A car will take you as far as Ayre, from where the fortress is a two-hour walk. From Paucartambo, in the dry season, you can go 44 km to **Tres Cruces**, along the Pilcopata road, turning left after 25 km. Señor Cáceres in Paucartambo will arrange this trip for you. Tres Cruces gives a wonderful view of the sunrise in June and July: peculiar climatic conditions make it appear as if three suns are rising. Tour operators in Cuzco (see page 114) can arrange transport and lodging.

Piquillacta Archaeological Park → For listings, see pages 228-230.

The Piquillacta Archaeological Park is 30 km southeast of Cuzco, off the main road to Sicuani. It has an area of 3421 ha and its nucleus is the remains of a lake, the Laguna de Huacarpay, around which are many pre-Columbian archaeological sites. The principal ones are Piquillacta, Choquepuquio, Kañarakay, Urpicancha and Rumicolca.

Piquillacta

ⓘ *Daily 0700-1730. Entry by BTC visitor ticket (see box, page 65), or US$3.60. Buses to Urcos from Av Huáscar in Cuzco will drop you at the entrance on the north side of the complex, though this is not the official entry.*

Piquillacta, which translates as the City of Fleas, is a large site, with some reconstruction in progress. It was an administrative centre at the southern end of the Huari Empire. The Huari, contemporaneous with the Tiahuanaco culture (AD 600-1000), were based near present-day Ayacucho in the Central Highlands, almost 600 km north of Cuzco by road. However, Huari influence covered most of what we now know as Peru, from Cajamarca and the Pacific coast in the north to the borders of the Tiahuanaco in the south. The Huari system of regional storehouses, irrigation, roads and government was similar to that of the Incas, who adopted it from them.

Archaeological evidence from Piquillacta is confusing, but mostly suggests that this was not a place for permanent residents but rather a base for storing supplies, housing itinerant groups of workers, gathering and distributing tributes, and conducting ceremonies. The whole site is surrounded by a wall, there are many enclosed compounds with buildings of over one storey and it appears that the walls were plastered and finished with a layer of lime. Going with a guide is recommended as the more interesting structures are not easy to find. Tiny turquoise figurines found at the site are on display in the Museo Inka in Cuzco.

Rumicolca

On the main road to Sicuani and Puno, shortly after the turn-off to Piquillacta, you will see, on the right, the huge gateway of Rumicolca. You can walk around it for free. This was a Huari aqueduct, built across a narrow stretch of the valley, which the Incas clad in fine stonework to create this gateway. If you look at the top you can see the original walls, four tiers high. It is now being 'restored', which in Cuzco means rebuilt – a highly controversial topic.

Rumicolca itself (the name means depository or storage site for rocks) was a control point and parallel set of gateways through which in Inca times all traffic between Cuzco and Collasuyo (the southeastern quarter of the Inca dominions) had to pass. It is very imposing. The wall through which the gates pass is of common enough composition, rough-hewn rock bound by a hardened clay mortar. There is evidence that this was covered in stucco and painted in ochres and reds. The gateways, though, are some of the finest Inca masonry. Large, perfectly cut, polished andesite ashlars fit together exactly, without mortar, demonstrating a quality of workmanship equal to anything in Cuzco, Ollantaytambo or Pisac. The finely dressed gateways probably date from the 14th century, contemporary with the monumental phase of Inca architecture in the era of Pachacútec or his successor Túpac Yupanqui. The wall which the gateway crosses is 600 to 800 years older and supported a Huari aqueduct which brought water to Piquillacta.

Laguna de Huacarpay

The lake, also known as **Laguna de Lucre**, is smaller now than it was in ancient times, when it was called Muyna. The basin of the lake lies at an altitude of 3200 m and is surrounded by several hills no higher than 3350-3400 m. Its shape is roughly circular and its circumference is presently about 8 km. Sections of the lake are overgrown with thick beds of *totora* reeds and other Andean lakeside vegetation. As the lake is gradually drying up, the reeds are spreading and fragmenting the open water, but several large sections of water remain. Water levels fluctuate between the dry and rainy seasons and as a result of other climatic events, such as El Niño. The village of Huacarpay, on its northern shore, can be subjected to damaging floods.

The Laguna de Huacarpay is the habitat of a variety of birdlife. In the open water, flocks of puna teals, pochards and pintails can be seen, as well as more scattered individual Andean ruddy ducks, with their conspicuous blue beaks. The *totora* reed banks are home to several varieties of gallinules and coots, the giant and the red-fronted being most noticeable. Along the shores of the lake and the neighbouring marshlands live puna ibis (though not in large numbers) and sometimes white-faced ibis; also some herons and occasional egrets. There are also lapwings, terns and Andean gulls. Most of these are present year-round. Huacarpay is the area most readily accessible from Cuzco in which to observe a typical Andean highland lake environment.

Around Laguna de Huacarpay

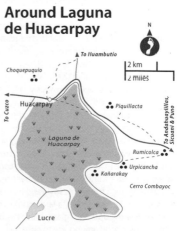

N

2 km
2 miles

To Huambutio
Choquepuquio
Huacarpay
Piquillacta
To Cuzco
Laguna de Huacarpay
To Andahuaylillas, Sicuani & Puno
Rumicolca
Urpicancha
Kañarakay
Cerro Combayoc
Lucre

Around Laguna de Huarcarpay

A good way to see both the ruins and some varied wildlife is to hike or cycle around the lake, on 8 km of level, paved minor road, which few motor vehicles use. The main focus of this basic circuit is birdwatching and only two or three secondary archaeological sites, but the hike can be lengthened to include the majority of the sites built on the surrounding hills. Some can be visited independently, but on an anticlockwise circuit of the lake basin they can easily be taken in.

From the main Cuzco–Urcos highway, take the turning south towards Lucre. At the southern end of the lake the road begins to swing slightly to the left (east) and soon splits: right to the town of Lucre and left around the lake. **Lucre** has been associated with textiles since Inca times. In the 1850s and 1860s, the area was owned by the Garmendia family who pioneered the first industrial production of textiles (worsteds, tweeds, alpaca and vicuña finished cloth) in this area, maybe in all Peru. To do this they imported a complete textile mill from England, the whole works, including the engineers and mechanics. It was shipped to Mollendo, thence to Arequipa and on over the Andes by mule. For many years it played a significant part in the local economy, but today there is no sign of it.

The left-hand fork continues east and shortly begins to climb a little and heads northeast. Here a really nice hike starts. On some maps this is marked Morada de Huascar, but its true name is **Kañarakay**. From this point, angling away and above the modern road, following the gently rising crest and the various converging trails and footpaths, you begin to glimpse the layers of history of this area. Looking north, some 5 km across the lake, as if moulded onto its hill, lies the rectilinear grid of Piquillacta. West of it and slightly lower are the less regular, but taller walls of Choqepuquio, while slightly lower but close by are the remains of a colonial hacienda, also named Choqepuquio. Much further away, 20-30 km north, is the unusual, stark profile of Cerro Pachatusan. Meanwhile, looking to the east of Piquillacta, the gates of Rumicolca are visible, the irrigation canals contouring the mountains from distant, forgotten sources. Also visible is the unmistakable architectural harmony between structure and environment that characterizes Inca building, in this case, the terraces of Urpicancha. That's the entire hike which lies ahead.

From Kañarakay start hiking northeastward. What at first sight appears to be arid, rocky country interspersed with crumbling ridges and strewn with loose rocks and scree, is in fact the remnants of a vast network of roads, passageways, buildings, retaining walls and stairways. Several cities lie scattered here, successively inhabited, abandoned and repopulated. This is also the realm of the cacti: *opuntia* predominate, but also thin, elongated prickly pears, enormously tall flat *nopales*, small barrel cacti, some with huge bright scarlet and yellow flowers. There are seven-pointed San Pedro cacti, with lily- white flowers which bud at dawn, blossom at noon and wither by sunset. *Epyphitic bromeliads*, most of them *tsillandsias* with bushy crowns of long thin leaves armed with sharp thorns, cling to ancient walls and grow in empty windows. There are also aloes and agave, and almost everywhere are blankets of Spanish moss. The fauna is limited to lizards and rodents, which keep the insect population under control. Most common are black widow spiders, which live under stones (it is best to leave rocks where they are and watch carefully where you sit down for a break!). Kestrels and hawks streak overhead, but the most typical of local birds are the Andean flicker, a large bright yellow-greenish speckled ground woodpecker, fond of lizards, and the giant hummingbirds – Patagonia gigas – with their nests strategically placed among the thick branches of a thorny cactus.

After 1 km of this jumble of stone, you come to the ruins of **Urpicancha** (*urpi* meaning dove, and *cancha* an enclosed field). Some legends say this was the birthplace of the Inca Huáscar, who waged war with his half-brother Atahualpa. Urpicancha is like a small oasis in the middle of the dusty environment surrounding the lake. It consists of a succession of a terraces on the hillside, descending almost to the lakeshore. At its base are two partial enclosures, made of well-fitted rocks which have acquired a striking orange hue from the lichen. A freshwater spring descends the hillside, partially piped, and there's an old colonial house, closed for some years now. It's a shady spot, with eucalyptus, willows and some mature elderberry trees (*sauco*).

From here, the hike climbs up to **Rumicolca** (see page 215). Several paths meander along the western slope of the large hill called Cerro Combayoc. All these trails will lead to Rumicolca but the routes closest to Urpicancha are the most scenic. The entire Muyna basin can be seen, and the eastern side of Combayoc, including 40 km of the Vilcanota river valley, Andahuaylillas and sections of the Rumicolca quarries. Rumicolca is a few metres from the modern Cuzco to Puno road. On the other side of the road, less than 50 m away, lies the entrance to the Huari adobe wall ruins of **Piquillacta** (see page 214).

From Piquillacta, head west into a valley through which runs the paved road from Cuzco to Paucartambo. Cross it and continue for about 50 m until you come to the remains of the old dirt road which runs parallel to the modern one for a short stretch and then veers left, crossing an old bridge. Over the bridge head west by southwest, past the site of a lime crusher (some houses, a small adobe factory); on the right is a marshy extension of Huacarpay lake. Here is some of the best birdwatching on the entire trek. Follow the main (or any secondary) path up the side of the valley, gaining the first ridge about 100 m beyond.

Look south and see the dark walls of **Choquepuquio**, perhaps the most mysterious of the archaeological sites on the trek. The walls suggest two-storeyed houses but also a redoubt, built to withstand siege and attack. Choquepuquio was erected as a stronghold in insecure times. Its drama derives from the fact that it is not being restored (unlike most other sites in the park). It is unkempt, there are thistles and brambles and, when seen up close, its walls appear even taller and more enigmatic than at first glance. From Choqepuquio follow any of the paths leading to the road which goes to Cuzco. You will emerge directly opposite the Lucre turn-off where the hike began.

Southeast towards Urcos → *For listings, see pages 228-230.*

Andahuaylillas

Continuing southeast towards Urcos you reach Andahuaylillas and the first of three fascinating 17th-century churches. This is a simple structure, but it has been referred to as the Andean Sistine Chapel because of its beautiful frescoes and internal architecture. Go in, wait for your eyes to adjust to the darkness, then turn to look at the two pictures either side of the splendid door. On the right is the path to heaven, which is narrow and thorny; on the left the way to hell, which is wide and littered with flowers. They are attributed to the artist Luis de Riaño. Above is the high choir, built in local wood, where there are two organs. Craning your neck further you will see the remarkable painted and carved ceiling. The main altar is gilded in 24-carat gold leaf and has symbols from both the Quechua and Christian religions, such as the sun and the lamb, respectively. Many of the canvases depict the lives of the church's patron saints, St Peter and St Paul. Ask for Sr Eulogio; he is a good guide, but speaks Spanish only. Outside, around the peaceful plaza, are massive pisonay trees dripping with red seeds and hanging moss.

Huaro

Before the next major town of Urcos is the quiet village of Huaro; turn left off the main road to reach the appalling main plaza, dominated by a concrete lookout tower. The church on this plaza is stunning inside. Walking in takes your breath away. The walls are plastered with frescoes used to evangelize the illiterate. Grinning skeletons compete with dragons and devils ushering the living into the afterlife and punishing them thereafter. Completed in 1802 by Tadeo Escalante, they are now mostly in a sad state of repair. Tour groups come here, but there is precious little money being spent on preservation. The first fresco on the right as you enter shows the torment of sinners in hell. A liar has his tongue torn out with pliers, a drunk has boiling alcohol poured down his throat through a funnel and others are impaled on a wheel. The torture is not confined to the masses. In a boiling cauldron, among the tortured, writhing, naked bodies are a priest, a cardinal and a bishop, identified by their hats.

Looking left of the door there is a priest giving absolution at the death of a girl in a poor house while below, a rich house plays host to a sumptuous banquet (with roasted guinea pig on the menu, of course). A woman here is choking and being led away by the skeleton of Death. The moral is clear. Right of the entrance, below another portrait of rich people having a feast, is the Tree of Life with good versus evil as Death wields an axe and Jesus sounds a bell.

To the right of this, on the left wall, is Judgement Day at its grimmest. Centre stage is a graveyard, the coffins of which are being yanked open by skeletons to drag the dead to either the underworld on the right (entered via the mouth of a dragon) or heaven (complete with Pearly Gates and musicians playing trumpets).

On the left are people being pulled from flames by angels. This is Purgatory and its inhabitants are those who have committed minor sins. Having paid their dues they will now be allowed into heaven. The democracy of the Catholic vision again allows these sinners to include cardinals and bishops.

To the right of this painting we see that Death is never far away. A huge skeleton containing the body of a woman (for we are all born of woman) has at its feet the paraphernalia of the rich, which cannot be taken into the next life. More skeletons stand behind people ignorant of their destiny. An angel sounds a trumpet from the top of a pillar at the moment of death. Meanwhile, the devil can be seen lurking under the bed of a person being given absolution. Again, look up at the wonderful ceiling.

Urcos

Beyond Huaro is Urcos. There are lodgings here, but they are basic to say the least. The **Laguna de Urcos** is a popular picnic spot and makes for a pleasant day out from Cuzco. There is a clear path from the town to the Laguna which can be seen from the road. A spectacular road runs from Urcos across the Eastern Cordillera to Puerto Maldonado in the jungle (see below and page 252).

Cordillera Vilcanota → *For listings, see pages 228-230. Colour map 2, B4.*

East of Cuzco lies the **Cordillera Vilcanota**, the greatest concentration of mountains and glaciers in southern Peru. With at least four great peaks towering above 6000 m (depending on which map you're looking at!) in densely packed icy masses, this area is reminiscent of the Cordillera Huayhuash further to the north. Viewed from the ruins of Sacsayhuaman above Cuzco, **Ausangate**, at 6384 m the range's loftiest peak, is impressive even from a distance of nearly 100 km, but in the Vilcanota mountains Ausangate is just the beginning.

Unlike both the Cordilleras of Vilcabamba and Urubamba, which plunge precipitously from sheer glaciers into lush subtropical valleys, the Vilcanota rises from the northern Altiplano, and treks into the region rarely, if ever, drop below 4000 m.

Life is harsh for the communities who live in the shadow of these great peaks. Knowledge of Spanish is often limited or non-existent and the people's respect of ancient ways and the power of the *apus* (mountain spirits), runs strong. Survival is eked from a meagre diet of potatoes, *cuy* (guinea pig) and the meat and wool of the large herds of domesticated llamas and alpacas that roam the valleys. In this land of wild and austere beauty the relatively sparse human population has allowed the continued survival of rare Andean wildlife. Vicuña are sometimes seen grazing on isolated mountain slopes, and viscacha, a relative of the chinchilla, are often seen in rocky areas. Sacred beasts to the Incas, the puma and the condor, though rarely seen, still inhabit this desolate kingdom.

The road to Puerto Maldonado
Some 82 km from Urcos, at the base of Ausangate, is the town of **Ocongate**, which has two hotels on the Plaza de Armas. The small town of **Tinqui**, east of Urcos is the traditional starting point for treks into the region and is a good place to find local guides and *arrieros* (mule drivers). Some 47 km after passing the snowline Hualla-Hualla pass, at 4820 m, the super-hot thermal baths of **Marcapata** ① *173 km from Urcos, entry US$0.10*, provide a relaxing break.

Ausangate circuit → *6 days.*
This is the most popular trekking route and involves fairly tough hiking around the peak itself, featuring icy mountain vistas, high passes (including two over 5000 m) and some beautiful turquoise lakes. As an added bonus, there are two geothermal springs to thaw out in at the beginning and end! In addition to the 'circuit', there is a great variety of other options, including treks around the range's northern peaks and routes to the magnificent **Laguna Sibinacocha**, a stunning 15-km-long lake set at 4800 m in remote territory to the east of Ausangate. Described below is the classic Ausangate Circuit, with an additional two-day extension to the isolated northern lake, **Laguna Singrenacocha**.

An alternative to the classic circuit is a new five-day trek that includes four mountain lodges for each night. The start of the Camino del Apu Ausangate is reached from Checacupe, where a side road goes to Pitumarca and the start of the trail near Chillca. Two indigenous communities of llama and alpaca herders have helped design the route with Auqui Mountain Spirit tour operator. For more details, Andean Lodges ① *José Gabriel Cosio 307, Urb Magisterial, Cuzco, T084-251578, www.andeanlodges.com.*

Preparations A standard fee for locals hired independently is US$8 per day for an *arriero* and US$6 per horse per day. You are also expected to provide sufficient food and a tent for the *arriero*. Tiofilo is a recommended guide/*arriero* who can be contacted through Tinqui's radio station, located just of the town's main plaza. The IGN 1:100,000 Ocongate map (available at **South American Explorers** in Cuzco) covers all trekking areas described below and is fairly accurate. Note that as you leave Tinqui you will be charged a community fee for using the Ausangate trail; at the time of writing this was S/.20 per person (about US$7.50).

Day one Four hours' walking in total. From Tinqui head southeast towards the radio and TV aerials on the hill overlooking town. This is **Concacancha**. A couple of families rent camping space up here, if you don't want to stay in one of Tinqui's cheap *hostales*. To get to

Concacancha you must cross a bridge to the south side of the Río Pinchimuro Mayo and climb the trail up the far bank. Ausangate's northern face dominates the landscape to the south on clear days. Just to the left of the small hill and radio masts a clear dirt road heads south towards the mountains. The road twists sharply in a small dip, then establishes itself on a heading of 150°, contained neatly between adobe walls. The landscape here is high-altitude *puna* with the occasional small dwelling. Don't be surprised, either here or further into the trek, if friendly, industrious locals, dressed in beautiful traditional clothing, track you down looking to sell alpaca goods and drinks. Please treat them with respect, they're just trying to make a living. After 1½ hours heading more or less south you cross a stream running across the trail, next to a Km 7 marker. A couple of minutes after the stream, turn right at the Y junction on a bearing of 220°. it's a good path, slightly less used than the previous one. After a further 10 minutes the trail fades a little, heading 150° again. You cross a second stream and keep your southeast course, crossing a small adobe bridge over an irrigation channel 2¼ hours after leaving Concacancha. Fifteen minutes more and you arrive at the crest of the hill, with spectacular views of Ausangate and a glacier tumbling into a narrow valley to the southeast. This valley and its hot springs are the destination for the day's hike.

Using trails contouring around the hills on the left side of the swampy **Upismayo** valley, head to the valley's eastern end and a small collection of buildings. This is **Upis**, reached after about three hours from Concacancha. The valley often contains interesting bird-life in addition to horses, llamas and alpacas. Bird species often spotted include Andean geese and puna ibis. From the settlement the glacial valley lies at 140°. Continue around the swamp and up the valley to the left of the stream that runs through its centre. About 30 minutes beyond the houses you pass the Upis hot springs. A further 20 minutes takes you to some decent camping areas with plenty of space. There seem to be several areas of hot pools, the cleanest being on the right hand side of the valley: soak in the pools and admire the snow.

Day two Five to six hours walking. Cross the stream to the far (right hand) side of the valley and hike towards the imposing north face of Ausangate. After 25 minutes the pass area comes into view, just to the right of a rocky triangular peak on a bearing of around 200°. The trail continues to ascend gradually to the right side of the valley, still holding roughly the same course, crossing areas of cushion moss after another 20 minutes or so, and all the time offering a stunning close-up of the craggy peaks and vast ice formations before you. After 1¼ hours take a sharp right, about 240°, up a grassy valley about 300 m before the black peak. Walking on the left side of this valley the route curves back to the left slightly, and, about 1¾ hours after leaving camp you reach the 4800 m **Arrapa Pass**. Fabulous desolate views surround you, with a deep valley to your right, and rugged, often snow-dusted hills beyond that.

From this point and for the next few days always keep Ausangate on your left. After the pass continue at 240° under a low line of hills. A little further and a huge, seemingly uninhabited valley opens out before you. This is the **Jalacocha Valley**, a place that, to this author at least, seems to possess a primeval, 'lost world' quality… let your imagination run wild! Turn hard left (140°) and descend gently across the top of the valley heading upstream; don't go down into the bottom of the valley. To the south, across the valley, rise the jagged spires of **Nevado Sorimani**. An hour from the *abra* you pass a small lake on your right. This is possibly **Yanacocha** on the IGN sheet, or perhaps a smaller unmarked lake. Just beyond this another much larger emerald lake comes into view, **Laguna Uchuy Pucacocha**, and this is your immediate destination. Steep winding paths take you south, down towards the lake. After 10 minutes you cross a flat pampa criss-crossed with clear streams, a decent snack or lunch stop. From here head south towards the stream and waterfall that flow from the lake's western end; 15 minutes should see you arrive at the crossing above the falls. Cross at this point to the right/southern side of the valley and climb up through interesting boulder-like rock formations before arcing around and emerging above Uchuy Pucacocha. You can now see yet another lake, the largest yet, **Jatun Pucacocha**, just beyond (to the east of) Uchuy and connected to it by another stream and waterfall. To the right of these connecting waterfalls lies a large rocky hill. Tonight's camp lies at the far end of Jatun Pucacocha and the easiest way of reaching it lies with the trails running to the right of the hill and down the valley, definitely the best option for those with pack animals.

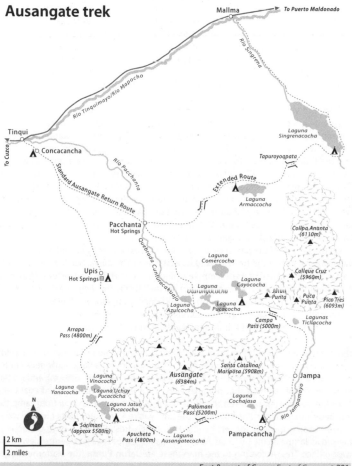

Ausangate trek

An alternative route passes some *campesino* houses beneath the hill, and contours around its left side, offering better views of the lake and the giant seracs and crevasses of the glacier tumbling down from Ausangate's southern flank towards the lakes. Keeping to the lake's southern side, once around the corner close to the falls, climb high to avoid some scrambling later and follow the lake to its eastern end. There's good flat ground for camping just to the north of the stream and the boggy ground. This campsite can be very exposed in windy weather.

Day three A long day, seven to eight hours with breaks. Walk east up the valley, crossing to the right side of the stream. After 10 minutes the trail turns to the right above some *campesinos'* houses, circumventing a steep rise in the valley floor. There are constant views of the great southern glaciers and, after about 50 minutes, views down to two small lakes on the left, one clear, the other milky turquoise. Forty minutes' more gentle climbing and you reach the first pass of the day, the 4800-m **Apucheta Pass**, named after the standing stones that crown the summit in honour of the surrounding *apus*. As you'd expect by now, there are great views of Ausangate and her snowfields, and from a little further down, **Ausangatecocha**, a beautiful, luminous lake (120° from the pass) nestled in the valley below. Head down into the valley below the lake, still heading east. This is a good place for a break, as the next couple of hours will see you climb to the highest pass on the route, the formidable 5200-m **Abra Palomani**.

From the valley floor the pass lies up a valley at about 70°, just to the right of Ausangate's huge glaciers threaded with crevasses and jutting seracs, and a black rocky outcrop just below the snow line. Twenty minutes' climb from the bottom the valley splits in two: take the left-hand route heading towards Ausangate. Another 10 minutes and the trail swings back to the right, climbing a ridge, crossing a small valley and resuming its initial 70°-80° course. Looking back, you're treated to spectacular views of **Nevado Sorimani**, **Nevado del Inca** and, far to the southeast, **Nevado Cóndor Tuco**. One and a half hours from the valley floor you reach the pass, exposed and crowded with *apuchetas*. There are fabulous views in both directions, as you'd expect, and now another peak reveals itself, **Santa Catalina** (5908 m), or Mariposa, as it is locally known, lying just to the east of the main Ausangate peak.

On the far side of the pass a clear trail descends over a desolate landscape into the valley below. At first the trail keeps to its east-northeast course, and then turns to the east in the second half of its descent, reaching the floor of this next valley just over an hour from the pass. Skirt the valley floor on its left side heading down for a further 45 minutes to its confluence with the larger **Jampamayo Valley**. Here lies Pampaconcha, a small indigenous community, and a couple minutes beyond this, northeast and to the left of the stream, is a sheltered camping spot.

Day four Five to six hours in total. Start the day hiking more or less northeast up the valley, always keeping to its left side. After about 30 minutes a huge snow peak comes into view at the head of the valley. This is **Señal Nevado Pico Tres** (6093 m), and it's this mountain's triple summit that dominates much of the day's walk. Jagged coal-black mountains on the right contrast sharply with the glaciers ahead. An hour from camp the trail begins to turn to the north and by the time you're 45 minutes further up the valley you're heading towards the left-hand edge of Pico Tres, passing a large community marked as **Jampa** on the IGN map. Above Jampa more great peaks edge into view to the west of Pico Tres. According to the map these are **Jatun Punta** (the Matterhorn-style peak to the left), **Puca Punta** just to the right and the massive **Collque Cruz** (5960 m) behind. Having said that, local names vary considerably and some refer to the entire massif that stretches to Laguna Armaccocha as **Ccallangate**. Continuing north you begin to climb higher on the left slope of the valley towards your immediate destination, the 5000-m **Campa Pass**. Just under three hours from last night's camp the trail swings sharply to the west, and it's this bearing that you'll more or less maintain for the rest of the day.

A chain of small lakes comes into view at the foot of the mountains across the valley to the north, the **Lagunas Ticllacocha**. Look out for wild vicuñas in this section of the valley, their delicate forms blending easily into the super-sized landscape. Keep to trails high on the left to avoid steeper terrain lower in the valley. Very soon the pass area begins to flatten out and a group of *apuchetas* are reached; slightly deceptive as the pass lies about 10 minutes further, with a second set of *apuchetas* about 3½ hours' walking time from the start of the day's hike. The pass rivals Palomani in terms of its beauty, with a vast wall of razor peaks, ridges and glaciers always to your right. Descending from the pass, many lakes come into view far below and to the west. The valley below is empty and lifeless with huge piles of boulders deposited close to the lakes, demonstrative of massive and continuing glacial retreat. Tonight's campsite, about an hour from the pass, lies on the far side of a small ridge, sheltered and directly south of the closest lake, **Laguna Cayococha**. The site boasts great views of Ausangate, the trekking peak of **Campa** (marked as María Huamantilla) and **Nevado Yanajaja**. Viscachas are easily observed by patient trekkers amongst the boulders near camp.

Day five Three to four hours in total. Leave camp heading west. After 10-15 minutes a large chain of lakes, each a different colour, comes into view: **Lagunas Pucacocha**, **Uturungococha** and **Minaparayoc**. On a clear day you can see the entire Urubamba range stretching across the horizon from La Verónica beyond Cuzco to its end in the east above the Manu National Park. Skirting the left side of the lakes, you cross an area of swampy ground (much favoured by the local alpacas) with the help of strategically placed local bridges. An unhindered view of Ausanagate's north face is visible above you. The path passes a tiny crystalline lake, **Cocha Otorongo** or Jaguar Lake, very clear even by Vilcanota standards. Locals say the lake is used in the ceremonies of traditional medicine men. Passing two smaller lakes on the right, the path turns north after just over an hour. Yet another large shallow lake reveals itself to the left, **Laguna Azulcocha**. Leaving the lakes behind you continue north over rough hilly country, dropping into a small valley after a further 40 minutes. Head northwest to the community marked on the IGN map as **Cullpaca**. At Cullpaca the valley joins the larger **Quebrada Cunturacahuajo**; follow this Quebrada north or north-northeast for 30 minutes until reaching the village of **Pacchanta**. This is positively a city by local standards, with a school, two-storey buildings, some super basic hostels if you're fed up with camping, and hot springs into the bargain!

Day six If you now want to head back to Tinqui on the 'standard' route leave Pacchanta following clear trails to the northwest. Cross the small range of hills above the town, then gently descend, crossing open *puna* towards Tinqui. In three hours you should be back in town.

Alternatively, to continue to the northern lakes, on leaving Pacchanta turn right/east. You're aiming for a pass lying just to the left/north of a large black hill (4800 m **Cerro Quimsa Puca Orjo**) which quickly comes into view ahead of you as you hike out above the village. The pass is reached after an hour's hiking from the village. If you feel inclined to climb to the hill's summit, you'll be rewarded with fabulous 360° views of

Ausangate to the south, the Collque Cruz/Ccallangate massif to the east and, far to the north, the range of mountains (also part of the Vilcanota range) that play host to the **Qoyllur Rit'i** festival each summer (see page 109). You'll also find a rustic altar for sacrifices in honour of the great peaks.

From the pass, descend into the **Quillhuahuayjo** valley below you to the east. You can see two *quebradas* (streams) entering the Quillhuahuayjo from the west. Don't take the valley immediately to the east of the pass; rather, on reaching the valley floor, head north past a small community, then, after 15-20 minutes, turn right up the **Quimsacocha Valley**. Heading roughly east, hike on the right side of the valley for 20 minutes before crossing a bridge to the left and continuing in the same direction. The valley is reminiscent of the Scottish highlands until the immense snow peaks poke over the horizon a few minutes later! Carry on following the main stream east, taking a slight left at the end of the valley. Fifteen minutes later pass just to the left of a *campesino*'s house, at which point the dark waters of **Laguna Armaccocha** come into view below you to the right, cradled beneath the icy peaks. Five minutes further and there's a good campsite in a flat 'step' high above the lake, with great views of both lake and mountains. If you want somewhere less windy there are also some good sites lower down, closer to the shore. Three or four hours in total.

Day seven About three hours relaxed hiking. Start the day hiking eastwards and upwards on a diagonal above the ash-grey Armaccocha lake. The sound of a small river entering the lake on its far side echoes up through the valley and seems disproportional to its size. After about 40 minutes the trail begins to swing more northeast and flattens out towards the top of the pass. Five more minutes and you reach the summit, known locally as **Tapuroyoqpata** for its location close to some ancient looted tombs. From this vantage point the Qoyllur Rit'i range becomes visible to the north once more. Continuing northeast over rocky country for a further 45 minutes brings you to a viewpoint over the fabulous turquoise **Laguna Singrenacocha**, 3.5 km long and perhaps the most impressive of all the lakes on the trek. Head down to the shore and make your way to the lake's southern end where there's a flat area ideal for camping. A powerful river enters here, with tumbling waterfalls flowing down from higher up the valley. Camp on the southern side or, if crossing, wade across where the river meets the lake and loses its power – be careful.

Day eight Follow trails north-northwest along the right-hand shore of the lake. Once at the far end after about 1½ hours, follow the Río Singrena and paths, then drivable roads, down to the small town of **Mallma**. Bank on a walk of around four hours. Mallma is on the Ocongate–Puerto Maldonado road, along which unscheduled trucks and, very occasionally, buses head towards Cuzco and the Sacred Valley. More reliable buses usually leave Tinqui and Ocongate for Cuzco in the afternoon or evening. Combis leave when they have enough passengers to cover the petrol and make a profit. Neither bus, truck nor combi makes for a particularly pleasant journey, so take a sleeping bag to fend off the frostbite at midnight!

Southeast from Urcos → *For listings, see pages 228-230.*

Southeast from Urcos, the main road passes through **Cusipata**, with an Inca gate and wall. Here the ornate bands for the decoration of ponchos are woven. Close by is the Huari hilltop ruin of **Llallanmarca**. Beyond Cusipata on the main road is **Checacupe** which has a fine church with good paintings and a handsome carved altar rail. Before you get there, however, it's worth heading west off the main road to visit the pretty village of Acomayo, the Inca bridge at Qeswachaka and four beautiful mountain lakes. You are advised to hire a 4WD or a vehicle with a driver for this side-trip but it is also feasible by combi, if you have more time. ▸▸ *For further details, see Transport, page 230.*

Acomayo and around

To get to Acomayo, take the road that branches off the main road between Cusipata and Checacupe, turning into a dirt track soon afterwards. At the first fork, just before **Lago Pomacanchi**, turn right to travel past a small community and on to Acomayo. The chapel here is decorated with mural paintings of the 14 Incas.

From Acomayo, you can walk to **Huáscar**, which takes one hour, and from there to **Pajlia**; a climb which leads through very impressive scenery. The canyons of the upper Río Apurímac are vast beyond imagination. Great cliffs drop thousands of metres into dizzying chasms and huge rocks balance menacingly overhead. This river, whose source is accepted as being the source also of the Amazon, rises in the mountains near Arequipa. The ruins of **Huajra Pucará** lie near Pajlia. They are small, but in an astonishing position.

Near Acomayo are four lakes. To reach them drive back along the dirt track from the village, as if you were going towards the main road. When you reach the first lake, Lago Pomacanchi, instead of continuing east, take a sharp right along the eastern shores of the lake. You will travel past three more beautiful lakes: Lago Acopia, Lago Asnacocha and Lago Pampamarca. Stop awhile beside **Lago Pampamarca**. It is absolutely quiet here and a great place to recharge your soul. Set against the pale green grass banks, serene waters reflect the red soil of the hills behind. The only sound is the occasional splash and hoot of a white-beaked Andean coot. The air is thin, clear and crisp.

Towards the Inca bridge

Beyond Pampamarca, the road continues to **Yanaoca**, where you'll find basic accommodation and restaurants. From here it is possible to head southeast to Sicuani but continuing to **Qeswachaka** and the grass Inca bridge 30 km away is well worth the effort. Just before you leave Yanaoca, turn right to join a road which, at times, is very rough. The way is marked with kilometre signs: turn right just after Km 22 where another road begins, marked with a Km 0. You will find steps down to the bridge shortly before Km 31, two bends from the bright orange road bridge.

The footbridge has been rebuilt every year for the past 400 years during a three-day festival, which starts on 10 June and is celebrated by the three communities who use the bridge. It is built entirely of *pajabrava* grass, woven and spliced to make six sturdy cables which are strung across the 15-m chasm. Look in the water at the far side and you will probably see the remains of the previous year's effort; the fibres last five months, after which they deteriorate and you should not attempt to cross.

About two hours before you reach Qeswachaka is the **Carañawi Cave** (at 4100 m). From Yanaoca find transport towards Livitaca and ask locals where to get off for Carañawi. There is also a large sign. You may only enter the cave between June and October as there is too much water at other times of the year. Camping is possible, but be prepared for extreme cold; there is no water available. It is certainly also possible to drive here in a rented car, but the road is terrible so taking a 4WD is a good idea.

Raqchi → *Colour map 2, B4.*

ⓘ *San Pedro de Cacha, 120 km southeast of Cuzco. Entry US$3.55. There is a basic shop at the site. The school next door greatly appreciates donations of books and materials.*

In the province of Canchis, in a fertile tributary valley of the Vilcanota, lies the colonial village of **San Pedro de Cacha**. Although unremarkable in itself, the village stands within Raqchi, one of the most important archaeological sites in Peru.

A few hundred metres beyond the village are the principal remains, the once great **Temple of Viracocha**, the pan-Andean god, creator of all living creatures. This is one of the only remaining examples of a two-storey Inca building. It was 90 m long and 15 m high and was probably the largest roofed building ever constructed by the Incas. Above walls of finely dressed masonry 3-4 m high – stonework equal to that found in Cuzco or Machu Picchu – rise the remains of another 5-6 m high wall of adobe brickwork of which only isolated sections remain. Similarly, of the 22 outer columns, which supported great sloping roofs, just one or two remain complete, the others being in various states of preservation. There are numerous other buildings, including *acllahuasi* (houses of chosen women, spinners and weavers of ceremonial cloth), barracks, granaries, reservoirs, baths and fountains. The burial site includes round *chullpa* tombs of the sort found around Lake Titicaca. Much of it was damaged and demolished by looters in search of treasure during or after the Spanish conquest. According to some accounts, the temple was built by Inca Viracocha in the late 14th century, but some chronicles attribute it to Pachacútec.

Archaeological research has shown that Raqchi was always a place associated with religious and ceremonial activity. This predates not only the Incas, but also the Canches (an ethnic group which flourished in the middle horizon of Tiahuanaco), who were conquered and incorporated into the Inca Empire. Since Raqchi was the principal religious site of the Canches, it was natural that the Incas should dedicate their own temple on their allies' hallowed ground. Perhaps the most significant reason behind the choice of this as a sacred site is that Raqchi stands on the slopes of the only dormant volcano in the Cuzco region, Kimsachata. The name in Quechua means 'three-cornered' or 'triplets'. Various myths of Viracocha's travels in the area tell of a hostile reception by local inhabitants, resulting in their destruction by fire and brimstone invoked by Viracocha; others show him taming and overcoming a devastating eruption of Kimsachata.

On the volcano's slopes are pure water springs and sulphurous thermal springs, salt and rich clay deposits. The clay provides the region's principal industry, pottery and ceramics (whence its other name, Raqchi, which in Quechua is a large vessel or pot used in the preparation of *chicha*), as well as building materials such as tiles and particularly strong bricks.

The village of Raqchi is also well known for its distinctive pottery featuring simple designs of animals and fish from the area. The daily market in the plaza now sells mostly mass-produced pottery brought from Cuzco, but if you ask for ceramics *al estilo Raqchi* you may be able to purchase pieces, or be taken to a local workshop.

Raqchi has also become something of a centre for **residential tourism projects** where tourists stay in the homes of local families, usually for one month, and share in their daily lives, including helping out with agricultural work. To get involved ask for the current leader of the *proyecto turismo vivencial*. You will need to speak at least some Spanish to get the most out of this experience. ▸▸ *For information on local festivals, see page 229.*

Sicuani → *Phone code: 084. Colour map 2, B4. Altitude: 3690 m.*

Sicuani is an important agricultural centre and an excellent place for items of llama and alpaca wool and skins. They are sold at the railway station and at the excellent Sunday morning market. The plaza is not as bad as the aberrations found in villages in the nearby mountains, but it is flanked along one entire side by a mirror-glass-fronted, purple-painted concrete monstrosity. On the other side are examples of what might have been much more appropriate colonial-style, balconied buildings. Around the plaza are several shops selling local hats. The bus terminal is in the newer part of town, which is separated from the older part and the Plaza de Armas by a pedestrian walkway and bridge. At the new end of the bridge, but also close to the centre of town, are several *hostales* advertising hot water and private bathrooms.

Beyond Sicuani the road continues 250 km to Puno. **La Raya Pass** (4321 m), the highest on this route, is 38 km beyond the town and marks the divide between Cuzco Department and the altiplano which stretches to Lake Titicaca.

South to Sicuani

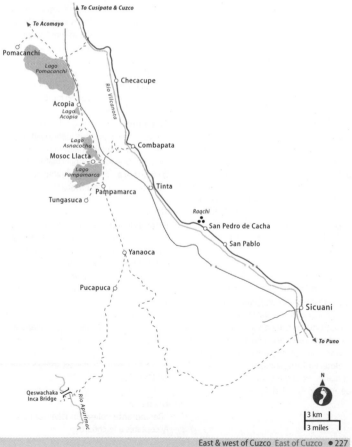

For Sleeping and Eating price codes and other relevant information, see pages 30-36.

⊜ Sleeping

San Jerónimo to Huanca *p208*
F Sanctuary of El Señor de Huanca.
Lodging and meals are available for pilgrims and hikers: a charge is made for bed and board, free for somewhere to sleep only (but you can cook). Both include full use of bath and toilet.

Paucartambo *p212*
G pp Albergue Municipal Carmen de la Virgen. Fairly basic.
G pp Quinta Rosa Marina, near the bridge. Similarly basic.

Andahuaylillas *p217*
E La Casa del Sol, close to the central plaza at Garcilaso 514. Relaxing, clean and bright hostal. Well-decorated rooms set around a courtyard, excellent value. Owned by Dr Gladys Oblitas, the hostal funds her project to provide medical services to poor campesinos. While staying you can take a course on natural and alternative medicine. She has a practice in Cuzco, T084-227264. Make reservations in Cuzco before going to Andahuaylillas as the *hostal* does not operate year round.

Urcos *p218*
G pp Hostal Luvic, on the plaza. Cheap, basic.
G pp Hostal Señor de Qoillurrit'i, on the main road on the central plaza. Best of a bad bunch. Dormitory rooms are very basic but clean; also a private double of similar quality. Showers are cold in a separate block outside.
   Hotel La Terraza in Urcos may look upmarket from the outside but should be avoided if at all possible.

Cordillera Vilcanota *p218*
If staying overnight in Tinqui, take earplugs as traffic on the Interoceánica highway runs through town all night long.
F Ausangate, Tinqui. Very basic but warm, friendly atmosphere.
F Hostal Tinqui Guide, Tinqui, on the right-hand side as you enter the village. Has safety deposit. Sr Crispin (or Cayetano), the owner, is knowledgeable and can arrange guides, mules, etc. He and his brothers can be contacted in Cuzco on F084-227768. All have been recommended as reliable sources of trekking and climbing information, for arranging trips and for being very safety conscious.

Southeast from Urcos *p224*
G Casa Comunal, Tinta. Clean dormitory accommodation and good food.

Camping
There are many places to camp wild by the lakes near **Acomayo**. Take warm clothing for night-time and plenty of water. At **Qeswachaca** there's good camping downstream, but take water.

Sicuani *p226*
E Hotel Obada, Jr Tacna 104, T084-351214. At the new end of the bridge. Has seen better days. Large, clean rooms with hot showers.
E Royal Inti, Av Centenario 116, T084-352730, on the west side of the old pedestrian bridge across the river. Modern, clean and friendly.
F Samary, Av Centenario 138 (next to Royal Inti), T084-352518. Offers good-value rooms with bathrooms.

⊘ Eating

Urcos *p218*
℻ **Restaurante Pollería**, on the main plaza. Acceptable and cheap.

Sicuani *p226*

There are several cafés on 2 de Mayo, running northeast from the plaza, which are good for snacks and breakfasts.

El Fogón, Zevallos, the main drag down from the plaza, smart, painted pink, on the left heading down. Serves up good chicken and chips.

Mijuna Wasi, Jr Tacna 146. Closed Sun. One of several *picanterías*, which prepares typical dishes such as *adobo* served with huge glasses of *chicha* in a dilapidated but atmospheric courtyard. Recommended.

Pizzería Bon Vino, 2 de Mayo 129, 2nd floor, off the east side of the plaza. Good for an Italian meal.

⊛ Festivals and events

Sanctuary of El Señor de Huanca *p210*
14-21 Sep Señor de Huanca celebrations. The pilgrimage continues throughout Oct.

Paucartambo *p212*
15-17 Jul Fiesta of the Virgen del Carmen (see page 213).

Towards the Inca bridge *p225*
10 Jun A 3-day festival is celebrated for the rebuilding of the grass Inca footbridge at Qeswachaka.

Raqchi *p226*
Raqchi is still a venue for ceremonial events. **24-29 Jun** Wiracocha festivities in San Pedro and neighbouring San Pablo start on 24 Jun. This date marks the dual Andean celebration of the ancient Inca festival of the sun, **Inti Raymi**, and the Christian feast day of **San Juan Bautista**, closely associated with water, streams and bathing, as well as being the patron saint of cattle and cattle breeders. It is the time of branding. On the eve of the fiesta, bonfires are lit across the Andes and fortunes are divined. Dancers come to Raqchi from all over Peru and through music and dance they illustrate everything from the ploughing of

fields to bull fights. This leads into the feast of **San Pedro** and **San Pablo** on 29th.

⊜ Transport

San Jerónimo to Huanca trek *p208*
Bus
The most convenient place in central Cuzco to board a bus to San Jerónimo is Av Sol 3rd block. Three services stop here: **ET León de San Jerónimo** (from Puquín District, on the road to Chinchero); **Santiago Express** (from plaza of Santiago district, a few blocks from La Virgen de Belén and the Antonio Lorena Hospital) and **Chaska** (from Villa El Sol-Independencia in the Santiago district). All services run 0530-2200 and go through the downtown area, Wanchac district and along Av de la Cultura all the way to San Jerónimo, US\$0.30.

Alight in front of San Jerónimo police station; C Clorinda Matto de Turner is 1½ blocks away, for the start of the trek. This street is also where the San Jerónimo main market is located and has the cemetery at its very end.

Sanctuary of El Señor de Huanca *p210*
Bus
Transport from Cuzco leaves from the Coliseo Cerrado and the back of the Social Security Hospital compound, 2 blocks beyond the Hospital Regional main bus stop, to the right on Av de la Cultura going southeast. Buses run 0700-1200 on weekends and daily during the Señor de Huanca celebrations and pilgrimage in Sep and Oct (see Festivals and events, above). Buses make the return trip 1200-1600.

The priests have their own private transport, which can be rented for a ride from the sanctuary to connect with transport to Cuzco or Pisac.

Taxis
Taxis from Cuzco to the sanctuary cost about US\$12-15 one way or US\$25-30 return with waiting time.

Humbutío to Pisac p212
Bus
Empresa de Transportes Paucartambo y Pitusiray, Av Tullumayo 202 (lower part), run from Cuzco to **San Salvador**, 0640 and 1300 Mon-Sat, 1½ hrs, US$1, returning to Cuzco at 0800 and 1330. There's also a bus from San Salvador to **Pisac** at 1400, 45 mins-1 hr, US$0.75.

Paucartambo p212
Private car hire for a round trip from Cuzco to **Paucartambo** on 15-17 Jul costs US$30 and can be arranged by tour operators in Cuzco. A minibus leaves for Paucartambo from Av Huáscar in Cuzco, every other day, 3-4 hrs, US$5; alternate days Paucartambo-Cuzco. Trucks and a private bus leave from the Coliseo, behind Hospital Segura in Cuzco; 5 hrs, US$3.

Piquillacta Archaeological Park p214
Buses to **Lucre** leave from the bus station on Av Huáscar in Wanchac district, on a side street ½ block from the market, 1 hr, US$0.50. Small cars wait at the start of the 8-km circuit around the Huacarpay lake charging US$2.50 (Ruperto Valencia and Ernesto Arredondo are recommended drivers). To go directly to **Piquillacta** and **Rumicola**, catch the Urcos bus from Av de la Cultura, see below.

Southeast to Urcos p217
Transportes Vilcanota depart daily 0500-2100 from the terminal on Av de la Cultura, Cuzco, at the Paradero Hospital Regional (on a side street) and run to **Urcos** (US$0.75) via **San Jerónimo**, **Saylla**, **Huasao**, **Tipón**, **Oropesa**, **Piquillacta/Huacarpay** and **Andahuaylillas**.

To **Andahuaylillas** you can also take a taxi, or the **Oropesa** bus from Av Huáscar in Cuzco, via Tipón, Piquillacta and Rumicolca. Taxi colectivos leave from block 17 of Av La Cultura, opposite the university in Cuzco.

Cordillera Vilcanota p219
Buses for **Tinqui** leave from Av Tomasatito Condemayta, at the corner of the Coliseo Cerrado in Cuzco, 1000 Mon-Sat, 6-7 hrs, US$3.50. **Huayna Ausangate** is a recommended company; they have a ticket office near the Coliseo Cerrado .

Southeast from Urcos p225
To get to **Acomayo**, take the Unancha bus from Calle Huáscar. They have services from 0500-0800, book in advance. Also you can take a combi from Cuzco to Sicuani (US$1.50, 1½ hrs), then a truck or bus to Acomayo (3 hrs, US$2). Alternatively, get off at Checacupe and take a truck on to Acomayo. To visit the 4 beautiful mountain lakes and Inca bridge, it's worthwhile renting a 4WD for 2 days. Giving locals a lift is fun and they will make sure you take the right road. Alternatively, hire a vehicle with a driver. It is just as feasible by combi. The bridge can also be reached from **Combapata** on the main Cuzco–Sicuani road. Combis and colectivos leave for the 30-km trip when full from the plaza for **Yanaoca** (US$0.75). Then hitchhike to **Quehue** (no accommodation), a 1½-hr walk from Qeswachaka, or to **Qeswachaka** itself, on the road to Livitaca. Be prepared for long waits on this road. On Wed and Sat there are direct buses to **Livitaca** from Cuzco with the **Warari** and **Olivares** companies that pass the site, returning on Mon and Thu.

❶ Directory

Sanctuary of El Señor de Huanca p210
Telephone A public telephone is at the Sanctuary.

Sicuani p226
Banks Banco de la Nación has a branch on the plaza, as does BCP, but the one cash machine takes only local cards.

West of Cuzco

West of Cuzco is the road to Abancay in the Department of Apurímac (195 km from Cuzco), where the principal overland route to Lima, via Nazca, heads west and another road continues through the highlands to Ayacucho. There are enough Inca sites on or near this road in the Department of Cuzco to remind us that the empire's influence spread to all four cardinal points. Add to this some magnificent scenery, especially in the canyon of the Río Apurímac, and you have the makings of some fascinating excursions away from the centre. One, to the ruins of Choquequirao, is a tough but rewarding trip; getting there requires an expedition of four days or more. ▸▸ *For listings, see pages 239-241.*

Ins and outs

All direct buses from Cuzco to Lima go via Abancay, 195 km, five hours (longer in the rainy season). There are also local buses between Cuzco and Abancay, which stop at places en route. The road is paved, but floods in the wet season may damage large sections of the highway. If prone to car sickness, be prepared, as there are many, many curves, but the scenery is magnificent (it also happens to be a great route for cycling). ▸▸ *For further details, see Transport, pages 122 and 241 .*

Anta to Abancay → *For listings, see pages 239-241.*

Anta to Limatambo

The Cuzco–Machu Picchu train follows the road west from the city through the Anta canyon for 10 km, and then, at a sharp angle, the Urubamba canyon, and descends along the river valley, flanked by high cliffs and peaks. In the town of **Anta**, felt trilby hats are on sale. Beyond Anta, heading towards Abancay, are the ruins of **Tarahuasi** ① *76 km west of Cuzco, 2 km before Limatambo, US$3.55.* A few hundred metres from the road is a very well-preserved Inca temple platform, with 28 tall niches, and a long stretch of fine polygonal masonry. The ruins are impressive, enhanced by the orange lichen which gives the walls a beautiful honey colour. Near here the Spanish *conquistadores* on their push towards the Inca capital of Cuzco suffered what could have been a major setback. Having crossed the Río Apurímac, the expeditionary force under the command of Hernando de Soto encountered an Inca army at Vilcaconga. On the first day of the battle, de Soto's men were almost routed, although only five were killed, but in the night reinforcements led by Almagro arrived. The following morning the Incas were demoralized to see a larger force than the one they had defeated the day before and, after renewed fighting, left the field to the Spaniards.

Apurímac canyon

One hundred kilometres from Cuzco along the Abancay road is the exciting descent into the **Apurímac canyon**. Nearby is the former Inca suspension bridge that inspired Thornton Wilder's *The Bridge of San Luis Rey* (see Books, page 345), which won the 1928 Pulitzer prize. The bridge itself was made of rope and was where the royal Inca road crossed the river. When the *conquistadores* reached this point on the march to Cuzco, they found the bridge destroyed. But luck was on their side since, it being the dry season, the normally fierce Río Apurímac was low enough for the men and horses to ford. In colonial times the bridge was rebuilt several times but it no longer exists.

Thornton Wilder (1897-1975) uses an imagined episode in the bridge's history to meditate upon individual destiny. His novel describes how, on 20 July 1714, five travellers are on the bridge when its ropes snap and it plummets into the river. A monk, Brother Juniper, witnesses their death and investigates the lives of each, trying to understand the role of divine providence in their demise. Three of the characters are fictional but the other two are the son and teacher of La Perricholi, the most famous actress in Peru at the time and one-time mistress of the Viceroy Amat. For his efforts, and for his questioning of God's purpose, Juniper is declared heretical by the Inquisition and burned at the stake.

Not far from the new road bridge over the Apurímac are the thermal baths of **Cconoc** ① *US$2*. An unmade road twists down to the river's edge where several pools and spouts are fed by warm water coming out of the cliffs. They are fairly clean, but watch out for the biting midges.

Curahuasi and around

The road continues to **Curahuasi**, which has several roadside restaurants and *hospedajes*. From here it's a good two-hour walk up Cerro San Cristóbal to **Capitán Rumi**, a huge rock overlooking the Apurímac canyon. The views are staggering, particularly if Salkantay and its snowy neighbours are free of cloud. Ask for directions, especially at the start.

About 20 minutes from Curahuasi at an altitude of 3500 m is the **Saywite Stone** ① *3 km from main road at Km 49, well signposted, entry US$4, students US$2*, a large carved rock that is said to represent the three regions of jungle, sierra and coast, with the associated animals and Inca sacred sites of each. It is now the centrepiece of a UNESCO World Heritage Site, consisting of six main areas falling away from the stone and its neighbouring group of buildings. There is a staircase beside an elegant watercourse of channels and pools, a group around a stone (split by lightning), called the Casa de Piedra or Rumi Huasi, an Usnu platform and another monolith, called the Intihuatana. The holes around the perimeter of the Saywite Stone suggest that it was once covered in gold. It is said to have been defaced by 'people from Lima' when they took a cast of it, breaking off many of the animals' heads. It is fenced in and clean; ask the guardian for a closer look.

Cachora

This village is the starting point for the trek to Choquequirao (see page 235). It lies in a magnificent location on the south side of the Apurímac, reached by a side road from the Cuzco–Abancay highway, shortly after Saywite. It is four hours by bus from Cuzco to the turn-off, then a two-hour descent from the road at 3695 m to Cachora at 2875 m. Accommodation, guides (Celestino Peña is the official guide) and mules for the trek are available here (about US$12 a day for guide and mule).

Choquequirao → *Colour map 2, B2.*

① *Entry US$13.50, students US$6.75; tickets may be bought online at www.machu picchu.gob.pe.*

Choquequirao is another 'lost city of the Incas', built on a ridge spur almost 1600 m above the Apurímac. Its Inca name is unknown, but research by US archaeologist Gary Ziegler suggests that it was built during the reign of Topa Inca. Although only 30% has been uncovered, it is believed to be a larger site than Machu Picchu, but with fewer buildings. The stonework is different from the classic Inca construction and masonry, simply because the preferred granite and andesite are not found in this region. A number of high-profile explorers and archaeologists, including Hiram Bingham, researched the site, but its importance has only recently been recognized. And now tourists are venturing in there, too. With new regulations being applied to cut congestion on the Inca Trail, Choquequirao is destined to replace the traditional hike as the serious trekker's alternative. The **Ministerio de Cultura** may introduce a fee to trek to the ruins, but it was not included in their 2010 prices.

Ins and outs The shortest route to Choquequirao is from **Cachora** (see above). The two-day hike from Cachora can be undertaken as part of the Vilcabamba traverse trek detailed on page 234. It is also possible to reach Choquequirao from either Huancacalle or Aguas Calientes by doing the trek in reverse, although this will take a minimum of eight days and require thorough preparation.

Exploring the site The main features of Choquequirao include the **Lower Plaza**, considered by most experts to be the focal point of the city. Double-jammed doorways and high-quality stonework suggest that the buildings were used by high-ranking members of Inca society. Three of the main buildings were two-storey structures. The **Upper Plaza**, reached by a huge set of steps or terraces, has what are possibly ritual baths. Some have speculated that this area was occupied by the priesthood of Choquequirao. The lesser quality of the stonework and the absence of double-jammed doorways suggest slightly lower status than the Lower Plaza. A beautiful set of slightly curved agricultural terraces runs for over 300 m east-northeast of the Lower Plaza.

The **Usnu** is a levelled hilltop platform, ringed with stones and giving awesome 360° views. Perhaps it was a ceremonial site, or was used for astronomical and solar observations. The **Ridge Group**, still shrouded in vegetation, is a large collection of buildings some 50-100 m below the Usnu. Unrestored, with some significant hall-like structures, this whole area makes for great exploring. Perhaps this extensive and complex set of buildings formed the living quarters for the site's residents.

The **Outlier Building**, isolated and surrounded on three sides by sheer drops of over 1500 m into the Apurímac Canyon, possesses some of the finest stonework within the Choquequirao site. The Outlier's separation from the other structures must also be significant in some way, but exactly how, like so many other questions regarding the Incas and their society, remains a mystery.

Choquequirao

N

100 metres
100 yards

1 Lower Plaza
2 Upper Plaza
3 Curved Terraces
4 Usnu
5 Ridge Group
6 Outlier Building

Capuliyoc (viewpoint), nearly 500 m below the Lower Plaza, is a great set of agricultural terraces, visible on the approach from the far side of the valley. These terraces enabled the Incas to cultivate plants from a significantly warmer climate in close geographical proximity to their ridge-top home. Further terraces decorated with llamas in white stone have been uncovered; ask if they are open to the public.

Abancay → *Phone code: 083. Colour map 2, B1.*

Nestled between mountains in the upper reaches of a glacial valley at 2378 m, this friendly town is a functional, commercial centre, growing in importance now that the paved Lima–Nazca–Cuzco road passes through it. It also hopes to benefit from the tourist trade to Choquequirao and much investment is taking place in hotels and generally improving the town. It celebrates the **Yawar Fiesta** in July. **Tourist office** ① *Lima 206, open 0800-1430*, or **Dircetur** ① *Av Arenas 121, p 1, T083-321664, apurimac@mincetur.gob.pe.*

Half-day tours are run to nearby sites such as the former haciendas of **Yaca** and **Illanya**. Near the former is a place where silkworms are bred. Also included is the colonial bridge at **Pachachaca**, the Mirador at **Taraccasa**, for good views over the city, and the thermal baths of **Santo Tomás**. The **Santuario Nacional de Ampay**, north of town, has lagoons called Angasccocha (3200 m) and Uspaccocha (3820 m), a glacier on Ampay moutain at 5235 m and flora and fauna typical of these altitudes. By public transport, take a colectivo to Tamburco and ask the driver where to get off. To reach the glacier requires two days of trekking, with overnight camping.

Vilcabamba traverse trek → *Colour map 2, B2.*

The Vilcabamba range was the last refuge of the Inca Empire and, under Manco Inca and his sons, resistance endured for decades after the initial conquest (see box, page 199). Hemmed in between two great rivers, the mountains form a natural fortress, and Inca ruins, many little known and unrestored, lie scattered across the entire region.

Described below is a trek across the mountains from Cachora to Choquequirao, continuing from there to the Yanama river valley and on to Santa Teresa or Machu Picchu

Vilcabamba traverse trek

itself. The full route crosses the entire Vilcabamba range, between the mighty canyons of the Apurímac and Urubamba rivers, connecting two of the most impressive archaeological sites in South America. For those with time this is an excellent alternative to the classic Inca Trail and in places follows well-preserved examples of Inca road. It passes the mines of La Victoria and involves an incredible number of strenuous ascents and descents. En route you are rewarded with fabulous views of the Sacsarayoc massif (also called Pumasillo), Salkantay, other snow peaks and the deep canyons of the Río Blanco and the Apurímac. You will also see condors and meet very friendly people, but the highlight is Choquequirao itself. Those with less time to spare can follow the first part of the route only, from Cachora to Choquequirao, and return via the same trail.

A third alternative splits from the main route in the Yanama Valley and goes to Huancacalle (see page 197), via the pass of Choquetacarpo, 4600 m high. From Huancacalle it's possible to continue on to Espíritu Pampa on the edge of the rainforest. Both routes can be undertaken in reverse.

Ins and outs
It is recommended that you hire a guide, either locally in Cachora (see page 232) or in Cuzco. Not only will you obtain local knowledge of the area and route, but also you will be helping to bring employment to an extremely isolated region of Peru and at the same time give an incentive to preserve the region's cultural and environmental resources. The 1:100,000 IGN sheet Machu Picchu completely covers the route, although in some places accuracy is not great. Maps are available at the **Instituto Geográfico Nacional** in Lima or at **South American Explorers** in Cuzco. Some agencies in Cuzco are beginning to offer organized treks on these routes.

Cachora to Choquequirao → 2 days.
Day one From Cachora take the road heading down, out of the village, through lush cultivated countryside and meadows. On a clear day you should have good views of the snow peak of **Padrayoc**, roughly to the north, on the far side of the Apurímac canyon. There are many trails close to the village; if uncertain of the trail, ask; the locals are very friendly. After 15 minutes of descent, a sign for Choquequirao points to a left-hand path, initially following the course of a small stream. Follow the trail and cross a footbridge to the other side of a large stream. From here the track becomes more obvious, with few paths diverging from the main route. The trail follows the left side of the valley, more or less flat, passing an old hacienda on the right-hand side. To your right is the Apurímac Canyon, the river flowing far beneath (although difficult to see at this point), and the Vilcabamba range.

After 9 km, two or 2½ hours from the start of the trek, is the wonderful *mirador* (viewpoint) of **Capuliyoc**, at 2800 m, with fantastic vistas of the Apurímac Canyon and the snowy Vilcabamba range across the river. (Many organized treks start here.) With a pair of binoculars it's just possible to recognize Choquequirao, etched into the forested hills to the west. Condors are sometimes seen in this area. Beyond Capuliyoc the trail begins to descend towards the river. Here, away from the village, there exist some excellent examples of dry forest, largely devoid of leaves in the dry season. Further down the valley lies **Cocamasana**, a rest spot with a rough covered roof. From this point the river is clearly visible, running emerald green when the water level is low, a rushing white torrent during the rains. At Km 16 is **Chiquisca** (1930 m), a lovely wooded spot and home to a local family. Chiquisca has a fairly clean water supply, so it's an opportunity to fill bottles. If you don't want to continue any further on the first day, this is a good campsite at US$1.50 per person, with flush toilets, a shower and drinks on sale. Another one-hour descent leads you to the suspension bridge crossing the Río Apurímac (1500 m). Currents are strong on the river, but a few sheltered spots are good for a refreshing dip. By the bridge, camping is possible at Playa Rosalina.

Crossing the bridge the path ascends very steeply for one and a half hours. **Santa Rosa**, a good area for camping, again near the property of a local family, is just after the Km 21 sign. The family at Santa Rosa also has a small shop and brew their own chicha, which your *arrieros* may be interested in! Clean water is available. If this area is occupied, another larger site is available 10 minutes further up the hill. Ask residents for directions.

Day two From Santa Rosa continue uphill on a steep zigzag for two hours to the *mirador* of **Marampata**, where the family sells hot meals. The **Huanpaca** waterfall can be seen on the far side of the valley. From Marampata the trail flattens out, following the right side of the canyon, downstream, towards Choquequirao. In the valley below the guard post and underneath the main site, you can see some excavated agricultural terraces. Far below, in a different warmer microclimate, these terraces enabled the inhabitants to cultivate lower-altitude fruits and vegetables in close proximity to their highland staples. After 1½ hours on this flatter trail you enter some beautiful stretches of cloudforest, before a final short climb and arrival at **Choquequirao** itself.

Most groups camp on the great set of terraces reached upon arrival at the site. The warden will show you where to camp. At an altitude of 3000 m the nights can be cold. If coming from Santa Rosa you should have the afternoon free to explore the complex. There is much more to Choquequirao than at first appears, so, given time, you could easily allow an extra day here. Many people find the unrestored buildings below the main plaza particularly enchanting, with the remains of terraces and living quarters still smothered in dense forest. They also give an impression of what the site must have looked like when first discovered, a great contrast to the restored Lower and Upper Plaza areas. To return to Cachora at this point, simply retrace the route, possibly camping at Chiquisca to give a nice break to the two-day return trek.

Choquequirao to Yanama → *2 days.*

Day three The third day, if completed in one day as described below, is almost certainly the toughest on the trek. It will keep you walking pretty much all day, and there's a steep ascent to the campsite, just to add to your pleasure!

Climb to the Upper Plaza complex roughly to the northwest of the Main Plaza and terraces. There are spectacular vistas of the canyon, the surrounding peaks, including Ampay to the west, and also over the central areas of Choquequirao itself. A rough and sometimes overgrown trail climbs steeply up the hill behind, following sections of old Inca trail and drainage channels, and passing some small ruins. The route traverses cloudforest, festooned with mosses, around the left side of the mountain for one hour, with some precipitous drops on the left. Beyond Choquequirao many sections of trail will prove a challenge to those with severe vertigo! The path then emerges into an area of alpine grassland and starts to descend steeply, zigzagging into the valley of the **Quebrada Victoria**. Towards the lower section of the grassland is a green glade, used to graze pack animals. It's possible to camp here, but water could be a problem in the dry season.

After the glade the path continues its descent, once again entering scrub and then dry forest. Note the contrast between the dry vegetation on this side of the valley, which receives sun for most of the day, and the damp and green forest on the far side, which is often in shadow. This is a vivid illustration of how mountain ranges such as the Vilcabamba create a vast range of microclimates and, therefore, biodiversity, in an extremely limited geographical area. After 30 minutes the trail passes close to the unrestored houses and terraces of **Pinchiunuyoc**. It's possible to obtain water here as the original Inca water channels are still flowing. After another 1½ or two hours of steep descent you reach the Quebrada Victoria at around 2000 m. The climate here is subtropical and, except for the large numbers of sandflies, this is a great spot for lunch and a bracing dip in the river. In the wet season or during flash floods the Quebrada Victoria could be impossible to cross; seek local information.

Continue downstream along the right-hand bank of the *quebrada* (ravine) for perhaps 200 m and you'll come to the beginning of the trail leading up the other side, running almost entirely through thick forest. This is a brutal ascent, climbing for three or four hours until reaching the campsite at roughly 3500 m. The campsite, which has a limited water supply, is, once again, on the land of a local family who live perched on the edge of the abyss, with the forest and towering glacial peak of Corihuaynachina as a backdrop. Several trails branch off the main route near the family's land and potentially this could be confusing. Perhaps the surest way to locate your home for the night is to listen for the sounds of domestic animals, the barking of dogs and crowing of cockerels coming from the family's home. It's a magnificent campsite, but cold at night. Enjoy the view from your tent!

Day four Carry on up the trail from camp, following the left side of the valley, roughly in the direction of Corihuaynachina. The **Abra San Juan** (San Juan Pass) is to the left of this peak. Continue through cloudforest for 2½ hours. The trail can be very muddy in places. There are some beautiful examples of mountain cedar in the area and the valley supports much wildlife, including spectacled bears. Birdlife is prolific and diverse, with many species of mountain tanager, solitary eagles in the valley's lower reaches, mountain caracaras, and sometimes condors soaring above the peaks. The route passes several abandoned mine shafts, which can be explored (at your own risk) with flashlights.

After the initial 2½ or three hours' hiking from camp, the forest fades, replaced by high Andean *puna* (grassland) studded with flowers and, in places, a strange blood-red lichen covering the rocks. The path follows a section of original Inca trail, arriving at the Abra San Juan (4200 m) roughly four hours after leaving camp. On a clear day there are magnificent views of the *nevados* (snowy peaks) of Choquetacarpo and Sacsarayoc (also known as Pumasillo). Below them is the valley of the Río Yanama. The alternative route to Huancacalle can be seen to the north on the far side of the Yanama. Follow the path roughly east-northeast, descending for 2½ or three hours, and this will bring you to the small traditional village of **Yanama**, at around 3500 m. On the way down to Yanama some of the drop-offs are very steep. The valley is full of wild flowers. In the village it's usually possible to camp in front of the school buildings and to buy basic food. It may also be possible to hire mules and guides. Yanama has no roads to the outside world and traditional cultures are still strong. Please respect these people's ways and don't offer children sweets, etc. Note the excellent quality of the stonework in many of the traditional dwellings, and also the fine grass roofing.

Yanama to La Playa → *2 days.*
Day five Ascend the Yanama Valley for 1½ hours, following the course of the Río Yanama, which runs on your left. Waterfalls can be seen on either side, snowmelt from

glaciers high above. Towards the head of the valley the trail starts to veer away from the river to the right, beginning the ascent to the 4800-m **Abra Apacheta** (Apacheta Pass). It's a hard climb of around three hours and the altitude can take its toll. To the right of Apacheta is **Padrayoc**, the mountain visible from Cachora, towering above the Apurímac. From the pass, in clear weather, it's possible to see **Salkantay**, at 6271 m the highest peak in the Vilcabamba range. The descent from the pass is long and some trails lead away from the main route to houses and farms – be careful, especially in foggy conditions. The path tends to veer to the right and leads into the valley of the **Quebrada Tortora**. This area is badly marked on the IGN 1:100,000 sheet, and a stream that you keep on your left, and that runs into the Quebrada Tortora, appears not to be marked. Once in the valley, you follow the Río Tortora for about an hour before crossing to the other side via a small bridge just before a metal-roofed house. Continue with the river on your right until you reach a flat grassy area with several houses. This is **Hornopampa**. From here you can see Tortora village, 1 km or so down the valley. Tortora appears to be marked too far up the valley on the IGN 1:100,000 sheet, which could cause confusion. In Tortora you can camp near the medical post. The biting insects here can be awful but, to make up for the bugs, there are lovely views of many tall peaks, including **Huamantay**, visible down the valley.

Day six Walk downhill through forest for two hours, staying on the right side of the river. Just before you come to a big wedge-shaped hill at the bottom of the valley cross to the other side. Tortora bridge lies just below a series of grassy meadows in this region. The trails in this area are often affected by landslides, so seek local information. On crossing the bridge follow the gently sloping trail through fairly undisturbed sections of forest for four or five hours until reaching the small community of **La Playa** where it is possible to camp. About halfway between the bridge and La Playa the trail crosses a rocky stream bed; the path doesn't continue directly on the other side. Climb about 50 m up the rocky stream bed and you'll see the trail continuing on the right. A short distance after this, a beautiful waterfall tumbles across the trail, perhaps 100 m high. Next to the trail, under the fall, is a pool that is perfect for bathing and a (very!) refreshing shower.

La Playa has a run-down feel and doesn't give the most welcoming impression to the passing hiker, so you may want to camp slightly before the village, for greater privacy. The town centre and the road (see below) are both located across the bridge on the right side of Río Santa Teresa. You can obtain basic supplies at a couple of small stores in the town centre.

La Playa to Aguas Calientes → *1 day*.
Day seven La Playa marks the beginning of a rough road that runs to Santa Teresa. To finish the hike, you can simply follow the road downhill to Santa Teresa, or catch the early morning *camión* if you're feeling lazy; *camiones* (trucks) leave for Santa Teresa at 0600 on most days, although the road may be closed in the wet season.

Alternatively, to continue the hike from La Playa, the more interesting route is to follow the Santa Teresa road for 30 minutes to the tiny settlement of **Lucmabamba**. On the right-hand side a restored section of Inca trail leads into the hills. Follow this trail uphill, towards the ruins of **Paltallacta**, which lie over the ridge in the next valley. From the road it's 2½ or three hours' climb through scrubby bush and sections of cloudforest until reaching the pass. The restored section of Inca road runs out after about 1 km and a narrow but clear trail takes its place. In one or two places it's possible to see small sections of the original Inca trail. At the summit of the hill is a magnificent area of virgin cloudforest, worth the climb in itself. Once you begin to descend on the other side it's possible, weather conditions allowing, to view Machu Picchu from a very interesting perspective, encircled by hills, and behind, the snow-covered peaks of the Urubamba range. The large waterfall you can see, spilling out from the mountain in front of Machu Picchu is La Hidroeléctrica, designed to generate power for the surrounding area. Half an hour below the summit you reach the dispersed ruins of **Paltallacta**, unrestored walls and terraces that must have once represented a substantial settlement. Recent expeditions in the area have uncovered many new finds, including one originally described by Hiram Bingham and subsequently lost for almost a century. Who knows what remains to be discovered? Just below the ruins, to the left of the trail, are some grassy areas which give a wonderful perspective on the whole scene.

From Paltallacta, a steep descent of at least one hour leads to **Ahobamba Valley** and a cable bridge crossing the Río Ahobamba. Take care crossing the bridge as the wooden planks have been known to break. Once on the other side follow the path along the river, past the waterfall (La Hidroeléctrica), keeping to the right, past some fenced facilities, presumably associated with the hydroelectric project. You're now in the valley of the **Río Urubamba**, having crossed the entire Vilcabamba range. From here there should be plenty of people to ask directions.

There are two levels of railway track in the area. To get the local train to Aguas Calientes you need to climb up the bank to reach the main, higher track. Here there is a small railway station from which trains normally leave in the afternoon for Aguas Calientes. Alternatively you can walk to Aguas Calientes, 9 km, two to three hours' walk, simply by following the railway tracks (see also box, page 166). At several points there are good views of Machu and Huayna Picchu, towering above the Urubamba. Be careful of speeding trains! Near the Hidroeléctrica train station are the well-preserved ruins of an Inca temple (ask the locals for directions). This site features an intricately carved sacred rock, similar to that at Machu Picchu, which almost perfectly mirrors the contour of the mountain on the other side of the valley. If you still have energy this is certainly worth a look before getting to Aguas Calientes.

▶▶ *For details of Sleeping, Eating and other facilities in Aguas Calientes, see pages 186-189.*

⊚ West of Cuzco listings

For Sleeping and Eating price codes and other relevant information, see pages 30-36.

⊜ Sleeping

Anta to Limatambo *p231*
F Hostal Central, Jr Jaquijahuanca 714, Anta. A basic, friendly place with motorbike parking; beware of water shortages.
F Hostal Rivera, near the river, Limatambo. An old stone house built round a courtyard, clean, quiet and full of character.

Curahuasi and around *p232*
F Hostal San Cristóbal, Curahuasi. Clean, nice decor, pleasant courtyard, shared bath,

cold shower. A new bathroom block is currently being built.
    Camping in Curahuasi is possible on the football pitch, but ask the police for permission first.

Cachora *p232*
B pp Los Tres Balcones, Jr Abancay s/n, www.choquequirau.com. Hostel designed as start and end-point for the trek to Choquequirao. Breakfast included, comfortable, hot showers, restaurant and pizza oven, camping. Shares information with the town's only internet café. They run a 5-day trek to Choquequirao, US$550, with camping gear (but not sleeping bag), all

meals and lunch at the hostel afterwards, entrance to the ruins, horses to carry luggage (US$650 including transport from Cuzco and bilingual tour guide).

D pp Casa de Salcantay, Prolongación Salcantay s/n, T084-984 397336 (mob), www.salcantay.com. Price includes breakfast, dinner available if booked in advance. Dutch-run hostel with links to community projects, comfortable, small, Dutch, English, German spoken, can help with arranging independent treks, or organize treks with tour operator.

F pp La Casona de Ocampo, San Martín 122, T084-237514, lacasonadeocampo@yahoo.es. With hot shower all day, free camping, owner Carlos Robles is friendly and knowledgeable, rents camping equipment, organizes treks to Choquequirao and beyond.

Abancay *p234*

B-C Turistas, Av Díaz Bárcenas 500, T083-321017, www.turismoapurimac.com. With bathroom, breakfast included. The original building is in colonial style, but there is a new block and the whole hotel has been refurbished, with new bedrooms, a bigger restaurant, gardens and a travel agency, **Apurimac Tours**, offering hiking packages to Choquequirao. Rooms are large and, in the old block, the better and more expensive ones are on the top floor. Quiet, clean, good restaurant, Wi-Fi, parking space.

E Imperial, Díaz Bárcenas 515, T083-321578, http://imperialhotel.galeon.com/. Rooms are around the central parking space in this hospitable, efficient and spotless hotel. Great beds, TV and hot water (also in the shared bathrooms), breakfast included, Wi-Fi, laundry service. Helpful and good value.

E Hostal Arenas, Av Arenas 192, T083-322107. A brand-new hotel is constructed beside the old one, with plain but well-appointed rooms, good beds, big showers, hot water, internet, restaurant, TV, parking and a lift to the top floor, which has good views. Hospitable.

F Apurímac Tours, Jr Cuzco 421, T083-321446. Another new building; rooms upstairs sleep 1-4, with tiny bathroom and hot water. Breakfast and lunch served in the courtyard, pay extra for either. Good value, helpful, laundry, TV, bar, café.

❶ Eating

Anta to Limatambo *p231*
¶ Tres de Mayo, Anta. Very good and popular, with top service.

There is also a good cheap restaurant in **Limatambo**, hidden from the road by trees.

Curahuasi and around *p232*
¶ La Amistad, Curahuasi. The best restaurant in town, popular, with good food and moderate prices, but has poor service.

Abancay *p234*
¶ Focarela Pizzería, Díaz Bárcenas 521, T083-322036. Simple but pleasant decor, pizza from a wood-burning oven, fresh, generous toppings, popular. Ask for *vino de la casa*!

¶ Pizzería Napolitana, Díaz Bárcenas 208. With a wood-fired clay oven and wide choice of toppings.

Cafés
Café Mundial, Arequipa 301. Open early for breakfast and also for evening snacks.

Dulce & Salad, Arequipa y 2 de Mayo. A pleasant café and *heladería*, 4 types of breakfast, daily salad specials, sandwiches, hot and cold drinks, cakes and a bar.

La Delicia, Díaz Bárcenas 210. A small vegetarian place serving breakfast, lunch buffet, juices, yoghurts and other products.

Natur Center, Díaz Bárcenas 211. An equally small vegetarian café with breakfast, lunch *menú*, juices and treatments.

Panadería Buen Gusto, Núñez 209. Good bread and cakes baked on the premises, also has a café.

Panadería Cynthia, Huancavelica 311.
With café serving enormous croissants.

▲▲ Activities and tours

Abancay p234
Apurimak Tours, at Hotel Turistas, see
Sleeping. Runs local tours and 1- and 2-day
trips to Santuario Nacional de Ampay: 1-day,
7 hrs. Also a 4-day trip to Choquequirao
including transport, guide, horses, tents
and food, just bring your sleeping bag.
Carlos Valer, guide in Abancay. Ask for him at
Hotel Turistas, very knowledgeable and kind.

⊖ Transport

Anta to Limbatambo p231
The bus fare to Anta from Cuzco is US$0.30.

Choquequirao p232
From Cuzco take the first Abancay bus of
the morning with Bredde which leaves the
Terminal Terrestre at 0600 and get off at
Cachora. Buy your ticket the night before
to make sure you get a seat. From Cachora
to Abancay, buses at 0630 and 1100, 2 hrs,
US$1.50; also colectivo taxis.

Abancay p234
The following bus companies (office
addresses are given in brackets) all
depart from the Terminal Terrestre, on
Av Pachacútec, on the west side of
Abancay. Cruz del Sur (Díaz Bárcenas 1151,

T083-323028), serves the whole country.
Companies running to Cuzco include:
Bredde (Gamarra 423, T083- 321643), 5 daily
including 0600, 1300; Los Chankas (Díaz
Bárcenas 1011, El Olivo, T083-321485);
Molina (Gamarra 422, T083-322646),
3 daily; San Jerónimo at 2130.

The terminal has a restaurant, internet
and phones, a *cambio*, toilets and shops.
Taxi to centre US$0.75, otherwise it's a steep
5 blocks up Av Juan Pablo Castro to Jr Lima,
another block to Jr Arequipa and cheap
hotels, and one more to hotels Turistas
and Imperial. Several bus companies have
offices on or near the El Olivo roundabout
at Av Díaz Bárcenas y Gamarra.

Buses to Cachora (for the Choquequirao
trek) depart from Jr Prado Alto, between
Huancavelica and Núñez (5 blocks uphill
from Díaz Bárcenas; it's not the first
Jr Prado you come to), 0500 and 1400,
2 hrs, US$1.50. Alternatively, hire a car
with driver from the Curahuasi terminal
on Av Arenas, next to the Wari office,
charge US$10.

⊕ Directory

Abancay p234
Banks BCP, Jr Arequipa 218, has ATM
outside, Visa and Amex. There are several
cambios on Jr Arequipa, opposite the
mercado central, including Machi, No 202
(also at Díaz Bárcenas 105) and Oro Verde
Internet The town is full of internet places.
Some have phone cabins.

Contents

Footprint features

Machu
Picchu
Cuzco

Southern jungle

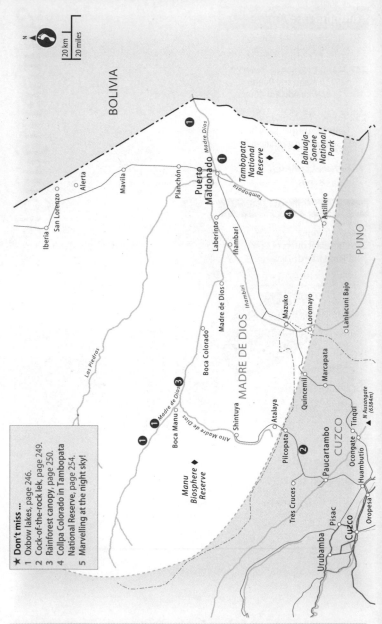

★ Don't miss ...
1 Oxbow lakes, page 246.
2 Cock-of-the-rock lek, page 249.
3 Rainforest canopy, page 250.
4 Collpa Colorado in Tambopata
   National Reserve, page 254.
5 Marvelling at the night sky!

BOLIVIA

N

20 km
20 miles

Iberia
San Lorenzo
Alerta
Mavila
Planchón
Puerto
Maldonado
Madre Dios
Tambopata
National
Reserve
Bahuaja-
Sonene National
Park
Astillero
Laberinto
Iñambari
Madre de Dios
Inambiri
Mazuko
Loromayo
Lanlacuni Bajo
PUNO
Boca Colorado
MADRE DE DIOS
Las Piedras
Madre de Dios
Alto Madre de Dios
Shintuya
Atalaya
Quincemil
Marcapata
Boca Manu
Manu
Biosphere
Reserve
N Ausangate
(6384m)
Tinqui
Ocongate
Huambutio
CUZCO
Pilcopata
Paucartambo
Tres Cruces
Oropesa
Pisac
Urubamba
CUZCO

The immense Amazon Basin covers a staggering 4 million sq km, an area roughly three quarters the size of the United States. But despite the fact that 60% of Peru is covered by this green carpet of jungle, less than 6% of its population lives there. This lack of integration with the rest of the country makes transportation difficult but does mean that much of Peru's rainforest is still intact.

The Peruvian jungles are home to a diversity of life unequalled anywhere on earth, and it is this great diversity which makes the Amazon Basin a paradise for nature lovers, be they scientists or simply curious amateurs. Overall, Peru's jungle lowlands contain some 10 million living species, including 2000 species of fish and 300 mammals. They also contain over 10% of the world's 8600 bird species and, together with the adjacent Andean foothills, 4000 butterfly species.

The southern part of Peru's Amazon jungle contains the Manu National Biosphere Reserve (2.04 million ha), the Tambopata National Reserve (254,358 ha) and the Bahuaja-Sonene National Park (1.1 million ha). These three great protected areas are in the department of Madre de Dios, adjoining the eastern edge of the department of Cuzco and extending to the borders of Brazil and Bolivia. They are far removed from the modern world and in fact most of Manu is off limits to tourists. The lack of hunting pressure in protected areas means that some larger mammals, like tapir, giant anteaters, otters and primates are fairly easy to spot, while the huge variety of forest types and diverse habitats have led to more bird species here than anywhere else on the planet. Many lodges in the area are close to the river port of Puerto Maldonado.

Background

The forest of this lowland region (altitude: 260 m) is technically called subtropical moist forest, which means that it receives less rainfall than tropical forest and is dominated by the flood plains of its meandering rivers. One of the most striking features is the former river channels that have become isolated as oxbow lakes (*cochas*). These are home to black caiman and giant otter and a host of other species. Other rare species living in the forest are jaguar, puma, ocelot and tapir. There are also capybara, 13 species of primate and many hundreds of bird species, including macaws, guans, currasows and the giant harpy eagle. If you include the cloudforests and highlands of the Manu Biosphere Reserve, the bird species count almost totals 1000.

The relative proximity to Cuzco of Manu in particular has made it one of the prime nature-watching destinations in South America. Despite its reputation, Manu is heavily protected, with visitor numbers limited and a large percentage of the park inaccessible to tourists. Nevertheless, there is no need to worry that this level of management is going to diminish your pleasure. There is more than enough in the way of birds, animals and plants to satisfy the most ardent wildlife enthusiast. Tambopata does have a town in the vicinity, Puerto Maldonado, and the area is under threat from exploitation and settlement. The suspension of oil exploration in 2000 led to a change of status for a large tract of this area, giving immediate protection to another of Peru's zones of record-breaking diversity.

Since 2003 the new emerging threat to the forests of Madre de Dios is the construction of the Interoceánica, a road linking the Atlantic and Pacific Oceans via Puerto Maldonado and Brazil. The paving of this road system, creating a high-speed link between the two countries, will certainly bring more uncontrolled colonization in the area, placing the forests of the Tambopata region under further pressure. The uncontrolled colonization of the Bahuaja-Sonene's southern border, in the Tambopata headwaters area is another cause for concern. On top of that is illegal logging and the issue of new oil exploration contracts for most of Madre de Dios outside of the conservation concessions. This, in spite of the fact that they overlap heavily with the indigenous territories concession, including the lands of indigenous peoples living in voluntary isolation.

Manu Biosphere Reserve

→ *Colour map 2, A3/4.*

No other rainforest can compare with Manu for the diversity of its life forms. It is one of the world's great wilderness experiences, with the best birdwatching as well as offering the best chance of seeing giant otters, jaguars, ocelots and several of the 13 species of primate that abound in this pristine tropical wilderness. The more remote areas of the reserve are home to uncontacted indigenous tribes and many other indigenous groups with very little knowledge of the outside world. Covering an area of 2,041,137 ha, Manu Biosphere Reserve is also one of the largest conservation units on Earth, encompassing the complete drainage of the Manu river, with an altitudinal range of 200-4100 m above sea level. ►► *For listings see pages 256-266.*

Ins and outs

Getting there The multiple-use zone of Manu Biosphere Reserve is accessible to anyone and several lodges exist in the area (see Lodges in Manu, page 256). The reserved zone is accessible by permit only and entry is strictly controlled (see below). The frontier town of Puerto Maldonado is the starting point for expeditions to the Tambopata National Reserve and is only a 30-minute flight from Cuzco. Almost all visitors go with a specialist tour operator (see list, page 262), with accommodation and transport – either a flight to the airstrip at Boca Manu or overland in a private vehicle – included in the tour price. ►► *For further information see Transport, page 264.*

Best time to visit The climate is warm and humid, with a rainy season from November to March and a dry season from April to October. A cool air mass descending from the Andes, called a *friaje*, is characteristic of the dry season, when temperatures drop to 15-16°C during the day, and 13°C at night. Always bring a sweater at this time. The best time to visit is during the dry season when there are fewer mosquitoes and the rivers are low, exposing the beaches. This is also a good time to see birds nesting and to view the animals at close range, as they stay close to the rivers. A pair of binoculars is essential and insect repellent is a must.

Visitor information **Manu National Park Office** ① *Av Micaela Bastidas 310, Cuzco, T084-240898, pqnmanu@terra.com.pe, 0800-1400*. They issue a permit for the former Reserved Zone, costing S/.150 per person (about US$54). This is included in package tour prices. For information on conservation issues: **Asociación Peruana para la Conservación de la Naturaleza (Apeco)** ① *Parque José Acosta 187, p 2, Magdalena del Mar, Lima 17, T01-264 0094, www.apeco.org.pe*; and **Pronaturaleza** ① *Alfredo León 211, Miraflores, Lima 18, T01-447 9032 and Jr Cajamarca, cuadra 1 s/n, Puerto Maldonado, T082-571585, www.pronaturaleza.org*. **Perú Verde** ① *Ricaldo Palma J-1, Santa Mónica, Cuzco, T084-226392, www.peruverde.org*, is a local NGO that can help with information and has free video shows about Manu National Park and Tambopata National Reserve. Staff are friendly and helpful and also have information on programmes and research in the jungle area of Río Madre de Dios.

Park areas

The biosphere reserve is divided into the **Manu National Park** (1,692,137 ha), where only government-sponsored biologists and anthropologists may visit with permits from the Ministry of Agriculture in Lima, the **Manu Reserved Zone** (257,000 ha) (within the Manu

National Park), set aside for applied scientific research and ecotourism, and the **Cultural Zone** (92,000 ha), containing acculturated native groups and colonists, where the locals still employ their traditional way of life. To enter these tourism and recreational areas visitors may only go under the auspices of an authorized operator with an authorized guide. Permits are limited and reservations should be made well in advance, though it is possible to book a place on a trip at the last minute in Cuzco. In the former Reserved Zone there are two lodges, the rustic **Casa Machiguenga** run by the Machiguenga communities of Tayakome and Yomibato with the help of a German NGO,

Manu Biosphere Reserve

Sleeping
1 Amazonia Lodge
2 Boca Manu &
   Yine Lodges
3 Casa Machiguenga
4 Cock of the Rock
   Lodge
5 Erika Lodge
6 Manu Cloud
   Forest Lodge
7 Manu Lodge
8 Manu Wildlife Center
9 Pantiacolla Lodge
10 Posada San Pedro
   Cloud Forest Lodge
11 Proyecto Selva Inca
12 Yanayaco Lodge

Cultural Zone

and the upmarket **Manu Lodge**. In the Cocha Salvador area, several companies have tented safari camp infrastructures, some with shower and dining facilities, but all visitors sleep in tents. Some companies have installed walk-in tents with cots and bedding.

The Cultural Zone is accessible to anyone and several lodges exist in the area. It is possible to visit these lodges under your own steam. Among the ethnic groups in the Cultural Zone (a system of buffer areas surrounding the core Manu area) are the Harakmbut, Machiguenga and Yine in the Amarakaeri Reserved Zone, on the east bank of the Alto Madre de Dios. They have set up their own ecotourism activities, which are entirely managed by indigenous people. Associated with Manu are other areas protected by conservation groups or local people, for example the Blanquillo reserved zone, a conservation concession in the adjacent Los Amigos river system and some cloudforest parcels along the road. The **Nuhua-Kugapakori Reserved Zone** (443,887 ha), set aside for these two nomadic groups, is the area between the headwaters of the Río Manu and headwaters of the Río Urubamba, to the north of the Alto Madre de Dios. ▶▶ *For details of lodges and other accommodation, see Sleeping, page 256.*

Birdwatching in Manu

Much of the Manu National Park is totally unexplored and the variety of birds is astounding: about 1000 species, significantly more than in the whole of Costa Rica and over a tenth of all the birds on earth. Although there are other places in the Manu area where you can see birdlife and an astonishing variety of other wildlife, an excellent place for the visiting birder with limited time is the **Manu Wildlife Center** (see page 257).

A typical trip starts in Cuzco and takes in the wetlands of Lake Huacarpay (to the south of the city – see page 215) where a variety of Andean waterfowl and marsh birds can be seen. Here, the beautiful and endemic mountaineer hummingbird can be seen feeding on tree tobacco. Then the route proceeds to the cloudforest of the eastern slopes of the Andes. Driving slowly down the road through the cloudforest, every 500 m loss in elevation produces new birds. This is the home of the Andean cock-of-the-rock, and a visit to one of their leks (courtship areas) is one of the world's top ornithological experiences. These humid montane forests are home to a mind-boggling variety of multicoloured birds, and a mixed flock of tanagers, honeycreepers and conebills turns any tree into a Christmas tree! There are two species of quetzal here, too.

Levelling out onto the forested foothills of the Andes, the upper tropical zone is then reached. This is a forest habitat that in many parts of South America has disappeared and been replaced by tea, coffee and coca plantations. In Manu, the forest is intact, and rare species such as the Amazonian umbrellabird and blue-headed and military macaws can be found.

Good places to base yourself for upper-tropical birding and an introduction to lowland Amazon species are **Amazonia**, **Erika** and **Pantiacolla** lodges, all on the Río Alto Madre de Dios. From here on, transport is by river and the beaches are packed with nesting birds in the dry season. Large-billed terns scream at passing boats and Orinoco geese watch warily from the shore. Colonies of hundreds of sand-coloured nighthawks roost and nest on the hot sand.

As you leave the foothills behind and head into the untouched forests of the western Amazon, you are entering forest with the highest density of birdlife per square kilometre on earth. Sometimes it seems as if there are fewer birds than in an English woodland; only strange calls betray their presence. Then a mixed flock comes through, containing maybe 70-plus species, or a brightly coloured group of, say, rock parakeets dashes out of a fruiting tree.

This forest has produced the highest day-list ever recorded anywhere in the world and holds such little-seen gems as black-faced cotinga and rufous-fronted ant-thrush. Antbirds and ovenbirds creep in the foliage and give tantalizing glimpses until they reveal themselves in a shaft of sunlight. Woodcreepers and woodpeckers climb tree-trunks and multicoloured tanagers move through the rainforest canopy. To get to this forest is difficult and not cheap, but the experience is well worth it.

Some good places for lowland birding are the **Manu Wildlife Center** and **Tambo Blanquillo**, both of which are located close to a large *collpa* (macaw lick) and to *cochas* (oxbow lakes) crammed with birds. There's an excellent walk-up canopy tower at the Manu Wildlife Center where rainforest canopy species can be seen with ease. There are many excellent areas; the entire **Lower Manu River** is superb, and **Cocha Salvador**, deep inside the pristine forests of the national park, is hard to beat.

A trip to Manu is one of the ultimate birding experiences and topping it off with a *collpa* is a great way to finish; hundreds of brightly coloured macaws and other parrots congregate to eat the clay essential to their digestion, in one of the world's great wildlife spectacles.

To Manu and Puerto Maldonado from Cuzco → *For listings, see pages 256-266.*

The arduous trip over the Andes from Cuzco to Pilcopata takes about 16-18 hours by bus or truck (20-40 hours in the wet season). On this route, the scenery is magnificent.

Leaving Cuzco

From Cuzco you climb up to the Huancarani pass before **Paucartambo** (3½ hours), before dropping down to this picturesque mountain village in the Mapacho Valley (see page 228) at the border between the departments of Cuzco and Madre de Dios. The road then ascends to the Ajcanacu pass (cold at night), after which it goes down to the cloudforest and then the rainforest. On the way you pass **Manu Cloudforest Lodge**, **Cock of the Rock Lodge** and the **San Pedro Biological Station** (owned by **Tapir Tours**, visited in their Manu programmes). After 12 hours you reach **Pilcopata** at 650 m.

Atalaya

After Pilcopata, the route is hair-raising and breathtaking. Even in the dry season this part of the road is appalling and trucks often get stuck en route to Atalaya, the first village on the Alto Madre de Dios river and about an hour away from Pilcopata. Atalaya consists of a few houses, and basic accommodation can be found here. Meals are available at the very friendly family home of Rosa and Klaus, where you can also camp. Boats here will take you across the river to **Amazonia Lodge**, see page 256. The village is also the jumping-off point for river trips further into the Manu. The route continues to **Salvación**, where a Manu Park office is situated. There are basic hostels and restaurants.

Shintuya and Itahuania

The road now bypasses Shintuya, a commercial and social centre, as wood from the jungle is transported from here to Cuzco. There are a few basic restaurants and you can camp (beware of thieves). The priest will let you stay in the dormitory rooms at the mission. Supplies are expensive. There are two Shintuyas: one is the port and mission and the other is the indigenous village. The next town is **Itahuania**, the starting point for river transport, but it won't be long before the port moves down river as the road is pushed through to Nuevo Edén, 11 km away, and on to Diamante. The road is one day planned to reach Boca Colorado. **Note** It is not possible to arrange trips to the Reserved Zone of the National Park from Itahuania, owing to park regulations; all arrangements must be made in Cuzco.

Boca Manu

Boca Manu is the connecting point between the rivers Alto Madre de Dios, Manu and Madre de Dios. It has a few houses, an airstrip and some food supplies. It is also the entrance to the Manu Reserve and to go further you must be part of an organized group. The park ranger station is located in **Limonal**, 20 minutes by boat from Boca Manu. You need to show your permit here; camping is allowed if you have a permit. There are no regular flights from Cuzco to Boca Manu. These are arranged the day before, if there are enough passengers. Check at Cuzco airport or with the tour operators in Cuzco.

To the Reserved Zone

Upstream on the Río Manu you pass the **Manu Lodge** (see page 257) on the Cocha Juárez, three to four hours by boat. You can continue to Cocha Otorongo, 2½ hours, and Cocha Salvador, 30 minutes, the biggest lake with plenty of wildlife where the **Casa Machiguenga Lodge** is located and several companies have safari camp concessions. From here it is two hours to **Pakitza**, the entrance to the National Park Reserved Zone. This is only for biologists and others with a special permit.

Boca Colorado

From Itahuania infrequent cargo boats sail (when fully laden, about six to eight a week) to the gold-mining centre of Boca Colorado on the Río Madre de Dios, via Boca Manu, passing several ecotourism lodges including **Pantiacolla Lodge** and **Manu Wildlife Center**, see page 257. The trip takes around nine hours, and costs US$15. Basic accommodation can be found here but is not recommended for lone women travellers. From Boca Colorado a road now runs to Puerto Maldonado, 4½ hours by colectivo and a ferry crossing (see Transport, page 265). Some lodges in the Manu area now use this route: flight to Puerto Maldonado, a vehicle to Boca Colorado and then a boat upstream to the lodge.

Between Boca Manu and Colorado is **Blanquillo**, a private reserve (10,000 ha). Bring a good tent with you and all food if you want to camp, or alternatively accommodation is available at the **Tambo Blanquillo** (full board or accommodation only). Wildlife is abundant, especially macaws and parrots at the macaw lick near Manu Wildlife Center. There are occasional boats to Blanquillo from Shintuya, six to eight hours.

Puerto Maldonado and around

→ Phone code: 082. Population: 45,000. Altitude: 250 m. Colour map 2, A6.

Puerto Maldonado is an important starting point for visiting the southeastern jungles of the Tambopata Reserve, or for departing to Brazil or Bolivia. Most visitors do not see much of the place because they are whisked through town on their way to a lodge on the Río Madre de Dios or the Río Tambopata. The city dwellers haven't been too pleased about this, preferring tourists to spend some time in town, which is a major timber, gold mining, Brazil nut and tourism centre. Its expansion is bound to continue as a bridge, part of the Interoceánica highway, is being built across the Río Madre de Dios. Even before its completion (in 2011 – at the time of writing two of the supports were in place) the town is becoming an increasingly active commercial centre for trade and business travellers from Lima and Brazil. Facilities to accommodate them are popping up in the form of more modern hotels with air-conditioning and cable TV, in contrast to the more traditional tourist jungle lodges. It's a safe place, with chicha music blaring out from most street corners. ▸▸ *For listings, see pages 256-266.*

Ins and outs

Getting there   The road from Cuzco to Puerto Maldonado is being upgraded as part of the Interoceánica highway. In late 2010 it was 85% paved and there are now regular bus services. When paving is complete (estimated mid-2011), it will be possible to travel from the jungle to Cuzco, or vice versa, in daylight and the road's susceptibility to bad weather will decrease. In its pre-upgrading state it was expertly described in Matthew Parris' book *Inka-Cola.*   (See www.southamericanpictures.com/collections/interoceanic-highway/interoceanic-highway.htm for a photo essay). The road passes through Ocongate and Marcapata before reaching **Quincemil**, 240 km from Urcos, a centre for alluvial gold-mining. Petrol is scarce here because most vehicles continue on 70 km to **Mazuko**, where it's cheaper. The changing scenery is magnificent. Take warm clothing for travelling through the sierra. For an alternative route, see page 251. ▸▸ *For further details, see Transport, page 265.*

Tourist office   There are tourist offices at the airport and at **Dircetur** ① *Urb Fonavi, take a mototaxi to the Posta Médica, which is next door.*

Sights

Puerto Maldonado overlooks the confluence of the rivers Tambopata and Madre de Dios. From the park at the end of Jirón Arequipa, across from the Capitanía, you get a good view of the two rivers, the ferries across the Madre de Dios (soon to be replaced by the new bridge) and the stacks of lumber at the dockside. The Brazil-nut harvest is from December to February and the crop tends to be good on alternate years. Nuts are sold on the street, plain or coated in sugar or chocolate. **El Mirador** ① *at the junction of Av Fitzcarrald and Av Madre de Dios, Mon-Fri 0700-1200, 1500-2100 (officially, not always obeyed), US$0.60*, is a 47-m-high tower with 250 steps and three platforms giving fine views over the city and surrounding rainforest. There is also a toilet at the top – no curtains – from which there is an equally fine view over the city! **Museo Huamaambi** ① *26 de Diciembre 360, US$1*, contains photos and artefacts pertaining to the Harakmbut culture of central Madre de Dios and is now also home to **Fenamad** ① *26 de Diciembre 276*, a local organization for the protection of the lands and cultures of people from jungle communities. **Inkaterra** is currently managing the **Mariposario (Butterfly House)** ⓘ *adjoining the airport entrance (a 5-min walk from the terminal building), open 0800-1330, US$5,* which breeds butterflies as part of a sustainable development project. Tours are self-guided and there are plaques with information about the butterflies and tortoises you will see. Worth a visit if you arrive early for your flight or if it is delayed. It's also worth noting that the entrance fee gets you a seat in the cool and breezy Inkaterra reception area with free internet; definitely more comfortable than waiting at the airport. Further along the road towards Puerto Maldonado is the **Serpentarium** (Snake Farm) where you can see boas, bushmasters and fer-de-lances.

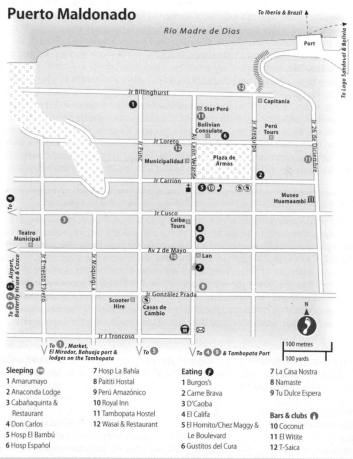

Puerto Maldonado

Sleeping 🛏
1 Amarumayo
2 Anaconda Lodge
3 Cabañaquinta & Restaurant
4 Don Carlos
5 Hosp El Bambú
6 Hosp Español
7 Hosp La Bahía
8 Paititi Hostal
9 Perú Amazónico
10 Royal Inn
11 Tambopata Hostel
12 Wasai & Restaurant

Eating 🍴
1 Burgos's
2 Carne Brava
3 D'Caoba
4 El Califa
5 El Hornito/Chez Maggy & Le Boulevard
6 Gustitos del Cura
7 La Casa Nostra
8 Namaste
9 Tu Dulce Espera

Bars & clubs 🍸
10 Coconut
11 El Witite
12 T-Saica

Around Puerto Maldonado

The beautiful and tranquil **Lago Sandoval** ① *US$9.50, you must go with a guide; this can be arranged by the boat driver*, is a one-hour boat ride (about US$25 a day, plus fuel, from the Madre de Dios port, minimum two people, don't pay the full cost in advance) along the Río Madre de Dios from Puerto Maldonado, and then a 5-km walk into the jungle. Parts of the first 3 km are a raised wooden walkway; boots are advisable. There is an interpretation centre at the start of the trail and a 35-m-high observation tower overlooking the lake. It is possible to see giant river otters early in the morning and several species of monkeys, macaws and hoatzin. There are two jungle lodges at the lake (see Sleeping, page 259). At weekends, especially on Sundays, the lake gets quite busy.

Upstream from Lago Sandoval, towards Puerto Maldonado, is the wreck of a steamer that resembles the *Fitzcarrald*. It lies a few metres from the Madre de Dios in the bed of a small stream. The German director, Werner Herzog, was inspired to make his famous film, *Fitzcarraldo*, by the story of Fitzcarrald's attempt to haul a boat from the Ucuyali to the Madre de Dios drainage basins (in what is now the Manu National Park).

For those interested in seeing a gold-rush town, a trip to **Laberinto** is suggested. There is one hotel and several poor restaurants. At Km 1.5 on the Cuzco road you will find the **Kapievi Ecoaldea**, www.kapievi.org, which has cultural workshops, a children's play area, vegetarian restaurant and some tourist bungalows. Further along at Km 11 is the **Amazon Shelter**, www.amazonshelter.org, a centre for the rehabilitation and conservation of wild animals. At Km 13 on the Cuzco road is a pleasant recreational centre with a restaurant and natural pools where it's possible to swim. It gets busy at weekends. It's US$2 each way by mototaxi from town. Trips can be made to **Lago Valencia**, 60 km away near the Bolivian border; four hours there, six hours back. It is an oxbow lake with lots of wildlife, and many excellent beaches and islands are located within an hour's boat ride. Mosquitoes are voracious. You can stay overnight with local families or at a refuge.

Tambopata National Reserve → *For listings, see pages 256-266. Colour map 2, A6.*

From Puerto Maldonado you can visit the Tambopata National Reserve by travelling up the Tambopata river or down the Madre de Dios. The area was first declared a reserve in 1990 and is a very reasonable alternative for those who do not have the time or money to visit Manu. It is a close rival in terms of seeing wildlife and boasts some superb oxbow lakes. There are a number of lodges here which are excellent for lowland rainforest birding. **Explorers' Inn** is perhaps the most famous, but the **Posada Amazonas/Tambopata Research Centre** and **Tambopata EcoLodge** are also good. In an effort to ensure that more tourism income stays in the area, a few local families have established their own small-scale *casas de hospedaje*, which offer more basic facilities and make use of the nearby forest.

Ins and outs

If not visiting the Reserve on a lodge package, you need to visit the **SERNANP office** ① *Av 28 de Julio 482, T082-573278, Mon-Fri 0830-1300, 1430-1800, Sat 0900-1200.* ▸▸ *For Transport, see page 266.*

Bahuaja-Sonene National Park

The **Bahuaja-Sonene National Park** runs from the Río Heath, which forms the Bolivian border, across to the Río Tambopata, 50-80 km upstream from Puerto Maldonado. It was expanded to 1,091,416 ha in August 2000, with the Tambopata National Reserve

(254,358 ha) created to form a buffer zone. The park is closed to visitors though those visiting the *collpa* (macaw lick) on the Tambopata or river rafting down the Tambopata will travel through it.

Río Las Piedras → For listings, see pages 256-266.

Lying to the northeast of, and running roughly parallel to the Río Manu, this drainage runs some 700 km from remote rainforest headwaters in the Alto Purús region. The lower, more easily accessible section of the river, closer to Puerto Maldonado and currently outside state protection, runs through rich tropical forests, very similar to those in the Manu and Tambopata areas. Close to 600 species of birds, at least eight primate species and some of the Amazon's larger mammals, jaguar, puma, tapir and giant anteater, are all present. Healthy populations of giant otters exist in the rivers and oxbow lakes, and there are several clay licks that attract parrots, macaws and, in some cases, larger mammals as well. Due to its lack of protected status it's also fairly straightforward to tailor your own itinerary in this part of the forest. The only real downside is that hunting pressure has resulted in wildlife being somewhat shyer and more secretive than in Manu or Tambopata. Nevertheless this remains an excellent wildlife destination.

Tambopata National Reserve & Bahuaja-Sonene National Park

Sleeping
1 Casa de Hosp Mejía
2 Casas de Hosp Baltimore
3 EcoAmazonia Lodge
4 El Corto Maltés
5 Explorer's Inn
6 Inkaterra Reserva Amazónica
7 Posada Amazonas
8 Refugio Amazonas
9 Sandoval Lake
10 Tambopata EcoLodge
11 Tambopata Research Centre
12 Wasaí Lodge

The giant otters of Río Madre de Dios

Giant otters (*Pteronura brasiliensis*) are the largest and most spectacular of the world's 13 otter species, sometimes reaching 1.8 m (6 ft) in length. The otters live and hunt in family groups and local people call them *lobos del río* (wolves of the river), as a mark of respect for their supreme hunting abilities.

The giant otters in the Peruvian Amazon are endangered. The species as a whole has been pushed to the very edge of extinction by the skin trade, and now perhaps less than 2000 remain in South America, the only continent in which they occur. Despite legal protection the otters now face a new threat, this time from uncontrolled tourism, as guides anxious to earn tips or under pressure from tourists, approach the otters too closely.

Giant otters are highly territorial and sensitive animals that require large areas of pristine lake and river habitat to survive. This habitat is shrinking fast owing to human encroachment, and areas such as Tambopata and Manu offer the best chance of the species' survival. According to studies carried out by the Frankfurt Zoological Society you should always maintain a distance of at least 70 m from giant otters. Keep quiet and move slowly. Approaching or chasing giant otters causes stress, which eventually can lead to the death of pups or to otters leaving their lake habitat entirely.

As a tourist visiting the protected areas of Madre del Dios or *cochas* (oxbow lakes) in the forest beyond, you MUST share the responsibility for preserving these magnificent predators. If your guide or other tourists in the group wish to approach the otters, please insist that they adhere to the above conditions and keep your distance; if you explain why, most tourists will be happy with your decision. By keeping to these simple rules you will be making a small but very significant contribution to the survival of giant otters in the wild.

◉ Southern jungle listings

For Sleeping and Eating price codes and other relevant information, see pages 30-36.

◉ Sleeping

Manu Biosphere Reserve
p247, map p248
The following lodges offer various packages:
Amazonia Lodge, on the Río Alto Madre de Dios just across the river from Atalaya, T084-816131, www.amazonialodge.com; in Cuzco at Matará 334, p 3, T/F084-231370. An old tea hacienda run by the Yabar-Calderón family, famous for its bird diversity and fine hospitality, a great place to relax, meals included, US$70 per person per night, birding or natural history tours available, contact in advance to arrange a pickup.

Casa Machiguenga, contact Manu Expeditions or the Apeco NGO, T084-225595. Near Cocha Salvador, upriver from Manu Lodge, Machiguenga-style cabins run by the local community of Tayakome with NGO help.
Cock of the Rock Lodge, www.tropical naturetravel.com. On the road from Paucartambo to Atalaya at San Pedro, at 1600 m, next to a Cock of the Rock lek, 10 private cabins with en suite bath, US$595 per person for 3 days/2 nights, including tours, guide and meals.
Erika Lodge, contact Manu Ecological Adventures, Plateros 356, Cuzco T084-261640, www.manuadventures.com (see Activities and tours, page 263). On the Alto Madre de Dios, 25 mins from Atalaya. Like

Amazonia Lodge, this is good place for birds. It offers basic facilities and is cheaper than the other, more luxurious lodges.

Manu Cloud Forest Lodge, owned by Manu Nature Tours (see Activities and tours, page 263). Located at Unión at 1800 m on the road from Paucartambo to Atalaya, 6 rooms with 16-20 beds.

Manu Lodge, run by Manu Nature Tours (see Activities and tours, page 263) and only bookable as part of a full-package deal with transport. Situated on the Manu river, 3 hrs upriver from Boca Manu towards Cocha Salvador. It's a fine location overlooking Cocha Juárez, an oxbow lake, which often plays host to a family of giant otters. The lodge has an extensive trail system, and stands of mauritia palms near the lake provide nesting sites for colonies of blue and yellow macaws.

Manu Wildlife Center, book through Manu Expeditions, which runs it in conjunction with the conservation group Peru Verde, www.manuwildlifecenter.com. 2 hrs down the Río Madre de Dios from Boca Manu, near the Blanquillo macaw lick. 22 double cabins, all with private bathroom and hot water. It also has a tapir lick and canopy tower for birdwatching.

Pantiacolla Lodge, www.pantiacolla.com. 14 rooms in bungalows, book through Pantiacolla Tours. 30 mins downriver from Shintuya. Owned by the Moscoso family. This lodge is located at the foot of the Pantiacolla Mountains, which boasts vast biological diversity, particularly with birds. There is a good trail system. Lots of tours available and all-inclusive packages with transport and guides. Also managed by Pantiacolla is the **Yine Lodge**, see below.

Yanayaco Lodge, Procuradores 46, Cuzco, T084-248122, www.yanayacolodge.com. About 1 hr by boat above Diamante village on the southern bank of the Madre de Dios, close to a small parrot *collpa* (mineral lick); claims to offer frequent sightings of large mammals. Using local river transport to arrive at the lodge rates are very reasonable, prices depend on length of stay. The lodge also offers several different itineraries in Manu.

To Manu and Puerto Maldonado from Cuzco *p250*

Posada San Pedro Cloud Forest Lodge, San Pedro, on the road from Paucartambo to Atalaya, before Pilcopata. 14 rooms. Included as an overnight stop in many tour operators' Manu programmes.

Proyecto Selva Inca, Av Sumar Pacha s/n, Pilcopata, T084-231625 or T084-984 756207 (mob), in Cuzco Urb Marcavalle C-25, Wanchac, www.selvainka.com. Run by Evelyne Vega Oblitas, this is a safe, friendly and inexpensive option in Pilcopata, staying at the **Albergue Turístico La Casa del Kshipaktona**. Due to its village position this is more a social project than an opportunity to see rare wildlife, but we've received several positive reports regarding their sustainable development programmes and work with local communities. Contact in advance to see what options are available.

Turismo Indígena Wanamei, Av 26 de Diciembre 276, Puerto Maldonado, T082-572539, and Av El Sol 814, p 2, of 212, Cuzco, T084-234608, T084-984 754708 (mob), www.ecoturismowanamei.com. 8 indigenous communities from the Amarakaeri Communal Reserve introduce visitors to their ancestral lands, located between Manu and Tambopata. Their 9-day trip, starting in Cuzco, costs US$2640 for 2 people. Accommodation includes lodges, communities and camping. The trips aim to offer not only excellent wildlife viewing opportunities but also an insight into the daily life of indigenous peoples in the early 21st century. To gain the most from this unusual experience you need to speak Spanish (or Harakmbut!) and to have some experience of hiking over difficult terrain. Tents can be hired in Cuzco. Porters can be hired at US$10 per day.

D Boca Manu Lodge, book through Emperadores Tours, Procuradores 190, Cuzco, T084-239987, empetcusco@hotmail.

com. Run by long-standing Manu resident Juan de Dios Carpio. Juan owns a general store in Boca, so if you're stranded in Boca Manu and you're looking for a reasonably priced place to stay this could be an option – just ask at the store.

G Hospedaje Manu, Boca Colorado, on street beside football field. Cell-like rooms, open windows and ceilings but comfy mattresses and mosquito netting.

G Hostal, Boca Manu, run by the community. Basic accommodation.

G The Mission, Shintuya. The priest will let you stay in the dormitory rooms. There are a few basic restaurants and you can camp (beware of thieves). Supplies are expensive.

G Sra Rubella, Pilcopata. This unnamed place is very basic, but friendly.

Lodges

Yine Lodge, next to the airstrip, Boca Manu. A smart cooperative project run by **Pantiacolla Tours**. Actually, the native Yine community of Diamante operates its own tours into the community and suroundings.

Puerto Maldonado *p252, map p253*
B Anaconda Lodge, 600 m from airport, T082-982 611039 (mob), www.anaconda junglelodge.com. **E** with shared bath, Swiss/Thai-owned bungalows, hot showers, swimming pool, Thai restaurant, tours arranged, has space for camping, very pleasant, family atmosphere.
B Don Carlos, Av León Velarde 1271, T082-571029, www.hotelesdoncarlos.com. Nice view over the Río Tambopata, a/c, restaurant, TV, phone, pool, good.
B Wasaí Maldonado, Billinghurst, opposite the Capitanía, T082-572290, www.wasai.com. Price includes breakfast, a/c, TV, shower. In a beautiful location overlooking the Madre de Dios, with forest surrounding cabin-style rooms that are built on a slope down to the river. The hotel may be affected because of its proximity to the new bridge. A/c, TV, shower, small pool with waterfall, good restaurant (local fish a speciality). Recommended. They

can organize local tours and have a lodge on the Tambopata River.
C Cabañaquinta, Jirón Cuzco 535, T082-571045, www.hotelcabanaquinta.com.pe. With buffet breakfast, bathroom, a/c, small pool, sauna, good restaurant, friendly, lovely garden, very comfortable, price includes airport transfer if needed. Recommended.
C Paititi Hostal, G Prada 290 y Av León Velarde, T082-574667, paititihostal@ hotmail.com. All mod-cons, executive and standard rooms, TV, a/c, breakfast included, Wi-Fi. Reserve in advance. Recommended.
C Perú Amazónico, Jr Ica 269, T082-571799, peruamazonico@hotmail.com. Brand new, modern, comfortable and good, cable TV, frigobar, a/c, Wi-Fi. No outdoor space, but popular with business travellers and those who need a break from the jungle.
E Amarumayo, Libertad 433, T082-573860, residenciamarumayo@hotmail.com. Price includes breakfast. Comfortable, with pool and garden, good restaurant, 10 mins from the centre. Recommended.
E Hospedaje Español, González Prada 670, T082-572381. Comfortable, set back from the road in a quiet part of town. Garden setting, clean, friendly.
E Hospedaje La Bahía, 2 de Mayo 710, T082-572127. Cheaper without bath or TV, large rooms, clean. Best of cheaper options.
E Royal Inn, Av 2 de Mayo 333, T082-573464, mitsukate4@hotmail.com. Modern and huge, clean, rooms at back are less noisy, rooms have ceiling fans and TV, secure parking.
F Hospedaje El Bambú, Jr Puno 837, T082-793880. New, basic and small but well-kept rooms with fan, family atmosphere, breakfast and juices not included in price but served in dining room. A good budget option.
F pp Tambopata Hostel, Av 26 de Diciembre 234, www.tambopatahostel.com. The only real backpacker hostel in town, dorm beds. Nice atmosphere, they also organize local tours.
F Hotel Toni, in Quincemil, on the road from Cuzco to Puerto Maldonado. Friendly, clean, cold shower, good meals.

Tambopata National Reserve (TNR)
p254, map p255

Most of the lodges in the Tambopata area use the term 'ecotourism', or something similar, in their publicity material, but it is applied pretty loosely. **Posada Amazonas'** collaboration with the local community is unique in the area, but fortunately no lodge offers trips where guests hunt for their meals. Wi-Fi and mobile phone access now seems to be standard in the larger, upmarket lodges along the Tambopata. To escape this you would need to stay somewhere smaller, such as a community-run lodge like **Baltimore**. Prices are given only for standard 3-day/2-night packages that include all transport links, accommodation on a full-board basis and guiding. Lodges on the Tambopata are reached by vehicle to Bahuaja port, 15 km upriver from Puerto Maldonado, by the community of Infierno, then by boat. Some of the lodges mentioned above also offer guiding and research placements to biology and environmental science graduates. For more details send an SAE to **TReeS: UK**, c/o J Forrest, PO Box 33153, London NW3 4DR, www.tambopata.org.uk. Long-term visitors should be aware that leishmaniasis exists in this area.

Río Madre de Dios

Casa de Hospedaje Mejía, book via **Ceiba Tours**, Av L Velarde 420 in Puerto Maldonado (see Activities and tours, page 264), T082-573567/571420, turismomejia@hotmail.com. A small, family-run, rustic lodge close to Lago Sandoval, with 10 double rooms, none en suite. Canoes available to explore the lake. An English-speaking guide can be arranged. 3 days/2 nights costs US$190.

Eco Amazonia Lodge, book through their office in Lima: Enrique Palacios 292, Miraflores, Lima, T01-242 2708; in Cuzco: Garcilazo 210, of 206, T084-236159, www.ecoamazonia.com.pe. On the Madre de Dios, 1 hr downriver from Puerto Maldonado (ofice Jr Lambayeque 774, T082-573491). 45 basic bungalows and

dormitories, good for birdwatching with viewing platforms and tree canopy access, has a pool and Monkey Island, with animals taken from the forest, US$210-230 for 3 days/2 nights including tours.

El Corto Maltés, in Puerto Maldonado, T082-573831, www.cortomaltes-amazonia.com. On the south side of the Madre de Dios river, one of the closest to Puerto Maldonado, halfway to Sandoval, the focus of most visits. Bungalows are very well spaced out and all have a river view. I lot water, huge dining room, well run, pool planned. Ayahuasca sessions can be arranged. US$240 for 3 days/2 nights.

Estancia Bello Horizonte, 20 km northwest of Puerto Maldonado, office in Puerto Maldonado, Jr José María Grain 105, T/F082-572748, www.estanciabellohorizonte.com. In a nice stretch of forest overlooking the Madre de Dios, a small lodge with bungalows for 20 people, with private bath, hammock and pool, transport and breakfast included, or book a package, 3 days/2 nights US$240 with all meals and tours with guide. The lodge belongs to APRONIA and profits fund a home for children with learning difficulties. Suitable for those wanting to avoid a river trip.

Inkaterra Reserva Amazónica Lodge, Rio Madre de Dios Km 15, Margen Izquierda, T082-573534, 45 mins by boat. To book: Inkaterra, Andalucía 174, Lima 18, T01-610 0400; Plaza Las Nazarenas 167, p 2, Cuzco T084-234010; or Cuzco 436, Puerto Maldonado, www.inkaterra.com. A hotel in the jungle with rooms and suites in 35 tastefully decorated, thatched-roof cabañas with solar electricity and hot water, good food in huge dining room supported by a big tree. Jungle tours available with multilingual guides in its own 10,000-ha reserve and to Lago Sandoval, plus a 350-m canopy walkway with a canopy treehouse, two 30-m canopy viewing towers and a Monkey Island (Isla Rolín), for the recovery of primates, which are readapted to their natural environment. 3 day/2 night packages from US$1080 all-inclusive; several packages and room-only otions available. Has the largest number of ant species recorded in a single location: 362. Also offers guided visits to the Hacienda Concepción research centre.

Sandoval Lake Lodge, to book, **InkaNatura**, Manuel Bañón 461, San Isidro, Lima, T01-440 2022, www.inkanatura.com/sandovallake lodge.asp. Also have offices in Cuzco, C Ricardo Palma J1, Santa Mónica, T084-255255, and Puerto Maldonado, Jr San Martín 755, T082-571037. 1 km beyond Mejía on Lago Sandoval, usually accessed by canoe across the lake after a 3-km walk or rickshaw ride along the trail, this lodge, on a *cocha*, is part-owned by local Brazil-nut collectors. It can accommodate 50 people in 25 rooms, bar and dining area, electricity, hot water. There is a system of trails nearby, guides are available in several languages. Price for 3 days/2 nights is US$278-298 per person based on 2 sharing.

Río Tambopata

Casas de Hospedaje Baltimore, several families in the community of Baltimore on the banks of the Río Tambopata, 60 km upriver. In Puerto Maldonado, Junín cuadra 1, Mz 2-Lote 10F, T082-572380, info@baltimore peru.org.pe. They offer the opportunity to experience the forest close-up, and an insight into daily life in the forest at a more economical price. US$165 double, 4 days/ 3 nights. The 1st night is spent camping, the next 2 staying in a family home. Guiding in Spanish; English-speaking guide can be arranged for US$25. Researchers and volunteers also welcomed by arrangement. **Explorer's Inn**, www.explorersinn.com, or book through **Peruvian Safaris**, Alcanfores 459, Miraflores, Lima, T01-447 8888, www.peruviansafaris.com. The office in Puerto Maldonado is at Fonavi H15, T/F082-572078. 7 thatched bungalows, candle lit at night, solar electricity only in the central building with dining room. The lodge is in the TNR, in the part where most research work has been done, 58 km from Puerto Maldonado. It's a 2½-hr ride up the Río

Tambopata (1½ hrs return, in the early morning, so take warm clothes and rain gear), one of the best places in Peru for seeing jungle birds (more than 580 species have been recorded here), butterflies (more than 1230 species), also giant river otters, but you probably need more than a 2-day tour to benefit fully from the location. Offers tours through the adjoining community of La Torre to meet local people and find out about their farms (*chacras*) and handicrafts.

Posada Amazonas Lodge, on the Tambopata river, 1½ hrs by vehicle and boat upriver from Puerto Maldonado. Book through **Rainforest Expeditions**, San Francisco de Paula Ugariza 813, Of 201, San Antonio-Miraflores, Lima, T01-241 4880, reservations at T01-997 903650 (mob), www.perunature.com. A collaboration between the tour agency and the local native community of Infierno. Attractive rooms with cold showers, visits to Lake Tres Chimbadas, with good birdwatching including the Tambopata Collpa. Offers trips to a nearby indigenous primary health care project where a native healer gives guided tours of the medicinal plant garden. Service and guiding is very good. Recommended. The **Tambopata Research Centre**, the company's more intimate, but comfortable lodge, is about 6 hrs further upriver. Rooms are smaller than Posada Amazonas, shared showers, cold water. The lodge is next to the famous Tambopata macaw clay lick. 2 hrs from Posada Amazonas, Rainforest Expeditions also has the **Refugio Amazonas**, close to Lago Condenados. It is the usual stopover for those visiting the collpa. 3 bungalows accommodate 70 people in en suite rooms, large, kerosene lit, open bedrooms with mosquito nets, well- designed and run, atmospheric. Prices for a 5 day/4 night package at the Posada or Refugio range from US$908-2127. There are many more packages at the different lodges and lots of add-ons.

Tambopata EcoLodge, on the Río Tambopata, make reservations at Nueva Baja 432, Cuzco, T084-245695, operations office at Jr Gonzales Prada 269, Puerto Maldonado, T082-571726, www.tambopatalodge.com. The lodge has rooms and suites with solar-heated water, accommodates 59. Good guides, excellent food. Trips go to Lake Condenados, some to Lake Sachavacayoc, and to the Collpa de Chuncho, guiding mainly in English and Spanish, package from US$307 per person for 3 days/2 nights. Naturalists programme provided.

Wasaí Lodge and Expeditions, on the Río Tambopata, 120 km (4½ hrs) upriver from Puerto Maldonado, T082-572290, 3 hrs return, same owners as **Hotel Wasaí** in town, www.wasai.com. Small lodge with 7 bungalows for 40 people, 20 km of trails around the lodge, guides in English and Spanish. 3 days/2 nights costs US$337; 5 days/4 nights costs US$596. See also Activities and tours, below.

Río Las Piedras *p255*

Amazon Rainforest Conservation Centre, Las Piedras Amazon Tours, Jr Los Cedros B-17, Los Castaños, Puerto Maldonado, T082-573655, www.laspiedrasamazontour.com. Roughly 8 hrs up Río Las Piedras, in a magnificent location overlooking Lago Soledad, a beautiful oxbow lake, which has a family of giant otters. Surrounding the lodge is a 7000-ha private reserve. 8 comfortable bungalows, with bath, hot water, small balcony. Activities include a viewing platform 35 m up an ironwood tree, a hide overlooking a macaw lick, and walks on the extensive trail network. Most trips break the river journey half way at Tipishca Camp, overlooking an oxbow lake with a family of otters. A 5-day/4-night package costs US$1055 (6-, 7- and 8-day tours available, cheaper for larger groups).

Las Piedras Biodiversity Station is, in effect, a *casa de hospedaje*, T/F082-573922, www.rainforestresearch.netfirms.com. A small lodge in a 4000-ha concession of 'primary' rainforest 90 km up Río Las Piedras. Visitors camp en route to the lodge. With only 20 beds in 10 rooms the lodge offers

a more personalized experience of the rainforest. Central dining room, shared bath, no electricity, library, guiding in English/Spanish. Owing to the remoteness of the lodge the minimum package is for 4 days/3 nights, US$470 per person based on a group of 2-3 people, falling to US$239 per person for groups of 10-14 people. Birdwatching trips cost more. They also offer volunteer placements.

🍴 Eating

Puerto Maldonado *p252, map p253*
The best restaurant in town is at the **Hotel Wasaí**, the best lunchtime menu is at the **Cabañaquinta** (see above).
₸-₸ Burgos's, Billinghurst 480 y Puno. An atmospheric restaurant with a lovely terrace overlooking the Madre de Dios, serves traditional dishes and has a good set lunch menu, creole buffet Tue-Sun. Good variety and good reputation among locals.
₸-₸ Carne Brava, on the Plaza de Armas. One of the smart places for a steak and chips. Similar, also on the Plaza, is **Vaka Loca**.
₸-₸ El Califa, Piura 266. Often has bushmeat, mashed banana and palm hearts.
₸-₸ El Hornito/Chez Maggy, on the plaza. Cosy atmosphere, busy at weekends, good pizzas, pasta dishes are not such good value.
₸ D'Caoba, Madre de Dios 439. Serves the most delicious *pollos a la brasa* in town.
₸ La Casa Nostra, Av León Velarde 515. The best place for snacks, cakes and coffee. Sells huge fruit juices, *tamales*, *papas rellenas* and enormous fancy cakes.
₸ Namaste, Av León Velarde 469. Moroccan and Indian food, sandwiches, breakfasts and set lunches, in chilled out surroundings.

Cafés

Gustitos del Cura, Loreto 258, Plaza de Armas. An ice cream parlour run by a project for homeless teenagers, offering an amazing range of delicious and unusual tropical juices. The "last delicatessen before the jungle".

Tu Dulce Espera, Av L Velarde 475. Good for evening juices and snacks.

🎵 Bars and clubs

Puerto Maldonado *p252, map p253*
Coconut, east side of the plaza. Disco.
El Witite, Av León Velarde 153. A popular, good disco, latin music, open Fri and Sat.
Le Boulevard, behind **El Hornito**.
Live music, popular.
T-Saica, Loreto 335. An atmospheric bar with live music at weekends.
Vikingo and **Juzal**, 26 de Diciembre y 2 de Mayo. Two popular bars/open-air discos.

⛰ Activities and tours

Manu Biosphere Reserve
p247, map p248
The tour operators listed below are situated in Cuzco, the gateway to the reserve. Beware of pirate operators on the streets of Cuzco who offer trips to the Reserved Zone of Manu and end up halfway through the trip changing the route 'due to emergencies', which in reality means they have no permits to operate in the area. The following companies organize trips into the Multiple Use and Reserved Zones. Contact them for more details.
Amazon Trails Peru, Tandapata 660, San Blas, Cuzco, T084-437374, T984-714148 (mob), www.amazontrailsperu.com. Small

agency owned and operated by ornithologist Abraham Huamán, who has many years' experience guiding in the region, and Ulrike (Ulla) Maennig. Mainly offers interesting itineraries into Manu National Park and to Manu Blanquillo, a private reserve adjoining the national park. Well-organized tours include visits to macaw and tapir licks. Guaranteed deperature dates with minimum 2 people. Recommended. Also operate trekking tours in the Cuzco area and run the **Amazon Hostel** next door to the office, T084-236770, www.amazonhostelcusco.com.
Bonanza Tours, Suecia 343, T084-507871, www.bonanzatoursperu.com. 3- to 8-day tours to Manu with local guides, jungle walks, rafting, kayaking and camp-based excursions. Tours go down the Madre de Dios as far as the Blanquillo clay lick, not to the Reserve area.
Expediciones Vilca, Plateros 359, T/F084-244751, www.manuvilcaperu.com. Manu jungle tours of 4-8 days. Will supply sleeping bags at no extra cost. Minimum 5 people, maximum 10 per guide. This is the only economical tour that camps at the Otorongo camp, which is supposedly quieter than Salvador where many agencies camp. There are discounts for students and SAE members. Very efficient, good service.
InkaNatura Travel, Manuel Bañón 461, San Isidro, Lima, T01-440 2022, www.inkanatura. com. Also in Cuzco. A non-profit organization with proceeds directed back into projects on sustainable tourism and conservation.

Arranges trips to the Manu Reserved Zone, Manu Wildlife Center, The Biotrip, 6 days/ 5 nights, which takes you through the Andes to lowland jungle, and **Sandoval Lake Lodge** in Tambopata. They sell a book called *Peru's Amazonian Eden – Manu*, US$80, proceeds go to the projects. The same title can be found in other bookshops at a much inflated price. **Manu Ecological Adventures**, Plateros 356, Cuzco, T084-261640, www.manuadventures. com. Manu jungle tours, either economical tour in and out overland, or in by land and out by plane, giving you longer in the jungle. Options include a mountain biking descent through the cloudforest and 3 hrs of whitewater rafting on the way to **Erika Lodge** on the upper Río Madre de Dios. Good for guides, food and value. They operate with

Manu Adventures
Jungle Specialist - Tour Operator
Manu National Park

Tambopata Reserve

Main Office:
356 Plateros Street.

Phones:
+51 84 261640/225562
www.manuadventures.com
www.tambopatadventures.com

a minimum of 4 people and a maximum of 10 people per guide.
Manu Expeditions, Clorinda Matto de Turner 330, Urb Magisterial, Cuzco, T084-225990, www.manuexpeditions.com. Mon-Fri 0900-1300, 1530-1900; Sat 0900-1300. English spoken. Run by ornithologist and British Consul Barry Walker of the **Cross Keys Pub**. 3 trips available to the reserve and Manu Wildlife Center. 2 of the trips on 1st Sun of every month visit a lodge run by Machiguenga people and cost an extra US$150.
Manu Nature Tours, Av Pardo 1046, T084-252721, www.manuperu.com. Owned by Boris Gómez Luna, English spoken. This company aims more for the luxury end of the market. Owns **Manu Lodge** (see page 257) and part-owns **Manu Cloudforest Lodge**. Tours are based around these sites, thus entailing less travel between different areas. Manu Lodge has an extensive trail system and also offers canopy climbing for an additional US$45 per person.
Oropéndola, Av Circunvalación s/n, Urb Guadalupe Mz A Lote 3, Cuzco, T084-241428, www.oropendolaperu.org. Guide Walter Mancilla Huamán is a flora and fauna expert. 5-, 7- and 9-day tours from US$800 per person plus park entrance of US$50. Tours finance the non-profit Oropéndola Project, which manages a 500-ha reserve and operates **Oropéndola Lodge** and **Manu Camping Lodge**.
Pantiacolla Tours, Saphi 554, Cuzco, T084-238323, www.pantiacolla.com. Manu jungle tours: 5- and 7-day trips include return flights, the 9-day trip is an overland return. Prices do not include park entrance fee. Guaranteed departure dates regardless of number, maximum 10 people per guide. The trips involve a combination of camping, platform camping and lodges. All clients are given a booklet entitled *Talking About Manu*, written by the Dutch owner, Marianne van Vlaardingen, who is a biologist. She is extremely friendly and helpful. Marianne and her Peruvian husband Gustavo Moscoso have recently opened an ecotourism lodge in

conjunction with the Yine native community of Diamante. Yine guides are used and community members are being trained in the various aspects of running the project.

Puerto Maldonado *p252, map p253*
All guides should have a carnet issued by the Ministry of Tourism (DIRCETUR), which verifies them as suitable for trips to other places and confirms their identity. Check that the carnet has not expired. Reputable guides are **Hernán Llave Cortez**, **Romel Nacimiento** and the **Mejía** brothers, all of whom can be contacted on arrival at the airport, if available. Also recommended: **Carlos Borja Gama**, a local guide offering specialist birdwatching and photography trips as well as traditional jungle tours, he speaks fluent English, French, Portuguese and Spanish; contact him through **Wasai** (see below) or see www.carlosexpeditions.com. **Víctor Yohamona**, T082-968 6279 (mob), victorguideperu@hotmail.com. Speaks English, French and German. Boat hire can be arranged through the Capitanía del Puerto (Río Madre de Dios), T082-573003. **Ceiba Tours**, Av L Velarde 420, T082-573567, turismomejia@hotmail.com. Organize local trips, including to their lodge at Lago Sandoval. **Perú Tours**, Loreto 176, T082-573244, perutours ytravel@hotmail.com. Organize local trips.

Tambopata National Reserve (TNR)
p254, map p255
Peruvian Safaris, Alcanfores 459, Miraflores, Lima 18, T01-447 8888, www.peruviansafaris. com. For reservations for the Explorer's Inn.
Tambo Tours, 4405 Spring Cypress Rd Suite 210, Spring, Texas, 77388, USA, T1-888-2-GO-PERU (246-7378), T001-281 528 9448, www.2GOPERU.com.
Wasaí Lodge and Expeditions, contact Las Higueras 257, Residencial Monterrico, La Molina, Lima 12, T01-436 8792, or Plaza Grau 1, Puerto Maldonado, T/F082-572290, www.wasai.com. Offering a variety of traditional and innovative tours including river trips, wildlife observation, birdwatching, canoeing, volunteer work, etc. Also offering budget tours for backpackers, see their website for details. For lodge, see page 261.

☉ Transport

Manu Biosphere Reserve
p247, map p248
Air
There is an airstrip at **Boca Manu**, but no regular flights from Cuzco. These are arranged the day before, usually by Manu tour operators, if there are enough passengers.

Road

From the Coliseo Cerrado in Cuzco 3 bus companies run to **Pilcopata** Mon, Wed, Fri, returning same night, US$10. They are fully booked even in low season. The best are **Gallito de las Rocas**; also **Unancha** from Calle Huáscar near the main plaza. Trucks to Pilcopata run on same days, returning Tue, Thu, Sat, 10 hrs in wet season, less in the dry. Only basic supplies are available after leaving Cuzco, so take all your camping and food essentials, including insect repellent. Transport can be disrupted in the wet season because the road is in poor condition although improvements are being made. *Camioneta* service runs between Pilcopata and **Salvación** to connect with the buses, Mon, Wed, Fri. The same *camionetas* run **Itahuania–Shintuya–Salvación** regularly, when there are sufficient passengers, probably once a day, and 2 trucks a day. On Sun, there is no traffic whatsoever. To **Boca Manu** you can hire a boat in Atalaya, be it a *peque-peque*, or a motorboat it will cost you several hundred dollars. It's cheaper to wait or hope for a boat going empty up to Boca Manu to pick up passengers, when the fare will be US$15 per passenger. Itahuania-Boca Manu in a shared boat with other passengers is US$7.50. A private chartered boat will also be over US$100. From Itahuania, cargo boats leave for **Boca Colorado** via Boca Manu, but only when the boat is fully laden; about 6-8 a week, 9 hrs, US$20. From Boca Colorado colectivos leave from near football field for Puerto Carlos, 1 hr, US$5, ferry across river 10 mins, US$1.65, then colectivos run to **Puerto Maldonado**, 3 hrs, US$10, rough road, lots of stops (in Puerto Maldonado Turismo Boca Colorado, Tacna 342, T082-573435, leave when full). Tour operators usually use their own vehicles for the overland trip from Cuzco to Manu.

Puerto Maldonado *p252, map p253*
Air

To **Lima**, daily with LAN and Star Perú, via Cuzco. Combis to the airport run along Av 2 de Mayo, 10-15 mins, US$0.75. A mototaxi from town to the airport is US$3.

Airline offices LAN, Av León Velarde y 2 de Mayo, T082-573677. Star Perú, Av León Velarde 151, T082-982 7074.

Bus

There are daily buses from the Terminal Terrestre in **Cuzco** with **Transportes Iguazú**, **Mendivil** and **Móvil Tours**. All are on Av Tambopata, blocks 3 and 5 in Puerto Maldonado. Fare is US$15, 8-10 hrs. **Móvil** (at No 529, T082-795785) 1830, 1930, US$16. All run at night from Puerto Maldonado until the Interoceánica is complete, then it is expected that there will be daytime services. **Móvil** also have daily service to **Rio Branco** (Brazil), 1200, US$35. There are also daily buses from **Mazuko** to Puerto Maldonado with **Transportes Bolpebra** and **Transportes Señor de la Cumbre**, US$3. To **Laberinto**, combis take 50 mins, US$1.50, uncomfortable (return in afternoon daily). To **Juliaca**, **Transportes Tambopata** and **Transportes Aguilas/Tahuamanu**, Fizcarrald 609, daily services via San Gabán, at 1700 and 1900 respectively, 18 hrs, US$17. These routes form part of the Interoceánica highway and are being upgraded and paved. More and more public transport companies are using tourist minibus-style vehicles on the Cuzco-Puerto Maldonado route; ask around for a colectivo, they usually leave from close to the bus station.

Motorcycles/taxis

Scooters and mopeds can be hired from **San Francisco**, and others, on the corner of Puno and G Prada for US$1.15 per hr or US$10 per day. No deposit is required but your passport and driving licence need to be shown. Mototaxis around town charge US$0.60; riding pillion on a bike is US$0.30.

Boat

For **Boca Manu** and **Itahuania** take a *colectivo* to **Boca Colorado** and then take a cargo boat (no fixed schedule). From

Itahuania there is transport to **Pilcopata** and **Cuzco** (see above under Manu Biosphere Reserve).

Tambopata National Reserve (TNR)
p254, map p255
Boat
A river taxi makes 2 journeys a week, Mon and Thu upriver, Tue and Fri down, up to 10 hrs, US$5 to travel as far as **Wasaí Lodge**. It leaves Puerto Maldonado between 0600 and 0900.

❶ Directory

Puerto Maldonado *p252, map p253*
Banks 0900-1300, 1700-1900. **BCP**, cash advances with Visa, ATM, no commission on TCs. **Banco de la Nación**, cash on MasterCard, quite good rates for TCs. Both on the south side of the plaza. Best rates for cash are at the casas de cambio/gold shops on Puno 6th block. **Internet** All over town. **Laundry** On block 4 of Av León Velarde, next to **Ceiba Tours** office. **Post** Serpost, Av León Velarde 6th block, 0800-2000 (0800-1500 Sun). **Telephone** Telefónica, west side of plaza, adjoining the Municipalidad. Phone office on the plaza, next to **El Hornito**.

Contents

Footprint features

■ Lima

Machu □
Picchu □ Cuzco

Lima

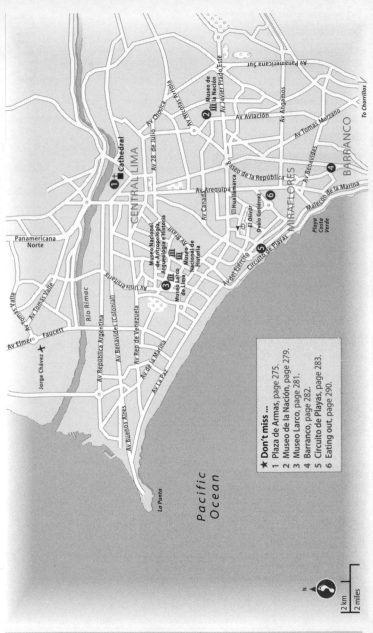

★ **Don't miss ...**

1 Plaza de Armas, page 275.
2 Museo de la Nación, page 279.
3 Museo Larco, page 281.
4 Barranco, page 282.
5 Circuito de Playas, page 283.
6 Eating out, page 290.

It is a well-established cliché to call Lima a city of contradictions and a rapid glance only reinforces that view. Here you'll encounter grinding poverty and conspicuous wealth in abundance. The hardships of the poor in this sprawling metropolis of 8.2 million inhabitants are all too evident in the lives of those struggling to get by in the crowded streets. Bus lanes are frantic and cars and taxis struggle to make progress on the congested thoroughfares. The drive from the airport to the city centre passes an array of urban landscapes, from the rubbish-strewn to the elegant, while the shanty towns on the outskirts emphasize the vast divisions within society. Most visitors, though, have the option of heading for Miraflores, San Isidro or Barranco, where smart restaurants and plush hotels rub shoulders with pre-Inca pyramids, and neat parks and the cliff-top Larcomar shopping centre overlook the ocean. Lima's image as a place to avoid or quickly pass through is enhanced by the thick grey blanket of cloud that descends in May and hangs around for the next seven months. Wait until the blanket is pulled aside in November to reveal bright blue skies and suddenly all Limeños descend on the city's popular coastal resorts. Weekends then become a raucous mix of sun, sea, salsa and *ceviche*. Lima can also entertain, excite and inform. It boasts some of the finest historical monuments and museums in the country. The colonial centre, with its grand Plaza de Armas, fine churches and beautiful wooden balconies, is one of Peru's 10 UNESCO World Heritage Sites and strenuous efforts are being made to refurbish the historical districts. The city's cuisine has earned it the title 'Gastronomic Capital of the Americas' and the bars, discos and *peñas* of Barranco and Miraflores ring to the sounds of everything from techno to traditional music. Scratch beneath that coating of grime and traffic fumes and you'll find one of the most vibrant and hospitable cities anywhere.

Getting there
From the airport
All **international flights** land at Jorge Chávez Airport, some 16 km from the centre of the city. It is a little further to Miraflores and Barranco. Transport into town is easy if a bit expensive. Remise taxis have desks outside International Arrivals and National Arrivals: **Taxi Green** ① *T01-484 4001, www.taxigreen.com.pe*, US$8 to San Miguel, US$13 to the city centre, US$11.50 to San Isidro, US$15 to Miraflores and Barranco; **Mitsui** ① *T01-349 7722, remisse@mitsuiautomotriz.com*, US$27 to centre, US$31 to San Isidro and Miraflores, US$36 to Barranco; and **CMV** ① *T01-422 4838, cmv@exalmar.com.pe*, a little cheaper. There are many taxi drivers offering their services outside Arrivals with similar or higher prices (more at night). The **Bus Super Shuttle** ① *T01-517 2556, www.supershuttle airport.com*, runs six-seater minibuses from the airport to San Miguel, the centre, San Isidro, Miraflores and Barranco for US$15 (six people sharing), or US$25 private hire. Alternatively, you can contact a taxi driver to meet you in advance, such as perufrienddrivers@hotmail.es, which offers fair prices and drivers who speak English.

1 Lima

➡ **Lima maps**
1 Lima orientation, page 270
2 Lima centre, page 276
3 San Isidro, page 281
4 Miraflores, page 282
5 Barranco, page 285

Pacific Ocean

N

2 km		
2 miles		

Sleeping 😊		
1 Chez Elizabeth	3 Hostal Bait Sababa	6 Pay Purix
2 Guest House Marfil	4 Hostal Res Victor	7 Ramada Costa del Sol
	5 Mami Panchita	8 Tambopacaya

Note To get to Miraflores by combi, take the 'Callao-Ate' with a big red 'S' ('La S'), the only direct connection between the airport and Miraflores. You catch it outside the airport, on Avenida Faucett, US$0.45. This is not a safe option, however. You should definitely not take the cheapest, stopping buses to the centre along Avenida Faucett. They are frequently robbed. Nor go to the car park exit and find a taxi outside the perimeter. Although much cheaper than those inside, they are not safe either.

The airport is the best and most cost-effective place to arrange car hire. The larger international chains – **Avis**, **Budget**, **Dollar**, **Hertz**, **Localiza**, **National** – are usually cheaper and tend to have better-maintained vehicles than local firms. If hiring a car at the airport with the intention of driving to a hotel in the city, be aware that driving in Lima requires patience, forcefulness and nerves of steel.

If staying in Lima after arriving by **bus**, you may arrive at one of the company terminals around Jirón Carlos Zavala, just south of the historic centre of Lima. Take a taxi to your hotel even if it's close, as this area is not safe day or night. Some of the high-class bus companies have terminals in safer areas, so check with the bus company where their Lima terminal is and try to get your bearings before you arrive.

Note If arriving on a flight which lands late at night and you have a connection to Cuzco early next morning, you can stay the night at the airport.

Airport facilities Global Net ATMs (accepting American Express, Visa, MasterCard and the Plus, Cirrus and Maestro systems), *casas de cambio* (money-changing kiosks) and a bank can be found in many parts of arrivals and departures. The exchange rates are marginally poorer than outside the terminal. There are public telephones around the airport and a **Teléfonica** *locutorio*, daily 0700-2300. Internet facilities are more expensive than in the city. There are postal services.

The airport has offices of **iperú**, T01-574 8000, daily 24 hours. Information desks can be found in the national foyer, the international foyer and on the 1st floor. There are also helpful desks in the international and national arrivals halls. There are many smart shops, places to eat and drink, including Starbucks, and, in international arrivals, mobile phone rentals. See listings below for hotels near Jorge Chávez.

Getting around

Downtown Lima can be explored on foot in the daytime, but take all the usual

SAN JUAN DE LURIGANCHO
Cerro San Cristóbal
Av Independencia
SANTA ANITA
Cerro El Agustino
ATE
Av N Ayllón
Av Nicolás Arriola
SAN BORJA
Museo de la Nación
Av Javier Prado Este
Vía de Evitamiento
LA MOLINA
Hipódromo de Monterrico
MONTERRICO
Av Panamericana Sur
Av Alonso de Molina
Av Primavera
mos
Museo de Oro del Perú
Av Tomás Marsano
To Chorrillos

Metropolitano bus line ▬▬▬

precautions. The central hotels are fairly close to the many of the tourist sites. At night taxis are a safer option. Many of the better hotels and restaurants are located in San Isidro, Miraflores and Barranco.

The Lima public transport system, at first glance very intimidating, is actually quite good. There are three different types of vehicle that will stop whenever flagged down: buses, combis, and colectivos. They can be distinguished by size: big and long; mid-size and minivans; or cars, respectively. The flat-rate fare for the first two types of vehicle is US$0.35, the third costs a little more. On public holidays, Sunday and from 2400 to 0500 every night, a small charge is added to the fare. Always try to pay with change to avoid hassles, delays and dirty looks from the *cobrador* (driver's assistant). Termini of public transport vehicles are posted above the windscreens, with the route written on the side. However good the public transport system or smart your taxi, one thing is unavoidable, the amount of traffic. Lima's roads are congested almost throughout the whole day. Allow plenty of time to get from A to B and be patient. A new **Metropolitano** bus service runs from Chorrillas in the south to the Estación Central outside the Sheraton, continuing to Comas in the north. A **tren eléctrico** will link various eastern districts, including San Borja, in 2011 and a new coastal **autopista** is also under construction. ➤ See Transport, page 301.

Best time to visit
Only 12° south of the equator, you would expect a tropical climate, but Lima has two distinct seasons. The winter is from May to October, when a damp *garúa* (sea mist) hangs over the city, making everything look greyer than it is already. It is damp and cold, 8-15°C. The sun breaks through around November and temperatures rise as high as 30°C. Note that the temperature in the coastal suburbs is lower than in the centre because of the sea's influence. You should protect yourself against the sun's rays when visiting the beaches around Lima, or elsewhere in Peru.

Tourist information
iperú has offices at **Jorge Chávez International Airport** ① *T01-574 8000, daily 24 hrs*; at **Casa Basadre** ① *Av Jorge Basadre 610, San Isidro, T01-421 1627, Mon-Fri 0830-1830*; and at **Larcomar shopping centre** ① *Módulo 10, Plaza Principal, Miraflores, T01-445 9400, Mon-Fri 1100-1300, 1400-2000*. There is a **Municipal tourist kiosk** on Pasaje Ribera el Viejo, behind the Municipalidad, near the Plaza de Armas, www.munlima.gob.pe. Ask about guided walks in the city centre. There are eight kiosks: Parque Central; Parque Salazar; Parque del Amor; González Prada y Avenida Petit Thouars; Avenida R Palma y Avenida Petit Thouars; Avenida Larco y Avenida Benivides; Huaca Pucllana; and Ovalo Gutiérrez.

South American Explorers ① *Piura 135, Miraflores, T01-444 2150, T800-274 0568 (USA), www.saexplorers.org, Mon-Fri 0930-1700 (Wed until 2000 for events) and Sat 0930-1300. Headquarters in the USA: 126 Indian Creek Rd, Ithaca, NY, 14850, T1-607 277 0488*, is a non-profit educational organization that functions as a travel resource centre for South America and is widely recognized as the best place to get the most up-to-date information regarding everything from travel advice to volunteer opportunities. A yearly membership is currently US$60 per person and US$90 per couple. Services include access to member-written trip reports, a full map room for reference, an extensive library in English and a book exchange. Members can store luggage as well as valuables in their very secure deposit space. SAE sells official maps from the **Instituto Geográfico Nacional**, SAE-produced trekking maps, used equipment and a wide variety of Peruvian crafts. They host regular presentations on various topics ranging from jungle trips to freedom of the press. Discounts are available for students, volunteers and nationals. If you're looking to study Spanish in Peru, hoping to travel down the Amazon or in search of a quality Inca Trail tour company, they have the information you'll need to make it happen. South American Explorers, apart from the services mentioned above, is simply a great place to step out of the hustle and bustle of Lima and delight in the serenity of a cup of tea, a magazine and good conversation with a fellow traveller. SAE has other clubhouses in Cuzco and Quito (Ecuador), Buenos Aires (Argentina) and Ithaca (New York State).

➤➤ For further sources of information, see Tourist information, page 56.

Background

Lima, originally named 'La Ciudad de Los Reyes' (City of Kings), in honour of the Magi, was founded on Epiphany in 1535 by Francisco Pizarro. From then until the independence of the South American republics in the early 19th century, it was the chief city of Spanish South America. The name Lima, a corruption of the Quechua name *Rimac* (speaker), was not adopted until the end of the 16th century.

At the time of the Conquest, Lima was already an important commercial centre. It continued to grow throughout the colonial years and by 1610 the population was 26,000, of whom 10,000 were Spaniards. This was the time of greatest prosperity. The commercial centre of the city was just off the Plaza de Armas in the Calle de Mercaderes (first block of Jirón de la Unión) and was full of merchandise imported from Spain, Mexico and China. All the goods from the mother country arrived at the port of Callao, from where they were distributed all over Peru and as far away as Argentina.

At this time South American trade with Spain was controlled by a monopoly of Sevillian merchants and their Limeño counterparts who profited considerably. It wasn't until the end of the 18th century that free trade was established between Spain and her colonies, allowing Peru to enjoy a period of relative wealth. Much of this wealth was reinvested in the country, particularly in Lima where educational establishments benefited most of all.

After Francis Drake made a surprise attack on Callao on the night of 13 February 1579, plans were made to strengthen the city's defences against the threat from English pirates. However, an argument raged during the following century between Spain and Lima as to what form the defences should take and who should pay. Finally, it was agreed to encircle the city with a wall, which was completed by 1687.

Life for the white descendants of the Spaniards was good, although *criollos* (Spaniards born in the colonies) were not allowed to hold public office in Peru. The indigenous people and those of mixed blood were treated as lesser citizens. Their movements were strictly controlled. They weren't allowed to live in the city centre; only in areas allocated to them, referred to as *reducciones*.

There were few cities in the Old World that could rival Lima's wealth and luxury, until the terrible earthquake of 1746. The city's notable elegance was instantly reduced to dust. Only 20 of the 3000 houses were left standing and an estimated 4000 people were killed. Despite the efforts of the viceroy, José Manso de Velasco, to rebuild the city, Lima never recovered her former glory. During the 19th century man-made disasters rather than natural ones wreaked havoc on the capital and its people. The population dropped from 87,000 in 1810 to 53,000 in 1842, after the wars of Independence, and the city suffered considerable material damage during the Chilean occupation that followed the War of the Pacific.

Lima was built on both banks of the Rímac river. The walls erected at the end of the 17th century surrounded three sides while the Rímac bordered the fourth. By the time the North American railway engineer, Henry Meiggs, was contracted to demolish the city walls in 1870, Lima had already begun to spread outside the original limits. Meiggs reneged on his contract by leaving much of the wall intact in the poor area around Cercado, where the ruins can still be seen.

By the beginning of the 20th century the population had risen to 140,000 and the movement of people to the coastal areas meant that unskilled cheap labour was readily available for the increasing numbers of factories. Around this time, major improvements were made to the city's infrastructure in the shape of paved streets, modern sanitation, new markets and plazas. For the entertainment of the middle classes, a modern racetrack was opened in what is now the Campo de Marte, as well as the municipal theatre, the Teatro Segura. At the same time, the incumbent president, José Pardo, dramatically increased government expenditure on education, particularly in Lima.

Large-scale municipal improvements continued under the dictatorship of Augusto Leguía and the presidency of Oscar Benavides, who focused on education for the masses, housing facilities for workers and low-cost restaurants in the slum areas that were growing up around Lima.

Lima, a city of some 8.2 million people, continues to struggle to live up to its former reputation as the City of Kings. This has involved drastic changes in the last few years. The commercial heart has moved away from the centre of town and has taken root in more upmarket districts such as Miraflores and San Isidro. After suffering serious decline, the old centre is benefiting from great efforts to clean it up and is re-establishing itself as a place to visit. The city can, however, be seriously affected by smog at certain times of the year. It is also surrounded by *pueblos jóvenes*, or shanty settlements of squatters who have migrated from all parts of Peru looking for work and education.

Sights

When Alberto Andrade Carmona became Mayor of Lima in 1995, he began a campaign to return the historic centre to its original beauty. This meant ejecting the ambulantes (street sellers), cleaning the streets and pavements, and rehabilitating the Plaza de Armas and Plaza San Martín. He also mounted a security force called Serenazgo to enforce public safety and order, whose members are recognizable by their dark jump-suits, long night sticks and riot gear. At least until 2010, when Mayor Luis Castañeda Cossio was to step down, these efforts have continued. An increasing number of buildings in the centre are being restored and the whole area is being given a new lease of life as the architectural beauty and importance of the Cercado (as it is known) is recognized. ▸▸ *For listings, see pages 286-305.*

Central Lima → *For listings, see pages 286-305.*

Plaza de Armas

One block south of the Río Rímac lies the Plaza de Armas, which has been declared a World Heritage Site by UNESCO. The plaza used to be the city's most popular meeting point and main market. Before the building of the Acho bullring in the 1760s, bullfights were traditionally held here.

Around the great Plaza de Armas stand the **Palacio de Gobierno**, the **cathedral**, the **Archbishop's Palace**, the **Municipalidad** and the **Club Unión**. In the centre of the plaza is a bronze fountain dating from 1650. The flower beds are planted with blooms whose colours reflect the city's celebrations, eg red and white at Independence in July, purple at El Señor de los Milagros in October.

Palacio de Gobierno

ⓘ *Plaza de Armas, T01-311 3908. Tours in Spanish and English Mon-Fri 0830-1300, 1400-1700, 45 mins, free; book 2 days in advance at the Oficina de Turismo, of 201 (ask guard for directions); foreigners must take passport. Shorts may not be worn.*

The Government Palace stands on the site of the original palace built by Pizarro. When the Viceroyalty was founded, it became the official residence of the representative of the crown. Despite the opulent furnishings inside, the exterior remained a poor sight throughout colonial times, with shops lining the front facing the plaza. The façade was remodelled in the second half of the 19th century, then transformed in 1921, following a terrible fire. In 1937, the palace was totally rebuilt. The changing of the guard is at 1200 daily.

The cathedral

ⓘ *Plaza de Armas, T01-427 9647, Mon-Fri 0900-1700, Sat 1000-1300, entry to cathedral US$3.65, ticket also includes Museo Arzobispado US$11.*

The cathedral stands on the site of two previous buildings. The first, finished in 1555, was partly paid for by Francisca Pizarro on the condition that her father, the *Conquistador*, was buried there. A larger church, however, was soon required to complement the city's status as an archbishopric. In 1625, the three naves of the main building were completed while work continued on the towers and main door. The new building was reduced to rubble in the earthquake of 1746 and the existing church, completed in 1755, is a reconstruction on the lines of the original.

2 Lima centre

To Panamericana Norte

RIMAC

Convento & Alameda de los Descalzos

To Cerro San Cristóbal

Madera
Purus
Yutay

Ramón Espinoza
Hector

Jr Cajamarca

Jr Ayabaca
Trujillo
Hurtado
Chiclayo
de Mendoza
Icayaue
Marañón
Julian Piñeyro

Alameda Chabuca Granda
Jr Conde de Superunda
Santuario de Santa Rosa
Río Rímac
Puente de Piedra
Palma

Jr Tayacaja
Jr Angaraes
Jr Cañete
Jr Chancay

Jr Huancavelica
Jr Callao

Santo Domingo
Casa Aliaga
Palacio de Gobierno
San Francisco
Parque de la Muralla

To Plaza 2 de Mayo

Av Tacna
Ica
Municipalidad
Plaza de Armas
Fertur
Casa de Las Trece Monedas
Pre Ricardo Rossi
Jr Ayacucho
Plaza Italia

Tacna
Cathedral
Plaza Bolívar
Jr Ancash

Rufino Torrico
Av Emancipación
Jr de la Unión
Palacio Torre Tagle
Congress

Jr Moquegua
La Merced
Museo del Tribunal de la Santa Inquisición
Jr Ucayali

Jr Ocoña
Augusto N Wiese
San Pedro
Jr Miró Quesada

To Cruz del Sur Terminal (150m)
Quilca
Lima Tours
Plaza San Martín
Jr Lampa
Mercado Central

Info Perú
Colmena
Jr Puno
Jr Andahuaylas
BARRIO CHINO

Plaza Francia
Contumazá
Parque Universitario
Jr Abancay
Jr Miró Quesada
Jr Cusco
Jr Huanta

Av Uruguay
Jr Pachitea
Jr Azángaro
Jr Puno
Leticia

Av Roosevelt
Av Nicolás de Piérola

To 3
Estación Central
Manco Cápac
Jr Leticia

Av España
Miguel
M Cuadros
Jr Sandia
Ormeño
Jr Montevideo

Paseo de la República (Wilson)
M Cotabambas
Carlos Zavala
Av Grau
Raimondi
G Naranjo

Plaza Grau
Polvos Azules
Cruz del Sur
Av 28 De Julio
Cromotex

9 de Diciembre
Museo de Arte
Gran Parque Cultural
Bauzate y Mesa
Humboldt

To Plaza Bolognesi (200m), Breña & Immigration
Parque Hernán Velarde
Estadio Nacional

To Parque de la Reserva, Miraflores & San Isidro
To San Isidro (Corpac), Miraflores & Barranco

Metropolitano

N

200 metres
200 yards

➡ Lima maps
1 Lima orientation, page 270
2 Lima centre, page 276
3 San Isidro, page 281
4 Miraflores, page 282
5 Barranco, page 285

Sleeping
1 Familia Rodríguez
2 Hostal España
3 Hostal Iquique
4 Hostal Posada del Parque
5 Hostal Roma & Café Carrara
6 Hostal San Francisco
7 Lima Sheraton
8 Maury
9 Pensión Ibarra

Eating
1 Acllahuasy
2 Antaño & L'Eau Vive
3 De César
4 Estadio Futbol Sports Bar
5 La Catedral del Pisco
6 La Choza Náutica
7 Machu Picchu
8 Natur
9 Salon Capon
10 San Paolo
11 Wa Lok

The interior is immediately impressive, with its massive columns and high nave. Also of note are the splendidly carved stalls (mid-17th century), the silver-covered altars surrounded by fine woodwork, mosaic-covered walls bearing the coats of arms of Lima and Pizarro and an allegory of Pizarro's commanders, the 'Thirteen men of Isla del Gallo'. The remains of Francisco Pizarro, found in the crypt, lie in a small chapel, the first on the right of the entrance. Notices give details of the bio-archaeological evidence proving the authenticity of the bones. There is a **Museo de Arte Religioso** in the cathedral, with sacred paintings, portraits, altar pieces and other items, as well as a café and toilets.

Next to the cathedral is the **Palacio Arzobispal** (Archbishop's Palace), rebuilt in 1924, with a superb wooden balcony. It also has a museum of religious art, **Museo Arzobispado** ① *T01-427 6463, www.palacioarzobispaldelima.com, opening times as for cathedral.*

Around the Plaza de Armas

Just behind the Municipalidad de Lima is **Pasaje Ribera el Viejo**, which has been restored and is now a pleasant place, with several good cafés with outdoor seating.

Casa Aliaga ① *Unión 224, T01-427 7736, www.casadealiaga.com, Mon-Fri 0900-1700, US$11, knock on the door and wait to see if anyone will let you in, or contact in advance for tour operators who offer guided visits,* is still occupied by the Aliaga family and is open to the public. Don Jerónimo de Aliaga was one of the 13 commanders to arrive with Francisco Pizarro, all of whom were given land around the main square to build their own houses when Lima was founded in 1535. It contains what is said to be the oldest ceiling in Lima and is furnished entirely in the colonial style. All the rooms on view are lovingly kept, from the private chapel to reception rooms and bedrooms.

Santo Domingo

① *Church and monastery on the 1st block of Jr Camaná, T01-427 6793, Mon-Sat 0900-1230, 1500-1800, Sun and holidays, mornings only, US$1.65.*

Built in 1549, the church is still as originally planned with a nave and two aisles covered by a vaulted ceiling, though the present ceiling dates from the 17th century. The cloister is one of the most attractive in the city and dates from 1603. The second cloister is much less elaborate. A chapel, dedicated to San Martín de Porres, one of Peru's most revered saints, leads off from a side corridor. Between the two cloisters is the Chapter House (1730), which was once the premises of the Universidad de San Marcos (1551). In the covent is a magnificent cedarwood ceiling. Beneath the sacristy are the tombs of San Martín de Porres and Santa Rosa de Lima, the first saint of the Americas and patron saint of Lima (Santuario de Santa Rosa, Av Tacna, 1st block, T01-425 1279, is open daily 0930-1300, 1500-1800, free entry to the grounds). In 1669, Pope Clement presented the alabaster statue of Santa Rosa in front of the altar. The Basílica de La Veracruz is open at lunchtime. The main hall has some interesting relics.

Behind Santo Domingo is **Alameda Chabuca Granda**, named after one of Peru's greatest singers and composers. In the evening there are free art and music shows and you can sample food and sweets from all over Peru.

Tours by minibus depart from in front of Santo Domingo (Camaná y Conde Superunda, daily 1000-2100, one hour, US$2). They go through the old *barrio* of Rímac, then pass the Alameda de los Descalzos, designed in the early 17th century as a restful place to stroll, but now a dangerous area to wander alone. On the Alameda is **Convento de los Descalzos** ① *T01-481 0441, Wed-Mon 1000-1300, 1500-1800, US$1, guided tour only, 45 mins in Spanish,* founded in 1592. It now contains over 300 paintings of the Cuzco, Quito and Lima schools, which line the four main cloisters and two ornate chapels. The minibus tour climbs through one of the city's oldest shanty towns with its brightly painted houses to the top of **Cerro San Cristóbal**. About half the tour is spent going to the summit, where there is a café, a small museum and a spectacular view of Lima. The other half is a historical tour. Check the cloud level first, otherwise you will see very little. **Urbanito** buses (T01-424 3650, www.urbanito.com.pe, three hours, weekends and holidays), also run from the Plaza de Armas on a tour of central Lima, which includes Cerro San Cristóbal.

San Francisco and around

ⓘ *Church and monastery stand on the 1st block of Jr Lampa, corner of Ancash, T01-427 1381, daily 0930-1645, guided tours only, US$1.65, US$0.50 children.*

The baroque church, which was finished in 1674, was one of the few edifices to withstand the 1746 earthquake. The nave and aisles are lavishly decorated in the Mudéjar style. The choir, which dates from 1673, is notable for its beautifully carved seats in Nicaraguan hardwood. There is a valuable collection of religious paintings by the Spanish artist, Francisco de Zubarán (1598-1664). The monastery is famous for the Sevillian tilework and panelled ceiling in the cloisters (1620). The 17th-century *retablos* in the main cloister are carved from cedar and represent scenes from the life of San Francisco, as do the paintings. A broad staircase leading down to a smaller cloister is covered by a remarkable carved wooden dome (nicknamed *la media naranja* – the half orange) dating from 1625. Next to this smaller cloister is the Capilla de la Soledad where a café is open to the public. The catacombs under the church and part of the monastery are well worth seeing. This is where an estimated 25,000 Limeños were buried before the main cemetery was opened in 1808.

Parque de la Muralla ⓘ *open 0900-2000*, on the south bank of the Rímac behind San Francisco, incorporates a section of the old city wall, fountains, stalls and street performers. There is a cycle track, toilets and places to eat both inside and near the entrance on Calle de la Soledad.

Two blocks down Ancash, at No 536, is **Casa de las Trece Monedas**, built in 1787 by counts from Genoa. It still has the original doors and window grilles.

Turn right down Avenida Abancay to the **Museo del Tribunal de la Santa Inquisición** ⓘ *Jr Junín 548, near the corner of Av Abancay, T01-311 7777, www.congreso.gob.pe/museo.htm, daily 0900-1700, free.* The main hall has a splendidly carved mahogany ceiling that remains untouched. The Court of Inquisition was first held here in 1584, after being moved from its first home opposite the church of La Merced. From 1829 until 1938 the building was used by the Senate. In the basement there is an accurate recreation in situ of the gruesome tortures. The whole tour is fascinating, if a little morbid. A description in English is available at the desk and students will offer to show you round for a tip.

The city's best surviving specimen of secular colonial architecture is **Palacio Torre Tagle** ⓘ *Jr Ucayali 363, access to the patio only Mon-Fri during working hours*, which was built in 1735 for Don José Bernardo de Tagle y Bracho, to whom King Philip V gave the title of First Marquis of Torre Tagle. The house remained in the family until it was acquired by the government in 1918. Today, it is still used by the Foreign Ministry, but visitors are allowed to enter courtyards to inspect the fine, Moorish-influenced woodcarving in the balconies, the wrought ironwork and a 16th-century coach, complete with commode.

The church of **San Pedro** ⓘ *on the 3rd block of Jr Ucayali, Mon-Sat 0930-1145, 1700-1800*, finished by Jesuits in 1638, has an unadorned façade, different from any other in the city. In one of the massive towers hangs a five-tonne bell called *La Abuelita* (the grandmother), first rung in 1590, which sounded the Declaration of Independence in

1821. The contrast between the sober exterior and sumptuous interior couldn't be more striking. The altars are marvellous, in particular the high altar, attributed to the skilled craftsman, Matías Maestro. The church also boasts Moorish-style balconies and rich, gilded woodcarvings in the choir and vestry, tiled throughout. The most important paintings in the church are hung near the main entrance. In the monastery, the sacristy is a beautiful example of 17th-century architecture. Also of note are La Capilla de Nuestra Señora de la O and the penitentiary. Several viceroys are buried below.

Southwest of the Plaza de Armas

The Jirón de la Unión, the main shopping street, runs from the Plaza de Armas. It has been converted into a pedestrian precinct that teems with life.

La Merced ① *Plazuela de la Merced, Unión y Miró Quesada, T01-427 8199, Mon-Sat 0800-1245, 1600-2000, Sun 0700-1300, 1600-2000; monastery daily 0800-1200 and 1500-1730*, was the first church to be built in Lima, and it is said that it was the site where the first Mass took place. At Independence, the Virgin of La Merced was made a marshal of the Peruvian army. The restored colonial façade is a fine example of baroque architecture. Inside are magnificent altars and some notable tilework on the walls. A door from the right of the nave leads into the monastery where you can see 18th-century religious paintings in the sacristy. The cloister dates from 1546.

South of Jirón de la Unión, the **Plaza San Martín** has a statue of the eponymous hero in the centre. The square has been remodelled with flowerbeds and trees and is now a nice place to relax. Taxis and colectivos line the north side, while Pasaje Quilca on the west side is lined with food stalls.

The **Gran Parque Cultural de Lima** (daily 0800-2030) was inaugurated in January 2000 by both the mayor of Lima, Alberto Andrade, and the then-president Alberto Fujimori. It has a medium-sized outdoor amphitheatre, Japanese garden, food court and children's activities. Relaxing strolls through this green, peaceful and safe oasis in the centre of Lima are recommended. Within the park is the **Museo de Arte** ① *9 de Diciembre (Paseo Colón) 125, T01-423 4732, http://museoarte.perucultural.org.pe, Thu-Tue 1000-1700, US$3.65, free guide, signs in English*, which was built in 1868 as the Palacio de la Exposición. The building was designed by Alexandre Gustave Eiffel. There are more than 7000 exhibits, giving a chronological history of Peruvian cultures and art from the Paracas civilization up to today. They include excellent examples of 17th- and 18th-century Cuzco paintings, a beautiful display of carved furniture, heavy silver and jewelled stirrups and also pre-Columbian pottery. A *filmoteca* (cinema club) is on the premises and shows films almost every night; consult the local paper for details, or look in the museum itself.

In **Parque de la Reserva** ① *block 8 of Av Arequipa and going up towards the centre, Santa Beatriz, www.circuitomagicodelagua.com.pe, Wed-Sun and holidays 1600-2200, US$1.40*, is the **Circuito Mágico del Agua**, a display of 13 fountains, the highest reaching 80 m, enhanced by impressive light and music shows four times a night, great fun and very popular. It has featured in the *Guiness Book of Records* as the largest fountain complex in the world.

San Borja and Surco

Museo de la Nación ① *Javier Prado Este 2465, San Borja, T01-476 9933, Tue-Sun 0900-1700, closed major public holidays, 4-hr tours available, US$2.50, 50% discount with ISIC card. See http://inc. perucultural.org.pe/agenda.asp for details of temporary exhibitions. It is cold in the museum.* This is the anthropological and archaeological museum for the exhibition and study of the art and history of the aboriginal races of Peru. There are good explanations in Spanish and English on Peruvian history, with ceramics, textiles and displays about many ruins in Peru. It is arranged so that you can follow the development of Peruvian pre-colonial history through to the time of the Incas. A visit is recommended before you go to see the archaeological sites themselves. There are displays on the tomb of the Señor de Sipán, artefacts from Batán Grande near Chiclayo (Sicán culture), reconstructions of the friezes found at Huaca La Luna and Huaca El Brujo, near Trujillo, and of Sechín and other sites. Temporary exhibitions are held in the basement, where there is also an Instituto de Cultura bookshop. The museum also has a cafeteria.

To get to the museum from downtown Lima, take a combi with a window sticker that says 'Javier Prado/Aviación' from Avenida Garcilaso de la Vega. Get off at the 21st block of Javier Prado at Avenida Aviación. To get there from Miraflores, take a bus down Avenida Arequipa to Avenida Javier Prado (27th block), then take a bus with a window sticker saying 'Todo Javier Prado' or 'Aviación'. A taxi from downtown Lima or from the centre of Miraflores costs US$3.20.

South and east of San Borja are the districts of **Santiago de Surco** and **Monterrico**, upper and middle-class residential districts. The **Museo de Oro del Perú** ① *Alonso de Molina 1100, Monterrico, Surco (between blocks 18 and 19 of Av Primavera), Lima 33, T01-345 1292, www.museoroperu.com.pe, daily 1130-1900, US$11.55, children under 11 US$5.60, multilingual audioguides*, houses an enormous collection of Peruvian gold, silver and bronze objects, together with an impressive international array of arms and military uniforms from Spanish colonial times to the present day and textiles from Peru and elsewhere. Allow plenty of time to appreciate all that is on view. It is directed by the **Fundación Miguel Mujica Gallo** (named after the businessman, diplomat and collector who created the museum) which, following a controversy over the authenticity of a number of pieces, is now conducting an inventory and registration of the collection with the **Ministerio de Cultura**. The museum remains a popular call on the capital's tourist circuit and 167 of its pieces can be seen in the **Sala Museo Oro del Perú**, in Larcomar (see below).

Lima suburbs

Pueblo Libre

Museo Nacional de Antropología, Arqueología e Historia ① *Plaza Bolívar, not to be confused with Plaza Bolívar in the centre, T01-463 5070, http://museonacional.peru cultural.org.pe, Tue-Sat 0900-1700, Sun and bank holidays 0900-1600, US$4, students US$1.20, guides available for groups*, is the original museum of archaeology and anthropology. On display are ceramics of the Chimú, Nazca, Mochica and Ichma (Pachacámac) cultures, various Inca curiosities, works of art and interesting textiles. The museum has a model of Machu Picchu.

Next door is the **Museo Nacional de Historia** ① *Plaza Bolívar, T01-463 2009, Tue-Sat 0900-1700, Sun and holidays 0900-1600, US$3.65*, housed in a mansion built by Viceroy Pezuela and occupied by San Martín (1821-1822) and Bolívar (1823-1826). The exhibits comprise colonial and early republican paintings, manuscripts, portraits, uniforms, etc.

To get to both museums from the centre, take any public transport on Avenida Brasil with the window sticker 'Todo Brasil.' Get off at the 21st block and walk about five blocks down Vivanco. The museums will be on your left. From Miraflores, take bus SM 18 Carabayllo–Chorrillos, marked 'Bolívar, Arequipa, Larcomar', get out at block eight of

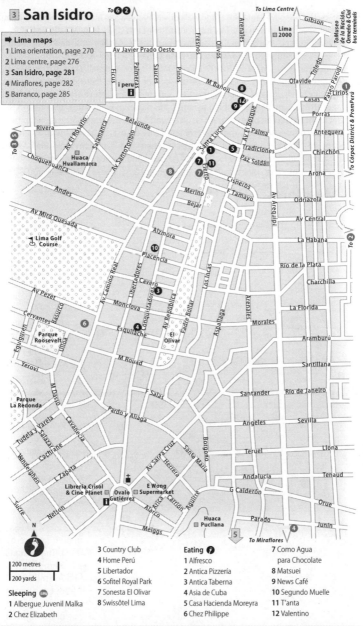

3 San Isidro

Lima maps
1 Lima orientation, page 270
2 Lima centre, page 276
3 **San Isidro, page 281**
4 Miraflores, page 282
5 Barranco, page 285

Sleeping
1 Albergue Juvenil Malka
2 Chez Elizabeth

3 Country Club
4 Home Perú
5 Libertador
6 Sofitel Royal Park
7 Sonesta El Olivar
8 Swissôtel Lima

Eating
1 Alfresco
2 Antica Pizzería
3 Antica Taberna
4 Asia de Cuba
5 Casa Hacienda Moreyra
6 Chez Philippe

7 Como Agua
para Chocolate
8 Matsuei
9 News Café
10 Segundo Muelle
11 T'anta
12 Valentino

Bolívar, by the Hospital Santa Rosa, and walk down Avenida San Martín five blocks till you see the 'blue line'; then turn left. Taxi from downtown Lima US$3; from Miraflores US$4.

A faded 'blue line' marked on the pavement links the Museo Nacional de Antropología, Arqueología e Historia to the **Museo Larco de Lima** ① *Av Bolívar 1515, T01-461 1312, www.museolarco.org, daily 0900-1800, US$11 (half price for students); texts in 6 languages, guides, tours in Spanish, English and French can be booked, there is disabled access; photography is not allowed*, a 15-minute walk. Located in an 18th-century mansion built on a seventh-century pre-Columbian pyramid, this museum houses the collection of the archaeologist Rafael Larco Herrera, which gives world-class overview of the development of Peruvian cultures through their pottery and other objects. It has the world's largest collection of Moche, Sicán and Chimú pieces. There is a five-room Gold and Jewels Gallery, a magnificent textile collection and a fascinating erotica section. Don't miss the storerooms with their overwhelming array of pottery, unlike anything you'll see

elsewhere. There is a library and computer room for your own research and the museum published its own fully-illustrated book on the collection. It is surrounded by flower-filled gardens, has a new entrance and park outside, a new boutique and the **Café del Museo** (see Eating, page 292).

To get there, take any bus to the 15th block of Avenida Brasil. Then take a bus down Avenida Bolívar. Or, from Miraflores, take the SM 18 Carabayllo-Chorrillos, see above, to block 15 of Bolívar. A taxi from downtown, Miraflores or San Isidro takes 15 minutes and costs US$4.

San Isidro → *See map, page 281.*

The district of San Isidro combines some upscale residential areas, many of Lima's fanciest hotels and restaurants and important commercial zones with a huge golf course smack in the middle. Along Avenida La República is **El Olivar**, an old olive grove

100 metres
100 yards

Sleeping 🛏
1 Adventures House *A2*
2 Albergue Turístico Juvenil Internacional *D3*
3 Albergue Verde *D2*
4 Alemán *A3*
5 Antigua Miraflores *B1*
6 Blue House *C1*
7 Casa Andina *D2*
8 Casa Andina Private Collection *C3*
9 Casa de Baraybar *A2*
10 Casa del Mochilero *A2*
11 Casa Rodas *B3*
12 Condor's House *A1*
13 Dragonfly *C1*
14 El Carmelo *B1*
16 Eurobackpackers *C1*
17 Explorer's House *A1*
18 Flying Dog *B2, C2*
19 Friend's House *C1*
20 Home Perú *A3*
21 Hostal El Patio *C2*
22 Hostal La Castellana *C2*
23 HQ Villa *A3*
24 Inka Frog *A2*
26 José Antonio *C1*
27 JW Marriott *D1*
28 La Casa Nostra *D2*

30 Lex Luthor's House & The Angels Inn *C1*
31 Lion Backpackers *C3*
32 Loki Backpackers *A1*
33 Mansión San Antonio *D3*
34 Miraflores Park *D1*
35 Pariwana *B3*
36 Perú Backpackers Miraflores Guesthouse *D1*
37 Pirwa *B3*
38 Pirwa B&B *A3*
39 San Antonio Abad *D3*
40 Señorial *D1*
43 Sonesta Posadas del Inca & Café La Máquina *C2*
44 Stop & Drop Backpacker Hotel & Guesthouse *B2*
45 The Lighthouse *A2*

Eating 🍴
1 Astrid y Gaston *C3*
2 Café Beirut *B2*
3 Café Café *B2*
4 Café de la Paz *B2*
5 Café Tarata & Mama Olla *C2*
6 Café Voltaire *B3*
7 Café Zeta *B2*
8 C'est si bon *A2*
9 Chef's Café *C2*
11 Dalmacia *D1*
12 El Huarike *B3*
13 El Kapallaq *B3*
14 El Parquetito *B2*
15 El Rincón Gaucho *D1*
16 El Señorío de Sulco *A2*
17 Govinda *D2*
18 Haiti *B3*

21 Las Brujas de Cachiche *B1*
22 Las Tejas *C2*
23 La Tiendecita Blanca *B3*
24 La Trattoria *C3*
25 La Trattoria *A3*
26 Lobo del Mar – Octavio Otani *C1*
27 Panchita *B3*
30 Pizza Street *B3*
32 Sandwich.com & Shehadi *B2*
33 Sí Señor *B1*

Bars & clubs 🍸
34 Bartinis *D1*
35 Media Naranja *B2*
36 Murphy's *C3*
37 The Old Pub *B2*
38 Treff Pub Alemán *C2*
39 Voluntarios Pub *B2*

➡ **Lima maps**
1 Lima orientation, page 270
2 Lima centre, page 276
3 San Isidro, page 281
4 **Miraflores, page 282**
5 Barranco, page 285

planted by the first Spaniards, which has been turned into a beautiful park. It's definitely worth a stroll either by day or night.

Between San Isidro and Miraflores, is **Huallamarca** ① *C Nicolás de Rivera 201 and Av Rosario, T01-222 4124, 0900-1700, closed Mon, US$1.75, take bus 1 from Av Tacna, or minibus 13 or 73 to Choquechaca, then walk.* This adobe pyramid of the Maranga culture is also known as the Pan de Azúcar and dates from AD 100-500. There is a small site museum.

Miraflores → *See map page 282.*

Miraflores, apart from being a nice residential part of Lima, is also home to a busy mercantile district full of fashionable shops, cafés, discos, fine restaurants and good hotels and guesthouses. As in the centre, there is a security force patrolling the streets, in trucks, on motorbikes or on foot.

In the centre of Miraflores is the beautiful **Parque Central de Miraflores (Parque Kennedy)** located between Avenida Larco and Avenida Oscar Benavides (locally known as Avenida Diagonal). This extremely well-kept park has a small open-air theatre with performances Thursday-Sunday, ranging from Afro-Peruvian music to comedy to rock'n'roll. Towards the bottom of the park is a nightly crafts market open 1700-2300.

At the end of Avenida Larco and running along the promenade is the renovated **Parque Salazar** and the very modern shopping complex called **Centro Comercial Larcomar**. The shopping centre's terraces, which have been carved out of the cliff, contain expensive shops, hip cafés and restaurants, an open-air internet café and discos. The balustrades have a beautiful view of the ocean and the sunset.

Huaca Pucllana ① *at the intersection of Gral Borgoño y Tarapacá, near the 45th block of Av Arequipa, T01-445 8695, http://pucllana.perucultural.org.pe/, Wed-Mon 0900-1600, US$2.50, includes a good 45-min tour in Spanish or English,* is a fifth- to eighth-century AD ceremonial and administrative centre of the pre-Inca Lima culture. The pyramid of small adobe bricks is 23 m high. Evidence of occupation of the site by the Wari culture has been found. It has a site museum, with some objects from the site itself, an area growing crops and raising animals, and a souvenir shop. See also Eating, page 293.

Barranco

South of Miraflores is Barranco, which was already a seaside resort by the end of the 17th century. During Spanish rule, it was a getaway for the rich who lived in or near the centre. Nowadays, Barranco is something of an intellectual haven, with artists' workshops and chic galleries.

The attractive public library, formerly the town hall, stands on the delightful plaza. Nearby is the interesting *bajada*, a steep path leading down to the beach, where many of Lima's artists live. The **Puente de los Suspiros** (Bridge of Sighs), leads towards the Malecón, with fine views of the bay.

Barranco is a quiet suburb during the day but comes alive at night when the city's young flock here to party at weekends. Squeezed together into a few streets are dozens of good bars and restaurants.

Lima beaches

Lima sits next to an open bay, with its two points at La Punta (Callao) and Punta La Chira (Chorrillos). During the summer (December to March), beaches get very crowded on weekdays as much as at weekends, even though all the beaches lining the Lima coast have been declared unsuitable for swimming. Most beaches have very strong currents

5 Barranco

➡ Lima maps
1 Lima orientation, page 270
2 Lima centre, page 276
3 San Isidro, page 281
4 Miraflores, page 282
5 Barranco, page 285

Pacific Ocean

100 metres
100 yards

Sleeping 🛏
1 Barranco's Backpackers Inn
2 Casa Barranco
3 Domeyer
4 Hosp La Casona de Barranco
5 Safe in Lima
6 San Mart Inn
7 The Point

Eating 🍴
1 Antica Trattoria
2 Canta Rana
3 Expreso Virgen de Guadalupe
4 Istanbul
5 La Cía
6 La Costa Verde
7 La Fonda de los Suspiros
8 Las Mesitas
9 Sóngoro Cosongo
10 Tío Mario

Bars & clubs 🍸
11 Ayahuasca
12 Déjà Vu
13 Del Carajo
14 De Rompe y Raja
15 El Dragón
16 Juanitos
17 La Candelaria
18 La Estación de Barranco
19 La Noche
20 La Posada del Angel
21 La Posada del Mirador
22 Las Terrazas
23 Mochileros
24 Santos Café & Espirituosos
25 Sargento Pimienta

Ⓜ Metropolitano

and extreme caution should be exercised. Lifeguards are not always present. A stroll on the beach is pleasant during daylight hours but, when the sun goes down, the thieves come out and it becomes very dangerous.

The beaches of Miraflores, Barranco and Chorrillos are very popular and sand and sea can get dirty. It's much better to take a safe taxi 40 km or more south to **Punta Rocas**, **Señoritas**, **El Silencio**, or **Punta Hermosa**, which has frequent surfing and volleyball tournaments.

◉ Lima listings

For Sleeping and Eating price codes and other relevant information, see pages 30-36.

● Sleeping

All hotels in the upper price brackets charge 19% state tax (IVA) and a service charge on top of prices. In hotels foreigners pay no IVA and the amount of service charged is up to the hotel. Neither is included in prices below, unless indicated otherwise.

Lima has several international, high-class chain hotels: Lima Sheraton, reservas@ sheraton.com.pe; Swissôtel Lima, www.lima.swissotel.com; Sofitel Royal Park, www.sofitel.com; JW Marriott, www.marriott.com. All are recommended.

The central colonial heart of Lima is not as safe at night as the more upmarket areas of San Isidro, Miraflores or Barranco. If you are only staying a short time in the city and want to see the main sights, the centre is convenient, but do take care. San Isidro is the poshest district, while Miraflores has a good mix of places to stay, great ocean views, bookstores, restaurants and cinemas. From here you can commute to the centre by bus (30-45 mins) or by taxi (20-30 mins). Barranco, which is more bohemian, is a little further out.

Near the airport *map p270*
L **Ramada Costa del Sol**, Av Elmer Faucett s/n, T01-711 2000, www.ramada.com. Within the airport perimeter. Offers day rates as well as overnights if you can't get into the city.
B-D **Hostal Residencial Víctor**, Manuel Mattos 325, Urb San Amadeo de Garagay, Lima 31, T01-569 4662, hostalvictor@ terra.com.pe. 5 mins from the airport by taxi,

or phone or email in advance for free pick-up, large comfortable rooms, with bath, hot water, cable TV, free luggage store, free internet and 10% discount for Footprint book owners, American breakfast, evening meals can be ordered locally, 2 malls with restaurants, shops, cinemas, etc nearby, very helpful. See also La Catedral del Pisco, page 292. For information, contact Víctor Melgar Morales, victortravelservice@terra.com.pe.
C **Pay Purix**, Av Bertello Bolatti, Mz F, Lote 5, Urb Los Jazmines, 1ra Etapa, Callao, T01-484 9118, www.paypurix.com. 3 mins from airport, can arrange pick-up (taxi US$6, US$2 from outside airport). Hostel with doubles and dorms (**E** pp), convenient, with breakfast, Wi-Fi, washingmachine, English spoken, CDs, DVDs, games and use of kitchen.

Central Lima *p275, map p276*
B **Maury**, Jr Ucayali 201, T01-428 8188, http://ekeko2.rcp.net.pe/hotelmaury. The most luxurious hotel in the historical centre, fancy, secure, breakfast included. The bar, all wood panels, is reputed to be the home of the first-ever pisco sour.
C **La Posada del Parque Hostal**, Parque Hernán Velarde 60, near 2nd block of Av Petit Thouars, Santa Beatriz, between centre and San Isidro, T01-433 2412, www.incacountry. com. A charmingly refurbished old house in a safe area, excellent bathrooms, cable TV, safe in room, breakfast US$2 extra, airport transfer 24 hrs, US$17 for up to 3 passengers, no credit cards, free internet 0830-2200. Always check the website for special offers and gifts. The owners speak good English. Recommended as excellent value.

D Hostal Iquique, Jr Iquique 758, Breña (discount for SAE members), T01-433 4724, www.hostal-iquique-lima.com. Rooms on top floor at the back are best, well-kept if a bit noisy and draughty, use of kitchen, warm water, storage facilities, safe, internet. Repeated recommendations.

D Hostal Roma, Jr Ica 326, T/F01-427 7576, www.hostalroma.8m.com. **E** without bath, cheaper in low season, hot water, basic, often full, internet extra, motorcycle parking. Roma Tours arranges city tours but shop around if you want to, flight reservations, Errol Branca speaks English.

F Hostal España, Jr Azángaro 105, T01-427 9196, www.hotelespanaperu.com. **E** with private bath (3 rooms), **G** per person in dorm, fine old building, shared bathroom, hot showers, French and English spoken, internet, motor-cycle parking, luggage store (free), laundry service, don't leave valuables in rooms, roof garden, good café, can be very busy.

F Hostal San Francisco, Jr Azángaro 127, T01-426 2735, hostalsf@lanpro.com.pe. Dormitories with and without bathrooms, safe, Italian/Peruvian owners, good service, internet and café.

G pp **Familia Rodríguez**, Av Nicolás de Piérola 730, p 2, T01-423 6465, jotajot@terra.com.pe. Breakfast, popular, some rooms noisy, will store luggage, also has dormitory accommodation with only 1 bathroom (same price), transport to airport, good information, secure.

G Pensión Ibarra, Av Tacna 359, p 14-16, T/F01-427 8603 (no sign), pensionibarra@ekno.com. Breakfast US$2, discount for longer stay, use of kitchen, balcony with views of the city, very helpful owner, hot water, full board available (good small café next door).

Lima suburbs

Pueblo Libre *p280, map p270*
F pp **Guest House Marfil**, Parque Ayacucho 126, at the 3rd block of Bolívar, T01-463 3161, cosycoyllor@yahoo.com. English spoken,

breakfast, kitchen facilities and laundry free of charge, internet, Spanish classes arranged, family atmosphere.

F pp **Hostal Bait Sababa**, Av San Martín 743, near the hospital, T01-261 4990, www.bait sababa.com. Home of a Jewish family who also speak Spanish and English, very helpful, Fri evening meal provided, restaurants, laundry, internet and phone nearby.

San Miguel and Magdalena del Mar
C Hostal Mami Panchita, Av Federico Gallessi 198 (ex-Av San Miguel), T01-263 7203, www.mami panchita.com. Dutch/Peruvian-owned, English, French, Dutch, Spanish and German spoken, includes breakfast and welcome drink, comfortable rooms with bath, hot water, living room and bar, patio, email service, book exchange, **Raymi Travel** agency (good service), 15 mins from airport, 15 mins from Miraflores, 20 mins from historical centre. Frequently recommended.

E Tambopacaya, Manco Capac 212 (block 31 of Av Brasil), T01-261 6122, www.tambopacaya.com. **F** in dorm, hot water, private rooms have bath, use of kitchen, internet, luggage store, laundry, convenient for airport and centre.

San Isidro *p283, maps p270 and p281*
LL Country Club, Los Eucaliptos 590, T01-611 9000, www.hotelcountry.com. Excellent hotel offering fine service, luxurious rooms, safes in rooms, cable TV, free internet for guests, good bar and restaurant, classically stylish.

LL Libertador Hotels Peru, Los Eucaliptos 550, T01-518 6300, www.libertador.com.pe (reservations: Las Begonias 441, office 240, T01-518 6500). Overlooking the golf course, full facilities for the business traveller, large comfortable rooms in this relatively small hotel, fine service, good restaurant. Member of a hotel group with recommended properties throughout Peru.

LL Sonesta El Olivar, Pancho Fierro 194, T01-712 6000, www.sonesta.com/lima.

One of the top 5-star hotels in Lima. Looking out onto El Olivar park, this first-rate modern hotel boasts many superb eating options. Very attentive staff, quiet, fine rooms with all amenities, bar, swimming pool, popular. Warmly recommended.

D Chez Elizabeth, Av del Parque Norte 265, T01-99 800 7557 (mob), http://chezelizabeth.typepad.fr. Family house in residential area 7 mins' walk from Cruz del Sur bus station. Shared or private bathrooms, TV room, laundry, luggage storage, Wi-Fi, breakfast included, airport transfers US\$17.50 for 3.

F Albergue Juvenil Malka, Los Lirios 165 (near 4th block of Av Javier Prado Este), T01-442 0162, hostelmalka@terra.com.pe. Youth hostel, 20% discount with ISIC card, dormitory style, 4-8 beds per room, English spoken, cable TV, laundry, kitchen, climbing wall, nice café.

Miraflores *p284, map p282*

LL Casa Andina Private Collection, Av La Paz 463, T01-213 4300, www.casa-andina.com. Top of the range hotel in this recommended Peruvian chain, modern, well-appointed large rooms with safe, cable TV, Wi-Fi, good bathrooms. Fine food in **Alma** restaurant and good value café, **Sama**, 1st-class service, bar, pool and gym.

LL Miraflores Park, Av Malecón de la Reserva 1035, T01-610 4000, www.miraflorespark.com. An **Orient Express** hotel, excellent service and facilities, beautiful views over the ocean, top class. Rooftop, open-air, heated pool and spa which looks out over the ocean, open to the public when you buy a spa treatment. Check with the hotel for monthly offers. Highly recommended.

L-A Mansión San Antonio, Av Tejada 531, T01-445 9665, www.mansionsanantonio.com. Bed and breakfast, 7 suites of varying standards on 3 floors in a quiet residential area, safe, bar, coffee shop, Wi-Fi in public areas, swimming pool, stylish, gay-friendly.

L-A Sonesta Posadas del Inca, Alcanfores 329, T01-241 7688, www.sonesta.com/

miraflores. Part of renowned chain of hotels, convenient location, cable TV, a/c, restaurant.

AL-A Antigua Miraflores, Av Grau 350 at C Francia, T01-241 6116, www.peru-hotels-inns.com. A small, elegant hotel in a quiet but central location, very friendly service, tastefully furnished and decorated, gym, cable TV, good restaurant. Recommended.

AL-A Casa Andina, Av 28 de Julio 1088, T01-241 4050, www.casa-andina.com. Also at Av Petit Thouars 5444, T01-447 0263, in Miraflores. These Classic hotels in this chain have similar facilities and decor (others in the Cuzco area, Puno and Lake Titicaca, Arequipa, Colca, Chincha and Nazca). Very neat, with many useful touches, comfortable beds, free internet and Wi-Fi, a/c, fridge, safe, laundry service, buffet breakfast, other meals available. Check website for discounts.

A José Antonio, 28 de Julio 398 y C Colón, T01-445 7743, www.hotelesjoseantonio.com. Good in all respects, including the restaurant, huge rooms, jacuzzis, internet, swimming pool, business facilities, helpful staff speak some English.

A San Antonio Abad, Ramón Ribeyro 301, T01-447 6766, www.hotelsanantonio abad.com. Secure, quiet, helpful, tasty breakfasts, 1 free airport transfer with reservation, justifiably popular and frequently recommended.

A-B Casa de Baraybar, Toribio Pacheco 216, T01-441 2160, www.casadebaraybar.com. 1 block from the ocean, discounts for cash and long stay, extra long beds, breakfast included, TV, 24-hr room service, laundry, airport transfers free for stays of 3 nights. Bilingual staff, internet. Recommended.

A-B Hostal El Patio, Diez Canseco 341, T01-444 2107, www.hostalelpatio.net. Includes breakfast, reductions for cash and long stays. The patio has a fountain, lots of flowers and bird cages; terraces for sitting outside. Very nice suites and rooms, comfortable, English and French spoken, convenient, *comedor*, gay-friendly. Airport pick-up available.

B Alemán, Arequipa 4704, T01-241 1500, www.hotelaleman.com.pe. No sign, comfortable, quiet, garden, excellent breakfast included, enquire about laundry service, smiling staff, free internet, Wi-Fi.

B Hostal La Castellana, Grimaldo del Solar 222, T01-444 4662, lacastellan@terra.com.pe. Pleasant, good value, nice garden, safe, expensive restaurant, laundry, English spoken, special price for SAE members.

C El Carmelo, Bolognesi 749, T01-446 0575, www.hostalelcarmelo.com.pe. With TV, great location a couple of blocks from the Parque del Amor, small restaurant downstairs serving *criolla* food and *ceviche*, price includes breakfast, good value, comfortable.

C La Casa Nostra, Av Grimaldo del Solar 265, T01-241 1718, www.lacasanostraperu.com. Variety of rooms (**E** per person in 4-bed room), good service, convenient, with breakfast, internet, safe, money exchange, laundry, tourist information. Popular.

C Señorial, José González 567, T01-445 0139, www.senorial.com. With breakfast, comfortable, nice garden, Wi-Fi, restaurant, good services. Recommended.

C-D pp Eurobackpackers, Manco Cápac 471, T01-654 4339, www.eurobackpackers.com. Under new management. Doubles with and without bath, dormitories including girls only **F** per person, breakfast included, kitchen, comfortable, internet, Wi-Fi (free). Airport (US$15) and bus terminal (US$8.50) transfers.

C-D Flying Dog, Diez Canseco 117, T01-445 6745, www.flyingdogperu.com. Also at Lima 457 and Olaya 280, all with dorms **F** per person. At Pershing 155 is a house for monthly rentals and they have hostels in Cuzco and Arequipa. All on or near Parque Kennedy, with kitchen, internet, lockers, but all with different features.

C-F Lion Backpackers, Grimaldo del Solar 139, T01-447 1827, www.lionbackpackers. com. 3 blocks from Parque Kennedy, doubles (**C**) and dorms (**E-F** per person), the hostal has a good atmosphere, clean rooms if a bit small, helpful staff, safe, use of kitchen, Wi-Fi.

D Inka Frog, Gral Iglesias 271, T01-445 8979, www.inkafrog.com. **E** with SAE discount. Renovated hostel, self-styled 'Exclusive B&B', comfortable, nice decor, lounge with huge TV, all rooms with bath and cable TV, rooftop terrace. Breakfast included, great value.

D The Lighthouse, Cesareo Chacaltana 162, T01-446 8397, www.thelighthouseperu.com. **F** in shared dorm. Near Plaza Morales Barros, British/Peruvian-run, relaxed, small dorm or private rooms with shared bath. Free internet and Wi-Fi, use of kitchen, small indoor patio. Breakfast included. Recommended.

D-E Casa Rodas, Av Petit Thouars 4712, T01-447 5761, and Tarapacá 250, T01-242 4872, www.casarodas.com. Both locations provide clean rooms for 2, 3 or 4, good beds, hot water, breakfast included, use of kitchen, cable TV and DVD player, free internet, Wi-Fi available, helpful staff.

D-E Friend's House, José González 427, T01-446 3521, friendshouse_peru@ yahoo.com.mx. Very popular, reserve in advance. Near **Larcomar** shopping centre, plenty of good information and help, family atmosphere, includes breakfast, use of kitchen, cable TV, internet and Wi-Fi. Highly recommended. They have another branch at Jr Manco Cápac 368, T01-446 6248, with dormitory accommodation with shared bath and hot water, **F** per person. Neither branch is signed, except on the bell at No 427. (Do not confuse with a signed hostel of the same name on J González, near Porta.)

D-E Home Perú, Av Arequipa 4501 (no sign), T01-241 9898, www.homeperu.com. In a 1920s mansion with huge rooms, with breakfast, **E-F** per person with shared bath, group discounts, very welcoming and helpful, use of kitchen, luggage store, English spoken, laundry service, internet. Can help with bus and plane tickets, connected to other *hostales* in Peru.

D-F Hitchhikers B&B Backpackers Hostel, Bolognesi 400, T01-242 3008, www.hhikers peru.com. Close to the ocean, dorms (including female only) and private rooms with bath, kitchen, nice patio, Wi-Fi, plenty of parking.

E-F pp **Perú Backpackers Miraflores Guesthouse**, José González 526, T01-447 7044, www.backpackersperu.com. **C** in double room, has a girls-only dorm, good breakfast included, good service, cooking facilities, internet, DVD, safe, book exchange.

E-F pp **Stop & Drop Backpacker Hotel & Guesthouse**, Berlín 168, p2, T01-243 3101, www.stopandrop.com. **C-D** Double rooms with private bath. Backpacker hotel and guesthouse, also surf and Spanish school. Bar, kitchen facilities, luggage store, laundry, TV, movies, internet, games, comfy beds, safe, hot showers 24 hrs, adventure sports (including diving, horse riding) and volunteer jobs. Airport pick-up.

F pp **Adventures House**, Jr Alfredo León 234, T01-241 5693, www.adventures house.com. Rooms for up to 4, also has doubles (**D**), with bath and hot water, free internet, national calls, pleasant, quiet, a short walk from all facilities, airport transfer, kitchen, bike rental US$15 per day. Associated with Fly Adventure, see Paragliding, page 299.

F pp **Albergue Turístico Juvenil Internacional**, Av Casimiro Ulloa 328, San Antonio, T01-446 5488, www.limahostell. com.pe. Dormitory accommodation, **C** in a double private room, basic cafeteria, travel information, cooking (minimal) and laundry facilities, swimming pool often empty, extra charge for kitchen facilities, safe, situated in a nice villa; 20 mins' walk from the beach. Bus No 2 or colectivos pass Av Benavides to the centre; taxi to centre, US$2.50.

F pp **Albergue Verde**, Grimaldo del Solar 459, T01-445 3816, www.albergue verde.com. Nice small hostal, comfortable beds, **D** per person in double, friendly owner, breakfast included, airport transfers US$15, bus terminal transfer US$4.

F pp **Condor's House**, Martín Napanga 137, T01-446 7267, www.condorshouse.com. Award-winning hostel in a quiet part of Miraflores, shared rooms with lockers, good bathrooms, also a twin and a matrimonial (**C**), with breakfast, good meeting place, TV room with films, book exchange, internet, Wi-Fi,

kitchen, *almuerzo criollo* and *parrillada* prepared once a week, bar, not a party hostel. Helpful manager, Arturo Luna, and staff; friendly dog, Chévere.

F pp **Dragonfly**, Av 28 de Julio 190, T01-654 3226, www.dragonflyhostels.com. Shared rooms with lockers, without bath, double room **D**, breakfast included, internet, Wi-Fi, kitchen, can arrange surfing, papapenting and other sports and tours, best to reserve a bed in advance.

F pp **Explorer's House**, Av Alfredo León 158, by 10th block of Av José Pardo, T01-241 5002, explorers_house@yahoo.es. No sign, but plenty of indications of the house number, with breakfast, dorm with shared bath, or double rooms with bath, hot water, use of kitchen, laundry service, Spanish classes, English spoken, very welcoming.

F pp **HQ Villa**, Independencia 1288, T01-221 3221, info@hqvilla.com. Peruvian/British-owned hostel with mixed and girls-only dorms and doubles (**C**) in a modern house, garden, lounge, double kitchen, receptionists speak 3 languages, airport pick-up, with breakfast, internet, Wi-Fi, spacious, nice atmosphere.

F pp **Lex Luthor's House**, Porta 550, T01-242 7059, www.thelexluthorshouse.com. Dormitories and doubles (**D** with and without bath), breakfast included, pleasant family house, small, clean, use of kitchen, book exchange, internet, Wi-Fi, good value. In the same entrance, owned by a cousin, is **The Angels Inn**, No 540, T01-241 4614, www.theangelsinnperu.com, rooms with and without bath, bunk rooms, kitchen, Wi-Fi, reserve in advance.

F pp **Loki Backpackers**, José Galvez 576, T01-651 2966, www.lokihostel.com. In a quiet area, the capital's sister to the party hostel of the same name in Cuzco, **D** in double room, good showers, with breakfast (cooked breakfast extra), Fri barbecues, use of kitchen, free internet, lockers, airport transfer extra.

F Pariwana, Av Larco 189, T01-242 4350, www.pariwana-hostel.com. New in 2009, party hostel with dorms and shared bath, individual lockers with power outlets so you can leave your gadgets charging in a safe place.

F pp **Pirwa**, González Prada 179, T01-444 1266 and Coronel Inclán 494, T01-242 4059, www.pirwahostelsperu.com. Members of a chain of hostels in Peru (Cuzco, Arequipa, Puno, Nazca); G Prada branch has shared rooms with shared bath, Inclán branch is B&B with bath (**D**). Prices include breakfast, lockers, internet, Wi-Fi, use of kitchen, transfers, bike rental.

G pp **Blue House**, José González 475, T01-445 0476, www.bluehouse.com.pe. A true backpacker hostel, most rooms with bath including a double (**F**), basic but good value for the location, breakfast included, internet, Wi-Fi, use of kitchen, *terraza* with *parrilla*, films to watch.

G pp **Casa del Mochilero**, Cesareo Chacaltana 130A, T01-444 9089, pilaryv@ hotmail.com. Ask for Pilar or Juan, dorms or **E** in double room on terrace, all with shared bath, breakfast and internet extra, hot water, Wi-Fi, use of kitchen. lots of information. Not to be confused with **Mochilero's Inn** at No 136, which also has dorms in **G** range.

Barranco p284, map p285

C Domeyer, C Domeyer 296, T01-247 1413, www.domeyerhostel.net. Friendly and clean, **E** in shared room, hot water 24 hrs, laundry service, secure and gay-friendly.

E pp **Barranco's Backpackers Inn**, Malecón Castilla 260, T01-247 1326. Ocean view, colourful rooms, all en suite, shared and private rooms with cable TV, free internet with Wi-Fi, kitchen facilities. Breakfast included. Discount for **SAE** members.

E Casa Barranco, Av Grau 982, T01-477 0984, www.lacasabarranco.8m.com. There is no sign on the street, so just ring the bell. All rooms have shared bath, dormitory costs **F**, also monthly rentals available. Has kitchen, DVD room, cable TV and PS1. Helpful owner, Felipe. Discount for SAE members.

E pp **Hospedaje La Casona de Barranco**, Av Bolognesi 271, T01-247 8835. By Bulevar metropolitano stop. With bath, hot water,

cable TV, comfortable and safe, no breakfast or internet. Nextdoor is **La Vieja Taberna** restaurant with lunch *menú*.

E Safe in Lima, Alfredo Silva 150, T01-252 7330, www.safeinlima.com. Quiet, Belgian-run hostal with family atmosphere, with breakfast, very helpful, airport pick-up US$16.50, good value, reserve in advance, lots of information for travellers. Also a travel agency and tour operator, see page 301.

F pp **The Point**, Malecón Junín 300, T01-628 7952, www.thepointhostels.com. Rooms range from doubles to large dormitories, all with shared bath, very popular with backpackers (book in advance at weekends), breakfast included, internet, cable TV, laundry, kitchen facilities, gay-friendly, party atmosphere most of the time, **The Pointless Pub** open 2000 till whenever, weekly barbecues, therapeutic massage next door, can arrange bungee jumping, flight tickets and volunteering. Also has hostels in Arequipa, Cuzco, Máncora and Puno.

F pp **San Mart Inn**, Av San Martín 135, T01-247 1522, www.sanmart-inn.com. Backpacker hostel, also has doubles (**D**, cheaper with shared bath), hot water, with breakfast, Wi-Fi.

🍴 Eating

19% state tax and 10% service will be added to your bill in middle- and upper-class restaurants.

Central Lima p275, map p276

🍴🍴🍴 **Wa Lok**, Jr Paruro 864, Barrio Chino, T01-427 2656. Good dim sum, cakes and fortune cookies (when you pay the bill). English spoken, very friendly. Also at Av Angamos Oeste 700, Miraflores, T01-447 1329.

🍴🍴 **Antaño**, Ucayali 332, opposite the Torre Tagle Palace, T01-426 2372. Good, typical Peruvian food, nice patio. Recommended.

🍴🍴 **La Choza Náutica**, Jr Breña 204 and 211 behind Plaza Bolognesi, Breña, T01-483 8087. Good *ceviche* and friendly service, with 2 branches on this street, consistently recommended.

¶¶ L'Eau Vive, Ucayali 370, also opposite the Torre Tagle Palace, T01-427 5612. Mon-Sat, 1230-1500 and 1930-2130. Run by nuns, fixed-price lunch menu, Peruvian-style in interior dining room, or à la carte in either of dining rooms that open onto the patio, excellent, profits go to the poor, *Ave María* is sung nightly at 2100.

¶¶ Salon Capon, Jr Paruro 819. Good dim sum, at this recommended *chifa*. Also has a branch at **Larcomar** shopping centre, which is **¶¶¶**, elegant and equally recommended.

¶¶-¶ De César, Ancash 300, T01-428 8740. Open 0700-2300. Old-fashioned atmosphere, apart from the 3 TVs. Offers breakfasts, snacks, seafood, including *ceviche* and *chicharrones de marisco*. Meat dishes, pastas, pizza, juices, coffees and teas. Good food.

¶¶-¶ San Paolo, Ancash 454, T01-427 4600. Open 0600-2400. Peruvian food, also has a good *menú diario* for US$3-4.

¶ Machu Picchu, Jr Ancash 312. Closed for breakfast. Huge portions, grimy bathrooms, yet very popular.

¶ Natur, Moquegua 132, 1 block from Jr de la Unión, T01-427 8281. The owner, Humberto Valdivia, is also president of the SAE's board of directors; the casual conversation, as well as his vegetarian restaurant, is certainly recommended.

Cafés

Accllahuasy, Jr Ancash 400. Daily 0700-2300. Around the corner from **Hostal España**, good Peruvian dishes.

Café Carrara, Jr Ica 330, attached to **Hostal Roma**. Open daily from breakfast until 2300, pancakes, sandwiches.

La Catedral del Pisco, Av Uruguay 114, T01-330 0079, lacatedraldelpisco@hotmail.com. Open 0800-2200 for *comida criolla*, drinks, free Peruvian coffee or pisco sour (both excellent) for Footprint guide owners, live music at night. See also **Víctor Travel Service**, page 301, travel agency and information service, includes online facilities for visitors.

Lima suburbs

Pueblo Libre *p280*
¶¶ Café del Museo, at the Museo Larco, Av Bolívar 1515, Pueblo Libre, T01-462 4757, www.cafedelmuseo.com. Daily 0900-1800. Seating inside and on the terrace. Specially designed interior, selection of salads, fine Peruvian dishes, pastas and seafood, a tapas bar of traditional Peruvian foods, snacks, desserts and cocktails. Highly regarded.

San Isidro *p283, map p281*
¶¶¶ Alfresco, Santa Lucía 295 (no sign), T01-422 8915. Best known for its tempting seafood and *ceviche*, also pastas and rice dishes, expensive wines.

¶¶¶ Antica Pizzería, Av Dos de Mayo 728, T01-222 8437, www.anticapizzeria.com.pe. Very popular, great ambience, excellent food, Italian owner. Also **Antica Trattoria** in Barranco at Alfonso Ugarte 242, and an excellent bar, **Antica Taberna**, with a limited range of food at Conquistadores 605, San Isidro, very good value, fashionable, get there early for a seat.

¶¶¶ Asia de Cuba, Conquistadores 780, T01-222 4940. Popular, serving a mix of Asian, Cuban and Peruvian dishes. It also has a reputation for its bar and nightclub; try the martinis.

¶¶¶ Casa Hacienda Moreyra, Av Paz Soldán 290, T01-444 4022, www.casahacienda moreyra.com. Closed Sun and 1600-1900. A beautifully restored colonial house offering a fabulous *criolla* food.

¶¶¶ Matsuei, C Manuel Bañón 260, T01-422 4323, www.matsueiperu.com. Sushi bar and Japanese dishes, very popular, among the best Japanese in Lima.

¶¶¶ Valentino, Manuel Bañón 215, T01-441 6174. One of Lima's best international restaurants, formal, look for the tiny brass sign.

¶¶ Chez Philippe, Av 2 de Mayo 748, T01-222 4953, www.chez-philippe.net. Pizza, pasta and crêpes, wood oven, rustic decor (same owners as **Pizza B&B** in Huaraz).

ŸŸ **Como Agua Para Chocolate**, Pancho Fierro 108, T01-222 0297, aguapachocolat@terra.com.pe. Dutch/Mexican-owned restaurant, specializing in Mexican food as the name suggests, also has a very amusing Dutch night once a month. SAE members get a discount.

ŸŸ **Segundo Muelle**, Av Conquistadores 490, T01-421 1206, and Av Canaval y Moreyra (aka Corpac) 605. Excellent *ceviche* and other seafood, popular with the younger crowd.

Cafés

News Café, Av Santa Luisa 110. Great salads and desserts, popular and expensive.

T'anta, Pancho Fierro 115 (1 block from Hotel El Olivar). Huge selection of entrées and desserts, very smart with prices to match.

Miraflores *p284, map p282*

C San Ramón, known as 'Pizza Street' (across from Parque Kennedy), is a pedestrian walkway lined with outdoor restaurants/bars/discos open until the wee small hrs. It's very popular, with good-natured touts trying to entice diners and drinkers with free offers.

ŸŸŸ **Astrid y Gaston**, Cantuarias 175, T01-242 5387, www.astridygaston.com. Exceptional local/Novo Andino and international cuisine, one of the best in Lima, owners are Gastón Acurio and his wife Astrid. Also has a bar.

ŸŸŸ **Café Voltaire**, Av Dos de Mayo 220, T01-447 4807. Closed Sun. International cuisine with emphasis on French dishes, beautifully cooked food, pleasant ambience, good service.

ŸŸŸ **El Kapallaq**, Av Petit Thouars 4844, T01-444 4149, www.elkapallaqrestaurant.blogspot.com. Mon-Fri 1200-1800. Prize-winning Peruvian restaurant specializing in seafood and fish, excellent *ceviches*.

ŸŸŸ **El Rincón Gaucho**, Av Armendáriz 580, T01-447 4778, www.rincongauchoperu.com. Renowned for its steaks.

ŸŸŸ **El Señorío de Sulco**, Malecón Cisneros 1470, T01-441 0183, www.senoriodesulco.com. Overlooking a clifftop park, with ocean views from upstairs. Forget the Footprint grading, this is a '5-fork' restaurant that some believe is the best in Lima, all Peruvian food, à la carte and buffet, piscos, wines, piano music at night.

ŸŸŸ **Huaca Pucllana**, Gral Borgoño cuadra 8 s/n, alt cuadra 45 Av Arequipa, T01-445 4042, www.resthuacapucllana.com. Facing the archaeological site of the same name, contemporary Peruvian fusion cooking, very good food in an unusual setting, popular with groups.

ŸŸŸ **Las Brujas de Cachiche**, Av Bolognesi 460, T01-447 1883, www.brujasdecachiche.com.pe. An old mansion converted into bars and dining rooms, traditional food (menu in Spanish and English), best *Lomo Saltado* in town, live *criollo* music.

ŸŸŸ **La Trattoria**, Manuel Bonilla 106, 1 block from Parque Kennedy, T01-446 7002. Italian cuisine, popular, good desserts. Has another branch, **La Bodeguita**, opposite entrance to Huaca Pucllana.

ŸŸŸ **Panchita**, Av 2 de Mayo 298, T01-242 5957. Another Gaston Acurio restaurant, specialising in *anticuchos* and *tamales*. Very good and popular, be prepared to queue as you cannot book in advance. Closed Sun.

ŸŸŸ **Rosa Náutica**, Espigón No 4, Circuito de Playas, T01-445 0149, www.larosanautica.com. Daily 1230-0200. Built on old British-style pier, in Lima Bay. Delightful opulence, finest fish cuisine, experience the atmosphere by buying an expensive beer in the bar at sunset.

ŸŸŸ **Sí Señor**, Jr Bolognesi 706, T01-445 3789, www.sisenor.org. Mexican food, cheerful, interesting decor, huge portions.

ŸŸŸ-ŸŸ **Las Tejas**, Diez Canseco 340, T01-444 4360. Daily 1100-2300. Good, Peruvian food, vegetarian dishes, recommended for *ceviche*.

ŸŸ **Café Tarata**, Pasaje Tarata 260, T01-446 6330. Good atmosphere, family-run, good varied menu including Argentine steaks.

ŸŸ **Dalmacia**, San Fernando 401, T01-445 7917. Spanish-owned, casual gourmet restaurant, excellent.

ŸŸ **El Huarike**, Enrique Palacios 140, T01-241 6086, www.elhuarike.com. Rub shoulders with Miraflores high-fliers at this hip, gourmet restaurant which serves delicious combinations of *ceviche* and sushi.

¶¶ **Lobo del Mar - Octavio Otani**, Colón 587, T01-242 1871. The basic apperance of this small seafood restaurant is deceptive. One of the oldest *cevicherías* in Miraflores, Octavio Otani makes a mean *ceviche* – and a good selection of other seafood dishes. Choose your fish from the display counter if you want to.

¶¶ **Mama Olla**, Pasaje Tarata 248. Charming café on a pedestrian walkway, with huge menu and big portions. There are several other places to eat on this street.

¶¶-¶ **Café Beirut**, Mártir Olaya 204. Excellent Middle Eastern restaurant, close to the centre of Miraflores, enthusiastic waiters, superb falafel and Arabic favourites, both sweet and savoury. Also a good selection of international dishes.

¶¶-¶ **Shehadi**, Av Diagonal 220. Facing Parque Kennedy, US-owned, brightly lit restaurant specializing in pizza but also serving typical Peruvian fare. Good-value daytime menus. Popular with locals and foreigners.

¶ **El Parquetito**, Diez Canseco 150. Good cheap menu, serves breakfast, eat either inside or out.

¶ **Govinda**, Schell 630. Vegetarian, from the Hare Krishna foundation, lunch *menú* US$3.

¶ **Madre Natura**, Chiclayo 815. Closes 2100. Natural foods shop and eating place, good.

¶ **Sandwich.com**, Av Diagonal 234. Good, cheap sandwiches with interesting combinations of fillings.

Cafés

Café Café, Martín Olaya 250, near the Parque Kennedy roundabout on the corner with Av Diagonal 598, T01-444 5579. Good atmosphere, over 100 different blends of coffee, good salads and sandwiches, very popular with 'well-to-do' Limeños, has Wi-Fi. Also in Larcomar.

Café de la Paz, Lima 351, middle of Parque Kennedy. Good outdoor café right on the park, expensive, great cocktails.

Café La Máquina, Alcanfores 323. Friendly small café and bar with good cocktails,

interesting sandwiches and great cakes. To while away the time there are hundreds of Rubik's cubes to set straight.

Café Zeta, Mcal Oscar R Benavides 598 y José Gálvez. American owned, excellent Peruvian coffee, teas, hot chocolate, and the best home-made cakes away from home, cheap.

C'est si bon, Av Cdte Espinar 663. Excellent cakes by the slice or whole, best in Lima.

Chef's Café, Av Larco 763. A smart place for a wide selection of sandwiches and light lunches, with good coffee.

Haiti, Av Diagonal 160, Parque Kennedy. Open almost round the clock daily, great for people watching, good ice cream.

La Tiendecita Blanca, Av Larco 111 on Parque Kennedy. One of Miraflores' oldest, expensive, good people-watching, very good cakes, European-style food and delicatessen.

Barranco p284, map p285

¶¶¶ **Canta Rana**, Génova 101, T01-247 7274. Sun-Mon 1200-1800, Tue-Sat 1200-2300. Good *ceviche*, expensive, small portions, but the most popular local place on Sun.

¶¶¶ **La Costa Verde**, on Barranquito beach, T01-441 3086. Daily 1200-2400. Excellent fish and wine, expensive but recommended as the best by Limeños. Sun buffet.

¶¶¶-¶¶ **La Fonda de los Suspiros**, Pedro de Osma 102. Restaurant/bar by the plaza, serving meat, pasta, fish and seafood dishes, with good reports.

¶¶¶-¶¶ **Tío Mario**, Jr Zepita 214, on the steps to the Puente de Suspiros. Excellent *anticuchería*, serving delicious Peruvian kebabs, always busy, fantastic service, varied menu and good prices.

¶¶¶ **Las Mesitas**, Av Grau 341, T01-477 4199. Open 1200-0200. Traditional tea rooms-cum-restaurant, serving Creole food and traditional desserts which you won't find anywhere else, lunch *menú* served till 1400, US$3.

¶¶-¶ **Expreso Virgen de Guadalupe**, San Martín y Ayacucho. Vegetarian buffet in an old railway carriage, also seating in the garden, more expensive at weekends, has Wi-Fi.

ᵀᵀ-ᵀ Sóngoro Cosongo, Ayacucho 281, T01-247 4730, at the top of the steps down to Puente de Suspiros. Good value *comida criolla*, 'un poco de todo'.

Cafés

Istanbul, Grau 310. Turkish café, new in 2010, with Wi-Fi.

La Cía, Grau 320. Colourful murals, young and trendy scene, friendly, good food such as lunch *menú* and desserts. Turns into a bar later at night.

🌓 Bars and clubs

Central Lima *p275, map p276*
The centre of town, specifically Jr de la Unión, has many bars and discos. It's best to avoid the nightspots around the intersection of Av Tacna, Av Piérola and Av de la Vega. These places are rough and foreigners will receive much unwanted attention.

For latest recommendations for gay and lesbian places, check out http://lima.queer city.info/index.html, www.deambiente. com/web and www.gayperu.com.

Estadio Futbol Sports Bar, Av Nicolás de Piérola 926 on the Plaza San Martín, T01-428 8866. Beautiful bar with a disco, football theme, with life-sized models of famous footballers, with whom you can have a drink! Good international and Creole food.

Miraflores *p284, map p282*
Bartinis, in Larcomar, 101-241 1299, www.bartini-larcomar.com. Good cocktails, trendy crowd, expensive.

La Tasca, Av Diez Canseco 117, very near Parque Kennedy, part of the **Flying Dog** group and underneath one of the hostels (see Sleeping, page 289). Spanish-style bar with cheap beer (for Miraflores). Attracts an eclectic crowd including ex-pats, travellers and locals. Gay-friendly. Small and crowded.

Media Naranja, Schell 130, at the bottom of Parque Kennedy. Brazilian bar with typical drinks and food.

Murphy's, Schell 619, T01-447 1082. Open Mon-Sat from 1600. Happy hours every day with different offers, lots of entertainment, very popular.

The Old Pub, San Ramón 295 (Pizza St), www.oldpub.com.pe. Cosy, with live music most days.

Treff Pub Alemán, Av Benavides 571-104, T01-444 0148, www.treff-pub-aleman.com (hidden from the main road behind a cluster of tiny houses signed "Los Duendes"). A wide range of German beers, plus cocktails, good atmosphere, darts and other games.

Voluntarios Pub, Independencia 131, T01-445 3939, www.voluntariospub.com.pe. All staff are volunteers from non-profit organizations who benefit by receiving 90% of the profits made. Good atmosphere, music and drinks; it's nice to know that other people are benefiting from your partying.

Barranco *p284, map p285*
Barranco is the capital of Lima nightlife. The following is a short list of some of the better bars and clubs. Pasaje Sánchez Carrión, right off the main plaza, used to be the heart of it all. Watering holes and discos line both sides of this pedestrian walkway. Av Grau, just across the street from the plaza, is also lined with bars, eg **Las Terrazas**, Av Grau 290, **Déjà Vu**, No 294. Many of the bars in this area turn into discos later on.

Ayahuasca, San Martín 130. In the stunning Berninzon House from the Republican era, chilled out lounge bar with several areas for eating, drinking and dancing. Food is expensive and portions are small, but go for the atmosphere.

El Dragón, N de Piérola 168, T01-797 1033, www.eldragon.com.pe. Popular bar and venue for music, theatre and painting.

El Grill de Costa Verde, part of the **Costa Verde** restaurant on Barranco beach. Young crowd, packed at weekends.

Juanitos, Av Grau, opposite the park. Open from 1600-0400. Barranco's oldest bar, where writers and artists congregate, a perfect spot to start the evening.

La Noche, Bolognesi 307, at Pasaje Sánchez Carrión. A Lima institution and high standard, live music, Mon is jazz night, all kicks off at around 2200.

La Posada del Angel, 3 branches, Pedro de Osma 164 and 218 and Av Prol San Martín 157, T01-247 5544. These are popular bars serving snacks and meals.

La Posada del Mirador, near the Puente de los Suspiros (Bridge of Sighs). Beautiful view of the ocean, but you pay for the privilege.

Mochileros, Av Pedro de Osma 135. Good pub in a beautiful house, weekend events.

Santos Café & Espirituosos, Jr Zepita 203, just above the Puente de Suspiros, T01-247 4609. Mon-Sat 1700-0100. Favourite spot for trendy young professionals who want to drop a few hundred soles, relaxed, informal but pricey.

Sargento Pimienta, Bolognesi 755. Live music, always a favourite with Limeños.

Del Carajo, San Ambrosio 328, Barranco, T01-241 7977, www.delcarajo.com.pe. All types of traditional music.

De Rompe y Raja, Manuel Segura 127, Barranco, T01-247 3271, www.derompey raja.net. Popular, Thu, Fri, Sat for music, dancing and *criolla* food.

La Candelaria, Av Bolognesi 292, Barranco, T01-247 1314, www.lacandelariaperu.com. Fri-Sat from 2130. A good Barranco *peña*,

La Estación de Barranco, at Pedro de Osma 112, Barranco, T01-477 5030, www.laestaciondebarranco.com. Open from Thu. Good, family atmosphere, varied shows.

Las Brisas de Titicaca, Pasaje Walkuski 168, at 1st block of Av Brasil near Plaza Bolognesi, T01-332 1901, www.brisasdeltiticaca.com. A Lima institution.

Sachun, Av del Ejército 657, Miraflores, T01-441 0123, www.sachunperu.com. Great shows on weekdays as well.

◉ Entertainment

Cinema

The newspaper *El Comercio* lists cinema information in the section called *Luces*. Tue is reduced price at most cinemas and Mon and Wed are cheaper than Thu-Sun. Most films are in English with subtitles and cost US$2 in the centre and around US$4-5 in Miraflores. The best cinema chains in the city are **Cinemark**, **Cineplanet** and **UVK Multicines**.

Theatre and concert tickets can be booked through **Teleticket**, T01-610 8888, Mon-Fri 0900-1900, www.teleticket.com.pe. Also in **Wong** supermarkets.

Peñas

De Cajón, C Merino 2nd block, near 6th block of Av del Ejército, Miraflores. Good *música negra*.

◉ Festivals and events

18 Jan The anniversary of the founding of Lima, with a Peruvian music festival on the previous night (17 Jan), culminating in the Plaza de Armas.

Semana Santa, or Holy Week, is a colourful spectacle with processions.

28-29 Jul Independence, has music and fireworks in the Plaza de Armas on the evening before.

30 Aug Santa Rosa de Lima.

Mid-Sep Mistura, www.mistura.pe, a huge gastronomy fair in Parque Exposición, with Peruvian foods to try, celebrity chefs, workshops and more. Fast gaining a reputation as one of the best food fairs in South America.

Oct This is the month of **Our Lord of the Miracles** with impressive processions starting at Las Nazarenas church on the 4th block of Av Tacna.

O Shopping

Alpaca and cotton

There are bargains in high-quality Pima cotton. Shops selling alpaca items include:

Alpaca 859, Av Larco 859, Miraflores. Good-quality alpaca and baby alpaca products.

Da Capo, Aramburú 920, dpto 402, San Isidro, T01-441 0714. Beautiful alpaca scarves and shawls in new designs.

Kuna by Alpaca 111, Av Larco 671, Miraflores, T01-447 1623, www.kuna.com.pe. High-quality alpaca, baby alpaca and vicuña items. Also at Av Jorge Basadre Grohmann 380, San Isidro, T01-440 2320, in **Larcomar** shopping centre, Local 1-07, at the airport, and in the Museo Larco Herrera.

Bookshops

Crisol, Ovalo Gutiérrez, Av Santa Cruz 816, San Isidro, T01-221 1010, below **Cine Planet**. Large bookshop with café, titles in English, French and Spanish. Also in **Jockey Plaza Shopping Center**, Av Javier Prado Este 4200, Surco, T01-436 0004, and other branches, www.crisol.com.pe.

Epoca, Av Cdte Espinar 864, Miraflores, T01-241 2951. Great selection of books, mostly in Spanish.

Ibero Librerías, Av Oscar R Benavides 500, T01-242 2798, Larco 199, T01-445 5520, and in **Larcomar**, Miraflores, www.iberolibros.com. Stocks Footprint books as well as a wide range of other titles.

Special Book Services, Av Angamos Oeste 301, Miraflores, T01-241 8490, www.sbs.com.pe. Holds stock of international books in several languages. Has a branch in **Larcomar** and others around the country.

Virrey chain has a great selection, but few in English: Pasaje Los Escribanos 107-115, Lima centre behind the Municipalidad, T01-427 5080, and Miguel Dasso 147, T01-440 0607, San Isidro, www.elvirrey.com.

Camping equipment

It's better to bring all camping and hiking gear from home. Camping gas (the most popular brand is **Doite**, which comes in small blue bottles) is available from any large hardware store or bigger supermarket, about US$3.

Alpamayo, Av Larco 345, Miraflores at Parque Kennedy, T01-445 1671. Mon-Fri 1000-1330, 1430-2000, Sat 1000-1400. Sleeping mats, boots, rock shoes, climbing gear, water filters, tents, backpacks, etc, very expensive but top-quality equipment. Owner speaks fluent English and offers good information.

Altamira, Arica 880, Parque Damert, behind Wong on Óvalo Gutiérrez, Miraflores, T01-445 1286. Sleeping bags, climbing gear, hiking gear and tents.

Camping Center, Av Benavides 1620, Miraflores, T01-242 1779, www.camping peru.com. Mon-Fri 1000-2000, Sat 1000-1400. Selection of tents, backpacks, stoves, camping and climbing gear.

Minex, Gral Borgoño 394 y Piura, Miraflores, T01-445 3923 (ring bell). Quality camping gear for all types of weather, made-to-order products as well.

Tatoo, CC Larcomar, locs 123-126, T01-242 1938 and CC Jockey Plaza loc 127, Av Javier Prado 4200, T01-436 6055, www.tatoo.ws. For top-quality imported ranges and own brands of equipment.

Todo Camping, Av Angamos Oeste 350, Miraflores, near Av Arequipa, T01-447 6279. Sells 100% deet, blue gas canisters, lots of accessories, tents, crampons and backpacks.

Handicrafts

Since so many artisans have come to Lima, it is possible to find any kind of handicraft in the capital. Miraflores is a good place for high-quality, expensive handicrafts; there are many shops on and around Av La Paz.

Agua y Tierra, Diez Canseco 298 y Alcanfores, Miraflores, T01-444 6980. Fine crafts and indigenous art.

Arte XXI, Av La Paz 678, Miraflores, T01-447 9777. Gallery and store for Peruvian handicrafts.

Artesanía Santo Domingo, Plaza Santo Domingo, by the church of that name, in centre, T01-428 9860. Good Peruvian crafts.

Centro Comercial El Alamo, corner of La Paz y Diez Canseco, Miraflores. *Artesanía* shops with good choice.

Dédalo, Paseo Sáenz Peña 295, Barranco, T01-477 0562. A labyrinthine shop selling furniture, jewellery and other items, as good as a gallery. It also has a nice coffee shop and has cinema shows.

Kuntur Huasi, Ocharan 182, Miraflores, opposite **Sol de Oro** hotel, look for the sign above the wall, T01-447 7173, kunturh@speedy.com.pe. English-speaking owners are very knowledgeable about Peruvian textiles; often have exhibitions of fine folk art and crafts.

La Casa de la Mujer Artesana, Juan Pablo Ferandini 1550 (Av Brasil cuadra 15), Pueblo Libre, T01-423 8840, www.casadela mujerartesana.com. Mon-Fri 0900-1300, 1400-1700. A cooperative run by the Movimiento Manuela Ramos, excellent quality work mostly from *pueblos jóvenes*.

Las Pallas, Cajamarca 212, Barranco, T01-477 4629. Mon-Sat 0900-1900. Very high-quality handicrafts, English, French and German spoken.

Luz Hecho a Mano, Berlín 399, Miraflores, T01-446 7098, www.luzhechoamano.com. Lovely handmade handbags, wallets and other leather goods including clothing that lasts for years and can be custom-made.

Jewellery

On C La Esperanza and on C La Paz, Miraflores, dozens of shops offer gold and silverware at very reasonable prices.
Ilaria, Av 2 de Mayo 308, San Isidro, T01-221 8575. Jewellery and silverware with interesting designs. There are other branches in Lima, Cuzco and Arequipa. Recommended.

Maps

Instituto Geográfico Nacional (IGN),
Av Aramburú 1190, Surquillo, T01-618 9800, ext 119, www.ign.gob.pe. Mon-Fri 0800-1730. It has topographical maps of the whole country, mostly at 1:100,000, political and physical maps of all departments and satellite and aerial photographs. They also have a new series of tourist maps for trekking, eg of the Cordillera Blanca, the Cuzco area, at 1:250,000. You may be asked to show your passport when buying these maps. **South American Explorers** (see page 272) also stocks a selection of the most popular maps.

Lima 2000, Av Arequipa 2625, Lince (near the intersection with Av Javier Prado), T01-440 3486, www.lima2000.com.pe. Mon-Fri 0900-1300 and 1400-1800. Has an excellent street map of Lima (the only one worth buying), US$10, or US$14 as booklet. Provincial maps and a country road map as well. Good for road conditions and distances, perfect for driving or cycling. **South American Explorers** also stocks these maps.

Markets

Av Petit Thouars, in Miraflores. At blocks 51-54 (near Parque Kennedy, parallel to Av Arequipa) is a crafts market area, popularly called Museo Inca, but made up of several sections, each named after a pre-Hispanic civilization. This is the largest crafts arcade in Miraflores. All are open 7 days a week until late(ish).

Parque Kennedy, the main park of Miraflores, hosts a daily crafts market open 1700-2300.

Polvos Azules, on García Naranjo, La Victoria, just off Av Grau in the centre of town. This is the official black market of Lima. The normal connotations of a black market do not apply here as this establishment is an accepted part of Lima society, condoned by the government and frequented by people of all economic backgrounds. It's good for cameras, hiking boots, music and personal stereos. This is not a safe area, so be alert and put your money in your front pockets.

Supermarkets

Supermarket chains include **E Wong**, **Metro**, **Plaza Vea**, **Tottus** and the upmarket **Vivanda**. They are all well stocked and carry a decent supply of imported goods.

▲ Activities and tours

Cycling

See www.ciclismoperu.com.
Best Internacional, Av Cdte Espinar 320, Miraflores, T01-446 4044. Mon-Sat 1000-1400, 1600-2000. Leisure and racing bikes, also repairs, parts and accessories.
Biclas, Av Conquistadores 641, San Isidro, T01-440 0890. Mon-Fri 1000-1300, 1600-2000, Sat 1000-1300. Knowledgeable staff, tours possible, good selection of bikes, repairs and accessories, cheap airline boxes.
BikeMavil, Av Aviación 4023, Surco, T01-449 8435. Mon-Sat 0930-2100. Rents mountain and racing bikes, repairs, tours.
Bike Tours of Lima, Bolívar 150, Miraflores, T01-445 3172, www.biketoursoflima.com. Offer a variety of day tours through the city of Lima by bike, also bicycle rentals.
Casa Okuyama, Manco Cápac 590, La Victoria, T01-330 9131. Mon-Fri 0900-1300, 1415-1800, Sat 0900-1300. Repairs, parts, try here for 28-in tyres, excellent service.
Cycloturismo Peru, Jr Emilio Fernández 640, Santa Beatriz; T01-433 7981, www.ciclo turismo peru.com. Offers good-value cycling trips around Lima and beyond, as well as bike rental. The owner, Aníbal Paredes, speaks good English, is very knowledgeable and is the owner of **Mont Blanc Gran Hotel**.
Perú Bike, T01-260 8225, www.perubike. com. Experienced agency leading tours, professional guiding, mountain bike school and workshop.
Willy Pro (Williams Arce), Av Angamos Este 2485, San Borja, T01-99-919 2514 (mob). Mon-Sat 0800-2000. Selection of specialized bikes, helpful staff.

Paragliding

Andean Trail Perú, T01-99-836 3436 (mob), www.andeantrailperu.com. For parapenting tandem flights, US$53, and courses, US$600 for 10 days. They also have a funday for US$120 to learn the basics of parapenting. Parapenting, trekking and kayaking in the Cuzco area can be arranged. Recommended.

Fly Adventure, Alfredo León 234, of 202, Miraflores, T01-241 5693, T01-99-754 2011 (mob), www.flyadventure.net. 15-min tandem flights over the cliffs, 1-day course and 7-day course. Also offer paragliding tours. Recommended.

Tour operators

Do not conduct business anywhere other than in the agency's office and insist on a written contract. Bus offices or the airport are not the places to arrange and pay for tours. You may be dealing with representatives of companies that either do not exist or who fall far short of what is paid for.

Most of those in Lima specialize in selling air tickets, or in setting up a connection in the place where you want to start a tour. Shop around and compare prices; also check all information carefully. It is best to use a travel agent in the town closest to the place you wish to visit; it is cheaper and they are more reliable.
Andean Tours, Schell 319, of 304-305, Miraflores, T01-241 1222, www.andean-tours.com. Recommended for bespoke arrangements.
AQP (Travex), Av Santa Cruz 621, Miraflores, T01-710 3900, www.saaqp.com.pe. Comprehensive service, tours offered throughout the country.
Aracari Travel Consulting, Schell 237, of 602, Miraflores, T01-651 2424, www.aracari.com. Regional tours throughout Peru, also 'themed' and activity tours, has a very good reputation.
Class Adventure Travel (CAT), San Martín 800, Miraflores, T01-444 1652, www.cat-travel.com/peru/information. Dutch-owned and run, CAT has offices in several Latin American countries and offers tailor-made travel solutions throughout the continent. Highly recommended.
Coltur, Av Reducto 1255, Miraflores, T01-615 5555, www.coltur.com.pe. Helpful, well- organized and experienced tours.
Condor Travel, Armando Blondet 249, San Isidro, T01-615 3000, www.condortravel.com.

Peruvian HQ of highly regarded, South America-wide travel company, offices in Cuzco, Arequipa, commitment to social responsibility with Misminay Project near Cuzco, and others.

Dasatariq, Jr Francisco Bolognesi 510, Miraflores, T01-513 4400, www.dasatariq.com. Also in Cuzco. Well-organized, helpful, with a good reputation.

Domiruth Travel Service, Av Petit Thouars 4305, T01-610 6022, www.domiruth.com.pe. Tours throughout Peru, from the mystical to adventure travel. See also **Peru 4x4 Adventures**, part of Domiruth, T01-610 6000, www.peru4x4adventures.com, for exclusive 4WD tours with German, English, Spanish, Italian and Portuguese-speaking drivers.

Ecocruceros, Av Arequipa 4964, of 202, Miraflores, T01-226 8530, www.islaspalomino.com. Daily departures at 1000 from Plaza Grau in Callao to see the sea lions at Islas Palomino, 30-40 mins wetsuit swimming with guide, snack lunch, US$35 (take ID). Transfer from Lima US$12 (US$24 for 1 person).

Explorandes, C San Fernando 320, Miraflores, T01-715 2323, www.explorandes.com. Award-winning company. Offers a wide range of adventure and cultural tours throughout the country. Also offices in Cuzco and Huaraz.

Fertur Peru Travel, C Schell 485, Miraflores, T01-445 1760, and Jr Junín 211, Plaza de Armas, T01-427 1958 (USA/Canada T1-877-247 0055 toll free, UK T020-3002 3811), www.fertur-travel.com. Open 0900-1900. Siduith Ferrer de Vecchio, CEO of this agency, is highly recommended; she offers up-to-date, correct tourist information on a national level, but also great prices on national and international flights, discounts for those with ISIC and Youth cards and **SAE** members. Other services include flight reconfirmations, hotel reservations and transfers to and from the airport or bus stations. Also tours.

Il Tucano Peru, Elías Aguirre 633, Miraflores, T01-444 9361, 24-hr number T01-975 05375. Personalized tours for groups or individuals

throughout Peru, also 4WD overland trips, 1st-class drivers and guides, good service. Recommended.

Info Perú, Jr de la Unión (Belén) 1066, of 102, T01-431 0117, www.infoperu.com.pe. Mon-Fri 0900-1800, Sat 0930-1400. Run by a group of women, ask for Laura Gómez, offering personalized programmes, hotel bookings, transport, free tourist information, sale of maps, books and souvenirs, English and French spoken.

InkaNatura Travel, Manuel Bañón 461, San Isidro, T01-203 5000, www.inkanatura.com. Also in Cuzco and Chiclayo, experienced company offering good tours with knowledgeable guides, special emphasis on both sustainable tourism and conservation, especially in Manu and Tambopata, also birdwatching, and on the archaeology of all of Peru. Very helpful. Recommended.

Lima Mentor, T01-275 2986, www.limamentor.com. Contact through web, phone or through hotels. An agency offering cultural tours of Lima using freelance guides in specialist areas (eg gastronomy, art, archaeology, Lima at night), entertaining, finding different angles from regular tours. Half-day tours US$50-55, full day US$90-110. Recommended.

Lima Tours, Jr Belén 1040, T01-619 6900, www.limatours.com.pe. Recommended for tours in the capital and around the country; new programmes include health and wellness tours.

Masi Travel Sudamérica, Porta 350, Miraflores, T01-446 9094, www.masitravel.com. Tours throughout Peru, plenty of information on the website. Contact Verónika Reategui for an efficient service.

Peru For Less, ASTA Travel Agent, Luis Garcia Rojas 240, Urb Humboldt, US office: T1-877-269 0309; UK office: T+44-203-002 0571; Peru (Lima) office: T273 2486, Cuzco T084-254800, www.peruforless.com. Will meet or beat any published rates on the internet from outside Peru. Good reports.

Peru Rooms, Av Dos de Mayo 1545, of 205, San Isidro, T422 3434, www.perurooms.com.

Internet-based travel service offering
3- to 5-star packages throughout Peru,
cultural, adventure and nature tourism.
Often recommended.

Rutas del Peru SAC, Av Enrique Palacios
1110, Miraflores, T01-445 7249,
www.rutasdelperu.com. Bespoke trips
and overland expeditions in trucks.

Safe in Lima, Alfredo Silva 150, Barranco,
T01-252 7330, www.safeinlima.com.
Tailor-made trips for individuals and groups.
Also a friendly hostel of the same name,
see page 291.

Viajes Pacífico (Gray Line), Av La Mar 163,
T01-610 1900, www.graylineperu.com.
Expanded service with tours throughout
Peru and within South America.

Víctor Travel Service, Jr de la Unión 1100,
esq Av Uruguay 114, T01-332 1064,
or T01-999 583303/T01-993 350095,
www.victortravelservice.com. Tours
throughout Peru, hotel, bus and air
reservations, English spoken, very helpful
with information, maps and plans (free), daily
0800-2000. Víctor Melgar Morales also acts
as a private guide, contact on T01-782 0104,
or through the above phone numbers,
or victormelgarmorales@hotmail.com.
See also **La Catedral del Pisco**, page 292.

Viracocha, Av Vasco Núñez de Balboa 191,
Miraflores, T01-445 3986, peruviantours@
viracocha.com.pe. Very helpful, especially
with flights, adventure, cultural, mystical
and birdwatching tours.

Private guides

The **MITINCI** (Ministry of Industry Tourism,
Integration and International Business)
certifies guides and can provide a list. Most
are members of **AGOTUR** (Asociación de
Guías Oficiales de Turismo), Av La Paz 678,
Miraflores (for correspondence only),
www.agotur.com. Book in advance. Most
guides speak a language other than Spanish.

⊖ Transport

Air

For information on international flights, see
Getting there, page 22. For information on
domestic flights, see Getting around, page 25.
For transport to and from Lima airport, see Ins
and outs page 270. To enquire about arrivals or
departures, T01-511 6055, www.lap.com.pe.

Airlines

Domestic LAN, Av José Pardo 513,
Miraflores, T01-213 8200, www.lan.com.
LC Busre, Los Tulipanes 218, San Eugenio-
Lince, T01-619 1300, www.lcbusre.com.pe.
Peruvian Airlines, Av José Pardo 495,
Miraflores, T01-716 6000, www.peruvian
airlines.pe. **Star Perú**, Av Cdte Espinar 331,
Miraflores, T01-705 9000, www.starperu.com.
TACA Perú, Av Cdte Espinar 331, Miraflores,
T01-511 8222, www.grupotaca.com.

International Aerolíneas Argentinas,
Carnaval y Moreyra 370, p 1, San Isidro, T01-
513 6565, ventasperu@aerolineasargentinas.
com.pe. Air France-KLM, Av Alvarez
Calderón 185, p 6, San Isidro, T01-415 0923,
www.klm.com. **American Airlines**, Las
Begonias 471, San Isidro, and Av Pardo 392 y
Jr Independencia, T01-211 7000. Avianca,
Av José Pardo 140, Miraflores, T01-445 6895
or T0800-51936. Continental, Av V A
Belaúnde Via Principal 110 of 101, Edificio
Real 5, San Isidro, and in the Hotel Marriott,
Av Larco 1325, Miraflores, T01-712 9230 or
T0800-70030. Copa, Canaval y Moreyra y
Los Halcones, Centro Empresarial Torre
Chocavento of 105, T01-610 0810. Delta, Av V
A Belaúnde 147 Via Principal 180, Edif Real 3,
of 701, San Isidro, T01-211 9211. Iberia, Av
Camino Real 390, p 9, San Isidro, T01-411
7800. Lacsa, Av 2 de Mayo 755, Miraflores,
T01-444 7818. LAN, see above. Lufthansa, Av
Jorge Basadre 1330, San Isidro, T01-442 4455,
lufthansa@hansaperu.com. TAME, Av La Paz
1631, Miraflores, T01-422 6600.

Bus
Local

Av Arequipa runs 52 blocks between downtown Lima and Parque Kennedy in **Miraflores**. There is no shortage of public transport on this avenue; they have 'Todo Arequipa' on the windscreen. When heading towards downtown from Miraflores the window sticker should say 'Wilson/Tacna'. To get to Parque Kennedy from downtown look on the windshield for 'Larco/Schell/Miraflores', 'Chorrillos/Huaylas' or 'Barranco/Ayacucho'.

Lima's only urban freeway, Vía Expresa, runs from Plaza Grau in the centre of town, to the northern tip of **Barranco**. This 6-lane thoroughfare, locally known as *El Zanjón* (The Ditch), with the **Metropolitano** bus lane in the middle, is the fastest way to cross the city. Buses downtown for the Vía Expresa can be caught on Av Tacna, Av Wilson (also called Garcilaso de la Vega), Av Bolivia and Av Alfonso Ugarte.

The **Metropolitano** is a system of articulated buses running on dedicated lanes of the Vía Expresa/Paseo de la República (T01-203 9000, www.metropolitano.com.pe). The **Estación Central** is in front of the **Sheraton** hotel. The southern section runs to Matellini in Chorrillos (estimated journey time 32 mins). For Miraflores take stations between Angamos and 28 de Julio; for **Barranco** the **Bulevar** station is 170 m from the plaza. The northern branch runs to Naranjal in Comas, a 34-min journey. Stations Estación Central to Ramón Castilla serve the city centre. Tickets are prepaid and rechargeable, from S/.5-100, each journey is S/.1.50 (US$0.55). Buses run from 0600-2150 daily. From 0700-0930, 1700-2030 Mon-Fri an express service between Estación Central and Matellini calls at just 10 stations. Buses are packed in rush hour.

Long distance

There are many different bus companies, but the larger ones are better organized, leave on time and do not wait until the bus is full. For approximate prices, frequency and duration of trip, see destinations. Also see Getting around in Essentials, page 26, for general points on bus travel. **Note** In the weeks either side of 28/29 Jul (Independence), and of the Christmas/New Year holiday, it is practically impossible to get bus tickets out of Lima, unless you book in advance. Bus prices double at these times.

Companies with nationwide coverage include: **Cruz del Sur**, T01-311 5050 (telephone sales), www.cruzdelsur.com.pe. The main terminal is at Av Javier Prado 1109, La Victoria, T01-225 6163, with *Cruzero* and *Cruzero Suite* services (luxury buses) and *Imperial* service (quite comfortable buses and periodic stops for food and bathroom breaks, a cheap option with a quality company) to most parts of Peru. Another terminal is at Jr Quilca 531, Lima centre, T01-431 5125, for *Imperial* and *Ideal* (economy) services to **Cuzco** and other cities. There are sales offices throughout the city, eg on Av 28 de Julio.

Ormeño and its affiliated bus companies depart from and arrive at Av Carlos Zavala 177, Lima centre, T01-427 5679; also Av Javier Prado Este 1059, Santa Catalina, T01-472 1710, www.grupo-ormeno.com.pe. **Ormeño** offers *Royal Class* and *Business Class* service to certain destinations. These buses are very comfortable with bathrooms, hostess, etc. They mostly arrive and depart from the Javier Prado terminal, but the Carlos Zavala terminal is the best place to get information and buy any Ormeño ticket. **Cial**, República de Panamá 2469, T01-265 8121, and Paseo de la República 646, T01-717 8322, www.expresocial.com, has national coverage.

Cromotex, Av Nicolás Arriola 898, Santa Catalina, Av Paseo de La República 659, T01-424 7575, www.cromotex.com.pe, offers services to **Cuzco** and **Arequipa**. **Warning** The area around the bus terminals is very unsafe; thefts and assaults are more common in this neighbourhood than elsewhere in the city. You are strongly advised either to take a bus from a company that has a terminal away from the Carlos Zavala area (eg **Cruz del Sur**, or to take a taxi to and from your bus. Make sure your luggage is well guarded and put on the right bus. It is also important not to assume that buses leave from the place where you bought the tickets. Finally, always check your change very carefully when paying in cash.

Car rental

Most companies have an office at the airport, where you can arrange everything and pick up and leave the car. It is recommended to test-drive before signing the contract as quality varies. It can be much cheaper to rent a car in Cuzco for a few days than to drive from Lima; also companies don't have a collection service. Cars can be hired from: **Budget**, T01-204 4400, www.budget peru.com; **Hertz**, www.hertz.com; **Localiza**, T01-447 7474, www.localiza.com; **National**, T01-578 7878, www.nationalcar.com.pe. **Paz Rent A Car**, Av Diez Canseco 319, of 15, Miraflores, T01-446 4395, T01-9993 9853 (mob), www.perupaz consortium.com. **VIP**, T01-434 1111, www.viperu.com. Prices range from US\$35 to US\$85 depending on type of car. Make sure that your car is in a locked garage at night.

Taxi

The following are taxi fares for some of the more common routes, give or take a sol. **From downtown Lima to:** Parque Kennedy (Miraflores), US\$3.55; San Isidro, US\$3.20; Museo de la Nación, US\$3.20. South American Explorers, US\$3.55. Barranco, US\$4.25.

From Miraflores (Parque Kennedy) to: Museo de la Nación, US\$2.50; Archaeology Museum, US\$3.20; Barranco, US\$4.

By law, all taxis must have the vehicle's registration number painted on the side. They are often white or yellow, but can come in any colour, size or make. Licensed and phone taxis are safest, but if hailing a taxi on the street, local advice is to look for an older driver rather than a youngster. There are several reliable phone taxi companies, which can be called for immediate service, or booked in advance; prices are 2-3 times more than ordinary taxis; eg to the airport US\$12.50-15, to suburbs US\$9-10. Some are **Taxi Real**, T01-470 6263, www.taxireal.com; **Taxi Seguro**, T01-241 9292, www.taxiseguro.com.pe; **TCAM**, run by Carlos Astacio, T99-983 9305, safe, reliable. If hiring a taxi by the hour, agree on price beforehand, eg US\$7-9.

Recommended, knowledgeable drivers: **Hugo Casanova Morella**, T01-485 7708 (he lives in La Victoria), for city tours, travel to the airport, etc. **Mónica Velásquez Carlich**, T01-425 5087, T99-943 0796 (mob), vc_monica@hotmail.com. For airport pick-ups, tours, Speaks English, most helpful. **Note** Drivers don't expect tips; give them small change from the fare.

❶ Directory

Banks

Main banks' services are given in Essentials, under Money (see page 48). **BCP**, Jr Lampa 499, Lima centre (main branch), Av Larco at Pasaje Tarata, Miraflores, and others. **BBVA Continental**, corner of Av Larco and Av Benavides, Miraflores, and corner of Av Larco and Pasaje Tarata (this branch changes TCs), Jr Cusco 286, Lima centre near Plaza San Martín. **Banco Financiero**, Av Ricardo Palma 278, near Parque Kennedy (main branch). Cash only, GlobalNet ATM. **Banco Santander Central Hispano (BSCH)**, Av Augusto Tamayo 120, San Isidro (main branch), Av Pardo 482 and Av Larco 479, Miraflores. ATM for Visa/Plus and MasterCard. **Citibank**, Av Javier Prado Oeste 127, Miraflores, Mon-Fri 0900-1800, Sat 0930-1300. Red Unicard and GlobalNet ATMs; cash withdrawals on Visa cards and changes cash. **HSBC**, 28 de Julio y Av Larco, Miraflores, T01-616 4722, Mon-Fri 0900-1800, Sat 0900-1230, changes cash, Red Unicard ATM. **Interbank** has agencies everywhere, open Mon-Fri till 1800, and these will exchange TCs, including in **Vivanda** supermarkets, open till 2100. **Scotiabank**, Av Diagonal 176 on Parque Kennedy, Av José Pardo 697, Miraflores, and others, for MasterCard cash withdrawals.

In Barranco there are branches of **Interbank**, **BBVA** and **Scotiabank** on Av Grau, with ATMs, and there is a **Scotiabank** ATM in the Municipalidad.

Exchange houses

There are many *casas de cambio* on and around Jr Ocoña off the Plaza San Martín. On the corner of Ocoña and Jr Camaná is a large concentration of *cambistas* (street changers) with huge wads of US$, euro and soles in one hand and a calculator in the other. They should be avoided. Changing money on the street should only be done with official street changers wearing an identity card with a photo. This card doesn't automatically mean that they are legitimate but you're less likely to have a problem. Around Parque Kennedy and down Av Larco in Miraflores are official *cambistas* with an ID card and a green vest. In 2010 there was no real advantage in changing money on the street. There are a few places on Jr de la Unión at Plaza San Martín that will accept worn, ripped and old bills, but the exchange will be terrible. A repeatedly recommended *casa de cambio* is **LAC Dolar**, Jr Camaná 779, 1 block from Plaza San Martín, p 2, T01-428 8127, also at Av La Paz 211, Miraflores, T01-242 4069. Open Mon-Sat 1000-1800, helpful, safe, fast, reliable, 2% commission on cash and TCs (Amex, Citicorp, Thomas Cook, Visa), will come to your hotel if you're in a group. Another recommended *casa de cambio* is **Virgen P Socorro**, Jr Ocoña 184, T01-428 7748. Open daily 0830-2000, safe, reliable and friendly. In Miraflores, *casas de cambio* include: Av Larco 657 (with internet, phones and Western Union); **Finserva**, Javier Prado Oeste 142; **MSB**, Av Larco y San Martín.

For credit card companies, see Essentials, page 49. **Moneygram**, Ocharan 260,

Miraflores, T01-447 4044. Safe and reliable agency for sending and receiving money. Locations throughout Lima and the provinces. Exchanges most world currencies and TCs.

Embassies and consulates

During the summer, most embassies open only in the morning. **Australia**, Av Víctor Andrés Belaúnde 147, Vía Principal 155, Ed Real 3, of 1301, San Isidro, Lima 27, T01-222 8281, info.peru@austrade.gov.au. **Austria**, Av República de Colombia 643, p 5, San Isidro, T01-442 0503, lima-ob@bmeia.gv.at. **Belgian Consulate**, Angamos Oeste 380, Miraflores, T01-241 7566, www.diplomatie. be/lima. Bolivian Consulate, Los Castaños 235, San Isidro, T01-442 3836, embajada@ boliviaenperu.com, 0900-1330, 24 hrs for visas (except those requiring clearance from La Paz). **Brazil**, José Pardo 850, Miraflores, T01-512 0830, www.embajadabrasil.org.pe, Mon-Fri 0930-1300. **Canada**, Libertad 130, Casilla 18-1126, Lima, T01-444 4015, lima@ dfaitmaeci.gc.ca. **Chilean Consulate**, Javier Prado Oeste 790, San Isidro, T01-710 2211, embchile@mail.cosapidata.com.pe, open 0900-1300, need appointment. **Ecuadorean Consulate**, Las Palmeras 356, San Isidro (6th block of Av Javier Prado Oeste), T01-212 4161, embajada@mecuador peru.org.pe. **French Embassy**, Arequipa 3415, San Isidro, T01-215 8400, www.ambafrance-pe.org. **Germany**, Av Arequipa 4202, Miraflores, T01-212 5016, emergency number T99-927 8338, www.lima.diplo.de. Israel, Natalio Sánchez 125, p 6, Santa Beatriz, T01-418 0500, http://lima.mfa. gov.il. **Italy**, Av Giusepe Garibaldi 298, Jesús María, T01-463 2727. **Japan**, Av San Felipe 356, Jesús María, T463 0000. **Netherlands Consulate**, Torre Parque Mar, Av José Larco 1301, p 13, Miraflores, T01-213 9800, info@nlgovlim.com, open Mon-Fri 0900-1200. **New Zealand Consulate**, Los Nogales 510, p 3, San Isidro, T01-422 7491, alfonsorey1@gmail.com, open Mon-Fri 0830-1300, 1400-1700. **Spain**, Jorge Basadre 498, San Isidro, T01-212 5155, open

0900-1300. **Sweden**, C La Santa María 130, San Isidro, T01-442 8905, konslima@ speedy.com.pe. **Switzerland**, Av Salaverry 3240, Magdalena, Lima 17, T01-264 0305, www.eda.admin.ch/lima. **UK**, Torre Parque Mar, p 22, T01-617 3000, www.british embassy.gov.uk/peru, open 1300-2130 (Dec-Apr to 1830 Mon and Fri, and Apr-Nov to 1830 Fri), good for security information and newspapers. **USA**, Av Encalada block 17, Surco, T01-618 2000, for emergencies after hours T01-434 3032, http://lima.usembassy. gov. The consulate is in the same building.

Emergencies
See page 41 in Essentials.

Immigration
Migraciones, Digemin, Av España 730, Breña, Lima, T01-417 6900/433 0731, www.digemin. gob.pe, Mon-Fri 0800-1300. Provides new entry stamps if passport is lost or stolen.

Internet
Lima is completely inundated with internet cafés, so you will have absolutely no problem finding one regardless of where you are. An hour will cost you US$0.60-0.90.

Post
The central post office is on Jr Camaná 195 in the centre of Lima near the Plaza de Armas. Open Mon-Fri 0730-1900 and Sat 0730-1600 Poste Restante is in the same building but is considered unreliable. In Miraflores the main post office is on Av Petit Thouars 5201 (same hours). There are many small branches around Lima, but they are less reliable. For express service: **EMS**, next to central post office in downtown Lima, T01-533 2020, is Serpost's courier service. **DHL, UPS** and **Federal Express** have branches throughout the city.

Telephone
Easiest to use are the many independent phone offices, *locutorios*, all over the city. They take phone cards, which can be bought in *locutorios*, or in the street nearby. There are payphones all over the city. Some accept coins, some only phone cards and some both.

Contents

Footprint features

Background

History

Inca Dynasty

The origins of the Inca Dynasty are shrouded in mythology. The best known story reported by the Spanish chroniclers talks about Manco Cápac and his sister rising out of Lake Titicaca, created by the Sun as divine founders of a chosen race. This was in approximately AD 1200. Over the next 300 years the small tribe grew to supremacy as leaders of the largest empire ever known in the Americas, the four territories of Tawantinsuyo, united by Cuzco as the umbilicus of the universe. The four quarters of Tawantinsuyo, all radiating out from Cuzco, were: Chinchaysuyo, north and northwest; Cuntisuyo, south and west; Collasuyo, south and east; Antisuyo, east.

At its peak, just before the Spanish Conquest, the Inca Empire stretched from the Río Maule in central Chile, north to the present Ecuador-Colombia border, containing most of Ecuador, Peru, western Bolivia, northern Chile and northwest Argentina. The area was roughly equivalent to France, Belgium, Holland, Luxembourg, Italy and Switzerland combined (980,000 sq km).

The first Inca ruler, Manco Cápac, moved to the fertile Cuzco region, and established Cuzco as his capital. Successive generations of rulers were fully occupied with local conquests of rivals, such as the Colla and Lupaca to the south, and the Chanca to the northwest. At the end of Inca Viracocha's reign the hated Chanca were finally defeated, largely thanks to the heroism of one of his sons, Pachacútec Inca Yupanqui, who was subsequently crowned as the new ruler.

From the start of Pachacútec's own reign in AD 1438, imperial expansion grew in earnest. With the help of his son and heir, Topa Inca, territory was conquered from the Titicaca basin south into Chile, and all the north and central coast down to the Lurin Valley. The Incas also subjugated the Chimú, their highly sophisticated rivals on the coast (see above). Typical of the Inca method of government, some of the Chimú skills were assimilated into their own political and administrative system, and some Chimú nobles were even given positions in Cuzco.

Perhaps the pivotal event in Inca history came in AD 1527 with the death of the ruler, Huayna Capac. Civil war broke out in the confusion over his rightful successor. One of his legitimate sons, Huáscar, ruled the southern part of the empire from Cuzco. Atahualpa, Huáscar's half-brother, governed Quito, the capital of Chinchaysuyo. In AD 1532, soon after Atahualpa had won the civil war, Francisco Pizarro arrived in Tumbes with 167 *conquistadores*, a third of them on horseback. Atahualpa's army was marching south, probably for the first time, when he clashed with Pizarro at Cajamarca.

Francisco Pizarro's only chance against the formidable imperial army he encountered at Cajamarca was a bold stroke. He drew Atahualpa into an ambush, slaughtered his guards, promised him liberty if a certain room were filled with treasure, and finally killed him on the pretext that another Inca army was on its way to free him. Pushing on to Cuzco, he was at first hailed as the executioner of a traitor: Atahualpa had ordered the death of Huáscar in AD 1533, while himself a captive of Pizarro, and his victorious generals were bringing the defeated Huáscar to see his half-brother. Panic followed when the *conquistadores* set about sacking the city, and they fought off with difficulty an attempt by Manco Inca to recapture Cuzco in AD 1536.

Children of the Sun

Like any agrarian society, the Incas were avid sky watchers, but their knowledge of astronomy was naturally limited to what could be of practical use to them with regard to their farming activities. In common with other cultures throughout the world, they realized that the seasons on which their subsistence depended were governed by the apparent movement of the sun, who they called Inti, and placed at the head of their pantheon of gods. As the Inca Garcilaso de la Vega explains in his Royal Commentaries (1609), the Incas gave the name *huata* to the sun's annual motion, which in Quechua can mean either 'year', or 'to attach'. They believed that the sun had been created by the supreme creator god Viracocha, who caused it to rise from an island on Lake Titicaca now known as Isla del Sol, and that the moon goddess, the sun's sister, called Mama Killa, rose from the nearby island of Coatí (known today as the Island of the Moon). Lake Titicaca is central to the creation legends of the Incas, having also been the birthplace of the first two Incas (also brother and sister) and the scene of a great flood sent, it is said, by Viracocha, to punish mankind for having disobeyed his teachings. Colourful as they may seem, such myths were also central to the political structure of the Inca State, in that they established the Inca's divine right to rule, as a direct descendant of the sun god Inti and, therefore, his representative on earth.

Any agrarian society learns over time when to sow and harvest its crops by observing the cycle of nature around it. But in a planned, centralized economy governed by a self-proclaimed elite, the seasons of the year must be anticipated and, if it is to remain in power, that elite must be seen to monopolize the knowledge required for such predictions. The Incas, therefore, recruited the high priests, or tarpuntaes, who made astronomical observations from the empire's many temples dedicated to the sun, from the ranks of their own nobility, who were essentially the Inca's extended family. These priests observed solar and lunar eclipses, which were variously interpreted as the sexual union of the two astral bodies or, more calamitously, manifestations of their anger with their chosen people, a warning of the imminent death of a public figure, or indications that they themselves were under attack.

These astronomer-priests divided the year into 12 lunar months, which they themselves realized fell short of the solar year. They corrected this discrepancy by carefully following the course of the sun using cylindrical stone columns erected on the hills around the city of Cuzco and measuring their shadows to calculate the solstices, placing their new year at the time of the summer solstice and their greatest celebration, Inti Raymi, during the winter solstice (June in the modern calendar). The equinoxes were calculated using a single stone pillar placed in the centre of each temple dedicated to the sun. At noon, when the stone barely cast a shadow, Inti was said to be sitting 'with all his light on the column'. As the Incas extended their empire towards present-day Ecuador, they realized that at the new temples they established, the further north they went, the more the shadow cast by the stones they erected was reduced. Quito's temple, therefore, just 22 km south of the equator, where the sun casts no shadow at midday, was held to be the favourite resting place of Inti, thereby rivalling the importance of the oldest and most venerated shrine in the empire at Qoricancha, in Cuzco.

Inca society

The people we call the Incas were a small aristocracy numbering only a few thousand, centred in the highland city of Cuzco. They rose gradually as a small regional dynasty, similar to others in the Andes of that period, starting around AD 1200. Then, suddenly, in the mid-1400s, they began to expand explosively under Pachacútec, a sort of Andean Alexander the Great, and later his son, Túpac. Less than 100 years later, they fell before the rapacious warriors of Spain. The Incas were not the first dynasty in Andean history to dominate their neighbours, but they did it more thoroughly and went further than anyone before them.

Empire building

Enough remains today of their astounding highways, cities and agricultural terracing for people to marvel and wonder how they accomplished so much in so short a time. They seem to have been amazingly energetic, industrious and efficient – and the reports of their Spanish conquerors confirm this hypothesis.

They must also have had the willing cooperation of most of their subject peoples, most of the time. In fact, the Incas were master diplomats and alliance-builders first, and military conquerors only second, if the first method of expansion failed. The Inca skill at generating wealth by means of highly efficient agriculture and distribution brought them enormous prestige and enabled them to 'out-gift' neighbouring chiefs in huge royal feasts involving ritual outpourings of generosity, often in the form of vast gifts of textiles, exotic products from distant regions, and perhaps wives to add blood ties to the alliance. The 'out-gifted' chief was required by the Andean laws of reciprocity to provide something in return, and this would usually be his loyalty, as well as a levy of manpower from his own chiefdom.

Thus, with each new alliance the Incas wielded greater labour forces and their mighty public works programmes surged ahead. These were administered through an institution known as *mit'a*, a form of taxation through labour. The state provided the materials, such as wool and cotton for making textiles, and the communities provided skills and labour.

Mit'a contingents worked royal mines, royal plantations for producing coca leaves, royal quarries and so on. The system strove to be equitable, and workers in such hardship posts as high altitude mines and lowland coca plantations were given correspondingly shorter terms of service.

Organization

Huge administrative centres were built in different parts of the empire, where people and supplies were gathered. Articles such as textiles and pottery were produced there in large workshops. Work in these places was carried out in a festive manner, with plentiful food, drink and music. Here was Andean reciprocity at work: the subject supplied his labour, and the ruler was expected to provide generously while he did so.

Aside from *mit'a* contributions there were also royal lands claimed by the Inca as his portion in every conquered province, and worked for his benefit by the local population. Thus, the contribution of each citizen to the state was quite large, but apparently, the imperial economy was productive enough to sustain this.

Another institution was the practice of moving populations around wholesale, inserting loyal groups into restive areas, and removing recalcitrant populations to loyal areas. These movements of *mitmakuna*, as they were called, were also used to introduce skilled farmers and engineers into areas where productivity had to be raised.

All roads lead to Cuzco

There was a time when roads of colossal dimensions and magnificent construction crossed the difficult Andean terrain, thousands and thousands of kilometres in the most amazing network ever seen in antiquity. Through the building and management of this complex system, the Inca empire achieved both its expansion and its consolidation.

Cuzco, navel of the world and capital of the powerful Tawantinsuyo, was where these roads began and ended. From the city's civic arena, Huacaypata (today's Plaza de Armas), the four trunk roads set out to each of the four (*tahua*) quarters (*suyus*) into which the empire was divided: Chinchaysuyo to the northwest as far as Quito and the Colombian border; Collasuyo to the south, incorporating the altiplano as far as Argentina and Chile; Cuntisuyu to the west, bound by the Pacific Ocean; and Antisuyu to the east and the Amazon lowlands.

The limits presented by sea and jungle made the roads to north and south into a great axis which came to be known as Capaq Ñan (Royal, or Principal Road). They became the Incas' symbol of power over men and over the sacred forces of nature. So marvellous were these roads that the Spaniards who saw them at the height of their glory said there was nothing comparable in all Christendom and that, for example, a young girl from court could run their length barefoot as they were even swept clean. Amazement was not the sole preserve of the Europeans, as an early chronicle reveals. A settler who lived a long way from the capital reached the road in his district and said, "At last, I have seen Cuzco."

Imperial life revolved around these roads. Via them the produce of the coastal valleys and Amazonia were collected in tribute, to be exchanged prudently with those of the sierra, or to be stored for times of shortage. Whole communities were moved along these roads, to keep rebellion in check or to take the skills they possessed to another corner of the empire. These people had been conquered by armies thousands strong who advanced, unstoppable, along the roads, their supplies guaranteed at the *tambos* (store-houses) that were placed at regular intervals. News and royal decrees travelled with all haste, delivered by the famous *chasquis*, a race of men dedicated exclusively to running in relay along the roads.

While the roadbuilding did not happen all at once, the speed with which Pachacútec and his successors transformed the Andean world was incredible. In scarcely a century the most important civilization of the southern hemisphere had been created, only to be destroyed as the Spaniards capitalized on the fratricidal war between Huáscar and Atahualpa. What happened to the roads after that parallels what happened to the civilization itself. For a while the Spaniards used the very same roads which had been used to feed this immense body, only to leave it weakened and lifeless. Then, the large populations which the roads connected were exiled to live in reductions in the valleys where they could be controlled more easily and the roads, now running from one ghost town to the next, faded into oblivion.

The Incas, however, built for eternity. Many sections of the great network can be found today, not only in good condition but still in use, like the Inca Trail to Machu Picchu. Many other sections are lost under vegetation. But today Inca roads are considered of national importance and there is a hope that work will begin on their conservation, especially the singularly important Capaq Ñan.

Communications

The huge empire was held together by an extensive and highly efficient highway system. There were an estimated 30,000 km of major highway, most of it neatly paved and drained, stringing together the major Inca sites. Two parallel highways ran north to south, along the coastal desert strip and the mountains, and dozens of east-west roads crossing from the coast to the Amazon fringes. These roadways took the most direct routes, with wide stone stairways zigzagging up the steepest mountain slopes and rope suspension bridges crossing the many narrow gorges of the Andes.

Every 12 km or so there was a *tambo*, or way station, where goods could be stored and travellers lodged. The *tambos* were also control points, where the Inca state's accountants tallied movements of goods and people. Even more numerous than *tambos*, were the huts of the *chasquis*, or relay runners, who continually sped royal and military messages along these highways.

The Inca state kept records and transmitted information in various ways. Accounting and statistical records were kept on skeins of knotted strings known as *quipus* (see box, page 314). Numbers employed the decimal system, and colours indicated the categories being recorded. An entire class of people, known as *quipucamayocs*, existed whose job was to create and interpret these. Neither the Incas nor their Andean predecessors had a system of writing as we understand it, but there may have been a system of encoding language into *quipus*.

Archaeologists are studying this problem today. History and other forms of knowledge were transmitted via songs and poetry. Music and dancing, full of encoded information which could be read by the educated elite, were part of every major ceremony and public event information was also carried in textiles, which had for millennia been the most vital expression of Andean culture.

Textiles

Clothing carried insignia of status, ethnic origin, age and so on. Special garments were made and worn for various rites of passage. It has been calculated that, after agriculture, no activity was more important to Inca civilization than weaving. Vast stores of textiles were maintained to sustain the Inca system of ritual giving. Armies and *mit'a* workers were partly paid in textiles. The finest materials were reserved for the nobility, and the Inca emperor himself displayed his status by changing into new clothes every day and having the previous day's burned.

Most weaving was done by women and the Incas kept large numbers of 'chosen women' in female-only houses all over the empire. Among their duties was to supply textiles to the elite and the many deities, to whom the weavings were frequently given as burned offerings. These women had other duties, such as making *chicha* – the Inca corn beer which was consumed and sacrificed in vast quantities on ceremonial occasions. They also became wives and concubines to the Inca elite and loyal nobles. And some may have served as priestesses of the moon, in parallel to the male priesthood of the sun.

Religious worship

The Incas have always been portrayed as sun-worshippers, but it now seems that they were just as much mountain-worshippers. Recent research has shown that Machu Picchu was at least partly dedicated to the worship of the surrounding mountains, and Inca sacrificial victims have been excavated on frozen Andean peaks at 6700 m. In fact, until technical climbing was invented, the Incas held the world altitude record for humans.

Human sacrifice was not common, but every other kind was, and ritual attended every event in the Inca calendar. The main temple of Cuzco was dedicated to the numerous deities: the Sun, the Moon, Venus, the Pleiades, the Rainbow, Thunder and Lightning, and the countless religious icons of subject peoples which had been brought to Cuzco, partly in homage, partly as hostage. Here, worship was continuous and the fabulous opulence included gold cladding on the walls, and a famous garden filled with life-size objects of gold and silver. Despite this pantheism, the Incas acknowledged an overall Creator God, whom they called Viracocha. A special temple was dedicated to him, at Raqchi, about 100 km southeast of Cuzco. Part of it still stands today.

Military forces

The conquering Spaniards noted with admiration the Inca storehouse system, still well-stocked when they found it, despite several years of civil war among the Incas. Besides textiles, military equipment, and ritual objects, they found huge quantities of food. Like most Inca endeavours, the food stores served a multiple purpose: to supply feasts, to provide during lean times, to feed travelling work parties, and to supply armies on the march.

Inca armies were able to travel light and move fast because of this system. Every major Inca settlement also incorporated great halls where large numbers of people could be accommodated, or feasts and gatherings held, and large squares or esplanades for public assemblies.

Inca technology is usually deemed inferior to that of contemporary Europe. Their military technology certainly was. They had not invented iron-smelting and basically fought with clubs, palmwood spears, slings, wooden shields, cotton armour and straw-stuffed helmets. They did not even make much use of the bow and arrow, a weapon they were well aware of. Military tactics, too, were primitive. The disciplined formations of the Inca armies quickly dissolved into melees of unbridled individualism once battle was joined.

This, presumably, was because warfare constituted a theatre of manly prowess, but was not the main priority of Inca life. Its form was ritualistic. Battles were suspended by both sides for religious observance. Negotiation, combined with displays of superior Inca strength, usually achieved victory, and total annihilation of the enemy was not on the agenda.

Architecture

Other technologies, however, were superior in every way to their 16th-century counterparts: textiles, settlement planning and agriculture in particular with its sophisticated irrigation and soil conservation systems, ecological sensitivity, specialized crop strains and high productivity under the harshest conditions.

Unlike modern cities, Inca towns, or *llaqtas*, were not designed to house large, economically active populations. Inca society was essentially agrarian and, among the common people, almost everyone worked and lived on the land. The towns and cities that the Incas did build were meant to serve as residential areas for the state's administrative and religious elite. Throughout Tawantinsuyo, the *llaqtas* were divided into two zones, along blood lines, between the two principal *ayllus*, of Hanan and Urin. The streets were laid out in a simple grid pattern, with the whole forming a trapezoid. The trapezoid was the fundamental basis of Inca architecture, from niches and doorways to buildings and entire towns, and has been called the Inca version of the arch.

Quipus: holding the strings of empire

Despite their extraordinary advances in the fields of government, agriculture, architecture, astronomy and engineering, it is generally agreed that the Incas never developed a written language. But given the phenomenal degree to which the Inca State was centrally planned and governed, it should come as no surprise to learn that they did employ a complex mnemonic device for the keeping of state records.

The *quipu*, an invention which predates the Incas, consisted of a series of strings with knots tied in them. Those *quipus* found so far by archaeologists vary in length from just a few centimetres to more than a metre. By varying the colour of the strings, and the position and type of knot, the Incas were able to record vast amounts of information related to the affairs of the empire in a series of censuses of its entire population of more than 10 million.

The *quipucamayocs*, an hereditary group trained in the art of compiling and deciphering the *quipus*, were charged with keeping a complete demographic record from births and deaths to age groups, the number of men-under-arms, marriages, and the material wealth of the empire, which comprised great storehouses like those discovered by the Spanish when they reached Cuzco in 1533. These huge rectangular sheds contained everything that was grown or manufactured in an empire where private ownership was almost unknown, including grain, cloth, military equipment, coca, metal, shoes and items of clothing. All of this vast treasure, which the gold-hungry Spanish completely ignored, would have been precisely documented using *quipus*.

The Inca social system of *ayllus*, or clans, was based on groups of multiples of 10, and its arithmetical system was therefore also decimal. Apparently the concept of zero was understood but had no symbol; on those *quipus* deciphered by researchers it is represented by the absence of a knot. The data recorded on a *quipu* was calculated using an abacus, or *yupana*, which was fashioned from a rectangular tablet divided into smaller rectangular blocks, upon which grains of quinoa and corn of different colours were used to add, subtract, multiply and divide complex sums. The Spanish chronicler José de Acosta (1590) was astonished by the dexterity and exactitude of the Incas' *yupanaca-mayocs*, who he claimed never made a mistake and were much faster and more accurate than the Spanish accountants who used pen and paper.

While most scholars maintain that *quipus* were only used to record numbers, some others assert that they were also utilized to record other kinds of information, and that they were therefore effectively written records, or books. Recent research has suggested that the Incas employed a decimal alphabet in which consonants were represented by numbers and vowels were omitted, enabling them to communicate, and conserve, abstract concepts like poetry and storytelling on both their *quipus* and in the geometric designs of their weavings.

If such theories can be proved, they would make the Incas the inventors of written language in South America, and the *quipucamayocs* their court historians and Peru's first chroniclers. See http://incas.homestead.com/quipu/index.html, for a selection of articles.

The Incas fell short of their Andean predecessors in the better-known arts of ancient America – ceramics, textiles and metalwork – but it could be argued that their supreme efforts were made in architecture, stoneworking, landscaping, road building, and the harmonious combination of these elements. These are the outstanding survivals of Inca civilization, which still remain to fascinate the visitor: the huge, exotically close-fit blocks of stone, cut in graceful, almost sensual curves; the astoundingly craggy and inaccessible sites encircled by great sweeps of Andean scenery; the rhythmic layers of farm terracing that provided land and food to this still-enigmatic people. The finest examples of Inca architecture can be seen in the city of Cuzco and throughout the Sacred Valley.

Ruling elite

The ruling elite lived privileged lives in their capital at Cuzco. They reserved for themselves and privileged insiders certain luxuries such as the chewing of coca, the wearing of fine vicuña wool, and the practice of polygamy. But they were an austere people, too. Everyone had work to do, and the nobility were constantly being posted to state business throughout the empire. Young nobles were expected to learn martial skills, besides being able to read the *quipus*, speak both Quechua and the southern language of Aymara, and know the epic poems.

The Inca elite belonged to royal clans known as *panacas*, which each had the unusual feature of being united around veneration of the mummy of their founding ancestor – a previous Inca emperor, unless they happened to belong to the *panaca* founded by the Inca emperor who was alive at the time. Each new emperor built his own palace in Cuzco and amassed his own wealth rather than inheriting it from his forebears, which perhaps helps to account for the urge to unlimited expansion.

This urge ultimately led the Incas to overreach themselves. Techniques of diplomacy and incorporation no longer worked as they journeyed farther from the homeland and met ever-increasing resistance from people less familiar with their ways. During the reign of Huayna Cápac, the last emperor before the Spanish invasion, the Incas had to establish a northern capital at Quito in order to cope with permanent war on their northern frontier. Following Huayna Cápac's death came a devastating civil war between Cuzco and Quito, and immediately thereafter came the Spanish invasion. Tawantisuyo, the empire of the four quarters, collapsed with dizzying suddenness.

Conquest and after

Peruvian history after the arrival of the Spaniards was not just a matter of *conquistadores* versus Incas. The vast majority of the huge empire remained unaware of the conquest for many years. The Chimú and the Chachapoyas cultures were powerful enemies of the Incas. The Chimú developed a highly sophisticated culture and a powerful empire stretching for 560 km along the coast from Tumbes south to present-day Lima. Their history was well-recorded by the Spanish chroniclers and continued through the conquest possibly up to about 1600. The Kuélap/ Chachapoyas people were not so much an empire as a loose-knit "confederation of ethnic groups with no recognized capital" (Morgan Davis *Chachapoyas: The Cloud People*, Ontario, 1988). But the culture did develop into an advanced society with great skill in roads and monument building. Their fortress at Kuélap was known as the most impregnable in Tawantinsuyo. It remained intact against Inca attack and Manco Inca even tried, unsuccessfully, to gain refuge here against the Spaniards.

Exploration of the Vilcabamba

The Peruvian Vilcabamba remained virtually unexplored until the 20th century, both because of its geographical isolation and a lack of interest. The few travellers who went there, like the Comte de Sartiges in 1833, concentrated on the southwestern fringes and the site of Choquequirao.

Then in 1910 Sir Clements Markham, the President of the Royal Geographical Society, published *The Incas of Peru*, which focused attention on the late 'neo-Inca' period when they fled from Cuzco deep into the Vilcabamba heartland after the Spanish invasion. This whetted the interest of a young American academic from Yale called **Hiram Bingham**.

Bingham's subsequent reporting of Machu Picchu in 1911 is so famous that it has at times obscured the other discoveries he made in the area: Vitcos, which the last Incas used as their capital in exile for 35 years after the Spanish had conquered the rest of their empire; and another mysterious site down below in the jungle, whose significance evaded Bingham at the time, in an area called Espíritu Pampa which he evocatively translated as 'the Plain of Ghosts'.

Over the course of two subsequent expeditions, in 1912 and 1914-1915, he went on to report many other sites and cover an awe-inspiring amount of ground. It is fair to say that almost a century later, many explorers and archaeologists are still just adding footnotes and elucidations to Bingham's pioneering work.

Another less heralded but important contribution came from the mining prospector **Christian Bües**, who roamed the area in the 1920s and left a meticulously detailed map which is still used by today's explorers. He was the first to visit the remote and well-preserved ruin of Inca Wasi in the Puncuyoc hills.

Significant discoveries were made in 1941 by an American expedition led by the film-maker and anthropologist **Paul Fejos**, which investigated the Inca Trail. They found the dramatic site of Wiñay Wayna ('forever young'), which was named after an orchid found locally, and the nearby Inti Pata. The expedition was accompanied by a young scholar called **John H Rowe**, who went on over a long career to become the most influential Andeanist of his generation.

Gene Savoy made a swashbuckling entrance into the exploring world in 1964 with his discovery that the Espíritu Pampa site Bingham had partially found down in the jungle 50 years before was actually far larger than had been suspected. It could now be properly identified as the site of Old Vilcabamba, the city the Incas escaped to right at the end of their 'kingdom in exile' when they were driven out of Vitcos. The Spanish burnt and looted it in 1572 before capturing Túpac Amaru.

Savoy's methods were often unorthodox and his work at Espíritu Pampa was cut short when a *denuncia* was issued against him by the local community. A search party was sent down from Lima to apprehend him, led by an American archaeologist called **Gary Ziegler**. Savoy escaped and has since concentrated very successfully on exploring Chachapoyas in the north.

In the 1980s, architect and ex-Marine called **Vince Lee** retraced much of Savoy's route and made positive identifications of many Inca fortresses along the way. Lee brought draughtsmanship and much-needed humour to the study of Inca ruins in the area, as the title of his entertaining book *Sixpac Manco* exemplifies.

My own introduction to exploration in the area came at roughly the same time, when I joined some of the reconnaissance groups organized by the Cusichaca Project, run by the British archaeologist Ann Kendall, who reported on the area around the Aobamba and Santa Teresa valleys.

The Vilcabamba became difficult to travel in during the height of the Sendero Luminoso years and it was not until 2002 that interest in the area was reawakened with the discovery of a hill-top Inca site on Cerro Victoria by a National Geographic team led by Peter Frost and Gary Ziegler – the same Ziegler who had chased after Gene Savoy several decades before.

This was followed in the same year by the discovery of another site by Ziegler and myself called Cota Coca, which lies in the lower Yanama Valley and has been concealed for many years because the sides of that valley have collapsed.

In 2003, another Thomson – of the Ziegler Research Expedition, this time supported by the Royal Geographical Society – used thermal imaging cameras to fly over the cloudforest and find the outlines of stone buildings beneath the vegetation. The main Inca site under investigation was called Llactapata – appropriately one of the very sites Bingham had first reported partially on, in 1912. As with Espíritu Pampa, Llactapata was found to be considerably larger than Bingham had initially realized.

The above is a short summary only of the many expeditions that have been made into the Vilcabamba. Unlike mountaineering and the climbing of summits, there is no 'registered log' for the discovery of Inca sites and, while I have tried to attribute each successive discovery in the area to the correct team, there may be some unpublished explorers of whom I am unaware. I apologize to anyone who may have been inadvertently omitted as a result. In the words of Vince Lee: "I don't know who you are. I wish I did."

Why are discoveries still being made here when the rest of the world is so well mapped? It is partly because the Vilcabamba is such a dense quadrant of twisting river canyons and thick cloudforest, making it easy to pass within 3 m of a ruin and miss it.

Both for aesthetic and strategic reasons, the Incas chose to build on remote, isolated sites, as even the most casual visitor to Machu Picchu can observe. They also often built settlements in sectors scattered at different levels on a hillside, so that while one sector may have been found, others remain hidden.

All these factors mean that it is highly likely more ruins will be found in the years to come. The Vilcabamba has by no means given up all its secrets.

For more information see Hugh Thomson's book *The White Rock: An Exploration of the Inca Heartland*, Phoenix (UK)/Overlook Penguin (USA) and the website www.thewhiterock. co.uk, which has up-to-date links with the most recent discoveries.

© Hugh Thomson 2003

In 1535, wishing to secure his communications with Spain, Pizarro founded Lima, near the ocean, as his capital. The same year Diego de Almagro set out to conquer Chile. Unsuccessful, he returned to Peru, quarrelled with Pizarro, and in 1538 fought a pitched battle with Pizarro's men at the Salt Pits, near Cuzco. He was defeated and put to death. Pizarro, who had not been at the battle, was assassinated in his palace in Lima by Almagro's son three years later.

For the next 27 years each succeeding representative of the Kingdom of Spain sought to subdue the Inca successor state of Vilcabamba, north of Cuzco, and to unify the fierce Spanish factions. Francisco de Toledo (appointed 1568) solved both problems during his 14 years in office: Vilcabamba was crushed in 1572 and the last reigning Inca, Túpac Amaru, put to death.

For the next 200 years the Viceroys closely followed Toledo's system, if not his methods. The Major Government – the Viceroy, the Audiencia (High Court), and *corregidores* (administrators) – ruled through the Minor Government (indigenous chiefs put in charge of large groups of natives), a rough approximation to the original Inca system.

Towards independence

There was an indigenous rising in 1780, under the leadership of an Inca noble who called himself Túpac Amaru II. He and many of his lieutenants were captured and put to death under torture at Cuzco. Another indigenous leader in revolt suffered the same fate in 1814, but this last flare-up had the sympathy of many of the locally born Spanish, who resented their status, inferior to the Spaniards born in Spain, the refusal to give them any but the lowest offices, the high taxation imposed by the home government, and the severe restrictions upon trade with any country but Spain.

Help came to them from the outside world. José de San Martín's Argentine troops, convoyed from Chile under the protection of Lord Cochrane's squadron, landed in southern Peru on 7 September 1820. San Martín proclaimed Peruvian independence at Lima on 28 July 1821, though most of the country was still in the hands of the Viceroy, José de La Serna. Bolívar, who had already freed Venezuela and Colombia, sent Antonio José de Sucre to Ecuador where, on 24 May 1822, he gained a victory over La Serna at Pichincha.

San Martín, after a meeting with Bolívar at Guayaquil, left for Argentina and a self-imposed exile in France, while Bolívar and Sucre completed the conquest of Peru by defeating La Serna at the battle of Junín (6 August 1824) and the decisive battle of Ayacucho (9 December 1824). For over a year there was a last stand in the Real Felipe fortress at Callao by the Spanish troops under General Rodil before they capitulated on 22 January 1826. Bolívar was invited to stay in Peru, but left for Colombia in 1826.

Post-independence Peru

Following independence Peru attempted a confederation with Bolivia in the 1830s but this proved temporary. Then, in 1879 came the disastrous War of the Pacific, in which Peru and Bolivia were defeated by Chile and Peru lost its southern territory.

Economic change

Peru's economic development since independence has been based upon the export of minerals and foodstuffs to Europe and the United States. Guano, a traditional fertilizer in Peru and derived from the manure of seabirds, was first shipped to Europe in 1841. In the three decades that followed it became an important fertilizer in Europe and by the early 1860s over 80% of the Peruvian government's revenues were derived from its export. Much of this income, though, went to pay off interest on the spiralling national debt. By the 1870s the richer deposits were exhausted and cheaper alternatives to guano were being discovered. One of these was nitrates, discovered in the Atacama desert, but Peru's defeat by Chile in the War of the Pacific ensured that she would lose her share of this wealth.

After the decline of guano, Peru developed several new exports. In the 1890s the demand in Europe and USA for Amazonian rubber for tyres and for use in electrical components led to a brief boom in both the Brazilian and Peruvian Amazon. The Peruvian industry was based around the port of Iquitos. This boom was short-lived as cheaper rubber was soon being produced from plantations in the East Indies. Peru's colonial mineral exports, gold and silver, were replaced by copper, although ownership was mainly under control of foreign companies, particularly the US-based Cerro de Pasco Copper Corporation and Northern Peru Mining. Oil became another important product, amounting to 30% of Peruvian exports by 1930. Further exports came from sugar and cotton, which were produced on coastal plantations.

Social change

Independence from Spanish rule meant that power passed into the hands of the Creole elite with no immediate alternation of the colonial social system. The *contribución de indíginas* (the colonial tribute collected from the native peoples) was not abolished until 1854, the same year as the ending of slavery.

Until the 1970s land relations in the sierra changed very little, as the older landholding families continued to exert their traditional influence over 'their' peones. The traditional elite, the so-called '44 families', were still very powerful, though increasingly divided between the coastal aristocracy with their interests in plantation agriculture and trade, and the serrano elite, more conservative and inward looking.

The pattern of export growth did, however, have major social effects on the coast. The expansion of plantation agriculture and mining led to the growth of a new labour force; this was supplied partially by Chinese indentured labourers, about 100,000 of whom arrived between 1855 and 1875, partly by the migration of indigenous people from the sierra and partly by the descendants of black slaves.

Modern Peru

Political developments

For much of the period since independence Peruvian political life has been dominated by the traditional elites. Political parties have been slow to develop and the roots of much of the political conflict and instability which have marked the country's history lie in personal ambitions and in regional and other rivalries within the elite.

The early years after independence were particularly chaotic as rival caudillos (political bosses) who had fought in the independence wars vied with each other for power. The increased wealth brought about by the guano boom led to greater stability, though political corruption became a serious problem under the presidency of José Rufino Echenique (1851-1854) who paid out large sums of the guano revenues as compensation to upper class families for their (alleged) losses in the Wars of Independence. Defeat by Chile in the War of the Pacific discredited civilian politicians even further and led to a period of military rule in the 1880s.

Early 20th century

Even though the voting system was changed in 1898, this did little to change the dominance of the elite. Voting was not secret so landowners herded their workers to the polls and watched to make sure they voted correctly. Yet voters were also lured by promises as well as threats. One of the more unusual presidents was Guillermo Billinghurst (1912-1914) who campaigned on the promise of a larger loaf of bread for five cents, thus gaining the nickname of 'Big Bread Billinghurst'. As president he proposed a publicly funded housing programme, supported the introduction of an eight hour day and was eventually overthrown by the military who, along with the elite, were alarmed at his growing popularity among the urban population.

The 1920s This decade was dominated by Augusto Leguía. After winning the 1919 elections Leguía claimed that Congress was plotting to prevent him from becoming president and induced the military to help him close Congress. Backed by the armed forces, Leguía introduced a new constitution which gave him greater powers and enabled him to be re-elected in 1924 and 1929. Claiming his goal was to prevent the rise of communism, he proposed to build a partnership between business and labour. A large programme of public works, particularly involving building roads, bridges and railways, was begun, the work being carried out by poor rural men who were forced into unpaid building work. The Leguía regime dealt harshly with critics: opposition newspapers were closed and opposition leaders arrested and deported. His overthrow in 1930 ended what Peruvians call the *Oncenio* or 11-year period.

The 1920s also saw the emergence of a political thinker who would have great influence in the future, not only in Peru but elsewhere in Latin America. José Carlos Mariátegui, a socialist writer and journalist, argued that the solution to Peru's problems lay in the reintegration of the indigenous people through land reform and the breaking up of the great landed estates.

The formation of APRA Another influential thinker of this period was Víctor Raúl Haya de la Torre, a student exiled by Leguía in 1924. He returned after the latter's fall to create the

Alianza Popular Revolucionaria Americana (APRA), a political party which called for state control of the economy, nationalization of key industries and protection of the middle classes, which, Haya de la Torre argued, were threatened by foreign economic interests.

In 1932 APRA seized control of Trujillo; when the army arrived to deal with the rising, the rebels murdered about 50 hostages, including 10 army officers. In reprisal the army murdered about 1000 local residents suspected of sympathizing with APRA. APRA eventually became the largest and easily the best-organized political party in Peru, but the distrust of the military and the upper class for Haya de la Torre ensured that he never became president.

A turning point in Peruvian history occurred in 1948 with the seizure of power by General Manuel Odría, backed by the coastal elite. Odría outlawed APRA and went on to win the 1950 election in which he was the only candidate. He pursued policies of encouraging export earnings and also tried to build up working class support by public works projects in Lima. Faced with a decline in export earnings and the fall in world market prices after 1953, plus increasing unemployment, Odría was forced to stand down in 1956.

In 1962 Haya de la Torre was at last permitted to run for the presidency. But although he won the largest percentage of votes he was prevented from taking office by the armed forces who seized power and organized fresh elections for 1963. In these the military obtained the desired result: Haya de la Torre came second to Fernando Belaúnde Terry. Belaúnde attempted to introduce reforms, particularly in the landholding structure of the sierra; when these reforms were weakened by landowner opposition in Congress, peasant groups began invading landholdings in protest.

At the same time, under the influence of the Cuban revolution, terrorist groups began operating in the sierra. Military action to deal with this led to the deaths of an estimated 8000 people. Meanwhile Belaúnde's attempts to solve a long-running dispute with the International Petroleum Company (a subsidiary of Standard Oil) resulted in him being attacked for selling out to the unpopular oil company and contributed to the armed forces' decision to seize power in 1968.

The 1968 coup

This was a major landmark in Peruvian history. Led by General Juan Velasco Alvarado, the Junta had no intention of handing power back to the civilians. A manifesto issued on the day of the coup attacked the 'unjust social and economic order' and argued for its replacement by a new economic system 'neither capitalist nor communist'. Partly as a result of their experiences in dealing with the insurgency, the coup leaders concluded that agrarian reform was a priority.

Wide-ranging land reform was launched in 1969, during which large estates were taken over and reorganized into cooperatives. By the mid-1970s, 75% of productive land was under cooperative management. The government also tried to improve the lives of shanty-town dwellers around Lima, as well as attempting to increase the influence of workers in industrial companies. At the same time efforts were made to reduce the influence of foreign companies. Soon after the coup, IPC was nationalized, to be followed by other transnationals including ITT, Chase Manhattan Bank and the two mining giants Cerro de Pasco and Marcona Mining. After a dispute with the US government, compensation was agreed.

Understandably, opposition to the Velasco government came from the business and landholding elite. The government's crack-down on expressions of dissent, the seizure of newspapers and taking over of TV and radio stations all offended sections of the urban middle class. Trade unions and peasant movements found that, although they agreed with many of the regime's policies, it refused to listen and expected their passive and unqualified support. As world sugar and copper prices dropped, inflation rose and strikes increased. Velasco's problems were further increased by opposition within the armed forces and by his own ill-health. In August 1975 he was replaced by General Francisco Morales Bermúdez, a more conservative officer, who dismantled some of Velasco's policies and led the way to a restoration of civilian rule.

Belaúnde returned to power in 1980 by winning the first elections after military rule. His government was badly affected by the 1982 debt crisis and the 1981-1983 world recession, and inflation reached over 100% a year in 1983-1984. His term was also marked by the growth of the Maoist movement **Sendero Luminoso** (Shining Path) and the smaller, Marxist **Movimiento Revolucionario Túpac Amaru** (MRTA).

Initially conceived in the University of Ayacucho, Shining Path gained most support for its goal of overthrowing the whole system of Lima-based government from highland indigenous and migrants to urban shanty towns. The activities of Sendero Luminoso and the MRTA were effectively curtailed after the arrest of both their leaders in 1992. Víctor Polay of MRTA was arrested in June and Abimael Guzmán of Sendero Luminoso was captured in September. Although Sendero did not capitulate, many of its members in 1994-1995 took advantage of the Law of Repentance, which guaranteed lighter sentences in return for surrender, and freedom in exchange for valuable information. Meanwhile, MRTA was thought to have ceased operations (see below).

In 1985 APRA, in opposition for over 50 years, finally came to power. With Haya de la Torre dead, the APRA candidate Alan García Pérez won the elections and was allowed to take office by the armed forces. García attempted to implement an ambitious economic programme intended to solve many of Peru's deep-seated economic and social problems. He cut taxes, reduced interest rates, froze prices and devalued the currency. However, the economic boom that this produced in 1986-1987 stored up problems as increased incomes were spent on imports. Moreover, the government's refusal to pay more than 10% of its foreign debt meant that it was unable to borrow. In 1988 inflation hit 3000% and unemployment soared. By the time his term of office ended in 1990 Peru was bankrupt and García and APRA were discredited.

Peru under Fujimori

In presidential elections held over two rounds in 1990, **Alberto Fujimori** of the Cambio 90 movement defeated the novelist **Mario Vargas Llosa** (see box, page 338), who belonged to the Fredemo (Democratic Front) coalition. Fujimori, without an established political network behind him, failed to win a majority in either the senate or the lower house. Lack of congressional support was one of the reasons behind the dissolution of congress and the suspension of the constitution on 5 April 1992. The president declared that he needed a freer hand to introduce market reforms and combat terrorism and drug trafficking, at the same time as rooting out corruption.

In elections to a new, 80-member Democratic Constituent Congress (CCD) in November 1992, Fujimori's Cambio 90/Nueva Mayoría coalition won a majority of seats. Though three major political parties – APRA, Acción Popular and the Movimiento de Libertad – boycotted the elections, they satisfied many aid donor's requirements for the resumption of financial assistance.

A new constitution drawn up by the CCD was approved by a narrow majority of the electorate in October 1993. Among the new articles were the immediate re-election of the president (previously prohibited for one presidential term), the establishment of a single-chamber congress, the designation of Peru as a market economy and the favouring of foreign investment. As expected, Fujimori stood for re-election on 9 April 1995 and the opposition chose as an independent to stand against him former UN General Secretary, Javier Pérez de Cuéllar. Fujimori was re-elected by a resounding margin, winning about 65% of the votes cast. The coalition that supported him also won a majority in Congress.

The government's success in most economic areas did not appear to accelerate the distribution of foreign funds for social projects. Rising unemployment and the austerity imposed by economic policy continued to cause hardship for many, despite the government's stated aim of alleviating poverty.

Dramatic events on 17 December 1996 thrust several of these issues into sharper focus: 14 Túpac Amaru terrorists infiltrated a reception at the Japanese Embassy in Lima, taking 490 hostages. Among the rebel's demands were the release of their imprisoned colleagues, better treatment for prisoners and new measures to raise living standards. Most of the hostages were released and negotiations were pursued during a stalemate that lasted until 22 April 1997. The president took sole responsibility for the successful, but risky assault that freed all the hostages (one died of heart failure) and killed all the terrorists. By not yielding to Túpac Amaru, Fujimori regained much popularity.

But this masked the fact that no steps had been taken to ease social problems. It also deflected attention from Fujimori's plans to stand for a third term following his unpopular manipulation of the law to persuade Congress that the new constitution did not apply to his first period in office. His chances of winning looked remote as demands grew for a more open, democratic approach, though opposition to his standing for a third term of office remained fragmented. Ultimately, his chances hinged on the economy, which looked to be improving until the worst El Niño of the 20th century hit Peru in late 1997, causing chaos, many deaths and devastating damage.

Fujimori's unpopularity was further driven home by Shell-Mobil's withdrawal from the multi-million dollar Camisea natural gas project, which was supposed to pull Peru out of its energy deficit. In July 1998, a 1.4 million-name petition was presented to the National Electoral Authority, requesting a referendum on whether Fujimori should be allowed to stand for a third term. In spite of the amendment to the constitution following Fujimori's auto golpe in 1993, allowing presidents to run for only two successive terms, the president had, in 1996, pushed through congress a law of 'authentic interpretation' of the constitution, allowing him to run for election once more on the grounds that the new constitution did not apply to his first term. All the same, until the last month of campaigning for the 2000 presidential elections, Fujimori had a clear lead over his rivals, who insisted that he should not stand. Moreover, local and international observers voiced increasing concern over the state domination of the media. Meanwhile, the popularity of a fourth candidate, Alejandro Toledo, a former World Bank official of humble origins, surged to such an extent that he and Fujimori were neck and neck in the first poll. Toledo, a pro-marketeer given to left-wing rhetoric, and his supporters claimed that Fujimori's slim majority was the result of fraud, a view echoed in the pressure put on the president, by the US government among others, to allow a second ballot. The run-off election, on 28 May 2000, was also contentious since foreign observers, including the Organization of American States, said the electoral system was unprepared and flawed, proposing a postponement. The authorities refused to delay. Toledo boycotted the election and Fujimori was returned unopposed, but with scant approval. Having won, he proposed "to strengthen democracy".

This pledge proved to be utterly worthless following the airing of a secretly shot video on 14 September 2000 of Fujimori's close aide and head of the National Intelligence Service (SIN), Vladimiro Montesinos, allegedly handing US$15,000 to a congressman, Alberto Kouri, to persuade him to switch allegiances to Fujimori's coalition. Fujimori's demise was swift. His initial reaction was to close down SIN and announce new elections, eventually set for 8 April 2001, at which he would not stand. Montesinos was declared a wanted man and he fled to Panama, where he was denied asylum. He returned to Peru in October and Fujimori personally led the search parties to find his former ally. Peruvians watched in amazement as this game of cat-and-mouse was played out on their TV screens. While Montesinos himself successfully evaded capture, investigators began to uncover the extent of his empire, which held hundreds of senior figures in its web. His activities encompassed extortion, money-laundering, bribery, intimidation, alleged arms and drugs dealing and possible links with the CIA and death squads. Swiss bank accounts in his name were found to contain about US$70 million, while other millions were discovered in accounts in the Cayman Islands and elsewhere. In early 2001 he was eventually captured in Venezuela and returned to Peru where he was tried on, and convicted of, a multitude of charges. Fujimori, on the other hand, fled to Japan from where, on 20 November 2000, he sent Congress an email announcing his resignation. Congress rejected this, firing him instead on charges of being "morally unfit" to govern. An interim president, Valentín Paniagua, was sworn in, with ex-UN Secretary General Javier Pérez de Cuéllar as Prime Minister, and the government set about uncovering the depth of corruption associated with Montesinos and Fujimori. In 2004, prosecutors sought to charge exiled Fujimori with authorizing death squads at Barrios Altos (1991) and La Cantuta (1992) in which 25 people died. This followed the Truth and Reconciliation Committee's report (2003) into the civil war of the 1980s and 1990s, which stated that over 69,000 Peruvians had been killed. With attempts to extradite Fujimori from Japan coming to nothing, prosecution could not proceed. Meanwhile Fujimori declared that he would be exonerated and stand again for the presidency in 2006. To this end he flew to Chile in November 2005 with a view to entering Peru, but the Chilean authorities jailed him for seven months and then held him on parole until an extradition request was finally approved in September 2007. In December that year the first of several trials began, Fujimori being charged with, but strenuously denying, the Barrios Altos and La Cantuta murders, kidnapping and corruption. He was found guilty of human rights abuses in 2009 and sentenced to 25 years in prison. As further convictions followed, he vowed to appeal and support for him was likely to continue as his daughter, Keiko, planned to stand for the presidency in 2011.

Post-Fujimori In the run-up to the 2001 elections, the front-runner was Alejandro Toledo, but with far from a clear majority. Ex-President Alan García emerged as Toledo's main opponent, forcing a second ballot on 3 June. This was won by Toledo with 52% of the vote. He pledged to heal the wounds that had opened in Peru since his first electoral battle with the disgraced Fujimori, but his presidency was marked by slow progress on both the political and economic fronts. With the poverty levels still high, few jobs created and a variety of scandals, Toledo's popularity plummeted. A series of major confrontations and damaging strikes forced the president to declare a state of emergency in May 2003 to restore order. Nor could Toledo escape charges of corruption being laid at his own door;

accusations that he and his sister orchestrated voter fraud in 2000 were upheld by a congressional commission in May 2005.

The April 2006 elections were contested by Alan García, the conservative Lourdes Flores and Ollanta Humala, a former military officer and unsuccessful coup leader who claimed support from Venezuela's Hugo Chávez and Evo Morales of Bolivia. García and Humala won through to the second round, which García won, in part because many were suspicious, even critical of the 'Chávez factor' and the latter's interference in Peruvian affairs. Many were equally suspicious of García's ability to overcome his past record as president, but prior to taking office he pledged to rein in public spending and not squander the benefits of a growing economy. Humala's Unión por el Perú-Partido Nacionalista Peruano (UPP-PNP) won 45 seats in Congress, compared with 36 for APRA, forcing García to forge allies with right-leaning parties in order to sustain a majority for his policies. His first cabinet included APRA members and independents, as well as an unprecedented number of women (six), to help tackle social problems.

Much depended upon García's ability to succeed where no previous government seems to have made significant progress, namely alleviating poverty. Congress' approval of a trade pact with the United States in 2006 became the focus of protests as many claimed that food exports were taking precedence over the domestic market, where prices for food began to rise sharply. US-Peru Trade Promotion Agreement (PTPA) came into force in 2009 and Peru has also entered into, or is negotiating similar agreements with a number of other countries, including Canada, China and the EU. Between 2005 and 2008 the economy grew strongly, but suffered in line with world recession and low commodity prices in 2009. García's free-market policies were judged to have failed to address the inequality of income distribution and major demonstrations were held through 2007 and 2008. Even worse events occurred in mid 2009 when indigenous protestors from near Bagua Grande (Amazonas) clashed with police over oil-drilling rights on their land. Many feared that Peru's mineral exploration policies would put areas of the Peuvian Amazon under threat of deforestation and the fact that this protest led to over 50 deaths and claims of human rights abuse highlighted the extreme sensitivity of the issue.

Constitution and government

Peru has a single chamber 120-seat congress. Men and women over 18 are eligible to vote, and registration and voting is compulsory until the age of 70. Those who do not vote are fined. The president, to whom is entrusted the executive power, is elected for five years. Peru is split into 25 regions (divided into 150 provinces, subdivided into 1321 districts), plus the province of Lima.

Society

The most remarkable thing about Peru is its people. For most Peruvians life is a daily struggle to survive in the face of seemingly insurmountable problems. Most people do get by, through a combination of ingenuity, determination and sheer hard work. Many work full time and study at night school. Those without work (and employment opportunities are few and far between) invent their own jobs.

Peru may not be the poorest country in South America and a thriving economy since 2002 has helped to reduce levels of poverty, but recent estimates put the number of poor at about 45% of the population, while almost a fifth of people live in extreme poverty.

Over a third of homes have no electricity or running water and a third of children suffer from chronic malnutrition.

Health

There have been major improvements in health care in recent years, but almost a third of the population has no access to public health services. The infant mortality rate is 21 deaths under age one per 1000 births (2005-2010, INEI – Instituto Nacional de Estadística e Informática); the figure rises steeply in some rural areas where one in 10 infants dies within a year of birth. Life expectancy is 73 years.

As only a small percentage of the population contributes to social security schemes, medical consultations are not necessarily free. People also have to pay for prescribed medicines, which are very expensive, and so rarely finish a course of treatment. As with other areas, there is a huge gulf between those who can afford to pay for health care and those who cannot. Lack of health education and limited primary health care also means that many women die in childbirth. Abortion is illegal in Peru, but those with cash can always find a private doctor. Those without the means to pay for a doctor run the risk of death or infection from botched abortions.

Education

Education is free and compulsory for both sexes between six and 14. Adult literacy in 2007 stood at 93%. There are public and private secondary schools and private elementary schools. There are 32 state and private universities, and two Catholic universities. But resources are extremely limited and teachers earn a pittance. Poorer schoolchildren don't have money to buy pencils and notebooks and textbooks are few and far between in state schools. Furthermore, many children have to work instead of attending school; a quarter of those who start primary school don't finish. This is also due to the fact that classes are taught in Spanish and those whose native tongue is Quechua, Aymara or one of the Amazonian languages find it difficult and give up.

Migration

The structure of Peruvian society, especially in the coastal cities, has been radically altered by internal migration. This movement began most significantly in the 1950s and 1960s as people from all parts of Peru sought urban jobs in place of work on the land. It was a time of great upheaval as the old system of labour on large estates was threatened by the peasant majority's growing awareness of the imbalances between the wealthy cities and impoverished sierra. The process culminated in the agrarian reforms of the government of General Juan Velasco (1968-1975). Province-to-city migration was given renewed impetus during the war between the state and Sendero Luminoso in the 1980s. Many communities that were depopulated in that decade are now beginning to come alive again.

Culture

People

Peruvian society today is a melting pot of Native Andeans, Afro-Peruvians, Spanish, immigrant Chinese, Japanese, Italians, Germans and, to a lesser extent, indigenous Amazon tribes. The total population in 2007 was 28.2 million (INEI census statistics), with an annual average growth rate of 1.6%. The INEI estimates the total at 29.5 million in 2010. The urban population represents 73% of the total.

Peru has a substantial indigenous population, only smaller as a percentage of the total than Bolivia and Guatemala of the Latin American republics. The literacy rate of the indigenous population is the lowest of any comparable group in South America and their diet is 50% below acceptable levels. The highland Indians bore the brunt of the conflict between Sendero Luminoso terrorists and the security forces, which caused thousands of deaths and mass migration from the countryside to provincial cities or to Lima. Many indigenous groups are also under threat from colonization, development and road-building projects. Long after the end of Spanish rule, discrimination, dispossession and exploitation is still a fact of life for many native Peruvians.

Quechua

According to Inca legend, the dynasty's forebears were a small group who originally lived near Lake Titicaca. They later moved to Cuzco, from where they expanded to create the Inca Empire. Their culture soon covered an area from the southernmost edge of present-day Colombia, through Quito and Ecuador, Peru and Bolivia to northern Chile and Argentina. Out of this rapid expansion grew the myth that the Quechua language originated with the Incas and spread along with their influence. But linguistic evidence points to Quechua being spoken in northern and central Peru long before the Incas arrived on the scene, even though the precise starting point of the language cannot be pinpointed. So the common idea that Quechua equals Inca is misleading (for more information on this issue, visit www.quechua.org.uk).

Quechua is spoken widely throughout the Andes by people of a predominantly agricultural society, growing potatoes and corn as their basic diet, largely outside the money economy. This society ranges from Bolivia to Ecuador (where the language is known as Quichua). According to some estimates, about two million Quechua-speakers cannot converse in Spanish, but there are many more Indians who now speak only Spanish. Though recognized as an official language, little effort is made to promote Quechua nationally. It is only the remoteness of many Quechua speakers which has preserved it in rural areas. This isolation has also helped preserve many ancient traditions and beliefs. It remains primarily a spoken, in-group language, strongly bound up with the distinct indigenous identity, but unlike the Aymara (see below), the seven million or so Quechua-speakers have generally been much less successful in asserting themselves. There is no real sense of unity between the disparate groups of speakers scattered through Ecuador, Peru and Bolivia. Some recent developments in these three countries have at last been more positive. The language is now increasingly written and is being fitfully introduced in primary education, though the impact of Spanish, and polemics about standardization, continue to have a very disruptive effect. See also Festivals, on page 336.

The ancient leaf

Coca flourishes in the subtropical valleys of the eastern Andes, as well as in the Sierra Nevada de Santa Marta in Colombia, and for millennia it has been central to the daily life and religious rituals of many of the indigenous cultures of South America. The coca plant (*Erythroxylum coca*) is an evergreen shrub found in warm, fertile valleys. Its leaves are oval, 3-5 cm long and resemble laurel or bay leaves. Chewed with lime, which acts as a catalyst, the leaf releases a mild dose of cocaine alkaloid, numbing the senses, dulling both hunger and pain and even providing some vitamins otherwise absent in the starch-heavy diet of the highland people.

Under the Incas, the use of coca was restricted to ceremonies involving the nobility and priesthood. After the conquest the Spanish promoted it among the half-starved slaves of the mines of Huancavelica and Potosí. It wasn't until 1862 that an Austrian chemist refined the leaf to produce pure cocaine, which was subsequently marketed as a cure for opium addiction, a local anaesthetic, a tonic and (as Coca Cola) a headache remedy. In the 1970s, with the drug's growth in popularity in the US and Europe, cocaine became big business, funding entire guerrilla movements and creating multi-billion dollar fortunes for men like Colombia's Pablo Escobar.

Some ethnobiologists estimate that coca has been cultivated in the Andes for at least 4000 years. Archaeological discoveries in Ecuador from the Valdivia Period (1500 BC) seem to provide early evidence of the use of coca: ceramic figurines have been found showing men with the bulges in the cheeks characteristic of the coca chewer. The traditional consumption of coca remains an important symbol of ethnic identity for the indigenous peoples of the highlands.

Under the Incas, coca was revered as a gift from the gods and was strictly controlled by the state. It was used in religious rites and burials and for divination. After the conquest, the role of coca in indigenous religious practices and divination provoked the Catholic extirpators of idolatry to ban its use. Diego de Robles began the Western-led demonization of coca which continues to this day when he declared that it was "a plant that the devil invented for the total destruction of the natives", and it was condemned outright at the first ecclesiastical council of Lima in 1551.

However, it did not take the Spanish long to recognize the enormous business potential. As the Uruguayan historian Eduardo Galeano writes: "In the mines of Potosí in the 16th century as much was spent on Euro-pean clothing for the oppressors as on coca for the oppressed. In Cuzco, 400 Spanish merchants made their living from trafficking coca, one hundred thousand baskets, containing a million kilos of coca leaves, entered the silver mines of Potosí annually. The Church extracted taxes from the traffic. Inca Garcilaso de la Vega tells us, in his *Royal Commentaries*, that "the greater part of the income of the bishop, canons and other church ministers came from the tithe on coca. ... With the few coins that they received for their work, the Indians bought coca leaves ... chewing the leaves they could stand better ... the inhuman tasks imposed upon them".

Today coca continues to play an important role in the lives of Peru's indigenous highlanders. The act of chewing coca is a form of social bonding; it can stave off hunger and fatigue, relieve the effects of altitude, help divine the future, or appease Mother Earth in ceremonies as old as the cultures that have guarded them so jealously through the centuries.

Aymara

High up in the Andes, in the southern part of Peru, lies a wide, barren and hostile plateau, the altiplano. Prior to Inca rule Tiahuanaco on Lake Titicaca was a highly organized centre for one the greatest cultures South America has ever witnessed: the Aymara people. Today, the shores of this lake and the plains that surround it remain the homeland of the Aymara. The majority live in Bolivia, the rest are scattered on the southwestern side of Peru and northern Chile. The climate is so harsh on the altiplano that, though they are extremely hardworking, their lives are very poor. They speak their own unwritten language, Aymara. More so than the scattered group of different peoples that speak Quechua, the Altiplano Aymara people form a compact group with a clear sense of their own distinct identity and in many respects have been able to preserve more of their indigenous traditions and belief system.

The Aymaras are a deeply religious people whose culture is permeated with the idea of the sacred. They believe that God, the Supreme Being, gives them security in their daily lives and this God of Life manifests him/herself through the deities, such as those of the mountains, the water, wind, sun, moon and *wa'qas* (sacred places). As a sign of gratitude, the Aymara give *wax'ta* (offerings), *wilancha* (llama sacrifices) and *ch'alla* (sprinkling alcohol on the ground) to the *achachilas* (the protecting spirits of the family and community), the Pachamama (Mother Earth), Kuntur Mamani and Uywiri (protecting spirits of the home).

The remote mountains of the bleak *altiplano* are of particular importance for the Aymara. The most sacred places are these high mountains, far from human problems. It is here that the people have built their altars to offer worship, to communicate with their God and ask forgiveness. The community is also held important in the lives of the Aymara. The achachila is the great-great grandfather of the family as well as the protector of the community, and as such is God's representative on earth.

The offerings to the sacred mountains take place for the most part in August and are community celebrations. Many different rituals are celebrated: there are those within the family; in the mountains; for the planting and the harvest; rites to ask for rain or to ask for protection against hailstorms and frosts; and ceremonies for Mother Earth.

All such rituals are led by Aymara Yatiris, who are male or female priests. The Yatiri is a wise person – someone who knows – and the community's spiritual and moral guide. Through a method of divination that involves the reading of coca leaves, they guide individuals in their personal decision-making.

Amazonian peoples

Before the arrival of the Europeans, an estimated six million people inhabited the Amazon Basin, comprising more than 2000 tribes or ethnic-linguistic groups who managed to adapt to their surroundings through the domestication of a great variety of animals and plants, and to benefit from the numerous nutritional, curative, narcotic and hallucinogenic properties of thousands of wild plants.

It's not easy to determine the precise origin of these aboriginal people. What is known, however, is that since the start of colonial times this population slowly but constantly decreased, mainly because of western diseases such as influenza and measles. This demographic decline reached dramatic levels during the rubber boom of the late 19th and early 20th centuries as a result of forced labour and slavery.

Today, at the basin level, the population is calculated at no more than two million inhabitants making up 400 ethnic groups, of which approximately 200,000 to 250,000 live in the Peruvian jungle. Within the basin it is possible to distinguish at least three large conglomerates of aboriginal societies: the inhabitants of the *varzea*, or seasonally flooded lands alongside the large rivers (such as the Omagua, Cocama and Shipibo people); the people in the interfluvial zones or firm lands (such as the Amahuaca, Cashibo and Yaminahua) and those living in the Andean foothills (such as the Amuesha, Asháninka and Machiguenga).

The Amazonian natives began to be decimated in the 16th century, and so were the first endangered species of the jungle. These communities still face threats to their traditional lifestyles, notably from timber companies, gold miners and multinational oil companies. There appears to be little effective control of deforestation and the intrusion of colonists who have taken over native lands to establish small farms. And though oil companies have reached compensation agreements with local communities, previous oil exploration has contaminated many jungle rivers, as well as exposing natives to risk from diseases against which they have no immunity.

Criollos and mestizos

The first immigrants were the Spaniards who followed Pizarro's expeditionary force. Their effect, demographically, politically and culturally, has been enormous. They intermarried with the indigenous population and the children of mixed parentage were called mestizos. The Peruvian-born children of Spanish parents were known as *criollos*, though this word is now used to describe people who live on the coast, regardless of their ancestry, and coastal culture in general.

Afro-Peruvians

Peru's black community is based on the coast, mainly in Chincha, south of Lima, and also in some working-class districts of the capital. Their ancestors were originally imported into Peru in the 16th century as slaves to work on the sugar and cotton plantations on the coast. Though small – between 2% and 5% of the total population – the black community has had a major influence on Peruvian culture, particularly in music and dancing and cuisine.

Asian immigrants

There are two main Asian communities in Peru, the Japanese and Chinese. Large numbers of poor Chinese labourers were brought to Peru in the mid-19th century to work in virtual slavery on the guano reserves on the Pacific Coast and to build the railroads in the central Andes. The culinary influence of the Chinese can be seen in the many *chifas* found throughout the country.

The Japanese community, now numbering some 100,000, established itself in the first half of the 20th century. The normally reclusive community gained prominence when Alberto Fujimori, one of its members, became the first president of Japanese descent outside Japan anywhere in the world. During Fujimori's presidency, many other Japanese Peruvians took prominent positions in business, central and local government. The nickname 'chino' is applied to anyone of Oriental origin.

Europeans

Like most of Latin America, Peru received many emigrés from Europe seeking land and opportunities in the late 19th century. The country's wealth and political power remains concentrated in the hands of this small and exclusive class of whites, which also consists of the descendants of the first Spanish families. There still exists a deep divide between people of European descent and the old colonial snobbery persists.

Religion

The Inca religion (described on page 312) was displaced by Roman Catholicism from the 16th century onwards, the conversion of the inhabitants of the 'New World' to Christianity being one of the stated aims of the Spanish *conquistádores*. Today, statistics vary between 81% and 89% of the population declaring itself Catholic.

One of the first exponents of Liberation Theology, under which the Conference of Latin American Bishops in 1968 committed themselves to the 'option for the poor', was Gustavo Gutiérrez, from Huánuco. This doctrine caused much consternation to orthodox Catholics, particularly those members of the Latin American church who had traditionally aligned themselves with the oligarchy. Gutiérrez, however, traced the church's duty to the voiceless and the marginalized back to Fray Bartolomé de las Casas.

The Catholic Church faced a further challenge to its authority when President Fujimori won the battle over family planning and the need to slow down the rate of population growth. Its greatest threat, however, comes from the proliferation of evangelical Protestant groups throughout the country. Some 6% of the population now declare themselves Protestant and one million or more people belong to some 27 different non-Catholic denominations.

Although the vast majority of the population ostensibly belongs to the Roman Catholic religion, in reality religious life for many Peruvians is a mix of Catholic beliefs imported from Europe and indigenous traditions based on animism, the worship of deities from the natural world such as mountains, animals and plants. Some of these ancient indigenous traditions and beliefs are described throughout this section.

Arts and crafts

Peru is exceptionally rich in handicrafts. Its geographic division into four distinct regions – coast, mountains, valleys and Amazon Basin – coupled with cultural differences, has resulted in numerous variations in technique and design. Each province, even each community, has developed its own style of weaving or carving.

The Incas inherited 3000 years of skills and traditions: gold, metal and precious stonework from the Chimú; feather textiles from the Nazca; and the elaborate textiles of the Paracas. All of these played important roles in political, social and religious ceremonies. Though much of this artistic heritage was destroyed by the Spanish conquest, the traditions adapted and evolved in numerous ways, absorbing new methods, concepts and materials from Europe while maintaining ancient techniques and symbols.

Textiles and costumes

Woven cloth was the most highly prized possession and sought after trading commodity in the Andes in pre-Columbian times. It is, therefore, not surprising that ancient weaving traditions have survived. **The Incas** inherited this rich weaving tradition. They forced the Aymaras to work in *mit'as* or textile workshops. The ruins of some enormous *mit'as* can be seen at the temple of Raqchi, south of Cuzco (see page 226). Inca textiles are of high quality and very different from coastal textiles, being warp-faced, closely woven and without embroidery. The largest quantities of the finest textiles were made specifically to

The family that weaves together ...

Historically, the women weave most of the men's garments and the men weave the women's, or at least a very important part of them: the men weave the women's skirts. It works like this: the women weave the fine warp-faced pieces like *llicllas* (*mantas*), ponchos, *chumpis* (belts), *ch'uspas*, and similar items. But the plainer elements, men's pantaloons, women's skirts, are woven by men on large treadle looms, imported from Europe soon after the conquest. The men also weave the thick blankets, but on heavier versions of the traditional backstrap loom (or waist loom). The men are also the knitters and crochet makers. There are a few elements of Andean garb that are not woven at all, the most important being the *chullo* (the classic wool cap with the earl flaps), but there are also *chullos* for children of either sex and, in some areas like Pitumarca, for young girls until puberty. All of these are knitted, the preferred alternative to the standard knitting needles being the spokes of bicycle wheels.

For a while, many of the traditional elements of weaving were under threat from synthetic threads and dyes, commercially produced garments and the need for men to leave their communities in search of work. But a resurgence is under way. Organizations such the Center for Traditional Textiles of Cusco (www.textilescusco.org), Awamaki (www.awamaki.org), Threads of Peru (www.threadsofperu.com) and others are seeking to rescue techniques and arts that were being lost. They are fostering individual creativity, a new sense of community and an understanding of how much the weavers' skills are valued in a global market. This is also encouraging a new family dynamic in that women are, often for the first time, bringing an income to the household, money which can be spent on the children and their well-being.

be burned as ritual offerings – a tradition which still survives. The Spanish, too, exploited this wealth and skill by using the *mit'as* and exporting the cloth to Europe.

Prior to Inca rule Aymara men wore a tunic (*llahua*) and a mantle (*llacata*) and carried a bag for coca leaves (*huallquepo*). The women wore a wrapped dress (*urku*) and mantle (*iscayo*) and a belt (*huaka*); their coca bag was called an *istalla*. The *urku* was fastened at shoulder level with a pair of metal *tupu*, the traditional Andean dress pins.

The Inca men had tunics (*unkus*) and a bag for coca leaves called a *ch'uspa*. The women wore a blouse (*huguna*), skirts (*aksu*) and belts (*chumpis*), and carried foodstuffs in large, rectangular cloths called *llicllas*, which were fastened at the chest with a single pin or a smaller clasp called a *ttipqui*. Women of the Sacred Valley now wear a layered, gathered skirt called a *pollera* and a *montera*, a large, round, red Spanish type of hat. Textiles continue to play an important part in society. They are still used specifically for ritual ceremonies and some even held to possess magical powers.

Textile materials and techniques

The Andean people used mainly alpaca or llama wool. The former can be spun into fine, shining yarn when woven and has a lustre similar to that of silk, though sheep's wool came to be widely used following the Spanish conquest.

A commonly used technique is the drop spindle. A stick is weighted with a wooden wheel and the raw material is fed through one hand. A sudden twist and drop in the spindle spins the yarn. This very sensitive art can be seen practised by women while herding animals in the fields. Spinning wheels were introduced by Europeans and are now prevalent owing to increased demand. Pre-Columbian looms were often portable and those in use today are generally similar. A woman will herd her animals while making a piece of costume, perhaps on a backstrap loom, or waist loom, so-called because the weaver controls the tension on one side with her waist with the other side tied to an upright or tree. The pre-Columbian looms are usually used for personal costume while the treadle loom is used by men for more commercial pieces.

The skills of **dyeing** were still practised virtually unchanged even after the arrival of the Spanish. Nowadays, the word *makhnu* refers to any natural dye, but originally was the name for cochineal, an insect which lives on the leaves of the nopal cactus. These dyes were used widely by pre-Columbian weavers. Today, the biggest centre of production in South America is the valleys around Ayacucho. Vegetable dyes are also used, made from the leaves, fruit and seeds of shrubs and flowers and from lichen, tree bark and roots.

Pottery

Inca ceramic decoration consists mainly of small-scale geometric and usually symmetrical designs. One distinctive form of vessel which continues to be made and used is the *arybola*. This pot is designed to carry liquid, especially *chicha*, and is secured with a rope on the bearer's back. It is believed that *arybolas* were used mainly by the governing Inca elite and became important status symbols. Today, Inca-style is very popular in Cuzco and Pisac.

With the Spanish invasion many indigenous communities lost their artistic traditions, others remained relatively untouched, while others still combined Hispanic and indigenous traditions and techniques. The Spanish brought three innovations: the potter's wheel, which gave greater speed and uniformity; knowledge of the enclosed kiln; and the technique of lead glazes. The enclosed kiln made temperature regulation easier and allowed higher temperatures to be maintained, producing stronger pieces. Today, many communities continue to apply pre-Hispanic techniques, while others use more modern processes.

Jewellery and metalwork

Some of the earliest goldwork originates from the Chavín culture – eg the *Tumi* knife found in Lambayeque. These first appeared in the Moche culture, when they were associated with human sacrifice. Five centuries later, the Incas used *tumis* for surgical operations such as trepanning skulls. Today, they are a common motif.

The Incas associated gold with the sun. However, very few examples remain as the Spanish melted down their amassed gold and silver objects. They then went on to send millions of Indians to their deaths in gold and silver mines.

During the colonial period gold and silver pieces were made to decorate the altars of churches and houses of the elite. Metalworkers came from Spain and Italy to develop the industry. The Spanish preferred silver and strongly influenced the evolution of silverwork during the colonial period. A style known as Andean baroque developed around Cuzco embracing both indigenous and European elements. Silver bowls in this style – *cochas* – are still used in Andean ceremonies.

Woodcarving

Wood is one of the most commonly used materials. Carved ceremonial objects include drums, carved sticks with healing properties, masks and the Incas' *keros* – wooden vessels for drinking *chicha*. *Keros* come in all shapes and sizes and were traditionally decorated with scenes of war, local dances, or harvesting coca leaves. The Chancay, who lived along the coast between 100 BC and AD 1200, used *keros* carved with sea birds and fish. Today, they are used in some Andean ceremonies, especially during **Fiesta del Cruz**, the Andean May festival.

Glass mirrors were introduced by the Spanish, although the Chimú and Lambayeque cultures used obsidian and silver plates, and Inca *chasquis* (messengers) used reflective stones to communicate between hilltop forts. Transporting mirrors was costly, therefore they were produced in Lima and Quito. Cuzco and Cajamarca then became centres of production. In Cuzco the frames were carved, covered in gold leaf and decorated with tiny pieces of cut mirror. Cajamarca artisans, meanwhile, incorporated painted glass into the frames.

Gourd-carving

Gourd-carving, or *mate burilado*, as it is known, is one of Peru's most popular and traditional handicrafts. It is thought even to predate pottery – engraved gourds found on the coast have been dated to some 3500 years ago. During the Inca empire gourd-carving became a valued art form and workshops were set up and supported by the state. Gourds were used in rituals and ceremonies and to make *poporos* – containers for the lime used while chewing coca leaves.

Music and dance

The music of Peru can be described as the very heartbeat of the country. Peruvians see music as something in which to participate, and not as a spectacle. Just about everyone, it seems, can play a musical instrument or sing. Just as music is the heartbeat of the country, so dance conveys the rich and ancient heritage that typifies much of the national spirit. Peruvians are tireless dancers and dancing is the most popular form of entertainment. Unsuspecting travellers should note that once they make that first wavering step there will be no respite until they collapse from exhaustion.

Each region has its own distinctive music and dance that reflects its particular lifestyle, its mood and its physical surroundings. The music of the sierra, for example, is played in a minor key and tends to be sad and mournful, while the music of the lowlands is more up-tempo and generally happier. Peruvian music divides at a very basic level into that of the highlands (*Andina*) and that of the coast (*Criolla*).

Highlands When people talk of Peruvian music they are almost certainly referring to the music of the Quechua- and Aymara-speaking Indians of the highlands which provides the most distinctive Peruvian sound. The highlands themselves can be very roughly subdivided into some half dozen major musical regions, of which perhaps the most characteristic are Ancash and the north, the Mantaro Valley, Cuzco, Puno and the Altiplano, Ayacucho and Parinacochas.

Urban and other styles Owing to the overwhelming migration of peasants into the barrios of Lima, most types of Andean music and dance can be seen in the capital, notably on Sundays at the so-called *Coliseos*, which exist for that purpose. This flood of migration to the cities has also meant that the distinct styles of regional and ethnic groups have become blurred. One example is **Chicha music**, which comes from the *pueblos jóvenes*, and was once the favourite dance music of Peru's urban working class. *Chicha* is a hybrid of Huayno music and the Colombian cumbia rhythm – a meeting of the highlands and the tropical coast.

Another recent phenomenon is **tecno-cumbia**, which originated in the jungle region with groups such as **Rossy War**, from Puerto Maldonado, and **Euforia**, from Iquitos. It is a vibrant dance music which has gained much greater popularity across Peruvian society than *chicha* music ever managed. There are now also many exponents on the coast such as **Agua Marina** and **Armonía 10**. Many of the songs comment on political issues and Fujimori used to join **Rossy War** on stage. Tecno-cumbia has evolved into a more sophisticated form with wider appeal across Peruvian society, with **Grupo 5**, from Chiclayo, one of the most popular exponents.

Música criolla, the music from the coast, could not be more different from that of the sierra. Here the roots are Spanish and African. The immensely popular **Valsesito** is a syncopated waltz that would certainly be looked at askance in Vienna and the **Polca** has also undergone an attractive sea change.

Reigning over all, though, is the **Marinera**, Peru's national dance, a splendidly rhythmic and graceful courting encounter and a close cousin of Chile's and Bolivia's *Cueca* and the Argentine *Zamba*, all of them descended from the *zamacueca*. The Marinera has its *Limeña* and *Norteña* versions and a more syncopated relative, the *Tondero*, found in the northern coastal regions, is said to have been influenced by slaves brought from Madagascar.

All these dances are accompanied by guitars and frequently the *cajón*, a resonant wooden box on which the player sits, pounding it with his hands. Great names of *música criolla* include the singer/composers **Chabuca Granda** and **Alicia Maguiña**, the singer **Jesús Vásquez** and the groups **Los Morochucos** and **Hermanos Zañartu**.

Afro-Peruvian Also on the coast is the music of the small but influential black community, the *Música Negroide* or *Afro-Peruano*, which had virtually died out when it was resuscitated in the 1950s, but has since gone from strength to strength, thanks to **Nicomedes and Victoria Santa Cruz** who have been largely responsible for popularizing this black music and making it an essential ingredient in contemporary Peruvian popular music. It has all the qualities to be found in black music from the Caribbean – a powerful, charismatic beat, rhythmic and lively dancing, and strong percussion provided by the *cajón* and the *quijada de burro*, a donkey's jaw with the teeth loosened. Its greatest star is the Afro-Peruvian diva **Susana Baca**. Her incredible, passionate voice inspired Talking Head's David Byrne to explore this genre further and release a compilation album in 1995, thus bringing Afro-Peruvian music to the attention of the world. Other notable exponents are the excellent **Perú Negro**, one of the best music and dance groups in Latin America, and the singer Eva Ayllón. **Novalima**, a group of internationally based Peruvian musicians, has produced new arrangements of many classic Afro-Peruvian tracks (see www.novalima.net).

Musical instruments Before the arrival of the Spanish in Latin America, the only instruments were wind and percussion. Although it is a popular misconception that Andean music is based on the panpipes, guitar and *charango*, anyone who travels through the Andes will realize that these instruments only represent a small aspect of Andean music. The highland instrumentation varies from region to region, although the harp and violin are ubiquitous. In the Mantaro area the harp is backed by brass and wind instruments, notably the clarinet. In Cuzco it is the *charango* and *quena* and on the altiplano the *sicu* panpipes.

The *quena* is a flute, usually made of reed, characterized by not having a mouthpiece to blow through. As with all Andean instruments, there is a family of *quenas* varying in length from around 15 cm to 50 cm. The *sicu* is the Aymara name for the *zampoña*, or panpipes. It is the most important pre-Hispanic Andean instrument, formed by several reed tubes of different sizes held together by knotted string. Virtually the only instrument of European origin is the *charango*. When stringed instruments were first introduced by the Spanish, the indigenous people liked them but wanted something that was their own and so the *charango* was born. Originally, they were made of clay, condor skeletons and armadillo or tortoise shells.

Dances

The highlands are immensely rich in terms of music and dance, with over 200 dances recorded. Every village has its fiestas and every fiesta has its communal and religious dances. *Comparsas* are organized groups of dancers who perform for spectators dances following a set pattern of movements to a particular musical accompaniment, wearing a specific costume. These dances have a long tradition, having mostly originated from certain contexts and circumstances and some of them still parody the ex-Spanish colonial masters.

Many dances for couples and/or groups are danced spontaneously at fiestas throughout Peru. These include indigenous dances which have originated in a specific region and ballroom dances that reflect the Spanish influence. One of the most popular of the indigenous dances is the **Huayno**, which originated on the altiplano but is now danced throughout the country. It involves numerous couples, who whirl around or advance down the street, arm-in-arm, in a *pandilla*. During fiestas, and especially after a few drinks, this can develop into a kind of uncontrolled frenzy.

Festivals

Fiestas (festivals) are a fundamental part of life for most Peruvians, taking place up and down the length and breadth of the country and with such frequency that it would be hard to miss one, even during the briefest of stays. This is fortunate, because arriving in any town or village during these inevitably frenetic celebrations is one of the great Peruvian experiences.

While Peru's festivals can't rival those of Brazil for fame or colour, the quantity of alcohol consumed and the partying run them pretty close. What this means is that, at some point, you will fall over, through inebriation or exhaustion, or both. After several days of this, you will awake with a hangover the size of the Amazon rainforest and probably have no recollection of what you did with your backpack.

The object of the fiesta is a practical one, such as the success of the coming harvest or the fertility of animals. Thus the constant eating, drinking and dancing serves the purpose of giving thanks for the Sun and Rain that makes things grow and for the fertility of the soil and livestock, gifts from *Pachamama* (Mother Earth), the most sacred of all gods. So, when you see a Peruvian spill a little *chicha* (maize beer) every time they refill, it's not because they're sloppy but because they're offering a *ch'alla* (sacrifice) to Pachamama.

Literature

The fact that the Incas had no written texts in the conventional European sense and that the Spaniards were keen to suppress their conquest's culture means that there is little evidence today of what poetry and theatre was performed in pre-conquest times. It is known that the Incas had two types of poet, the *amautas* – historians, poets and teachers who composed works that celebrated the ruling class' gods, heroes and events – and *haravecs* – who expressed popular sentiments. Written Quechua today is less common than works in the oral tradition. Although Spanish culture has had some influence on Quechua, the native stories, lyrics and fables retain their own identity. Not until the 19th century did Peruvian writers begin seriously to incorporate indigenous ideas into their art, but their audience was limited. Nevertheless, the influence of Quechua on Peruvian literature in Spanish continues to grow.

Colonial period

In 16th-century Lima, headquarters of the Viceroyalty of Peru, the Spanish officials concentrated their efforts on the religious education of the new territories and literary output was limited to mainly histories and letters.

Chroniclers such as **Pedro Cieza de León** (*Crónica del Perú*, published from 1553) and **Agustín de Zárate** (*Historia del descubrimiento y conquista del Perú*, 1555) were written from the point of view that Spanish domination was right. Their most renowned successors, though, took a different stance. **Inca Garcilaso de la Vega** was a mestizo, whose *Comentarios reales que tratan del origen de los Incas* (1609) were at pains to justify the achievements, religion and culture of the Inca Empire. He also commented on Spanish society in the colony. A later work, *Historia general del Perú* (1617), went further in condemning Viceroy Toledo's suppression of Inca culture. Through his work, written in Spain, many aspects of Inca society, plus poems and prayers have survived.

Writing at about the same time as Inca Garcilaso was **Felipe Guaman Poma de Ayala**, whose *El primer nueva corónica y buen gobierno* (1613-1615) is possibly one of the most reproduced of Latin American texts (eg on T-shirts, CDs, posters and carrier bags). Guaman Poma was a minor provincial Inca chief whose writings and illustrations, addressed to King Felipe III of Spain, offer a view of a stable pre-conquest Andean society (not uniquely Inca), in contrast with the unsympathetic colonial society that usurped it.

In the years up to Independence, the growth of an intellectual elite in Lima spawned more poetry than anything else. As *criollo* discontent grew, satire increased both in poetry and in the sketches which accompanied dramas imported from Spain. The poet **Mariano Melgar** (1791-1815), who wrote in a variety of styles, died in an uprising against the Spanish but played an important part in the Peruvian struggle from freedom from the colonial imagination.

After Independence

After Independence, Peruvian writers imitated Spanish *costumbrismo*, sketches of characters and lifestyles from the new Republic. The first author to transcend this fashion was **Ricardo Palma** (1833-1919), whose inspiration, the *tradición*, fused *costumbrismo* and Peru's rich oral traditions. Palma's hugely popular *Tradiciones peruanas* is a collection of pieces which celebrate the people, history and customs of Peru through sayings, small incidents in mainly colonial history and gentle irony.

Much soul-searching was to follow Peru's defeat in the War of the Pacific. **Manuel González Prada** (1844-1918), for instance, wrote essays fiercely critical of the state of the nation: *Páginas libres* (1894), *Horas de lucha* (1908). **José Carlos Mariátegui**, the foremost Peruvian political thinker of the early 20th century, said that González Prada represented the first lucid instant of Peruvian consciousness.

Mario Vargas Llosa

The best known of Peru's writers, Mario Vargas Llosa, was born in 1936 in Arequipa and educated in Cochabamba (Bolivia), from where his family moved to Piura. After graduating from the Universidad de San Marcos, he won a scholarship to Paris in 1958 and, from 1959 to 1974, lived first in Paris then in London in voluntary exile. In 2010, while teaching at Princeton University in the US, he was awarded the Nobel Prize for Literature, "for his cartography of structures of power and his trenchant images of the individual's resistance, revolt and defeat". At the time of winning, he said "This Nobel goes to Latin American literature. It is a recognition of everything that surrounds me." Much has been written about his personal life, and his political opinions have been well documented, but, as befits an author of the highest international standing and one of the leading figures in the so-called 'Boom' of Latin American writers in the 1960s, it is for his novels that Vargas Llosa the writer is best known.

The first three – *La ciudad y los perros* (1963), *La casa verde* (1966) and *Conversación en la Catedral* (1969) – with their techniques of flashback, multiple narrators and different interwoven stories, are an adventure for the reader. Meanwhile, the humorous books, like *Pantaleón y las visitadoras* and *La tía Julia y el escribidor* cannot be called lightweight. *La guerra del fin del mundo* marked a change to a more direct style and an intensification of Vargas Llosa's exploration of the role of fiction as a human necessity, extending also to political ideologies. *La fiesta del chivo* (2000) is another fictionalized account of historical events, this time the assassination of President Trujillo of the Dominican Republic in 1961 and the intrigue and fear surrounding his period in office. It is a gripping story, widely regarded as one of his best. More recently he has written *Travesuras de la niña mala* (2006 – The Bad Girl), which the author called his first 'love story', and, due out at the time of going to press in 2010, *El sueño del celta*, about the Irishman, Roger Casement.

Vargas Llosa has always maintained that in Peruvian society the writer is a privileged person who should be able to mix politics and literature as a normal part of life. This drive for authenticity led to his excursion into national politics. He stood as a presidential candidate in 1990, losing to Alberto Fujimori. He has since taken up Spanish citizenship (2007) with homes in Lima, Paris, Madrid and London.

20th century

Mariátegui himself (1895-1930), after a visit to Europe in 1919, considered deeply the question of Peruvian identity, writing about politics, economics, literature and the Indian question from a Marxist perspective (see *Siete ensayos de interpretación de la realidad peruana*, 1928). Other writers had continued this theme. **Clorinda Matto de Turner** (1854-1909), with *Aves sin nido* (1889), was the forerunner by several years of the 'indigenist' genre in Peru and the most popular of those who took up González Prada's cause. Other prose writers continued in this vein at the beginning of the 20th century, but it was **Ciro Alegría** (1909-1967) who gave major, fictional impetus to the racial question. Of his first three novels, *La serpiente de oro* (1935), *Los perros hambrientos* (1938) and *El mundo es ancho y ajeno* (1941), the latter is his most famous.

Contemporary with Alegría was **José María Arguedas** (1911-69), whose novels, stories and politics were also deeply rooted in the ethnic question. Arguedas, though not Indian, had a largely Quechua upbringing and tried to reconcile this with the hispanic world in which he worked. This inner conflict was one of the main causes of his suicide. His books include *Agua* (short stories, 1935), *Yawar fiesta* (1941), *Los ríos profundos* (1958) and *Todas las sangres* (1964).

In the 1950s and 1960s, there was a move away from the predominantly rural and indigenist to an urban setting. At the forefront were, among others, **Mario Vargas Llosa** (see Box), **Julio Ramón Ribeyro**, **Enrique Congrains Martín**, **Oswaldo Reynoso**, **Luis Loayza**, **Sebastián Salazar Bondy** and **Carlos E Zavaleta**. They explored all aspects of the city, including the influx of people from the sierra. These writers incorporated new narrative techniques in the urban novel, which presented a world where popular culture and speech were rich sources of literary material, despite the difficulty in transcribing them.

Alfredo Bryce Echenique (born 1939) has enjoyed much popularity following the success of *Un mundo para Julius* (1970), a brilliant satire on the upper and middle classes of Lima. Other contemporary writers of note are **Rodolfo Hinostrozo** (born 1941), novelist, playwright and poet, **Mario Bellatín** (born 1960 – see *Salón de belleza* and *Damas chinas*), and **Jaime Bayly**, who is also a journalist and TV presenter. His novels include *Fue ayer y no me acuerdo*, *Los últimos días de la prensa*, *La noche es virgen* and *Ya de repente, un angel*. Most recently, writers are confronting the violence and the after-effects of the Sendero Luminoso/MRTA and Fujimori/Montesinos period, with powerful, neorrealist novels and stories. Among the best examples are **Alonso Cueto** (born 1954): *Grandes miradas* (2003), *La hora azul* (2005); **Santiago Roncagliolo** (born 1975): *Abril rojo* (2006); and **Daniel Alarcón** (born Lima 1977), who lives in the USA and writes in English: *War by Candlelight* (2005) and *Lost City Radio* (2007).

Without doubt, the most important poet in Peru, if not Latin America, in the first half of the 20th century, was **César Vallejo**, born in 1892 in Santiago de Chuco (Libertad). In 1928 he was a founder of the Peruvian Socialist Party, then he joined the Communist Party in 1931 in Madrid. From 1936 to his death in Paris in 1938 he opposed the fascist takeover in Spain. His first volume was *Los heraldos negros* in which the dominating theme of all his work, a sense of confusion and inadequacy in the face of the unpredictability of life, first surfaces. *Trilce* (1922), his second work, is unlike anything before it in the Spanish language. *Poemas humanos* and *España, aparta de mí este cáliz* (written as a result of Vallejo's experiences in the Spanish Civil War) were both published posthumously, in 1939.

In addition to Clorinda Matto de Turner (see above), modern women writers worth checking out are: **Blanca Varela** (1926-2009), who published volumes of poetry from 1959 (*Ese puerto existe*) to her anthology *Como Dios en la nada* (covering 1949-1998). **Carmen Ollé** (born 1947) introduced a style of writing that is regarded as feminist and confessional. Her best-known poetry collection is *Noches de adrenalina* (1981), while her prose includes *Las dos caras del deseo* (1994) and *Una muchacha bajo su paraguas* (2002). **Giovanna Pollarolo** is a poet, short storywriter and screenwriter (born 1952) whose collections include *Huerto de olivos*, 1982, *Entre mujeres solas*, 1996, and *Atado de nervios*, 1999. **Laura Riesco's** (1940-2008) *Ximena de dos caminos* (1994), an episodic tale of a young girl growing up in the sierra in the 1940s, is considered one of the best, late 20th-century Peruvian novels.

Painting

The Catholic Church was the main patron of the arts during the colonial period. The innumerable churches and monasteries that sprang up in the newly conquered territories created a demand for paintings and sculptures, met initially by imports from Europe of both works of art and of skilled craftsmen, and later by home-grown products. An essential requirement for the inauguration of any new church was an image for the altar and many churches in Lima preserve fine examples of sculptures imported from Seville during the 16th and 17th centuries. But sculptures were expensive and difficult to import, and as part of their policy of relative frugality the Franciscan monks tended to favour paintings. The Jesuits, too, tended to commission paintings and several major works by Sevillian artists can be seen in Lima's churches.

Painters and sculptors soon made their way to Peru in search of lucrative commissions including several Italians who arrived during the later 16th century. The Jesuit **Bernardo Bitti** (1548-1610), for example, trained in Rome before working in Lima, Cuzco, Juli and Arequipa. European imports, however, could not keep up with demand and local workshops of creole, mestizo and Indian craftsmen flourished from the latter part of the 16th century. As the Viceregal capital and the point of arrival into Peru, the art of Lima was always strongly influenced by European, especially Spanish models, but the old Inca capital of Cuzco became the centre of a regional school of painting which developed its own characteristics. A series of paintings of the 1660s, now hanging in the Museo de Arte Religioso in Cuzco, commemorate the colourful Corpus Christi procession of statues of the local patron saints through the streets of Cuzco. These paintings document the appearance of the city and local populace, including Spanish and Inca nobility, priests and laity, rich and poor, Spaniard, Indian, African and mestizo. Many of the statues represented in this series are still venerated in the local parish churches. They are periodically painted and dressed in new robes, but underneath are the original sculptures, executed by native craftsmen. Some are of carved wood while others use the pre-conquest technique of maguey cactus covered in sized cloth.

One of the most successful native painters was **Diego Quispe Tito** (1611-81) who claimed descent from the Inca nobility and whose large canvases, often based on Flemish engravings, demonstrate the wide range of European sources that were available to Andean artists in the 17th century. But the **Cuzco School** is best known for the anonymous devotional works where the painted contours of the figures are overlaid with flat patterns in gold, creating highly decorative images with an underlying tension between the two- and three-dimensional aspects of the work. The taste for richly decorated surfaces can also be seen in the 17th- and 18th-century frescoed interiors of many Andean churches, as in Chinchero, Andahuaylillas and Huaro, and in the ornate carving on altarpieces and pulpits throughout Peru.

Land and environment

Geography

Peru is the third largest South American country, the size of France, Spain and the United Kingdom combined, and presents formidable difficulties to human habitation. Virtually all of the 2250 km of its Pacific Coast is desert. From the narrow coastal shelf the Andes rise steeply to a high plateau dominated by massive ranges of snow-capped peaks and gouged with deep canyons. The heavily forested and deeply ravined Andean slopes are more gradual to the east. Further east, towards Brazil and Colombia, begin the vast jungles of the Amazon Basin.

Highlands

The highlands, or sierra, extend inland from the coastal strip some 250 km in the north, increasing to 400 km in the south. The average altitude is about 3000 m and 50% of Peruvians live there. Essentially, it is a plateau dissected by dramatic canyons and dominated by some of the most spectacular mountain ranges in the world.

In spite of these ups and downs which cause great communications difficulties, the presence of water and a more temperate climate on the plateau has attracted people throughout the ages. Present day important population centres in the Highlands include Cajamarca in the north, Huancayo in central Peru and Cuzco in the south, all at around 3000 m. Above this, at around 4000 m, is the 'high steppe' or *puna*, with constant winds and wide day/night temperature fluctuations. Nevertheless, fruit and potatoes (which originally came from the *puna* of Peru and Bolivia) are grown at this altitude and the meagre grasslands are home to the ubiquitous llama.

Eastern Andes and Amazon Basin

Almost half of Peru is on the eastern side of the Andes and about 90% of the country's drainage is into the Amazon system. It is an area of heavy rainfall with cloudforest above 3500 m and tropical rainforest lower down. There is little savanna, or natural grasslands, characteristic of other parts of the Amazon Basin.

There is some dispute on the Amazon's source. Officially, the mighty river begins as the Marañón, whose longest tributary rises just east of the Cordillera Huayhuash. However, the longest journey for the proverbial raindrop, some 6400 km, probably starts in southern Peru, where the headwaters of the Apurímac (Ucayali) flow from the snows on the northern side of the Nevado Mismi, near Cailloma.

With much more rainfall on the eastern side of the Andes, rivers are turbulent and erosion dramatic. Although vertical drops are not as great – there is a whole continent to cross to the Atlantic – valleys are deep, ridges narrow and jagged and there is forest below 3000 m. At 1500 m the Amazon jungle begins and water is the only means of surface transport available, apart from three roads which reach Saramериza (on the Marañón), Yurimaguas (on the Huallaga) and Pucallpa (on the Ucayali), all at about 300 m above the Atlantic which is still 4000 km or so downstream. The vastness of the Amazon lowlands becomes apparent and it is here that Peru bulges 650 km northeast past Iquitos to the point where it meets Colombia and Brazil at Leticia. Oil and gas have recently been found in the Amazon, and new finds are made every year, which means that new pipelines and roads will eventually link more places to the Pacific Coast.

Climate

In the highlands, April to October is the dry season. It is hot and dry during the day, around 20° to 25°C, and cold and dry at night, often below freezing. From November to April is the wet season, when it is dry and clear most mornings, with some rainfall in the afternoon. There is a small temperature drop (18°C) and not much difference at night (15°C). In the Amazonian lowlands April to October is the dry season, with temperatures up to 35°C. In the jungle areas of the south a cold front can pass through at night. November to April is the wet season. It is humid and hot, with heavy rainfall at any time.

Wildlife and vegetation

Peru is a country of great biological diversity. It contains 84 of the 117 recognized life zones and is one of the eight 'mega-diverse countries' on earth. The fauna and flora are to a large extent determined by the influence of the Andes, the longest uninterrupted mountain chain in the world, and the mighty Amazon river, which has by far the largest volume of any river in the world.

Andes

From the desert rise the steep Andean slopes. In the deeply incised valleys Andean fox and deer may occasionally be spotted. Herds of llamas and alpacas graze the steep hillsides. Mountain caracara and Andean lapwing are frequently observed soaring, and there is always the possibility of spotting flocks of mitred parrots or even the biggest species of hummingbird in the world (*Patagonia gigas*).

The Andean zone has many lakes and rivers and countless swamps. Exclusive to this area short-winged grebe and the torrent duck which feeds in the fast flowing rivers, and giant and horned coots. Chilean flamingo frequent the shallow soda lakes.

The *puna*, a habitat characterized by tussock grass and pockets of stunted alpine flowers, gives way to relict elfin forest and tangled bamboo thicket in this inhospitable windswept and frost-prone region. Occasionally the dissected remains of a *Puya* plant can be found; the result of the nocturnal foraging of the rare spectacled bear. There are quite a number of endemic species of rodent including the viscacha, and it is the last stronghold of the chinchilla. Here also pumas roam preying on the herbivores which frequent these areas, mountain-pudu, Andean deer or guemal and the mountain tapir.

Tropical Andes

The elfin forest grades into mist enshrouded cloudforest at about 3500 m. In the tropical zones of the Andes, the humidity in the cloudforests stimulates the growth of a vast variety of plants particularly mosses and lichens. The cloudforests are found in a narrow strip that runs along the eastern slopes of the spine of the Andes. It is these dense, often impenetrable, forests clothing the steep slopes that are important in protecting the headwaters of all the streams and rivers that cascade from the Andes to form the mighty Amazon as it begins its long journey to the sea.

This is a verdant world of dripping epiphytic mosses, lichens, ferns and orchids which grow in profusion despite the plummeting overnight temperatures. The high humidity resulting from the 2 m of rain that can fall in a year is responsible for the maintenance of the forest and it accumulates in puddles and leaks from the ground in a constant trickle that combines to form myriad icy, crystal-clear tumbling streams that cascade over precipitous waterfalls.

In secluded areas the flame-red Andean cock-of-the-rock give their spectacular display to females in the early morning mists. Woolly monkeys are also occasionally sighted as they descend the wooded slopes. Mixed flocks of colourful tanagers are commonly encountered, and the golden-headed quetzal and Amazon umbrella bird are occasionally seen.

Amazon Basin

At about 1500 m there is a gradual transition to the vast lowland forests of the Amazon Basin, which are warmer and more equable than the cloudforests clothing the mountains above. The daily temperature varies little during the year with a high of 23° to 32°C falling slightly to 20° to 26°C overnight. This lowland region receives some 2 m of rainfall per year most of it falling from November to April. The rest of the year is sufficiently dry, at least in the lowland areas to inhibit the growth of epiphytes and orchids which are so characteristic of the highland areas. For a week or two in the rainy season the rivers flood the forest. The zone immediately surrounding this seasonally flooded forest is referred to as *terre firme* forest.

The vast river basin of the Amazon is home to an immense variety of species. The environment has largely dictated the lifestyle. Life in or around rivers, lakes, swamps and forest depend on the ability to swim and climb and amphibious and tree-dwelling animals are common. Once the entire Amazon Basin was a great inland sea and the river still contains mammals more typical of the coast, eg manatees and dolphins.

Here, in the relatively constant climatic conditions, animal and plant life has evolved to an amazing diversity over the millennia. It has been estimated that 3.9 sq km of forest can harbour some 1200 vascular plants, 600 species of tree, and 120 woody plants. In these relatively flat lands, a soaring canopy some 50 m overhead is the power-house of the forest. It is a habitat choked with strangling vines and philodendrons among which mixed troupes of squirrel monkeys and brown capuchins forage. In the high canopy small groups of spider monkeys perform their lazy aerial acrobatics, whilst lower down, clinging to epiphyte-clad trunks and branches, groups of saddle-backed and emperor tamarins forage for blossom, fruit and the occasional insect prey.

The most accessible part of the jungle is on or near the many great meandering rivers. At each bend of the river the forest is undermined by the currents during the seasonal floods at the rate of some 10 m or 20 m per year leaving a sheer mud and clay bank, whilst on the opposite bend new land is laid down in the form of broad beaches of fine sand and silt.

A succession of vegetation can be seen. The fast growing willow-like *tessaria* first stabilizes the ground enabling the tall stands of *caña brava gynerium* to become established. Within these dense almost impenetrable stands the seeds of rainforest trees germinate and over a few years thrust their way towards the light. The fastest growing is a species of *cercropia* which forms a canopy 15 m to 18 m over the *caña* but even this is relatively short-lived. The gap in the canopy is quickly filled by other species. Two types of mahogany outgrow the other trees forming a closed canopy at 40 m with a lush understory of shade-tolerant *heliconia* and ginger. Eventually even the long-lived trees die off to be replaced by others providing a forest of great diversity.

Jungle wildlife

The meandering course of the river provides many excellent opportunities to see herds of russet-brown capybara – a sheep-sized rodent – peccaries and brocket deer. Of considerable ecological interest are the presence of oxbow lakes, or *cochas*, since these provide an abundance of wildlife which can be seen around the lake margins. The best way to see the wildlife is to get above the canopy. Ridges provide elevated viewpoints for excellent views over the forest. From here, it is possible to look across the lowland flood plain to the very foothills of the Andes, possibly some 200 km away. Flocks of parrots and macaws can be seen flying between fruiting trees and noisy troupes of squirrel monkeys and brown capuchins come very close.

The lowland rainforest of Peru is particularly famous for its primates and giant otters. Giant otters were once widespread in Amazonia but came close to extinction in the 1960s owing to persecution by the fur trade. The giant otter population in Peru has since recovered and is now estimated to be at least several hundred. Jaguar and other predators are also much in evidence. Although rarely seen their paw marks are commonly found along the forest trails. Rare bird species are also much in evidence, including fasciated tiger-heron and primitive hoatzins.

The (very) early morning is the best time to see peccaries, brocket deer and tapir at mineral licks (*collpa*). Macaw and parrot licks are found along the banks of the river. Here at dawn a dazzling display arrives and clambers around in the branches overhanging the clay lick. At its peak there may be 600 birds of up to six species (including red and green macaws, and blue-headed parrots) clamouring to begin their descent to the riverbank where they jostle for the mineral rich clay, a necessary addition to their diet which may also neutralize the toxins in their leaf and seed diet. Rare game birds such as razor-billed curassows and piping guans may also be seen.

A list of over 600 bird species has been compiled. Particularly noteworthy species are the black-faced cotinga, crested eagle, and the spectacular Harpy eagle, perhaps the world's most impressive raptor, easily capable of taking an adult monkey from the canopy. Mixed species flocks are commonly observed containing from 25 to over 100 birds of perhaps more than 30 species including blue dacnis, blue-tailed emerald, bananaquit, thick-billed euphoria and the paradise tanager. Each species occupies a slightly different niche, and since there are few individuals of each species in the flock, competition is avoided. Mixed flocks foraging in the canopy are often led by a white-winged shrike, whereas flocks foraging in the understorey are often led by the bluish-slate ant shrike. (For more information on the birds of Peru, see page 14.)

Books

Culture and history

Bingham, Hiram *Lost City of the Incas*, (new illustrated edition, with introduction by Hugh Thomson, Weidenfeld & Nicolson, London, 2002).

Bowen, Sally *The Fujimori File. Peru and its President 1990-2000* (2000). A very readable account of the last decade of the 20th century; it ends at the election of that year so the final momentous events of Fujimori's term happened after publication. Bowen has also written, with **Jane Holligan**, *The Imperfect Spy: the Many Lives of Vladimiro Montesinos* (2003), Peisa.

Hemming, John *The Conquest of the Incas* (1970). The one, invaluable book on the period of the conquest.

MacQuarrie, Kim *The Last Days of the Incas*, a thrilling account of the events that led to the Incas' final resistance and of the explorers who have tries to uncover the secrets of their civilization (2007) Piatkus.

Morrison, Tony *Qosqo. The Navel of the World* (1997) Condor Books. Cuzco's past and present with an extensive section of photographs of the city and its surroundings. *Pathways to the Gods: The Mystery of the Andes Lines* (1978), Michael Russell, obtainable in Lima; and *The Mystery of the Nasca Lines* (1987), nonesuch Expeditions, with an intro by Marie Reiche.

Mosely, Michael F *The Incas and their Ancestors: The Archaeology of Peru* (2001) Thames and Hudson.

Muscutt, Keith *Warriors of the Clouds: A Lost Civilization in the Upper Amazon of Peru* (1998) New Mexico Press. Excellent coffee table book and Chachapoyas memoir; also refer to its website (www.chachapoyas.com).

Starn, Orin, Carlos Iván Degregori, and **Robin Kirk**, *The Peru Reader* (2nd edition, 2005), Duke Univeristy Press. A good collection on history, culture and politics.

Urton, Gary, *The Social Life of Numbers* (1997), University of Texas Press, on the significance and philosophy of numbers in Andean society. Related to Urton's other studies on khipus and Inca mythology.

Capaq Ñan, the Royal Inca Road

Espinosa, Ricardo, *La Gran Ruta Inca, The Great Inca Route* (2002), Petróleos del Perú. A photographic and textual record of Espinosa's walk the length of the Camino Real de los Incas, in Spanish and English. He has also walked the length of Peru's coast, described in *El Perú a toda Costa* (1997) Editur. The same company has published *Zarzar, Omar, Por los Caminos del Perú en Bicicleta.*

Muller, Karin *Along the Inca Road. A Woman's Journey into an Ancient Empire* (2000), National Geographic.

Portway, Christopher *Journey Along the Andes* (1993) Impact Books. An account of the Andean Inca road.

Non-Peruvian Fiction

Matthiessen, Peter *At Play in the Fields of the Lord* (1965).

Shakespeare, Nicholas *The Vision of Elena Silves* (1989).

Thubron, Colin *To the Last City* (2002) Chatto & Windus.

Vltchek, Andre *Point of No Return* (2005) Mainstay Press.

Wilder, Thornton *The Bridge of San Luis Rey* (1941) Penguin.

Travel

Murphy, Dervla *Eight Feet in the Andes* (1983).

Parris, Matthew *Inca-Kola* (1990).

Shah, Tahir *Trail of Feathers* (2001).

Thomson, Hugh *The White Rock* (Phoenix, 2002), describes Thomson's own travels in the Inca heartland, as well as the journeys of earlier explorers. *Cochineal Red: Travels through Ancient Peru* (Weidenfeld & Nicolson, 2006), explores pre-Inca civilizations.

Trekking and climbing

Biggar, John *The Andes. A Guide for Climbers* (1999) Andes Publishing.

Gómez, Antonio, and Tomé, Juan José *La Cordillera Blanca de Los Andes* (1998) Desnivel, Spanish only, climbing guide with some trekking and general information, available locally. Also *Escaladas en los Andes. Guía de la Cordillera Blanca* (1999) Desnivel (Spanish only), a climbing guide.

Ricker, John F *Yuraq Janka, Cordilleras Blanca and Rosko* (1977), The Alpine Club of Canada, The American Alpine Club.

Sharman, David *Climbs of the Cordillera Blanca of Peru* (1995) Whizzo. A climbing guide, available locally, from South American Explorers, as well as from Cordee in the UK and Alpenbooks in the USA.

Simpson, Joe *Touching the Void* (1997) Vintage. A nail-biting account of Simpson's accident in the Cordillera Huayhuasah.

Wildlife

Clements, James F and Shany, Noam *A Field Guide to the Birds of Peru* (2001) Ibis.

Schulenberg, Thomas S, Stotz, Douglas F, et al *Birds of Peru* (2007), Helm. A comprehensive field guide.

TReeS (see under Jungle tours from Puerto Maldonado: Tambopata, for address) publish *Tambopata – A Bird Checklist, Tambopata – Mammal, Amphibian & Reptile Checklist* and *Reporte Tambopata*; they also produce tapes and CDs of *Jungle Sounds* and *Birds of Southeast Peru* and distribute other books and merchandise.

Valqui, Thomas, *Where to Watch Birds in Peru* (2004), www.granperu.com/bird watchingbook/. Describes 151 sites, how to get there and what to expect once there.

Walker, Barry, and Jon Fjeldsa *Birds of Machu Picchu*.

Contents

Footnotes

Spanish words and phrases

Volumes of dictionaries, phrase books or word lists will not provide the same enjoyment as being able to communicate directly with the people of the country you are visiting. Learning Spanish is a useful part of the preparation for a trip to Peru and you are encouraged to make an effort to grasp the basics before you go. As you travel you will pick up more of the language and the more you know, the more you will benefit from your stay. The following section is designed to be a simple point of departure.

Whether you have been taught the 'Castilian' pronunciation (z, and c followed by i or e are pronounced as the th in think) or the 'American' pronunciation (they are pronounced as s), you will encounter little difficulty in understanding either. Regional accents and usages vary, but the basic language is essentially the same everywhere. For a basic guide to pronunciation, see page 353.

Greetings, courtesies

good afternoon/evening/night	*buenas tardes/noches*
good morning	*buenos días*
goodbye	*adiós/chao*
hello	*hola*
How are you?	*¿cómo está?¿cómo estás?*
I do not understand	*no entiendo*
leave me alone	*déjeme en paz/no me moleste*
no	*no*
please	*por favor*
pleased to meet you	*mucho gusto/encantado/encantada*
see you later	*hasta luego*
thank you (very much)	*(muchas) gracias*
What is your name?	*¿cómo se llama? ¿cómo te llamas?*
yes	*sí*
I speak...	*Hablo...*
I speak Spanish	*Hablo español*
I don't speak Spanish	*No hablo español*
Do you speak English?	*¿habla inglés?*
Please speak slowly	*hable despacio por favor*
I am very sorry	*lo siento mucho/disculpe*
I'm fine, thanks	*estoy muy bien gracias*
I'm called...	*me llamo...*
What do you want?	*¿qué quiere?*
I want	*quiero*
I don't want it	*No lo quiero*
long-distance phone call	*una llamada de larga distancia*
good/bad	*bueno/malo*

Nationalities and languages

American *americano/a*	British *británico/a*
Australian *australiano/a*	Canadian *canadiense*
Austrian *austriaco/a*	Danish *danés/danesa*

Dutch *holandés/holandesa*
English *inglés/inglesa*
French *francés/francesa*
German *alemán/alemana*
Irish *irlandés/irlandesa*
Italian *italiano/a*
New Zealand *neozelandés/neozelandesa*

Norwegian *noruego/a*
Portuguese *portugués/portuguesa*
Scottish *escocés/escocesa*
Swedish *sueco/a*
Swiss *suizo/a*
Welsh *galés/galesa*

Basic questions

Have you got a room for two people?
  ¿Tiene una habitación para dos personas?
How do I get to_? *¿cómo llego a_?*
How much does it cost? *¿cuánto cuesta?*
How much is it? *¿cuánto es?*
When does the bus leave (arrive)?
  ¿a qué hora sale (llega) el autobús?

When? *¿Cuándo?*
Where is_? *¿Dónde está?*
Where is the nearest petrol station?
  ¿dónde está el grifo más cerca?
Why? *¿por qué?*

Basics

bank *el banco*
bathroom/toilet *el baño*
bill *la factura/la cuenta*
cash *el efectivo*
cheap *barato*
church/cathedral *La iglesia/catedral*
exchange house *la casa de cambio*
exchange rate *el tipo de cambio*
expensive *caro*
internet café *cibercafé*

market *el mercado*
notes/coins *los billetes/las monedas*
police (policeman) *la policía (el policía)*
post office *el correo*
supermarket *el supermercado*
telephone office *el centro de llamadas*
ticket office *la boletería/la taquilla*
travellers' cheques *los travelers/*
  los cheques de viajero

Getting around

aeroplane/airplane *el avión*
airport *el aeropuerto*
bus station *la terminal de autobús*
bus *el bus/el autobús*
minibus *la combi*
motorcycle taxi *el mototaxi*
bus route *el corredor*
first/second class *primera/segunda clase*

on the left/right *a la izquierda/derecha*
second street on the left *la segunda calle*
  a la izquierda
ticket *el boleto*
to walk *caminar*
Where can I buy tickets? *¿dónde se puede*
  comprar boletos?
Where can I park? *¿dónde se puede parquear?*

Orientation and motoring

arrival *la llegada*
avenue *la avenida*
block *la cuadra*
border *la frontera*
fixed route taxi *el colectivo*
corner *la esquina*
customs *la aduana*
departure *la salida*

east *el este, el oriente*
empty *vacío*
full *lleno*
highway, main road *la carretera*
immigration *la inmigración*
insurance *el seguro*
the insured *el asegurado/la asegurada*
to insure yourself against *asegurarse contra*

luggage *el equipaje*
motorway, freeway *el autopista/la carretera*
north *el norte*
oil *el aceite*
passport *el pasaporte*
petrol/gasoline *la gasolina*
puncture *el pinchazo*
south *el sur*

street *la calle*
that way *por allí/por allá*
this way *por aquí/por acá*
tourist card *la tarjeta de turista*
tyre *la llanta*
unleaded *sin plomo*
visa *el visado*
west *el oeste/el poniente*

Accommodation

air conditioning *el aire acondicionado*
all-inclusive *todo incluido*
blankets *las mantas*
clean/dirty towels *las toallas limpias/sucias*
dining room *el comedor*
double bed *la cama matrimonial*
guesthouse *la casa de huéspedes*
hot/cold water *el agua caliente/fría*
hotel *el hotel*
Is service included? *¿está incluido el servicio?*
Is tax included? *¿están incluidos los impuestos?*
noisy *ruidoso*
pillows *las almohadas*

power cut *el apagón/corte*
restaurant *el restaurante*
room *el cuarto/la habitación*
sheets *las sábanas*
shower *la ducha*
single/double *sencillo/doble*
soap *el jabón*
to clean *limpiar*
toilet *el sanitario*
toilet paper *el papel higiénico*
with private bathroom *con baño privado*
with two beds *con dos camas*

Health

aspirin *la aspirina*
blood *la sangre*
chemist *la farmacia*
condoms *los preservativos, los condones*
contact lenses *los lentes de contacto*
contraceptive *anticonceptivo*
  (pill) *(la píldora anticonceptiva)*
diarrhoea *la diarrea*

doctor *el médico*
fever/sweat *la fiebre/el sudor*
(for) pain *(para) dolor*
head *la cabeza*
period/towels *la regla/las toallas*
stomach *el estómago*
altitude sickness *el soroche*

Time

at one o'clock *a la una*
at half past two *a las dos y media*
at a quarter to three *a cuarto para las tres*
  or *a las tres menos quince*
it's one o'clock *es la una*
it's seven o'clock *son las siete*
it's six twenty *son las seis y veinte*
it's five to nine *son cinco para las nueve/*
  son las nueve menos cinco
in ten minutes *en diez minutos*
five hours *cinco horas*
does it take long? *¿tarda mucho?*

Monday *lunes*
Tuesday *martes*
Wednesday *miércoles*
Thursday *jueves*
Friday *viernes*
Saturday *sábado*
Sunday *domingo*

January *enero*
February *febrero*
March *marzo*
April *abril*

May *mayo*	September *septiembre*
June *junio*	October *octubre*
July *julio*	November *noviembre*
August *agosto*	December *diciembre*

Numbers

one *uno/una*	sixteen *dieciséis*
two *dos*	seventeen *diecisiete*
three *tres*	eighteen *dieciocho*
four *cuatro*	nineteen *diecinueve*
five *cinco*	twenty *veinte*
six *seis*	twenty-one *veintiuno*
seven *siete*	thirty *treinta*
eight *ocho*	forty *cuarenta*
nine *nueve*	fifty *cincuenta*
ten *diez*	sixty *sesenta*
eleven *once*	seventy *setenta*
twelve *doce*	eighty *ochenta*
thirteen *trece*	ninety *noventa*
fourteen *catorce*	hundred *cien/ciento*
fifteen *quince*	thousand *mil*

Family

aunt *la tía*	grandmother *la abuela*
brother *el hermano*	husband *el esposo/marido*
cousin *el/la primo/a*	married *casado/a*
daughter *la hija*	single/unmarried *soltero/a*
family *la familia*	sister *la hermana*
father *el padre*	son *el hijo*
fiancé/fiancée *el novio/la novia*	uncle *el tío*
friend *el amigo/la amiga*	wife *la esposa*
grandfather *el abuelo*	

Food

Avocado *la palta*	chilli pepper or green pepper *el ají*
baked *al horno*	clear soup, stock *el caldo*
bakery *la panadería*	cooked *cocido*
beans *los frijoles/las habichuelas*	dining room *el comedor*
beef *la carne de res*	egg *el huevo*
beef steak or pork fillet *el bistec*	fish *el pescado*
boiled rice *el arroz blanco*	fork *el tenedor*
bread *el pan*	fried *frito*
breakfast *el desayuno*	fritters *las frituras*
butter *la mantequilla*	garlic *el ajo*
cassava, yucca *la yuca*	goat *el chivo*
casserole *la cazuela*	grapefruit *el pomelo*
chewing gum *el chicle*	grill *la parrilla*
chicken *el pollo*	grilled/griddled *a la plancha*

guava *la guayaba*
ham *el jamón*
hamburger *la hamburguesa*
hot, spicy *picante*
ice cream *el helado*
jam *la mermelada*
knife *el cuchillo*
lime *el limón*
lobster *la langosta*
lunch *el almuerzo*
margarine, fat *la manteca*
meal, supper, dinner *la comida*
meat *la carne*
minced meat *el picadillo*
mixed salad *la ensalada mixta*
onion *la cebolla*
orange *la naranja*
pepper *el pimiento*
plantain, green banana *el plátano*
pasty, turnover *la empanada/el pastelito*
pork *el cerdo*
potato *la papa*
prawns *los camarones*
raw *crudo*

restaurant *el restaurante*
roast *el asado*
salad *la ensalada*
salt *la sal*
sandwich *el bocadillo*
sauce *la salsa*
sausage *la longaniza*
scrambled eggs *los huevos revueltos*
seafood *los mariscos*
small sandwich, filled roll *el bocadito*
soup *la sopa*
spoon *la cuchara*
squash *la calabaza*
squid *los calamares*
supper *la cena*
sweet *dulce*
sweet potato *la batata*
to eat *comer*
toasted *tostado*
turkey *el pavo*
vegetables *los legumbres/vegetales*
without meat *sin carne*
yam *el camote*

Drink

beer *la cerveza*
boiled *hervido*
bottled *en botella*
camomile tea *la manzanilla*
canned *en lata*
cocktail *el coctel*
coconut milk *la leche de coco*
coffee *el café*
coffee, small, strong *el cafecito*
coffee, white *el café con leche*
cold *frío*
condensed milk *la leche condensada*
cup *la taza*
drink *la bebida*
drunk *borracho*
firewater *el aguardiente*
fruit milkshake *el batido*
glass *el vaso*
glass of liquer *la copa de licor*
hot *caliente*

ice *el hielo*
juice *el jugo*
lemonade *la limonada*
milk *la leche*
mint *la menta*
orange juice *el jugo de naranja*
pineapple milkshake *el batido de piña con leche*
rum *el ron*
soft drink *el refresco*
soft fizzy drink *la gaseosa/cola*
sugar *el azúcar*
tea *el té*
to drink *beber/tomar*
water *el agua*
water, carbonated *el agua mineral con gas*
water, still mineral *el agua mineral sin gas*
wine, red *el vino tinto*
wine, white *el vino blanco*

Key verbs

To **go** *ir*	We have *tenemos*
I go *voy*	They, you (plural) have *tienen*
you go (familiar) *vas*	(Also used in 'I am hungry' *tengo hambre*)
he, she, it goes, you (formal) go *va*	There is/are *hay*
we go *vamos*	There isn't/aren't *no hay*
they, you (plural) go *van*	To **be** (in a permanent state) **ser**
To **have** (possess) *tener*	*soy; eres; es; somos; son*
I have *tengo*	To **be** (positional or temporary state) **estar**
You (familiar) have *tienes*	*estoy; estás; está ; estamos; están*
He, she, it, you (formal) have *tiene*	

This section has been assembled on the basis of glossaries compiled by André de Mendonça and David Gilmour of South American Experience, London, and the Latin American Travel Advisor, No 9, March 1996

Spanish pronunciation

The stress in a Spanish word conforms to one of three rules: 1) if the word ends in a vowel, or in n or **s**, the accent falls on the penultimate syllable (*ventana, ventanas*); 2) if the word ends in a consonant other than **n** or **s**, the accent falls on the last syllable (*hablar*); 3) if the word is to be stressed on a syllable contrary to either of the above rules, the acute accent on the relevant vowel indicates where the stress is to be placed (*pantalón, metáfora*). Note that adverbs such as *cuando*, 'when', take an accent when used interrogatively: *¿cuándo?*, 'when?'

Vowels: **a** not quite as short as in English 'cat'; **e** as in English 'pay', but shorter in a syllable ending in a consonant; **i** as in English 'seek'; **o** as in English 'cot' (North American 'caught'), but more like 'pope' when the vowel ends a syllable; **u** as in English 'food'; after 'q' and in 'gue', 'gui', u is unpronounced; in 'güe' and 'güi' it is pronounced; **y** when a vowel, pronounced like 'i'; when a semiconsonant or consonant, it is pronounced like English 'yes'; **ai**, **ay** as in English 'write'; **ei**, **ey** as in English 'eight'; **oi**, **oy** as in English 'voice'

Unless listed below **consonants** can be pronounced in Spanish as they are in English. **b**, **v** have an interchangeable sound and both are a cross between the English 'b' and 'v', except at the beginning of a word or after 'm' or 'n' when it is like English 'b'; **c** like English 'k', except before 'e' or 'i' when it is as the 's' in English 'sip'; **g** before 'e' and 'i' it is the same as j; **h** when on its own, never pronounced; **j** as the 'ch' in the Scottish 'loch'; **ll** as the 'g' in English 'beige'; sometimes as the 'lli' in 'million'; **ñ** as the 'ni' in English 'onion'; **rr** trilled much more strongly than in English; **x** depending on its location, pronounced as in English 'fox', or 'sip', or like 'gs'; **z** as the 's' in English 'sip'.

Food glossary

Food has always played an important role in Peruvian culture. The country's range of climates has also made it internationally famed for its cuisine.

Savoury dishes

Ají (hot pepper)
Ají is found in many varieties and is used to add 'spice' to everything from soup to fish to vegetable dishes. It is a staple in Peruvian kitchens from the coast to the most remote jungle villages. These peppers can be extremely spicy, so the inexperienced palate should proceed with caution!

Papa (potato)
The potato is as Peruvian as the Inca himself. There are more than 2000 varieties of tuber although only a fraction are edible. *The International Potato Institute* is located on the outskirts of metropolitan Lima so those with a potato fetish might wish to visit. The *papa amarilla* (yellow potato) is by far the best-tasting of the lot.

Causa
A casserole served cold with a base of yellow potato and mixed with hot peppers, onion, avocado, with either chicken, crab or meat. A fantastic starter.

Estofado
A mild chicken stew, with lots of potatoes and other vegetables, served with rice.

Lomo saltado
Strips of sirloin sautéed with tomato, onion, *ají amarillo* (a spicy orange pepper) and french fried potatoes served with rice.

Papa Ocopa
A typical dish from the Arequipa region. A spicy peanut sauce served over cold potatoes with a slice of hard boiled egg.

Papa a la Huancaína
A dish which originated in the central department of Huancayo. This creamy cheese sauce served over cold potatoes is a common starter for set menus everywhere.

Papa rellena (stuffed potato)
First baked then fried, the potato is stuffed with meat, onions, olives, boiled egg and raisins. *Camote* (yams) can be substituted for potatoes.

Choclo (corn)
Another staple in the Peruvian diet. The large kernels are great with the fresh cheese produced all over the country.

Maíz morado (purple corn)
This type of corn is not edible for humans. It's boiled and the liquid is used to make *chicha*, a sweet and very traditional Peruvian refreshment.

Chicha de Jora
A strong fermented beverage mostly found in mountain communities. The people who make it use their saliva to aid in the fermenting process.

Granos (grains)
Kiwicha and *quinoa* are very high sources of protein and staples of the Inca diet. *Quinoa* is wonderful in soups and *kiwicha* is a common breakfast food for children throughout the country.

Arroz (rice)
Another major staple in Peruvian cooking.

Anticuchos (beef heart kebabs)
Beef heart barbecued and served with cold potato and a wonderful assortment of spicy sauces.

Cuy (guinea pig)
Prepared in a variety of ways from stewed to fried.

Cau cau
Tripe and potatoes.

Rocoto relleno (stuffed hot peppers)
Stuffed with meat and potatoes, then baked.

Pachamanca
Typical mountain cuisine, so popular it's now prepared everywhere. Beef, pork and chicken mixed with a variety of vegetables, and cooked together over heated stones in a hole in the ground.

Seco de cabrito
A favorite dish from the north coast. Roasted goat marinated with fermented *chicha*, served with beans and rice.

Ají de gallina
A rich mix of creamed, spicy chicken over rice and boiled potatoes.

Ceviche
The national dish of Peru. Raw fish or seafood marinaded in a mixture of lime juice, red onions and hot peppers, usually served with a thick slice of boiled yam (*camote*) and corn. With a coastline of more than 1800 km, the fruits of the sea are almost limitless. Sea bass, flounder, salmon, red snapper, sole and many varieties of shellfish are all in abundance. Keep in mind that *ceviche* is a dish served for lunch. Most *cevicherías* close around 1600.

Postres (desserts)

Arroz con leche
Rice pudding.

Manjar blanco
A caramel sweet made from boiled milk and sugar.

Picarones
Deep-fried donut batter bathed in a honey sauce.

Suspiro a la limeña
Manjar blanco with baked egg white.

Turrón
This popular sweet, shortbread covered in molasses or honey, is sold everywhere during the October celebrations of *Señor de los Milagros* (Lord of Miracles) in Lima.

Fruta (fruit)

There's a great selection of fruit in Peru. Apart from common fruits such as mandarins, oranges, peaches and bananas, there are exotic tropical fruits to choose from.

Chirimoya
Custard apple. In Quechua means 'the sweet of the gods'.

Lúcuma
Eggfruit.

Maracuyá
Passionfruit, often served as a juice.

Tuna
Prickly pear.

Bebidas (drinks)

The national beers include *Cristal, Cusqueña, Barena* and *Pilsen*. There are also some dark beers.

Although not known as a great wine-producing country, there are many wineries (*bodegas*) in the Ica region. The best are Tabernero, Tacama (especially its Selección Especial and Terroix labels), Ocucaje and Santiago Queirolo (in particular its Intipalka label).

Pisco, a strong brandy made from white grapes, is produced in the departments of Ica, Moquegua and Tacna. *Pisco sour*, the national drink, is made with lime juice, egg white, sugar and a dash of cinnamon.

Index → Entries in bold refer to maps.

Advertisers' index

Notes

Acknowledgements

This edition of the *Cuzco & the Inca Heartland* has been produced on the strength of researches for both the 2011 edition of Footprint's *South American Handbook* and the eighth edition of the *Peru Handbook*. Ben Box and Sarah Cameron visited Peru in 2009 and Ben was there again in 2010. Acknowledgements for the invaluable assistance received on those research trips are given in the *South American* and *Peru Handbooks*. However, special mention must be given here to Mary Finn of South American Explorers in Cuzco for her updates on treks around the city and on hotels and restaurants.

The authors should also like to thank the following travellers: Karim Malamoud, Georgie Stone and Pieter van de Sype, as well as all those who have written to the *South American Handbook* and Footprint's website, www.footprinttravelguides.com.

We should also like to acknowledge the previous authors of this book, especially Steve Frankham, who researched many of the treks and adventures that are described.

Finally, Ben and Sarah are most grateful to the Footprint team who have worked on this edition, especially Nicola Gibbs, Alan Murphy, Emma Bryers and Kevin Feeney.

Credits

Footprint credits

Project editor: Nicola Gibbs
Layout and production: Emma Bryers
Cover and colour section: Pepi Bluck
Maps: Ben Box, Kevin Feeney

Managing Director: Andy Riddle
Commercial Director: Patrick Dawson
Publisher: Alan Murphy
Publishing Managers: Felicity Laughton, Nicola Gibbs
Digital Editors: Jo Williams, Jen Haddington
Marketing and PR: Liz Harper
Advertising: Renu Sibal, Elizabeth Taylor
Finance and administration: Elizabeth Taylor

Photography credits
Front cover: Sacsayhuaman, Hervé Hughes / hemis.fr
Back cover: Moray, Hervé Hughes / hemis.fr

Manufactured in India by Nutech Print Services.

Every effort has been made to ensure that the facts in this guidebook are accurate. However, travellers should still obtain advice from consulates, airlines etc about travel and visa requirements before travelling. The authors and publishers cannot accept responsibility for any loss, injury or inconvenience however caused.

Publishing information
Footprint Cuzco and the Inca Heartland
5th edition
© Footprint Handbooks Ltd
April 2011

ISBN: 978 1 907263 361
CIP DATA: A catalogue record for this book is available from the British Library

® Footprint Handbooks and the Footprint mark are a registered trademark of Footprint Handbooks Ltd

Published by Footprint
6 Riverside Court
Lower Bristol Road
Bath BA2 3DZ, UK
T +44 (0)1225 469141
F +44 (0)1225 469461
footprinttravelguides.com

Distributed in the USA by Globe Pequot Press, Guilford, Connecticut

Colour section photography credits
Page 1: Hervé Hughes/hemis.fr. Pages 2-3: Hervé Hughes/hemis.fr. Page 6: (clockwise from top) Hervé Hughes/hemis.fr; Eye Ubiquitous/photolibrary.com; Arco Images GmbH/Alamy; Alexey Stiop/Shutterstock; James Brunker/Alamy. Page 7: (clockwise from top) Hervé Hughes/hemis.fr; Steve Allen Travel Photography/Alamy; Ckchiu/Dreamstime.com; Konrad Wothe/Minden Pictures/FLPA. Page 8: Mirmoor/Dreamstime.com.

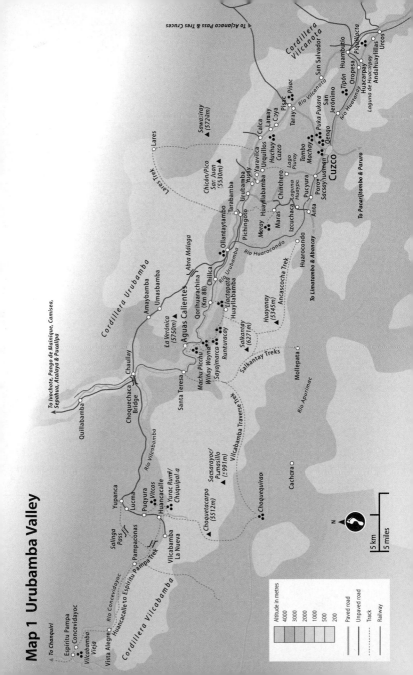

Map 1 Urubamba Valley

Map 2 Cuzco region

To Camisea, Shepahua, Atalaya & Pucallpa

Pongo de Mainique

Ivochote

Manu Biosphere Reserve

A

Koshirena
Kiteni
Echarate
Ocobamba

Urubamba

Quillabamba
Chaullay

Espíritu Pampa

Vilcabamba Vieja

Yupanca
Lucma
Huancacalle

Vilcabamba La Nueva

Aguas Calientes

Machu Picchu

Abra Málaga

Cordillera Urubamba

Lares
Tres Cruces
Acjanaco Pass

Ollantaytambo
Yucay
Calca
Paucartambo

Río Apurímac

Cordillera Vilcabamba

Huayllabamba
▲ *Salkantay (6271m)*
Moray
Urubamba
Chinchero
Pisac
San Salvador

CUZCO

Choquequirao
Limatambo
Mollepata
Tarahuasi
Cachora
Curahuasi
Anta
Sacsayhuaman

Cuzco
San Jerónimo
Huambutío
Riquillacta
Oropesa
Urcos

Abancay
Saywite

Talavera
Andahuaylas

Cotabambas
Pacarijtambo

Río Santo Tomás

Cusipata
Checacupe

Lago Pomacanchi

Acomayo
Combapa

B

Colcabamba

APURIMAC

Tambobamba

El Progreso
Chuquibambilla

Quehui

Pampachiri
Chalhuanca

Livitaca

Antabamba

Santo Tomás

Challa

AYACUCHO

C

Incuyo
L Parinacochas

Puica
Cotahuasi

Valle de los Volcanes

Caylloma

Calhua
Orcopampa

AREQUIPA

▲ *Corupana (6425m)*
Andagua
Cabanaconde
Chivay

Colca

1   **2**   **3**

Administration

☐ Capital city
○ Other city, town
Ⅎ International border
Regional border
Disputed border

Roads and travel

══ Motorway
── Main road (National highway)
── Minor road
---- Track
······ Footpath
⊷▬ Railway with station
✈ Airport
🚌 Bus station
Ⓜ Metro station
---- Cable car
⧓⧓⧓ Funicular
⛴ Ferry

Water features

▭ River, canal
◯ Lake, ocean
ᵛᵥᵛ Seasonal marshland
▦ Beach, sandbank
💧 Waterfall
〜 Reef

Topographical features

◯ Contours (approx)
▲ Mountain, volcano
⇌ Mountain pass
⌐ Escarpment
⟟⟟ Gorge
▦ Glacier
▦ Salt flat
▦ Rocks

Cities and towns

═ Main through route
═ Main street

Minor street
Pedestrianized street
Ⅎ Ⅎ Tunnel
→ One-way street
▥ Steps
⊨ Bridge
▲▲▲ Fortified wall
▦ Park, garden, stadium
● Sleeping
𝗣 Eating
♫ Bars & clubs
▭ Building
▫ Sight
♱ Cathedral, church
🏮 Chinese temple
🏛 Hindu temple
🕍 Meru
🕌 Mosque
△ Stupa
✿ Synagogue
🛈 Tourist office
🏛 Museum
✉ Post office
® Police
Ⓢ Bank
@ Internet
♪ Telephone
🏪 Market
✚ Medical services
🅿 Parking
⛽ Petrol
⛳ Golf
▣ A Detail map
◁ A Related map

Other symbols

∴ Archaeological site
♦ National park, wildlife reserve
✿ Viewing point
⛺ Campsite
⌂ Refuge, lodge
🏰 Castle, fort
🤿 Diving
🌳 Deciduous, coniferous, palm trees
⌂ Hide
🍇 Vineyard, winery
△ Distillery
⛵ Shipwreck
✕ Historic battlefield

Join us online...

Follow us on **Twitter** and **Facebook** – ask us questions, speak to our authors, swap your stories, and be kept up to date with travel news and exclusive discounts and competitions.

Upload your travel pics to our **Flickr** site – inspire others on where to go next, and have your photos considered for inclusion in Footprint guides.

And don't forget to visit us at **footprint**travelguides.com